# Lecture Notes in Artificial Intelligence    1986

Subseries of Lecture Notes in Computer Science
Edited by J. G. Carbonell and J. Siekmann

# Lecture Notes in Computer Science

Edited by G. Goos, J. Hartmanis and J. van Leeuwen

T0237737

**Springer**
*Berlin*
*Heidelberg*
*New York*
*Barcelona*
*Hong Kong*
*London*
*Milan*
*Paris*
*Singapore*
*Tokyo*

Cristiano Castelfranchi    Yves Lespérance (Eds.)

# Intelligent Agents VII

## Agent Theories Architectures and Languages

7th International Workshop, ATAL 2000
Boston, MA, USA, July 7-9, 2000
Proceedings

Springer

Series Editors

Jaime G. Carbonell,Carnegie Mellon University, Pittsburgh, PA, USA
Jörg Siekmann, University of Saarland, Saarbrücken, Germany


Volume Editors

Cristiano Castelfranchi
University of Siena
Department of Communication Sciences, "Cognitive Science"
piazza S. Francesco 8, 53100 Siena, Italy
E-mail: castelfranc@unisi.it

Yves Lespérance
York University, Department of Computer Science
4700 Keele Street, Toronto, Onatrio, Canada M3J 1P3
E-mail: lesperan@cs.yorku.ca

Cataloging-in-Publication Data applied for

Die Deutsche Bibliothek - CIP-Einheitsaufnahme

Intelligent agents VII : agent theories, architectures, and languages ; 7th
international workshop ; proceedings / ATAL 2000, Boston, MA, USA, July 7 -
9, 2000. Christiano Castelfranchi ; Yves Lespérance (ed.). - Berlin ;
Heidelberg ; New York ; Barcelona ; Hong Kong ; London ; Milan ; Paris ;
Singapore ; Tokyo : Springer, 2001
　(Lecture notes in computer science ; Vol. 1986 : Lecture notes in
　artificial intelligence)
　ISBN 3-540-42422-9


CR Subject Classification (1998): I.2.11,I.2, C.2.4, D.2, F.3

ISBN 3-540-42422-9 Springer-Verlag Berlin Heidelberg New York

Springer-Verlag Berlin Heidelberg New York
a member of BertelsmannSpringer Science+Business Media GmbH

http://www.springer.de

© Springer-Verlag Berlin Heidelberg 2001
Printed in Germany

Typesetting: Camera-ready by author, data conversion PTP Berlin, Stefan Sossna
Printed on acid-free paper　　　SPIN 10781933　　　06/3142　　　5 4 3 2 1 0

# Preface

Intelligent agents are one of the most important developments in computer science of the past decade. Agents are of interest in many important application areas, ranging from human-computer interaction to industrial process control. The ATAL workshop series aims to bring together researchers interested in the core/micro aspects of agent technology. Specifically, ATAL addresses issues such as theories of agency, software architectures for intelligent agents, methodologies and programming languages for realizing agents, and software tools for applying and evaluating agent systems. One of the strengths of the ATAL workshop series is its emphasis on the synergies between theories, languages, architectures, infrastructures, methodologies, and formal methods.

This year's workshop continued the ATAL trend of attracting a large number of high quality submissions. In more detail, 71 papers were submitted to the ATAL 2000 workshop, from 21 countries. After stringent reviewing, 22 papers were accepted for publication and appear in these proceedings.

As with previous workshops in the series, we chose to emphasize what we perceive as important new themes in agent research. This year's themes were both associated with the fact that the technology of intelligent agents and multi-agent systems is beginning to migrate from research labs to software engineering centers. As agents are deployed in applications such as electronic commerce, and start to take over responsibilities for their human users, techniques for controlling their autonomy become crucial. As well, the availability of tools that facilitate the design and implementation of agent systems becomes an important factor in how rapidly the technology will achieve widespread use. Consequently, the ATAL 2000 program included two special tracks on *Autonomy — Theory, Dimensions, and Regulation* and *Agent Development Tools*. Besides papers in each of these special tracks, the program also featured two associated panels (organized by Cristiano Castelfranchi and Keith Decker respectively). Another highlight of this year's program was the invited talks by leading exponents of agent research:

| | | |
|---|---|---|
| ARCHITECTURES | Craig Boutilier | Structured Online and Offline Solution of Decision-Theoretic Planning Problems |
| THEORIES | Phil Cohen | On Group Communication |

It is both our hope and our expectation that this volume will be as useful to the agent research and development community as its six predecessors have proved to be. We believe that ATAL and the *Intelligent Agents* series, of which these proceedings form a part, play a crucial role in a rapidly developing field, by focusing specifically on the relationships between the theory and practice of agents. Only through understanding these relationships can agent-based computing mature and achieve its widely predicted potential.

March 2001

Cristiano Castelfranchi
Yves Lespérance

# Workshop Organization

## Organizing Committee

| | |
|---|---|
| Cristiano Castelfranchi | University of Siena, Italy |
| Yves Lespérance | York University, Canada |

## Steering Committee

| | |
|---|---|
| Nicholas R. Jennings | University of Southampton, UK |
| Yves Lespérance | York University, Canada |
| Jörg P. Müller | Siemens Research, Germany |
| Munindar P. Singh | North Carolina State University, USA |
| Michael Wooldridge | University of Liverpool, UK |

## Program Committee

| | | | |
|---|---|---|---|
| Chitta Baral | (USA) | Suzanne Barber | (USA) |
| Michael Beetz | (Germany) | Stefan Bussmann | (Germany) |
| Lawrence Cavedon | (Australia) | Paolo Ciancarini | (Italy) |
| Phil Cohen | (USA) | Rosaria Conte | (Italy) |
| Giuseppe De Giacomo | (Italy) | Keith Decker | (USA) |
| Frank Dignum | (The Netherlands) | Alexis Drogoul | (France) |
| Jacques Ferber | (France) | Klaus Fischer | (Germany) |
| Michael Fisher | (UK) | Stan Franklin | (USA) |
| Fausto Giunchiglia | (Italy) | Piotr Gmytrasiewicz | (USA) |
| Keith Golden | (USA) | Barbara Grosz | (USA) |
| Henry Hexmoor | (USA) | Wiebe van der Hoek | (The Netherlands) |
| Marc Huber | (USA) | Mark d'Inverno | (UK) |
| Nick Jennings | (UK) | David Kinny | (Australia) |
| Sarit Kraus | (Israel) | Michael Luck | (UK) |
| John-Jules Meyer | (The Netherlands) | Jörg Müller | (Germany) |
| Anand Rao | (UK) | Murray Shanahan | (UK) |
| Onn Shehory | (Israel) | Carles Sierra | (Spain) |
| Munindar Singh | (USA) | Liz Sonenberg | (Australia) |
| Katia Sycara | (USA) | Milind Tambe | (USA) |
| Jan Treur | (The Netherlands) | Manuela Veloso | (USA) |
| Tom Wagner | (USA) | Wayne Wobcke | (UK) |
| Mike Wooldridge | (UK) | Eric Yu | (Canada) |

## Additional Reviewers

| | | |
|---|---|---|
| Jaelson Castro | Rino Falcone | Anuj Goel |
| Claudia V. Goldman | John Graham | Daniel Gross |
| Pu Huang | Luke Hunsberger | Manuel Kolp |
| Dung Lam | Foster McGeary | Wieke de Vries |
| Wei Yang | | |

# Table of Contents

## Section IX: Panel Summary: Autonomy — Theory, Dimensions, and Regulation

# Introduction

Like its predecessors [5,6,3,4,2,1], this volume of the Intelligent Agents series focuses on the relationships between the theory and the practice of intelligent autonomous agents. The volume is divided into eight sections. Sections I and III present work on agent theories. Section II discusses work on development tools and platforms for agents and multiagent systems. Section IV presents work on models of agent communication and coordination. Section V deals with the issue of autonomy and presents additional work on agent coordination. Section VI deals with programming and specification languages for agents. Section VII focuses on issues in agent architectures, such as how to support planning, decision making, and learning. Finally, Sections VIII and IX provide summaries of the discussions held at the two ATAL panels, one on Agent Development Tools and the other on Autonomy — Theory, Dimensions, and Regulation.

## Section I: Agent Theories I

*Wooldridge and Dunne* develop a formal model of the problem of designing an agent that achieves and/or maintains given goals and prove some new results about the complexity of the agent design problem under various assumptions. They look at optimistic agent design, where the agent is only required to achieve/maintain its goals for *some execution* of the specified environment. They also look at disjunctive design, where the agent is allowed to achieve/maintain only one among a set of alternative goals.

*Dragoni et al.* develop a formal framework for modeling how agents' mental states are updated as a consequence of communication acts. Mental states are modeled as multi-context propositional theories. An abductive account of mental state change is developed for the framework. The use of the framework is illustrated by formalizing the "inform" speech act and showing how its effects on the hearer's mental state can be captured.

*Zimmerbaum and Scherl* propose a generalized version of a framework for reasoning about how knowledge is affected by action, to deal with concurrent actions and time. The framework, which is based on the situation calculus, captures the knowledge effects of both sensing and non-sensing actions. Indexical knowledge of time and absolute knowledge of time are both handled.

## Section II: Agent Development Tools and Platforms

*DeLoach and Wood* present their MaSE methodology for multiagent system development and a tool that supports its use. The methodology is comprehensive, covering both the analysis and design phases. Diagram-based notations are provided for developing detailed models of the behaviors associated with roles and conversations.

*Riley et al.* present their *layered disclosure* approach to supporting the debugging and fine tuning of complex agent systems. In layered disclosure, the system designer defines an information hierarchy, which is then used to control the level of detail of the information provided in response to queries about the agent's internal state and why it acted in a particular way. The implementation and use of the approach in a simulated robot soccer playing system is discussed.

*Bryson and Stein* propose a meta-methodology for reducing the cost of the proliferation of architectures and methodologies. They propose the use of "idioms" to compare architectures and methodologies. An idiom is a compact, regularized way of expressing a frequently used set of ideas or functionality. As an example, they describe the "Basic Reactive Plan" idiom and compare various agent architectures in terms of how they can express this idiom.

*Bellifemine et al.* present JADE, a software framework that facilitates the development of agent applications in compliance with the FIPA specifications for multiagent systems. They discuss the advantages of this agent platform, for instance, flexible and efficient messaging, and its limitations, such as the primitive character of the basic agent model used.

## Section III: Agent Theories II

*Shanahan and Witkowski* present a logic-based agent programming framework that allows the interleaving of planning, plan execution, and perception, and preserves reactivity. The framework is based on the event calculus. Planning and observation assimilation are viewed as abductive theorem proving tasks and are implemented in a logic programming meta-interpreter. Simple application programs for robot navigation and map building are provided as examples.

*Terán et al.* present an approach for analyzing the behavior of multiagent systems through constraint-based search of possible system trajectories. The approach can be viewed as doing a model-based proof that the under the given constraints, the system's behavior satisfies certain properties. They describe a method for compiling a system specification into one that is more efficiently searchable.

## Section IV: Models of Agent Communication and Coordination

*Norman and Reed* study delegation and responsibility by analyzing the delegation of a task from one autonomous agent to another in terms of the performance of some imperative communication act, and the creation of a normative state of affairs. They distinguish between an agent doing something, being responsible for getting something done, and being responsible for bringing about a state of affairs. In their framework, it is possible to evaluate the coherence of an agent's action with respect to the agent's commitments.

*Dignum et al.* present an architecture for agents that can discuss the formation of a team, construct a collective plan by dialogue, and work as a team member until the collective goal has been fulfilled. They explain how fixed protocols like contract net do not suffice for this, and propose the use of *structured dialogues*, with an emphasis on persuasion.

The dialogues in which agents engage are described formally using modal logic and speech acts.

*Nodine et al.* explore issues related to the coordination of complex and long running tasks in systems involving unreliable agents. Their analysis of coordination issues uses three crucial categories: tasks, roles, and conversations. They claim that current agent communication languages make certain assumptions about the agent system, such as stability or intelligence, that are not always justified in information-centric applications. They discuss what additional requirements agent communication languages should satisfy for this, and propose changes to fulfill them.

## Section V: Autonomy and Models of Agent Coordination

*Luck and d'Inverno* introduce the notion of *sociological agents*, agents who can model their social environment and in particular the social relationships in which they participate, for instance, autonomy, dependence, and power relations. They explain how by making use of this information, the agents can enhance their performance by exploiting social opportunities and exerting power over others. The models of social relationships used are not limited to characterizing problem situations, such as dependencies, or the notion of "owned resource", but also provide the agents with solutions, for example, through self-sufficient plans.

In their paper, *Sierra et al.* present a new approach to landmark-based robot navigation based on the use of bidding mechanisms to coordinate the actions requested by a group of agents in charge of guiding a robot towards a specified target in an unknown environment. The approach uses a qualitative (fuzzy) representation of landmark information.

*Clement and Durfee*, working on the complexity of the coordination problem, show how coordinating CHiPs, i.e. individually formed concurrent hierarchical plans, at a higher level is still exponentially cheaper than at lower levels, in spite of the possibly exponential growth of the associated summary information. The paper also proposes heuristics that take advantage of summary information to smartly direct the search for a global plan. Experiments that confirm the effectiveness of the proposed heuristics are described.

## Section VI: Agent Languages

*Hindriks et al.* address a fundamental deficiency in existing agent programming languages, namely that their notions of goal are more like procedure calls than true declarative goals. They propose a simple agent programming language that supports declarative goals. The language incorporates simple mechanisms for selecting actions based on the agent's beliefs and goals and for goal revision. A programming logic is also proposed for reasoning about programs in this language.

*Shapiro and Lespérance* present the latest version of their CASL language for specifying multiagent systems. CASL supports the specification of complex agent behaviors and how they depend on agents' knowledge and goals. The new version has a simpler model of goals and encrypted communication actions. Use of the language is illustrated by modeling a fairly complex multiagent system that resolves feature interactions in telecommunications.

*van Eijk et al.* present enhancements to their multiagent programming framework inspired from work on the semantics of concurrent programming. To better support the programming of open and complex agent systems, they incorporate notions drawn from object-oriented programming, such as agent classes, and agent communication interfaces defined in terms of question templates.

*Marini et al.* propose a metalanguage for specifying agent architectures and multiagent system configurations. The metalanguage allows specifications to be given in a procedural format. Concrete architectures can be specified as instances of abstract architecture classes. A formal semantics is provided for the specification metalanguage.

## Section VII: Planning, Decision Making, and Learning

*Antunes et al.* present a novel approach for decision making, an alternative to classical utilitarian theories. Their BVG agent architecture relies on the use of *values*, i.e. multiple dimensions against which to evaluate a situation, to perform choice among a set of candidate goals. In the BVG model, agents adjust their scale of values by feeding back evaluative information about the consequences of their decisions. In the paper, new experiments are presented where the agents have to make decisions without having all relevant information.

*Koenig* addresses the problem of synthesizing optimal plans for agents, e.g. delivery robots, in the presence of uncertainty and immediate soft deadlines. He does this by introducing the additive and multiplicative planning-task transformations: fast representation changes that transform planning tasks with convex exponential utility functions to planning tasks that can be solved with variants of standard deterministic or probabilistic AI planners. Advantages of such representations include that they are context insensitive, fast, scale well, allow for optimal or near-optimal planning, and are grounded in utility theory.

In his paper, *Weiß* presents M-Dyna-Q, a multiagent coordination framework that integrates joint learning, planning, and reacting. M-Dyna-Q is an extension of Dyna-Q, which is an instantiation of Dyna, a single-agent architectural framework that integrates learning, planning, and reacting. M-Dyna-Q bridges the gap between plan-based and reactive coordination in multiagent systems. After summarizing the key Dyna features, M-Dyna-Q is described in detail, and experimental results on its use are provided. Benefits and limitation of the framework are discussed.

# Panel Summaries

*Bryson et al.* describes the questions that the panel on *Agent Development Tools* attempted to address, the essence of the panelists' statements, and the general conclusions that were drawn.

*Castelfranchi*, who chaired the other panel on *Autonomy — Theory, Dimensions, and Regulation*, introduces the topics that were discussed at this panel. This is followed by statements by the panelists.

March 2001                                    Cristiano Castelfranchi (Siena, Italy) and
                                              Yves Lespérance (Toronto, Canada)

# References

1. N.R. Jennings and Y. Lespérance, editors. *Intelligent Agents VI — Agent Theories, Architectures, and Languages, 6th International Workshop, ATAL'99, Orlando, Florida, USA, July 15–17, 1999, Proceedings*, volume 1757 of *Lecture Notes in Artificial Intelligence*. Springer-Verlag, Berlin, 2000.
2. J.P. Müller, M.P. Singh, and A.S. Rao, editors. *Intelligent Agents V — Agent Theories, Architectures, and Languages, 5th International Workshop, ATAL'98, Paris, France, July 4-7, 1998, Proceedings*, volume 1555 of *Lecture Notes in Artificial Intelligence*. Springer-Verlag, Berlin, 1999.
3. J.P. Müller, M.J. Wooldridge, and N.R. Jennings, editors. *Intelligent Agents III — Agent Theories, Architectures, and Languages, ECAI'96 Workshop (ATAL), Budapest, Hungary, August 12-13, 1996, Proceedings*, volume 1193 of *Lecture Notes in Artificial Intelligence*. Springer-Verlag, Berlin, 1997.
4. M.P. Singh, A. Rao, and M.J. Wooldridge, editors. *Intelligent Agents IV — Agent Theories, Architectures, and Languages, 4th International Workshop, ATAL'97, Providence, Rhode Island, USA, July 24-26, 1997, Proceedings*, volume 1365 of *Lecture Notes in Artificial Intelligence*. Springer-Verlag, Berlin, 1998.
5. M. Wooldridge and N.R. Jennings, editors. *Intelligent Agents — ECAI-94 Workshop on Agent Theories, Architectures, and Languages, Amsterdam, The Netherlands, August 8-9, 1994. Proceedings*, volume 890 of *Lecture Notes in Artificial Intelligence*. Springer-Verlag, Berlin, 1995.
6. M. Wooldridge, J. Müller, and M. Tambe, editors. *Intelligent Agents II — Agent Theories, Architectures, and Languages, IJCAI'95-ATAL Workshop, Montreal, Canada, August 19-20, 1995 Proceedings*, volume 1037 of *Lecture Notes in Artificial Intelligence*. Springer-Verlag, Berlin, 1996.

# Optimistic and Disjunctive Agent Design Problems

Michael Wooldridge and Paul E. Dunne

Department of Computer Science
University of Liverpool
Liverpool L69 7ZF
United Kingdom
{M.J.Wooldridge, P.E.Dunne}@csc.liv.ac.uk

**Abstract.** The *agent design* problem is as follows: Given an environment, together with a specification of a task, is it possible to construct an agent that can be guaranteed to successfully accomplish the task in the environment? In previous research, it was shown that for two important classes of tasks (where an agent was required to either achieve some state of affairs or maintain some state of affairs), the agent design problem was PSPACE-complete. In this paper, we consider several important generalisations of such tasks. In an *optimistic* agent design problem, we simply ask whether an agent has at least *some* chance of bringing about a goal state. In a *combined* design problem, an agent is required to achieve some state of affairs while ensuring that some invariant condition is maintained. Finally, in a *disjunctive* design problem, we are presented with a number of goals and corresponding invariants — the aim is to design an agent that on any given run, will achieve one of the goals while maintaining the corresponding invariant. We prove that while the optimistic achievement and maintenance design problems are NP-complete, the PSPACE-completeness results obtained for achievement and maintenance tasks generalise to combined and disjunctive agent design.

## 1 Introduction

We are interested in building agents that can autonomously act to accomplish tasks on our behalf in complex, unpredictable environments. Other researchers with similar goals have developed a range of software architectures for agents [17]. In this paper, however, we focus on the underlying decision problems associated with the deployment of such agents. Specifically, we study the *agent design* problem [16].

The agent design problem may be stated as follows: Given an environment, together with a specification of a task that we desire to be carried out on our behalf in this environment, is it possible to construct an agent that can be guaranteed to successfully accomplish the task in the environment? The *type* of task to be carried out is crucial to the study of this problem. In previous research, it was shown that for two important classes of tasks (achievement tasks, where an agent is required to achieve some state of affairs, and maintenance tasks, where an agent is required to maintain some state of affairs), the agent design problem is PSPACE-complete in the most general case [16].

In this paper, we consider several important variations of such tasks. First, in an *optimistic* agent design problem, we simply ask whether there exists an agent that has

C. Castelfranchi, Y. Lespérance (Eds.): Intelligent Agents VII, LNAI 1986, pp. 1–14, 2001.

at least *some chance* of achieving the goal or maintaining the condition respectively. In a *combined* agent design problem, the task involves achieving some state of affairs *while at the same time* ensuring that some invariant condition is maintained. In a *disjunctive* design problem, we are presented with a number of goals and corresponding invariants — the aim is to design an agent that on any given run, will achieve one of the goals while maintaining the corresponding invariant. We prove that for optimistic achievement and maintenance tasks, the agent design problem is NP-complete, while the PSPACE-completeness results obtained for achievement and maintenance tasks generalise to combined and disjunctive agent design problems.

We begin in the following section by setting up an abstract model of agents and environments, which we use to formally define the decision problems under study. We then informally motivate and introduce the various agent design problems we study, and prove our main results. We discuss related work in section 6, and present some conclusions in section 7.

*Notation:* We use standard set theoretic and logical notation wherever possible, augmented as follows. If $S$ is a set, then the set of finite sequences over $S$ is denoted by $S^*$. If $\sigma \in S^*$ and $s \in S$, then the sequence obtained by appending $s$ to $\sigma$ is denoted $\sigma \cdot s$. We write $s \in \sigma$ to indicate that element $s$ is present in sequence $\sigma$, and write $last(\sigma)$ to denote the final element of $\sigma$. Throughout the paper, we assume some familiarity with complexity theory [12].

## 2  Agents and Environments

In this section, we present an abstract formal model of agents and the environments they occupy; we then use this model to frame the decision problems we study. The systems of interest to us consist of an agent situated in some particular environment; the agent interacts with the environment by performing actions upon it, and the environment responds to these actions with changes in state. It is assumed that the environment may be in any of a finite set $E = \{e, e', \ldots\}$ of instantaneous states. Agents are assumed to have a repertoire of possible actions available to them, which transform the state of the environment. Let $Ac = \{\alpha, \alpha', \ldots\}$ be the (finite) set of actions.

The basic model of agents interacting with their environments is as follows. The environment starts in some state, and the agent begins by choosing an action to perform on that state. As a result of this action, the environment can respond with a number of possible states. However, only one state will *actually* result — though of course, the agent does not know in advance which it will be. On the basis of this second state, the agent again chooses an action to perform. The environment responds with one of a set of possible states, the agent then chooses another action, and so on.

A *run*, $r$, of an agent in an environment is thus a sequence of interleaved environment states and actions:

$$r : e_0 \xrightarrow{\alpha_0} e_1 \xrightarrow{\alpha_1} e_2 \xrightarrow{\alpha_2} e_3 \xrightarrow{\alpha_3} \cdots \xrightarrow{\alpha_{u-1}} e_u \cdots$$

Let $\mathcal{R}$ be the set of all such possible runs. We use $r, r', \ldots$ to stand for members of $\mathcal{R}$.

In order to represent the effect that an agent's actions have on an environment, we introduce a *state transformer* function (cf. [5, p154]):

$$\tau : \mathcal{R} \to 2^E$$

Thus a state transformer function maps a run (assumed to end with the action of an agent) to a set of possible environment states. There are two important points to note about this definition.

First, environments are allowed to be *history dependent* (or non-Markovian). In other words, the next state of an environment is not solely determined by the action performed by the agent and the current state of the environment. The previous actions performed by the agent, and the previous environment states also play a part in determining the current state. Many environments have this property. For example, consider the well-known travelling salesman problem [12, p13]: history dependence arises because the salesman is not allowed to visit the same city twice. Note that it is often possible to transform a history dependent environment into a history independent one, by encoding information about prior history into an environment state. However, this can only be done at the expense of an exponential increase in the number of environment states. Intuitively, given a history dependent environment with state set $E$, which has an associated set of runs $\mathcal{R}$, we would need to create $|\mathcal{R} \times E|$ environment states. Since $|\mathcal{R}|$ is easily seen to be exponential in the size of $Ac \times E$ (even if we assume a polynomial bound on the length of runs), this implies that the transformation is not likely to be possible in polynomial time (or space). Hence although such a transformation is possible in principle, it is unlikely to be possible in practice.

Second, note that this definition allows for non-determinism in the environment. There is thus *uncertainty* about the result of performing an action in some state.

If $\tau(r) = \emptyset$, (where $r$ is assumed to end with an action), then there are no possible successor states to $r$. In this case, we say that there are *no allowable actions*, and that the run is *complete*. One important assumption we make is that every run is guaranteed to complete with length polynomial in the size of $Ac \times E$. This assumption may at first sight appear restrictive, and so some justification is necessary. Our main point is that exponential (or worse) runs *are of no practical interest whatsoever*: the *only* tasks of interest to us are those that require a polynomial (or better) number of actions to achieve. To see this, suppose we allowed runs that were exponential in the size of $Ac \times E$; say $O(2^{|Ac \times E|})$. Now consider a trivial environment, with just 10 states and 10 actions. Then in principle, such an environment would allow tasks that require $2^{100} = 1.2 \times 10^{30}$ actions to accomplish. Even if our agents could perform a $10^9$ actions per second[1] then such a task would require more time to carry out than there has been since the universe began. The exponential length of runs will rapidly eliminate any advantage we gain by multiplying the speed of our agent by a constant factor. The polynomial restriction on run length is, therefore, entirely reasonable if we are concerned with tasks of practical interest.

Before proceeding, we need to make clear a couple of assumptions about the way that transformer functions are *represented*. To understand what is meant by this, consider that

---

[1] A high performance desktop computer can carry out about this many operations per second.

the input to the decision problems we study will include some sort of representation of the behaviour of the environment, and more specifically, the environment's state transformer function $\tau$. Now, one possible description of $\tau$ is as a table that maps run/action pairs to the corresponding possible resulting environment states:

$$r_1, \alpha_1 \rightarrow \{e_1, e_2, \ldots\}$$
$$\ldots \quad \rightarrow \ldots$$
$$r_n, \alpha_n \rightarrow \{\ldots\}$$

Such a "verbose" encoding of $\tau$ will clearly be exponentially large (in the size of $E \times Ac$), but since the length of runs will be bounded by a polynomial in the size of $E \times Ac$, it will be finite. Once given such an encoding, finding an agent that can be guaranteed to achieve a set of goal states will, however, be comparatively easy. Unfortunately, of course, no such description of the environment will usually be available. In this paper, therefore, we will restrict our attention to environments whose state transformer function is described as a two-tape Turing machine, with the input (a run and an action) written on one tape; the output (the set of possible resultant states) is written on the other tape. It is assumed that to compute the resultant states, the Turing machine requires a number of steps that is at most polynomial in the length of the input. We refer to such environment representations as *concise*. In the remainder of this paper, we will assume that all state transformer functions are concisely represented.

Formally, we say an environment *Env* is a triple *Env* $= \langle E, \tau, e_0 \rangle$ where $E$ is a set of environment states, $\tau$ is a state transformer function, represented concisely, and $e_0 \in E$ is the initial state of the environment.

We now need to introduce a model of the agents that inhabit systems. Many architectures for agents have been reported in the literature [17], and one possibility would therefore be to directly use one of these models in our analysis. However, in order to ensure that our results are as general as possible, we choose to model agents simply as functions that map runs (assumed to end with an environment state) to actions (cf. [14, pp580–581]):

$$Ag : \mathcal{R} \rightarrow Ac$$

Notice that while environments are implicitly non-deterministic, agents are assumed to be deterministic.

We say a *system* is a pair containing an agent and an environment. Any system will have associated with it a set of possible runs; we denote the set of complete runs of agent $Ag$ in environment *Env* by $\mathcal{R}(Ag, Env)$. Formally, a sequence $(e_0, \alpha_0, e_1, \alpha_1, e_2, \ldots)$ represents a run of an agent $Ag$ in environment *Env* $= \langle E, \tau, e_0 \rangle$ iff

1. $e_0 = \tau(\epsilon)$ and $\alpha_0 = Ag(e_0)$ (where $\epsilon$ is the empty sequence); and
2. for $u > 0$,

$$e_u \in \tau((e_0, \alpha_0, \ldots, \alpha_{u-1})) \quad \text{where}$$
$$\alpha_u = Ag((e_0, \alpha_0, \ldots, e_u))$$

# 3   Agent Design Tasks

We build agents in order to carry out *tasks* for us. We can identify many different *types* of tasks. The two most obvious of these are *achievement tasks* and *maintenance tasks*, as follows [16]:

1. Achievement tasks are tasks with the general form "achieve state of affairs $\varphi$".
2. Maintenance tasks are tasks with the general form "maintain state of affairs $\varphi$".

Intuitively, an achievement task is specified by a number of "goal states"; the agent is required to bring about one of these goal states. Note that we do not care *which* goal state is achieved — all are considered equally good. Achievement tasks are probably the most commonly studied form of task in artificial intelligence. Many well-known AI problems (such as the towers of Hanoi) are instances of achievement tasks. An achievement task is specified by some subset $\mathcal{G}$ (for "good" or "goal") of environment states $E$. An agent is *successful* on a particular run if the run results in one of the states in $\mathcal{G}$, that is, if every run of the agent in the environment results in one of the states $\mathcal{G}$. We say an agent *Ag* succeeds in an environment *Env* if every run of the agent in that environment is successful. An agent thus succeeds in an environment if it can *guarantee* to bring about one of the goal states.

We refer to a tuple $\langle Env, \mathcal{G} \rangle$, where *Env* is an environment and $\mathcal{G} \subseteq E$ is a set of environment states as a *task environment*. We can identify the following agent design problem for achievement tasks:

ACHIEVEMENT AGENT DESIGN
*Given*: task environment $\langle Env, \mathcal{G} \rangle$.
*Answer*: "Yes" if there exists an agent *Ag* that succeeds in $\langle Env, \mathcal{G} \rangle$, "No" otherwise.

This decision problem amounts to determining whether the following second-order formula is true, for a given task environment $\langle Env, \mathcal{G} \rangle$:

$$\exists Ag \cdot \forall r \in \mathcal{R}(Ag, Env) \cdot \exists e \in \mathcal{G} \cdot e \text{ occurs in } r.$$

We emphasise that achievement tasks are emphatically *not* simply graph search problems. Because the environment can be *history dependent*, the solution to an achievement design problem must be a strategy, which dictates not simply which action to perform for any given environment state, but which action to perform *for any given history*. Such strategies will be exponentially large in the size of $E \times Ac$.

*Example 1.*  Consider the environment whose state transformer function is illustrated by the graph in Figure 1; the initial state is $e_0$. In this environment, an agent has just four available actions ($\alpha_1$ to $\alpha_4$ respectively), and the environment can be in any of six states ($e_0$ to $e_5$). History dependence in this environment arises because the agent is not allowed to execute the same action twice. Arcs between states in Figure 1 are labelled with the actions that cause the state transitions — note that the environment is non-deterministic. Now consider the achievement problems determined by the following goal sets:

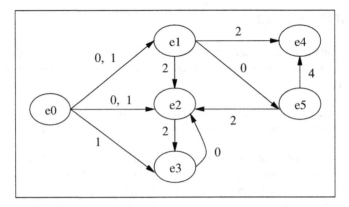

**Fig. 1.** The state transitions of an example environment: Arcs between environment states are labelled with the sets of actions corresponding to transitions. Note that this environment is *history dependent*, because agents are not allowed to perform the same action twice. So, for example, if the agent reached state $e_2$ by performing $\alpha_0$ then $\alpha_2$, it would not be able to perform $\alpha_2$ again in order to reach $e_3$.

 - $\mathcal{G}_1 = \{e_2\}$
   An agent can reliably achieve $\mathcal{G}_1$ by performing $\alpha_1$, the result of which will be either $e_1$, $e_2$, or $e_3$. If $e_1$ results, the agent can perform $\alpha_0$ to take it to $e_5$ and then $\alpha_2$ to take it to $e_2$. If $e_3$ results, it can simply perform $\alpha_0$.
 - $\mathcal{G}_2 = \{e_3\}$
   There is no agent that can be guaranteed to achieve $\mathcal{G}_2$. If the agent performs $\alpha_1$, then any of $e_1$ to $e_3$ might result. In particular, if $e_1$ results, the agent can only get to $e_3$ by performing $\alpha_2$ twice, which is not allowed.

A useful way to think about ACHIEVEMENT AGENT DESIGN is as the agent *playing a game* against the environment. In the terminology of game theory [2], this is exactly what is meant by a "game against nature". The environment and agent both begin in some state; the agent takes a turn by executing an action, and the environment responds with some state; the agent then takes another turn, and so on. The agent "wins" if it can *force* the environment into one of the goal states $\mathcal{G}$. The achievement design problem can then be understood as asking whether or not there is a *winning strategy* that can be played against the environment *Env* to bring about one of $\mathcal{G}$. This class of problem — determining whether or not there is a winning strategy for one player in a particular two-player game — is closely associated with PSPACE-complete problems [12, pp459–474].

Just as many tasks can be characterised as problems where an agent is required to bring about some state of affairs, so many others can be classified as problems where the agent is required to *avoid* some state of affairs, that is, to maintain some invariant condition. As an extreme example, consider a nuclear reactor agent, the purpose of which is to ensure that the reactor never enters a "meltdown" state. Somewhat more mundanely, we can imagine a software agent, one of the tasks of which is to ensure that a particular file is never simultaneously open for both reading and writing. We refer to such task environments as *maintenance* task environments.

A maintenance task environment is formally defined by a pair $\langle Env, \mathcal{B} \rangle$, where $Env$ is an environment, and $\mathcal{B} \subseteq E$ is a subset of $E$ that we refer to as the "bad", or "failure" states — these are the environment states that the agent must avoid. An agent is successful with respect to a maintenance task environment $\langle Env, \mathcal{B} \rangle$ if no state in $\mathcal{B}$ occurs on any run in $\mathcal{R}(Ag, Env)$.

*Example 2.* Consider again the environment in Figure 1, and the maintenance tasks defined by the following bad sets:

- $\mathcal{B}_1 = \{e_5\}$
  There is clearly an agent that can avoid $e_5$. After the agent performs its first action (either $\alpha_0$ or $\alpha_1$), one of the three states $e_1$ to $e_3$ will result.
  If the state that results is $e_1$, then the agent can perform $\alpha_2$, after which either $e_4$ or $e_2$ will result; there will be no allowable moves in either case.
  If the state that results is $e_2$, then the agent can only perform $\alpha_2$, which will transform the environment to $e_4$. The only allowable move will then be $\alpha_0$ (if this has not already been performed — if it has, then there are no allowable moves); if the agent performs $\alpha_0$, then environment state $e_2$ will result, from where there will be no allowable moves.
  Finally, if the state that results is $e_3$, then the agent can only perform $\alpha_0$ and then $\alpha_2$, which returns the environment to state $e_3$ from where there are no allowable moves.
- $\mathcal{B}_1 = \{e_2\}$
  No agent can be guaranteed to avoid $e_2$. Whether or not the first action is $\alpha_0$ or $\alpha_1$, it is possible that $e_2$ will result.

Given a maintenance task environment $\langle Env, \mathcal{B} \rangle$, the MAINTENANCE AGENT DESIGN decision problem simply involves determining whether or not there exists some agent that succeeds in $\langle Env, \mathcal{B} \rangle$. It is again useful to think of MAINTENANCE AGENT DESIGN as a game. This time, the agent wins if it manages to *avoid* $\mathcal{B}$. The environment, in the role of opponent, is attempting to force the agent into $\mathcal{B}$; the agent is successful if it has a winning strategy for avoiding $\mathcal{B}$. It is not hard to see that the MAINTENANCE AGENT DESIGN problem for a given $\langle Env, \mathcal{B} \rangle$ amounts to determining whether or not the following second-order formula is true:

$$\exists Ag \cdot \forall r \in \mathcal{R}(Ag, Env) \cdot \forall e \in \mathcal{B} \cdot e \text{ does not occur in } r.$$

Intuition suggests that MAINTENANCE AGENT DESIGN must be *harder* that ACHIEVEMENT AGENT DESIGN. This is because with achievement tasks, the agent is only required to bring about $\mathcal{G}$ *once*, whereas with maintenance tasks environments, the agent must avoid $\mathcal{B}$ *indefinitely*. However, this turns out not to be the case.

**Theorem 1 (From [16]).** *Both* ACHIEVEMENT AGENT DESIGN *and* MAINTENANCE AGENT DESIGN *are* PSPACE-*complete in the case where environments may be history dependent, and any run is at most polynomial in the size of* $E \times Ac$.

We remark that although the precise relationship of PSPACE-complete problems to, for example, NP-complete problems is not (yet) known, it is generally believed that they are much harder in practice. For this reason, PSPACE-completeness results are interpreted as much more negative than "mere" NP-completeness.

## 4  Optimistic Agent Design

In this paper, we focus on some variations of ACHIEVEMENT AGENT DESIGN and MAIN-TENANCE AGENT DESIGN. These variations allow us to consider weaker requirements for agent design, and also progressively more complex types of tasks for agents. The first variation we consider is *optimistic* agent design (cf. [8]). The intuition is that, in our current agent design problems, we are looking for an agent that can be *guaranteed* to carry out the task. That is, the agent is required to succeed with the task on *every possible* run. This is a rather severe requirement: after all, when we carry out tasks in the real world, there is frequently some possibility — even if rather remote — that we will fail. We would still be inclined to say that we have the capability to carry out the task, even though we know that, in principle at least, it is possible that we will fail.

This consideration is our motivation for a more relaxed notion of agent design. If $P$ denotes either the ACHIEVEMENT AGENT DESIGN or MAINTENANCE AGENT DESIGN, then by OPTIMISTIC $P$ we mean the variant of this problem in which an agent is deemed to succeed if there is *at least one run* of the agent in the environment that succeeds with respect to the task. So, for example, an instance of OPTIMISTIC ACHIEVEMENT AGENT DESIGN (OAD) is given by a tuple $\langle Env, \mathcal{G} \rangle$, as with ACHIEVEMENT AGENT DESIGN. The goal of the problem is to determine whether or not there exists an agent $Ag$ such that at least one member of $\mathcal{G}$ occurs on at least one run of $Ag$ when placed in $Env$. Formally, an OAD problem can be understood as determining whether the following second-order formula is true:

$$\exists Ag \cdot \exists r \in \mathcal{R}(Ag, Env) \cdot \exists e \in \mathcal{G} \cdot e \text{ occurs in } r.$$

Notice the difference between the pattern of quantifiers in this expression and that for ACHIEVEMENT AGENT DESIGN.

*Example 3.* Consider again the environment in Figure 1, and the optimistic achievement design problems defined by the following sets:

- $\mathcal{G}_3 = \{e_1\}$
  Recall that no agent can *guarantee* to bring about $e_1$. However, there clearly exists an agent that can optimistically achieve $e_1$: the agent simply performs $\alpha_0$.

Intuition tells us that optimistic variants of ACHIEVEMENT and MAINTENANCE AGENT DESIGN are easier than their regular variants, as we are proving an existential rather than a universal (one run rather than all runs). And for once, intuition turns out to be correct. We can prove the following.

**Theorem 2.** *Both* OAD *and* OMD *are* NP-*complete.*

*Proof. We do the proof for* OAD: *the* OMD *case is similar. We need to show that (i) the problem is in* NP; *and (ii) some known* NP-*complete problem can be reduced to* OAD *in polynomial time. Membership of* NP *is established by the following non-deterministic algorithm for* OAD. *Given an instance* $\langle Env, \mathcal{G} \rangle$ *of* OAD, *begin by guessing a run* $r \in \mathcal{R}$ *such that this run ends with a member of* $\mathcal{G}$, *and verify that the run is consistent with the state transformer function* $\tau$ *of Env. Since the length of the run will be at most polynomial in the size of Ac × E, guessing and verifying can be done in non-deterministic polynomial time. Given such a run, extracting the corresponding agent is trivial, and can be done in (deterministic) polynomial time.*

*To prove completeness, we reduce the* DIRECTED HAMILTONIAN CYCLE (DHC) *problem to* OAD *[6, p199]:*

DIRECTED HAMILTONIAN CYCLE (DHC):
*Given: A directed graph $G = (V, F \subseteq V \times V)$*
*Answer: "Yes" if G contains a directed Hamiltonian cycle, "No" otherwise.*

*The idea of the reduction is to encode the graph G directly in the state transformer function $\tau$ of the environment: actions correspond to edges of the graph, and success occurs when a Hamiltonian cycle has been found.*

*Formally, given an instance $G = (V, F \subseteq V \times V)$ of* DHC, *we generate an instance of* OAD *as follows. First, create the set of environment states as follows:*

$$E = V \cup \{succeed\}$$

*We then define the initial state of the environment as follows:*

$$e_0 = v_0$$

*We create an action $\alpha_{i,j}$ corresponding to every arc in G:*

$$Ac = \{\alpha_{i,j} \mid \langle v_i, v_j \rangle \in F\}$$

*We define $\mathcal{G}$ to be a singleton:*

$$\mathcal{G} = \{succeed\}$$

*And finally, we define the state transformer function $\tau$ in two parts. The first case deals with the first action of the agent:*

$$\tau(\epsilon \cdot \alpha_{0,j}) = \begin{cases} \{v_j\} & \text{if } \langle v_0, v_j \rangle \in F \\ \emptyset & \text{otherwise.} \end{cases}$$

*The second case deals with subsequent actions:*

$$\tau(r \cdot v_i \cdot \alpha_{i,j}) = \begin{cases} \emptyset & \text{if } v_j \text{ occurs in } r \cdot v_i \text{ and } v_j \neq v_0 \\ \{succeed\} & \text{if } v_j = v_0 \text{ and every } v \in V \text{ occurs in } r \cdot v_i \\ \{v_j\} & \text{if } \langle v_i, v_j \rangle \in F \end{cases}$$

*An agent can only succeed in this environment if it visits every vertex of the original graph. An agent will fail if it revisits any node. Since the construction is clearly polynomial time, we are done.*

As an aside, note that this proof essentially involves interpreting the Hamiltonian cycle problem as a game between a deterministic, history dependent environment, and an agent. The objective of the game is to visit every vertex of the graph exactly once. The game is history dependent because the "player" is not allowed to revisit vertices. Also note that for deterministic environments, optimistic and "regular" design problems coincide (there will only be one possible run of any given agent in a deterministic environment). An immediate corollary of the above result is thus that for deterministic environments, the achievement and maintenance design problems are NP-complete.

One could argue that simply knowing there exists an agent that has some non-zero probability $p$ of achieving its design objectives is not very useful unless we actually know the value of $p$. This begs for the analysis of a related problem, *probabilistic agent design*: is there an agent that achieves some design objectives with probability at least $p$? We leave consideration of such problems for future work.

## 5   Disjunctive Agent Design

The next variations of agent design that we consider involve *combining* achievement and maintenance problems. The idea is that we specify a task by means of *both* a set $G \subseteq E$ and a set $B \subseteq E$. A run will be said to satisfy such a task if it contains at least one state in $G$, and contains no states in $B$. As before, we say an agent $Ag$ succeeds in an environment $Env$ with such a task if every run of the agent in the environment satisfies the task, i.e., if every run contains at least one state in $G$ and no states in $B$. Note that we do not require the *same* states to be achieved on different runs — all states in $G$ are considered equally good.

*Example 4.* With respect to the environment in Figure 1, consider the following combined design tasks:

- $G_4 = \{e_2\}$ and $B_3 = \{e_4\}$.
  There is clearly an agent that can be guaranteed to succeed with this task. The agent simply uses the strategy described above for the achievement task of $e_2$; this strategy avoids $e_4$.
- $G_5 = \{e_2\}$ and $B_4 = \{e_5\}$.
  There is no agent that can be guaranteed to bring about $e_2$ while avoiding $e_5$.

We refer to a triple $\langle Env, G, B \rangle$, where $Env$ is an environment, and $G, B \subseteq E$, as a *combined task environment*. Obviously, if $G \subseteq B$, then no agent will exist to carry out the task.

It turns out that the COMBINED AGENT DESIGN problem is in fact no harder than either ACHIEVEMENT AGENT DESIGN or MAINTENANCE AGENT DESIGN. (The problem is of course no easier, as any ACHIEVEMENT AGENT DESIGN problem $\langle Env, G \rangle$ can trivially be reduced to a COMBINED AGENT DESIGN problem $\langle Env, G, \emptyset \rangle$.) We will see that it is in fact a special case of a yet more general type of problem, called *disjunctive* agent design. The idea in a disjunctive task is that we give an agent a number of *alternative* goals to achieve, where each goal is associated with a corresponding invariant condition.

An agent is successful with such a task if, on every possible run, it brings about one of the goals without invalidating the corresponding invariance.

To make this more precise, a disjunctive agent design problem is specified using a set of pairs with the form:

$$\{\langle \mathcal{G}_1, \mathcal{B}_1 \rangle, \ldots, \langle \mathcal{G}_n, \mathcal{B}_n \rangle\}$$

Here, $\mathcal{G}_i$ is a set of goal states and $\mathcal{B}_i$ is the invariant corresponding to $\mathcal{G}_i$. A run will be said to satisfy such a task if every run satisfies at least one of the pairs $\langle \mathcal{G}_i, \mathcal{B}_i \rangle \in \{\langle \mathcal{G}_1, \mathcal{B}_1 \rangle, \ldots, \langle \mathcal{G}_n, \mathcal{B}_n \rangle\}$. In other words, a run $r$ satisfies task $\{\langle \mathcal{G}_1, \mathcal{B}_1 \rangle, \ldots, \langle \mathcal{G}_n, \mathcal{B}_n \rangle\}$ if it satisfies $\langle \mathcal{G}_1, \mathcal{B}_1 \rangle$ or it satisfies $\langle \mathcal{G}_2, \mathcal{B}_2 \rangle$ or ... or it satisfies $\langle \mathcal{G}_n, \mathcal{B}_n \rangle$.

Formally, this problem involves asking whether the following second-order formula is true:

$$\exists Ag \cdot \forall r \in \mathcal{R}(Ag, Env) \cdot \exists i \cdot [(\exists e \in \mathcal{G}_i \cdot e \text{ is in } r) \text{ and } (\forall e \in \mathcal{B}_i \cdot e \text{ is not in } r)]$$

Notice the following subtleties of this definition:

- An agent is *not* required to bring about the *same* goal on each run in order to be considered to have succeeded. Different goals on different runs are perfectly acceptable.
- If an agent brings about some state in $\mathcal{G}_i$ on a run $r$ and no state in $r$ is in $\mathcal{B}_i$, then the fact that some states in $\mathcal{B}_j$ occur in $r$ (for $i \neq j$) is not relevant — the agent is still deemed to have succeeded on run $r$.

We can prove the following.

**Theorem 3.** DISJUNCTIVE AGENT DESIGN *is* PSPACE-*complete.*

*Proof. As before, we need to establish that* DISJUNCTIVE AGENT DESIGN *(i) is in* PSPACE, *and (ii) is* PSPACE-*hard.* PSPACE-*hardness follows immediately from Theorem 1: any instance of* ACHIEVEMENT AGENT DESIGN *or* MAINTENANCE AGENT DESIGN *can be immediately reduced to an instance of* DISJUNCTIVE AGENT DESIGN. *We therefore focus on establishing membership of* PSPACE.

*We give the design of a non-deterministic polynomial space Turing machine M that accepts instances of the problem that have a successful outcome, and rejects all others. The inputs to the algorithm will be a task environment* $\langle Env, \{\langle \mathcal{G}_1, \mathcal{B}_1 \rangle, \ldots, \langle \mathcal{G}_n, \mathcal{B}_n \rangle\}\rangle$ *together with a run* $r = (e_0, \alpha_0, \ldots, \alpha_{k-1}, e_k)$ — *the algorithm actually decides whether or not there is an agent that will succeed in the environment given this current run. Initially, the run r will be set to the empty sequence* $\epsilon$. *The algorithm for M is as follows:*

1. *if r ends with an environment state in* $\mathcal{G}_i$, *for some* $1 \leq i \leq n$, *then check whether any member of* $\mathcal{B}_i$ *occurs in r — if the answer is no, then M accepts;*
2. *if there are no allowable actions given r, then M rejects;*
3. *non-deterministically choose an action* $\alpha \in Ac$, *and then for each* $e \in \tau(r \cdot \alpha)$ *recursively call M with the run* $r \cdot \alpha \cdot e$;
4. *if all of these accept, then M accepts, otherwise M rejects.*

*The algorithm thus non-deterministically explores the space of all possible agents. Notice that since any run will be at most polynomial in the size of $E \times Ac$, the depth of recursion stack will be also be at most polynomial in the size of $E \times Ac$. Hence M requires only polynomial space. Hence* DISJUNCTIVE AGENT DESIGN *is in non-deterministic polynomial space (*NPSPACE*). But since* PSPACE = NPSPACE *[12, p150], it follows that* DISJUNCTIVE AGENT DESIGN *is also in* PSPACE.

Note that in DISJUNCTIVE AGENT DESIGN, we require an agent that, on every run, both achieves some state in $\mathcal{G}_i$ while avoiding all states in $\mathcal{B}_i$. We can consider a variant of DISJUNCTIVE AGENT DESIGN, as follows. The idea is that on every run, an agent must *either* achieve some state in $\mathcal{G}_i$, *or* avoid all states in $\mathcal{B}_i$. This condition is given by the following second-order formula:

$$\exists Ag \cdot \forall r \in \mathcal{R}(Ag, Env) \cdot \exists i \cdot [(\exists e \in \mathcal{G}_i \cdot e \text{ is in } r) \text{ or } (\forall e \in \mathcal{B}_i \cdot e \text{ is not in } r)]$$

We refer to this problem as WEAK DISJUNCTIVE AGENT DESIGN. It is not difficult to prove that this problem is also PSPACE-complete.

**Theorem 4.** WEAK DISJUNCTIVE AGENT DESIGN *is* PSPACE-*complete.*

*Proof.* PSPACE-*hardness follows from Theorem 1. To show membership, we give the design of a non-deterministic polynomial space Turing machine M that will decide the problem — the idea is similar to Theorem 3:*

1. *if r ends with an environment state in $\mathcal{G}_i$, for some $1 \le i \le n$, then M accepts;*
2. *if there are no allowable actions given r, and there is some $1 \le i \le n$ such that no element of $\mathcal{B}_i$ occurs on r, then M accepts;*
3. *if there are no allowable actions given r, then M rejects;*
4. *non-deterministically choose an action $\alpha \in Ac$, and then for each $e \in \tau(r \cdot \alpha)$ recursively call M with the run $r \cdot \alpha \cdot e$;*
5. *if all of these accept, then M accepts, otherwise M rejects.*

*The remainder of the proof is as Theorem 3.*

## 6    Related Work

Probably the most relevant work from mainstream computer science to that discussed in this paper has been on the application of temporal logic to reasoning about systems [9, 10]. Temporal logic has been particularly applied to the specification of *non-terminating* systems. Temporal logic is particularly appropriate for the specification of such systems because it allows a designer to succinctly express complex properties of infinite sequences of states.

We identified several decision problems for agent design, and closely related problems have also been studied in the computer science literature. Perhaps the closest to our view is the work of Manna, Pnueli, Wolper, and colleagues on the automatic synthesis of systems from temporal logic specifications [4,11,13]. In this work, tasks are specified as formulae of temporal logic, and constructive proof methods for temporal logic are used to construct model-like structures for these formulae, from which the desired system can then be extracted. The main difference with our work is that research on the synthesis of programs from temporal logic specifications has focussed on much richer specification languages than those considered here, but in much simpler environmental settings. It is generally assumed that environments are deterministic, for example. However, our results can be seen as establishing asymptotic bounds on the complexity of the associated synthesis problems: see the discussion in [16].

In artificial intelligence, the planning problem is most closely related to our achievement tasks [1]. Bylander was probably the first to undertake a systematic study of the complexity of the planning problem; he showed that the (propositional) STRIPS decision problem is PSPACE-complete [3]. Building on his work, many other variants of the planning problem have been studied — a recent example is [8]. The main differences between our work and this are as follows:

- Most complexity results in the planning literature assume *declarative specifications* of goals and actions — the STRIPS representation is commonly used. In some cases, it is therefore not clear whether the results obtained reflect the complexity of the decision task, or whether they are an artifact of the chosen representation. Some researchers, noting this, have considered "flat" representations, where, as in our work, goals are specified as sets of states, rather than as logical formulae [8].
- Most researchers have ignored the properties of the environment; in particular, we are aware of no work that considers history dependence. Additionally, most research assumes deterministic environments.
- As far as we are aware, no other research in AI planning has considered complex task specifications — the focus appears to be almost exclusively on achievement goals.

Recently, there has been renewed interest by the artificial intelligence planning community in *Partially Observable Markov Decision Processes* (POMDPs) [7]. Put simply, the goal of solving a POMDP is to determine an optimal policy for acting in an environment in which there is uncertainty about the environment state, and which is non-deterministic. Finding an optimal policy for a POMDP problem is similar to our agent design problem.

## 7    Conclusions

In this paper, we have investigated the computational complexity of two important classes of agent design problem. In a combined agent design problem, we define a task via a set of goal states and a set of states corresponding to an invariant; we ask whether there exists an agent that can be guaranteed to achieve the goal while maintaining the invariant. In a disjunctive agent design problem, a task is specified by a set of goals and corresponding invariants; we ask whether there exists an agent that will bring about a goal state while maintaining the corresponding invariant. We have demonstrated that both of these problems are PSPACE-complete, and are hence no worse than the (intuitively simpler) achievement and maintenance problems discussed in [16].

We are currently investigating one obvious generalisation of agent design problems, to allow for arbitrary boolean combinations of tasks, rather than simple disjunctions.

Cases where the PSPACE-completeness results collapse to NP or P are also being investigated. Finally, multi-agent variants seem worthy of study (cf. [15]).

**Acknowledgments.** We thank the reviewers for their detailed, insightful, and extremely helpful comments.

# References

1. J. F. Allen, J. Hendler, and A. Tate, editors. *Readings in Planning*. Morgan Kaufmann Publishers: San Mateo, CA, 1990.
2. K. Binmore. *Fun and Games: A Text on Game Theory*. D. C. Heath and Company: Lexington, MA, 1992.
3. T. Bylander. The computational complexity of propositional STRIPS planning. *Artificial Intelligence*, 69(1-2):165–204, 1994.
4. E. M. Clarke and E. A. Emerson. Design and synthesis of synchronization skeletons using branching time temporal logic. In D. Kozen, editor, *Logics of Programs — Proceedings 1981 (LNCS Volume 131)*, pages 52–71. Springer-Verlag: Berlin, Germany, 1981.
5. R. Fagin, J. Y. Halpern, Y. Moses, and M. Y. Vardi. *Reasoning About Knowledge*. The MIT Press: Cambridge, MA, 1995.
6. M. R. Garey and D. S. Johnson. *Computers and Intractability: A Guide to the Theory of NP-Completeness*. W. H. Freeman: New York, 1979.
7. L. P. Kaelbling, M. L. Littman, and A. R. Cassandra. Planning and acting in partially observable stochastic domains. *Artificial Intelligence*, 101:99–134, 1998.
8. M. L. Littman, J. Goldsmith, and M. Mundhenk. The computational complexity of probabilistic planning. *Journal of AI Research*, 9:1–36, 1998.
9. Z. Manna and A. Pnueli. *The Temporal Logic of Reactive and Concurrent Systems*. Springer-Verlag: Berlin, Germany, 1992.
10. Z. Manna and A. Pnueli. *Temporal Verification of Reactive Systems — Safety*. Springer-Verlag: Berlin, Germany, 1995.
11. Z. Manna and P. Wolper. Synthesis of communicating processes from temporal logic specifications. *ACM Transactions on Programming Languages and Systems*, 6(1):68–93, January 1984.
12. C. H. Papadimitriou. *Computational Complexity*. Addison-Wesley: Reading, MA, 1994.
13. A. Pnueli and R. Rosner. On the synthesis of a reactive module. In *Proceedings of the Sixteenth ACM Symposium on the Principles of Programming Languages (POPL)*, pages 179–190, January 1989.
14. S. Russell and D. Subramanian. Provably bounded-optimal agents. *Journal of AI Research*, 2:575–609, 1995.
15. M. Tennenholtz and Y. Moses. On cooperation in a multi-entity model: Preliminary report. In *Proceedings of the Eleventh International Joint Conference on Artificial Intelligence (IJCAI-89)*, Detroit, MI, 1989.
16. M. Wooldridge. The computational complexity of agent design problems. In *Proceedings of the Fourth International Conference on Multi-Agent Systems (ICMAS-2000)*, pages 341–348, Boston, MA, 2000.
17. M. Wooldridge and N. R. Jennings. Intelligent agents: Theory and practice. *The Knowledge Engineering Review*, 10(2):115–152, 1995.

# Updating Mental States from Communication

A.F. Dragoni[1], P. Giorgini[2], and L. Serafini[3]

[1] University of Ancona, 60131, Ancona, Italy. dragon@inform.unian.it
[2] DISA, University of Trento, 38100, Trento, Italy. pgiorgini@cs.unitn.it
[3] ITC-IRST, 38050, Trento, Italy. serafini@irst.itc.it

**Abstract.** In order to perform effective communication agents must be able to foresee the effects of their utterances on the addressee's mental state. In this paper we investigate the update of the mental state of a hearer agent as a consequence of the utterance performed by a speaker agent. Given an agent communication language with a STRIPS-like semantics, we propose a set of criteria that allow the binding of the speaker's mental state to its uttering of a certain sentence. On the basis of these criteria, we give an abductive procedure that the hearer can adopt to partially recognize the speaker's mental state, on the basis of its utterances. This procedure can be adopted by the hearer to update its own mental state and its image of the speaker's mental state.

## 1 Introduction

In multi agent systems, if agents are not designed with embeddeda pre-compiled knowledge about the beliefs, intentions, abilities and perspective of other agents, they need to exchange information to improve their social activities. However, in real application domains, communication might be a limited resource (limited bandwidth, low signal/noise ratio etc.). In such cases, it is very important that, when deciding whether to send a message, agents consider their expected benefits vs. the costs of communication.

BDI agents (namely agents able to have Beliefs, Desires and Intentions) [23,24,25, 18,8,28] are supposed to have a, so called, *mental state* which contains beliefs, desires and intentions about the environment, and about the other agents' beliefs, desires and intentions. The strong assumprion underlying such a model is that agents' behaviour strongly depends on their mental state. Under this assumption an agent can influence the behaviour of another agent by trying to change its mental state. Communication is the main road for agents to affects the behavior of other agents by exchanging information about the environment and their beliefs, desires and intentions.

Communication is also supposed to be intentional, i.e. activated by the speaker's reasoning about its own beliefs, desires and intentions. In other words, it is generally possible to regard utterances as the consequence of the speaker's being in a particular mental state, that provokes its desire to influence the hearer's mental state. This position is very general and is independent of the particular class of speech acts (assertive, commissive, directive, declarative or expressive). If utterances are the effects of mental conditions, it seems natural to suppose that the hearer tries to recognize the speaker's mental state through some form of backward reasoning (e.g., abduction) from the kind and the content of the received communication to the hypothetical mental state that

C. Castelfranchi, Y. Lespérance (Eds.): Intelligent Agents VII, LNAI 1986, pp. 15–30, 2001.

originated it. If this were possible, then we could develop logical theories that partially predict dialogue.

The main goal of this paper is to provide some methods that a hearer can adopt to recognize the speaker's mental state on the basis of its utterances. We propose:

1. a formal representation of agents' mental states based on the theory of contexts [3];
2. a causal relation between the mental state of an agent and its utterances, based on the plan-based theory of speech acts [4];
3. an abductive method that allows an agent to find a set of explanations of an utterance in terms its causes in the speaker's mental states.
4. a formal characterization of the updating of a mental state, formalized as a set of contexts.

The novelty of the paper stands in the fact that, not only do we devise an abductive theory for revising the mental state of an agent, but we also relate this theory to the semantics of agent communication languages.

The paper is structured as follows. In section 2 we present the theory of contexts used to formalize agents' mental states. Section 3 describes a simple explanatory scenario. Section 4 illustrates how the plan-based theory of speech acts can be used to correlate the speaker's mental state to its utterances. In section 5 we extend Konolige's definition of abduction, to the context framework. On the basis of contextual abduction, we define three basic operations on mental states: abductive expansion, abductive contraction and abductive revision. Section 6 applies the theory to an example. Finally, section 7 discusses the related work, and section 8 presents some conclusions and future work.

## 2   Mental States

Each agent is supposed to be characterized by a *mental state*. A mental state is a structure based on two primitive mental attitudes: *beliefs* and *desires*[1].

Following [3,11,12,13], we use *propositional contexts* to formalize agents' mental states. Roughly speaking a context can be though as a set of formulas of a logical language, closed under logical consequence (i.e., a theory) with a unique identifier. For any agent $i$, its sets of beliefs and intentions are represented by the contexts named $B_i$ and $I_i$, respectively. A formula $\phi$ in the context $B_i$ (denoted by the pair $B_i : \phi$) represents the fact that $i$ believes $\phi$ and, analogously, a formula $\phi$ in the context $I_i$ ($I_i : \phi$) represents the fact that $i$ has the intention to bring about $\phi$. In general beliefs and intentions of the agents might be expressed in different languages. Although contexts support it, multiple languages is not the main focus of this paper, we, therefore ,consider the simple case in which the languages for beliefs and intentions of all the agents coincide. The language of the beliefs and intention of each agent contains a set of proposition $p_1, p_2, \ldots$, used to

---

[1] Intuitively, intentions represent what the agent desires to be true (or false) and also believes could be true (or false). The "could" means that the agent is able to act in order to change the external world and/or the other agents mental states to reach the desired state of affairs. Of course, this opens many critical questions which are far aside the scope of this paper. However, although we distinguished between the two, we still continue the tradition of calling "intention" what should be better defined "desire".

represent the state of the environment, and a set of atomic formulas to represents beliefs and intentions of other agents. In particular the language is closed under the following condition:

If $\phi$ is a formula, then $B_j\phi$ and $I_j\phi$ are atomic formulas, for any agent $j$.

Formulas of the form $B_j\phi$ and $I_j\phi$ are called BDI atoms [2]. Reasoning capabilities of an agent $i$ on its beliefs and intentions, are represented in the contexts $B_i$ and $I_i$ by two sets of inference rules. Examples of reasoning capabilities could be any set of logical inference rules. Reasoning capabilities are supposed to be general purpose reasoning machineries, which do not contain special inference rules for BDI atoms. For the sake of this paper we suppose that any inference machinery is the set of rules for propositional logic. BDI atoms are considered as any other atomic formula. This implies, for instance, that $B_j\phi$ and $B_j(\phi \vee \phi)$ are considered as completely independent formulas. On the other hand, if agent $i$ ascribes to the agent $j$ enough reasoning capabilities, then either $i$ believes that $j$ believes both $\phi$ and $\phi \vee \phi$, or $i$ believes that $j$ believes neither $\phi$ nor $\phi \vee \phi$. This means that the context for $i$'s beliefs (namely $B_i$), either contains both $B_j\phi$ and $B_j\phi \vee \phi$, or it does not contain ether of them. The relation among BDI atoms in $B_i$ and $I_i$, therefore, depends on the reasoning capabilities that $i$ ascribes to $j$. The beliefs, the intentions, and the reasoning capabilities that $i$ ascribes to another agent $j$ are explicitly modeled by means of a mental state, called $i$'s *image of $j$'s mental state*. In particular, $i$'s beliefs about the beliefs and the intentions of $j$, are represented by the contexts $B_iB_j$ and $B_iI_j$, respectively. The same representation is used to formalize $i$'s intentions regarding $j$'s beliefs and intentions, that is the contexts $I_iB_j$ and $I_iI_j$. Analogously, $i$'s beliefs about $j$'s beliefs about another agent $k$ are formalized by the pair of contexts $B_iB_jB_k$ and $B_iB_jI_k$. This iteration can go on infinitely, but, in the cases of artificial agents with finite resources, it is more adequate to consider a finite amount of iterations. On the other hand, we do not put any upper-bound on the limit of nested beliefs and intentions. For the sake of the explanation we consider only three levels of nesting.

The intuitive interpretation of a formula depends on the context. For instance, as already said, the formula $\phi$ in the context $B_i$, denoted by $B_i : \phi$, expresses the fact that agent $i$ believes $\phi$. The same formula in the context $B_iB_jI_i$, denoted by $B_iB_jI_i : \phi$, expresses the fact that $i$ believes that $j$ believes that $i$ intends $\phi$. On the other hand, different formulas in different contexts can represent the same fact. For instance, the formulas $\phi$ in the context $B_iI_j$ and the formula $I_j\phi$ in the context $B_i$ have the same meaning. The effect of this "meaning overlapping" is that, contexts cannot be considered as isolated theories, and that the set of theorems of a context might affect the set of theorems in another context. The interaction among contexts is formalized by *bridge rules*. In particular, we use the following bridge rules between contexts in a mental state and contexts in images of mental state:

$$\frac{\alpha : B_i\phi}{\alpha B_i : \phi}\ \mathcal{R}_{dn.B} \qquad \frac{\alpha B_i : \phi}{\alpha : B_i\phi}\ \mathcal{R}_{up.B} \qquad \frac{\alpha : I_i\phi}{\alpha I_i : \phi}\ \mathcal{R}_{dn.I} \qquad \frac{\alpha I_i : \phi}{\alpha : I_i\phi}\ \mathcal{R}_{up.I}$$

where $\alpha$ is any context name. $\mathcal{R}_{dn.B}$ and $\mathcal{R}_{dn.I}$ are called *reflection down*, whereas $\mathcal{R}_{up.B}$ and $\mathcal{R}_{up.I}$ *reflection up*. The beliefs and the intentions of an agent are not independent. The relation between the beliefs and the intentions of an agent can also be

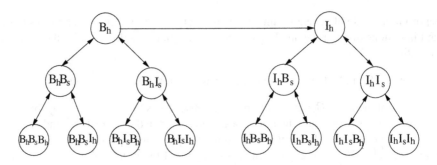

**Fig. 1.** Contexts for agent $h$

represented by bridge rules from the context of its beliefs to that of its intentions. For instance, the bridge rule:

$$\frac{B_i : raining}{I_i : bring\_umbrella} \ B2I$$

formalizes the fact that, if agent $i$ believes that *it is raining*, then $i$ intends *to bring an umbrella*.

Since we are interested in formalizing the effects of an utterance performed by a speaker on the beliefs and intentions of a hearer, we consider the two agents $s$ and $h$ denoting the speaker and hearer, respectively. Furthermore, we focus only on the effects of the utterance on the hearer's mental state. We therefore consider only the contexts for the hearer's beliefs and intentions (namely $B_h$ and $I_h$), the contexts for the hearer's beliefs and intentions regarding the speaker's beliefs and intentions (namely $B_h B_s$, $B_h I_s$, $I_h B_s$, and $I_h I_s$), and the contexts for the hearer's beliefs and intentions regarding the speaker's beliefs and intentions regarding the hearer's beliefs and intentions. Of course, this nesting could be extended indefinitely (for more details see [9,10,14]), but three levels (as depicted in figure 1, where circles represent contexts and arrows represent bridge rules) are sufficient to illustrate the abductive methods for the inference of mental states from communicative acts.

The logical systems that formalize the reasoning with a set of contexts connected by bridge rules are called multi-context systems [13].[2] Roughly speaking, a multi context system is a set of context connected by a set of bridge. rules. In the following we do not give a formal definition of multi-context system, we rather define a specific multi-context system suitable for our special case.

Let MC be the multi-context system composed of the contexts shown in figure 1 connected by the bridge rules $\mathcal{R}_{up.}$ and $\mathcal{R}_{dn.}$, and by a set of bridge rules $B2I$ from $B_h$ to $I_h$.

Deductions in MC are trees of wffs starting from a finite number of formulas (either axioms or assumptions), possibly belonging to distinct contexts, and applying a finite number of inference and bridge rules. A very common pattern of deduction in MC can

---

[2] In [13], multi-context systems are called multi-language systems to stress the fact that they allow for multiple distinct languages

be obtained by a combination of reflection down and reflection up. For instance, to prove $B_j\phi \supset B_j(\phi \vee \phi)$ in the context of its beliefs, $i$ can perform the following deduction:

$$\cfrac{\cfrac{\cfrac{\cfrac{B_i : B_j\phi}{B_iB_j : \phi} \, \mathcal{R}_{dn.B}}{B_iB_j : \phi \vee \psi} \, \vee I}{B_i : B_j(\phi \vee \psi)} \, \mathcal{R}_{up.B}}{B_i : B_j\phi \supset B_j(\phi \vee \psi)} \, \supset I$$

Notice that reflection down allows an agent $i$ to convert the belief $B_j\phi$, into a simpler, but equivalent, format in the context of the beliefs it ascribes to $j$. $i$ can therefore reason starting from $\phi$ in this context. Reflection up is used by $i$ to lift up, in its beliefs, the result of such a reasoning. This reasoning pattern allows $i$ to prove relations among BDI atoms.

A wff $\alpha : \phi$ is derivable from a set of axioms AX in MC (in symbols, $AX \vdash_{MC} \alpha : \phi$), if there is a deduction that ends with $\alpha : \phi$ and whose axioms are in AX. For a detailed description on the proof theory of MC we refer the reader to [13]. Given a set of axioms AX, for each context $\alpha$, let $\alpha^* = \{\phi \mid AX \vdash_{MC} \alpha : \phi\}$.

The *mental state* of the agent $h$ is defined as the pair of sets containing $h$'s beliefs and $h$'s intentions which are derivable in MC. In symbols $ms(h) = \langle B_h^*, I_h^* \rangle$. Analogously *$h$'s image of $s$' mental state* is composed of the set of $h$'s beliefs on $s$' beliefs and the set of $h$'s beliefs on $s$' intentions. In symbols $ms(h, s) = \langle B_h B_s^*, B_h I_s^* \rangle$. Finally $ms(h, s, h) = \langle B_h B_s B_h^*, B_h B_s I_h^* \rangle$, which stands for $s$'s image of $h$'s image of $s$'s image of $h$'s mental state. This definition can be straightforwardly generalized for any belief nesting.

According to the definition above, in MC hearer's mental states and hearer's images of mental states are completely determined by the set of axioms AX. The effects of the receipt of a message from the hearer, on its mental state and on its images of mental states, can be represented by a suitable change of the set of axioms AX into a new set of axioms AX'. For each context $\alpha$, we define the set $\alpha'^* = \{\phi \mid AX' \vdash_{MC} \alpha : \phi\}$. Analogously, we can provide the definition of the updated (due to the utterance) mental state and images of mental states $ms'(\ldots)$.

## 3 Working Example

Let consider the multi-context system MC represented in figure 2 (the labels indicate both the formulae that belong to the contexts and the bridge rules) and characterized by the following $B2I$ bridge rule and set of axioms AX.

$$\frac{B_h : temp\_higher\_20°}{I_h : air\_conditioning\_on} \, B2I \qquad\qquad (1)$$

If the hearer believes that the temperature is higher than 20 degrees, then it has the intention of switching conditioning on.

$$AX = \{B_h : (2), B_h : (3), B_h : (4), B_h B_s : (5)\}$$

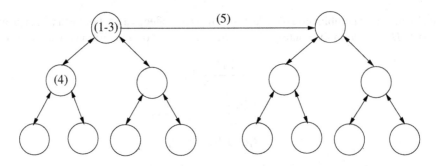

**Fig. 2.** Initial $h$'s mental state

$$\frac{\dfrac{B_h \,:\, B_s \neg air\_conditioning\_on}{B_h B_s \,:\, \neg air\_conditioning\_on}\mathcal{R}_{dn.B} \quad B_h B_s \,:\, (5)}{\dfrac{\dfrac{B_h B_s \,:\, temp\_higher\_20°}{B_h \,:\, B_s \, temp\_higher\_20°}\mathcal{R}_{up.B} \qquad\qquad B_h \,:\, (2)}{\dfrac{B_h \,:\, temp\_higher\_20°}{I_h \,:\, air\_conditioning\_on}B2I}\supset E}} \supset E$$

**Fig. 3.** The formula $I_h \,:\, air\_conditioning\_on$ is derivable, by axioms (5) and (2), from the assumption $B_h \,:\, B_s \, temp\_higher\_20° \supset temp\_higher\_20°$.

where:

$$B_s \, temp\_higher\_20° \supset temp\_higher\_20° \tag{2}$$

If $s$ believes that the temperature is higher than 20 degrees, then the temperature is higher than 20 degrees.

$$air\_conditioning\_on \supset \neg temp\_higher\_20° \tag{3}$$

If the conditioning is on, then the temperature is lower than 20 degrees.

$$B_s(temp\_higher\_20° \wedge air\_conditioning\_on) \supset I_s \, stop\_working \tag{4}$$

If $s$ believes that the temperature is higher than 20 degrees and that the conditioning is on, then $s$ intends to stop working.

$$\neg air\_conditioning\_on \supset temp\_higher\_20° \tag{5}$$

If the conditioning is off, then the temperature is higher than 20 degrees.

With the set of axioms AX, $h$ infers that, if $s$ believes that the conditioning is off, then $h$ adopts the intention of switching it on. In symbols:

$$AX, B_h \,:\, B_s \neg air\_conditioning\_on \vdash_{MC} I_h \,:\, air\_conditioning\_on$$

The corresponding deduction in MC is shown in figure 3.

## 4   Plan-Based Model of Speech Acts

The plan-based vision of *speech acts* [4], which treats them as actions and represents them as STRIPS-like operators, offers us an intuitive way to correlate the speaker's mental state to its utterances. The "trick" is in the modeling of the speech acts' preconditions. To illustrate this idea we use a simplified and revised version of the INFORM operator which is the prototypical member of the assertive speech act class [26].

In a plan-based theory of speech acts, INFORM$(s, h, \phi)$ is generally defined to be an action whose main effect on hearer's mental state is that the hearer believes that the speaker believes the propositional content $\phi$, and its prerequisite is that the speaker believes $\phi$ (sincerity).

| Speech act | Preconditions | Main effects |
|---|---|---|
| INFORM$(s, h, \phi)$ | $\phi \in B_s^*$ | $\phi \in B_h B_s^*$ |

The structure of this simple operator is closely related to the one by Cohen and Perrault [4]. We envisage, however, a larger range of effects described in the following:

1. The effects of the INFORM operator given by Cohen and Perrault [4] are the main effects here. The complete effects of a speech act on the hearer's mental state are beyond the speaker's control. We think that part of these *perlocutionary effects* are the result of some kind of abductive reasoning performed by the hearer from the received communication and from his actual mental state (which is in general different from the speaker's image of the hearer's mental state).
2. The precondition of the INFORM operator does not include the speaker's goal to perform such a speech act. As we see later, the speaker's actual intentions which leads to the execution of the speech act, are ascribed by the hearer to the speaker, again with some kind of abductive reasoning.

The basic assumption in this paper is that there is a causal relationship between an agent's mental state and its possible uttering of a sentence. We may say that $s$ plans an INFORM$(s, h, \phi)$ because of the facts that:

**I1.** $s$ *has the intention* to bring $h$ in a mental state where a formula $\psi$ (which might differ from $\phi$ itself) is either believed or intended by $h$; i.e., either $\psi \in I_s B_h'^*$ or $\psi \in I_s I_h'^*$.

**I2.** $s$ *doesn't believe* that $h$ is already in that mental state: $\psi \notin B_s B_h^*$ (resp. $\psi \notin B_s I_h^*$).

**I3.** $s$ *believes* that if it performs the INFORM act, then $h$ will be in a mental state in which it believes (resp. intends) $\psi$; i.e., $\psi \in B_s B_h'^*$ (resp. $\psi \in B_s I_h'^*$).

**I4.** $s$ can perform the INFORM; that is, INFORM's precondition holds before and after $s$ performs the speech act; i.e., $\phi \in B_s^*$ and $\phi \in B_s'^*$.

## 5   Contextual Abduction and Revision

Before introducing abduction for contexts, let us briefly recall the main concepts of causal theories, abduction, and abductive explanation introduced by Konolige in [16]. Roughly speaking, abduction is an abstract hypothetical inferential schema that, given a causal theory of the domain, and an observation on a set of observable effects, looks for an explanation for them. An explanation for an observation is a minimal set of hypotheses, chosen among a set of possible causes, which if "added" to the causal theory, justify the observation. Syntactic propositional accounts of abduction formalize *causes* and *effects* as literals of a finite propositional language $L$, and the causal theory of the domain (*domain theory*) as a propositional theory of $L$.

A *simple causal theory* on a finite propositional language $L$, is a tuple

$$T = \langle C, E, \Sigma \rangle$$

where $C$ and $E$ are sets of literals of $L$, and $\Sigma$ is a theory on $L$. An *abductive explanation* (*ABE*) of an observation $O \subseteq E$, under a domain theory $\Sigma$, is a finite set $A \subseteq C$ such that:

- $\Sigma \cup A \nvdash \bot$ ($A$ is consistent with $\Sigma$)
- $\Sigma \cup A \vdash O$
- $A$ is subset-minimal over sets satisfying the first two conditions.

A *Simple Multi-Context Causal Theory* MT for a multi-context MC[3] is a family, $\{T_\alpha = \langle C_\alpha, E_\alpha, \Sigma_\alpha \rangle\}$ composed of a Simple Causal Theory $T_\alpha$ for each context $\alpha$ of MC. We introduce the extra hypothesis that for all $\alpha$, $E_\alpha \subseteq C_\alpha$. This is because we accept the fact that each effect can be regarded as the explanation of itself.

We define

$$\mathbf{C} \overset{\triangle}{=} \{\alpha : \sigma \mid \sigma \in C_\alpha\}$$

$$\mathbf{\Sigma} \overset{\triangle}{=} \{\alpha : \sigma \mid \sigma \in \Sigma_\alpha\}$$

respectively, the *causes* and the *domain theory* of MT. An *Abductive Explanation* (ABE) for an observation $O \subseteq E_\alpha$ in a context $\alpha$ under the domain theory $\mathbf{\Sigma}$, is a set $\mathbf{A} \subseteq \mathbf{C}$, such that:

1. $\forall \beta, \ \mathbf{\Sigma} \cup \mathbf{A} \nvdash_{\mathsf{MC}} \beta : \bot$: $\mathbf{A}$ is consistent with $\mathbf{\Sigma}$ in any context.
2. $\mathbf{\Sigma} \cup \mathbf{A} \vdash_{\mathsf{MC}} \alpha : O$: the observation $O$ can be derived in $\alpha$ from the set of axioms $\mathbf{A}$ and the domain theory $\mathbf{\Sigma}$.
3. $\mathbf{A}$ is the minimal set satisfying conditions 1 and 2. I.e., for any set $\mathbf{B} \subseteq \mathbf{C}$ satisfying condition 1 and 2, $\mathbf{B} \not\subset \mathbf{A}$.

From the decidability of MC (see [13]), and the fact that the set of possible explanations is finite, we can conclude that the problem of finding an ABE of an observation $O$ under the domain theory $\mathbf{\Sigma}$ is decidable.

*Example 1.* Let us consider the situation where the domain theory is composed by the set of axiom $\mathbf{\Sigma} = \{(2)-(5)\}$, and the set of causes and effects of the Simple Causal Theory of each context of MT are defined as follows:

- $E_{B_h} = E_{B_h B_s} = E_{B_h B_s B_h} = \{air\_conditioning\_on, temp\_higher\_20°\}$
  beliefs and nested beliefs about temperature and about the conditioning are considered observable effects.

---

[3] In the rest of the paper, the reference to the multi-context MC is left implicit.

- $E_{I_h} = E_{B_h I_s} = \{air\_conditioning\_on, stop\_working\}$
  intentions and beliefs about the speaker's intention regarding the conditioning and working are considered observable effects.
- For any other context $\alpha$, $E_\alpha = \emptyset$
  we are not interested in effects in contexts different from the one mentioned above.
- $C_{B_h} = C_{B_h B_s} = C_{B_h B_s B_h} = \{air\_conditioning\_on, temp\_higher\_20°\}$
  beliefs and nested beliefs about the temperature and about the conditioning are considered possible causes of the observable effects.
- $C_{I_h} = C_{B_h I_s} = \{air\_conditioning\_on, stop\_working\}$
  beliefs and intentions regarding the speaker's intention regarding the conditioning and working are considered possible causes of the observable effects.
- For any other context $\alpha$, $C_\alpha = \emptyset$
  we are not interested in causes in contexts different from the one mentioned above.

An ABE of the observation $I_h : air\_conditioning\_on$ is:

$$\{B_h B_s : \neg air\_conditioning\_on\}$$

Indeed we have that:

1. $\Sigma, B_h B_s : \neg air\_conditioning\_on \nvdash_{\mathsf{MC}} \beta : \bot$, for any context $\beta$ of MC;
2. $\Sigma, B_h B_s : \neg air\_conditioning\_on \vdash_{\mathsf{MC}} I_h : air\_conditioning\_on$, see deduction in Figure 3;
3. $\{B_h B_s : \neg air\_conditioning\_on\}$ is minimal.

An ABE of the observation $B_h I_s : stop\_working$ is

$$\{B_h B_s : temp\_higher\_20°, B_h B_s : air\_conditioning\_on\} \tag{6}$$

$B_h B_s : temp\_higher\_20°$ can be derived from $B_h B_s : \neg air\_conditioning\_on$ (by axiom (5); and therefore $B_h B_s : temp\_higher\_20°$ in the above explanation could be replaced by $B_h B_s : \neg air\_conditioning\_on$ in (6) in order to obtain a second ABE for $B_h I_s : stop\_working$. On the other hand we cannot accept

$$\{B_h B_s : \neg air\_conditioning\_on, B_h B_s : air\_conditioning\_on\}$$

as an ABE since it violates the consistency condition.

Let us now describe how contextual abduction and revision can be exploited by the hearer to update its mental state. When the hearer receives a message, it can do a number of observations on the speaker's mental state; these observations concern the conditions that have induced $s$ to send such a message. For instance, when $h$ receives an INFORM from $s$, $h$ can observe that the conditions I1–I4 on the speaker's mental state, described in Section 4, must hold. Such observations, however, are not unconditionally accepted by the hearer, rather it looks for a set of explanations for them, and only if it finds satisfactory explanations, it updates its mental state accordingly.

As described in Section 2, the hearer's mental state can be represented by a set of axioms AX in a multi-context system MC . In order to explain observations deriving from communication, the hearer must be provided with a simple multi-context causal theory on MC . The domain theory of MC is always part of $h$'s mental state, in symbols $\Sigma \subseteq AX$. The domain theory is never revised by the hearer. On the other hand AX contains other revisable belief and intentions, which can change along the dialogue. As argued above, these changes are the result of accepting the explanations of some observation. As a consequence the portion of AX which is not in $\Sigma$ must be a subset of the causes; in symbols $AX = \Sigma \cup \mathbf{X}$, where $\mathbf{X} \subseteq \mathbf{C}$ is the only part that can be modified by the reception of the speech act (i.e., $AX' = \Sigma \cup \mathbf{X}'$). We call $\mathbf{X}$ the set of *current explanations*. $\mathbf{X}$ can be changed by applying three basic operations: *abductive expansion*, *abductive contraction*, and *abductive revision*.

*Abductive Expansion.* Abductive Expansion, denoted by $+$, is applied when $\mathbf{X}$ must be extended to make possible to derive the observation $\phi$ in a context $\alpha$:

$$\mathbf{X} + \alpha : \phi \stackrel{\triangle}{=} \mathbf{X} \cup \mathbf{A}$$

where $\mathbf{A}$ is an ABE of $\alpha : \phi$ under the domain theory $\Sigma \cup \mathbf{X}$. Expansion does not specify how $\mathbf{A}$ is chosen among the set of minimal explanations. This choice might be based on a partial order on ABEs. In this paper we do not consider the effect and the specific definition of such an order. This order strictly depends on the application domain and on the meaning and the degree of plausibility of the explanations. Similarly we do not consider methods to represent and compute such a partial order.

*Abductive Contraction.* The operation of contraction, denoted by $-$, is applied if $\mathbf{X}$ is inconsistent with the new observation, hence we need to contract by $\phi$ which is the negation of the inconsistent observation. So, some formulas must be removed from $\mathbf{X}$. For any formula $\phi$ in a context $\alpha$:

$$\mathbf{X} - \alpha : \phi \stackrel{\triangle}{=} \mathbf{X} \setminus \mathbf{Y}$$

where $\mathbf{Y}$ is a minimal hitting set[4] of $\{\mathbf{A}_1, \ldots, \mathbf{A}_n\}$, where $\{\mathbf{A}_1, \ldots, \mathbf{A}_n\}$ is the set of all the ABEs of $\phi$ in the context $\alpha$ under the domain theory $\Sigma$, which are contained in $\mathbf{X}$. Again we have not specified how the hitting set is chosen in all the $\mathbf{A}_i$. As before, this will be related to the ordering on the ABEs.

*Abductive Revision.* The operation of revision, denoted by $*$, must be performed when $\mathbf{X}$ explains something which is inconsistent with the observation. For any formula $\phi$ in a context $\alpha$, we define the operator:

$$\mathbf{X} * \alpha : \phi = (\mathbf{X} - \alpha : \neg\phi) + \alpha : \phi$$

The definition of this operation comes from the Levi's identity (see [7,5]).

---

[4] Given a collection of sets $S = \{\mathbf{A}_1, \ldots, \mathbf{A}_n\}$, a set $\mathbf{H}$ is a hitting set of $S$ if for each $\mathbf{A}_i$, $\mathbf{H} \cap \mathbf{A}_i \neq \emptyset$. A hitting set is minimal if for any other hitting set $\mathbf{H}'$, $\mathbf{H}' \not\subseteq \mathbf{H}$.

# 6   Update from INFORM

*Checking preconditions (Condition I4).* Suppose that $s$ performs an INFORM($s, h, \phi$). Being aware of the fact that condition **I4** holds, $h$ may update its image of the speaker's mental state by imposing that the precondition of INFORM($s, h, \phi$) holds on its images of speaker's beliefs[5]:

$$\phi \in B_h B'_s{}^*$$

The new mental state is obtained by updating the set of current explanations $\mathbf{X}$ to $\mathbf{X}'$ as follows:

$$\mathbf{X}' = \mathbf{X} * B_h B_s : \phi$$

We can distinguish two cases: either $\Sigma \cup \mathbf{X}$ is consistent with $B_h B_s : \phi$, (i.e., $\neg\phi \notin B_h B_s^*$) or it is inconsistent with $B_h B_s : \phi$ (i.e., $\neg\phi \in B_h B_s^*$). In the first case $h$ just expands $\mathbf{X}$ with an explanation of $B_h B_s : \phi$; in the second case, $h$ computes $\mathbf{X}'$ first by contracting $\mathbf{X}$, in order to have a new set $\mathbf{Y} = \mathbf{X} - B_h B_s : \neg\phi$, such that $\Sigma \cup \mathbf{Y} \nvdash_{\mathsf{MC}} B_h B_s : \neg\phi$, and then expands $\mathbf{Y}$ into a set $\mathbf{X}' = \mathbf{Y} + B_h B_s : \phi$, by adding an explanation of $B_h B_s : \phi$. In the resulting mental state we have, therefore, that $\phi \in B_h B'_s{}^*$.

*Example 2.* Suppose that $s$ performs INFORM($s, h, temp\_higher\_20°$) when the current explanations $\mathbf{X} = \emptyset$. It is easy to see that $\mathbf{X}' = \mathbf{X} * B_h B_s : temp\_higher\_20° = \{B_h B_s : \neg air\_conditioning\_on\}$. Indeed, since $\neg temp\_higher\_20° \notin B_h B_s^*$ the hearer computes the following minimal ABE:

$$\mathbf{A} = \{B_h B_s : \neg air\_conditioning\_on\}$$

and expands $\mathbf{X}$ accordingly, resulting in $\mathbf{X}' = \{B_h B_s : \neg air\_conditioning\_on\}$. Notice that, in this new mental state, $h$ has the intention to switch the conditioning on, as we have $\Sigma \cup \mathbf{X}' \vdash_{\mathsf{MC}} I_h : air\_conditioning\_on$.

*Intention recognition (condition I1).* By intention recognition we mean the hearer's ability to recognize the intention that caused the speaker to perform the speech act. Condition (**I1**) states that a motivation for $s$ to perform an INFORM($s, h, \phi$) is its intention to change $h$'s mental state so that $h$ believes or intends some new formula. To discover this intention, $h$ checks the differences between its mental state before and after $s$ executes INFORM($s, h, \phi$) ($\mathbf{X}$ and $\mathbf{X}'$ respectively) and then it extends $\mathbf{X}'$ to include the fact that $s$ has the intention of causing those differences. For instance suppose that for the context $B_h B_s$[6] there is formula $\psi$ such that:

$$\psi \notin B_h^* \quad \text{and} \quad \psi \in B_h'^* \tag{7}$$

This intuitively means that one of the effect that the speaker has obtained by its utterance is that, the hearer believes $\psi$. Therefore the hearer might suppose that this was an intention

---

[5] Notice that this coincides also with the main effects of INFORM($s, h, \phi$) on the mental state of $h$.

[6] $h$ could be interested only in the effects yielded in some particular contexts.

of the speaker. Namely the hearer makes the observation $B_h I_s B_h : \phi$. Then $h$ revises $\mathbf{X}'$ by the observation $B_h I_s B_h : \psi$, i.e. $h$ tries to find an explanation of the fact that the speaker has the intention to make itself to believe $\psi$. To do this $h$ revises $\mathbf{X}'$ to obtain a new set of explanations $\mathbf{X}''$ defined as follows:

$$\mathbf{X}'' = \mathbf{X}' * B_h I_s B_h : \psi$$

Similar revision can be done on any other context of the hearer's belief state.

*Example 3.* Let us consider our example restricting the recognition problem to the possible speaker's intentions regarding hearer's beliefs and intentions. Suppose that $s$ performs INFORM($s, h, temp\_higher\_20°$) and $\mathbf{X}'$ is computed as in Example 2. We have that $h$ finds that $temp\_higher\_20°$ is not in $B_h^*$ but it is in $B_h'^*$. So $h$ revises $\mathbf{X}'$ as follows:

$$\mathbf{X}'' = \mathbf{X}' * B_h I_s B_h : temp\_higher\_20°$$

Moreover $h$ finds that $air\_conditioning\_on$ is a formula that does not belong to $\mathbf{X}$, but belongs to $\mathbf{X}'$. As before $h$ revises $\mathbf{X}'$ as follows:

$$\mathbf{X}'' = \mathbf{X}' * B_h I_s I_h : air\_conditioning\_on$$

This means that $h$ believes that $s$ intends to make $h$ itself to believe $temp\_higher\_20°$ and to intend to bring about $air\_conditioning\_on$.

*A final update (Condition I3).* A further observation that the hearer can do as a consequence of itself getting to believe $\phi$ (see condition (7)) is that now $s$ is in a mental state in which $s$ believes that its intention has been satisfied; namely that $s$ believes that $h$ believes $\psi$. (conditioning **I3**). As a consequence $h$ can can expand $\mathbf{X}''$ in order to verify that $\psi \in B_h B_s B_h^*$ as follows:

$$\mathbf{X}''' = \mathbf{X}'' * B_h B_s B_h : \psi$$

## 7   Related Work

The work presented in this paper relates to four main research areas: agent's internal structure, agent communication language, abduction, and belief revision. Concerning agent internal models, we based our approach on previous work [13,2,4].

Concerning the semantics of agent communication languages, there are a number of proposals of a speech act based semantics for KQML and FIPA ACL (the two main agent communication Languages), however, all these languages do not specify how this semantics must be used by the agents involved in a dialog. In contrast, in our approach we have defined a concrete and computationally feasible way for an agent to treat a specific set of communicative acts. In other words, given a set of communicative acts with a semantics expressed in terms of preconditions and main effects, we have defined a set of revision policies that an agent can follow to update its mental state whenever it receives a message.

Despite the fact that belief revision and abduction are well developed research areas, there have been few attempts at combining them. In [17], Lobo and Uzcátegui define an abductive version of a large class of theory change operators. For any operator $*$ they define its abductive version $*_a$. Lobo's and Uzcátegui's objective is to define general abductive change operators (on the basis of existing theory change operators), while our work has as its main goal to define a *specific* set of theory change operators suitable for observations generated by a communicative act.

Aravidian and Dung, in [1], state a number of rationality postulates for the contraction of a knowledge basew.r.t. a sentence, and they define an abduction based algorithm for its computation. Their algorithm (based on hitting sets) is very close to the definition of abductive contraction given in this paper. As a matter of fact, our definition of contraction fulfills their basic rationality postulates. A second important similarity is the fact that they suppose that the knowledge base is composed of two subset: an "immutable theory" and an "updatable theory" which are the analogues of the $\Sigma$ and $X$ defined in this paper. The main difference is that we extend this idea to the case of abductive extension and revision, and we have specialized the operators to a logic for belief and intentions.

Analogously, Pagnucco et al. [21,22] introduce some rationality postulates for abductive expansion and, [20] argue that the notion of abduction corresponds to an attempt to determine an initial belief state from a contracted belief state and an epistemic input under certain conditions. In all these the revision process is limited to the agent's beliefs. Introducing mental states, we extend the revision process to the agent's intentions. In multi-agent systems this is very important because it allows an agent to revise its intentions whenever new beliefs are acquired. Moreover, the use of images of mental states allows to maintain its beliefs about the mental state of the other agents always updated.

Hindriks et al. in [15] provide an operational semantics for two pairs of communicative operators, **ask** and **tell**, and **request** and **offer**, based on transition systems. As in our approach, in their approach each agent contains a mental state, which is composed of two sets: beliefs and goals. In addition, each mental state contains a set of rules describing its evolution. The mental state of an agent refers to a particular moment during the agent evolution. The semantics of communicative operators is given in terms of a transition of an agent from a belief state to another. A first difference between their and our approachs is that they do not allow agents to have images of the others' mental states. A more radical difference regards the fact that, in their semantics, communicative acts do not have either preconditions or effects on the beliefs of an agent. In other words, the semantics does not contain an explicit relationship between the agent's beliefs and its communications. The main consequence of this choice is that the reception of a message does not necessarily yield the revision of the agent's mental state. Belief revision is considered as any other action. An agent can decide to revise its beliefs independently from the communication with other agents. Moreover, [15] does not provide any criteria for belief revision, which is assumed to be a pre-compiled function. Our proposal is therefore complementary to this approach as we provide a well founded and executable methods for revising beliefs after communication. Finally, Hindriks et al. deal with synchronous communication while we consider asynchronous communication. Synchronous communication means that a **tell** from agent $A$ to agent $B$ is necessarily preceded by an **ask** from agent $B$ to agent $A$, and vice-versa any **ask** from $B$ to $A$ is followed by a **tell** in the opposite direction. This is true also for the other pair of communicative acts, namely request and offer. Deduction and abduction are not used to enlarge and/or modify agents beliefs. Rather, in our work deduction is a reasoning pattern which is used by an agent to generate an answer (tell) of an information request (ask); similarly abduction is used to generate an offers (offer) that fulfill a request (request). In contrast in our approach, which considers asynchronous communication, deduction and abduction are performed not only to generate the answer to a specific request, but to process the reception and the sending of any message.

There are two main differences between our work and the other approaches contained in this volume for formalizing cooperative agents [29,30,19,6]. The first difference is that we consider a *subjective perspective* rather than a *global objective perspective*. Agents mental states are described as perceived by a single agent and not from an external absolute point of view. The formal system MC defined in Section 2 represents the beliefs and the intentions of the hearer about the state of the world and the speaker's mental state, rather than the actual state of the world and the actual hearer's mental state. Differently, the situation calculi proposed in [30] and [27], and the modal logics proposed in [6] describe agent's mental attitudes from the perspective of an external observer. The second difference concerns the fact that we explicitly introduce for any agent a *model of the mental state of the other agents*. Agents coordination can be reached via communication only in the sense that communication is just a way to update each agent's model of the other's mental state.

## 8  Conclusion

In this paper we have made the fundamental assumption that there is a causal relationship between a speaker's mental state and its uttering a sentence. Following this idea, we have developed some abductive methods to recognize the speaker's mental state and then to update the hearer's image of the speaker's mental state. Inspiration for the causal relationship has been taken from the classical "Speech Acts Theory", namely we have adopted the plan-based vision of speech acts in representing them as STRIPS-like operators. We have investigated how it is possible to use both the preconditions and the effects of the speech act in order to update the addressee's image of the speaker's belief and intentions. Our work is based upon the use of multi-context systems for which we have extended the notion of casual theories, abduction and revision. The definition of an efficient and implementable algorithm that computes the set of all abductive explanations for an observation will be the object of our future work.

## References

1. C. Aravindan and P.M. Dung. Knowledge revision, abduction and database updates. *Journal of Applied Non-Classical Logics*, 5(1):51–76, 1995.
2. M. Benerecetti, F. Giunchiglia, and L. Serafini. Model Checking Multiagent Systems. *Journal of Logic and Computation, Special Issue on Computational & Logical Aspects of Multi-Agent Systems*, 8(3):401–423, 1998.

3. A. Cimatti and L. Serafini. Multi-Agent Reasoning with Belief Contexts II: Elaboration Tolerance. In *Proceedings of the 1st International Conference on Multi-Agent Systems (ICMAS-95)*, pages 57–64, 1996.

4. P.R. Cohen and C.R. Perrault. Elements of a plan-based theory of speech acts. *Cognitive Science*, 3(3):177–212, 1979.

5. A.F. Dragoni and P. Giorgini. Revising beliefs received from multiple source. In M A Williams and H Rott, editors, *Frontiers of Belief Revision*, Applied Logic. Kluwer, 2000.

6. F. Dignum B. Dunin-Kęplicz and R. Verbrugge. Agent theory for team formation by dialogue. In C. Castelfranchi and Y. Lesperance, editors, *Proceedings of the Seventh International Workshop on Agent Theories, Architectures, and Languages (ATAL-2000)*, LNAI. Springer Verlag, 2001.

7. P. Gärdenfors. *Knowledge in Flux: Modeling the Dynamics of Epistemic States*. MIT Press., Cambridge Mass., 1988.

8. M. Georgeff. Communication and interaction in multiagent planning. In *Proceedings of the 3th National Conference on Artificial Intelligence*, pages 125–129, 1983.

9. C. Ghidini. Modelling (Un)Bounded Beliefs. In P. Bouquet, L. Serafini, P. Brezillon, M. Benerecetti, and F. Castellani, editors, *Modelling and Using Context – Proceedings of the 2nd International and Interdisciplinary Conference, Context'99*, volume 1688 of *LNAI*, pages 145–158. Springer Verlag - Heidelberg, 1999.

10. E. Giunchiglia and F. Giunchiglia. Ideal and Real Belief about Belief. *Journal of Logic and Computation*, 2000. To appear.

11. F. Giunchiglia. Contextual reasoning. *Epistemologia, special issue on I Linguaggi e le Macchine*, XVI:345–364, 1993.

12. F. Giunchiglia and C. Ghidini. Local Models Semantics, or Contextual Reasoning = Locality + Compatibility. In *Proceedings of the Sixth International Conference on Principles of Knowledge Representation and Reasoning (KR'98)*, pages 282–289. Morgan Kaufmann, 1998.

13. F. Giunchiglia and L. Serafini. Multilanguage hierarchical logics (or: how we can do without modal logics). *Artificial Intelligence*, 65:29–70, 1994.

14. P.J. Gmytrasiewicz and E.H. Durfe. A rigorous, operational formalization of recursive modeling. In *Proceedings of the First International Conference on Multi-Agent Systems (ICMAS)*, pages 125–132, 1995.

15. K.V. Hindriks, F.S. de Boer, W. van der Hoek, and J.J.Ch. Meyer. Semantics of communicating agents based on deduction and abduction. In *Proceedings of IJCAI'99 Workshop on ACL*, 1999.

16. K. Konolige. Abduction versus closure in causal theories. *Artificial Intelligence*, 53:255–272, 1992.

17. J. Lobo and C. Uzcátegui. Abductive change oprators. *Fundamenta Informaticae*, 27(4):319–418, 1996.

18. J.S. Rosenschein M.R. Gensereth, M.L. Ginsberg. Cooperation without communication. In *AAAI 86*, pages 51–57, 1986.

19. T.J. Norman and C. Reed. Delegation and respnsability. In C. Castelfranchi and Y. Lesperance, editors, *Proceedings of the Seventh International Workshop on Agent Theories, Architectures, and Languages (ATAL-2000)*, LNAI. Springer Verlag, 2001.

20. M. Pagnucco and N.Y. Foo. The relationship between abduction and changes in belief states. In *Proceedings of the ICLP93 Postconference Workshop on Abductive Reasoning*, pages 75–83, Budapest, Hungary, 1993.

21. M. Pagnucco, A.C. Nayak, and N.Y. Foo. Abductive expansion: The application of abductive inference to the process of belief change. In *Proceedings of the Seventh Australian Joint Conference on Artificial Intelligence*, pages 70–77, Armidale, Australia, 1994.

22. M. Pagnucco, A.C. Nayak, and N.Y. Foo. Abductive reasoning, belief expansion and non-monotonic consequence. In *Proceedings of the ICLP'95 Joint Workshop on Deductive Databases and Logic Programming and Abduction in Deductive Databases and Knowledge-based Systems*, pages 143–158, Shonan Village Center, Japan, 1995.

23. A.S. Rao and M. Georgeff. BDI agents: from theory to practice. In *Proceedings of the First International Conference on Multi-Agent Systems (ICMAS-95)*, pages 312–319, S. Francisco, CA, 1995.

24. A.S. Rao, M. Georgeff, and E.A. Sonenberg. Social plans: A preliminary report. In E. Werner and Y. Demazeau, editors, *Decentralized AI - Proceedings of the Third European Workshop on Modeling Autonomous Agents in a Multi-Agent World (MAAMAW-91)*, pages 57–76, Amsterdam, The Netherlands, 1992. Elsevier Science Publishers B.V.

25. J.S. Rosenschein and M.R. Genesereth. Communication and cooperation. *Stanford Heuristic Programming Rep*, 1984.

26. J.R. Searle and D. Vanderveken. *Foundations of illuctionary Logic*. Cambridge University Press, 1985.

27. S. Shapiro and Y. Lespérance. Modelling multiagent systems with casl–a feature interaction resolution application. In C. Castelfranchi and Y. Lesperance, editors, *Proceedings of the Seventh International Workshop on Agent Theories, Architectures, and Languages (ATAL-2000)*, LNAI. Springer Verlag, 2001.

28. E. Werner. Toward a theory of communication and cooperation for multiagent planning. In *Proceedings of the Second Conference on Theoretical Aspects of Reasoning About Knowledge*, Los Altos, CA, 1988. Morgan Kaufmann Publisher.

29. M. Wooldridge and P.E. Dunne. Optimistic and disjunctive agent design problems. In C. Castelfranchi and Y. Lesperance, editors, *Proceedings of the Seventh International Workshop on Agent Theories, Architectures, and Languages (ATAL-2000)*, LNAI. Springer Verlag, 2001.

30. S. Zimmerbaum and R. Scherl. Sensing actions, time, and concurrency in the situation calculus. In C. Castelfranchi and Y. Lesperance, editors, *Proceedings of the Seventh International Workshop on Agent Theories, Architectures, and Languages (ATAL-2000)*, LNAI. Springer Verlag, 2001.

# Sensing Actions, Time, and Concurrency in the Situation Calculus

Stephen Zimmerbaum and Richard Scherl*

Department of Computer and Information Science
New Jersey Institute of Technology
University Heights
Newark, New Jersey
07102-1982
szimmerb@cis.njit.edu scherl@cis.njit.edu

**Abstract.** A formal framework for specifying and developing agents/robots must handle not only knowledge and sensing actions, but also time and concurrency. Researchers have extended the situation calculus to handle knowledge and sensing actions. Other researchers have addressed the issue of adding time and concurrent actions. We combine both of these features into a unified logical theory of knowledge, sensing, time, and concurrency. The result preserves the solution to the frame problem of previous work, maintains the distinction between indexical and objective knowledge of time, and is capable of representing the various ways in which concurrency interacts with time and knowledge.

## 1 Introduction

We propose a unified logical theory of knowledge, sensing, time, and concurrency. Actions have preconditions which may include knowledge preconditions. Sensing actions alter knowledge. The knowledge produced depends upon the relative time at which sensing actions occur and also whether or not other sorts of actions occur concurrently. All of this interacts with the agent's evolving knowledge of time.

Sensing interacts with time in many ways. Certainly, the results of sensing occur at a particular point in time. For many purposes, the results of sensing actions that occur at the same time are significant. Depth perception in vision is an important example. Not only do we have the need for two distinct concurrent sensing actions in binocular stereopsis, but also in the simultaneous use of other features such as texture gradients and shading to achieve knowledge of depth relationships. The information produced by the sensing actions is different depending on which sensing actions occurred concurrently.

Relative time also interacts with perception and knowledge. The perception of motion depends upon the result of sensing actions at distinct time intervals. Yet, knowledge of the absolute time is not required to perceive the motion. It is only knowledge of the relative time between perceptual acts.

Many sensing actions require concurrent non-sensing actions in order to have their intended effect. For example, it may be necessary to hold the shutter open and sense

---

* Corresponding Author

C. Castelfranchi, Y. Lespérance (Eds.): Intelligent Agents VII, LNAI 1986, pp. 31–45, 2001.

concurrently in order for an image to be perceived. Additionally, the knowledge prerequisites of executing two actions concurrently may be different from the knowledge required to execute each individually.

Furthermore, specification of an agent's ability to achieve a goal in general involve requiring that the agent know what to do to arrive at a goal state [13,5]. As the ability to achieve particular goals will often involve the ability to perform concurrent actions, the integration of knowledge and concurrency is an important step in fully formalizing these aspects of ability.

We develop our framework within the situation calculus – a first-order formalism for representing and reasoning about the effects of actions. The language is based upon the dialect of the situation calculus used in the *Cognitive Robotics Group* at the University of Toronto. Previously, researchers have extended the situation calculus to incorporate knowledge and knowledge-producing actions [19]. Other researchers have added time and concurrent actions to the framework [17]. But the two aspects not been previously combined. This combination of sensing and knowledge with concurrent actions and continuous time is the main contribution of this paper.

By working in the situation calculus, we are able to extend previous work on reasoning (by regression and theorem proving) to cover the language developed here as well. Furthermore, our work is suitable to be incorporated into the robot programming language GOLOG. It can then be used to specify agents that must reason about the interactions of time, knowledge, and concurrent actions (including sensing actions).

The situation calculus [9] is a language for modeling dynamically changing worlds. Changes to the world are the results of *actions*, while possible world histories consisting of sequences of actions are represented by *situations*. The situation calculus can be used for agent planning via goal regression. Reiter [16] proposed a simple solution to the frame problem, an approach to axiomatization within the situation calculus. Although this approach to the frame problem requires certain simplifying assumptions, it has proven to be useful and is the foundation for both goal regression [16] and the programming language GOLOG [7]. Goal regression was extended by Scherl and Levesque to apply to an agent who can sense the world (read numbers on paper [9], determine the shape of an object). Furthermore, other authors have explored relaxations of the simplifying assumptions [8,11]. A related framework is used in [22] as the basis for a method of modeling multiagent systems.

This paper combines and extends the work of Scherl and Levesque [19] incorporating the model of *concurrency* and *time* presented by Reiter [17]. At the same time, Reiter's simple solution to the frame problem is preserved. Furthermore, it is shown that the solution preserves the distinction between indexical and objective time [4]. If the agent currently knows the absolute time, then he knows the absolute time after executing an action. But if he doesn't know the absolute time, then he only knows that he began executing the action some number of time units ago, unless of course he reads a clock. While maintaining these properties, our work allows the representation of the various ways in which actions (including sensing actions and possibly other concurrent actions) interact with time and knowledge. We also extend the method of regression to our augmented language.

In this paper, we only consider a single agent situation. The issues addressed in this paper become even more prominent in a multi-agent context. Once we allow multiple agents, then we different agents acting concurrently (possibly known or unknown to the others). Each will have his own knowledge of the world and of time. It is important to get the basic issues down before addressing them in the more complex multi-agent environment.

Section 2 gives a quick introduction to the situation calculus and Section 3 does the same for the foundational axioms. The representation of knowledge and sensing actions are covered in Section 4. Concurrency is integrated into the framework in Section 5. Section 6 covers some additional constructs of the language and then illustrates the representational power of the language with two examples. A number of properties of the formulation are discussed in Section 7. Finally, in Section 8, the paper is summarized, aspects of the work not covered here are mentioned, and future work is discussed.

## 2   Situation Calculus and the Frame Problem

The situation calculus (following [16,18]) is a many-sorted first-order language for representing dynamically changing worlds in which all changes are the result of named *actions* performed by some agent. The sort *action* is for primitive actions.

Terms are used to represent states of the world, i.e., *situations*. The unique situation constant symbol, $S_0$, is a member of the sort *situation*. Additional situations are generated by the binary function DO : $action \times situation \rightarrow situation$.

The result of performing action $\alpha$ in situation $s$ is represented by DO $(\alpha, s)$. The constant $S_0$ denotes the initial situation. Relations whose truth values vary from situation to situation, called *fluents*, are denoted by a predicate symbol taking a situation term as the last argument.

It is assumed that the axiomatizer has provided for each action $\alpha(x)$, an *action precondition axiom* of the form given in 1, where $\pi_\alpha(s)$ is the formula for $\alpha(x)$'s action preconditions.

$$\text{Poss}(\alpha(x), s) \equiv \pi_\alpha(x, s) \tag{1}$$

An action precondition axiom for the action *drop* is given below.

$$\text{Poss}(\text{DROP}(x), s) \equiv \text{HOLDING}(x, s) \tag{2}$$

Our axiomatization utilizes successor state axioms to represent the effects of actions. If this style of axiomatization is followed, then there is no frame problem. Reiter [16] has shown that under certain simplifying assumptions (absence of state constraints), such axioms may be automatically compiled from the usual positive and negative effect axioms. Other authors have relaxed these simplifying assumptions, in particular allowing for the presence of ramifications [8,11].

The form of the axioms are as follows:

$$\text{Poss}(a, s) \rightarrow [\text{F}(\text{DO}(a, s)) \equiv \gamma_\text{F}^+(a, s) \vee (\text{F}(s) \wedge \neg\gamma_\text{F}^-(a, s))] \tag{3}$$

Here $\gamma_F^+(a, s)$ is a formula describing under what conditions doing the action $a$ in situation $s$ leads the fluent F to become true in the successor situation $\mathrm{DO}(a, s)$ and similarly $\gamma_F^-(a, s)$ is a formula describing the conditions under which performing action $a$ in situation $s$ results in the fluent F becoming false in situation $\mathrm{DO}(a, s)$.

As an example of a successor state axiom, consider such an axiom for the fluent BROKEN given below:

$$\mathrm{Poss}(a, s) \rightarrow [\mathrm{BROKEN}(y, \mathrm{DO}(a, s)) \equiv a = \mathrm{DROP}(y) \wedge \mathrm{FRAGILE}(y) \tag{4}$$
$$\vee (\exists b) a = \mathrm{EXPLODE}(b) \wedge \mathrm{NEXTO}(b, y, s)$$
$$\vee \mathrm{BROKEN}(y, s) \wedge a \neq \mathrm{REPAIR}(y)]$$

## 3   Foundational Axioms

On analogy with the Peano axioms for number theory, a set of foundational axioms for elements of the sort *situation* have been developed [8,18]. The axioms are as follows:

$$S_0 \neq do(a, s) \tag{5}$$
$$do(a_1, s_1) = do(a_2, s_2) \supset a_1 = a_2 \wedge s_1 = s_2 \tag{6}$$
$$(\forall P).P(S_0) \wedge [(\forall a, s).[P(s) \supset P(do(a, s))]] \supset (\forall s)P(s) \tag{7}$$

There are two additional axioms:

$$\neg s \prec S_0 \tag{8}$$
$$s \prec do(a, s') \equiv \mathrm{Poss}(a, s') \wedge s \preceq s' \tag{9}$$

where $s \preceq s'$ is shorthand for $s \preceq s' \vee s = s'$. These five axioms are *domain independent*. They will provide the basic properties of situations in any domain specific axiomatization of particular fluents and actions.

We want to reason about situations reachable by an executable sequence of actions. The intuition is that if $s \preceq s'$, then there is a sequence of zero or more executable actions that move from $s$ to $s'$. An action is executable if the action's preconditions are true in the situation in which the action is to be performed. $S_0 \preceq s$ means that $s$ is reachable from the initial situation by a sequence of executable actions. Such situations are a (possibly proper) subset of the set of all situations, some of which are not accessible from the initial situation.

Sentence(10) provides an explicit second order definition of $\preceq$.

$$(\forall s, s').s \preceq s' \equiv (\forall P).\{[(\forall s_1)P(s_1, s_1)] \wedge$$
$$[(\forall a, s_1, s_2).\mathrm{Poss}(a, s_2) \wedge P(s_1, s_2) \tag{10}$$
$$\supset P(s_1, do(a, s_2))]\}$$
$$\supset P(s, s').$$

It says that $\preceq$ is the smallest binary relation on situations $(\sigma, \sigma')$ such that:

1. $\sigma \preceq \sigma$, and
2. $\sigma \preceq do(a, \sigma')$ whenever action $a$ is possible in situation $\sigma'$ and $\sigma \preceq \sigma'$.

Although the details are not covered here, these axioms can be extended to include the presence of knowledge as well as concurrency [3,18].

## 4   An Epistemic Fluent

Scherl and Levesque adapt the standard possible-world model of knowledge to the situation calculus, as first done by Moore[13]. Informally, we think of there being a binary accessibility relation over situations, where a situation $s'$ is understood as being accessible from a situation $s$ if as far as the agent knows in situation $s$, he might be in situation $s'$. So something is known in $s$ if it is true in every $s'$ accessible from $s$, and conversely something is not known if it is false in some accessible situation.

To treat knowledge as a fluent, we introduce a binary relation $K(s', s)$, read as "$s'$ is accessible from s" and treat it the same way we would any other fluent. In other words, from the point of view of the situation calculus, the last argument to K is the official situation argument (expressing what is known in situation $s$), and the first argument is just an auxiliary like the $y$ in BROKEN$(y, s)$.[1]

We can now introduce the notation **Knows**$(P(\text{now}), s)$ (read as P is known in situation $s$) as an abbreviation for a formula that uses K. For example

$$\textbf{Knows}(\textsc{Broken}(y, \text{now}), s) \stackrel{\text{def}}{=} \forall s'\, K(s', s) \rightarrow \textsc{Broken}(y, s').$$

The special indexical now is instantiated with a situation variable upon expansion.

We may also consider actions that make known the denotation of a term. For this case, we introduce the notation **Kref**$(\textsc{t}(\text{NOW}), s)$ defined as follows:

$$\textbf{Kref}(\textsc{t}(\text{NOW}), s) \stackrel{\text{def}}{=} \exists x \textbf{Knows}(\textsc{t}(\text{NOW}) = x, s)$$
$$\textit{where x does not appear in } \textsc{t}.$$

In general, there may be many knowledge-producing actions. Associated with each action that makes known the truth value of a formula is an expression of the form $\varphi_i(s) \equiv \varphi_i(s')$. In the case of an action that makes known the denotation of a term, the formula is of the form $\tau_i(s) = \tau_i(s')$, where $\tau_i$ is a situation-dependent term. Elaborating upon the presentation in [6], we introduce SENSED FLUENT CONDITION AXIOMS and and SENSED TERM CONDITION AXIOMS which allow simplification of the successor state axiom for K.

A binary sensing action tells an agent whether or not some condition $\phi_a$ holds in the current situation. For each sensing action $a$, it is assumed that the domain theory entails a sensed fluent condition axiom of the form

$$SFC(a, s, s') \equiv (\phi_a(s) \equiv \phi_a(s')) \tag{11}$$

where $SFC$ is a predicate relating the action to the fluent. In the case of a SENSEP action which determines the truth of predicate P in situation $s$,

$$SFC(\textsc{sensep}, s, s') \equiv (P(s) \equiv P(s')) \tag{12}$$

For each sensing action $a$ that makes known the denotation of a term, it is assumed that the domain theory entails a sensed term condition axiom of the form

$$STC(a, s, s') \equiv (\tau(s) = \tau(s')) \tag{13}$$

---

[1] Note that using this convention means that the arguments to K are reversed from their normal modal logic use.

where $STC$ is a predicate relating the action to the term. In the case of a READ$_{\text{NUMBER}}$ action which makes known the denotation of the term NUMBER in situation $s$,

$$STC(\text{READ}_{\text{NUMBER}}, s, s') \equiv (\text{NUMBER}(s) = \text{NUMBER}(s')) \tag{14}$$

It is also assumed that for every action $a$ that does not make known the truth value of a formula (both non-sensing actions as well as sensing actions that make known the denotation of a term) $[SFC(a, s, s') \equiv True]$. Additionally, for every action $a$ that does not make known the denotation of a term (both non-sensing actions as well as sensing actions that make known the truth value of a formula) $[STC(a, s, s') \equiv True]$.

The form of the successor state axiom for K without concurrency is as follows:

$$\begin{aligned}
\text{Poss}(a, s) \rightarrow K(s'', (\text{DO}(a, s))) \equiv \\
(\exists s') \, s'' = \text{DO}(a, s') \wedge \ K(s', s) \wedge \text{Poss}(a, s') \\
\wedge SFC(a, s, s') \wedge \ STC(a, s, s')
\end{aligned} \tag{15}$$

The relation K at a particular situation DO$(a, s)$ is completely determined by the relation at $s$ and the action $a$.

# 5   Concurrency

As originally defined in the situation calculus [9], actions had to occur sequentially, with one action completed before another could begin. Furthermore, there was no facility to deal with the continuous passage of time. This contrasted with other formalisms such as the event calculus [20] which could naturally handle concurrent actions and continuous time. In fact, it was commonly believed that expressive power of the situation calculus was limited and unable to represent such features. This was shown to be false by [1], but the problem still remained to maintain the solution to the frame problem while extending the situation calculus.

## 5.1   Concurrency with Knowledge

The work of Pinto [14] and Reiter [17] proposed an approach to dealing with concurrency, natural actions and continuous time while still maintaining the solution to the frame problem. Reiter [17] defined a new sort *concurrent*, sets of simple actions. Variables $a, a', ..$ represent the sort *actions* and $c, c', ...$ represent the sort *concurrent*. In Reiter's notation, the time of an action's occurrence is the value of that action's temporal argument. Thus an action has the form $A(x, t)$ and for each action an axiom of the form TIME$(A(x, t)) = t$ is required to indicate the time of the action. An axiom of the form:

$$\text{START}(\text{DO}(a, s)) = \text{TIME}(a) \tag{16}$$

is needed to relate the time of the action to the start of a situation. There may also be an axiom giving the start time of the initial situation $S_0$. We also use a variant notation:

$$\text{TIME}(\text{DO}(a, s)) = \text{TIME}(a) \tag{17}$$

Concurrent actions are sets of ordinary actions that are taken to represent instantaneous acts. An action with duration is represented by two instantaneous actions — a start action and an end action. Additionally, the foundational axioms are modified to rule out the possibility of prior actions having later times.

If we introduced this definition of actions without change into the successor state axiom for K, it would require the agent to know the time after any action, even if it was unknown in the previous situation. To avoid this, we can not represent time as an argument to the instantaneous actions.

Instead, we represent the instantaneous actions and associated times as a tuple of the form $< a, t >$ with functions ACTION and TIME defined, returning the first and second elements of the tuple:

$$\text{ACTION}(< a, t >) = a \tag{18}$$

$$\text{TIME}(< a, t >) = t \tag{19}$$

These pairs, represented by variables $p, p', \dots$ are elements of the sort *action-time pairs*. Concurrent Actions are now a set of such tuples. The sort *action* contains actions without a temporal argument.

We also adopt, without significant change, Reiter's requirement that concurrent actions be coherent, that is there is at least one action-time pair $p$ in the collection, and the time of all pairs in the collection is the same:

$$\text{COHERENT}(c) \equiv (\exists p)\, p \, \epsilon \, c \wedge (\exists t)(\forall p')[p' \, \epsilon \, c \rightarrow \text{TIME}(p') = t]. \tag{20}$$

A set of action-time pairs are coherent if each of them have the same time component.

The definition of *time* can readily be extended to sets of concurrent actions and this allows us to define the function *start* of a situation resulting from the execution of a concurrent action.

$$\begin{aligned} \text{COHERENT}(c) \rightarrow \\ [\text{TIME}(c) = t \equiv \exists p\, (p \in c \wedge \text{TIME}(p) = t)] \\ \wedge \text{START}(do(c, s)) = \text{TIME}(c). \end{aligned} \tag{21}$$

The predicate Poss$(c, s)$ means that it is possible to execute concurrent action $c$ in situation $s$.

$$\text{Poss}(a, s) \rightarrow \text{Poss}(< a, t >, s), \tag{22}$$

$$\text{Poss}(p, s) \rightarrow \text{Poss}(\{p\}, s), \tag{23}$$

$$\text{Poss}(c, s) \rightarrow \text{COHERENT}(c) \wedge (\forall p)\, [p \, \epsilon \, c \rightarrow \text{Poss}(p, s)]. \tag{24}$$

Concurrent actions can interact in ways that affect both the possibility of performing the individual actions (*precondition interaction problem*) and in ways that alter the effects that the actions would have if executed individually (*effects interaction problem*) [17, 15]. Consideration of such issues involving sensing actions is left for future work.

In order to simplify the presentation in this paper, we assume the following axiom, which rules out the precondition interaction problem.

$$\text{COHERENT}(c) \wedge (\forall p)\, [p \, \epsilon \, c \rightarrow \text{Poss}(p, s)] \rightarrow \text{Poss}(c, s) \tag{25}$$

It is possible to execute a set of concurrent actions (i.e., action-time pairs) if each of the actions is individually possible, and also if the entire set is coherent.

In the presentation to follow, we implicitly assume an additional sort ranging over time points which in this paper are assumed to be integers. The standard Arabic numerals representing integers points are interpreted as integers. Additionally, the symbols for addition and subtraction are interpreted as the usual operations on integers.

## 5.2   Successor State Axiom for K with Concurrency

The Successor State Axiom for K using concurrency can be stated in several alternative ways depending on what conditions one wishes to apply regarding the agent's knowledge of time. We continue to require that the relation K at a particular situation $DO(c, s)$ is completely determined by the relation at $s$ and the set of concurrent actions $c$.

The following successor state axiom models an agent who knows how much time is passing. This is an agent who has an accurate clock.

$$
\begin{aligned}
\text{Poss}(c, s) \rightarrow K(s'', (\text{DO}(c, s))) \equiv \\
(\exists s', c') \, s'' = \text{DO}(c', s') \wedge \ K(s', s) \wedge \ \text{Poss}(c', s') \\
\wedge \ (\forall p') \, p' \in c' \ (\exists p) \, p \in c \\
\wedge \ \text{ACTION}(p') = \text{ACTION}(p) \\
\wedge \ (\forall p) \, p \in c \ (\exists p') \, p' \in c' \\
\wedge \ \text{ACTION}(p) = \text{ACTION}(p') \\
\wedge \ \text{START}(s'') = \text{START}(s') + (\text{TIME}(c) - \text{START}(s)) \\
\wedge \ (\forall p) \, p \in c \rightarrow \\
SFC(\text{ACTION}(p), s, s') \wedge STC(\text{ACTION}(p), s, s')
\end{aligned}
\tag{26}
$$

After executing a set of concurrent actions $c$ in situation $s$, as far as the agent knows, it could be in a situation $s''$ iff $s''$ is the result of performing $c'$ in some previously accessible situation $s'$, provided that $c$ is possible in $s'$ and that $s'$ is identical to $s$ in terms of what is being sensed. Furthermore, it is required that the concurrent action $c'$ being performed in all situations accessible from $s$ be identical to $c$ in terms of the individual actions that make up the set.

It is not required that the TIME of the actions be identical. (If this were the case, it would force the agent to know the objective time after executing any action.) Rather, it is only required that the difference between the *start* of $s'$ and the *start* of $s''$ be the same as the difference between the *start* of $s$ and the *start* of $do(c, s)$ (same as the *time* of $c$). The requirement that is made does ensure that the agent knows how much time is passing. Even though the agent does not know the time since the *start* of the various accessible situations are different, the difference between the *start* of those situations and the *start* of the situations resulting from the performance of a concurrent action in those situations will be the same.

Other formulations are possible. Agents can be modeled who have clocks of various degrees of accuracy. The passage of time is then known by the agent within certain bounds. At the extreme end is an agent who does not have any idea of how much time is passing. But these options are not explored in this paper.

# 6   The Language and Examples

## 6.1   Further Constructs

We need some way to refer to the current time without specifying the value of the current time. To achieve this we use the special indexical term now. Upon expansion the term is replaced with the appropriate situation term. So, START(now) can be used to refer to the current time. Here we illustrate by example. The agent's knowing the objective time is expressed as $\exists t$ **Know**(start(now) $= t, s$). This expands into

$$\exists t \, \forall s' (K(s', s) \rightarrow \text{START}(s') = t).$$

We augment our language with a number of additional expressions. These are based on ideas developed by Lesperance and Levesque [4] and require the use of the notion of precedence of situations as defined earlier. Note that we distinguish between the $<$ relation on integers used to represent time points and the $\prec$ relations on situations as defined in the foundational axioms for the situation calculus.

### Happened

An action occurred prior to s and it was time t at some point during the action's duration:

$$\begin{aligned}
\textbf{Happened}(t, Act, s) &\overset{\text{def}}{=} (\exists c, s', s'') \, (s'' = \text{DO}(c, s') \wedge \exists p \, \epsilon \, c \\
&\wedge \text{ACTION}(p) = Act \wedge \text{TIME}(p) = t \wedge s'' \preceq s \wedge s' \prec s'')
\end{aligned} \tag{27}$$

### Wasat

P held at s' and t was the time of s' or s' preceded t and no other situation after s' preceded t:

$$\begin{aligned}
\textbf{Wasat}(t, P(\text{then}), s) &\overset{\text{def}}{=} \\
(\exists s')((P(\text{then})&\{s'/\text{then}\} \wedge t = \text{START}(s')) \vee \\
(t > \text{START}(s') &\wedge \neg(\exists s'')(s' \prec s'' \prec s \wedge \text{START}(s'') \leq t)))
\end{aligned} \tag{28}$$

Here we introduce another special indexical then which is needed to ensure that the correct situation is substituted into the situation argument of the predicate which is the middle argument to **Wasat**.

## 6.2   Example 1

Our initial example illustrates the use of concurrency along with the notions of indexical versus absolute time, but does not involve a sensing action. We have a robot Rob which is very poorly constructed. When it moves its arm (as in picking up an object), it is advisable that all people near by move a good distance away. Therefore the designers of the robot built certain warning signals into Rob. When it performs some potentially dangerous maneuvers, it can be programmed to whistle and it must blink a warning light before it lifts an object off the floor.

It can always whistle and it can stop whistling if it is in the process of whistling.

$$\text{POSS}(\text{START\_WHISTLE}, s) \equiv T \tag{29}$$

$$\text{POSS}(\text{END\_WHISTLE}, s) \equiv \text{WHISTLING}(s) \tag{30}$$

When it is in the process of picking up an object, a light can be blinked.

$$\text{POSS}(\text{BLINK\_LIGHT}, s) \equiv \exists x \text{PICKING\_UP}(x) \tag{31}$$

It is possible for Rob to start picking up an object $x$ if Rob is located where object $x$ is, and Rob is not holding object $x$. Rob can finish picking up if he is in the process of picking up.

$$\text{POSS}(\text{START\_PICKUP}(x), s) \equiv \text{AT}(x, s) \wedge \neg\text{HOLDING}(x, s) \tag{32}$$

$$\text{POSS}(\text{END\_PICKUP}(x), s) \equiv \text{PICKING\_UP}(x, s) \tag{33}$$

It is possible for Rob to drop object $x$ if the object is currently being held.

$$\text{POSS}(\text{DROP}(x), s) \equiv \text{HOLDING}(x, s) \tag{34}$$

The fluent $\text{AT}(x, s)$ holds when the agent is located at the location of object $x$ in situation $s$. To be where an object is located, the agent must have moved there, or been there in the previous situation and not moved away.

$$\begin{aligned}
\text{Poss}(a, s) \rightarrow [&\text{AT}(x, \text{DO}(c, s)) \equiv \\
&(\exists p)\,(p \,\epsilon\, c \wedge \text{ACTION}(p) = \text{MOVETO}(x) \\
&\vee (\text{AT}(x, s) \ \wedge \neg(\exists p \,\epsilon\, c)\text{ACTION}(p) = \text{MOVETO}(y)))]
\end{aligned} \tag{35}$$

The fluent $\text{WHISTLING}(s)$ holds after a START_WHISTLE action has been executed and until an END_WHISTLE action has taken place.

$$\begin{aligned}
\text{Poss}(a, s) \rightarrow [&\text{WHISTLING}(\text{DO}(c, s)) \equiv \\
&(\exists p)\,(p \,\epsilon\, c \wedge \text{ACTION}(p) = \text{START\_WHISTLE} \\
&\vee (\text{WHISTLING}(s) \wedge \\
&\neg(\exists p \,\epsilon\, c)\text{ACTION}(p) = \text{END\_WHISTLE}(y)))]
\end{aligned} \tag{36}$$

The fluent ON_FLOOR(x,s) holds after a drop action, or if the object $x$ was already on the floor and the blink-light action has not occurred.

$$\begin{aligned}
\text{Poss}(a, s) \rightarrow [&\text{ON\_FLOOR}(x, \text{DO}(c, s)) \equiv \\
&(\exists p)\,(p \,\epsilon\, c \wedge \text{ACTION}(p) = \text{DROP}(x) \\
&\vee (\text{ON\_FLOOR}(x, s) \wedge \\
&\neg(\exists p \,\epsilon\, c)\text{ACTION}(p) = \text{BLINK\_LIGHT}(x)))]
\end{aligned} \tag{37}$$

The fluent PICKING_UP(x,s) holds after Rob has started picking up or if it already held and an end pick up action has not occurred.

$$\begin{aligned}
\text{Poss}(a, s) \rightarrow [&\text{PICKING\_UP}(x, \text{DO}(c, s)) \equiv \\
&(\exists p)\,(p \,\epsilon\, c \wedge \text{ACTION}(p) = \text{START\_PICKUP}(x) \\
&\vee (\text{PICKINGUP}(x, s) \wedge \\
&\neg(\exists p \,\epsilon\, c)\text{ACTION}(p) = \text{END\_PICKUP}(x)))]
\end{aligned} \tag{38}$$

To be holding an object, either it was just picked up, or it was previously picked up and has not been dropped.

$$\begin{aligned}
\text{Poss}(c, s) \rightarrow [\text{HOLDING}(x, do(c, s)) \equiv \\
(\exists p)\, (p \,\epsilon\, c \wedge \text{ACTION}(p) = \text{END\_PICKUP}(x) \\
\vee\, \text{HOLDING}(x, s) \wedge \\
\neg(\exists p)\, p \,\epsilon\, c \wedge \text{ACTION}(p) = \text{DROP}(x))]
\end{aligned} \tag{39}$$

In the initial situation, Rob knows that he is not holding an object and is located next to an object which is on the floor. We distinguish between the situation where Rob does not know the time

$$\begin{aligned}
\mathbf{Knows}(\neg(\exists x\, \text{OBJ}(x) \wedge \text{HOLDING}(x, \text{now})) \wedge \\
\exists y\, (\text{OBJ}(y) \wedge \text{AT}(y, \text{now}) \wedge \text{ON\_FLOOR}(x, \text{now}), s_0))
\end{aligned} \tag{40}$$

from the case where he knows the time:

$$\begin{aligned}
\mathbf{Knows}(\neg(\exists x\, \text{OBJ}(x) \wedge \text{HOLDING}(x, \text{now})) \wedge \exists y\, (\text{OBJ}(y) \wedge \text{AT}(y, \text{now}) \wedge \\
\text{ON\_FLOOR}(x, \text{now}) \wedge \text{TIME}(\text{now}) = t, s_0))
\end{aligned} \tag{41}$$

We then represent the proposition that in the situation resulting from first starting to whistle and starting to pickup a coffee cup at time 5, then blinking the light at time 7, and then ending the pickup action and the whistling at time 9, Rob knows that the object he is holding is the one that was on the floor when he began singing.

$$\begin{aligned}
\mathbf{Knows}[(\exists x, \exists t_1)(\text{HOLDING}(x, \text{now}) \wedge \\
\mathbf{Wasat}(t_1, \text{ON\_FLOOR}(x, \text{then}), \text{now}) \\
\wedge\, \mathbf{Happened}(t_1, \text{START\_WHISTLE}, \text{now}) \wedge t_1 < \text{TIME}(\text{now}) \\
\text{DO}(\{< \text{END\_WHISTLE}, 9 >< \text{END\_PICKUP}(\text{COFFEE\_CUP}), 9 >\}, \\
\text{DO}(\{< \text{BLINK\_LIGHT}, 7 >\}, \\
\text{DO}(\{< \text{START\_WHISTLE}, 5 > \\
< \text{START\_PICKUP}(\text{COFFEE\_CUP}), 5 >\}, s_0))))]
\end{aligned} \tag{42}$$

As above, Rob knows that the object he is holding is the one that was on the floor when he began singing, but he also knows the current time.

$$\begin{aligned}
\exists t\, \mathbf{Knows}[(\exists x, \exists t_1)(\text{HOLDING}(x, \text{now}) \wedge \\
\mathbf{Wasat}(t_1, \text{ON\_FLOOR}(x, \text{then}), \text{now}) \\
\wedge\, \mathbf{Happened}(t_1, \text{START\_WHISTLE}, \text{now}) \\
\wedge\, \text{TIME}(\text{now}) = t \wedge t_1 < t \\
\text{DO}(\{< \text{END\_WHISTLE}, 9 >< \text{END\_PICKUP}(\text{COFFEE\_CUP}), 9 >\}, \\
\text{DO}(\{< \text{BLINK\_LIGHT}, 7 >\}, \\
\text{DO}(\{< \text{START\_WHISTLE}, 5 > \\
< \text{START\_PICKUP}(\text{COFFEE\_CUP}), 5 >\}, s_0))))]
\end{aligned} \tag{43}$$

Our axiomatization guarantees that Equation 40 $\models$ Equation 42. We also have Equation 41 $\models$ Equation 43. However, Equation 40 $\not\models$ Equation 43.

## 6.3   Example 2

This example involves a very unusual door. It requires the user to first turn the key (assumed to be in the door) and read the combination off of a display at exactly the same time. Then 5 seconds later, this combination should be entered, then after another 5 seconds the door can be pulled open. All the while the key needs to be turned as it will spring back when the turning is ended.

To be able to pull a door, the agent must be located in front of a door.

$$\text{POSS}(\text{PULLDOOR}(x), s) \equiv \text{AT}(x, s) \wedge \text{DOOR}(x, s) \tag{44}$$

It is possible for the agent to start turning the key in $x$ if he is at $x$ and he is holding the key.

$$\text{POSS}(\text{START\_TURN\_KEY}(x), s) \equiv \\ \text{AT}(x, s) \wedge \text{DOOR}(x, s) \wedge \neg\text{KEY\_TURNED}(s) \tag{45}$$

It is possible for the agent to stop turning the key if the key is turned.

$$\text{POSS}(\text{END\_TURN\_KEY}(x), s) \equiv \text{KEY\_TURNED}(s) \tag{46}$$

In order to enter the combination of the door at a particular time, the object must be a door, the agent must be next to the door, and the agent must know the combination. Note that the combination of the door changes over time and so the combination entered must be the combination of the door at a particular time point. In order for it to be possible to enter the combination associated with a time $i$ seconds ago, the agent must know the combination associated with a time $i$ seconds prior to the current time, but does not need to know the value of the current time.

$$\text{POSS}(\text{ENTER\_COMBO}(x, (\text{START}(s) - i)), s) \equiv \\ \text{DOOR}(x, s) \wedge \text{AT}(x, s) \wedge \\ \mathbf{Kref}(\text{COMBO}(x, (\text{START}(\mathsf{now}) - i), s) \tag{47}$$

It is possible for the agent to read the combination if the agent is at the door

$$\text{POSS}(\text{READ}_{\text{COMBO}}(x), s) \equiv \text{AT}(x, s) \wedge \text{DOOR}(x, s) \tag{48}$$

and the result of doing so is that the agent will then know the combination for the time that the read action occurred.

$$STC(\text{READ}_{\text{COMBO}}(x), s) \equiv \\ \text{COMBINATION}(\text{START}(s), s) = \text{COMBINATION}(\text{START}(s'), s') \tag{49}$$

The successor state axiom for the key to be turned is as follows:

$$\text{Poss}(c, s) \rightarrow [\text{KEY\_TURNED}(x, do(c, s)) \equiv \\ (\exists p)(p \in c \wedge \text{ACTION}(p) = \text{START\_TURN\_KEY}(x) \vee \\ (\text{KEY\_TURNED}(x, s) \wedge \\ \neg(\exists p) p \in c \wedge \text{ACTION}(p) = \text{END\_TURN\_KEY}(x)))] \tag{50}$$

The successor state axiom for the fluent OPENED (i.e. be open) is as follows:

$$
\begin{aligned}
\text{Poss}(c, s) \to [\text{OPENED}(x, \text{DO}(c, s) \equiv \\
\exists t_1 t_2 \ \ t_1 = \text{START}(s) - 10 \ \wedge t_2 = \text{START}(s) - 5 \\
\textbf{KEY\_TURNED}(x, s) \wedge \\
\textbf{Happened}(t_1, \text{START\_TURN\_KEY}(x), s) \wedge \\
(\exists p)\, p \,\epsilon\, c \wedge \text{ACTION}(p) = \text{PULLDOOR}(x) \wedge \\
\textbf{Happened}(t_2, \text{ENTER\_COMBO}(x, (\text{START}(s) - 10)), s) \\
\vee (\text{OPENED}\ (x, s) \wedge \\
\neg (\exists p)\, p \,\epsilon\, c \wedge \text{ACTION}(p) = \text{CLOSEDOOR}(x))]
\end{aligned}
\tag{51}
$$

For the door to open, it is necessary to pull the door after having first turned the key, waited 5 seconds, entered the the combination from the time the key was turned, and then waited another five seconds without having released the key.

Our axiomatization entails that after carrying out this sequence of actions, the door is open.

$$
\begin{aligned}
\text{OPENED}(\text{DOOR}_1, \text{DO}(\{< \text{PULLDOOR}(\text{DOOR}_1), 105 >\}, \\
\text{DO}(\{< \text{ENTER\_COMBO}(\text{DOOR}_1, 95), 100 >\}, \\
\text{DO}(\{< \text{READ}_{\text{COMBO}}(\text{DOOR}_1), 95 >, < \text{START\_TURN\_KEY}, 95 >\}, s_0)))))
\end{aligned}
\tag{52}
$$

## 7   Properties of the Formulation

We can then prove a number of results about this representation. First of all, we show that the distinction between indexical and objective time is preserved.

**Theorem 1 (Default Persistence of Ignorance of Objective Time).** *For all situations s, if* $\neg \exists t$ **Know**$(\text{start}(\text{now}) = t, s)$ *then in* $do(c, s)$ *where c is any concurrent action it is also be the case that* $\neg \exists t$ **Know**$(\text{start}(\text{now}) = t, s)$ *unless there is some* $a \in c$ *defined in the successor state axiom for K as producing knowledge of time.*

**Theorem 2 (Persistence of Knowledge of Objective Time).** *For all situations s, if* $\exists t$ **Know**$(\text{start}(\text{now}) = t, s)$ *then in* $do(c, s)$ *where c is any concurrent action it is also be the case that* $\exists t$ **Know**$(\text{start}(\text{now}) = t, s)$

We also show (using **Happened** and **Wasat**) that even if agents do not know the objective time, they do know how much time has passed since the last occurrence of a particular action or the last time at which a particular fluent was true. Additionally, our results preserve the solution to the frame problem for knowledge. Analogues of theorems from [19] carry over to the framework considered here. Actions only affect knowledge in the appropriate way.

## 8   Conclusions

Our paper presents a unified logical theory of knowledge, sensing, time, and concurrency. The language is based upon the dialect of the situation calculus used by the *Cognitive*

*Robotics Group* at the University of Toronto. Therefore, the work reported here can be combined with the robot programming languages GOLOG[7] and CONGOLOG[2] to specify agents that perform sensing and concurrent actions and need to reason about the interaction of the two.

In a companion paper [23], a regression operator $\mathcal{R}$ is defined relative to a set of successor state axioms. The existence of the regression operator is the basis for efficient methods for answering the projection problem, as well as utilization of the language GOLOG and the possible development of planning methods for use with this language.

There are a variety of potential applications for the work discussed here. These include the verification and modeling of multi-agent systems [22], high-level robot control [21], and the formalization of testing actions in the context of diagnosis [10,12].

**Acknowledgments.** We thank Yves Lespérance for helpful discussions on many of the topics covered in this paper. Research for this paper was partially supported by NSF grants SES-9819116 and CISE-9818309, by the New Jersey Institute of Technology under SBR grant 421250, and by the New Jersey Commission on Science and Technology.

# References

1. M. Gelfond, V. Lifschitz, and A. Rabinov. What are the limitations of the situation calculus? In *Automated Reasoning: Essays in Honor of Woody Bledsoe*, pages 167–179. Kluwer Academic Publishers, Dordrecht, 1996.
2. G. De Giacomo, Y. Lespérance, and H. J. Levesque. Reasoning about concurrent execution, prioritized interrupts, and exogeneous actions in the situation calculus. In *Proceedings of the Fifteenth International Joint Conference on Artificial Intelligence*, Nagoya, Japan, 1997.
3. G. Lakemeyer and H.J. Levesque. AOL: A logic of acting, sensing, knowing and only-knowing. In *Principles of Knowledge Representation and Reasoning: Proceedings of the Sixth International Conference (KR-98)*, pages 316–327. Morgan Kaufmann Publishing, 1998.
4. Yves Lespérance and Hector Levesque. Indexical knowledge and robot action—a logical account. *Artificial Intelligence*, 73(1-2):69–115, February 1995.
5. Yves Lespérance, Hector J. Levesque, Fangzhen Lin, and Richard B. Scherl. Ability and knowing how in the situation calculus. *Studia Logica*, 2000. To appear.
6. Hector Levesque. What is planning in the presence of sensing? In *AAAI-96*, 1996.
7. Hector Levesque, Raymond Reiter, Yves Lespérance, Fangzhen Lin, and Richard B. Scherl. Golog: A logic programming language for dynamic domains. *Journal of Logic Programming*, 1997.
8. Fangzhen Lin and Raymond Reiter. State constraints revisited. *Journal of Logic and Computation*, 4(5):655–678, 1994.
9. J. McCarthy and P. Hayes. Some philosophical problems from the standpoint of artificial intelligence. In B. Meltzer and D. Michie, editors, *Machine Intelligence 4*, pages 463–502. Edinburgh University Press, Edinburgh, UK, 1969.
10. Sheila McIlraith and Richard B. Scherl. What sensing tells us: Towards a formal theory of testing for dynamical systems. In *Proceedings, Seventeenth National Conference on Artificial Intelligence*, pages 483–490, 2000.
11. Sheila A. McIlraith. Integrating actions and state constraints: A closed-form solution to the ramification problem (sometimes). *Artificial Intelligence*, pages 87–121, January 2000.
12. Sheila Ann McIlraith. *Towards a Formal Account of Diagnostic Problem Solving*. PhD thesis, University of Toronto, 1997.

13. R.C. Moore. Reasoning about knowledge and action. Technical Note 191, SRI International, October 1980.
14. J.A. Pinto. *Temporal Reasoning in the Situation Calculus*. PhD thesis, Department of Computer Science, University of Toronto, Toronto, Ontario, 1994. Available as technical report KRR-TR-94-1.
15. Javier A. Pinto. Concurrent actions and interacting effects. In *Principles of Knowledge Representation and Reasoning: Proceedings of the Sixth International Conference (KR-98)*, pages 292–303. Morgan Kaufmann Publishing, 1998.
16. Raymond Reiter. The frame problem in the situation calculus: A simple solution (sometimes) and a completeness result for goal regression. In Vladimir Lifschitz, editor, *Artificial Intelligence and Mathematical Theory of Computation: Papers in Honor of John McCarthy*, pages 359–380. Academic Press, San Diego, CA, 1991.
17. Raymond Reiter. Natural actions, concurrency and continuous time in the situation calculus. In L.C. Aiello, J. Doyle, and S.C. Shapiro, editors, *Principles of Knowledge Representation and Reasoning: Proceedings of the Fifth International Conference on Principles of Knowledge Representation and Reasoning (KR'96)*, pages 2–13, San Francisco, CA, 1996. Morgan Kaufmann Publishing.
18. Raymond Reiter. Knowledge in action: Logical foundations for describing and implementing dynamical systems. Unpublished book draft, 1999.
19. Richard B. Scherl and Hector J. Levesque. The frame problem and knowledge producing actions. In *Proceedings, Eleventh National Conference on Artificial Int elligence*, pages 689–695, 1993.
20. Murray Shanahan. A circumscriptive calculus of events. *Artificial Intelligence*, 77(2):249–284, September 1995.
21. Murray Shanahan and Mark Witkowski. High-level robot control through logic. In C. Castelfranchi and Y. Lespérance, editors, *Intelligent Agents VII. Agent Theories, Architectures, and Languages — 7th. International Workshop, ATAL-2000, Boston, MA, USA, July 7–9, 2000, Proceedings*, Lecture Notes in Artificial Intelligence. Springer-Verlag, Berlin, 2001. In this volume.
22. Steven Shapiro and Yves Lespérance. Modeling multiagent systems with CASL — a feature interaction resolution application. In C. Castelfranchi and Y. Lespérance, editors, *Intelligent Agents VII. Agent Theories, Architectures, and Languages — 7th. International Workshop, ATAL-2000, Boston, MA, USA, July 7–9, 2000, Proceedings*, Lecture Notes in Artificial Intelligence. Springer-Verlag, Berlin, 2001. In this volume.
23. Stephen Zimmerbaum and Richard Scherl. Reasoning about knowledge, time, and concurrency in the situation calculus. In *ECAI Workshop Notes: Cognitive Robotics*, pages 86–95, 2000.

# Developing Multiagent Systems with agentTool

Scott A. DeLoach and Mark Wood

Department of Electrical and Computer Engineering
Air Force Institute of Technology
2950 P Street, Wright-Patterson AFB, OH 45433-7765
scott.deloach@afit.edu

**Abstract.** The advent of multiagent systems has brought together many disciplines and given us a new way to look at intelligent, distributed systems. However, traditional ways of thinking about and designing software do not fit the multiagent paradigm. This paper describes the Multiagent Systems Engineering (MaSE) methodology and agentTool, a tool to support MaSE. MaSE guides a designer from an initial system specification to implementation by guiding the designer through a set of inter-related graphically based system models. The underlying formal syntax and semantics of clearly and unambiguously ties them together as envisioned by MaSE.

## 1 Introduction

The advent of multiagent systems has brought together many disciplines in an effort to build distributed, intelligent, and robust applications. They have given us a new way to look at distributed systems and provided a path to more robust intelligent applications. However, many of our traditional ways of thinking about and designing software do not fit the multiagent paradigm. Over the past few years, there have been several attempts at creating tools and methodologies for building such systems. Unfortunately, many of the methodologies have focused on single agent architectures [9, 13] or have not been adequately supported by automated toolsets [5, 17]. In our research, we have been developing both a complete-lifecycle methodology and a complimentary environment for analyzing, designing, and developing heterogeneous multiagent systems. The methodology we are developing is called Multiagent Systems Engineering (MaSE) while the tool we are building to support that methodology is called agentTool.

In this research, we view agents as a specialization of the objects. Instead of objects whose methods that are invoked directly by other objects, agents coordinate their actions via conversations to accomplish individual and community goals. Interestingly, this viewpoint sidesteps the issues regarding what is or is not an agent. We view agents merely as a convenient abstraction, which may or may not possess intelligence. In this way, we can handle intelligent and non-intelligent system components equally within the same framework. This view also justifies our use object-oriented tools and techniques. Since agents are specializations of objects, we can tailor general object-oriented methods and apply them to the specification and design of multiagent systems.

C. Castelfranchi, Y. Lespérance (Eds.): Intelligent Agents VII, LNAI 1986, pp. 46–60, 2001.
© Springer-Verlag Berlin Heidelberg 2001

## 2  Multiagent Systems Engineering Methodology

The general flow of MaSE follows the seven steps shown in Figure 1.  The rounded rectangles on the left side denote the models used in each step.  The goal of MaSE is to guide a system developer from an initial system specification to a multiagent system implementation.  This is accomplished by directing the designer through this set of inter-related system models.  Although the majority of the MaSE models are graphical, the underlying semantics clearly and unambiguously defines specific relationships between the various model components.

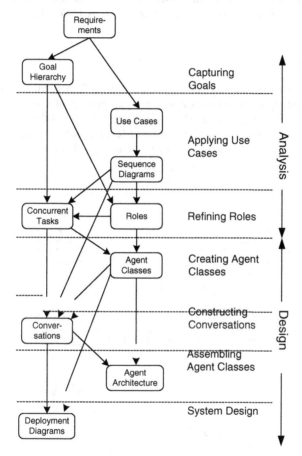

**Fig. 1.** MaSE Methodology

MaSE is designed to be applied iteratively.  Under normal circumstances, we would expect a designer to move through each step multiple times, moving back and forth between models to ensure each model is complete and consistent.  While this is common practice using most design methodologies, MaSE was specifically designed to support this process by formally capturing the relationships between the models.  By automating the MaSE models in our agentTool environment, these relationships are captured and enforced thus supporting the designer's ability to freely move between steps. The result is consistency between the various MaSE models and a system design that satisfies the original system goals.

MaSE, as well as agentTool, is independent of a particular multiagent system architecture, agent architecture, programming language, or communication framework. Systems designed using MaSE can be implemented in a variety ways. For example, a system could be designed and implemented that included a heterogeneous mix of agent architectures and used any one of a number of existing agent communication frameworks. The ultimate goal of MaSE and agentTool is the automatic generation of code that is correct with respect to the original system specification. With such a capability, MaSE and agentTool could work hand in hand with flexible and efficient runtime environments such as JADE [1].

## 2.1 Capturing Goals

The first step in the MaSE methodology is *Capturing Goals*, which takes the initial system specification and transforms it into a structured set of system goals, depicted in a *Goal Hierarchy Diagram*, as shown in Figure 2. In MaSE, a *goal* is always defined as a system-level objective. Lower-level constructs may inherit or be responsible for goals, but goals always have a system-level context.

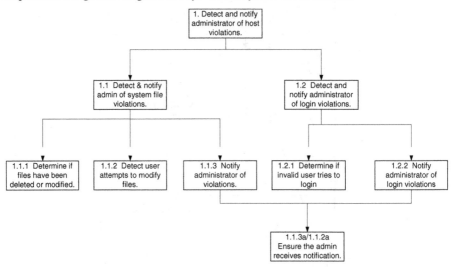

**Fig. 2.** Goal Hierarchy Diagram

There are two steps to *Capturing Goals*: identifying the goals and structuring goals. Goals are identified by distilling the essence of the set of requirements. These requirements may include detailed technical documents, user stories, or formalized specifications. Once these goals have been captured and explicitly stated, they are less likely to change than the detailed steps and activities involved in accomplishing them [7]. Next, the identified goals are analyzed and structured into a Goal Hierarchy Diagram. In a Goal Hierarchy Diagram, goals are organized by importance. Each level of the hierarchy contains goals that are roughly equal in scope and sub-goals are necessary to satisfy parent goals. Eventually, each goal will be associated with roles and agent classes that are responsible for satisfying that goal.

## 2.2  Applying Use Cases

The *Applying Uses Cases* step is a crucial step in translating goals into roles and associated tasks. *Use cases* are drawn from the system requirements and are narrative descriptions of a sequence of events that define desired system behavior. They are examples of how the system should behave in a given case.

To help determine the actual communications required within a multiagent system, the use cases are restructured as Sequence Diagrams, as shown in Figure 3. A *Sequence Diagram* depicts a sequence of events between multiple roles and, as a result, defines the minimum communication that must take place between roles. The roles identified in this step form the initial set of roles used to fully define the system roles in the next step. The events identified here are also used later to help define tasks and conversations since all events between roles will require a conversation between the agent classes if the roles are played by different agent classes.

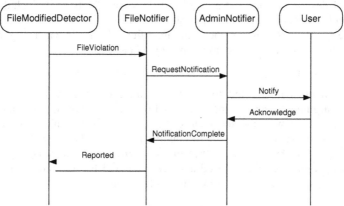

**Fig. 3.** Sequence Diagram

## 2.3  Refining Roles

The third step in MaSE is to ensure we have identified all the necessary roles and to develop the tasks that define role behavior and communication patterns. Roles are identified from the Sequence Diagrams developed during the Applying Use Cases step as well as the system goals defined in Capturing Goals. We ensure all system goals are accounted for by associating each goal with a specific role that is eventually played by at least one agent in the final design. A *role* is an abstract description of an entity's expected function and is similar to the notion of an actor in a play or an office within an organization [6]. Each goal is usually mapped to a single role. However, there are many situations where it is useful to combine multiple goals in a single role for convenience or efficiency. We base these decisions on standard software engineering concepts such as functional, communicational, procedural, or temporal cohesion. Other factors include the natural distribution of resources or special interfacing issues. Roles are captured in a Role Model as shown in Figure 4.

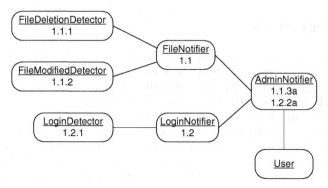

**Fig. 4.** Role Model

Once roles have been defined, tasks are created. A set of concurrent tasks provide a high-level description of what a role must do to satisfy its goals including how it interacts with other roles. An example of a MaSE *Concurrent Task Diagram*, which defines the Notify User task of the AdminNotifier role, is shown in Figure 5. The syntax of a transition follows the notation shown below [3].

```
trigger(args1) [ guard ] / transmission(args2)
```

The statement is interpreted to say that if an event *trigger* is received with a number of arguments *args1* and the condition *guard* holds, then the message *transmission* is sent with the set of arguments *args2*. All items are optional. For example, a transition with just a guard condition, *[guard]*, is allowed, as well as one with a received message and a transmission, *trigger / transmission*. Multiple transmission events are also allowed and are separated by semi-colons (;). Actions may be performed in a state and are written as functions.

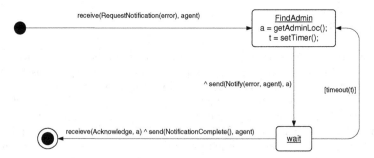

**Fig. 5.** MaSE Task

## 2.4  Creating Agent Classes

In *Creating Agent Classes*, agent classes are identified from roles and documented in an Agent Class Diagram, as shown in Figure 6. Agent Class Diagrams depict agent classes as boxes and the conversations between them as lines connecting the agent classes. As with goals and roles, we generally define a one-to-one mapping between roles, which are listed under the agent class name, and agent classes. However, the designer may combine multiple roles in a single agent class or map a single role to multiple agent classes. Since agents inherit the communication paths between roles, any paths between two roles become conversations between their respective classes. Thus, as the designer assigns roles to agent classes, the overall organization of the system is defined. To make the organization more efficient, it is often desirable to combine two roles that share a high volume of message traffic. When determining which roles to combine, concepts such as cohesion and the volume of message traffic are important considerations.

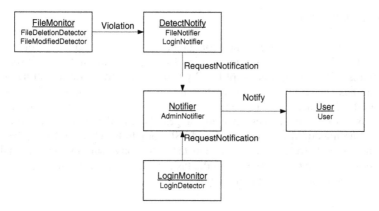

**Fig. 6.** Agent Class Diagram

## 2.5  Constructing Conversations

*Constructing Conversations* is the next step of MaSE, which is often performed almost in parallel with the succeeding step of Assembling Agents. The two steps are closely linked, as the agent architecture defined in Assembling Agents must implement the conversations and methods defined in Constructing Conversations. A MaSE conversation defines a coordination protocol between two agents. Specifically, a conversation consists of two Communication Class Diagrams, one each for the initiator and responder. A *Communication Class Diagram* is a pair of finite state machines that define a conversation between two participant agent classes. One side of a conversation is shown in Figure 7. The initiator always begins the conversation by sending the first message. The syntax for Communication Class Diagrams is very similar to that of Concurrent Task Diagrams. The main difference between conversations and concurrent tasks is that concurrent tasks may include multiple conversations between many different roles and tasks whereas conversations are binary exchanges between individual agents.

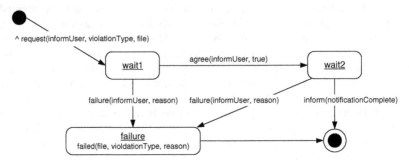

**Fig. 7.** Communication Class Diagram

## 2.6   Assembling Agents

In this step of MaSE, the internals of agent classes are created. Robinson [15] describes the details of assembling agents from a set of standard or user-defined architectures. This process is simplified by using an architectural modeling language that combines the abstract nature of traditional architectural description languages with the Object Constraint Language, which allows the designer to specify low-level details. When combined, these two languages provide the same capabilities as the text based architectural language of HEMASL found elsewhere in this volume [11]. A current research focus is how to map tasks to conversations and internal agent architectures. The actions specified in the tasks and conversations must be mapped to internal functions of the agent architecture.

## 2.7   System Deployment

The final step of MaSE defines the configuration of the actual system to be implemented. To date, we have only looked at static, non-mobile systems although we are currently investigating the specification and design of dynamic and mobile agent systems. In MaSE, we define the overall system architecture using Deployment Diagrams to show the numbers, types, and locations of agents within a system as shown in Figure 8. The three dimensional boxes denote individual agents while the lines connecting them represent actual conversations. A dashed-line box encompasses agents that are located on the same physical platform.

The agents in a Deployment Diagram are actual instances of agent classes from the Agent Class Diagram. Since the lines between agents indicate communications paths, they are derived from the conversations defined in the Agent Class Diagram as well. However, just because an agent type or conversation is defined in the Agent Class Diagram, it does not necessarily have to appear in a Deployment Diagram.

System Deployment is also where all previously undefined implementation decisions, such as programming language or communication framework, must be made. While in a pure software engineering sense, we want to put off these decisions until this step, there will obviously be times when the decision are made early, perhaps even as part of the requirements.

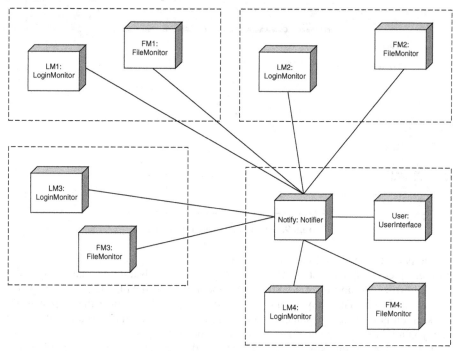

**Fig. 8.** Deployment Diagram

# 3  agentTool

The agentTool system is our attempt to implement a tool to support and enforce MaSE. Currently agentTool implements three of the seven steps of MaSE: Creating Agent Classes, Constructing Conversations, and Assembling Agent Classes. We are adding support for the analysis phase.

The agentTool user interface is shown in Figure 9. The menus across the top allow access to several system functions, including a persistent knowledge base [14], conversation verification [10], and code generation. The buttons on the left add specific items to the diagrams while the text window below them displays system messages. The different MaSE diagrams are accessed via the tabbed panels across the top of the main window. When a MaSE diagram is selected, the designer can manipulate it graphically in the window. Each panel has different types of objects and text that can be placed on them. Selecting an object in the window enables other related diagrams to become accessible. For example, in Figure 9, two agents have been added with a conversation between them. When the user selects the *Advertise* conversation (by clicking on the line), the *Conv:Advertise Initiator* and *Conv:Advertise Responder* tabbed panes become visible. The user may then access those diagrams by selecting the appropriate tab.

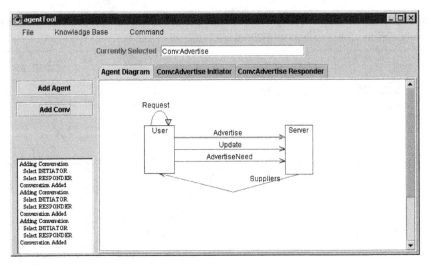

**Fig. 9.** Agent Class Diagram Panel

The part of agentTool that is perhaps the most appealing is the ability to work on different pieces of the system and at various levels of abstraction interchangeably, which mirrors the ability of MaSE to incrementally add detail. The "tabbed pane" operation of agentTool implements this capability of MaSE since the step you are working on is always represented by the current diagram and the available tabs show how you might move up and down through the methodology.

It is easier to envision the potential of this capability by considering the implementation of the entire MaSE methodology in agentTool. During each step of system development, the various analysis and design diagrams would be available through tabs on the main window. The ordering of the tabs follows the MaSE steps, so selecting a tab to the left of the current pane would move "back" in the methodology while selecting a tab to the right would move "forward." The available diagrams (tabs) are controlled by the currently selected object. The available diagrams include those that can be reached following valid MaSE steps. For instance, by selecting a conversation, tabs for the associated Communication Class Diagrams become available while selecting an agent would cause a tab for the Agent Architecture Diagram to appear.

## 3.1   Building a Multiagent System Using agentTool

Constructing a multiagent system using agentTool begins in an Agent Class Diagram as shown above in Figure 9. Since a conversation can only exist between agent classes, agent classes are generally added before conversations. While we can add all the agent classes to the Agent Class Diagram before adding any conversations, we can also add "sections" of the system at a time, connecting appropriate agent classes with conversations, and then moving onto the next section. Either method is supported and is generally a matter of personal choice.

## 3.2  Constructing Conversations in agentTool

Once we have defined agent classes and conversations, we can define the details of the conversations using Communication Class Diagrams. The "Add State" button adds a state to the panel while the "Add Conversation" button adds a conversation between the two selected states. A conversation can be verified at any point during its creation by using the *Verify Conversations* command from the Command menu [10]. The agentTool verification process ensures conversation specifications are deadlock free. If any errors exist, the verification results in a highlighted piece or pieces of a conversation, as shown in Figure 10 on the "Ack" transition (highlights are yellow in the application). Each highlight indicates a potential error as detected by the verification routine.

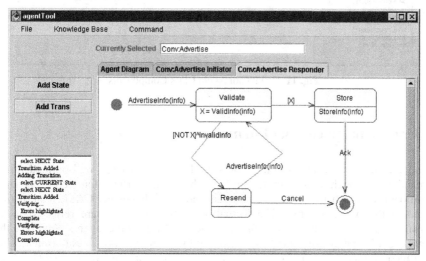

**Fig. 10.**  agentTool Conversation Error

## 3.3  Assembling Agent Class Components in agentTool

Agent classes in agentTool have internal components that can be added, removed, and manipulated in a manner similar to the other panels of agentTool. Agent classes do have an added layer of complexity however, since all of their components can have Component State Diagrams associated with them and additional sub-components beneath them. The agent class components shown in Figure 11 are the details of the "User" agent class from Figure 9.

Details can also be added to lower levels of abstraction. In Figure 11, the *Component Stat Diag* and *MessageInterface Architecture* tabs lead to a Component State Diagram and Sub-Architecture Diagram respectively. The Component State Diagram defines the dynamic behavior of the component while the Sub-Architecture Diagram contains additional components and connector that further define the component.

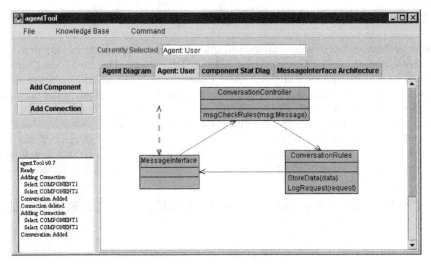

**Fig. 11.** agentTool Agent Class Components

## 4   Underlying agentTool Formalisms

Although graphical in nature, the models used in MaSE have a well-defined formal semantics, although space limitations prohibit their introduction here. A more traditional approach toward a formal agent modeling language, CASL, can also be found in this volume [16]. The formal semantics of MaSE are reflected in the transformations from one abstraction to the next. For example, agents *play* roles that *capture* goals and conversations have exactly two participants. These semantics are both incorporated and enforced by agentTool. In a future version of agentTool that incorporates the entire MaSE methodology, a role could be mapped "backward" to the set of goals from which it was created or "forward" to the agent class that plays it.

The agentTool system is based on an object hierarchy that mimics the objects in MaSE. The current agentTool object model is shown in Figure 12. In agentTool, each *System* is composed of a set of *Agents* and *Conversations*. As described above each Agent may have an *Architecture*, which is composed of *Components* and *Connectors*. Likewise, a Conversation is composed of two *State Tables*, which consist of a set of *States* and *Transitions*. Since the internal object model of agentTool only allows the configurations permitted by MaSE, we claim that it formally enforces the MaSE diagram structure and interrelationships.

Since we do not currently have MaSE entirely implemented in agentTool, it is difficult to see how the diagrams from different parts of the methodology are tied together. In our current work, we are extending the agentTool object model to incorporate Goals, Roles, and Tasks. Figure 13 shows this extension to the object model. In the new object model an *Agent* plays at least one *Role*, which consists of one or more *Tasks*. Likewise, all *Roles* must be played by at least one *Agent*. Each Role also captures one or more *Goals* and each *Goal* is captured by exactly one *Role*. This object model makes it easy to see that if the user selects a particular agent, it is not difficult to determine exactly what *Roles*, *Tasks*, *Goals*, and *Conversations* may be affected by any changes to that *Agent*. What may be even more important is that the user can select a *Goal* and easily determine what *Roles*, *Tasks*, *Agents*, and *Conversations* might be affected by changes to the goal.

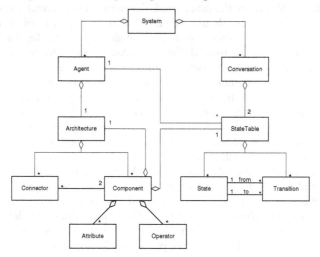

**Fig. 12.** Current MaSE Object Model

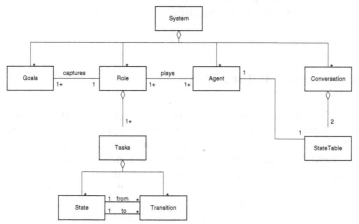

**Fig. 13.** Extended MaSE Object Model

## 5  Related Work

There have been several proposed methodologies for analyzing, designing, and building multiagent systems [5]. The majority of these are based on existing object-oriented or knowledge-based methodologies. The most widely published methodology is Gaia methodology [17], which we will use for comparison.

While Gaia and MaSE take a similar approach in analyzing multiagent system, MaSE is more detailed and provides more guidance to system designer. The first step in Gaia is to extract roles from the problem specification without real guidance on how this is done. MaSE, on the other hand, develops Goal Hierarchy and Use Cases to help define what roles should be developed. The use of roles by both methodologies is similar. They are used to abstractly define the basic behaviors within the system. In Gaia, roles define functionality in terms *responsibilities.* In MaSE, similar functionality is defined in Concurrent Task Diagram; however, concurrent tasks provide communication detail not found in Gaia. Gaia *permissions* define the use of resources by a particular role, which is not yet defined in MaSE. Gaia uses *activities* to model computations performed within roles and *protocols* to define interactions with other roles. These are captured with MaSE tasks, which once again provide more detail about when actions are performed, data input and output, and how the actions relate to the interaction protocols.

In the design phase, Gaia only provides a high-level design. It consists of an Agent Model, which identifies the agent types (and the roles from which they were derived) and their multiplicity within the system. This information is captured in MaSE Agent Class Diagrams and Deployment Diagrams. The Gaia Services Model identifies the main services of the agent type in terms of the inputs, outputs, and pre- and post-conditions. This does not have a direct parallel in MaSE although services and the details of the interactions (inputs and outputs) are defined in MaSE tasks and conversations. Finally, the Gaia acquaintance model identifies lines of communications between agent types. In MaSE, this information is captured in the Agent Class Diagram, which also identifies the types of interactions as individual conversations.

## 6   Conclusions and Future Work

The Multiagent Systems Engineering methodology is a seven-step process that guides a designer in transforming a set of requirements into a successively more concrete sequence of models. By analyzing the system as a set of roles and tasks, a system designer is naturally lead to the definition of autonomous, pro-active agents that coordinate their actions to solve the overall system goals.

MaSE begins in the analysis phase by capturing the essence of an initial system context in a structured set of goals. Next, a set of use cases are captured and transformed into Sequence Diagrams so desired event sequences will be designed into the system. Finally, the goals are combined to form roles, which include tasks that describe how roles satisfy their associated goals. In the design phase, roles are combined to define agent classes and tasks are used to identify conversations between the classes. To complete the agent design, the internal agent architecture is chosen and actions are mapped to functions in the architecture. Finally, the run-time structure of the system is defined in a Deployment Diagram and implementation choices such as language and communication framework are made.

MaSE, and our current version of agentTool, has been used to develop five to ten small to medium sized multiagent systems ranging from information systems [8, 12] and mixed-initiative distributed planners [2] to biologically based immune systems [4]. The results have been promising. Users tell us that following MaSE is relatively simple, yet is flexible enough to allow for a variety of solutions. We are currently using MaSE and agentTool to develop larger scale multiagent systems that are both mobile and dynamic in nature.

From our research on MaSE and agentTool, we have learned many lessons. First, it is clear that developing a methodology with an eye towards automation and formally defined relationships between the various models simplifies the semantics and makes implementation much easier. Secondly, using object-oriented principles as a basis for our methodology was the right choice. We consider MaSE a domain specific instance of the more general object-oriented paradigm. This also simplifies the underlying formal model as well as code generation. Instead of dealing with a general association, we have just one – a conversation between agents. While agents are not equivalent to an object, they are a specialization. Once again, we can focus our methodology and tool thus making the entire process less complex. Finally, we have shown that you can develop a methodology and tool to support multiple types of agent architectures, languages, and communications frameworks.

As stated throughout this paper, MaSE and agentTool are works in progress. We are currently extending MaSE to handle mobility and dynamic systems (in terms of agents being able to enter and leave the system during execution). We are also looking more closely at the relationship between tasks, conversations, and the internal design of agents. As for agentTool, we are extending it to handle all aspects of MaSE including code generation. We currently have a code generator that generates complete conversations for a single communication framework.

**Acknowledgements.** This research was supported by the Air Force Office of Scientific Research (AFOSR) and the Dayton Area Graduate Studies Institute (DAGSI). The views expressed in this article are those of the authors and do not reflect the official policy or position of the United States Air Force, Department of Defense, or the US Government.

# References

1. F. Bellifemine, A. Poggi, and G. Rimassa. Developing Multi-Agent Systems with JADE. In C. Castelfranchi and Y. Lespérance, editors, *Intelligent Agents VII. Agent Theories, Architectures, and Languages - 7th. International Workshop, ATAL-2000, Boston, MA, USA, July 7-9, 2000, Proceedings*, Lecture Notes in Artificial Intelligence. Springer-Verlag, Berlin, 2001. In this volume.

2. M. Cox, B. Kerkez, C. Srinivas, G. Edwin, and W. Archer. Toward Agent-Based Mixed-Initiative Interfaces. *Proceedings of the International Conference on Artificial Intelligence (IC-AI) 2000*. pages 309-316. CSREA Press, 2000.

3. S. DeLoach. Multiagent Systems Engineering: a Methodology and Language for Designing Agent Systems. *Proceedings of Agent Oriented Information Systems '99*. pages 45-57, 1999.

4. P. Harmer and G. Lamont. An Agent Architecture for a Computer Virus Immune System. *Workshop on Artificial Immune Systems at Genetic and Evolutionary Computation Conference*, Las Vegas, Nevada, July 2000.

5.   C. Iglesias, M. Garijo, and J. Gonzalez. A Survey of Agent-Oriented Methodologies. In: Müller, J.P., Singh, M.P., Rao, A.S., (Eds.): *Intelligent Agents V. Agents Theories, Architectures, and Languages*. Lecture Notes in Computer Science, Vol. 1555. Springer-Verlag, Berlin Heidelberg, 1998.

6.   E. Kendall. Agent Roles and Role Models: New Abstractions for Multiagent System Analysis and Design. *Proceedings of the International Workshop on Intelligent Agents in Information and Process Management*, Bremen, Germany, September 1998.

7.   E. Kendall, U. Palanivelan, and S. Kalikivayi. Capturing and Structuring Goals: Analysis Patterns. *Proceedings of the Third European Conference on Pattern Languages of Programming and Computing*, Bad Irsee, Germany, July 1998.

8.   S. Kern, M. Cox, and M. Talbert. A Problem Representation Approach for Decision Support Systems. *Proceedings of the Eleventh Annual Midwest Artificial Intelligence and Cognitive Science Conference*, pages 68-73. AAAI, 2000.

9.   D. Kinny, M. Georgeff, and A. Rao. A Methodology and Modelling Technique for Systems of BDI Agents. *Agents Breaking Away: Proceedings of the Seventh European Workshop on Modelling Autonomous Agents in a Multi-Agent World, MAAMAW '96*. LNAI volume 1038, pages 56-71, Springer-Verlag, 1996.

10.  T. Lacey, S. DeLoach. Automatic Verification of Multiagent Conversations. *Proceedings of the Eleventh Annual Midwest Artificial Intelligence and Cognitive Science Conference*, pages 93-100. AAAI, 2000.

11.  S. Marini, M. Martelli, V. Mascardi, and F. Zini. Specification of heterogeneous agent architectures. In C. Castelfranchi and Y. Lespérance, editors, *Intelligent Agents VII. Agent Theories, Architectures, and Languages - 7th. International Workshop, ATAL-2000, Boston, MA, USA, July 7-9, 2000, Proceedings*, Lecture Notes in Artificial Intelligence. Springer-Verlag, Berlin, 2001. In this volume.

12.  J. McDonald, M. Talbert, and S. DeLoach. Heterogeneous Database Integration Using Agent Oriented Information Systems. *Proceedings of the International Conference on Artificial Intelligence (IC-AI) 2000*. pages 1359-1366, CSREA Press, 2000.

13.  H. Nwana, D. Ndumu Leel, and J. Collis. ZEUS: A Toolkit for Building Distributed Multi-Agent Systems. *Applied Artificial Intelligence Journal*. **13** (1), pages 129-185, 1999.

14.  M. Raphael. *Knowledge Base Support for Design and Synthesis of Multi-agent Systems*. MS thesis, AFIT/ENG/00M-21. School of Engineering, Air Force Institute of Technology (AU), Wright-Patterson Air Force Base Ohio, USA, March 2000.

15.  D. Robinson. *A Component Based Approach to Agent Specification*. MS thesis, AFIT/ENG/00M-22. School of Engineering, Air Force Institute of Technology (AU), Wright-Patterson Air Force Base Ohio, USA, March 2000.

16.  S. Shapiro and Y. Lespérance. Modeling multiagent systems with CASL - a feature interaction resolution application. In C. Castelfranchi and Y. Lespérance, editors, *Intelligent Agents VII. Agent Theories, Architectures, and Languages - 7th. International Workshop, ATAL-2000, Boston, MA, USA, July 7-9, 2000, Proceedings*, Lecture Notes in Artificial Intelligence. Springer-Verlag, Berlin, 2001. In this volume.

17.  M. Wooldridge, N. Jennings, and D. Kinny. The Gaia Methodology for Agent-Oriented Analysis and Design. *Journal of Autonomous Agents and Multi-Agent Systems*, 3(3), 2000.

# Layered Disclosure: Revealing Agents' Internals

Patrick Riley[1], Peter Stone[2], and Manuela Veloso[1]

[1] Computer Science Department
Carnegie Mellon University
Pittsburgh, PA 15213-3891
{pfr, veloso}@cs.cmu.edu
[2] AT&T Labs — Research
180 Park Ave., room A273
Florham Park, NJ 07932
pstone@research.att.com

**Abstract.** A perennial challenge in creating and using complex autonomous agents is following their choices of actions as the world changes dynamically and understanding why they act as they do. This paper reports on our work to support human developers and observers to better follow and understand the actions of autonomous agents. We introduce the concept of *layered disclosure* by which autonomous agents have included in their architecture the foundations necessary to allow them to disclose upon request the specific reasons for their actions. Layered disclosure hence goes beyond standard plain code debugging tools. In its essence it also gives the agent designer the ability to define an appropriate information hierarchy, which can include agent-specific constructs such as internal state that persists over time. The user may request this information at any of the specified levels of detail, and either retroactively or while the agent is acting. We present layered disclosure as we created and implemented it in the simulated robotic soccer domain. We contribute the detailed design to support the application of layered disclosure to other agent domains. Layered disclosure played an important role in our successful development of the undefeated RoboCup champion CMUnited-99 multiagent team.

## 1 Introduction

A perennial challenge in creating and using complex autonomous agents is following their choices of actions as the world changes dynamically, and understanding why they act as they do. Our work focuses on environments in which agents have complex, possibly noisy, sensors and actuators. In such scenarios, even the human who develops an agent is often unable to identify what exactly caused the agent to act as it did in a given situation. This paper reports on our work to support human developers and observers to better follow and understand the actions of autonomous agents.

To this end, we introduce the concept of *layered disclosure* by which autonomous agents include in their architecture the foundations necessary to allow them to disclose to a person upon request the specific reasons for their actions. Whereas standard debugging tools allow one to trace function calls with inputs and outputs automatically,

C. Castelfranchi, Y. Lespérance (Eds.): Intelligent Agents VII, LNAI 1986, pp. 61–72, 2001.

layered disclosure gives the programmer the ability to define a specific information hierarchy, which can include agent-specific constructs such as internal state that persists over time. However, the information hierarchy must be created for the specific domain. Past agent explanation paradigms (e.g. [2,3]) have dealt with symbolic agent representations. Layered disclosure has been implemented and tested in a non-symbolic, real-time, multiagent environment.

A key component of layered disclosure is that the relevant agent information is organized in *layers*. In general, there is far too much information available to display all of it at all times. The imposed hierarchy allows the user to select at which level of detail he or she would like to probe into the agent in question. A person may then request information at any level of detail, and either retroactively or while the agent is acting. We say that the person is *probing* for information, while the agent is explicitly *disclosing* the information.

When an agent does something unexpected or undesirable, it is particularly useful to be able to isolate precisely *why* it took such an action. Using layered disclosure, a developer can probe inside the agent at any level of detail to determine precisely what needs to be altered in order to attain the desired agent behavior. For example, if a software agent is left to perform some action overnight, but fails to complete its assigned task, the developer could use layered disclosure to trace the precise reasons that the agent took each of its actions, and identify which parts of the agent need to be altered.

This paper describes our implementation of layered disclosure in the simulated robotic soccer domain. It played an important role in our successful development of the 1999 RoboCup simulator-league champion CMUnited-99 team. While the prototype implementation, including the information layers, is tailored to this domain, the layered disclosure methodology can be applied to any agent, provided that the developer defines and implements the required information hierarchy.

The remainder of this paper is organized as follows. Section 2 introduces the technical details of layered disclosure. Section 3 introduces our implementation of layered disclosure in the robotic soccer domain. Section 4 provides two detailed examples illustrating the effectiveness of layered disclosure. Sections 5 and 6 contain discussion and conclusions.

## 2   Layered Disclosure

In developing layered disclosure, we began with the assumption that agents' actions and the actual states of the world over time are generally observable. On the other hand, several agent characteristics are generally unobservable, including:

- The agents' sensory *perceptions*
- The agents' *internal states* (current role in team, current task assignment, etc.)
- The agents' *perceived current world states*
- The agents' *reasoning processes*

The goal of layered disclosure is to make these unobservable characteristics observable, either retroactively, or in real-time as an agent is acting. Furthermore, to avoid being overwhelmed with data, the observer must be able to probe into the agent at an arbitrary level of detail or abstraction.

There are four main steps to realizing this goal.

1. The developer must organize the agent's perception-cognition-action process in different levels of detail.
2. The agent must store a log of all relevant information from its internal state, world model, and reasoning process.
3. This log must be synchronized with a recording of the observable world (or generated in real-time).
4. An interface is needed to allow the developer to probe a given agent's internal reasoning at any time and any level of detail.

## 2.1 Layered Organization

The first step to implementing layered disclosure is the generation of a layered organizational structure of information to be stored for a given domain. To be the most useful, the hierrachy should contain information beyond the agent's reasoning process such as its perceptions, its internal state, and anything else that might influence its decision-making.

In particular, not all relevant information is necessarily present in an agent's action trace. For example, if an agent executes action with precondition $x > 45$ at time $t$, then one can conclude that at time $t$ the variable $x$ had a value greater than 45. However, one might want to know exactly what the value of $x$ was at time $t$ and how it got to be so. $x = 46$ may be a qualitatively different symptom from $x = 10,000$. Layered disclosure allows one to probe into an agent to determine the value of $x$ at time $t$, and, if probing more deeply, the agent's exact sensory perceptions and/or past states which caused $x$ to be set to its actual value at time $t$.

How the information hierarchy is constructed depends strongly on the architecture of the agent. For example, in our robotic soccer implementation, we use the following, where layers with greater numbers represent information that is stored at a deeper layer (scale 1–50):

**Levels 1–10:** The agent's abstract high-level goals.
**Levels 11–20:** The agent's action decisions, perhaps organized hierarchically.
**Levels 21–30:** Lower-level details regarding the specifics of these actions including all variable bindings.
**Levels 31–40:** The agent's internal state.
**Levels 41–50:** The agent's sensory perceptions.

If the agents uses a system which already includes a hierarchy, such as the operator hierarchy in hierarchical task network (HTN) planning [7], then this forms a nice basis on which to organize the layers. However, as argued above, just seeing which operators were executed does not always provide enough information. Therefore, more would need to be added to the information layers in order to make disclosure as useful as possible.

As another example, in a rule-based system, one would probably want to record which rules fired, what the exact values of the relevant variables were, what other rules also met their preconditions, and how any such ties were broken. In some cases, one may also want to include information on why certain rules did *not* meet their preconditions, though recording information about perceptions and internal state may allow the developer to reconstruct that information.

## 2.2    The Log File

Each agent's log file is its repository for all useful information that one might want to examine, either as the agent is acting or after the fact. It is generated and stored locally by the agent, or sent directly to the interface for immediate display. Each piece of information is time-stamped and tagged with its corresponding layer indicating its depth within the agents' reasoning process. The interface program can then display this information appropriately.

In general, the log file is of the format

```
<time> (<level ind>) <Text>
```

where
<time>        is the agent's conception of the current time.
<level ind> is the information's layer.
<Text>        is arbitrary agent information to be displayed.

Note that in a distributed or asynchronous environment, the agent does not in general have access to the "real world" or global time.

## 2.3    Synchronization

The agent's log files, which record what would otherwise be unobservable, must be synchronized with a recording of the *observable* world. That is, the human observer needs to be able to identify what point of the log file corresponds to a given point in the recording of the world. The more exact a correspondence can be determined, the more useful the disclosure will be.

In some domains, synchronization may be difficult to achieve. Without synchronization, layered disclosure can still be used retrospectively to understand what an agent was doing given its perception of the world. However, to understand the entire loop, that is to understand whether an agent's action was appropriate to what was really going on, and to access the agent's state from a recording of the world, synchronization is needed.

In order to synchronize, the recording of the real world must contain cues or time-stamps which match up with cues or time-stamps in the agents' log files. In environments such that agents have accurate knowledge of the global system or real-world time, the synchronization can be based on this time. Otherwise, the agent must actively transmit its internal time in such a way that it is visible to the recorder in conjunction with the agent's actions. For example, in a robotics domain, one could attach lights to the robots which flash in a given sequence in order to create a visual cue to line up the agent's log file and recording of the real world. It is then the job of the interface to display to the user both the recording and the requested layered disclosure information.

### 2.4   Interface

The interface includes a representation of the agents' actions in the form of a recording. In addition, the interface includes a method for the user to specify an agent (if there are multiple agents) and an information layer. The interface then displays the specified layer of information for the specified agent at the moment in question. The interface can also visually separate the layers to aid the human observer.

In general, there is far too much information available to display all of it at all times. The imposed hierarchy allows the user to select at which level of detail he or she would like to probe into the agent in question.

## 3   Layered Disclosure in Robotic Soccer

Our prototype layered disclosure implementation is in the simulated robotic soccer domain, in particular, in the RoboCup soccer server [1,4]. In this domain, there are 22 agents, each acting 10 times every second. Each agent gets local, incomplete perceptory information, making it impossible to determine an agent's impression of the world state based only upon the actual world state. Furthermore, it is possible for the agents to store internal state over time that can also affect their action decisions.

As laid out in Section 2 the actual world state and an agent's actions are observable (via the soccer monitor program which shows an overhead view of the soccer field), but the agents' sensory perceptions, internal states, perceived current world states, and reasoning processes are in general not observable. This lack of observability often makes it impossible to determine *why* agents acted as they did.

For example, whenever a robotic soccer agent kicks the ball towards its own goal, it is common to hear the agent's developer wondering aloud whether the agent was mistaken about its own location in the world, whether it was mistaken about the ball's or other agents' locations, or if it "meant" to kick the ball where it did, and why. Due to the dynamic, uncertain nature of the environment, it is usually impossible to reconstruct the situation exactly in order to retroactively figure out what happened. Indeed, our development of layered disclosure was inspired in part by our own inability to trace the reasons behind the actions of our own CMUnited-98 simulated agents [6].

Our layered disclosure implementation is publicly available.[1] It can and has been easily adapted for use with other RoboCup simulator teams. It works as follows.

During the course of a game, our agents store detailed records of selected information in their perceived world states, their determination of their short-term goals, and their selections of which actions will achieve these goals, along with any relevant intermediate decisions that lead to their action selections.

For example, the log file corresponding to the interface output shown in Figure 3 for agent 5 at time 838 looks like:

```
838 (35) Invalidating ball vel:0.36>0.36, vel was (1.73, -0.70)
838 (35) PB vel. est.: gpos(-32.1 -23.4),prev_seen(-33.5 -23.1)
838 (45) Sight 838.0:  B_ team:_____opp:_____9__
838 (5) Mode: AM_With_Ball
```

---

[1] http://www.cs.cmu.edu/afs/cs/usr/pstone/mosaic/RoboCup/CMUnited99-sim.html

**Fig. 1.** The layered disclosure tool. The terminal window (top right) shows layered information for the instant shown in the graphical game display (left). On the control bar (bottom right), the "P" buttons control which player is being examined and the "L" buttons control the level of displayed information.

```
838 (12) Handling the ball
838 (20) OurBreakaway() == 0
838 (25) CanDribbleTo (-22.05, -20.52): TRUE No players in cone
838 (17) handle_ball: dribbling to goal (2) -- have room
```

The content of these lines is chosen so as to be enlightening to the developer.

After the game is over, it can be replayed using the standard "logplayer" program which comes with the soccer server. Our layered disclosure module, implemented as an extension to this logplayer, makes it possible to stop the game at any point and inspect the details of an individual player's decision-making process. In this domain, the agents have an internal notion of the global time. Although it is not guaranteed to be accurate, it is sufficient for layered disclosure synchronization. Figure 1 shows our robotic soccer layered disclosure interface. For each time step, the interface strips off the times, but displays the layer and the text. The layer can be represented graphically as a series of dashes ("---") corresponding to the layer's depth.

The log file of the player being examined in Figure 1 contains the following lines. Notice that in Figure 1, only the lines at level 20 and below are displayed.

```
881 (35) My Pos: (15.85, -3.73)   angle: -24.00
881 (35) Ball Pos: (17.99, -4.87)conf: 0.95
881 (45) Sight at 880: Bv team:_  opp: 1
881 (5) Mode: AM_Offense_Active (I'm fastest to ball)
881 (15) get_ball: going to the moving ball (5) pow 100.0
881 (25) go_to_point: dash 100.0
881 (20) go_to_point 3 (21.1 -6.2)
881 (30) dashing 100.0
881 (45) Heard message of type 1 from 11
```

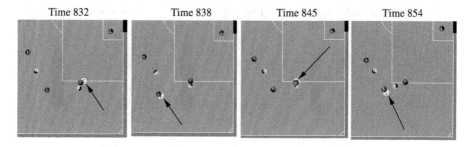

**Fig. 2.** Undesired passing behavior. The arrows point to the ball.

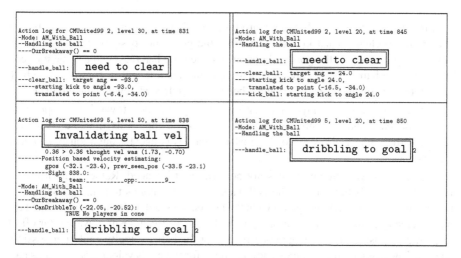

**Fig. 3.** Layered disclosure for the passing example (the boxes have been added for emphasis).

## 4  Layered Disclosure Examples

In this section we provide two examples illustrating the usefulness of layered disclosure. Both examples are drawn from the simulated robotic soccer domain.

### 4.1  Discovering Agent Beliefs

When observing an agent team performing, it is tempting, especially for a person familiar with the agents' architectures, to infer high level beliefs and intentions from the observed actions. Sometimes, this can be helpful to describe the events in the world, but misinterpretation is a significant danger.

Consider the example in Figure 2. Here, two defenders (the darker colored players) seem to pass the ball back and forth while quite close to their own goal. In general, this sort of passing back and forth in a short time span is undesirable, and it is exceptionally dangerous near the agents' own goal. Using the layered disclosure tool, we get the information displayed in Figure 3. Note that each dash '-' represents 5 levels.

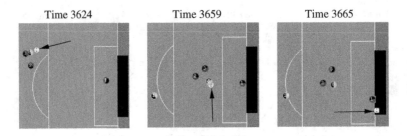

**Fig. 4.** Poorly performing defenders. The arrows point to the ball.

First, we see that in both cases that player number 2 was in control of the ball, it was trying to clear it (just kick it away from the goal), not pass to player number 5. Given the proximity of the goal and opponents, clearing is a reasonable behavior here. If a teammate happens to intercept a clear, then our team is still in control of the ball. Therefore, we conclude that this agent's behavior matches what we want and expect.

Next, we can see that player number 5 was trying to dribble towards the opponent's goal in both cases that he controlled the ball. There are no opponents immediately around him, and the path on the way to the goal is clear. This agent's intention is certainly reasonable.

However, player number 5 does not perform as it intended. Rather than dribbling forward with the ball, it kicked the ball backwards. This points to some problem with the dribbling behavior. As we go down in the layers, we see that the agent invalidated the ball's velocity. This means that it thought the ball's observed position was so far off of its predicted position that the agent's estimate for the ball's velocity could not possibly be right. The agent then computed a new estimate for the ball's velocity based on its past and current positions.

Given this estimation of the ball's velocity (which is crucial for accurate ball handling), we are led to look further into how this velocity is estimated. Also, we can compare the estimate of the velocity to the recorded world state. In the end, we find that the ball collided with the player. Therefore, it was invalid to estimate the ball's velocity based on position. In fact, this led us to more careful application of this velocity estimation technique.

Notice how useful the layering of information was here. One can first make a high level pass to understand the intentions of the agents, then examine whether thos intentions were fulfilled. If not, one can probe more deeply to discover what caused the agent to not fulfill its intention.

In this case, inferring the intentions of the players was extremely challenging given their behaviors. Without layered disclosure, the natural place to look to correct this undesirable behavior would have been in the passing decisions of the players. It would have been difficult or impossible to determine that the problem was with the estimation of the ball's velocity.

| Time | Player 2 | Player 3 |
|------|----------|----------|
| 3624 | -Defense_Active(poss=?) | *-Offense_Active* |
| 3625 | -Defense_Active(poss=l) | *-Offense_Active* |
| 3626 | -Defense_Active(poss=?) | *-Offense_Active* |
| 3627 | -Defense_Active(poss=l) | *-Offense_Active* |
| 3628 | *-Offense_Active* | -Defense_Active(poss=?) |
| 3629 | *-Offense_Active* | *-Offense_Active* |
| 3630 | *-Offense_Active* | -Defense_Active(poss=l) |
| 3631 | *-Offense_Active* | -Defense_Active(poss=l) |
| 3632 | *-Offense_Active* | -Defense_Active(poss=l) |
| 3633 | *-Offense_Active* | -Defense_Active(poss=l) |
| 3634 | *-Offense_Active* | -Defense_Active(poss=l) |
| 3635 | *-Offense_Active* | -Defense_Active(poss=l) |
| 3636 | -Defense_Active(poss=l) | *-Offense_Active* |
| 3637 | -Defense_Active(poss=l) | *-Offense_Active* |
| 3638 | -Defense_Active(poss=l) | *-Offense_Active* |
| 3639 | *-Offense_Active* | -Defense_Active(poss=l) |
| 3640 | *-Offense_Active* | -Defense_Active(poss=?) |
| 3641 | -Defense_Active(poss=l) | -Defense_Active(poss=l) |
| 3642 | -Defense_Active(poss=?) | -Defense_Active(poss=l) |
| 3643 | *-Offense_Active* | *-Offense_Active* |
| 3644 | *-Offense_Active* | -Defense_Active(poss=l) |
| 3645 | *-Offense_Active* | -Defense_Active(poss=l) |
| 3646 | -Defense_Active(poss=l) | -Defense_Active(poss=l) |
| 3647 | *-Offense_Active* | *-Offense_Active* |
| 3648 | -Defense_Active(poss=?) | *-Offense_Active* |
| 3649 | *-Offense_Active* | *-Offense_Active* |
| 3650 | -Defense_Active(poss=l) | *-Offense_Active* |
| 3651 | *-Offense_Active* | -Defense_Active(poss=l) |
| 3652 | *-Offense_Active* | -Defense_Active(poss=l) |
| 3653 | *-Offense_Active* | -Defense_Active(poss=?) |
| 3654 | *-Offense_Active* | -Defense_Active(poss=?) |
| 3655 | *-Offense_Active* | -Defense_Active(poss=?) |
| 3656 | *-Offense_Active* | -Defense_Active(poss=?) |
| 3657 | *-Offense_Active* | *-Offense_Active* |
| 3658 | *-Offense_Active* | *-Offense_Active* |
| 3659 | *-Offense_Active* | *-Offense_Active* |

**Fig. 5.** Layered disclosure for the defending example (the bold italics have been added for emphasis).

## 4.2 The Usefulness of Layers

The fact that the agents' recordings are layered is quite important. One important effect is that the layers allow the observer to look at just higher levels, then explore each case more deeply as required.

Consider the example depicted in Figure 4. Here, two defenders (the darker colored players) are unable to catch up and stop one offensive player with the ball, even though the defenders were in a good position to begin with.

Since this is a scenario that unfolds over many time steps, we need to be able to understand what happens over that time sequence. The first pass at this is to just look at the highest level decision. The first decision our agents make is in which "action mode" they are [6]. This decision is based on which team is controlling the ball, current location, role in the team structure, etc. Usually, the player fastest to the ball will be in "Offense_Active" mode, meaning they will try to get to the ball as quickly as possible. In a defensive situation, the second fastest player will be in "Defense_Active" mode, which means basically to get in the way of the player with the ball, without actively trying to steal it.

The output of just the highest level from the layered disclosure tool is depicted in Figure 5. There are two things to notice. First, the agents change roles many times over this sequence. Secondly, the agents' are often unsure about which side is in control of the ball (the 'poss=' field).

This constant changing of mode causes a problem for the agents. "Offense_Active" and "Defense_Active" modes lead the players to move to different spots on the field. By switching back and forth, the agents will waste a great deal of time turning to face the direction they want to go instead of actually going. Therefore, the agents do not catch up.

Noticing that the 'poss=' field is also in flux allows further diagnosis of the problem. The decision about what mode to go into is sometimes affected by which team the agent believes is controlling the ball. Realizing that this value is often unknown should lead to changes in the way that value is determined, or changes in the manner in which it is used.

In this case, making use of layered disclosure to examine just the high-level reasoning decisions of a pair of agents allows us to focus on a problem that would have otherwise been easily overlooked.

## 5   Discussion

Most existing debugging tools aim to automatically provide details of a program's execution. One common method is to store the entire program call stack with the arguments to each function call. In agent-based applications, it is also possible to automatically store either (i) the agent's entire reasoning process that leads directly to its actions, or (ii) just the agent's perceptions and internal state at every action opportunity.

For example, if behaviors are generated by planning operators such as in an HTN planner, (i) could be accomplished by storing the preconditions and effects of all selected operators. However, as argued in Section 2.1, the preconditions of selected actions do not necessarily disclose all relevant information pertaining to the agent.

Option (ii) allows one to recreate the agent's reasoning process and resulting actions by stepping through the program after the fact. While this option might be appropriate for agents with small states, in domains such as robotic soccer in which a large amount of information is relevant to each decision, our approach is more efficient both in terms of storage space and amount of information that needs to be conveyed to a human being; the developer can identify precisely what information is likely to be useful. In addition, storing only the internal state for subsequent reconstruction of the agent's behaviors does not allow for the agent also being able to disclose its internal state in real time as the action is proceeding.

As opposed to these automatic debugging options, layered disclosure requires a step on the part of the developer, namely the explicit definition and inclusion of an information hierarchy within the agent. In return, the developer gets full control over what information is disclosed by the agent. Our use of layered disclosure in the robotic soccer domain represents an efficient middle ground between storing the agents' entire internal states and storing just their actions.

Layered disclosure is potentially applicable in any agent-based domain. While our application is in a multiagent environment, it is inherently implemented on an individual agent: each agent discloses its own internal state. In order to take advantage of layered disclosure, one only needs to provide support for agents to store and disclose their perceptions, internal states, perceived current world states, and reasoning processes; as well as a method for synchronization between the agent's logfile and a recording of the world.

## 6   Conclusion and Future Work

Layered disclosure has proven to be very useful to us in our development of simulated robotic soccer agents. In particular, we used it as an integral part of our development of the 1999 RoboCup champion CMUnited-99 simulated robotic soccer team [5].

CMUnited-99 was built upon the CMUnited-98 team which won the RoboCup-98 simulator competition [6]. CMUnited-98 became publicly available after the 1998 competition so that other people could build upon our research. Thus, we expected there to be several teams at RoboCup-99 that could beat CMUnited-98, and indeed there were.

With this expectation, we knew that CMUnited-99 needed to improve upon CMUnited-98. However, even when we observed undesirable behaviors in CMUnited-98, it was not always clear what was going wrong. Using layered disclosure, we were able to identify and implement several significant improvements. CMUnited-99 was able to consistently beat CMUnited-98 by a significant margin and it went on to win the RoboCup-99 championship, outscoring its opponents by a combined score of 110–0.

While the prototype layered disclosure implementation is designed for a multi-agent system, it only allows the user to probe one agent at a time. A useful extension would be to allow the user to select any subset of agents and probe them all simultaneously. Coordination procedures could then be more easily understood.

Another interesting extension would be to allow the user more power in exploring the hierarchy. Currently, the user can select a layer of information to display. However, there may be only a small fraction of the information at that layer which is relevant for the current situation. Making the information hierarchy into a tree or a DAG could allow the user to further limit the amount of information displayed. However, one must be careful to keep it easy and efficient for the user to access all of the information.

Layered disclosure also has the potential to be used as a vechicle for interactive agent control. When coupled with an interface for influencing agent behaviors, layered disclosure could be used to allow the interleaving of autonomous and manual control of agents. Giving the user the power of reasonable abstractions allows them to effectively intercede in the agents' behaviors. For example, given a set of robots autonomously cleaning the floors in a large building, a person might want to monitor agents' perceptions of which floors are in most urgent need of attention. Upon noticing that one of the agents is ignoring an area that is particularly dirty, the person could determine the cause of the agent's oversight and manually alter the internal state or goal stack within the agent in real time.

We envision that layered disclosure will continue to be useful in agent development projects, particularly with complex agents acting in complex, dynamic environments. We also plan to begin using layered disclosure in interactive semi-autonomous agent-control scenarios.

## References

1. Emiel Corten, Klaus Dorer, Fredrik Heintz, Kostas Kostiadis, Johan Kummeneje, Helmut Myritz, Itsuki Noda, Patrick Riley, Peter Stone, and Travlex Yeap. Soccer server manual, version 5.0. Technical Report RoboCup-1999-001, RoboCup, 1999. At URL http://ci.etl.go.jp/˜noda/soccer/server/Documents.html.
2. Adele E. Howe, Robert St. Amant, and Paul R. Cohen. Integrating statistical methods for characterizing causal influences on planner behavior over time. In *Proceedings of the Sixth IEEE International Conference on Tools with AI*, 1994.
3. W. Lewis Johnson. Agents that learn to explain themselves. In *Proceedings of the Twelfth National Conference on Artificial Intelligence*, pages 1257–1263, 1994.
4. Itsuki Noda, Hitoshi Matsubara, Kazuo Hiraki, and Ian Frank. Soccer server: A tool for research on multiagent systems. *Applied Artificial Intelligence*, 12:233–250, 1998.
5. Peter Stone, Patrick Riley, and Manuela Veloso. The CMUnited-99 champion simulator team. In Manuela Veloso, Enrico Pagello, and Hiroaki Kitano, editors, *RoboCup-99: Robot Soccer World Cup III*, Berlin, 2000. Springer Verlag.
6. Peter Stone, Manuela Veloso, and Patrick Riley. The CMUnited-98 champion simulator team. In Minoru Asada and Hiroaki Kitano, editors, *RoboCup-98: Robot Soccer World Cup II*. Springer Verlag, Berlin, 1999.
7. David E. Wilkins. Domain-independent planning: Representation and plan generation. *Artificial Intelligence*, 22:269–301, 1984.

# Architectures and Idioms: Making Progress in Agent Design

Joanna Bryson and Lynn Andrea Stein*

Artificial Intelligence Laboratory, MIT
545 Technology Square, Cambridge MA 02139,USA
joanna@ai.mit.edu and las@ai.mit.edu

**Abstract.** This chapter addresses the problem of producing and maintaining progress in agent design. New architectures often hold important insights into the problems of designing intelligence. Unfortunately, these ideas can be difficult to harness, because on established projects switching between architectures and languages carries high cost. We propose a solution whereby the research community takes responsibility for re-expressing innovations as idioms or extensions of one or more standard architectures. We describe the process and provide an example — the concept of a Basic Reactive Plan. This idiom occurs in several influential agent architectures, yet in others is difficult to express. We also discuss our proposal's relation to the the roles of architectures, methodologies and toolkits in the design of agents.

## 1 Introduction

Design is the central problem of developing artificial intelligence. Even systems that learn or reason, learn or reason better when enabled by good design. Both experience and formal arguments have shown that structure and bias are necessary to these processes, in order to reduce the search space of their learning or reasoning algorithms to a tractable size [8, 29, 34, 35, 36]. Agent technology is itself a major design innovation which harnesses the innate ability of human designers to reason about societies of actors [19].

The importance of design explains the focus of our community on agent architectures. Agent architectures are essentially design methodologies: they are technological frameworks and scaffolding for developing agents. Of course, viewed as methodology, no architecture can be called complete. A complete architecture could automatically generate an intelligent agent from a specification.

Because the development of production-quality agents to date has always required the employment of human designers, there is a high cost associated with switching architectures. In fact, there is a high cost even for making changes to an architecture. The engineers responsible for building systems in an upgraded architecture require time to learn new structures and paradigms, and their libraries of existing solutions must be

---

* LAS: also Computers and Cognition Group, Franklin W. Olin College of Engineering, 1735 Great Plain Avenue, Needham, MA 02492 las@olin.edu

C. Castelfranchi, Y. Lespérance (Eds.): Intelligent Agents VII, LNAI 1986, pp. 73–88, 2001.

ported to or rewritten under the new version. These problems alone deter the adoption of new architectures. They are further exacerbated by the cost, for the architect, of creating documentation and maintaining a production-level architecture, and for the project manager, of evaluating new architectures. Nevertheless, new architectures often hold important insights into the problems of designing intelligence.

In this chapter we propose a meta-methodological strategy for the problem of incorporating the advances of new architectures into established development efforts. Our proposal is simple: a researcher, after having developed a new architecture, should express its major contributions in terms of one or more of the current "standard" architectures. The result of this process is a set of differences that can be rapidly understood by and absorbed into established user communities.

The next section presents this meta-methodological contribution in more detail. The bulk of the chapter then consists of an extended example of one such contribution, the Basic Reactive Plan (BRP), drawn not only from our own work [5, 6] but also from other architectures [10, 12, 26], We describe implementing it in three different architectures — Ymir [30], PRS-CL [23] and JAM [18], a Java-based extension of UM-PRS; we also discuss such an implementation in Soar. We conclude with a discussion of the roles of architecture, methodology, and toolkit in the problem of intelligent agent design.

## 2    Architecture Analysis by Reduction to Idiom

Consider the problem of expressing a feature of one architecture in another. There are two possible outcomes. A feature $f_1$, of architecture $A_1$ may be completely expressible in $A_2$. Assuming that this expression is not trivial (e.g. one line of code) then $A_1$ *constrains* $A_2$ in some way. On the other hand, if $f_1$ cannot be expressed in $A_2$ without altering the latter architecture, then $A_1$ *extends* $A_2$. These conditions are not mutually exclusive — two architectures generally both constrain and extend each other, often in multiple ways. Identifying these points of difference allows one architecture to be described in terms of another.

When we speak of the relative expressive power of two architectures, we are not really comparing their linguistic expressibility in the classical sense. Almost all agent architectures are Turing-complete; that is, a universal computing machine can be constructed within almost any agent architecture. This universal computing machine can then be used as an implementation substrate for another agent architecture. So, in the formal sense, all agent architectures are inter-reducible. We are concerned instead with the kinds of computational idioms that are *efficaciously expressible*[1] in a particular ar-

---

[1] In computational complexity theory, the notion of reducibility is augmented with the asymptotic worst case complexity of the reduction. So, for example, in the theory of NP-completeness, polynomial-time reducibility plays a crucial role. Our notion of efficacious expressibility does not rely on any criterion so sharply defined as the computational complexity of the reduction computation, but is intended to evoke a similar spectrum of reduction complexity.

chitecture. In this sense, an architecture $A_1$ may be considered to extend $A_2$ when there is no way to express reasonably succinctly the attributes of $A_1$ in $A_2$.

If, on the other hand, a feature $f_1$ of $A_1$ can be translated into a coding $i^{f_1}$ of $A_2$ with reasonable efficiency, then we call that coding $i^{f_1}$ an *idiom*. As we explained above, the existence of such an idiom means $A_1$ constrains $A_2$. This notion of constraint may seem counterintuitive, because new features of an architecture are usually thought of as extensions. However, as we argued in the introduction, extending the capabilities of the developer often means reducing the expressibility of the architecture in order to biases the search for the correct solution to the problem of designing an agent.

Although in our example $A_1$ is constrained relative to $A_2$ due to feature $f_1$ of $A_1$, adding the idiom $i^{f_1}$ is unlikely to constrain $A_2$. $A_2$ retains its full expressive power so long as the use of $i^{f_1}$ is not mandatory. For an example, consider object oriented programming. In a strictly object-based language such as smalltalk, OOP is a considerable constraint, which can consequently lead to effective and elegant program design. In contrast, C++ has added the features of objects, but still allows the full expression of C. Thus, for the C++ programmer, the elegance of OOP is an option, not a requirement.

An idiom is a compact, regularized way of expressing a frequently useful set of ideas or functionality. We borrow the notion of idiom both from natural language and computer science, though in computer science, the term 'idiom' (or 'design pattern') is sometimes used for a less rigorous mapping than we mean to imply. An architecture can be expressed as a set of idioms, either on programming languages or sometimes on other architectures. Researchers seeking to demonstrate that their architecture makes a contribution to agent design might do well to express their architecture in terms of idioms in familiar architectures. In this way, the architecture can be both readily understood and examined. We demonstrate this approach in the following two sections.

It is important to observe that this meta-methodology is different from though related to the practice of publishing extensions of architectures. First, we do not discourage the practice of building entirely new architectures. If an architecture has been built as an entity, it is more likely to have significant variation from standard architectures, potentially including vastly different emphases and specializations for particular tasks. These specializations may turn out to be generally useful contributions, or to be critical to a particular set of problems. Second, the idiomatic approach emphasizes the search for generally applicable strategies. Generality here does not necessarily mean across all possible problems, but it should mean an idiomatic solution relevant across a number of different underlying architectures. Thus even if an idiom is developed in the context of a well known architecture, it would be useful if, on publication, the researcher describes it in terms of general applicability.

## 3   Discovering an Idiom: The Basic Reactive Plan

We now illustrate our suggestions with an idiom that we will call a *Basic Reactive Plan* (BRP). In this section we will introduce the idiom, its functionality and the reasons we consider it to be a useful idiom. In the next we demonstrate its idiomaticity by expressing it in several agent architectures. We begin by situating the BRP within reactive planning and reactive AI.

## 3.1   Reactive AI, Reactive Planning, and Reactive Plans

The terms 'reactive intelligence', 'reactive planning' and 'reactive plan' appear to be closely related, but actually signify the development of several very different ideas. *Reactive intelligence* is what controls a reactive agent — one that can respond very quickly to changes in its situation. Reactive intelligence has sometimes been equated with statelessness, but that association is exaggerated. Intelligence of any kind requires state: for learning, perception, and complex control [4]. Reactive intelligence is however associated with minimal representations and the lack of deliberation.

*Reactive planning* is something of an oxymoron. It describes the way reactive systems handle the problem traditionally addressed by conventional planning — that is, action selection. Action selection is the ongoing problem for an autonomous agent of deciding what to do next. Conventional planning assumes the segmentation of intelligent behavior into the achievement of discrete goals. A conventional planner constructs a sequence of steps guaranteed to move an agent from its present state to a goal state. Reactive planning, in contrast, chooses only the immediate next action, and bases this choice on the current context. In most architectures utilizing this technique, reactive planning is facilitated by the presence of *reactive plans*. Reactive plans are stored structures which, given the current context, determine the next act.

## 3.2   Basic Reactive Plans

The BRP is an idiom relating to the form of the structure for a reactive plan. The simplest reactive plan possible is a simple sequence of primitive actions $\iota_1, \iota_2, \ldots \iota_n$. Executing a sequential plan involves priming or activating the sequence, then releasing for execution the first primitive act $\iota_1$. The completion of any $\iota_i$ releases the following $\iota_{i+1}$ until no active elements remain. Notice that this is *not* equivalent to the process of *chaining*, where each element is essentially an independent production, with a precondition set to the firing of the prior element. A sequence is an additional piece of control state; its elements may also occur in different orders in other sequences. Depending on implementation, the fact that sequence elements are released by the *termination* of prior elements can be significant in real time environments, and the fact that they are actively repressed by the existence of their prior element can increase plan robustness (see [39] for further discussion on time). This definition of sequence is derived from biological models of serial ordering (e.g. [14]).

A BRP is a more complicated plan structure for circumstances when the exact ordering of steps cannot be predetermined. For example, a BRP is useful in cases where some requirements of a goal might have already been met, might become unset during the procedure, or might require arbitrary repetitions of steps or sets of steps.

A *BRP step* is a triple $\langle \pi, \rho, \alpha \rangle$, where $\pi$ is a priority, $\rho$ is a releaser, and $\alpha$ is an action. A *BRP* is a small set (typically 3–7) of plan steps $\{\langle \pi_i, \rho_i, \alpha_i \rangle *\}$ associated with achieving a particular goal condition. The releaser $\rho_i$ is a conjunction of boolean perceptual primitives which determine whether the step can execute. Each priority $\pi_i$ is drawn from a total order. Each action $\alpha_i$ may be either another BRP or a sequence as described above. Hierarchies are controversial in reactive control because they generally involve maintaining a stack and can consequently become a control bottleneck. In this chapter we discuss hierarchical BRPs only briefly (see Section 4.1).

The order of expression of plan steps is determined by two means: the releaser and the priority. If more than one step is currently operable, then the priority determines which step's $\alpha$ is executed. If more than one step is released with the same priority, then the winner is determined arbitrarily. Normally the releasers $\rho_i$ on steps with the same priority are mutually exclusive. If no step can fire, then the BRP terminates. The top priority step of a BRP is often, though not necessarily a goal condition. In that case, its releaser, $\rho_1$, recognizes that the BRP has succeeded, and its action, $\alpha_1$ terminates the BRP.

### 3.3 An Example BRP

The details of the operation of a BRP are best explained through an example. BRPs occur in a number of architectures, and have been used to control such complex systems as flight simulators and mobile robots [1, 6, 25]. However, for clarity we draw this example from blocks world. Assume that the world consists of stacks of colored blocks, and that we want to enable an agent to meet the goal of holding a blue block[2]. A possible plan would be:

| Priority | Releaser | Action |
|---|---|---|
| 4 | (holding block) (block blue) | *goal* |
| 3 | (holding block) | drop-held-object, lose-fixation |
| 2 | (fixated-on blue) | grasp-top-of-stack |
| 1 | (blue-in-scene) | fixate-blue |

For this plan, we will assume that priority is strictly ordered and represented by position, with the highest priority step at the top. We refer to the steps by their priority.

Consider the case where the world consists of a stack with a red block sitting on the blue block. If the agent has not already fixated on the blue block before this plan is activated (and it is not holding anything), then the first operation to be performed would be element **1** because it is the only one whose releaser is satisfied. If, as a part of some previous plan, the agent has already fixated on blue, **1** would be skipped because the higher priority step **2** has its releaser satisfied. Once a fixation is established, element **2** will trigger. If the grasp is successful, this will be followed by element **3**, otherwise **2**

---

[2] This problem is from [33]. The perceptual operations in this plan are based on the visual routine theory of [32], as implemented by [17].

will be repeated. Assuming that the red block is eventually grasped and discarded, the next successful operation of element **2** will result in the blue block being held, at which point element **4** should recognize that the goal has been achieved, and terminate the plan.

This single reactive plan can generate a large number of expressed sequential plans. In the context of a red block on a blue block, we might expect the plan 1–2–3–1–2–4 to execute. But if the agent is already fixated on blue and fails to grasp the red block successfully on first attempt, the expressed plan would look like 2–1–2–3–1–2–4. If the unsuccessful grasp knocked the red block off the blue, the expressed plan might be 2–1–2–4. A basic reactive plan is both robust and opportunistic.

If a grasp fails repeatedly, the above construction might lead to an infinite number of retries. This can be prevented through several means: either through habituation at the step level, timeouts at the level of the BRP, or through a separate attentional mechanism which is triggered by repeated attempts or absence of change. This last mechanism requires another part of the architecture to provide for controlling attention; as is discussed immediately below, this is a common feature of reactive architectures.

### 3.4   Identifying a Valuable Idiom

How does one find a useful architectural feature, and how does one distinguish whether it is worth expressing as an idiom? Features are distinguished by the methodology described in Section 2, by comparison and reduction of an architecture to one or more others. Features can be idioms if they can be expressed in other architectures. Idioms are valuable within an architecture if they perform useful functions; they are valuable to the community if they are not yet regular features of existing architectures or methodologies. In this section, we illustrate the process of identification by going through the history of the identification of the BRP in our own research. We also give two counter-examples from the same source.

We first developed a BRP as one of three elements of the reactive planning system for the architecture Edmund [5, 6]. Edmund was initially conceived in the early nineties in response to the Subsumption Architecture [3]. Subsumption is a strictly behavior-based architecture with minimal internal state. Because the individual behaviors are intended to act primarily in response to their environment, only very limited communication is allowed between them. Developing action selection within this framework is very complicated. In Edmund, we attempt to maintain the advantages of the behavior-based system while simplifying the design of behavior arbitration. This is done with reactive plans.

The three structural elements of Edmund's reactive plans are action patterns, competences and drive collections. Action patterns are the simple sequences described in Section 3.2. Competences are BRPs. Drive collections are special forms of the BRP with extra state. In Edmund, a drive collection serves as the root of a BRP hierarchy, providing both motive force and an "alarm" system [28] for switching attention to urgent needs or salient events. To illustrate the search for valuable idioms, we consider a reduction of each of these three features of Edmund's reactive plans in the context of Subsumption Architecture (SA) [3], the Agent Network Architecture (ANA) [21], the Procedural Reasoning System (PRS) [13] and Soar [24].

Although deceptively simple, action patterns actually required extensions to the original versions of each of the above architectures except PRS. Within SA, a sequence can only be expressed within a single behavior, as part of its FSM. When the need for behavior sequencing was discovered, a mechanism for suppressing all but the currently active behavior was developed [9]. ANA explicitly represents the links of plans through chains of pre- and post-conditions, but with no privileged activation of a particular plan's elements. This sequencing strategy is inadequate [31], and has been improved in more recent derivative architectures [2, 27]. Soar initially represented sequences only as production chains. As mentioned in Section 3.2, this mechanism is insufficient in real-time applications. This problem has now been addressed with a dedicated sequencing mechanism that monitors durations [20]. PRS has a reactive plan structure, the Act, which allows for the coding not only of sequences, but of partial plans. Although an action pattern could therefore be seen as an idiom on an Act, we have no strong reason to argue that this particular reduction in power is useful. In conclusion, we have evidence from the history of multiple architectures that an action pattern is an important feature. However, it is not one that can easily be implemented as an idiom, because it generally extends rather than constrains architectures that lack a trivial way to express it.

As for a parallel mechanism for allowing attention shifts, some implementation of this feature is ubiquitous in reactive architectures. SA assumes that all behaviors operate in continuous parallel, and can always grasp attention. The difficulty in controlling this mechanism was the main motivation for Edmund. ANA has similar features and control problems: each behavior is always evaluated as a possible next act. PRS addresses both control and reactivity on each cycle: it first persists on the currently active plan, then engages meta-reasoning to check whether a different plan deserves top priority. Soar also seems to have struck a balance between persistence and reactivity. Being production based, it is naturally distributed and reactive, similarly to SA and ANA. Persistence is encouraged not only by the new seriating mechanism mentioned above, but primarily by clustering productions into *problem spaces*. A problem space is actually somewhat like a BRP in that it focuses attention on a subset of possible productions. Because all of these architectures have means for monitoring the environment and switching attention, introducing drive collections on top of these mechanisms does not have demonstrable utility.

The BRP is a different matter. First, there are several examples of structures like it in the planning literature, yet it is not present as a single feature in any of these four architectures. BRPs are similar in effect, though not in construction, to the "triangle tables" built to make STRIPS plans more robust [12]. They are also similar to teleo-reactive plans [26] and what Correia and Steiger-Garção [10] call "fixed action patterns" (a term that seems inappropriate given their flexibility in ordering expressed behavior). We therefore have evidence not only from our own experience, but also from several other architecture research communities of the utility of the BRP. Nevertheless, the BRP, unlike the simple sequence, is not in general use. In fact, to implement them in SA or ANA would require extensions, for much the same reason as the implementation of sequences requires extensions. There is no intrinsic way to favor or order a set of expressed actions in either architecture except by manipulating the environment. PRS and Soar, on the other hand, contain sufficient ordering mechanisms that implementing a BRP idiom should be tractable.

In summary, the value of an idiom is dependent on two things. It must be expressible but not trivially present in some interesting set of architectures, and it must be useful. Utility may be indicated by one's own experience, but also by the existence of similar features in other architectures. With respect to the BRP, it is present in several archi- tectures in the literature, and we have independently found its programming advantages sufficient to lead us to implement it in several architectures besides our own. The next section documents these efforts.

## 4    Expressing BRPs in Other Architectures

In the previous section, we introduced an architectural feature we called the Basic Re- active Plan. In this section, we document the implementation of this feature as an idiom on a number of architectures. In Section 5 we will discuss how to best exploit this sort of advance in agent design.

### 4.1   Ymir

Our first effort to generalize the benefits of Edmund's action selection was not in a widely-used standard architecture, but was rather in another relatively recent one, Ymir ([30] see also [7]). Ymir is designed to build complex agents capable of engaging in multi-modal dialog. A typical Ymir agent can both hear a human conversant and observe their gestures. The agent both speaks and provides non-verbal feedback via an animated character interface with a large number of degrees of freedom. Ymir is a reactive and behavior-based architecture. Its technical emphasis is on supporting interpretation of and responses to the human conversant on a number of different levels of time and abstraction. These levels are the following:

- a "reactive layer", for process-related back-channel feedback and low-level func- tional analysis. To be effective, this layer must be able operate within 100 millisecond constraints,
- a "process control layer", which deals with the reconstruction of dialogue structure and monitoring of process-related behaviors by the user, and
- a "content layer", for choosing, recognizing, and determining the success of content level dialogue goals.

Ymir also contains a key feature, the *action scheduler*, that autonomously determines the exact expression of behaviors chosen by the various layers. This serves to reduce the cognitive load, accelerate the response rate, and ensure that expressed behavior is smooth and coherent.

Although Ymir excels at handling the complexity of multimodality and human conversations, it does not have a built in capacity for motivation or long-term planning. Ymir is purely reactive, forming sentences for turn taking when prompted by a human user.

Because of Ymir's action scheduler, the implementation of drives, action patterns and BRPs was significantly different from that in Edmund. The scheduler could be relied on to "clean up" behaviors that had been triggered but were not expressed after a timeout, but it could also be signaled to allow their lifetimes to be renewed. In the case of action patterns, all of the elements were posted to the schedule, each with a unique tag, and all but the first with a precondition requiring that its predecessor complete before it began operating.

The BRP is implemented as an Ymir behavior object which is posted to the action-scheduler. When executed, the BRP selects a step (as per Section 3.2) and adds the step to the scheduler. The BRP then adds itself to the scheduler with the termination of its child as a precondition. The original copy of the BRP then terminates and is cleaned up by the scheduler. If the child or its descendents maintain control for any length of time, the 'new' parent BRP will also be cleaned up (see further [5] on reactive hierarchies). Otherwise, the BRP persists in selecting plan elements until it either terminates or is terminated by another decision process.

## 4.2  PRS-CL

Our next implementation of BRPs came during a project exploring the use of reactive planning in dialogue management. Because this was a relatively large-scale project, a well-established architecture, PRS, was chosen for the reactive planning. Because of other legacy code, the language of the project was Lisp. Consequently, we used the SRI implementation of PRS, PRS-CL [23]. PRS-CL provides not only an implementation of PRS, but also documentation and a set of GUI tools for developing and debugging PRS-CL agent systems. These tools are useful both for creating and debugging the main plan elements, the Act graphs.

Acts are roughly equivalent to action patterns described above, but significantly more powerful, allowing for parallel or alternative routes through the plan space and for cycles. We initially thought that a BRP would be best expressed within a single Act. However, there is no elegant way to express the inhibition of lower priority elements on an Act choice node. Instead, we implemented the BRP as a collection of Acts which are activated in response to the BRP's name being asserted as a goal. This results in the activation of all the Acts (steps) whose preconditions have been met.

PRS-CL has no built-in priority attribute for selecting between Acts. Selection is handled by meta-rules, which operate during the second half of the PRS control cycle (as mentioned in Section 3.4). We created a special function for the meta-rule that selects which of the Acts that have been triggered on a cycle is allowed to persist. This function is shown in Figure 1.

```
(defun BRP (list-of-ACTs)
  (let* ((comp-list (consult-db '(prs::speaker-competence prs::x.1)))
         (current-BRP (BRP-name (first comp-list)))
         (current-priorities (priorities-from-name current-BRP)))

    ; loop over priorities in order, terminate on first one available
    ; to fire (as indicated by presence in list-of-ACTs)
    (do ((priorities current-priorities (rest priorities))
         (result))
        ; this is the 'until' condition in a lisp 'do' loop ---
        ; if it is true, the 'do' returns a list containing ''result''
        ((setf result (BRP-find-ACT (first priorities) list-of-ACTs))
         (list result))
      ; if we have no priorities, we return something random
      (unless (and priorities list-of-ACTs)
        (return (set-randomly list-of-ACTs))))
                      ))
 )) ; defun BRP
```

**Fig. 1.** BRP prioritization implemented as a function for PRS-CL meta-reasoning. Since relative priority is situation dependent, the BRP function must query the database to determine the current competence context. Priorities are maintained as a list of Act names, each associated with a BRP name.

The BRP function we have built for PRS-CL depends on a list of priority lists, where each priority list is associated with the name of the BRP. This is somewhat unfortunate, because it creates redundant information. The Act graphs contain similar information implicitly. Any such replication often leads to bugs caused by inconsistencies in long-term maintenance. Ideally, the priority lists would be edited and maintained within the same framework as the Acts are edited and maintained, so that consistency could be checked automatically.

The fact that PRS-CL and its associated tool set emphasize the construction of very complex plan elements in the form of Acts, but provide relatively little support for the construction of metarules or the manipulation of plans as hierarchies, would seem to reflect an expectation that switching attention during plans is an unusual exception. Normal behavior is based on the execution of the elaborate Act plans. This puts PRS-CL near the opposite end of the reactive planning spectrum from architectures such as Subsumption (SA). As described in Section 3.4, SA assumes that unpredictability in action scheduling is the norm, and predictably sequenced actions are the exception. The BRP reflects a moderation between these two extremes. The BRP expects and handles the unexpected, but provides for the specification of solutions that require multiple, ordered steps.

### 4.3   JAM / UM-PRS

We have not been entirely happy with PRS-CL, so have been exploring other architectures for our dialogue project. JAM is a Java based extension of UM-PRS, which is in turn a C++ version of PRS that is more recently developed than PRS-CL. The control cycle in all three languages is similar. JAM and UM-PRS have somewhat simplified their analog of the Act so that it no longer allows cycles, but it is still more powerful than Edmund's action patterns. The JAM Act analog is called simply a "plan"; for clarity, we will refer to these as JAM-plans.

JAM-plans do have a notion of priority built in, which is then used by the default meta-reasoner to select between the JAM-plans that have been activated on any particular cycle. Our current implementation of BRPs in JAM is consequently a simplified version of the BRP in PRS-CL. A JAM BRP also consists primarily of a set of JAM-plans which respond to an "achieve" goal with the name of the BRP. However, in JAM, the priority of a step within the BRP is specified by hand-coding priority values into the JAM-plans. This is simpler and neater than the PRS-CL solution described above (and works more reliably). On the other hand, losing the list structure results in the loss of a single edit point for all of the priorities of a particular competence. This again creates exposure to potential software bugs if a competence needs to be rescaled and some element's priority is accidently omitted.

Both PRS implementations lack the elegance of the Ymir and Edmund solutions in that Acts or JAM-plans contain both local intelligence in their plan contents, and information about their parent's intelligence, in the priority and goal activation. In Edmund, all local information can be reused in a number of different BRPs, potentially with different relative priorities. The Ymir BRP implementation also allows for this, because the BRP (and sequence) information is present in wrapper objects, rather than in the plans themselves. We have not yet added this extra level of complexity in either PRS-CL or JAM, but such an improvement should be possible in principle.

### 4.4   Soar

We have not actually implemented a BRP in Soar yet, but for completeness with relation to the previous section, we will make a short description of the expected mechanism. Much as in PRS, we would expect each currently operable member element of the BRP to trigger in response to their mutual goal. This could be achieved either by preconditions, or exploiting the problem space mechanism. In Soar, if more than one procedure triggers, this results in an impasse which can be solved via meta-level reasoning. We assume it would be relatively simple to add a meta-level reasoning system that could recognize the highest priority element operable, since Soar is intended to be easily extendible to adapt various reasoning systems. This should operate correctly with or without chunking.

The Soar impasse mechanism is also already set for monitoring lack of progress in plans, a useful feature in BRPs mentioned in Section 2. In Edmund, retries are limited by setting "habituation" limits on the number of times a particular plan step will fire during a single episode. Ymir also supplies its own monitoring system; we have not yet addressed this problem in our PRS-CL or JAM implementations.

## 5   Discussion: Architecture, Methodology, or Tool?

An agent architecture has been defined as a methodology by which an agent can be constructed [37]. However, for the purpose of this discussion, we will narrow this definition to be closer to what seems to be the more common usage of the term. For this discussion, an *architecture* is a piece of software that allows the specification of an agent in an executable format. This actually moves the definition of architecture closer to the original definition of agent language, as a collection of "the right primitives for programming an intelligent agent" [38]. A *methodology* is a set of practices which is appropriate for constructing an agent. A *tool* is a GUI or other software device which creates code suitable for an architecture (as defined above), but code which may still be edited. In other words, the output of an architecture is an agent, while the output of a tool is code for an agent. A methodology has no output, but governs the use of architectures and tools.

In this chapter, we are emphasizing the use of idioms to communicate new concepts throughout the community regardless of architecture. In natural language, an idiom can be recognized as a phrase whose meaning cannot be deduced from the meanings of the individual words. If an idiom is built directly into an architecture, as a feature, there may be an analogous loss. Some features may be impossible to express in the same architecture, such as the BRP and fully autonomous behavior modules. Features implemented directly as part of an architecture reduce its flexibility. However, if a feature is implemented as an idiom, that can be overridden by direct access to the underlying code, then the problem of conflicting idioms can be dealt with at a project management level, rather than through architectural revision.

Accessibility to different idioms may explain why some architectures, such as SA or ANA, despite wide interest, have not established communities of industrial users, while others, such as Soar and PRS, have. Soar and PRS are sufficiently general to allow for the expression of a number of methodologies. However, as we said earlier, generality is not necessarily the most desirable characteristic of an agent development approach. If it were, the dominant agent "architectures" would be lisp and C. Bias towards development practices that have proven useful accelerates the development process.

We believe GUI toolkits are therefore one of the more useful ways to communicate information. They are essentially encoded methodologies: their output can be generalized to a variety of architectures (see further [11]). A toolkit might actually be an assemblage of tools chosen by a project manager. Each tool might be seen as supporting a particular idiom or related set of idioms. A GUI tool that would support the BRP would need to be able to parse files listing primitive functions, and existing sequential plans and BRPs.

A new BRP could then be created by assembling these items into a prioritized list with preconditions. This assemblage can then be named, encoded and stored as a new BRP. Such a tool might also facilitate the editing of new primitive elements and preconditions in the native architecture.

Of course, not all idioms will necessarily support or require GUI interfaces. Ymir's action scheduler, discussed in Section 4.1, is a structure that might easily be a useful idiom in any number of reactive architectures if they are employed in handling a large numbers of degrees of freedom. In this case, the "tool" is likely to be a stand-alone module that serves as an API to the agent's body. Its function would be to simplify control by smoothing the output of the system, much as the cerebellum intercedes between the mammalian forebrain and the signals sent to the muscular system.

What then belongs in an architecture? We believe architectures should only contain structures of extremely general utility. Program structures which might be best expressed as architectural attributes are those where professional coding of an attribute assists in the efficiency of the produced agents. This follows the discussion of agent languages given in [22]. Examples of such general structures are the interpreter cycle in PRS or the production system and RETE algorithm in Soar. Other structures, such as the BRP, should be implemented via idioms, and tools developed to facilitate the correct generation of those idioms.

Again, we do not discourage the development of novel architectures. An architecture may be a useful level of abstraction for developing specialized ideas and applications. However, when distributing these inventions and discoveries to the wider community, tools and idioms may be a more useful device. Note that a specialist in the use of a particular tool could be employed on a number of projects in different languages or architectures with no learning overhead, provided the tool's underlying idioms have already been expressed in those languages or architectures.

## 6    Conclusion

In this chapter we have argued that methodology is the main currency of agent design. Novel architectures are useful platforms for developing methodology, but they are not very useful for communicating those advances to the community at large. Instead, the features of the architecture should be distilled through a process of reduction to more standard architectures. This allows for the discovery of both extensions and idioms. Idioms are particularly useful, because they allow for methodological advances to be absorbed into established communities of developers. Given that this is the aim, we consider the development of tools for efficiently composing these idioms to often be a better use of time than attempting to bring an architecture to production quality.

As an ancillary point, our discussion of reactivity in Section 4.2 above demonstrates that this process of reduction is a good way to analyze and describe differences in architectures. This process is analogous to the process of "embedding" described in [15] (see also [16]). We have elsewhere used this approach to do a rough cross-paradigm analysis of useful features for agent architectures [4]. The reductions in that article were not particularly rigorous. Doing such work with the precision of [15] might be very illuminating, particularly if the reductions were fully implemented and tested. A particularly valuable unification might be one between a BDI architecture such as UM-PRS or JAM and Soar, since these are two large communities of agent researchers with little overlapping work.

Our community's search for agent methodology is analogous to evolution's search for the genome. When we find a strategy set which is sufficiently powerful, we can expect an explosion in the complexity and utility of our agents. While we are searching, we need both a large variety of novel innovations, and powerful methods of recombination of the solutions we have already found. In this chapter, we have demonstrated a mechanism for recombining the attributes of various architectures. We have also contributed some material in the form of the Basic Reactive Plan (BRP). It is our hope that contributions such as these can help the community as a whole develop, and discover through automated development, the agents we wish to build.

**Acknowledgements.** Thanks to Greg Sullivan and our anonymous reviewers for many excellent suggestions on this chapter. The work on Ymir was conducted with Kris Thórisson, who also contributed to this chapter with early discussions on the role of alternative architectures. The dialogue work was conducted at The Human Communication Research Centre in the University Edinburgh Division of Informatics under Prof. Johanna Moore.

# References

[1] Scott Benson. *Learning Action Models for Reactive Autonomous Agents.* PhD thesis, Stanford University, December 1996. Department of Computer Science.

[2] Bruce Mitchell Blumberg. *Old Tricks, New Dogs: Ethology and Interactive Creatures.* PhD thesis, MIT, September 1996. Media Laboratory, Learning and Common Sense Section.

[3] Rodney A. Brooks. A robust layered control system for a mobile robot. *IEEE Journal of Robotics and Automation*, RA-2:14–23, April 1986.

[4] Joanna Bryson. Cross-paradigm analysis of autonomous agent architecture. *Journal of Experimental and Theoretical Artificial Intelligence*, 12(2):165–190, 2000.

[5] Joanna Bryson. Hierarchy and sequence vs. full parallelism in reactive action selection architectures. In *From Animals to Animats 6 (SAB00)*, Cambridge, MA, 2000. MIT Press.

[6] Joanna Bryson and Brendan McGonigle. Agent architecture as object oriented design. In Munindar P. Singh, Anand S. Rao, and Michael J. Wooldridge, editors, *The Fourth International Workshop on Agent Theories, Architectures, and Languages (ATAL97)*, pages 15–30, Providence, RI, 1998. Springer.

[7] Joanna Bryson and Kristinn R. Thórisson. Dragons, bats & evil knights: A three-layer design approach to character based creative play. *Virtual Reality*, page in press, 2000.

[8] David Chapman. Planning for conjunctive goals. *Artificial Intelligence*, 32:333–378, 1987.

[9] Jonathan H. Connell. *Minimalist Mobile Robotics: A Colony-style Architecture for a Mobile Robot.* Academic Press, Cambridge, MA, 1990. also MIT TR-1151.

[10] Luis Correia and A. Steiger-Garção. A useful autonomous vehicle with a hierarchical behavior control. In F. Moran, A. Moreno, J.J. Merelo, and P. Chacon, editors, *Advances in Artificial Life (Third European Conference on Artificial Life)*, pages 625–639, Berlin, 1995. Springer.

[11] Scott A. DeLoach and Mark Wood. Developing multiagent systems with agentTool. In C. Castelfranchi and Y. Lespérance, editors, *Intelligent Agents VII. Agent Theories, Architectures, and Languages — 7th. International Workshop, ATAL-2000, Boston, MA, USA, July 7–9, 2000, Proceedings*, Lecture Notes in Artificial Intelligence. Springer-Verlag, Berlin, 2001. In this volume.

[12] Richard E. Fikes, Peter E. Hart, and Nils J. Nilsson. Learning and executing generalized robot plans. *Artificial Intelligence*, 3:251–288, 1972.

[13] M. P. Georgeff and A. L. Lansky. Reactive reasoning and planning. In *Proceedings of the Sixth National Conference on Artificial Intelligence (AAAI-87)*, pages 677–682, Seattle, WA, 1987.

[14] R. N. A. Henson and N. Burgess. Representations of serial order. In J. A. Bullinaria, D. W. Glasspool, and G. Houghton, editors, *Proceedings of the Fourth Neural Computation and Psychology Workshop: Connectionist Representations*, London, 1997. Springer.

[15] K. Hindriks, F. De Boer, W. Van Der Hoek, and J.-J. C. Meyer. Control structures of rule-based agent languages. In J.P. Müller, M.P. Singh, and A.S. Rao, editors, *The Fifth International Workshop on Agent Theories, Architectures, and Languages (ATAL98)*, pages 381–396, 1999.

[16] Koen V. Hindriks, Frank S. de Boer, Wiebe van der Hoek, and John-Jules Ch. Meyer. Agent programming with declarative goals. In C. Castelfranchi and Y. Lespérance, editors, *Intelligent Agents VII. Agent Theories, Architectures, and Languages — 7th. International Workshop, ATAL-2000, Boston, MA, USA, July 7–9, 2000, Proceedings*, Lecture Notes in Artificial Intelligence. Springer-Verlag, Berlin, 2001. In this volume.

[17] Ian D. Horswill. Visual routines and visual search. In *Proceedings of the 14th International Joint Conference on Artificial Intelligence*, Montreal, August 1995.

[18] Marcus J. Huber. JAM: A BDI-theoretic mobile agent architecture. In *Proceedings of the Third International Conference on Autonomous Agents (Agents'99)*, pages 236–243, Seattle, May 1999.

[19] Nicholas R. Jennings. On agent-based software engineering. *Artificial Intelligence*, 117: 277–296, 2000.

[20] John E. Laird and Paul S. Rosenbloom. The evolution of the Soar cognitive architecture. Technical Report CSE-TR-219-94, Department of EE & CS, University of Michigan, Ann Arbor, September 1994. also in *Mind Matters*, Steier and Mitchell, eds.

[21] Pattie Maes. The agent network architecture (ANA). *SIGART Bulletin*, 2(4):115–120, 1991.

[22] John-Jules Ch. Meyer. Agent languages and their relationship to other programming paradigms. In J.P. Müller, M.P. Singh, and A.S. Rao, editors, *The Fifth International Workshop on Agent Theories, Architectures, and Languages (ATAL98)*, pages 309–316, Paris, 1999. Springer.

[23] Karen L. Myers. *Procedural Reasoning System User's Guide*. Artificial Intelligence Center, SRI International, Menlo Park, CA, USA, 1.96 edition, 1997,1999.

[24] Alan Newell. *Unified Theories of Cognition*. Harvard University Press, Cambridge, Massachusetts, 1990.

[25] Nils Nilsson. Shakey the robot. Technical note 323, SRI International, Menlo Park, California, April 1984.

[26] Nils Nilsson. Teleo-reactive programs for agent control. *Journal of Artificial Intelligence Research*, 1:139–158, 1994.

[27] Bradley Rhodes. PHISH-nets: Planning heuristically in situated hybrid networks. Master's thesis, Media Lab, Learning and Common Sense, 1996.

[28] Aaron Sloman. Models of models of mind. In Aaron Sloman, editor, *AISB'00 Symposium on Designing a Functioning Mind*, 2000.

[29] Peter Stone and Manuela Veloso. A layered approach to learning client behaviors in the robocup soccer server. *International Journal of Applied Artificial Intelligence*, 12:165–188, 1998.

[30] Kristinn R. Thórisson. A mind model for multimodal communicative creatures & humanoids. *International Journal of Applied Artificial Intelligence*, 13(4/5):519–538, 1999.

[31] Toby Tyrrell. *Computational Mechanisms for Action Selection*. PhD thesis, University of Edinburgh, 1993. Centre for Cognitive Science.

[32] Shimon Ullman. Visual routines. *Cognition*, 18:97–159, 1984.

[33] Steven D. Whitehead. Reinforcement learning for the adaptive control of perception and action. Technical Report 406, University of Rochester Computer Science, Rochester, NY, Feb 1992.

[34] David H. Wolpert. The existence of a priori distinctions between learning algorithms. *Neural Computation*, 8(7):1391–1420, 1996.

[35] David H. Wolpert. The lack of a priori distinctions between learning algorithms. *Neural Computation*, 8(7):1341–1390, 1996.

[36] Michael Wooldridge and Paul E. Dunne. Optimistic and disjunctive agent design problems. In C. Castelfranchi and Y. Lespérance, editors, *Intelligent Agents VII. Agent Theories, Architectures, and Languages — 7th. International Workshop, ATAL-2000, Boston, MA, USA, July 7–9, 2000, Proceedings*, Lecture Notes in Artificial Intelligence. Springer-Verlag, Berlin, 2001. In this volume.

[37] Michael Wooldridge and Nicholas R. Jennings. Intelligent agents: Theory and practice. *Knowledge Engineering Review*, 10(2):115–152, 1995.

[38] Michael J. Wooldridge and Nicholas R. Jennings, editors. *Intelligent Agents: the ECAI-94 workshop on Agent Theories, Architectures and Languages*, Amsterdam, 1994. Springer.

[39] Stephen Zimmerbaum and Richard Scherl. Sensing actions, time, and concurrency in the situation calculus. In C. Castelfranchi and Y. Lespérance, editors, *Intelligent Agents VII. Agent Theories, Architectures, and Languages — 7th. International Workshop, ATAL-2000, Boston, MA, USA, July 7–9, 2000, Proceedings*, Lecture Notes in Artificial Intelligence. Springer-Verlag, Berlin, 2001. In this volume.

# Developing Multi-agent Systems with JADE

Fabio Bellifemine[1], Agostino Poggi[2], and Giovanni Rimassa[2]

[1] CSELT S.p.A.
Via G. Reiss Romoli, 274, 10148, Torino, Italy
bellifemine@cselt.it

[2] Dipartimento di Ingegneria dell'Informazione, University of Parma
Parco Area delle Scienze, 181A, 43100, Parma, Italy
(poggi,rimassa}@ce.unipr.it

**Abstract.** JADE (Java Agent Development Framework) is a software framework to make easy the development of multi-agent applications in compliance with the FIPA specifications. JADE can then be considered a middle-ware that implements an efficient agent platform and supports the development of multi agent systems. JADE agent platform tries to keep high the performance of a distributed agent system implemented with the Java language. In particular, its communication architecture tries to offer flexible and efficient messaging, transparently choosing the best transport available and leveraging state-of-the-art distributed object technology embedded within Java runtime environment. JADE uses an agent model and Java implementation that allow good runtime efficiency, software reuse, agent mobility and the realization of different agent architectures.

## 1. Introduction

Nowadays, agent-based technologies are considered the most promising means to deploy enterprise-wide and worldwide applications that often must operate across corporations and continents and inter-operate with other heterogeneous systems. It is because they offer the high-level software abstractions needed to manage complex applications and because they were invented to cope with distribution and interoperability [2,9,12,19,24,36].

However, agent-based technologies are still immature and few truly agent-based systems have been built. Agent-based technologies cannot keep their promises, and will not become widespread, until standards to support agent interoperability are in place and adequate environments for the development of agent systems are available. However, many people are working on the standardisation of agent technologies (see, for example, the work done by Knowledge Sharing Effort [27], OMG [22] and FIPA [7]) and on development environments to build agent systems (see, for example, DMARS [28], RETSINA [34] MOLE [1]).

Such environments provide some predefined agent models and tools to ease the development of systems. Moreover, some of them try to inter-operate with other agent systems through a well-known agent communication language, that is, KQML [6]. However, a shared communication language is not enough to support interoperability

C. Castelfranchi, Y. Lespérance (Eds.): Intelligent Agents VII, LNAI 1986, pp. 89–103, 2001.
© Springer-Verlag Berlin Heidelberg 2001

between different agent systems, because common agent services and ontology are also needed. The standardisation work of FIPA acknowledges this issue and, beyond an agent communication language, specifies the key agents necessary for the management of an agent system and the shared ontology to be used for the interaction between two systems.

In this paper, we present JADE (Java Agent Development Framework), a software framework to write agent applications in compliance with the FIPA specifications for interoperable intelligent multi-agent systems. The next section introduces FIPA specifications. Section three introduces related work on software frameworks to develop agent systems. Section four describes JADE main features. Section five describes the architecture of the agent platform, the communication subsystem. Section six presents JADE agent model. Finally, section seven concludes with a brief description about JADE main features, the use of JADE to realise applications and the relationships between JADE and some other agent software frameworks.

## 2.  FIPA Specifications

The Foundation for Intelligent Physical Agents (FIPA) [7] is an international non-profit association of companies and organisations sharing the effort to produce specifications for generic agent technologies. FIPA does not just promote a technology for a single application domain but a set of general technologies for different application areas that developers can integrate to make complex systems with a high degree of interoperability.

The first output documents of FIPA, named FIPA97 specifications, state the normative rules that allow a society of agents to exist, operate and be managed. First of all they describe the reference model of an agent platform: they identify the roles of some key agents necessary for managing the platform, and describe the agent management content language and ontology. Three mandatory roles were identified into an agent platform. The Agent Management System (AMS) is the agent that exerts supervisory control over access to and use of the platform; it is responsible for maintaining a directory of resident agents and for handling their life cycle. The Agent Communication Channel (ACC) provides the path for basic contact between agents inside and outside the platform. The ACC is the default communication method, which offers a reliable, orderly and accurate message routing service. FIPA97 mandates ACC support for IIOP in order to inter-operate with other compliant agent platforms. The Directory Facilitator (DF) is the agent that provides yellow page services to the agent platform.

The specifications also define the Agent Communication Language (ACL), used by agents to exchange messages. FIPA ACL is a language describing message encoding and semantics, but it does not mandate specific mechanisms for message transportation. Since different agents might run on different platforms on different networks, messages are encoded in a textual form, assuming that agents are able to transmit 7-bit data. ACL syntax is close to the widely used communication language KQML. However, there are fundamental differences between KQML and ACL, the most evident being the existence of a formal semantics for FIPA ACL, which should eliminate any ambiguity and confusion from the usage of the language.

FIPA supports common forms of inter-agent conversations through *interaction protocols*, which are communication patterns followed by two or more agents. Such protocols range from simple query and request protocols, to more complex ones, as the well-known contract net negotiation protocol and English and Dutch auctions.

The remaining parts of the FIPA specifications deal with other aspects, in particular with agent-software integration, agent mobility, agent security, ontology service, and human-agent communication. However they are not described here because they have not yet been considered in the JADE implementation. The interested reader should refer directly to the FIPA Web page [7].

## 3.   Related Work

A lot of research and commercial organisations are involved in the realisation of agent applications and a considerable number of agent construction tools has been realised [29]. Some of the most interesting are AgentBuilder [30], AgentTool [4], ASL [16], Bee-gent [15], FIPA-OS [23], Grasshopper-2 [10], MOLE [1], the Open Agent Architecture [20], RETSINA [34] and Zeus [25].

AgentBuilder [30] is a tool for building Java agent systems based on two components: the Toolkit and the Run-Time System. The Toolkit includes tools for managing the agent software development process, while the Run-Time System provides an agent engine, that is, an interpreter, used as execution environment of agent software. AgentBuilder agents are based on a model derived by the Agent-0 [32] and PLACA [35] agent models.

AgentTool [4] is a graphical environment to build heterogeneous multi-agent systems. It is a kind of CASE tool, specifically oriented towards agent-oriented software engineering, whose major advantages are the complete support for the MaSE methodology (developed by the same authors together with the tool) and the independence from agent internal architecture (with MaSE and agentTool it is possible to build multi agent systems made of agents with different internal architectures).

ASL [16] is an agent platform that supports the development in C/C++, Java, JESS, CLIPS and Prolog. ASL is built upon the OMG's CORBA 2.0 specifications. The use of CORBA technology facilitates seamless agent distribution and allows adding to the platform the language bindings supported by the used CORBA implementations. Initially, ASL agents used to communicate through KQML messages, now the platform is FIPA compliant supporting FIPA ACL.

Bee-gent [15] is a software framework to develop agent systems compliant to FIPA specification that has been realised by Toshiba. Such a framework provides two types of agents: wrapper agents used to agentify existing applications and mediation agents supporting the wrappers coordination by handling all their communications. Bee-gent also offers a graphic RAD tool to describe agents through state transition diagrams and a directory facility to locate agents, databases and applications.

FIPA-OS [23] is another software framework to develop agent systems compliant to FIPA specification that has been realised by NORTEL. Such a framework provides the mandatory components realising the agent platform of the FIPA reference model (i.e., the AMS, ACC and DF agents, and an internal platform message transport system), an agent shell and a template to produce agents that communicate taking advantage of FIPA-OS agent platform.

Grasshopper-2 [10] is a pure Java based Mobile Agent platform, conformant to existing agent standards, as defined by the OMG - MASIF (Mobile Agent System Interoperability Facility) [22] and FIPA specifications. Thus Grasshopper-2 is an open platform, enabling maximum interoperability and easy integration with other mobile and intelligent agent systems. The Grasshopper-2 environment consists of several Agencies and a Region Registry, remotely connected via a selectable communication protocol. Several interfaces are specified to enable remote interactions between the distinguished distributed components. Moreover, Grasshopper-2 provides a Graphical User for user-friendly access to all the functionality of an agent system.

MOLE [1] is an agent system developed in Java whose agents do not have a sufficient set of features to be considered truly agent systems [9,33]. However, MOLE is important because it offers one of the best supports for agent mobility. Mole agents are multi-thread entities identified by a globally unique agent identifier. Agents interact through two types of communication: through RMI for client/server interactions and through message exchanges for peer-to-peer interactions.

The Open Agent Architecture [20] is a truly open architecture to realise distributed agent systems in a number of languages, namely C, Java, Prolog, Lisp, Visual Basic and Delphi. Its main feature is its powerful facilitator that coordinates all the other agents in their tasks. The facilitator can receive tasks from agents, decompose them and award them to other agents.

RETSINA [34] offers reusable agents to realise applications. Each agent has four modules for communicating, planning, scheduling and monitoring the execution of tasks and requests from other agents. RETSINA agents communicate through KQML messages.

Zeus [25] allows the rapid development of Java agent systems by providing a library of agent components, by supporting a visual environment for capturing user specifications, an agent building environment that includes an automatic agent code generator and a collection of classes that form the building blocks of individual agents. Agents are composed of five layers: API layer, definition layer, organisational layer, coordination layer and communication layer. The API layer allows the interaction with non-agentized world.

## 4.  JADE

JADE (Java Agent Development Environment) is a software framework to make easy the development of agent applications in compliance with the FIPA specifications for interoperable intelligent multi-agent systems. JADE is an Open Source project, and the complete system can be downloaded from JADE Home Page [11]. The goal of JADE is to simplify development while ensuring standard compliance through a comprehensive set of system services and agents. To achieve such a goal, JADE offers the following list of features to the agent programmer:

-   FIPA-compliant Agent Platform, which includes the AMS (Agent Management System), the default DF (Directory Facilitator), and the ACC (Agent Communication Channel). All these three agents are automatically activated at the agent platform start-up.

- Distributed agent platform. The agent platform can be split on several hosts. Only one Java application, and therefore only one Java Virtual Machine, is executed on each host. Agents are implemented as one Java thread and Java events are used for effective and lightweight communication between agents on the same host. Parallel tasks can be still executed by one agent, and JADE schedules these tasks in a cooperative way.
- A number of FIPA-compliant additional DFs (Directory Facilitator) can be started at run time in order to build multi-domain environments, where a domain is a logical set of agents, whose services are advertised through a common facilitator.
- Java API to send/receive messages to/from other agents; ACL messages are represented as ordinary Java objects.
- FIPA97-compliant IIOP protocol to connect different agent platforms.
- Lightweight transport of ACL messages inside the same agent platform, as messages are transferred encoded as Java objects, rather than strings, in order to avoid marshalling and unmarshalling procedures.
- Library of FIPA interaction protocols ready to be used.
- Support for agent mobility within a JADE agent platform.
- Library to manage user-defined ontologies and content languages.
- Graphical user interface to manage several agents and agent platforms from the same agent. The activity of each platform can be monitored and logged. All life cycle operations on agents (creating a new agent, suspending or terminating an existing agent, etc.) can be performed through this administrative GUI.

The JADE system can be described from two different points of view. On the one hand, JADE is a runtime system for FIPA-compliant Multi Agent Systems, supporting application agents whenever they need to exploit some feature covered by the FIPA standard specification (message passing, agent life-cycle management, etc.). On the other hand, JADE is a Java framework for developing FIPA-compliant agent applications, making FIPA standard assets available to the programmer through object oriented abstractions. The two following subsections will present JADE from the two standpoints, trying to highlight the major design choices followed by the JADE development team. A final discussion section will comment on JADE actual strengths and weaknesses and will describe the future improvements envisaged in the JADE development roadmap.

## 5.  JADE Runtime System

A running agent platform must provide several services to the applications: when looking at the parts 1 and 2 of the FIPA97 specification, is can be seen that these services fall into two main areas, that is, message passing support with FIPA ACL and agent management with life-cycle, white and yellow pages, etc.

## 5.1 Distributed Agent Platform

JADE complies with the FIPA97 specifications and includes all the system agents that manage the platform that is the ACC, the AMS, and the default DF. All agent communication is performed through message passing, where FIPA ACL is the language used to represent messages.

While appearing as a single entity to the outside world, a JADE agent platform is itself a distributed system, since it can be split over several hosts with one among them acting as a front end for inter-platform IIOP communication. A JADE system is made by one or more *Agent Container*, each one living in a separate Java Virtual Machine and communicating using Java RMI. IIOP is used to forward outgoing messages to foreign agent platforms. A special, *Front End* container is also an IIOP server, listening at the official agent platform ACC address for incoming messages from other platforms. Figure 1 shows the architecture of a JADE Agent Platform.

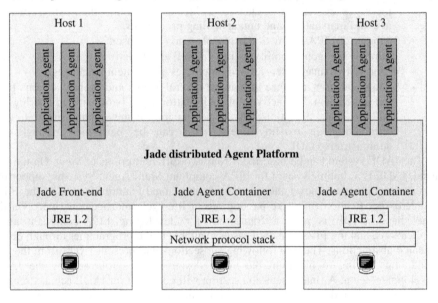

**Fig. 1.** Software architecture of a JADE Agent Platform

## 5.2 Message Delivery Subsystem

FIPA agent communication model is peer-to-peer though multi-message context is provided by interaction protocols and conversation identifiers. On the other hand, JADE uses transport technologies such as RMI, CORBA and event dispatching which are typically associated with reactive systems. Clearly, there is some gap to bridge to map the explicitly addressed FIPA message-passing model into the request/response communication model of distributed objects. This is why in JADE ordinary agents are not distributed objects, but agent containers are.

A software agent, in compliance to FIPA agent model, has a *globally-unique identifier (GUID)*, that can be used by every other agent to address it with ACL messages; likewise, an agent will put its GUID into the *:sender* slot of ACL messages it sends around. So, JADE must figure out receiver location by simply looking at *:receiver* message slot. Since a FIPA97 GUID resembles an email address, it has the form: *<agent name>* @ *<platform address>*, it is fairly easy to recover the agent name and the platform address from it.

When an ACL message is sent to a software agent, three options are given:

- *Receiver on the same container of the same platform:* Java events are used, the *ACLMessage* is simply cloned.
- *Receiver on a different container of the same platform:* Java RMI is used, the message is serialised at sender side, a remote method is called and the message is unserialised at receiver side.
- *Receiver on a different platform:* IIOP is used, the *ACLMessage* is converted into a *String* and marshalled at sender side, a remote CORBA call is done and an unmarshalling followed by ACL parsing occurs at receiver side.

### 5.3   Address Management and Caching

JADE tries to select the most convenient of the three transport mechanisms above according to agents location. Basically, each container has a table of its local agents, called the *Local-Agent Descriptor Table (LADT)*, whereas the front-end, besides its own LADT, also maintains a *Global-Agent Descriptor Table (GADT)*, mapping every agent into the RMI object reference of its container. Moreover, JADE uses an address caching technique to avoid querying the front-end continuously for address information.

Besides being efficient, this is also meant to support agent mobility, where agent addresses can change over time (e.g. from local to RMI); transparent caching means that messaging subsystem will not be affected when agent mobility will be introduced into JADE. Moreover, if new remote protocols will be needed in JADE (e.g. a wireless protocol for nomadic applications), they will be seamlessly integrated inside the messaging and address caching mechanisms.

### 5.4   Mobility

The new JADE version adds the support for agent mobility. Exploiting Java Serialization API and dynamic class loading, it is now possible to move or clone a JADE agent over different containers but within the same JADE agent platform. Our current implementation is completely proprietary and does not allow inter-platform mobility over the FIPA IIOP standard message transport service. While a more complete mobility support could be possible, we feel that it would not be worth the effort, because FIPA specifications for mobility support is still incomplete and a proprietary, JADE-only mobility service would not help standardization and interoperability.

Rather, some more general proposals should be submitted to FIPA, undergoing public discussion and evaluation. Then, an effective and interoperable implementation could be built.

## 5.5    User-Defined Ontologies and Content Languages

According to the FIPA standard, achieving agent level interoperability requires that different agents share much more than a simple on-the-wire protocol. While FIPA mandates a single agent communication language, the *FIPA ACL*, it explicitly allows application dependent content languages and ontologies. The FIPA specifications themselves now contain a *Content Language Library*, whereas various mandatory ontologies are defined and used within the different parts of the FIPA standard.

The last version of JADE lets application programmers create their own content languages and their ontologies. Every JADE agent keeps a capability table where the known languages and ontologies are listed; user defined codecs must be able to translate back and forth between the *String* format (according to the content language syntax) and a frame based representation.

If a user-defined ontology is defined, the application can register a suitable Java class to play an ontological role, and JADE is able to convert to and from frames and user defined Java objects. Acting this way, application programmers can represent their domain specific concepts as familiar Java classes, while still being able to process them at the agent level (put them within ACL messages, reasoning about them, etc.).

## 5.6    Tools for Platform Management and Monitoring

Beyond a runtime library, JADE offers some tools to manage the running agent platform and to monitor and debug agent societies; all these tools are implemented as FIPA agents themselves, and they require no special support to perform their tasks, but just rely on JADE AMS.

The general management console for a JADE agent platform is called *RMA* (*Remote Monitoring Agent*). The RMA acquires the information about the platform and executes the GUI commands to modify the status of the platform (creating agents, shutting down containers, etc.) through the AMS. The Directory Facilitator agent also has a GUI, with which it can be administered, configuring its advertised agents and services.

JADE users can debug their agents with the *Dummy Agent* and the *Sniffer Agent*.

The Dummy Agent is a simple tool for inspecting message exchanges among agents, facilitating validation of agent message exchange patterns and interactive testing of an agent.

The Sniffer Agent allows to track messages exchanged in a JADE agent platform: every message directed to or coming from a chosen agent or group is tracked and displayed in the sniffer window, using a notation similar to UML *Sequence Diagrams*.

# 6.  JADE Agent Development Model

FIPA specifications state nothing about agent internals, but when JADE was designed and built they had to be addressed. A major design issue is the execution model for an agent platform, both affecting performance and imposing specific programming styles on agent developers. As will be shown in the following, JADE solution stems from the balancing of forces from ordinary software engineering guidelines and theoretical agent properties.

## 6.1   From Agent Theory to Class Design

A distinguishing property of a software agent is its *autonomy*; an agent is not limited to react to external stimuli, but it's also able to start new communicative acts of its own. A software agent, besides being autonomous, is said to be *social*, because it can interact with other agents in order to pursue its goals or can even develop an overall strategy together with its peers.

FIPA standard bases its *Agent Communication Language* on *speech-act theory* [31] and uses a mentalistic model to build a formal semantic for the *performatives* agents exchange. This approach is quite different from the one followed by distributed objects and rooted in *Design by Contract* [21]; a fundamental difference is that invocations can either succeed or fail but a *request* speech act can be refused if the receiver is unwilling to perform the requested action.

Trying to map the aforementioned agent properties into design decisions, the following list was produced:

- *Agents are autonomous,* then they are active objects.
- *Agents are social,* then intra-agent concurrency is needed.
- *Messages are speech acts,* then asynchronous messaging must be used.
- *Agents can say "no",* then peer-to-peer communication model is needed.

The autonomy property requires each agent to be an *active object* [17] with at least a Java thread, to proactively start new conversations, make plans and pursue goals. The need for sociality has the outcome of allowing an agent to engage in many conversations simultaneously, dealing with a significant amount of concurrency.

The third requirement suggests asynchronous message passing as a way to exchange information between two independent agents, that also has the benefit of producing more reusable interactions [33]. Similarly, the last requirement stresses that in a Multi Agent System the sender and the receiver are equals (as opposed to client/server systems where the receiver is supposed to obey the sender). An autonomous agent should also be allowed to ignore a received message as long as he wishes; this advocates using a *pull consumer* messaging model [26], where incoming messages are buffered until their receiver decides to read them.

## 6.2   JADE Agent Concurrency Model

The above considerations help in deciding how many threads of control are needed in an agent implementation; the autonomy requirement forces each agent to have at least a thread, and the sociality requirement pushes towards many threads per agent. Unfortunately, current operating systems limit the maximum number of threads that can be run effectively on a system. JADE execution model tries to limit the number of threads and has its roots in actor languages.

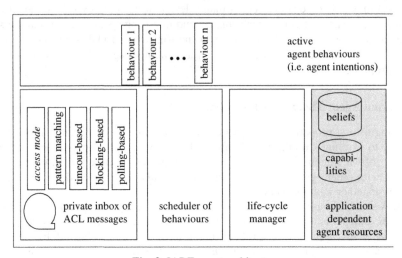

**Fig. 2.** JADE agent architecture.

The *Behaviour* abstraction models agent tasks: a collection of behaviours are scheduled and executed to carry on agent duties (see figure 2). Behaviours represent logical threads of a software agent implementation. According to *Active Object* design pattern [17], every JADE agent runs in its own Java thread, satisfying autonomy property; instead, to limit the threads required to run an agent platform, all agent behaviours are executed cooperatively within a single Java thread. So, JADE uses a *thread-per-agent* execution model with cooperative intra-agent scheduling.

JADE agents schedule their behaviour with a *"cooperative scheduling on top of the stack"*, in which all behaviours are run from a single stack frame (*on top of the stack*) and a behaviour runs until it returns from its main function and cannot be pre-empted by other behaviours (*cooperative scheduling*).

JADE model is an effort to provide fine-grained parallelism on coarser grained hardware. A likewise, stack based execution model is followed by Illinois Concert runtime system [14] for parallel object oriented languages. Concert executes concurrent method calls optimistically on the stack, reverting to real thread spawning only when the method is about to block, saving the context for the current call only when forced to.

Choosing not to save behaviour execution context means that agent behaviours start from the beginning every time they are scheduled for execution. So, behaviour state that must be retained across multiple executions must be stored into behaviour instance variables. A general rule for transforming an ordinary Java method into a JADE behaviour is:

1.  *Turn the method body into an object whose class inherits from Behaviour.*
2.  *Turn method local variables into behaviour instance variables.*
3.  *Add the behaviour object to agent behaviour list during agent start-up.*

The above guidelines apply the *reification technique* [13] to agent methods, according to *Command* design pattern [18]; an agent behaviour object reifies both a method and a separate thread executing it. A new class must be written and instantiated for every agent behaviour, and this can lead to programs harder to understand and maintain. JADE application programmers can compensate for this shortcoming using Java *Anonymous Inner Classes*; this language feature makes the code necessary for defining an agent behaviour only slightly higher than for writing a single Java method.

JADE *thread-per-agent* model can deal alone with the most common situations involving only agents: this is because every JADE agent owns a single message queue from which ACL messages are retrieved. Having multiple threads but a single mailbox would bring no benefit in message dispatching. On the other hand, when writing agent wrappers for non-agent software, there can be many interesting events from the environment beyond ACL message arrivals. Therefore, application developers are free to choose whatever concurrency model they feel is needed for their particular wrapper agent; ordinary Java threading is still possible from within an agent behaviour.

### 6.3  Using Behaviours to Build Complex Agents

The developer implementing an agent must extend *Agent* class and implement agent-specific tasks by writing one or more *Behaviour* subclasses. User defined agents inherit from their superclass the capability of registering and deregistering with their platform and a basic set of methods (e.g. send and receive ACL messages, use standard interaction protocols, register with several domains). Moreover, user agents inherit from their *Agent* superclass two methods: *addBehaviour(Behaviour)* and *removeBehaviour(Behaviour)*, to manage the behaviour list of the agent.

JADE contains ready made behaviours for the most common tasks in agent programming, such as sending and receiving messages and structuring complex tasks as aggregations of simpler ones. For example, JADE offers a so-called *JessBehaviour* that allows full integration with JESS [8], a scripting environment for rule programming offering an engine using the Rete algorithm to process rules.

*Behaviour* is an abstract class that provides the skeleton of the elementary task to be performed. It exposes three methods: the *action()* method, representing the "true" task to be accomplished by the specific behaviour classes; the *done()* method, used by the agent scheduler, that must return *true* when the behaviour has finished and *false* when the behaviour has not and the *action()* method must be executed again; the *reset()* method, used to restart a behaviour from the beginning.

JADE follows a compositional approach to allow application developers to build their own behaviours out of the simpler ones directly provided by the framework. Applying the *Composite* design pattern, *ComplexBehaviour* class is itself a *Behaviour*, with some sub-behaviours or *children*, defining two methods *addSubBehaviour(Behaviour)* and *removeSubBehaviour(Behaviour)*. This permits agent writers to implement a structured tree with behaviours of different kinds. Besides *ComplexBehaviour*, JADE framework defines some other subclasses of *Behaviour*: *SimpleBehaviour* can be used to implement atomic steps of the agent work. A behaviour implemented by a subclass of *SimpleBehaviour* is executed by JADE scheduler in a single time frame. Two more subclasses to send and receive messages are *SenderBehaviour* and *ReceiverBehaviour*. They can be instantiated passing appropriate parameters to their constructors. *SenderBehaviour* allows sending a message, while *ReceiverBehaviour* allows receiving a message, which can be matched against a pattern; the behaviour blocks itself (without stopping all other agent activities) if no suitable messages are present.

JADE recursive aggregation of behaviour objects resembles the technique used for graphical user interfaces, where every interface widget can be a leaf of a tree whose intermediate nodes are special container widgets, with rendering and children management features. An important distinction, however, exists: JADE behaviours reify execution tasks, so task scheduling and suspension are to be considered, too.

Thinking in terms of software patterns, if *Composite* is the main structural pattern used for JADE behaviours, on the behavioural side we have *Chain of Responsibility*: agent scheduling directly affects only top-level nodes of the behaviour tree, but every composite behaviour is responsible for its children scheduling within its time frame.

## 7.   Conclusions

JADE design tries to put together abstraction and efficiency, giving programmers easy access to the main FIPA standard assets while incurring into runtime costs for a feature only when that specific feature is used. This *"pay as you go"* approach drives all the main JADE architectural decisions: from the messaging subsystems that transparently chooses the best transport available, to the address management module, that uses optimistic caching and direct connection between containers.

Since JADE is a middleware for developing distributed applications, it must be evaluated with respect to scalability and fault tolerance, which are two very important issues for distributed robust software infrastructures.

When discussing scalability, it is necessary to first state with respect to which variable; in a Multi Agent System, the three most interesting variables are the number of agents in a platform, the number of messages for a single agent and the number of simultaneous conversations a single agent gets involved in.

JADE tries to support large Multi Agent Systems as possible; exploiting JADE distributed architecture, clusters of related agents can be deployed on separate agent containers in order to reduce both the number of threads per host and the network load among hosts.

JADE scalability with respect to the number of messages for a single agent is strictly dependent on the lower communication layers, such as the CORBA ORB used for IIOP and the RMI transport system. Again, the distributed platform with decentralised connection management tries to help; when an agent receives many messages, only the ones sent by remote agents stress the underlying communication subsystem, while messages from local agents travel on a fast path of their own.

JADE agents are very scalable with respect to the number of simultaneous conversations a single agent can participate in. This is in fact the whole point of the two level scheduling architecture: when an agent engages in a new conversation, no new threads are spawned and no new connections are set up, just a new behaviour object is created. So the only overhead associated to starting conversations is the behaviour object creation time and its memory occupation; agents particularly sensitive to these overheads can easily bound them a priori implementing a behaviour pool.

From a fault tolerance standpoint, JADE does not perform very well due to the single point of failure represented by the Front End container and, in particular, by the AMS. A replicated AMS would be necessary to grant complete fault tolerance of the platform. Nevertheless, it should be noted that, due to JADE decentralised messaging architecture, a group of cooperating agents could continue to work even in the presence of an AMS failure. What is really missing in JADE is a restart mechanism for the front-end container and the FIPA system agents.

Even if JADE is a young project, it has been designed with criteria more academics than industrials, and even if only recently it has been released under Open Source License, it has been already used into some of projects.

FACTS [5] is a project in the framework of the ACTS programme of the European Commission that has used JADE in two application domains. In the first application domain, JADE provides the basis for a new generation TV entertainment system. The user accesses a multi-agent system to help him on the basis of his profile that is able to capture, model, and refine over-time through the collaboration of agents with different capabilities. The second application domain deals with agents collaborating, and at the same time competing, in order to help the user to purchase a business trip. A Personal Travel Assistance represents the user interests and cooperates with a Travel Broker Agent in order to select and recommend the business trip.

CoMMA [3] is a project in the framework of the IST programme of the European Commission that is using JADE to help users in the management of an organisation corporate memory and in particular to facilitate the creation, dissemination, transmission and reuse of knowledge in the organisation.

JADE offers an agent model that is more "primitive" than the agents models offered, for example, by AgentBuilder, dMARS, RETSINA and Zeus; however, the overhead due to such sophisticated agent models might not be justified for agents that must perform some simple tasks. Starting from FIPA assumption that only the external behavior of system components should be specified, leaving the implementation details and internal architectures to agent developers, we realize a very general agent model that can be easily specialized to implement, for example, reactive or BDI architectures or other sophisticated architectures taking also advantages of the separation between computation and synchronization code inside agent behaviours through the use of guards and transitions. In particular, we can realize a system composed of agents with different architectures, but able to interact because on the top of the "primitive" JADE agent model. Moreover, the behavior abstraction of our agent model allows an easy integration of external software. For example, we realized a *JessBehaviour* that allows the use of JESS [8] as agent reasoning engine.

**Acknowledgements.** Thanks to all the people that contributed to development of JADE. The work has been partially supported by a grant from CSELT, Torino.

# References

1. J. Baumann, F. Hohl, K. Rothermel and M. Straßer. Mole - Concepts of a Mobile Agent System, World Wide Web,1(3):123-137, 1998.
2. J.M. Bradshaw. Software Agents. MIT Press, Cambridge, MA, 1997.
3. CoMMA Project Home Page. Available at
http://www.ii.atos-group.com/sophia/comma/HomePage.htm.
4. S.A. DeLoach and M. Wood, Developing Multiagent Systems with agentTool. In C. Castelfranchi and Y. Lespérance, editors, Intelligent Agents VII. Agent Theories, Architectures, and Languages - 7th International Workshop, ATAL-2000, Boston, MA, USA, July 7-9, 2000, Proceedings, Lecture Notes in Artificial Intelligence. Springer-Verlag, Berlin, 2001. In this volume.
5. FACTS Project Home Page: http://www.labs.bt.com/profsoc/facts/.
6. T. Finin and Y. Labrou. KQML as an agent communication language. In: J.M. Bradshaw (ed.), Software Agents, pp. 291-316. MIT Press, Cambridge, MA, 1997.
7. Foundation for Intelligent Physical Agents. Specifications. 1999. Available at
http://www.fipa.org.
8. E.J. Friedman-Hill. Java Expert System Shell. 1998. Available At
http://herzberg.ca.sandia.gov/jess.
9. M.R. Genesereth and S.P. Ketchpel. Software Agents. Comm. of ACM, 37(7):48-53.1994.
10. Grasshopper Home Page. Available at http://www.ikv.de/products/grasshopper.
11. The JADE Project Home Page, 2000. Available at http://sharon.cselt.it/projects/jade.
12. N.R. Jennings and M. Wooldrige. Agent Technology: Foundations, Applications, and Markets. Stringer, Berlin, Germany, 1998.
13. R.E. Johnson and J.M. Zweig. Delegation in C++. The Journal of Object Oriented Programming, 4(7):31-34, 1991.
14. V. Karamcheti, J. Plevyak and A. Chien. Runtime Mechanisms for Efficient Dynamic Multithreading. Journal of Parallel and Distributed Computing, 37:21-40, 1996.
15. T. Kawamura, N. Yoshioka, T. Hasegawa, A. Ohsuga and S. Honiden. Bee-gent : Bonding and Encapsulation Enhancement Agent Framework for Development of Distributed Systems. Proceedings of the 6th Asia-Pacific Software Engneering Conference, 1999.
16. D. Kerr, D. O'Sullivan, R. Evans, R. Richardson and F. Somers. Experiences using Intelligent Agent Technologies as a Unifying Approach to Network and Service Management. Proceedings of IS&N 98, Antwerp, Belgium. 1998.
17. G. Lavender and D. Schmidt. Active Object: An object behavioural pattern for concurrent programming. In J.M. Vlissides, J.O. Coplien, and N.L. Kerth, Eds. Pattern Languages of Program Design. Addison-Wesley, Reading, MA, 1996.
18. D. Lea. Concurrent Programming in Java: Design Principles and Patterns. Addison Wesley, Reading, MA, 1997.
19. P. Maes. Agents that reduce work and information overload. Comm. of ACM, 37(7):30-40. 1994.
20. D.L. Martin, A.J. Cheyer and D.B. Moran. The Open Agent Architecture: A Framework for Building Distributed Software Systems. Applied Artificial Intelligence 13:91-128. 1998.
21. B. Meyer. Object Oriented Software Construction, 2$^{nd}$ Ed. Prentice Hall, 1997
22. D. Milojicic, M. Breugst, I. Busse, J. Campbell, S. Covaci, B. Friedman, K. Kosaka, D. Lange, K. Ono, M. Oshima, C. Tham, S. Virdhagriswaran, and J. White. MASIF - The OMG Mobile Agent System Interoperability Facility. In K. Rothermel and F. Hohl, Eds. – Proc. 2nd Int. Workshop Mobile Agents (MA '98), Lecture Notes in Computer Science, 1477, pp. 50-67, Springer, Stuttgart, Germany, 1998.
23. FIPA-OS Home Page. Available at
http://www.nortelnetworks.com/products/announcements/fipa/index.html.
24. H.S. Nwana. Software Agents: An Overview. The Knowledge Engineering Review, 11(3):205-244, 1996.

25. H.S. Nwana, D.T. Ndumu and L.C. Lee. ZEUS: An advanced Tool-Kit for Engineering Distributed Mulyi-Agent Systems. In: Proc of PAAM98, pp. 377-391, London, U.K., 1998.
26. Object Management Group. 95-11-03: Common Services. 1997. Available at http://www.omg.org.
27. R.S. Patil, R.E. Fikes, P.F. Patel-Scheneider, D. McKay, T. Finin, T. Gruber and R. Neches. The DARPA knowledge sharing effort: progress report. In: Proc. Third Conf. on Principles of Knowledge Representation and Reasoning, pp 103-114. Cambridge, MA, 1992.
28. A.S. Rao and M. P. Georgeff. BDI agents: from theory to practice. In Proc. of the First Int. Conf. On Multi-Agent Systems, pp. 312-319, San Francisco, CA, 1995.
29. Reticular Systems. Agent Construction Tools. 1999. Available at http://www.agentbuilder.com.
30. Reticular Systems. AgentBuilder - An integrated Toolkit for Constructing Intelligence Software Agents. 1999. Available at http://www.agentbuilder.com.
31. J.R. Searle. Speech Acts: An Essay in the Phylosophy of language. Cambridge University Press, 1970.
32. Y. Shoham. Agent-oriented programming. Artificial Intelligence, 60(1):51-92. 1993.
33. Munindar P. Singh. Write Asynchronous, Run Synchronous. IEEE Internet Computing, 3(2):4-5. 1999.
34. K. Sycara, A. Pannu, M. Williamson and D. Zeng. Distributed Intelligent Agents. IEEE Expert, 11(6):36-46. 1996.
35. S.R. Thomas. The PLACA Agent Programming Language. In M.J. Wooldrige & N.R. Jennings (Eds.), Lecture Notes in Artificial Intelligence, pp. 355-370. Springer-Verlag, Berlin. 1994.
36. M. Wooldrige and N.R. Jennings. Intelligent Agents: Theory and Practice, The Knowledge Engineering Review, 10(2):115-152, 1995.

# High-Level Robot Control through Logic

Murray Shanahan and Mark Witkowski

Department of Electrical and Electronic Engineering,
Imperial College,
Exhibition Road,
London SW7 2BT,
England.
m.shanahan@ic.ac.uk, m.witkowski@ic.ac.uk

**Abstract.** This paper presents a programmable logic-based agent control system that interleaves planning, plan execution and perception. In this system, a program is a collection of logical formulae describing the agent's relationship to its environment. Two such programs for a mobile robot are described — one for navigation and one for map building — that share much of their code. The map building program incorporates a rudimentary approach to the formalisation of epistemic fluents, knowledge goals, and knowledge producing actions.

## 1 Introduction

Contemporary work in *cognitive robotics* has demonstrated the viability of logic-based high-level robot control [5], [2], [1], [12]. Building on the progress reported in [12], this paper describes an implemented logic-based, high-level robot control system in the cognitive robotics style. The controller is programmed directly in logic, specifically in the event calculus, an established formalism for reasoning about action. The controller's underlying computational model is a sense-plan-act cycle, in which both planning and sensor data assimilation are abductive theorem proving tasks.

Two small application programs written in this language are described in detail, one for navigation and one for map building. In navigation, the abductive processing of sensor data results in knowledge of the status (open or closed) of doors, while in map building (during which all doors are assumed to be open), it results in knowledge of the layout of rooms and doorways.

Both these programs have been deployed and tested on a Khepera robot. The Khepera is a miniature robotic platform with two drive wheels and a suite of eight infra-red proximity sensors around its circumference. The robot inhabits a miniaturised office-like environment comprising six rooms connected by doors which can be either open or closed (Figure 1). The robot cannot distinguish a closed door from a wall using its sensors alone, but has to use a combination of sensor data and abductive reasoning.

High-level control of the robot is the responsibility of an off-board computer, that communicates with the robot via an RS232 port. The high-level controller can initiate

C. Castelfranchi, Y. Lespérance (Eds.): Intelligent Agents VII, LNAI 1986, pp. 104–121, 2001.

low-level routines that are executed on-board, such as wall following, corner turning, and so on. Upon termination, these low-level routines communicate the status of the robot's sensors back to the high-level controller, which then decides how to proceed. The implementation details of the low-level actions are outside the scope of this paper, whose aim is to present the high-level controller.

It should be noted that the aim of the paper is not to present advances in any particular sub-area of AI, such as planning, knowledge representation, or robotics, but rather to show how techniques from these areas can be synthesised and integrated into an agent architecture, using logic as a representational medium and theorem proving as a means of computation.

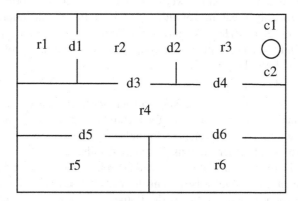

**Fig. 1.** The Robot's Environment

## 2 Theoretical Background

A high-level control program in our system is a set of logical formulae describing actions and their effects, those of both the robot and other agents. The formalism used to represent actions and their effects is the event calculus, and the frame problem is overcome using circumscription, as set out in [8].

The ontology of the event calculus includes *fluents*, *actions* (or *events*), and *time points*. The standard axioms of the event calculus (whose conjunction is denoted EC) serve to constrain the predicate HoldsAt, where HoldsAt( , ) represents that fluent holds at time . Here are two examples of these axioms.

HoldsAt(f,t3)
   Happens(a,t1,t2)   Initiates(a,f,t1)
     t2 < t3   Clipped(t1,f,t3)

Clipped(t1,f,t4)
    a,t2,t3 [Happens(a,t2,t3)   t1 < t3   t2 < t4
    Terminates(a,f,t2)]

A particular *domain* is described in terms of Initiates and Terminates formulae. Initiates( , , ) represents that fluent   starts to hold after action   at time  . Conversely, Terminates( , , ) represents that   starts not to hold after action   at  .

A particular *narrative* of events is described in terms of Happens and Initially formulae. The formulae Initially$_P$( ) and Initially$_N$( ) respectively represent that fluent   holds at time 0 and does not hold at time 0. Happens( , 1 , 2 ) represents that action or event   occurs, starting at time 1 and ending at time 2. Happens( , ) is equivalent to Happens( , , ).

Both planning and sensor data assimilation can be viewed as abductive tasks with respect to the event calculus [8], [11]. First, we need to construct a theory   of the effects of the robot's actions on the world and the impact of the world on the robot's sensors. Then, roughly speaking (omitting details of the circumscriptions), given a conjunction   of goals (HoldsAt formulae), and a conjunction $_I$ of formulae describing the initial state, a plan is a consistent conjunction   $_P$ of Happens and temporal ordering formulae such that,

$$_I \quad _P \quad EC \quad ^a \quad .$$

In order to interleave planning, sensing and acting effectively, we need to carry out hierarchical planning. The logical story for hierarchical planning is more or less the same, with the addition to   of Happens formulae describing how a compound action decomposes into its constituent actions. For more details, see [11].

A similar abductive account of sensor data assimilation (SDA) can be constructed. The need for such an account arises from the fact that sensors do not deliver facts directly into the robot's model of the world. Rather, they provide raw data from which facts can only be inferred. Given a conjunction   $_N$ of Happens and temporal ordering formulae describing the actions already carried out by the robot, and a description   of the sensor data received, an explanation of that sensor data is a consistent   such that,

$$_N \quad EC \quad ^a \quad .$$

The predicates allowed in   depend on the task at hand, either map building or navigation.

In the present system, both these abductive tasks — planning and SDA — are implemented by a single logic programming meta-interpreter. This meta-interpreter is sound and complete for a large class of domain theories. For more details, see [11].

## 3   Robot Programming in the Event Calculus

This section describes the robot's control system in more detail. In essence, it is a general purpose high-level agent control system, programmable directly in the event calculus. Although the focus of the present discussion is on robotics, the technology is applicable to other types of agent as well (c.f., [3], [13]).

The system executes a sense-plan-act cycle. The execution of this cycle has the following features.

- Planning and sensor data assimilation are both resolution-based *abductive* theorem proving processes, working on collections of event calculus formulae. These processes conform to the logical specifications sketched in the previous section.

- Planning and SDA are both *resource-bounded* processes. They are subject to constant suspension to allow the interleaving of sensing, planning and acting. The abductive meta-interpreter is made resource-bounded using techniques similar to those described in [4], where a meta-interpreter is described which is parameterised by the maximum number of resolution steps it can take before suspension. In the present implementation, each of the planning and SDA processes carries out just a single step of resolution on each iteration of the sense-plan-act cycle.

- To permit reactivity, planning is *hierarchical*. This facilitates planning in progression order, which promotes the rapid generation of a first executable action.

- The results of sensor data assimilation can expose conflicts with the current plan, thus precipitating *replanning*.

An event calculus robot program comprises the following five parts.

A.  A set of Initiates and Terminates formulae describing the effects of the robot's primitive, low-level actions.

B.  A set of Happens formulae describing the causes of robot sensor events.

C.  A set of Initiates and Terminates formulae describing the effects of high-level, compound actions.

D.  A set of Happens formulae defining high-level, compound actions in terms of more primitive ones. These definitions can include sequence, choice, and recursion.

E.  A set of declarations, specifying, for example, which predicates are abducible.

The formulae in A to D figure in the sense-plan-act cycle in the following way. Initially, the system has an empty plan, and is presented with a goal    in the form of a HoldsAt formula. Using resolution against formulae in C, the planning process identifies a high-level action    that will achieve   . (If no such action is available, the planner uses the formulae in A to plan from first principles.) The planning process then decomposes    using resolution against formulae in D. This decomposition may yield any combination of the following.

- Further sub-goals to be achieved (HoldsAt formulae).

- Further sub-actions to be decomposed (Happens formulae).

- Executable, primitive actions to be added to the plan (Happens formulae).

- Negated Clipped formulae, analogous to protected links in partial-order planning, whose validity must be preserved throughout subsequent processing.

As soon as a complete but possibly not fully decomposed plan with an executable first action is generated, the robot can act. Success is only guaranteed with this "act whenever you can" strategy, even in a benign world, if the set of compound actions has the *downward solution property* — for every compound action    that initiates a fluent   , there exists a decomposition of    which is a plan for   .

Meanwhile, the SDA process is also underway. This receives incoming sensor events in the form of Happens formulae. Using resolution against formulae in B, the SDA process starts trying to find an explanation for these sensor events. This may yield any combination of Happens, HoldsAt and negated Clipped formulae, which are subject to further abductive processing through resolution against formulae in A, taking into account the actions the robot itself has performed.

In many tasks, such as navigation, the SDA process ultimately generates a set of abduced Happens formulae describing external actions (actions not carried out by the robot itself) that explain the incoming sensor data. Using resolution against formulae in A, it can be determined whether these external events threaten the validity of the negated Clipped formulae (protected links) recorded by the planning process. If they do, the system replans from scratch.

In the context of this sense-plan-act cycle, the event calculus can be regarded as a logic programming language for agents. Accordingly, event calculus programs have both a *declarative* meaning, as collections of sentences of logic, and a *procedural* meaning, given by the execution model outlined here. The following sections present two robotic applications written as event calculus programs, namely navigation and map building.

Although neither of the robot programs presented here exhibits much reactivity, the system does facilitate the construction of highly reactive control programs. The key to achieving reactivity is to ensure that the program includes high-level compound actions that quickly decompose, in as many situations as possible, to a first executable action. Although each unexpected event will precipitate replanning from scratch, this replanning process then very rapidly results in an appropriate new action to be executed.

## 4   A Navigation Program

Appendices A and C of the full paper contain (almost) the complete text of a working event calculus program for robot navigation. This section describes the program's construction and operation. (Throughout the sequel, fragments of code will be written using a Prolog-like syntax, while purely logical formulae will retain their usual syntax.)

The robot's environment (Figure 1) is represented in the following way. The formula connects(D,R1,R2) means that door D connects rooms R1 and R2, inner(C) means that corner C is a concave corner, door(D,C1,C2) means corners C1 and C2 are door D's door-posts, and next_corner(R,C1,C2) means that C2 is the next corner from C1 in room R in a clockwise direction, where C1 and C2 can each be either convex or concave. A set of such formulae (a *map*) describing the room layout is a required background theory for the navigation application, but is not given in the appendices.

The robot has a repertoire of three primitive actions: follow_wall, whereby it proceeds along the wall to the next visible corner, turn(S), whereby it turns a corner in direction S (either left or right), and go_straight, whereby it crosses a doorway. For simplicity, we'll assume the robot only proceeds in a clockwise direction around a room, hugging the wall to its left. The navigation domain comprises just two fluents. The term `in(R)` denotes that the robot is in room R, while the term `loc(corner(C),S)` denotes that the robot is in corner C. The S parameter, whose value is either `ahead` or `behind`, indicates the relative orientation of the robot to C.

The program comprises the five parts mentioned in Section 3. To begin with, let's look at the formulae describing high-level, compound actions (parts C and D, according to Section 3). Let's consider the high-level action `go_to_room(R1,R2)`. The effect of this action is given by an `initiates` formula.

```
initiates(go_to_room(R1,R2),in(R2),T)  :-          (A1)
   holds_at(in(R1),T).
```

In other words, `go_to_room(R1,R2)` puts the robot in R2, assuming it was in R1. The `go_to_room` action is recursively defined in terms of `go_through` actions.

```
happens(go_to_room(R,R),T,T).                      (A2)

happens(go_to_room(R1,R3),T1,T4)  :-               (A3)
   towards(R2,R3,R1), connects(D,R1,R2),
   holds_at(door_open(D),T1),
   happens(go_through(D),T1,T2),
   happens(go_to_room(R2,R3),T3,T4),
   before(T2,T3),
   not(clipped(T2,in(R2),T3)).
```

In other words, `go_to_room(R1,R3)` has no sub-actions if R1 = R3, but otherwise comprises a `go_through` action to take the robot through door D into room R2 followed by another `go_to_room` action to take the robot from R2 to R3. Door D must be open. The `towards` predicate supplies heuristic guidance for the selection of the door to go through.

Notice that the action is only guaranteed to have the effect described by the `initiates` formula if the room the robot is in doesn't change between the two sub-actions. Hence the need for the negated `clipped` conjunct. The inclusion of such negated `clipped` conjuncts ensures that the sub-actions of overlapping compound actions cannot interfere with each other.

The `go_through` action itself decomposes further into `follow_wall`, `go_straight` and `turn` actions that the robot can execute directly (see Appendix A).

Now let's consider the formulae describing the effects of these primitive executable actions (part A of the program, according to Section 3). The full set of these formulae is to be found in Appendix C. Here are the formulae describing the `follow_wall` action.

```
initiates(follow_wall,                             (S1)
     loc(corner(C2),ahead),T)  :-
   holds_at(loc(corner(C1),behind),T),
   next_visible_corner(C1,C2,left,T).
```

```
terminates(follow_wall,                                    (S2)
    loc(corner(C),behind),T).
```

A `follow_wall` action takes the robot to the next visible corner in the room, where the next visible corner is the next one that is not part of a doorway whose door is closed. The effects of `go_straight` and `turn` are similarly described. The formulae in Appendix C also cover the fluents `facing` and `pos` which are used for map building but not for navigation.

Next we'll take a look at the formulae describing the causes of sensor events, which figure prominently in sensor data assimilation (part B of the program, according to Section 3). Three kinds of sensor event can occur: `left_and_front`, `left_gap` and `left`.

The `left_and_front` event occurs when the robot's left sensors are already high and its front sensors go high, such as when it's following a wall and meets a concave corner. The `left_gap` event occurs when its left sensors go low, such as when it is following a corner and meets a convex corner such as a doorway. The `left` event occurs when its front and left sensors are high and the front sensors go low, such as when it turns right in a concave corner.

In the formulae of Appendix C, each of these sensor events has a single parameter, which indicates the distance the robot thinks it has traveled since the last sensor event, according to its on-board odometry. This parameter is used for map building and can be ignored for the present. Here's the formula for `left_and_front`.

```
happens(left_and_front(X),T,T)  :-                         (S3)
    happens(follow_wall,T,T),
    holds_at(co_ords(P1),T),
    holds_at(facing(W),T),
    holds_at(loc(corner(C1),behind),T),
    next_visible_corner(C1,C2,left,T),
    inner(C2),
    displace(P1,X,W,P2),  pos(C2,P2).
```

The second, third, and final conjuncts on the right-hand-side of this formula are again the concern of map building, so we can ignore them for now. The rest of the formula says that a `left_and_front` event will occur if the robot starts off in corner C1, then follows the wall to a concave corner C2. Similar formulae characterise the occurrence of `left` and `left_gap` events (see Appendix C).

## 5   A Worked Example of Navigation

These formulae, along with their companions in Appendices A and C, are employed by the sense-plan-act cycle in the way described in Section 3. To see this, let's consider an example. The system starts off with an empty plan, and is presented with the initial goal to get to room r6.

```
holds_at(in(r6),T)
```

The planning process resolves this goal against clause (A1), yielding a complete, but not fully decomposed plan, comprising a single `go_to_room(r3,r6)` action.

Resolving against clause (A3), this plan is decomposed into a go_through(d4) action followed by a go_to_room(r4,r6) action. Further decomposition of the go_through action yields the plan: follow_wall, go_through(d4), then go_to_room(r4,r6). In addition, a number of protected links (negated clipped formulae) are recorded for later re-checking, including a formula of the form,

not(clipped( 1 ,door_open(d4), 2 )).

The system now possesses a complete, though still not fully decomposed, plan, with an executable first action, namely follow_wall. So it proceeds to execute the follow_wall action, while continuing to work on the plan. When the follow_wall action finishes, a left_and_front sensor event occurs, and the SDA process is brought to life. In this case, the sensor event has an empty explanation — it is just what would be expected to occur given the robot's actions.

Similar processing brings about the subsequent execution of a turn(right) action then another follow_wall action. At the end of this second follow_wall action, a left_and_front sensor event occurs. This means that a formula of the form,

happens(left_and_front( ), )

needs to be explained, where   is the time of execution of the follow_wall action. The SDA process sets about explaining the event in the usual way, which is to resolve this formula against clause (S3). This time, though, an empty explanation will not suffice. Since door d4 was initially open, a left_gap event should have occurred instead of a left_and_front event.

After a certain amount of work, this particular explanation task boils down to the search for an explanation of the formula,

next_visible_corner(c2,C, ), inner(C)

(The C is implicitly existentially quantified.) The explanation found by the SDA process has the following form.

happens(close_door(d4), '), before( ', )

In other words, an external close_door action occurred some time before the robot's follow_wall action. Since this close_door action terminates the fluent door_open(d4), there is a violation of one of the protected links recorded by the planner (see above). The violation of this protected link causes the system to replan, this time producing a plan to go via doors d2 and d3 , which executes successfully.

## 6  Map Building with Epistemic Fluents

The focus of the rest of this paper is map building. Map building is a more sophisticated task than navigation, and throws up a number of interesting issues, including how to represent and reason with knowledge producing actions and actions with knowledge preconditions, the subject of this section.

During navigation, explanations of sensor data are constructed in terms of open door and close door events, but for map building we require explanations in terms of the relationships between corners and the connectivity of rooms. So the first step in turning our navigation program into a map building program is to declare a different set of abducibles (part E of a robot program, according to Section 3). The abducibles will now include the predicates next_corner, inner, door, and connects. Map building then becomes a side effect of the SDA process.

But how are the effects of the robot's actions on its knowledge of these predicates to be represented and reasoned with? The relationship between knowledge and action has received a fair amount of attention in the reasoning about action literature. (See [6] and [14], for just two examples.) All of this work investigates the relationship between knowledge and action on the assumption that knowledge has a privileged role to play in the logic.

In the present paper, the logical difficulties consequent on embarking on such an investigation are to some degree sidestepped by according epistemic fluents, that is to say fluents that concern the state of the robot's knowledge, exactly the same status as other fluents. What follows is in no way intended as a contribution to the literature on the subject of reasoning about knowledge. But it's enough to get us off the ground with logic-based map building.

Before discussing implementation, let's take a closer look at this issue from a logical point of view. To begin with, we'll introduce a generic epistemic fluent Knows. The formula HoldsAt(Knows( ), ) represents that the formula    follows from the robot's knowledge (or, strictly speaking, from the robot's beliefs) at time  . (More precisely, to distinguish object- from meta-level, the formula *named by*    follows from the robot's knowledge. To simplify matters, we'll assume every formula is its own name.)

Using epistemic fluents, we can formalise the knowledge producing effects of the robot's repertoire of actions. In the present domain, for example, we have the following.

r,c2 [Initiates(FollowWall,
    Knows(NextCorner(r,c1,c2)),t)]
HoldsAt(Loc(Corner(c1),Behind),t)

In other words, following a wall gives the robot knowledge of the next corner along. This formula is true, given the right set of abducibles, thanks to the abductive treatment of sensor data via clause (S3). In practise, the abductive SDA process gives a new name to that corner, if it's one it hasn't visited before, and records whether or not it's an inner corner.

Similar formulae account for the epistemic effects of the robot's other actions. Then, all we need is to describe the initial state of the robot's knowledge, using the Initially$_N$ and Initially$_P$ predicates, and the axioms of the event calculus will take care of the rest, yielding the state of the robot's knowledge at any time.

Epistemic fluents, as well as featuring in the descriptions of the knowledge producing effects of actions, also appear in knowledge goals. In the present example, the overall goal is to know the layout of corners, doors and rooms. Accordingly, a new epistemic fluent KnowsMap is defined as follows.

HoldsAt(KnowsMap,t)
  [Door(d,c1,c2)
     r1,r2 [HoldsAt(Knows(Connects(d,r1,r2)),t)]]
  [Pos(c1,p)
     r,c2 [HoldsAt(Knows(NextCorner(r,c1,c2)),t)]]

Note the difference between

  r1,r2 [HoldsAt(Knows(Connects(d,r1,r2)),t)]

and

  r1,r2 [Connects(d,r1,r2)].

The second formula says that there are rooms connected by door d, while the first formula says that the robot knows what those rooms are. The robot's knowledge might include the second formula while not including the first. Indeed, if badly programmed, the robot's knowledge could include the first formula while not including the second. (There's no analogue to modal logic's axiom schema T (reflexivity).)

The top-level goal presented to the system will be HoldsAt(KnowsMap,t). Now suppose we have a high-level action Explore, whose effect is to make KnowsMap hold.

  Initiates(Explore,KnowsMap,t)

Given the top-level goal HoldsAt(KnowsMap,t), the initial top-level plan the system will come up with comprises the single action Explore. The definition of Explore is, in effect, the description of a map building algorithm. Here's an example formula.

Happens(Explore,t1,t4)                           (L1)
  HoldsAt(In(r1),t1)   HoldsAt(Loc(Corner(c1),s),t1)
    c2 [HoldsAt(Knows(NextCorner(r1,c1,c2)),t1)]
    d, c2, c3 [Door(d,c2,c3)
        r2 [HoldsAt(Knows(Connects(d,r1,r2)),t1)]]
  Happens(GoThrough(d),t1,t2)
  Happens(Explore,t3,t4)   Before(t2,t3)

This formula tells the robot to proceed through door d if it's in a corner it already knows about, where d is a door leading to an unknown room. Note the use of epistemic fluents in the third and fourth lines. A number of similar formulae cater for the decomposition of Explore under different circumstances.

# 7 A Map Building Program

Appendices B and C of the full paper present (almost) the full text of a working event calculus program for map building. This section outlines how it works. The three novel issues that set this program apart from the navigation program already discussed are,

1. the use of epistemic fluents,

2.   the need for integrity constraints, and

3.   the need for techniques similar to those used in constraint logic programming (CLP).

The first issue was addressed in the previous section. The second two issues, as we'll see shortly, arise from the robot's need to recognise when it's in a corner it has already visited. First, though, let's see how the predicate calculus definition of the Explore action translates into a clause in the actual implementation. Here's the implemented version of formula (L1) at the end of the previous section.

```
happens(explore,T1,T4) :-                                    (B1)
    holds_at(loc(corner(C1),S),T1),
    not(unexplored_corner(C1,T1)),
    unexplored_door(D,T1),
    happens(go_through(D),T1,T2),
    happens(explore,T3,T4), before(T2,T3).
```

Instead of using epistemic fluents explicitly, this clause appeals to two new predicates unexplored_corner and unexplored_door. These are defined as follows.

```
unexplored_corner(C1,T) :-                                   (B2)
    pos(C1,P), not(next_corner(R,C1,C2)).
```

```
unexplored_door(D,T) :-                                      (B3)
    door(D,C1,C2), not(connects(D,R1,R2)).
```

The formula pos(C,P) represents that corner C is in position P, where P is a co-ordinate range (see below).

By defining these two predicates, we can simulate the effect of the existential quantifiers in formula (L1) using negation-as-failure. Furthermore, we can use negation-as-failure as a substitute for keeping track of the Knows fluent. (This trick renders the predicates' temporal arguments superfluous, but they're retained for elegance.) Operationally, the formula,

```
not(next_corner(R,C1,C2))
```

serves the same purpose as the predicate calculus formula,

$$r,c2 \; [HoldsAt(Knows(NextCorner(r,c1,c2)),t1)]].$$

The first formula uses negation-as-failure to determine what is provable from the robot's knowledge, while the second formula assumes that what is provable is recorded explicitly through the Knows fluent.

The final issue to discuss is how, during its exploration of a room, the robot recognises that it's back in a corner it has already visited, so as to prevent the SDA process from postulating redundant new corners.

Recall that each sensor event has a single argument, which is the estimated distance the robot has traveled since the last sensor event. Using this argument, the robot can keep track of its approximate position. Accordingly, the program includes a suitable set of initiates and terminates clauses for the co_ords fluent, where co_ords(P) denotes that P is the robot's current position. A *position* is actually a list [X1,X2,Y1,Y2], representing a rectangle, bounded by X1 and X2 on the x-axis and Y1 and Y2 on the y-axis, within which an object's precise co-ordinates are known to fall.

Using this fluent, explanations of sensor data that postulate redundant new corners can be ruled out using an *integrity constraint*. (In abductive logic programming, the use of integrity constraints to eliminate possible explanations is a standard technique.) Logically speaking, an integrity constraint is a formula of the form,

$$[P_1 \quad P_2 \quad \ldots \quad P_n]$$

where each $P_i$ is an atomic formula. Any abductive explanation must be consistent with this formula. In meta-interpreter syntax, the predicate `inconsistent` is used to represent integrity constraints, and the abductive procedure needs to be modified to take them into account. In the present case, we need the following integrity constraint.

```
inconsistent([pos(C1,P1), pos(C2,P2),          (B4)
    same_pos(P1,P2),
    room_of(C1,R), room_of(C2,R),
    diff(C1,C2)]).
```

The formula `same_pos(P1,P2)` checks whether the maximum possible distance between `P1` and `P2` is less than a predefined threshold. The formula `diff(X,Y)` represents that X    Y. If the meta-interpreter is trying to prove `not(diff(X,Y))`, it can do so by abducing that X = Y, and rename them accordingly. (Terms that can be renamed in this way have to be declared.) In particular, to preserve consistency in the presence of this integrity constraint, the SDA process will sometimes equate a new corner with an old one, and rename it accordingly.

Having determined, via (B4), that two apparently distinct corners are in fact one and the same, the robot may have two overlapping positions for the same corner. These can be subsumed by a single, more narrowly constrained position combining the range bounds of the two older positions.

This motivates the addition of the final component of the system, namely a rudimentary constraint reduction mechanism along the lines of those found in constraint logic programming languages. This permits the programmer to define simple constraint reduction rules whereby two formulae are replaced by a single formula that implies them both. In the present example, we have the following rule.

```
common_antecedent(pos(C,[X1,X2,Y1,Y2]),
    pos(C,[X3,X4,Y3,Y4]),
    pos(C,[X5,X6,Y5,Y6]) :-
  max(X1,X3,X5), min(X2,X4,X6),
  max(Y1,Y3,Y5), min(Y2,Y4,Y6).
```

The formula `common_antecedent(P1,P2,P3)` represents that `P3` implies both `P1` and `P2`, and that any explanation containing both `P1` and `P2` can be simplified by replacing `P1` and `P2` by `P3`.

# 8  Concluding Remarks

The work reported in this paper and its companion [12] is part of an ongoing attempt to develop robot architectures in which logic is the medium of representation, and theorem proving is the means of computation. The hope is that such architectures, having a deliberative component at their core, are a step closer to robots that can reason, act, and communicate in a way that mimics more closely human high-level cognition [10]. The preliminary results reported here are promising. In particular, it's encouraging to see that event calculus programs for navigation and map building can be written and deployed on real robots that are each less than 100 lines long and, moreover, that share more than half their code.

However, the work presented has many shortcomings that need to be addressed in future work. Most important is the issue of scaling up. The robot environment used in the experiments described here is simple, highly engineered (compared to a real office) and static, and the robots themselves have extremely simple sensors. It remains to be seen, for example, what new representational techniques will be required to accommodate the proposed theory of sensor data assimilation to complex, dynamic environments and rich sensors, such as vision.

In addition, a number of logical issues remain outstanding. First, as reported in [11], the formal properties of the event calculus with compound actions are poorly understood. Second, the topic of knowledge producing actions in the event calculus needs to be properly addressed, and the limitations of the naive approach employed here need to be assessed.

**Acknowledgements.** This work was carried out as part of EPSRC project GR/N13104 "Cognitive Robotics II". Thanks to the ATAL 2000 anonymous referees.

# References

1.  C.Baral and S.C.Tran, Relating Theories of Actions and Reactive Control, *Linköping Electronic Articles in Computer and Information Science*, vol. 3 (1998), no. 9.
2.  G. De Giacomo, Y.Lespérance, and H.Levesque, Reasoning about Concurrent Execution, Prioritized Interrupts, and Exogenous Actions in the Situation Calculus, *Proceedings 1997 International Joint Conference on Artificial Intelligence (IJCAI 97)*, Morgan Kaufmann, pp. 1221–1226.
3.  K.V.Hindriks, F.S.de Boer, W.van der Hoek, and J-J.Ch.Meyer, Agent Programming with Declarative Goals, this volume.
4.  R.A.Kowalski, Using Meta-Logic to Reconcile Reactive with Rational Agents, in *Meta-Logics and Logic Programming*, ed. K.R.Apt and F.Turini, MIT Press (1995), pp. 227–242.
5.  Y.Lespérance, H.J.Levesque, F.Lin, D.Marcu, R.Reiter, and R.B.Scherl, A Logical Approach to High-Level Robot Programming: A Progress Report, in *Control of the Physical World by Intelligent Systems: Papers from the 1994 AAAI Fall Symposium*, ed. B.Kuipers, New Orleans (1994), pp. 79–85.
6.  H.Levesque, What Is Planning in the Presence of Sensing? *Proceedings AAAI 96*, pp. 1139–1146.

7.  N.J.Nilsson, ed., *Shakey the Robot*, SRI Technical Note no. 323 (1984), SRI, Menlo Park, California.

8.  M.P.Shanahan, *Solving the Frame Problem: A Mathematical Investigation of the Common Sense Law of Inertia*, MIT Press (1997).

9.  M.P.Shanahan, Noise, Non-Determinism and Spatial Uncertainty, *Proceedings AAAI 97*, pp. 153–158.

10. M.P.Shanahan, What Sort of Computation Mediates Best Between Perception and Action?, in *Logical Foundations for Cognitive Agents: Contributions in Honor of Ray Reiter*, eds. H.J.Levesque & F.Pirri, Springer-Verlag (1999), pages 352-368.

11. M.P.Shanahan, An Abductive Event Calculus Planner, *The Journal of Logic Programming*, vol. 44 (2000), pp. 207–239.

12. M.P.Shanahan, Reinventing Shakey, in *Logic Based Artificial Intelligence*, ed. J.Minker, Kluwer, to appear.

13. S.Shapiro and Y.Lespérance, Modeling Multiagent Systems with CASL — A Feature Interaction Resolution Application, this volume.

14. S.Zimmerbaum and R.Scherl, Sensing Actions, Time, and Concurrency in the Situation Calculus, this volume.

# Appendix A: Navigation Code

```
/* Navigation Compound Actions */

happens(go_to_room(R,R),T,T).

happens(go_to_room(R1,R3),T1,T4) :-
     towards(R2,R3,R1), connects(D,R1,R2),
     holds_at(door_open(D),T1), happens(go_through(D),T1,T2),
     happens(go_to_room(R2,R3),T3,T4),
     before(T2,T3), not(clipped(T2,in(R2),T3)).

happens(go_to_room(R1,R3),T1,T4) :-
     connects(D,R1,R2), holds_at(door_open(D),T1),
     happens(go_through(D),T1,T2),
     happens(go_to_room(R2,R3),T3,T4), before(T2,T3),
     not(clipped(T2,in(R2),T3)).

initiates(go_to_room(R1,R2),in(R2),T) :-
     holds_at(in(R1),T).

happens(go_through(D),T1,T2) :-
     holds_at(loc(corner(C1),ahead),T1), door(D,C1,C2),
     happens(turn(left),T1), happens(turn(left),T2),
     before(T1,T2), not(clipped(T1,door_open(D),T2)).

happens(go_through(D1),T1,T3) :-
     holds_at(loc(corner(C1),ahead)),T1), door(D2,C1,C2),
     diff(D1,D2), holds_at(door_open(D2),T1),
     happens(go_straight,T1), happens(go_through(D1),T2,T3),
     before(T1,T2).
```

```
happens(go_through(D),T1,T3) :-
     holds_at(loc(corner(C),behind),T1),
     happens(follow_wall,T1),
     happens(go_through(D),T2,T3), before(T1,T2),
     not(clipped(T1,door_open(D),T2)).

happens(go_through(D),T1,T3) :-
     holds_at(loc(corner(C),ahead),T1), inner(C),
     happens(turn(right),T1), happens(go_through(D),T2,T3),
     before(T1,T2), not(clipped(T1,door_open(D),T2)).

/* Navigation Heuristics */

towards(R1,R1,R2).

towards(R1,R2,R3) :- connects(D,R1,R2).

towards(R1,R2,R3) :- connects(D1,R1,R4), connects(D2,R4,R2).

/* External Actions */

terminates(close_door(D),door_open(D),T).

initiates(open_door(D),door_open(D),T).
```

## Appendix B: Map Building Code

```
/* Map Building Compound Actions */

happens(explore,T1,T6) :-
     holds_at(loc(corner(C1),ahead),T1), inner(C1),
     unexplored_corner(C1,T1), happens(turn(right),T1,T2),
     happens(follow_wall,T3,T4), before(T2,T3),
     happens(explore,T5,T6), before(T4,T5).

happens(explore,T1,T4) :-
     holds_at(loc(corner(C1),ahead),T1), not(inner(C1)),
     unexplored_corner(C1,T1), happens(go_straight,T1,T2),
     happens(explore,T3,T4), before(T2,T3).

happens(explore,T1,T4) :-
     holds_at(loc(corner(C1),behind),T1),
     unexplored_corner(C1,T1), happens(follow_wall,T1,T2),
     happens(explore,T3,T4), before(T2,T3).

happens(explore,T1,T4) :-
     holds_at(loc(corner(C1),S),T1),
     not(unexplored_corner(C1,T1)), unexplored_door(D,T1),
     happens(go_through(D),T1,T2),
     happens(explore,T3,T4), before(T2,T3).

initiates(explore,knows_map,T).

holds_at(knows_map,T) :-
     not(unexplored_door(D,T)), not(unexplored_corner(C,T)).
```

```
unexplored_corner(C1,T) :-
    pos(C1,P), not(next_corner(R,C1,C2)).

unexplored_door(D,T) :-
    door(D,C1,C2), not(connects(D,R1,R2)).

/* Integrity constraints */

inconsistent([pos(C1,P1), pos(C2,P2), same_pos(P1,P2),
    room_of(C1,R), room_of(C2,R), diff(C1,C2)]).

inconsistent([next_corner(R,C1,C2),
    next_corner(R,C1,C3), not(eq(C2,C3))]).

inconsistent([next_corner(R1,C1,C2),
    next_corner(R2,C1,C2), not(eq(R1,R2))]).

/* Constraints */

common_antecedent(pos(C,[X1,X2,Y1,Y2]),
        pos(C,[X3,X4,Y3,Y4]), pos(C,[X5,X6,Y5,Y6]) :-
    max(X1,X3,X5), min(X2,X4,X6), max(Y1,Y3,Y5), min(Y2,Y4,Y6).
```

## Appendix C: Shared Code

```
/* Primitive Actions */

initiates(follow_wall,loc(corner(C2),ahead),T) :-
    holds_at(loc(corner(C1),behind),T),
    next_visible_corner(C1,C2,left,T).

terminates(follow_wall,loc(corner(C),behind),T).

next_visible_corner(C1,C2,left,T) :-
    holds_at(in(R),T), next_corner(R,C1,C2),
    not(invisible_corner(C2,T)).

next_visible_corner(C1,C3,left,T) :-
    holds_at(in(R),T), next_corner(R,C1,C2),
    invisible_corner(C2,T), next_visible_corner(C2,C3,left,T).

invisible_corner(C1,T) :-
    door(D,C1,C2),holds_at(neg(door_open(D)),T).

invisible_corner(C1,T) :-
    door(D,C2,C1),holds_at(neg(door_open(D)),T).

initiates(go_straight,loc(corner(C2),behind),T) :-
    holds_at(loc(corner(C1),ahead),T), door(D,C1,C2).

terminates(go_straight,loc(corner(C1),ahead),T) :-
    holds_at(loc(corner(C1),ahead),T), door(D,C1,C2).

initiates(turn(left),loc(door(D),in),T) :-
    holds_at(loc(corner(C1),ahead),T),
    door(D,C1,C2), holds_at(door_open(D),T).
```

```
terminates(turn(left),loc(corner(C1),ahead),T) :-
    holds_at(loc(corner(C1),ahead),T),
    door(D,C1,C2), holds_at(door_open(D),T).

initiates(turn(left),loc(corner(C2),behind),T) :-
    holds_at(loc(door(D),in),T), holds_at(in(R1),T),
    connects(D,R1,R2), door(D,C1,C2), next_corner(R2,C1,C2).

terminates(turn(left),loc(door(D),in),T) :-
    holds_at(loc(door(D),in),T).

initiates(turn(left),in(R2),T) :-
    holds_at(loc(door(D),in),T),
    holds_at(in(R1),T),  connects(D,R1,R2).

terminates(turn(left),in(R1),T) :-
    holds_at(loc(door(D),in),T), holds_at(in(R1),T).

initiates(turn(right),loc(corner(C),behind),T) :-
    holds_at(loc(corner(C),ahead),T), inner(C).

terminates(turn(right),loc(corner(C),ahead),T) :-
    holds_at(loc(corner(C),ahead),T), inner(C).

initiates(turn(right),facing(W1),T) :-
    holds_at(facing(W2),T), plus_90(W2,W1).

terminates(turn(right),facing(W),T) :- holds_at(facing(W),T).

initiates(turn(left),facing(W1),T) :-
    holds_at(facing(W2),T), minus_90(W2,W1).

terminates(turn(left),facing(W),T) :- holds_at(facing(W),T).

initiates(follow_wall,co_ords(P),T) :-
    holds_at(loc(corner(C1),behind),T),
    next_visible_corner(C1,C2,left,T), pos(C2,P).

terminates(follow_wall,co_ords(P),T) :- holds_at(co_ords(P),T).

initiates(go_straight,co_ords(P),T) :-
    holds_at(loc(corner(C1),ahead),T),
    door(D,C1,C2), pos(C2,P).

terminates(go_straight,co_ords(P),T) :- holds_at(co_ords(P),T).

initiates(turn(left),co_ords(P),T) :-
    holds_at(loc(door(D),in),T),
    holds_at(in(R1),T), connects(D,R1,R2),
    door(D,C1,C2), next_corner(R2,C1,C2), pos(C2,P).

terminates(turn(left),co_ords(P),T) :-
    holds_at(loc(door(D),in),T), holds_at(co_ords(P),T).

/* Sensor events */

happens(left_and_front(X),T,T) :-
    happens(follow_wall,T,T), holds_at(co_ords(P1),T),
    holds_at(facing(W),T), holds_at(loc(corner(C1),behind),T),
    next_visible_corner(C1,C2,left,T),
    inner(C2), displace(P1,X,W,P2), pos(C2,P2).
```

```
happens(left(X),T,T) :-
     happens(turn(right),T,T),
     holds_at(loc(corner(C),ahead),T), inner(C).

happens(left(X),T,T) :-
     happens(turn(left),T,T), holds_at(loc(door(D),in),T),
     holds_at(in(R1),T), connects(D,R1,R2), connects(D,R2,R1),
     holds_at(co_ords(P1),T), holds_at(facing(W1),T),
     next_corner(R2,C3,C2), door(D,C3,C2),
     wall_thickness(Y1), displace(P1,Y1,W1,P2),
     pos(C2,P2), door_width(Y2), plus_90(W1,W2),
     displace(P2,Y2,W2,P3), pos(C3,P3).

happens(left(X),T,T) :-
     happens(go_straight,T,T), holds_at(co_ords(P1),T),
     holds_at(facing(W),T), holds_at(loc(corner(C1),ahead),T),
     holds_at(in(R),T), next_corner(R,C1,C2), door(D,C1,C2),
     displace(P1,X,W,P2), pos(C2,P2).

happens(left_gap(X),T,T) :-
     happens(follow_wall,T,T), holds_at(co_ords(P1),T),
     holds_at(facing(W),T), holds_at(loc(corner(C1),behind),T),
     next_visible_corner(C1,C2,left,T),
     not(inner(C2)), displace(P1,X,W,P2), pos(C2,P2).
```

# Determining the Envelope of Emergent Agent Behaviour via Architectural Transformation

Oswaldo Terán[1,2], Bruce Edmonds[1], and Steve Wallis[1]

[1]Centre for Policy Modelling, Manchester Metropolitan University,
Aytoun Building, Aytoun Street, Manchester, M1 3GH, UK.
*Tel.* +44 161 247 6478 *Fax.* +44 161 247 6802
{o.teran,b.edmonds,s.wallis}@mmu.ac.uk
[2]Department of Operation Research and Centre for Simulation
and Modelling, Universidad de Los Andes. Venezuela

**Abstract.** In this paper we propose a methodology to help analyse tendencies in MAS to complement those of simple inspection, Monte Carlo and syntactic proof. We suggest an architecture that allows an exhaustive model-based search of possible system trajectories in significant fragments of a MAS using forward inference. The idea is to identify tendencies, especially emergent tendencies, by automating the search through possible parameterisations of the model and the choices made by the agents. Subsequently, a proof of these tendencies could be attempted over all possible conditions using syntactic proof procedures. Additionally, we propose and exemplify a computational procedure to help implement this. The strategy consists of: "un-encapsulating" the MAS so as to reveal and then exploit the maximum information about logical dependencies in the system. The idea is to make possible the complete exploration of model behaviour over a range of parameterisations and agent choices.

## 1 Introduction: Understanding MAS

MAS can (and frequently do) exhibit very complex behaviour – in this fact lies their promise but it also means that they can be difficult to understand and predict. Broadly there are two means by which we can seek to understand MAS: through design and through observation. Careful design procedures based on well-understood formal models of agent behaviour help us to understand the behaviour of individual agents and, in special cases, larger parts of MAS. However understanding the behaviour of interacting groups of autonomous agents by formal design methods has its limitations, and even the most carefully designed MAS can exhibit emergent behaviour unforeseen by its designers. This is hardly surprising as half the *point* of autonomous agents is that they should be able to deal with circumstances unforeseen by their designers.

Thus a second important way in which we can control MAS (after careful design) is by inspecting and analysing the behaviour of MAS in a *post hoc* manner, so that this can inform our future design and control of them. In other words, just like any software development environment, to effectively deploy MAS one needs both design *and* debugging tools. The most common methods of such post hoc analysis are:

C. Castelfranchi, Y. Lespérance (Eds.): Intelligent Agents VII, LNAI 1986, pp. 122–135, 2001.
© Springer-Verlag Berlin Heidelberg 2001

*firstly*, by detailed scenario analysis, where a single MAS trajectory at a time is examined and analysed and *secondly*, using a Monte Carlo approach where the MAS is repeatedly run and statistics collected about general trends over a sample of trajectories.

The scenario analysis provides the *richest* source of information, typically providing far more detail than the programmer can possibly cope with. It is also inherently contingent and it can be difficult to separate out what can be taken as representative behaviour and what is exceptional. After examining and interacting with several such runs of the system it is up to programmers to abstract an understanding of the MAS's behaviour using their intuition; the scenario analysis only conclusively demonstrates possibilities.

A Monte Carlo approach can be used to separate out the exceptional from the representative in some cases, but has a number of drawbacks including: the sort of behaviour one is investigating may not be satisfactorily summarised using numerical devices (for example in safety critical systems it may be insufficient to know that a certain parameter *probably* stays within an acceptable range, on would want to *know* it does); and   the use of statistics inevitably involves the use of certain assumptions, which may not always be appropriate.

In this paper we discuss the use of a constraint-based search of possible models which can be deployed on significant subspaces of the total space of MAS possibilities. Like the Monte Carlo approach this can be seen as falling half-way between syntactic proof procedures and single scenario analyses. Unlike the Monte Carlo approach it produces definite answers to questions relative to the chosen subspace of possibilities – it can be seen as model-based proof w.r.t. subsets of the possibilities. It does not magically solve the problems in understanding all emergent MAS behaviour but is a useful addition to our menu of tools because it embodies a different trade-off between semantic richness and computational efficiency.

We will begin in section 2, by outlining the main idea.  The implementational concerns of the technique, i.e., the proposed architecture for doing the constraint-based model search in a "hunt" of tendencies is described in section 3. Following this (section 4), we will give an example of applying this architecture. Then in section 5, we will compare this procedure with a couple of related approaches. In section 6 we briefly position this approach with respect to single simulation inspection and general theorem proving. Finally, some conclusions are made.

## 2   Exploring the Envelope of Emergent MAS Behaviour

We want  to be able to establish a more general type of knowledge of emergent behaviour than can be gained from the inspection of individual runs of a system. In particular we want to know whether a particular emergent behaviour is a *necessary* consequence of the system or merely a *contingent* one. Thus we propose to *translate* the system from an agent formulation into a form whereby the *envelope* of system possibilities can be determined, under a wider range of conditions. The target we have chosen is a constraint-based architecture: the MAS, *modulo a range of parameterisations and nondeterministic agent choices*, are translated into a set of positive constraints and the inference engine then searches for a model (i.e., a representation of a possible simulation in the original MAS with a particular parameterisation and set of choices) that satisfies these. This establishes the *consistency* of the positive constraints[1]. Postulated formulations of *general* emergent behaviour can be tested as to their *necessity* over the range of parameterisations and nondeterministic choices by negating them and adding them as a further constraint followed by getting the system to check that there is now no possible model.

The idea is to do this in a way which makes it possible to translate the MAS into the constraint-based one in an automatic or near automatic way without changing the *meaning* of the rules that make it up. In this way a user can program the system using the agent-based paradigm with all its advantages, inspect single runs of the system to gain an intuitive understanding of the system and then check the generality of this understanding for fragments of the system via this translation into a constraint-based architecture.

# 3   Implementing a Suitable Constraint-Based Architecture

The main goal of the programming strategy to be described is to increase the efficiency in terms of simulation time, thus making the constraint search possible. The improvements will be achieved by making the rules and states more context-specific. This enables the inference engine to exploit more information about the logical dependencies between rules and thus increase the efficiency. Thus this can be seen as a sort of "practical compilation" process which *undoes* the agent encapsulation on an implemented MAS system in order to allow the more efficient exploration of its behaviour. In particular we split the transition rules into one per simulation period, and also by the initial parameters. This necessitates a dynamic way of building rules. This is done via a controller which generates the rules at the beginning of the simulation.

## 3.1   Time Discrete Simulation Approach

In synchronous simulations, time is taken as a discrete variable, given here as a set of positive numbers. In our case, we will call any of these numbers where the state variables are recalculated, a simulation time instant (STI) and the amplitude of the interval between two consecutive numbers, a simulation time step (STS). The transition function determines the state variables for STIs using the known values of the state variables in previous STIs. It is assumed that the state variables remain constant between two consecutive time instants.

In this architecture the structure of the simulated system is more than the one usually described in simulation formalisations [11], e.g., it allows certain forms of structural change. A meta-agent as a controller in MAS could guide not only quantitative changes, but also qualitative ones admitting its introduction into an evolutionary environment in a modular and transparent manner.

---

[1] Relative to the logic of the inference engine and range of parameters and choices allowed

### 3.2 What Is New in This Model-Constrained Methodological Approach

It is our goal in this paper to propose an alternative approach for exploring and analysing simulation trajectories. It will allow the entire exploration and subsequent analysis of a subspace of all simulation trajectories. We are suggesting the generation of trajectories in a semantically constrained way. Constrictions will be context-dependent (over the semantics of the trajectory itself) and will be driven via the introduction of a controller or meta-module.

Like Scenario Analysis, the idea is to generate individual trajectories for different parameterisations and agents' choices but unlike Scenario Analysis the exploration is constrained to only certain range of parameters and choices.

Akin to Monte Carlo techniques it explores only part of the total range of possible trajectories. But, unlike Monte Carlo studies it explores an entire subspace of (rather than some randomly generated sample) trajectories and is able to give *definitive* answers for inquires related to the dynamics of the simulation in that subspace.

### 3.3 Overview of the Architecture

We implemented the proposed architecture in three parts, let us call them *model*, *prover* and *meta-prover* (we happen to have implemented these as agents but that is not important). The following illustrates this:

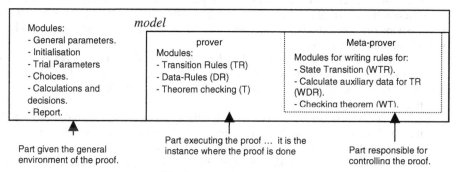

**Fig. 1.** Illustration of the system parts

### 3.4 Program Dynamics

The system fires the rules in the following order:
1. *model*: initialising the environment for the proof (setting parameters, etc..)
2. *meta-prover*: creating and placing the transition rules in *prover*.
3. *prover*: carrying on the simulation using the transition rules and backtracking while a contradiction is found.

The program backtracks from a path once the conditions for the negated theorem are verified, then a new path with different choices is picked up. The next figure describes a transition step.

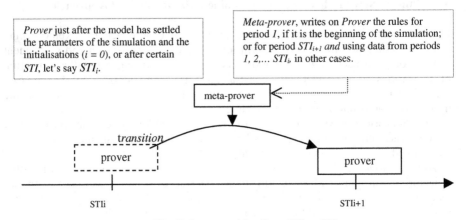

**Fig. 2.** State transition from $STI_i$ to $STI_{i+1}$

### 3.5   Description of System Modules

*General Parameters (GP)*. This will be placed in the *model* (see figure 1). Its task will be to set the general parameters of the simulation.

*Initialising (I)*. This creates the entities (e.g., agents) given the static structure of the simulation and initialises the state variables for the first STI. It will be in *model*, as it is responsible for initialising parameters to be instantiated by *meta-prover* when writing the transition rules.

*Trial Parameters (TP)*. To be placed in the *model*. Its task is to set up parameters to be fixed during one simulation trial. In general these are parameters for which the agents do not have to take decisions every STI (as for GP). They would be fixed before creating the transition rules.

*Choices (CH)*. It will place alternatives for the choices the agents have every STI and the conditions under which each choice could be made. Choices will be mainly responsible for the splitting of the simulation and the rise of simulation branches.

*Data Rules (DR), and Calculations and Decision rules (C&D)*. The first module would contain the set of rules responsible for doing calculations required by the transition rules and which is worthy to keep in the database (they could evolve like the TR). The second one is a sort of function generating a numerical or a truth value as a result of consulting the database and usually consists of backward chaining rules.

*Theorem (Constraints)(T)*. These are the conditions for checking the theorem. The theorem will be examined by a rule written by *meta-prover* in *prover*.

*Reports (R)*. The purpose of this module seems to be simple: to give the user outputs about what is going on in the dynamic of the simulation. This module will allows the user to know facts about the branch being tested as well as about branches already tested.

*Transition Rules (TR)*. This is the set of rules will be context dependent and will include explicitly syntactical manipulation to make more straightforward the linking among them.

### 3.6  Split of the Rules: A Source of Efficiency

A graphical illustration of the split procedure is shown in fig. 3.

In forward chaining simulation the antecedent retrieves instance data from the past in order to generate data for the present (and maybe the future):

past facts → present and future facts

Traditionally, the set of transition rules are implemented to be general for the whole simulation. A unique set of transition rules is used at any STI.

As the simulation evolves, the size of the database increases and the antecedents have to discriminate among a growing amount of data. At $STI_i$, there would be data from $(i-1)$ alternative days matching the antecedent. As the simulation evolves it becomes slower because of the discrimination the program has to carry out among this (linearly) growing amount of data.

Using the proposed technique, we would write a transition rule for each simulation time. The specific data in the antecedent as well as in the consequent could be instanced. Where possible, a rule for each datum, the original rule will generate, would be written. This will be better illustrated in the example of the next section.

This technique represents a step forward in improving the efficiency of declarative programs, one could, in addition, make use of partitions and time levels. Partitions permit the system to order the rules to fire in an efficient way according to their dependencies. Time levels let us discriminate among data lasting differently. The *splitting of rules lets us discriminate among the transition rules for different simulation times given a more specific instancing of data at any STI.*

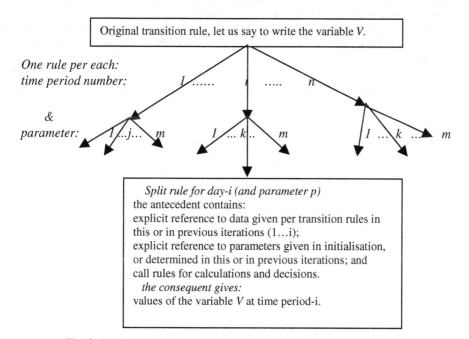

**Fig. 3.** Splitting of rules by time period and a combination of parameters

### 3.7 Measuring the Efficiency of the Technique

Comparing the two programs, the original MAS simulation and the constraint-based translation we obtain a *speed up* by a factor of $O(NM)$, where $N$ is the average number of agents instantiated by a rule and $M$ is the number of STIs. SDML [7] already has facilities for discriminating among STIs, but their use is not convenient for the sort of simulation we are doing (exploring scenarios and/or proving) because of the difficulties for accessing data from any time step at any time. If we had used this facility still the simulation would have been speeded up by $N$. Notice that all these values are only estimations because a program stops intending to fire a rule as soon as it finds out that one of its clauses is false.

It is clear that the greater the number of entities in the simulation or the number of STIs, the larger the benefits from the technique. We must notice that the speeding up of the simulation is only one dimension of the efficiency given by the technique.

### 3.8 Translating a Traditional MAS Architecture into a Efficient Model-Exploration Architecture

Before splitting the rules the original MAS is reduced in a sort of *unencapsulation* of the hierarchy of agents into the architecture shown in figure 1. Additional variables must be added into predicates and functions in order to keep explicit the reference to the "owner" agent of any instance of a variable. This will facilitate the check for tendencies, the testing of the theorem and any other data manipulation. It is as if the agent where replaced by its rulebase, see figure 4.

In the original architecture, each agent has its own rulebase (RB) and database (DB). The agent's structure is given by its set <RB, DB> as well as by the structure of any subagents.

Using the technique, the initialisation of the static structure is accomplished by the module "Initialising", as explained above. The transition rules (dynamic structure)

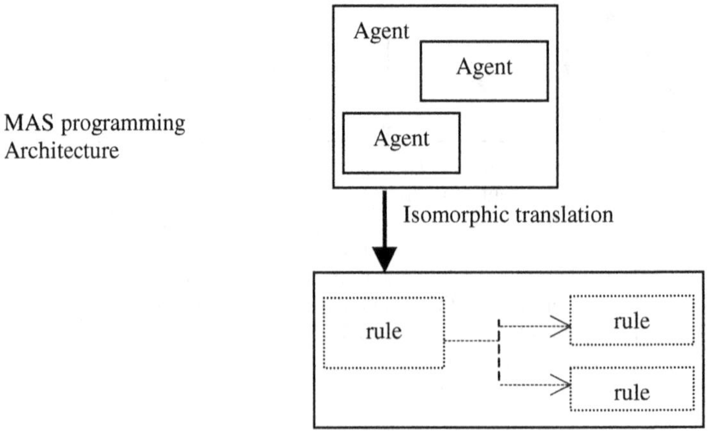

**Fig. 4.** Transformation of MAS system into a single rulebase-database pair

will be situated in the module "Transition Rules". There is still a hierarchy, both in the structure of the model and in the dynamics of the simulation – it is given by the precedence in the rulebase partition (figure 4).

Now we turn to show a way of implementing the technique automatically. After adding variables to associate data with agents, the task is to write it modularly, as illustrated in figure 4. One of the key issues is to determine dependencies among rules and then choose appropriate data structures to allow the meta-prover to build the TR. A procedure to do it would be:

1. Identify parameters and entities for splitting (agents and/or objects) as well as the dependencies among rules. Look for a "general" description of the dependencies. E.g., a Producer's price at $STI_i$ depends on Producers' sales and prices at $STI_{i-1}$.
2. Create a list of references or links to each datum used in dependencies. Taking the previous example, a list containing the names of the clauses for prices and sales is created ($[Price_1, Price_2 ..., Price_n], [Sale_1, Sale_2, ..., Sale_n]$ ($Price_i$, refers to price at $STI_i$). This list could be also specified by producer, if necessary.
3. Initialise parameters (GP and TP) and data at $STI_1$. It would be a task of module I (see above). It creates data used by module WTR at *meta-prover* and which are input for TR at $STI_2$.
4. Provide the values for the choices the agents have.
5. Using these data structure and our knowledge about dependencies, we must be able to write the WTR, WDT, and WT at *meta-prover*. If TR at $STI_i$ depend on data at $STI_{i-1}$ then the list named in 2. would allow to make such a reference automatically accessing the appropriate elements in the list.
6. Modules like R, C&D are auxiliary and do not need special attention.

*Constraints* in the search are applied in different ways, for example when theorem is adapting (maybe relaxing conditions for a tendency) and as WTR and WDR take into account the past and present dynamic of the system (for instance, when restricting choices for the agents or objects, constraining the space of simulation paths).

### 3.9 The Platform Used

We implemented the systems described entirely within the SDML programming language[2]. Although this was primarily designed for single simulation studies, its assumption-based backtracking mechanism which automatically detects syntactic logical dependencies also allows its use as a fairly efficient constraint-based inference system. SDML also allows the use of "meta-agents", which can read and write the rules of other agents. Thus the use of SDML made the procedures described much easier to experiment with and made it almost trivial to preserve the meaning and effect of rules between architectures. The use of a tailor-made constraint-satisfaction engine could increase the effectiveness and range of the techniques described once a suitable translation were done, but this would make the translation more difficult to perform and verify.

---

[2] Information about SDML can be found at http://www.cpm.mmu.ac.uk/sdml or [4]

## 4  An Example

A simple system of producers and consumers, which was previously built in SDML and in the Theorem Prover OTTER, was rebuilt using the proposed modelling strategy. In the new model the exploration of possibilities is speeded up by a factor of 14.

Some of the split transition rules were the ones for creating (per each STI) producers' prices and sales, consumers' demand and orders, warehouses' level and factories' production. Among the rules for auxiliary data split were the ones for calculating: total-order and total-sales (a sum of the orders for all producers), total-order and total-sales per producer, and total-order and total-sales per consumer.

### 4.1  Example of a Split Rule: Rule for Prices

This rule calculates a new price for each producer at each STI (which we called *day*), according to its own price and sales, and the price and sales of a chosen producer, at the immediately previous STI.

The original rule in SDML was like this:

```
for all (producer)
for all (consumer)
for all (day)
(
price(producer,myPrice,day)                                        and
totalSales(totalSales,day)                                         and
sales(producer,mySales,day)                                        and
choiceAnotherProducer(anotherProducer)                             and
price(anotherProducer,otherPrice, day)                            and
calculateNewPrice(mySales,totalSales, otherPrice, myPrice,newPrice)
   implies
price(producer, newPrice, day + 1)
)
```

The new rule (in the efficient program) will be "broken" making explicit the values of prices and sales per each day.

In the following, we show the rule per *day-i* and *producer-j*:

```
for all (consumer)
(
price(producer-j, myPrice, day-i)                                 and
totalSales(totalSales, day-i)                                     and
sales(producer, mySales, day-i)                                   and
choiceAnotherProducer(anotherProducer)                            and
price(anotherProducer, otherPrice, day-i)                         and
calculateNewPrice(mySales,totalSales,otherPrice,myPrice,newPrice)
   implies
price(producer-j, newPrice, (day-i) + 1)
)
```

If the name of price is used to make explicit the day, the rule will have the following form. It is important to observe that *only one instance of newPrice in the consequent is associated with only one transition rule and vice verse*:

```
for all (consumer)
(
price-i(producer-j, myPrice)                                              and
totalSales-i(totalSales)                                                  and
sales-i(producer-j, mySales)                                             and
choiceAnotherProducer(anotherProducer)                                    and
price-i(anotherProducer, otherPrice)                                      and
calculateNewPrice(mySales,totalSales, otherPrice, myPrice,newPrice)
   implies
price-(i+1)(producer-j, newPrice)
)
```

## 4.2  What the Technique Enables

In this example, we used the technique to prove that the size of the interval of prices (that is: *biggest price - smaller price*, each day) decreased over time during the first six time intervals over a range of 8 model parameterisations. An exponential decrease of this interval was observed in all the simulation paths. All the alternatives were tested for each day - a total of 32768 simulation trajectories. It was not possible to simulate beyond this number of days because of limitations imposed by computer memory. There was no restriction because of the simulation time, as the technique makes the simulation program quite fast – it had finished this search in 24 hours.

This technique is useful not only because of the speeding up of the simulation but also for its appropriateness when capturing and proving emergence. On one hand, it let us write the transition rules and the rule for testing the theorem at the beginning of the simulation in accordance to the tendency we want to prove. And, on the other hand, if the meta-prover is able to write the rules while the simulation is going on, it could adapt the original theorem we wanted to prove according to the results of the simulation. For example, if it is not possible to prove the original theorem then it could relax constraints and attempt to show that a more general theorem holds. Moreover, the technique could be implemented so that we have only to give the program hints related to the sort of proof we are interested in, then the meta-prover could adapt a set of hypotheses over time according to the simulation results. At best, such a procedure would find a hypothesis it could demonstrate and, at worst, such output could then be useful to guide subsequent experimentation.

## 5  Some Other Approaches

In OTTER (and similar Theorem Provers) the set of simulation rules and facts (atoms) is divided into two sets (this strategy is called *support strategy)* [6]:

One set with "support" and the other without it. The first one is placed in a list called "SOS" and, the second one, in the list "USABLE". Data in USABLE is "ungrounded" in the sense that the rules would not fire unless at least one of the antecedents is taken from the SOS list. Data inferred using the rules in USABLE are placed in SOS when they are not redundant with the information previously contained in this list, and then used for generating new inferences. The criteria for efficiency are basically subsumption and weighting of clauses.

Rules are usually fired in forward chaining but backward chaining rules and numerical manipulations are allowed in the constructs called "demodulators" [10].

In simulation strategies like event-driven simulation or partition of the space of rules, in declarative simulation, are used. The criteria for firing rules is well understood, and procedures like weighting and subsumption usually are not necessary. Additionally, redundant data could be avoided in MAS with a careful programming.

The advantages given for the weighting procedure in OTTER are yielded in MAS systems like SDML by procedures such as *partitioning*, where chaining of the rules allows firing the rules in an efficient order according to their dependencies.

Among other approaches for the practical proof of MAS properties, the more pertinent might be the case conducted by people working in DESIRE [4]. They propose the hierarchical verification of MAS properties, and succeeded in doing this for a system.

However, their aim is limited to verification of the computational program – it is proved that the program behaves in the intended way. It does not include the more difficult task, which we try to address, of establishing general facts about the dynamics of a system when run or comparing them to the behaviour observed in other systems [1].

DeLoach et al. [3] suggest building a MAS going by through a hierarchy of architectural transformations. A methodology, "Multiagent Systems Engineering (MaSE)", and a tool to support it, "agentTool", are proposed. The idea is to build a "more concrete" sequence of models in a "top-down" hierarchy of architectural levels starting from the level of goals. They argue that goals capture the context and the more abstract specification of the MAS. This methodology is aimed to help with the MAS verification, facilitating its building in accordance to some abstract specification, but not to assist in the understanding of the dynamics of a MAS.

Shapiro et al. [9] suggest using a language, "Cognitive Agents Specification Language (CASL)", for specifying and verifying a MAS. They claim that this language allows a formal specification allowing abstraction over an agent's preferences and over agents' interaction (messaging) mechanism. This formal representation is also meant to support a modeller when checking aspects of the agent's design but not to help in the understanding of the behaviour of a MAS.

Koen et al. [5] use contextual information for adding flexibility in behaviour of agents' using preference models. In particular they propose building agents able to "adapt" their plans in an environment with uncertainty and soft deadlines by using a context-sensitive planning. He claims these agents have more "realistic" preference models than those commonly used in other approaches. Their idea of a context sensitive planning is comparable to our idea of context driven exploration of simulation trajectories proposed in the second level of architectural transformations.

The Riley et al. [8]' paper is related with understanding MAS and observing aspects of their dynamics -in this sense related to the work presented in this article. Concretely, they propose a "layered disclosure by which autonomous agents have included in their architecture the foundations necessary to allow them to display upon request the specific reasons for their actions". In fact, this mechanism permits a modeller to check the state of the internal model of an agent at certain simulation time. This sort of mechanism is programmable in SDML by writing the specific rules for required reports, or, stopping the simulation and then writing the consulting rules in the "Experiment tag" of the appropriated agent. In addition, SDML allows us to go browse or return to previous states in the simulation. The analysis of the dynamics of a simulation they propose is quite simple and not so useful for understanding aspects of the simulation related with the theory implicit in the simulation. They do not address the more fundamental aspect of analysing tendencies (regularities over time) but rather aspects at certain isolated simulation instants.

## 6    A Sequence of Architectures for Modelling Behaviour and Proving Theorems in MAS

The architecture we describe could be used after single simulations have been run to suggest useful properties to test for. *Subsequently* one could employ a syntactically oriented architecture for proving those tendencies outright.   Thus the proposed technique can be seen as falling in between inspecting single runs and syntactic theorem proving. This is illustrated in figure 5.

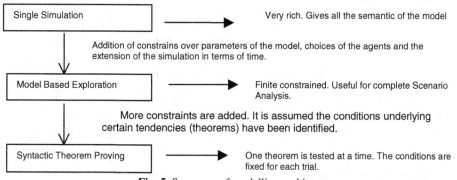

**Fig. 5.** Sequence of modelling architectures

The step to theorem proving from model-based exploration would involve a further translation step. The conditions established by experimenting with model-based exploration would need to be added to the MAS specification and all this translated into axioms for the theorem prover to work upon. The main aspects of the three architectures are summarised in Table 1, which is a comparison of these different approaches.

## 7    Conclusion

The proposed methodology is as follows: *firstly*, identify candidate emergent tendencies by inspection of single runs; *secondly*, explore and check these using the techniques of constraint-based model-search in significant fragments of the MAS; and *finally*, attempt to prove theorems of these tendencies using syntactic proof procedures. This methodology is oriented towards identifying interesting tendencies and emergence in MAS an area little explored but of considerable importance.

**Table 1.** A Comparison of Architectures

| Architecture:<br><br>Aspect: | SCENARIO ANALYSIS | MODEL-EXPLORATION | SYNTACTIC PROOF |
|---|---|---|---|
| Typical paradigm | Imperative. | Constraint | Declarative |
| Typical deduction system | (Forward Chaining) | Forward Chaining using efficient backtracking | Backward chaining or resolution-based |
| Nature of the manipulations | Possible Semantic | Range of Semantics | Syntactic |
| Limitations | Not constrained.<br>- Very rich. Too much information could mislead | - Finite constrained. Still quite rich.<br>- Suitable for Scenario Analysis. | -Constrained.<br>- Valuable for proving specific tendencies. |
| Search style. | Attempts to explore all simulation paths. | Limits the search by constraining the range of parameters and agent choices | Can be efficient in suitably constrained cases, typically impractical |

In addition, we have proposed a framework for improving the efficiency of MAS to enable the second of these. It has been implemented in an ideal example, resulting in a significant increase in the speed of the program. However, the notions are valid independently of the example and could be implemented in many different systems. In summary, the strategy consists of: unencapsulating the MAS system to allow the maximum amount of dependency information to be exploited; partitioning of the space of rules and splitting of transition rules by STI and some parameters, using the appropriate modularity of the simulation program, and specially initialising parameters and choices.

The technique perhaps presages a time when programmers routinely translate their systems between different architectures for different purposes, just as a procedural programmer may work with a semi-interpreted program for debugging and a compiled and optimised form for distribution. In the case of agent technology we have identified three architectures which offer different trade-offs and facilities, being able to automatically or semi-automatically translate between these would bring substantial benefits.

**Acknowledgements.** SDML has been developed in VisualWorks 2.5.2, the Smalltalk-80 environment produced by ObjectShare. Free distribution of SDML for use in academic research is made possible by the sponsorship of ObjectShare (UK) Ltd. The research reported here was funded by CONICIT (the Venezuelan Governmental Organisation for promoting Science), by the University of Los Andes, and by the Faculty of Management and Business, Manchester Metropolitan University.

# References

1. Axtell, R., R. Axelrod, J. M. Epstein, and M. D. Cohen, "Aligning Simulation Models: A Case of Study and Results", Computational Mathematical Organization Theory, 1(2), pp. 123-141, 1996.
2. Castelfranchi, C. and Y. Lesperance (Editors), Intelligent Agents VII. Agent Theories, Architectures, and Languages. --- 7$^{th}$ International Workshop, ATAL-2000, Boston, MA, USA, July 7--9, 2000, Proceedings, Lecture Notes in Artificial Intelligence, Springer-Verlag, Berlin (this volume).
3. DeLoach Scott and Mark Wood, "Developing Multiagent Systems with agentTool", in [2].
4. Engelfriet, J., C. Jonker and J. Treur, "Compositional Verification of Multi-Agent Systems in Temporal Multi-Epistemic Logic", Artificial Intelligence Group, Vrije Universiteit Amsterdam, The Netherlands, 1998.
5. Koen, V.Hindriks, Frank S. de Boer, Wiebe van der Hoek and John-Jules Ch. Meyer, "Agent Programming with Declarative Goals", in [2].
6. McCune, W., OTTER 3.0 Reference Manual Guide, Argonne National Laboratory, Argonne, Illinois, 1995.
7. Moss, S., H. Gaylard, S. Wallis, B. Edmonds, "SDML: A Multi-Agent Language for Organizational Modelling", Computational Mathematical Organization Theory, 4(1), 43-69, 1998.
8. Riley, Patrick, Peter Stone and Manuela Veloso, "Layered Disclosure: Revealing Agents' Internals", in [2].
9. Shapiro, Steven and Yves Lesperance, "Modeling Multiagent Systems with CASL -A Feature Interaction Resolution Application", in [2].
10. Wos, L., Automated Reasoning: 33 Basic Research Problems, Prentice Hall, New Jersey, USA, 1988.
11. Zeigler, B.,,, Theory of Modelling and Simulation, Robert E. Krieger Publishing Company, Malabar, Fl, USA, 1976.

# Delegation and Responsibility

Timothy J. Norman[1] and Chris Reed[2]

[1] Department of Computing Science, University of Aberdeen,
Aberdeen, AB24 3UE, Scotland, U.K.
`tnorman@csd.abdn.ac.uk`
[2] Department of Applied Computing, University of Dundee,
Dundee, DD1 4HN, Scotland, U.K.
`Chris.Reed@computing.dundee.ac.uk`

**Abstract.** An agent may decide to delegate tasks to others. The act of delegating a task by one autonomous agent to another can be carried out by the performance of one or more imperative communication acts. In this paper, the semantics of imperatives are specified using a language of actions and states. It is further shown how the model can be used to distinguish between whole-hearted and mere extensional satisfaction of an imperative, and how this may be used to specify the semantics of imperatives in agent communication languages.

## 1 Introduction

To delegate is to entrust a representative to act on your behalf. This is an important issue for agents that may be forced to rely on others. Although autonomous agents have a high degree of self-determination, they may be required to achieve a goal that is made easier, satisfied more completely or only possible with the aid of other, similarly autonomous, agents. For delegation to be successful, there must be a relationship between the agent delegating the goal or task and the agent to whom it is delegated. Furthermore, after successful delegation, responsibility for the task concerned is now shared. For example, the manager of a business unit, in delegating a task, will no longer be solely responsible for that task. The manager must, however, ensure that the employee to whom the task has been delegated acts appropriately (e.g. by completing the task, asking for help or further delegating the task).

A number of questions are immediately apparent from the short characterisation of delegation and responsibility given above:

1. What is the nature of the relationship on which the ability to delegate is predicated?
2. Through what communicative acts can an agent delegate tasks, and how are they specified?
3. Under what conditions can it be said that delegation was successful?

In this paper, primary consideration is given to questions 2 and 3 (a reader interested in question 1 is referred to the model of roles and relationships proposed by Panzarasa *et al.* [18] and to the work of Castelfranchi [4]). Given that an agent has some rationale for attempting to delegate a task, how can this delegation be carried out and how can it be

C. Castelfranchi, Y. Lespérance (Eds.): Intelligent Agents VII, LNAI 1986, pp. 136–149, 2001.
© Springer-Verlag Berlin Heidelberg 2001

considered a success? In answering these questions, the action-state semantics of imperatives proposed by Hamblin [11] is summarised, and the link between imperatives and normative positions is discussed. With this grounding, it is shown how the notion of delegation can be captured and how a clear distinction can be made between whole-hearted and mere extensional satisfaction. First, however, it is important to place imperatives in the context of other types of communicative acts, and relate this to existing literature on agent communication languages.

## 2   Imperatives and Agent Communication

Knowledge level [17] communication between agents through speech act based [2,21] agent communication languages (ACLs) is both an active area of research [24,20] and of standardisation [9,8]. These languages typically include *indicatives* (or assertions) such as 'tell' (KQML) and 'inform' (FIPA); for example, "It's raining". Queries or questions are also common (i.e. *interrogatives*) such as 'ask-if' (KQML) and 'query-if' (FIPA); for example, "Is it raining?". In addition to these, *imperatives* are used to issue commands, give advice or request action; for example, "bring the umbrella". Examples of imperative message types in ACLs are 'achieve' (KQML) and 'request' (FIPA). An intuitive explanation of these message types is that the sender is attempting to influence the recipient to act in some way. In fact, an attempt to influence the mental state of the hearer (or recipient of a message) is common to all knowledge level communication. For example, an agent utters an indicative such as "It's raining" with the intention of inducing a belief by means of the recognition of this intention [10]. In other words, the speaker is attempting to influence the hearer to adopt a belief about the weather.

Similarly, the imperative "bring the umbrella" is an attempt to influence the hearer's future actions by means of the hearer recognising that this is the intention of the speaker. Following Searle's [21] description of the types of illocutionary (or communicative) act, Cohen and Levesque [6] provide a model in which such acts are construed as attempts by the speaker to change the mental state of the hearer. For example, a request for the hearer to do some action, $a$, is an attempt to change the hearer's mental state in such a way that it becomes an intention of the hearer to do $a$. The hearer, being an autonomous agent, may refuse. This is, of course, different from misunderstanding the speaker.

With this in mind, Cohen and Levesque [6] distinguish the goal of the speaker in performing the act and their intention. The goal, in the case of an imperative, is that the hearer believes that the speaker intends the hearer to act and the hearer acts accordingly. The intention, however, is that the hearer believes that this is the intention of the speaker. If the intention of the speaker is not understood by the hearer, then the communicative act is unsuccessful. A communicative act is then an attempt to achieve the goal, but at least to satisfy the intention that the hearer believes that this is what the speaker wants. Through this definition of 'attempts', Cohen *et al.* [6,24] provide a concrete characterisation of the communicative acts that are common in ACLs, and go on to specify conversations. For example, one agent offers a service to another, which may be responded to with acceptance, rejection or silence (cf. Barbuceanu and Fox [3]). This extension of an agent communication language to capture typical conversations between agents is the approach taken by the FIPA specification [9], and it is the specification of imperatives within FIPA that is returned to in section 5.

The grounding of agent communication languages in such formal models is essential to ensure that the meaning of communicative acts are clear to those designing agents for practical applications. Without such a grounding, agent communication languages can suffer from inherent ambiguity which, when implemented, can lead to unexpected, undesirable and counter-intuitive results. The work presented in this paper focuses on imperatives, aims to present an account of delegation, and show how this may be better understood by considering both existing models of imperatives [11,26] and normative positions [15,22].

### 2.1   The Nature of Imperatives

Numerous proposals have been laid out in both philosophical and computational literature for classification of utterance types, or, more specifically, of illocutionary acts. Austin [2, p. 150] and Searle [21, pp. 66–67] are perhaps the two most prominent.

Though there are a range of similarities and dissimilarities, these schemes have at least one thing in common: not all utterances are indicative. This is not in itself remarkable, until it is considered that the logics employed to handle and manipulate utterances are almost always exclusively based upon the predominant formal tradition of treating only the indicative. The interrogative and imperative utterances (which figure amongst Austin's Exercitives and Expostives, and include Searle's Request, Question, Advise and Warn) rarely benefit from the luxury of a logic designed to handle them.

Interrogative logics for handling questions have been proposed by Åqvist [1] and Hintikka *et al.* [13] among others, and these form an interesting avenue for future exploration. The focus of the current work, however, is on imperative logic. Hamblin's [11] book *Imperatives* represents the first thorough treatment of the subject, providing a systematic analysis not only of linguistic examples, but also of grammatical structure, semantics and the role imperatives play in dialogue.

His classification goes into some detail, but one key distinction is drawn between imperatives which are *wilful*, and those which are not. The former class are characterised by advantage to the utterer, the latter by advantage to the hearer. Thus commands, requests, and demands are all classed as wilful; advice, instructions, suggestions, recipes and warnings are all classed as non-wilful.

The distinction is useful because it highlights the importance of the contextual environment of the utterance: commands would fail to have an effect if the utterer was not in a position of authority over the hearer; advice would fail if the hearer did not trust the utterer, and so on. Any logic of imperatives must both be able to cope with this wide range of locutionary acts, but also be insensitive to any of the extralinguistic (and thereby extralogical) factors affecting the subsequent effect of issuing imperatives.

### 2.2   Action State Semantics

Hamblin [11] offers an elegant investigation into imperatives, examining their role and variety, and developing an expressive syntax and semantics. Hamblin states [11, p. 137] that to handle imperatives there are several features, "usually regarded as specialised", which are indispensable: (1) a time-scale; (2) a distinction between actions and states; (3) physical and mental causation; (4) agency and action-reduction; and (5) intensionality. It is clear that any semantics, which competently integrates these five aspects should hold some significant appeal for those concerned with formalising the process by which agreements between agents are negotiated, specified, serviced, and verified.

The aim here is to equip the reader with a working grasp of action state semantics, so before the presentation of a formal summary, a brief overview is necessary. The first unusual feature of Hamblin's model is the explicit representation of both events and states — that is, a world comprises a series of states connected by events. The states can be seen as collections of propositions; the events are of two types: deeds, which are performed by specific agents, and happenings, which are world effects. This distinction gives the model an unusual richness: most other formal systems have explicit representation of one or other, defining either states in terms of the sequences of events (true of most action and temporal deontic logics), or else, less commonly, events in terms of a succession of states (classical AI planning makes this assumption). It is interesting to note that the situation calculus [16] admits explicit representation of both states and events, but the commonly adopted "axioms of arboreality" [23] restrict the flexibility such that states can be defined as event sequences.[1]

This rich underlying model is important in several respects. First, it allows, at a syntactic level, the expression of demands both that agents bring about states of affairs, and that they perform actions. Secondly, it avoids both ontological and practical problems of having to interrelate states and events — practical problems often become manifest in having to keep track of 'Done events' in every state [7]. Finally, this construction of a world as a chain of states connected by deeds and happenings, makes it possible to distinguish those worlds in which a given imperative $i$ is satisfied (in some set of states). Thus the imperative "Shut the door" is satisfied in those worlds in which the door is shut (given appropriate deixis). This 'extensional' satisfaction, however, is contrasted with a stronger notion, of 'whole-hearted' satisfaction, which characterises an agent's involvement and responsibility in fulfilling an imperative. Such whole-hearted satisfaction is based upon the notion of a strategy: an assignment of a deed to each time point for the specified agent. A partial $i$-strategy is then a set of incompletely specified strategies, all of which involve worlds in which $i$ is extensionally satisfied. The whole-hearted satisfaction of an imperative $i$ by an agent $x$, is then defined as being $x$'s adoption of a partial strategy and execution of a deed from that strategy at every time point after the imperative is issued.

The summary presented below is the core of Hamblin's model. For a more complete set-theoretic précis, the reader is referred to the appendix of Walton and Krabbe [26]. A world $w$ in $W$ is defined such that an assignment is made to every time point from $T$, (1) a state from the set of states $S$, (2) a member of the set $H$ of 'big happenings' (each

---

[1] This conflation arises from associating a given sequence of events with a single, unique situation: even if all the fluents in two situations have identical values, under the axioms of arboreality, those two situations are only the same if the events leading to them have also been the same. In Hamblin's work, there can be several different histories up to a given state and the histories are not themselves a part of those states.

of which collect together all happenings from one state to the next) and (3) a deed (in $D$) for every agent (in $X$), i.e. an element from $D^X$. The set $W$ of worlds is therefore defined as $(S \times H \times D^X)^T$.

The states, happenings and deed-agent assignments of a given world $w$ are given by $S(w)$, $H(w)$ and $D(w)$. Let $j_t$ be a history of a world up to time $t$, including all states, deeds and happenings of the world up to $t$. Thus $j_t$ is equivalent to a set of worlds which have a common history up to (at least) time $t$. $J_t$ is then the set of all possible histories up to $t$; i.e. all the ways by which the world could have got to where it is. A strategy $q_t$ is then an allocation of a deed to each $j_{t'} \in J_{t'}$ for every $t' \geq t$.[2]

Let the possible worlds in which the deeds of agent $x$ are those specified by strategy $q_t$ be $W_{strat}(x, q_t)$, and the worlds in which an imperative, $i$, is extensionally satisfied be $W_i$. A strategy for the satisfaction of an imperative $i$ (i.e. an $i$-strategy) can, therefore, be defined as follows.

**Definition 1.** A strategy $q_t \in Q_t$ is an $i$-strategy for agent $x$ if and only if the worlds in which $x$ does the deeds specified by $q_t$ are also worlds in which $i$ is extensionally satisfied: $W_{strat}(x, q_t) \subseteq W_i$.

In practice, however, it is not feasible for an agent to select a particular strategy in $Q_t$ at time $t$ that specifies every deed for every time $t'$ after $t$. For this reason, and agent will adopt a *partial i-strategy*.

**Definition 2.** A partial $i$-strategy is a disjunction of $i$-strategies, $Q'_t \subseteq Q_t$, and the world set for $x$ adopting this partial $i$-strategy is $W_{strat}(x, Q'_t)$.

With this grounding, the whole-hearted satisfaction of an imperative, $i$, can now be defined.

**Definition 3.** An agent $x$ may be said to whole-heartedly satisfy an imperative $i$ issued at $t$ if and only if for every $t' \geq t$:

(a)  $x$ has a partial $i$-strategy, $Q'_{t'}$; and
(b)  $x$ does a deed from the set of deeds specified by that $Q'_{t'}$.

## 3   The Action Component

With this grounding in Hamblin's action-state semantics, the syntax is now extended to explicitly refer to agents performing actions and achieving goals. With the sets of deeds, $\alpha, \beta, \ldots \in D$, states[3] $A, B, \ldots \in S$ and agents $x, y, \ldots \in X$, action modalities for bringing about states of affairs and performing actions can be defined (section 3.2). Before this is done, however, it is useful to summarise Jones and Sergot's [14] action modality $E_x$ on which the work reported here is based.

---

[2] This notion of a strategy has an intensional component, since it prescribes over a set of possible $w$, rather than picking out, at this stage, the actual world.

[3] In principle, states describe the entire universe at a given moment, so the elements referred to here are in fact portions of states; sets of propositions from which states are composed. The syntactic convenience adopted here is not important to the discussion.

## 3.1  The Action Modality $E_x$

In their model of institutionalised power, Jones and Sergot [14] specify an action modality $E_x$ (read "$x$ sees to it that. . ."). $E_x$ as the smallest system containing propositional logic and closed under the rule $RE$, with additional axiom schema $T$ (necessary for a logic of successful action), and the rule of inference $R\neg N$ which is intended to capture the notion that an agent is somehow responsible for its actions.

$$RE \qquad \frac{A \leftrightarrow B}{E_x A \leftrightarrow E_x B}$$

$$T \qquad E_x A \rightarrow A$$

$$R\neg N \qquad \frac{A}{\neg E_x A}$$

In the context of specifying imperatives, the single most important shortcoming of the action modality $E_x$, as proposed by Jones and Sergot, is that it relies upon a state-based semantics. Events are viewed through what Hamblin terms 'pseudo states', such as the state of something having happened or of something having been done [11, p. 143]. Jones and Sergot themselves do not offer a precise characterisation of the reading of $E_x A$ — they typically refer to it as "$x$ seeing to it that state of affairs $A$ holds" or "$x$'s act of seeing to it that $A$." They remark [14, p. 435]: "we employ the same action modality $E_x$ both for expressing that agent $x$ creates/establishes states of affairs, and for expressing that $x$ performs designated acts [...] We have found reasons to be uneasy regarding this kind of dual employment, and leave development to further work."

A clean resolution to the issue of how to deal syntactically with both states of affairs and actions, while retaining the clear E-type properties and the seamless integration with deontic constructs, is crucial for providing a language of imperatives.

## 3.2  The Action Modalities $S_x$ and $T_x$

Two new modalities, $S_x$ and $T_x$, are proposed for a coherent action logic which can distinguish actions and states. $S_x A$ indicates that agent $x$ sees to it that state of affairs $A$ holds. Similarly, $T_x \alpha$ indicates that agent $x$ sees to it that action $\alpha$ is carried out.[4] Notice that in neither case is a specific action demanded of $x$ — $T_x \alpha$ does not specify that $x$ should necessarily perform action $\alpha$, though clearly this would be one way in which it might be true. Each operator follows the relativised modal logic of type $E$ [5], closed under rule $RE$: rule 1 being $RE$ for the modal operator $S_x$ and rule 2 being that for $T_x$.

$$\frac{A \leftrightarrow B}{S_x A \leftrightarrow S_x B} \tag{1}$$

$$\frac{\alpha \leftrightarrow \beta}{T_x \alpha \leftrightarrow T_x \beta} \tag{2}$$

---

[4] The modalities draw their names from von Wright's distinction in his seminal work on deontic logic [25, p. 59] between Seinsollen and Tunsollen, *ought to be* and *ought to be done*. Some of the links between the current work and deontic logic are explored below.

Following Jones and Sergot's exposition of the modality $E_x$, both $S_x$ and $T_x$ use the additional axiom schema $T$: axiom schema 3 being $T$ for the modal operator $S_x$ and axiom schema 4 being that for $T_x$.

$$S_x A \to A \tag{3}$$

$$T_x \alpha \to \alpha \tag{4}$$

These modalities are defined in terms of the action-state semantics summarised in section 2.2. Using the fact that, for a particular world, $w$, the states of that world are given by $S(w)$ and the deed-agent assignments are given by $D(w)$, the action modalities $S_x$ and $T_x$ are understood in the following way:

*The modality $S_x$ is tied to $S(w)$.*

(a) If $A \in S(w) \leftrightarrow B \in S(w)$ then $S_x A \in S(w) \leftrightarrow S_x B \in S(w)$.
(b) If $S_x A \in S(w)$ then $A \in S(w)$.

*The modality $T_x$ is tied to both $S(w)$ and $D(w)$.*

(a) If $\alpha \in D(w) \leftrightarrow \beta \in D(w)$ then $T_x \alpha \in S(w) \leftrightarrow T_x \beta \in S(w)$.
(b) If $T_x \alpha \in S(w)$ then $\alpha \in D(w)$.

Note that no equivalent to the rule of inference R¬N is defined here (R¬N was included by Jones and Sergot [14] to capture the notion that an agent is somehow responsible for its actions). In contrast, responsibility for seeing to it that states of affairs hold (for $S_x$) and actions are done (for $T_x$) is captured by the definition of whole-hearted satisfaction. An agent's responsibility for bringing about a state of affairs or for seeing to it that an action is done is therefore defined by both the maintenance of a partial $i$-strategy, $Q'_t$, and the selection of deeds specified by this $Q'_t$ (see definitions 2 and 3).

It is worth re-emphasising at this point that there might be a temptation to "simplify" the logic, and define one of the two action modalities in terms of the other; to do so, however, would lose the attractive distinction provided by the semantic model, and thereby spoil the possibility of reasoning about commitment and the satisfaction of imperatives.

## 4    Delegation

There are two simple developments leading from the foundation introduced above that facilitate the introduction of machinery to handle delegation in a straightforward manner. First, the recognition that deontic statements can themselves be seen as states of affairs (see, for example Pörn [19]). Such states of affairs, like any other, can be the subject of the $S_x$ modality. Second, imperatives can be constructed using the resulting deontic action logic.[5]

---

[5] Note that it is not being claimed that deontic logic can be reduced to imperatives or vice versa (cf. Hamblin, 1987, pp. 113-127). It is however, claimed that normative positions where both normative (obligation, permission, etc.) and action components are involved can be seen as imperatives.

In this way, the statement $S_x O T_y \alpha$, can be read as "$x$ sees to it that the state of affairs holds in which it is obligatory for $y$ to see to it that $\alpha$ is performed". Further, the statement might be issued as an imperative by some third party to $x$. A linguistic example of such an imperative might be: "Make sure your sister cleans her teeth!" There may be a range of means by which $x$ might bring about this state of affairs (as with any other) but one obvious alternative is for $x$ to issue an imperative to $y$ of the form $T_y \alpha$ (e.g. "Clean your teeth, sis!").

Thus, in general, the act of uttering an imperative can, in the right situation, bring about a normative state of affairs. Clearly, both the form and type of locutionary act employed, and the imperative's overall success, will be partly dependent upon a variety of contextual factors, including in particular the relationship between the utterer and hearer, and existing normative positions either personal or societal. The general form of the interaction, though, is that the utterer attempts to introduce a new norm (and it is this act which counts as the utterer working towards whole-hearted satisfaction at this point); this attempt, if combined successfully with contextual parameters will generate a new normative position (or a modification of an existing position).

$$utter(S, H, I) \wedge \langle context \rangle \rightarrow O\,I \tag{5}$$

Here, 'utter' is an appropriate communicative primitive, such as 'request'. $S$ is the speaker, $H$ the hearer and $I$ an imperative formed using the $S$ and $T$ action modalities. The consequent is then that the addressee is obliged with respect to the content of the imperative $I$.

As mentioned above, the imperatives $S_x A$ and $T_x \alpha$ implicitly admit the possibility that $x$ delegates responsibility for their achievement. This implicit assumption is based on the simple deontic inter-definition between obligation and permission.

$$P p \leftrightarrow \neg O \neg p \tag{6}$$

This, combined with some notion of negation as failure, licenses any agent to bring about normative states of affairs (in the right context), unless expressly prohibited from so doing. This represents something of a simplification of Lindahl's [15] theory of normative position (see also Sergot [22]). In fact, there are seven distinct normative positions of an individual with respect to a state of affairs: an agent may have the freedom (or not) to bring about $p$, the freedom (or not) to bring about $\neg p$ and the freedom (or not) to remain passive towards $p$. The work presented in this paper does not address the range of freedoms described by Lindahl, but is consistent with it. The focus is on the distinction between an agent being free to act and being free to delegate a task.

In fact, it may be necessary to restrict the freedom of an agent to delegate, and to ensure that it carries out some action or brings about a state by his own, direct, intervention. Equally, there are, rarer, cases in which delegation is demanded. Taking this second and simpler case first, the imperative $S_x O T_y \alpha$ captures this enforced delegation: that x brings it about that the state of affairs holds in which y is responsible for ensuring that the action $\alpha$ is performed.

The first case is slightly more complex. The implicit freedom of $T_x$ (and identically for $S_x$) must be restricted by ensuring that $x$ does not delegate. There are three important problems with an interpretation of this restriction:

1. Delegation is not a specified action — there are many ways of delegating, and it is inappropriate for a logic to be founded upon some arbitrary action definition for delegation. Thus, it is undesirable to specify prohibition of a delegation action.
2. As explained above, the distinction between states and events is a key component of action state semantics and to tie states to event postconditions would conflate this distinction, loosing much of the power of the semantics. Therefore, it is also undesirable to prohibit a state of affairs which can be uniquely identified with the postcondition of delegation.
3. The agent to whom an action may be delegated may himself be subject to a number of imperatives, the status of which should not be impinged upon by restrictions on $x$'s power to delegate. Thus, if $y$ has an obligation towards action i.e. $O\,T_y\alpha$ then $x$'s inability to delegate responsibility for $\alpha$ should not be expressed using $\forall y\neg O\,T_y\alpha$.

The solution relies upon Hamblin's notion of whole-hearted satisfaction, and, in particular, upon interpreting the locutionary act, of $T_x\alpha$, as a request for whole-hearted satisfaction of the imperative. Trivially, the locution $\neg T_x\alpha$ is a request for not satisfying the imperative $T_x\alpha$ whole-heartedly; i.e. not adopting partial $i$-strategies at each $t$, and avoiding deeds that ensure extensional satisfaction of $T_x\alpha$. Crucially, extensional satisfaction of $\alpha$ is not thereby precluded ($x$ may not 'whole-heartedly bring it about', but it may happen any way). This negated imperative can then be used to restrict the license to delegate: $\neg S_x P\,T_y\alpha$. Thus $x$ must not whole-heartedly satisfy the imperative that the state of affairs is reached in which some $y$ is permitted to be responsible for the performance of $\alpha$. This not only avoids problems (1) and (2) by referring to a range of states of affairs after delegation, but also circumvents (3) by leaving open the possibility that $P\,T_y\alpha$, or even $O\,T_y\alpha$, is (or will) in fact be the case — but not as a result of anything $x$ has done (this, after all, is the definition of extensional satisfaction). To enjoinder $x$ to perform some action $\alpha$ which he does not have the power to delegate can therefore be expressed as $T_x\alpha \wedge \forall y\neg S_x P\,T_y\alpha$.

The characterisation is isomorphic for $S_x A$. The basic semantic interpretation permits delegation, and that power can be restricted where necessary, resulting in the conjunction of imperatives $S_x A \wedge \forall y\neg S_x P\,S_y A$.

## 4.1   Worked Examples

A couple of examples will serve to demonstrate not only the syntax of imperatives, the normative positions they engender, and the means by which whole-hearted satisfaction can be determined, but also to show clearly that the formalisation is intuitive and uncluttered.

*Example 1.* A lecturer is told by her head of department to prepare copies of her lecture notes for her class. She may then (a) copy the notes herself (b) request that the departmental secretary copy the notes.

The initial request concerns actions, so the appropriate modality is $T_x$, and the whole imperative is specified in equation 7.

$$i_1 = T_{lecturer}\text{copy\_notes} \tag{7}$$

The worlds in which this imperative is extensionally satisfied, $W_{i_1}$ are given by equation 8.

$$W_{i_1} = \{w \mid \exists x \cdot \text{copy\_notes}^x \in D(w)\} \tag{8}$$

That is, all those worlds in which anyone (any $x$) is assigned the deed of copy\_notes ($D(w)$ gives deed-agent assignments, see section 2.2).

Thus a world in which the deed-agent assignment copy\_notes$^{lecturer}$ is present would represent one in which $i_1$ is extensionally satisfied.

Alternatively, following example (1)b, the lecturer could issue the imperative $i_2$ to the secretary:

$$i_2 = T_{secretary}\text{copy\_notes} \tag{9}$$

This should, in the given context, lead to a normative state of affairs in which

$$O\,T_{secretary}\text{copy\_notes} \tag{10}$$

i.e. in which the secretary is obliged to see to it that the copy\_notes action is carried out. The action of the secretary carrying out copy\_notes would fulfil the definition of extensional satisfaction not only of $i_2$, but also of $i_1$ in (4) (of course, the worlds of extensional satisfaction of $i_2$ are identical to those of $i_1$ in this case). Notice also that the secretary could further delegate the task to the tea-boy, etc.

Whole-hearted satisfaction of $i_1$ is defined as usual using $W_{i_1}$ — the lecturer must select a deed from a partial $i_1$-strategy, i.e. a partial allocation of deeds at time points to ensure that at least some of the worlds $W_{i_1}$ remain possible. Both direct action and delegation thus keep extensional satisfaction within the bounds of possibility, and could thus figure in whole-hearted satisfaction of $i_1$.

A similar situation holds for the secretary, and the tea-boy (presumably there would eventually be only the option of performing the task, since any alternative would lead to the imperative lapsing).

*Example 2.* A lecturer is told by her mentor that she must, herself, write an exam paper.

The initial request again concerns action, so the positive part of the imperative is captured by

$$i_3 = T_{lecturer}\text{write\_exam} \tag{11}$$

There is, however, the non delegation component, captured by the second conjunct:

$$i_3 = T_{lecturer}\text{write\_exam} \wedge \forall y \neg S_{lecturer} P\,T_y\text{write\_exam} \tag{12}$$

Thus the lecturer may not be responsible for bringing about that any other agent is permitted to write her exam for her. Of course, it is conceivable that if, for example, she were to fall ill, her head of department might grant exam-writing permission to someone else in her place. Or, at a stretch of the imagination, there might be a role in a higher echelon of exam administration in which someone has the authority to write any exam paper they choose. Thus the normative position $P\,T_y write\_exam$ may either exist or come into existence for some agent $y$ — this is extensional satisfaction. It may not, however, come about as the result of whole hearted satisfaction on the part of the lecturer.

*Example 3.* A colleague asks the lecturer to get hold of a paper for him. She may be able to download the paper right away, or, if it is not available online, to delegate the task of getting hold of the paper via an Inter-Library Loan request to a secretary.

The imperative issued to the lecturer concerns a state of affairs, having a copy of the paper, and can be captured thus:

$$i_4 = S_{lecturer} \text{has\_paper} \tag{13}$$

If the paper is on-line, the deed-agent assignment download\_paper$^{lecturer}$ is sufficient to introduce has\_paper into the state of the world, thereby extensionally (and whole-heartedly) satisfying the imperative $i_4$.

The alternative is to delegate the task to the secretary, perhaps by issuing the imperative $i_5$

$$i_5 = S_{secretary} \text{has\_paper} \tag{14}$$

The secretary would then be responsible (through the new normative position $O\, S_{secretary} \text{has\_paper}$) for getting hold of the paper by whatever means she might see fit - by filling in an inter library loan form, by ringing the British Library or whatever. It is of no concern to the lecturer how her secretary finds the paper; the lecturer's task is (in this case) done on creating the obligation on her secretary.

Alternatively, the lecturer may decide to specify not the state of affairs that is desired, but rather the means by which they might be achieved. There are two key reasons why she might do this: (i) to avoid informing the secretary of her goal; (ii) to provide the secretary with more detailed instructions (as might be appropriate if the secretary had been recently appointed, say). Delegating the action is formulated, as can be seen from (5), in as natural a way as delegating states of affairs — in this case, the lecturer would utter $i_6$:

$$i_6 = T_{secretary} \text{complete\_ILL} \tag{15}$$

## 5   Specifying Communicative Acts

It now remains to discuss the consequences of using the model described in this paper in the practical task of specifying the primitives of an agent communication language. Following the distinction between actions and states, which has proven so useful in this discussion of imperatives, it is proposed that the primitives of an agent communication language should reflect this distinction. The FIPA ACL [9] provides four primitives that can be clearly understood as imperatives: 'request', 'request-when', 'request-whenever' and 'request-whomever'. Each of these primitives refer to actions to be performed. The rationale for this choice being that they may refer to other communication primitives.

The informal description of 'request-whomever' (no formal definition is provided within the 1997 FIPA specification [9]) and the difference between this primitive and 'request' is of particular interest here. The primitive 'request-whomever' is described as "The sender wants an action performed by some agent other than itself. The receiving agent should either perform the action or pass it on to some other agent." Ignoring the ambiguity of these two sentences, an interpretation of the 'request-whomever' primitive could be that the message is an attempted delegation of an action where the freedom to further delegate the action is unrestricted. Presumably, this means that the recipient can: (1) not understand the message; (2) refuse the request; (3) accept the request and perform the action itself; (4) accept the request and 'request' some other agent to perform it; or (5) accept the request and 'request-whomever' some other agent to perform it. The fact that agents can continue to "pass the buck" by forwarding this 'request-whomever' means that determining whether the request (or the imperative) has been satisfied is difficult. A further problem arises: What if agent $x$ requests that $y$ or whomever does $a$, then $y$ requests that $z$ or whomever does $a$ and then $z$ requests $x$ to do $a$. Neither $y$ nor $z$ has refused the request, and both have passed it on to an agent other than the agent that requested that they do $a$, but the buck has passed back to $x$! The action-state semantics of the model of imperatives presented in this paper provides a means to tie down this *delegation*.

In common with the majority of action languages, the formal specification of the primitive 'request', and all other communicative acts within the FIPA specification, provides a set of 'feasibility preconditions' (FP) and a set of 'rational effects' (RE). The definition of request is reproduced here:[6]

$$\langle i, \text{Request}(j, a) \rangle$$
$$\text{FP} : B_i \, \text{Agent}(j, a) \land \neg B_i \, I_j \, \text{Done}(a)$$
$$\text{RE} : \text{Done}(a)$$

There are two issues in this definition that are important to this discussion. First, the model relies on 'pseudo-states': the state of some action $a$ having been done. As discussed, the model presented in this paper avoids this problem: it provides a means through which the primitives of an agent communication language can refer to the delegation of both *actions* and *goals*. Second, and more importantly, to capture the notion of responsibility for satisfying the request, the preconditions include the belief of the message sender that the recipient is the agent of the action to which the request refers! Through the notion of whole-hearted satisfaction, the model presented in this paper provides a more justifiable and robust characterisation of *responsibility*.

## 6  Conclusions and Future Work

There are several key advantages that can be gained through adopting the model presented in this paper. First, it becomes possible, in a single formalism, to distinguish an agent

---

[6] There is a further feasibility condition defined in the FIPA specification [9], but this refers to the feasibility conditions of the action $a$. Although this is itself problematic, it is not relevant to this discussion, and is therefore omitted.

doing something, being responsible for getting something done, and being responsible for bringing about a state of affairs. This model provides a clear semantic interpretation for each. Second, it becomes possible to consider an agent's actions with regard to its commitment to a future obligation, and to determine whether or not it is behaving reasonably with respect to that commitment. Suppose that $x$ accepts the delegated task of doing $\alpha$; i.e. it involves the imperative $T_x\alpha$. Under this agreement, $x$ is at all times obliged to perform deeds which ensure that it can carry out $\alpha$, or at least it is forbidden from performing deeds which will remove the extensional satisfaction of $T_x\alpha$ from the bounds of possibility.

In the discussion on delegation, it is assumed that getting someone else to act on your behalf is a valid means to the satisfaction of a commitment. This avoids the need to restrict the action component, and hence tie ends to sets of means. The restriction that delegation is forbidden (it is forbidden because the agent is obliged not to delegate) must then be explicitly stated within an agreement. This has some parallel with the notion of the protective perimeter of rights [12,15]. The protective perimeter contains those actions that can be used to fulfil an obligation. This requires that the action component is extended to indicate that set of acceptable methods of achieving the goal. However, in parallel with Jones and Sergot [14], it is essential that an account of delegation is not dependent upon the detailed choices for the logic of the underlying action component.

The work presented in this paper has shown the application of the elegant action-state semantics proposed by Hamblin [11] to agent communication. Building on this, the paper contributes by: (1) giving a clear account of the distinction between doing and achieving through the introduction of the modalities $S_x$ and $T_x$; and (2) showing how delegation and responsibility can be cleanly captured using this novel framework.

# References

1. L. Åqvist. *A new approach to the logical theory of interrogatives.* Tubingen, TBL Verlag Gunter Barr, 1975.
2. J.L. Austin. *How to do things with words.* Oxford University Press, 1962.
3. M. Barbuceanu and M. S. Fox. Integrating communicative action, conversations and decision theory to coordinate agents. In *Proceedings of the Second International Conference on Autonomous Agents*, pages 47–58, 1997.
4. C. Castelfranchi. Modelling social action for AI agents. *Artificial Intelligence*, 103:157–182, 1998.
5. B. F. Chellas. *Modal logic: An introduction.* Cambridge University Press, 1980.
6. P. R. Cohen and H. J. Levesque. Communicative actions for artificial agents. In *Proceedings of the First International Conference on Multi-Agent Systems*, pages 65–72, 1995.
7. F. Dignum. Using transactions in integrity constraints: Looking forward or backwards, what is the difference? In *Proceedings of the Workshop on Applied Logics*, 1992.
8. T. Finin, D. McKay, R. Fritzson, and R. McEntire. KQML: An information and knowledge exchange protocol. In K. Funchi and T. Yokoi, editors, *Knowledge Building and Knowledge Sharing*. Ohmsha and IOS Press, 1994.
9. Foundation for Intelligent Physical Agents. *FIPA specification part 2: Agent communication language*, 1997. http://www.fipa.org/.
10. H. P. Grice. Meaning. *Philosophical review*, 66:377–388, 1957.
11. C. L. Hamblin. *Imperatives.* Basil Blackwell, Oxford, 1987.

12. H. L. A. Hart. Bentham on legal rights. In A. W. B. Simpson, editor, *Oxford Essays in Jurisprudence*, 2, pages 171–201. Oxford University Press, 1973.

13. J. Hintikka, I. Halonen, and A. Mutanen. Interrogative logic as a general theory of reasoning. unpublished manuscript, 1996.

14. A. I. J. Jones and M. J. Sergot. A formal characterisation of institutionalised power. *Journal of the IGPL*, 4(3):429–445, 1996.

15. L. Lindahl. *Position and change: A study in law and logic*. D. Reidel Publishing Company, Dordrecht, 1977.

16. J. McCarthy and P. Hayes. Some philosophical problems from the standpoint of artificial intelligence. In D. Michie and B. Meltzer, editors, *Machine Intelligence*, volume 4, pages 463–502. Edinburgh University Press, 1969.

17. A. Newell. The knowledge level. *Artificial Intelligence*, 18:87–127, 1982.

18. P. Panzarasa, T. J. Norman, and N. R. Jennings. Modeling sociality in the BDI framework. In J. Lui and N. Zhong, editors, *Proceedings of the First Asia-Pacific Conference on Intelligent Agent Technology*. World Scientific Publishing, 1999.

19. I. Pörn. *The logic of power*. Basil Blackwell, 1970.

20. C. A. Reed. Dialogue frames on agent communication. In *Proceedings of the Third International Conference on Multi-Agent Systems*, pages 246–253, 1998.

21. J. R. Searle. *Speech acts: An essay in the philosophy of language*. Cambridge University Press, 1969.

22. M. J. Sergot. Normative positions. In P. McNamara and H. Prakken, editors, *Norms, Logics and Information Systems*. ISO Press, 1998.

23. M. Shanahan. *Solving the frame problem*. MIT Press, 1997.

24. I. A. Smith, P. R. Cohen, J. M. Bradshaw, M. Greaves, and H. Holmback. Designing conversation policies using joint intention theory. In *Proceedings of the Third International Conference on Multi-Agent Systems*, pages 269–276, 1998.

25. G. H. von Wright. *An essay in deontic logic and the general theory of action*, volume 21 of *Acta philosophica Fennica*. North-Holland, Amsterdam, 1968.

26. D. N. Walton and E. C. W. Krabbe. *Commitment in dialogue: Basic concepts of interpersonal reasoning*. SUNY, New York, 1995.

# Agent Theory for Team Formation by Dialogue

Frank Dignum[1], Barbara Dunin-Kęplicz[2], and Rineke Verbrugge[3]

[1] Institute of Information and Computing Sciences, Utrecht University
P.O. Box 80.089, 3508 TB Utrecht, The Netherlands
`dignum@cs.uu.nl`
[2] Institute of Informatics, Warsaw University
Banacha 2, 02-097 Warsaw, Poland
`keplicz@mimuw.edu.pl`
[3] Cognitive Science and Engineering, University of Groningen
Grote Kruisstraat 2/1, 9712 TS Groningen, The Netherlands
`rineke@tcw2.ppsw.rug.nl`

**Abstract.** The process of cooperative problem solving can be divided into four stages. First, finding potential team members, then forming a team followed by constructing a plan for that team. Finally, the plan is executed by the team. Traditionally, protocols like the Contract Net protocol are used for performing the first two stages of the process. In an open environment however, there can be discussion among the agents in order to form a team that can achieve the collective intention of solving the problem. For these cases fixed protocols like contract net do not suffice. In this paper we present a theory for agents that are able to discuss the team formation and subsequently work as a team member until the collective goal has been fulfilled. We also present a solution, using structured *dialogues*, with an emphasis on persuasion, that can be shown to lead to the required team formation. The dialogues are described formally using modal logics and speech acts.

## 1 Introduction

The area of Distributed Problem Solving (DPS) has been occupied for more than ten years already with solving complex problems by teams of agents. Although in this field the problem might be solved in a distributed way, the control of solving it usually lies with one agent. This means that the team of agents is either already available or can be created on demand by the controlling agent. Also, these teams of agents are collaborative by nature. Thus they are designed to participate in the team to solve the problem.

We are concerned with problems that have to be solved by a number of existing agents that are not designed to solve this particular problem together. In this case, getting the right team of agents and controlling them is of prime interest. In this setting Contract Net [18] is often proposed as a simple but effective and efficient way to distribute tasks over a number of agents in order to achieve a common goal. It basically makes use of the market mechanism of task demand and supply to match tasks with agents that are willing to perform them. The reason of the success of this approach is the fact that it uses a fixed protocol with a limited number of steps and thus is easy to implement.

C. Castelfranchi, Y. Lespérance (Eds.): Intelligent Agents VII, LNAI 1986, pp. 150–166, 2001.

In our opinion, however, this functions only in cases where the market mechanism works, namely if several agents are willing to do the task (and these can compete), and if the tasks are all well described beforehand. We will concentrate on cases where these conditions are usually not met. Either because there is only one agent capable of performing a task and that one should be negotiated with or because the task cannot be described precisely at the beginning.

A good candidate to make conversation between agents during Cooperative Problem Solving (CPS) more flexible is the theory of Dialogue [21]. This theory gives rules for appropriate moves within different types of dialogues. The rules direct the dialogue without completely fixing the order of the moves. These moves themselves depend on particular stages of CPS. In fact, all of them are rather complex, both from the MAS and the AI perspective. Additionally, the cooperative process takes place in a dynamic and often unpredictable environment. Our intention is to present formal means allowing realisation of some relevant forms of dialogue. These dialogue types follow a formal theory of dialogue (see [21]) and speech acts (see [19]). In this way, it will be possible to prove that in given circumstances the dialogue results in a certain outcome. This is of prime importance if you want to construct a MAS for automated CPS.

We base our investigation on a formal model of teamwork. Thus, four stages of CPS are distinguished according to Wooldridge and Jennings' paper [22]. We define the stages somewhat differently, however (see [9] for a discussion). The first stage is *potential recognition* in which the agent that takes the initiative tries to find out which agents are potential candidates for achieving a given overall goal and how these can be combined in a team. The second stage is *team formation*. The result of this stage is a *collective intention* among a team to achieve the overall goal to solve the problem. This is the team that will try to actually achieve the goal. The third stage is *plan formation*. Here the team divides the goal into subtasks, associates these with actions and allocates these actions to team members. In terms of motivational attitudes the end result of this stage is a *collective commitment* to perform the social plan that realizes the goal. The last stage is *plan execution* in which the team members execute the allocated actions and monitor the appropriate colleagues. If necessary a *reconfiguration* of the plan can be constructed [9].

We concentrate on the first two stages of the process and show how the collective intention resulting from team formation is built up during the dialogues. It turns out that the main type of dialogue needed is persuasion. The running example in this paper is about team formation for achieving the following overall goal (further abbreviated as $\varphi$): "to arrange a trip of three weeks to Australia for a certain famous family; the trip should satisfy (specific) constraints on costs, times, places and activities". The initiative for teamwork is taken by travel agent $a$, who cannot arrange the whole trip on his own. The trip will be extensively publicized, so it has to be a success, even if circumstances change. Thus, he does not simply ask airline companies, hotels, and organizers of activities to deliver a number of fixed services. Instead, he believes that real teamwork, where all members are interested in the achievement of the overall goal, gives the best chances of a successful trip. This paper discusses the first two stages of cooperative problem solving only; plan formation and team action for this example will be described in further work.

The paper is structured in the following manner. A brief typology of dialogue is given in Section 2. Section 3 presents the logical background and briefly describes an agent architecture for the first two stages of CPS. Sections 4 and 5 investigate different dialogue types during potential recognition and team formation, respectively. Finally, in section 6 conclusions and further research are discussed. This paper is a revised and extended version of [5].

## 2   Conversations in CPS

In this section we will briefly discuss some theory to describe conversations.

Conversations are sequences of messages between two (or more) agents. These sequences can be completely fixed as is done by the use of a fixed protocol which states exactly which message should come next. Conversations can also be seen as completely free sequences of messages. In this case the agents can decide at any moment what will be the next message they send. We have already argued that fixed protocols are too rigid for the situation that we describe. However, complete freedom of choosing the next message would also be impractical. This would put a heavy burden on the agent that has to choose at each point in time which message it might send.

This is the reason that we choose for a form in between the two extremes sketched above. Dialogue theory structures conversations by means of a number of dialogue rules. These rules limit the number of possible responses at each point, while not completely fixing the sequence of messages. The agents speak in turn, for example asking questions and giving replies, and take into account, at each turn, what has occurred previously in the dialogue.

Krabbe and Walton [21] provide a typology of dialogue types between two agents, with an emphasis on the persuasion dialogue. They create a *normative model*, representing the ideal way reasonable, cooperative agents participate in the type of dialogue in question. For each type of dialogue, they formulate *an initial situation, a primary goal*, and *a set of rules*. Below, their typology is briefly explained and adapted to the CPS. In the course of communication among agents, there often occurs a shift from one type of dialogue to another, in particular *embedding* occurs when the second dialogue is functionally related to the first one.

A *persuasion dialogue* arises from a conflict of opinions. It may be that one agent believes $\varphi$ while some others either believe a contrary proposition $\psi$ (where $\varphi \land \psi$ is inconsistent) or just have doubt about $\varphi$. The goal of a persuasion dialogue is to resolve the conflict by verbal means, in such a way that a stable agreement results, corresponding to a collective informational attitude. In contrast to [21], we allow persuasion also with respect to motivational attitudes.

The initial situation of *negotiation* is a conflict of interests, together with a need for cooperation. The main goal is to make a deal. Thus, the selling and buying of goods and services, that is often described in the MAS literature, is only one of the many contexts where negotiation plays a role. Negotiation and persuasion are often not distinguished adequately.

The initial situation of *information seeking* occurs when one agent is ignorant about the truth of a certain proposition and seeks information from other agents. Two other important types of dialogue are *inquiry* and *deliberation*, but they play a role mainly during the stage of plan formation, which will be considered in a forthcoming paper. The last type of dialogue, *eristics* (verbal fighting between agents), is not relevant as we focus on teamwork.

In general, Krabbe and Walton [21] are not interested in informational and motivational attitudes of agents involved in dialogue, if these attitudes are not communicated explicitly. In contrast to them, our goal is to make the whole process of dialogue among computational agents transparent. For this reason, at each step of team formation the agents' internal attitudes need to be established, and then updated and revised when necessary.

## 3    Logical Background and Agent Architecture

We view individual beliefs, goals, and intentions as primitive notions and use well-known modal logics to formalize them. For the epistemic operator BEL, referring to agent's belief, the standard modal system KD45$_n$ for $n$ agents is used [12]. For the motivational operators GOAL and INT, referring to agent's goals and intentions, respectively, the axioms include the axiom system $K_n$. As to possible additional axioms, we assume that an agent's goals need not be consistent with each other. It chooses a limited number of its goals to be intentions, in such a way that consistency is preserved. This can be formulated by the well-known axiom $D$:

$$\neg \text{INT}(i, \bot) \text{ for } i = 1, \dots, n \text{ Intention Consistency Axiom}$$

Thus, for intentions (but not for goals, in contrast to [20]), the resulting system is $KD_n$.

As for Kripke semantics, formulas are evaluated with respect to pairs $(M, w)$ of a model $M$ and a world $w$, using binary accessibility relations $B_i, D_i, I_i$ between such model-world pairs, corresponding to each agent $i$'s beliefs, goals, and intentions in the standard way. The relations $B_i$ and $I_i$ are serial, as characterized by axiom $D$. Moreover, the $B_i$ are also transitive and euclidean, corresponding to axioms 4 and 5 for positive and negative introspection, respectively.

In this paper, intentions, goals, and beliefs all refer to agents' attitudes towards *propositions* $\psi$. (In other work, motivational attitudes are also defined with respect to actions [8,10].) We formalize the fact that agents are correct about their own intentions by the axiom BEL$(i, \text{INT}(i, \psi)) \rightarrow \text{INT}(i, \psi)$, which characterizes the frames in which for all worlds $u, v$, if $uI_iv$, then there is a $w$ such that $uB_iw$ and $wI_iv$. We also find it useful to formalize the fact that the set of an agent's intentions is a subset of its goals, as expressed by the axiom INT$(i, \psi) \rightarrow \text{GOAL}(i, \psi)$, which characterizes the Kripke frames for which $D_i \subseteq I_i$.

### 3.1    Collective Beliefs and Collective Intentions

To model teamwork, individual attitudes naturally do not suffice. In other work we discussed the pairwise notion of social commitments, as well as collective notions like collective belief, collective intention, and collective commitment [10]. In the first two stages of CPS, the essential notions are those of collective belief and collective intention.

In order to model group beliefs, a few axioms and rules need to be added to the System $KD45_n$. First, the formula E-BEL$_G(\varphi)$ is meant to stand for "every agent in group $G$ believes $\varphi$", axiomatized as follows:

(1) E-BEL$_G(\varphi) \leftrightarrow \bigwedge_{i \in G}$ BEL$(i, \varphi)$

A stronger operator is the one for collective belief, which is similar to the more usual common knowledge. C-BEL$_G(\varphi)$ is meant to be true if everyone in $G$ believes $\varphi$, everyone in $G$ believes that everyone in $G$ believes $\varphi$, etc. (Note that even collective beliefs need not be true, so C-BEL$_G(\varphi)$ need not imply $\varphi$.) Collective belief is axiomatized by the following axiom and rule. Note that the rule may only be applied if the antecedent $\varphi \rightarrow$ E-BEL$_G(\psi \wedge \varphi)$ is a theorem.

(2) C-BEL$_G(\varphi) \leftrightarrow$ E-BEL$_G(\varphi \wedge$ C-BEL$_G(\varphi))$
(3) From $\varphi \rightarrow$ E-BEL$_G(\psi \wedge \varphi)$ infer $\varphi \rightarrow$ C-BEL$_G(\psi)$ (Induction Rule)

The resulting system is called $KD45_n^C$, and it is sound and complete with respect to Kripke models where all $n$ accessibility relations are transitive, serial and euclidean [12].

The establishment of collective beliefs among a group is problematic. In [12, Chapter 11] it is shown that bilateral sending of messages does not suffice to determine collective belief if communication channels may be faulty. Some possible practical solutions are also given. We abstract from these problems by assuming collective beliefs can be achieved by global announcements.

The definition of *collective intention* is rather strong, because we focus on strictly cooperative groups. There, a necessary condition for a collective intention is that all members of the group have the associated individual intention INT$(i, \varphi)$. Moreover, to exclude the case of competition, all agents should *intend* all members to have the associated individual intention, as well as the intention that all members have the individual intention, and so on; we call such a mutual intention M-INT$_G(\varphi)$. Furthermore, all members of the group are aware of this mutual intention, that is, they have a collective belief about this (C-BEL$_G$(M-INT$_G(\varphi)$)).

In order to formalize the above two conditions, E-INT$_G(\varphi)$ (standing for "everyone intends") is defined by the following axiom, analogous to (1) above:

(4) E-INT$_G(\varphi) \leftrightarrow \bigwedge_{i \in G}$ INT$(i, \varphi)$.

The mutual intention M-INT$_G(\varphi)$ is axiomatized by an axiom and rule analogous to (2) and (3):

(5) M-INT$_G(\varphi) \leftrightarrow$ E-INT$_G(\varphi \wedge$ M-INT$_G(\varphi))$
(6) From $\varphi \rightarrow$ E-INT$_G(\psi \wedge \varphi)$ infer $\varphi \rightarrow$ M-INT$_G(\psi)$ (Induction Rule)

The system resulting from adding (4), (5), and (6) to $KD_n$ is called $KD_n^{\text{M-INT}_G}$, and it is sound and complete with respect to Kripke models where all $n$ accessibility relations are serial (by a proof analogous to the one for common knowledge in [12]). Finally, the collective intention is defined by the following axiom:

(7) $\text{C-INT}_G(\varphi) \leftrightarrow (\text{M-INT}_G(\varphi) \land \text{C-BEL}_G(\text{M-INT}_G(\varphi)))$

Note that this definition is different from the one given in [8,10]; the new definition will be extensively discussed and compared with others in a forthcoming paper. Let us remark that, even though $\text{C-INT}_G(\varphi)$ seems to be an infinite concept, a collective intention with respect to $\varphi$ may be established in a finite number of steps: according to (6) and (7), it suffices that all agents in $G$ intend $\varphi \land \text{M-INT}_G(\varphi)$ and that this fact is announced to the whole group by which a collective belief is established.

### 3.2 Agent Architecture for Team Formation by Dialogue

In order to ensure the proper realization of team formation by dialogue, we postulate that an agent architecture should contain a number of specific modules. The heart of the system is, as usual, the **reasoning** module. When realizing the consecutive stages leading ultimately to team formation, interaction with the **planning, communication,** and **social reasoning** modules is necessary. All these modules contain a number of specific *reasoning rules* which will be introduced formally in the sequel. Each rule refers to a specific aspect of the reasoning process; very often they can be viewed as rules bridging different modules.

The **reasoning** module contains rules creating agents' individual beliefs, intentions, and goals, as well as the collective informational and motivational attitudes established during potential recognition and team formation. The **communication** module contains rules leading to speech acts, but also some auxiliary rules or mechanisms organizing the *information seeking* and *persuasion* dialogues. In this paper we abstract from the latter, rather technical, ones. The **social reasoning** module contains rules allowing to reason about other agents. In this paper we only illustrate a number of rules in this module in as far as they relate directly to the conversation taking place. However, this module will also contain knowledge about multi-agent planning and capabilities etc. of the other agents. That is, it contains knowledge about the social impact of each plan. We assume the module to have at least the type of knowledge as illustrated in [15], but refer to that paper for reasoning about multi-agent plans to establish a team and before constructing/adopting a social plan. The **planning** module will be used for preplanning during the potential recognition stage. In fact, it will be more busy during higher stages of CPS, i.e. when generating a social plan and possibly during the reconfiguration process (see [9,11]).

## 4    Potential Recognition

Potential recognition is about finding the set of agents that may participate in the formation of the team that tries to achieve the overall goal. These agents are grouped into several potential teams with whom further discussion will follow during *team formation*. For simplicity, we assume that one agent takes the initiative to realize the overall goal, which is given.

## 4.1 The End Result of Potential Recognition

The first task of the *initiator* is to form a partial (abstract) plan for the achievement of the overall goal. On the basis of the (type of) subgoals that it recognizes it will determine which agents might be most suited to form the team. In order to determine this match the initiator tries to find out the properties of the agents, being interested in three aspects, namely their *abilities*, *opportunities*, and their *willingness* to participate in team formation.

The aspect of ability considers whether the agents can perform the right type of tasks. It does not depend on the situation, but may be viewed as an inherent property of the agent itself. The aspect of opportunity takes into account the possibilities of task performance in the present situation, involving resources and possibly other properties. The aspect of willingness considers their mental attitudes towards participating towards the overall goal. Very capable agents that do not want to do the job are of no use. The components of the agent's suitability are represented as follows (cf. [14] where formal definitions are given for ability and opportunity based on dynamic logic):

1. the individual ability of agent $b$ to achieve a goal $\psi$ is denoted by $able(b, \psi)$, meaning that $\psi$ is in a pre-given set of agent $b$'s abilities.
2. the resources available to agent b are reflected by the opportunity that agent $b$ has to achieve $\psi$, denoted by $opp(b, \psi)$. This is true in a world and a state if there is a branch through that state such that at a later point on that branch, agent $b$ has just seen to it that $\psi$.
3. the willingness of agent $b$ to participate towards the overall goal is denoted by $willing(b, \varphi)$. This stands for "agent $b$ believes that at some branch, at some point in future, it intends $\varphi$".

## 4.2 Towards a Potential of Cooperation

In the previous subsection we have described what type of information the initiating agent tries to gather in order to start team formation. Now, we will describe how the information is collected, leading to the formal outcome.

The output at this stage is the "potential for cooperation" that the initiator $a$ sees with respect to $\varphi$, denoted as $\text{POTCOOP}(a, \varphi)$. This means that $\varphi$ is a goal of $a$ ($\text{GOAL}(a, \varphi)$), and there is a group $G$ such that $a$ believes that $G$ can collectively achieve $\varphi$ (formalized as $\text{C-CAN}_G(\varphi)$) and are willing to participate in team formation; and either $a$ cannot or doesn't desire to achieve $\varphi$ in isolation. This is expressed by the following definitions (see [9] for more discussion):

$$\text{POTCOOP}(a, \varphi) \leftrightarrow \text{GOAL}(a, \varphi) \wedge$$
$$\exists G \subseteq \mathit{T}\text{BEL}(a, \text{C-CAN}_G(\varphi) \wedge \forall i \in G\, willing(i, \varphi)) \wedge$$
$$(\neg \text{CAN}(a, \varphi) \vee \neg \text{GOAL}(a, stit(\varphi)))$$

$$\text{CAN}(a, \varphi) \leftrightarrow able(a, \varphi) \land opp(a, \varphi).$$

$\text{POTCOOP}(a, \varphi)$ is derived from the information collected from the individual agents. To derive $\text{C-CAN}_G(\varphi)$ the initiator compares the information obtained about the other agents against a partial abstract plan for the overall goal $\varphi$. For this purpose $\varphi$ is split into a number of subgoals $\varphi_1, \ldots, \varphi_n$, which can be viewed as instrumental to the overall goal. Together they *realize* $\varphi$ and are compared with the individual abilities and opportunities that the agents are believed to have:

$$\text{C-CAN}_G(\varphi) \leftrightarrow \exists \varphi_1, \ldots, \exists \varphi_n (realize(< \varphi_1, \ldots, \varphi_n >, \varphi) \land$$
$$\forall i \leq n \exists j \in G(able(j, \varphi_i) \land opp(j, \varphi_i)))$$

Here, $realize(< \varphi_1, \ldots, \varphi_n >, \varphi)$ intuitively means: "if $\varphi_1, \ldots, \varphi_n$ are achieved, then $\varphi$ holds". Technically, one may need some extra-logical, context-dependent, reasoning to show the implication. In the reasoning module of the agent architecture, there is a formal rule corresponding to: "if $< \varphi_1, \ldots, \varphi_n >$ is a result of pre-planning to achieve $\varphi$, then $realize(< \varphi_1, \ldots, \varphi_n >, \varphi)$ holds".

### 4.3  Information Seeking Dialogue

Ultimately, the initiator has to form beliefs about the abilities, opportunities, and willingness of the individual agents in order to derive $\text{POTCOOP}(a, \varphi)$. The possible strategies for organizing this information seeking part remain out of our interest. For example, $a$ may first investigate the willingness of particular agents, and on this basis then ask the interested ones about their abilities and opportunities. Depending on the specific situation we deal with, another organization of this process may be more adequate. In any case, the questions in this stage form part of an *information seeking* dialogue. This can be done by $a$ asking every agent about its properties and the agent responding with the requested information.

Formally this can be expressed as follows, where $\psi$ may stand for any of the aspects $opp(i, \varphi_i)$, $able(i, \varphi_i)$, $willing(i, \varphi)$, etc.

$$[\text{REQ}_{a,i}( \textbf{if } \psi \textbf{ then } \text{ASS}_{i,a}(\psi) \textbf{ else } \text{ASS}_{i,a}(\neg\psi))]$$
$$[\text{ASS}_{i,a}(\psi)](\text{TRUST}(a, i, \psi) \to \text{BEL}(a, \psi))$$

The above formula is based on the formal theory on *speech acts* developed in [19] and [7]. It is expressed as a dynamic logic formula of the form $[\alpha_1][\alpha_2]\psi$, meaning that if $\alpha_1$ is performed then always a situation arises such that if $\alpha_2$ is performed then in the resulting state $\psi$ will always hold. In the above case $\alpha_1$ is the complex action $\text{REQ}_{a,i}( \textbf{if } \psi \textbf{ then } \text{ASS}_{i,a}(\psi) \textbf{ else } \text{ASS}_{i,a}(\neg\psi))$, where $\text{REQ}_{a,i}(\alpha)$ stands for agent $a$ requesting agent $i$ to perform the action $\alpha$. After this request $i$ has three options.

1. It can simply ignore $a$ and not answer at all.
2. It can state that it is not willing to divulge this information:
   $\text{ASS}_{i,a}(\neg( \textbf{if } \psi \textbf{ then } \text{ASS}_{i,a}(\psi) \textbf{ else } \text{ASS}_{i,a}(\neg\psi)))$.
3. It can state that it does not have enough information:
   $\text{ASS}_{i,a}(\neg(\text{BEL}(i, \psi) \land \neg\text{BEL}(i, \neg\psi)))$.

4. It can either assert that $\psi$ is the case (as described above) or that it is not, in which case $a$ believes $\psi$ is not true:

$$[\text{ASS}_{i,a}(\neg\psi)](\text{TRUST}(a, i, \neg\psi) \rightarrow \text{BEL}(a, \neg\psi)).$$

Of course in case 2, agent $a$ can already derive that $i$ is not willing to achieve $\varphi$ as part of a team; only in case 4 will $a$ have a resulting belief about $\psi$.

An important notion here is whether $a$ trusts the other agent's answer; we use $\text{TRUST}(a, i, \psi)$ to mean "agent $a$ trusts agent $i$ with respect to proposition $\psi$". Trust is a complex concept that has been defined in many ways, from different perspectives (see [3] for some current work in this area). We will not try to define trust in any way in this paper, but simply use its intuitive meaning. We suppose that the module social reasoning contains rules giving a number of conditions (e.g. "$a$ has observed that agent $i$ is generally trustworthy") implying $\text{TRUST}(a, i, \psi)$.

In an analogous way, an information seeking dialogue about all ingredients of $\text{POTCOOP}(a, \varphi)$ takes place. In principle, the schema of all necessary questions may be rather complex. For example, when recognizing the ability to achieve a specific sub-goal $\varphi_i$, agent $a$ should repeat this question for all the subgoals it distinguished to every agent, but this solution is apparently not acceptable from the AI perspective. Of course it is more effective for agent $a$ to ask each agent $i$ to divulge all the abilities it has with respect to achieving this set of goals. These are, however, strategic considerations, not related to the theory of dialogue.

A next strategic point is about case 1. To avoid agent $a$ waiting indefinitely for an answer, we assume that every speech act has an implicit deadline for reaction incorporated. After this deadline, the silent agent will not be considered as a potential team member anymore. The logical modeling of these types of deadlines is described in [6] and will not be pursued here.

Finally, the formal result of the potential recognition stage is that agent $a$ has the belief that it is possible to form a team to achieve the overall goal or that it is not. In some applications, like scientific research projects, the outcome of this stage is communicated to the agents who replied positively. In the context of services like travel agencies this may not be necessary.

## 5   Team Formation

At the stage of potential recognition, individual properties of agents were considered. These could play a role in different types of cooperation, where some services are exchanged but there is no interest in other agent's activities, and more specifically, there is no collective intention to achieve a goal as a team. At the stage of team formation, however, the conditions needed for teamwork in a strict sense are created. The main condition of teamwork is the presence of a collective intention, defined in subsection 3.1.

Note that this concept of teamwork requires agents that have a type of "social conscience". We do not consider a set of agents as a team if they cooperate by just achieving their own predefined part of a common goal. If agents are part of a team they should be interested in the performance of the other team members and willing to adjust their task on the basis of the needs of others.

At the beginning, the initiator has a sequence of groups in mind that could be suitable to form a team for achieving the goal. Although we do not go into details here, the organization of the groups into a sequence is important for the case that the most desirable group can not be formed.

All agents in these potential teams have expressed their willingness to participate towards the overall goal, but do not necessarily have the individual intention to contribute towards it yet. (Note that this situation is almost complementary to the one assumed in [16] in which tasks are delegated and the willingness of the other agent to perform the task is not considered). In this situation, the initiator tries to persuade them to take on the intention to achieve the overall goal as well as to act as a team with the other members. Note that task division and task allocation only come to the fore at the next stage, plan formation.

## 5.1  Persuasion Dialogue

The goal of a persuasion dialogue is to establish a collective intention within a group $G$ to reach the overall goal $\varphi$ (C-INT$_G(\varphi)$, see subsection 3.1). Axiom (7) makes evident that a crucial step for the initiator is to persuade all members of a potential team to take the overall goal as an individual intention. To establish the higher levels of the mutual intention, the initiator also persuades each member to take on the intention that all members of the potential team have the mutual intention, in order to strengthen cooperation from the start. It suffices if the initiator persuades all members of a potential team $G$ to take on an individual intention towards $\varphi$ (INT$(i, \varphi)$) and the intention that there be a mutual intention among that team (INT$(i, \text{M-INT}_G(\varphi))$. This results in INT$(i, \varphi \wedge \text{M-INT}_G(\varphi))$ for all $i \in G$, or equivalently by axiom (4): E-INT$_G(\varphi \wedge \text{M-INT}_G(\varphi))$, which in turn implies by axiom (5) that M-INT$_G(\varphi)$. When all the individual motivational attitudes are established within the team, the initiator broadcasts the fact M-INT$_G(\varphi)$, by which the necessary collective belief C-BEL$_G(\text{M-INT}_G(\varphi))$ is established and the collective intention is in place.

This will be achieved during a persuasion dialogue, which according to [21] consists of three main stages: information exchange, rigorous persuasion and completion. In our case the information exchange already started in the potential recognition stage. Let us remind the reader that we extended the concept of persuasion to include also intentions, and not only beliefs. The final result of the team formation stage is reached when for one potential team all the persuasion dialogues have been concluded successfully.

**Information exchange.** During the information exchange the agents make clear their initial stand with respect to the overall goal and to form part of a certain team to achieve it. These issues are expressed partly in the form of intentions and beliefs. Other beliefs supporting or related to the above issues might also be exchanged already. Only when a conflict arises about these issues a persuasion dialogue has to take place. In each persuasion there are two parties or roles; the proponent (P) and the opponent (O). In our case the proponent is the initiator and the opponent the other agent.

The stands the other agents take about the above issues are seen as its initial *concessions*. Concessions are beliefs and intentions that an agent takes on for the sake of argument, but need not be prepared to defend. The agents will also have private attitudes that may only become apparent later on during the dialogue. The stand of the initiator is seen as the initial thesis that it is prepared to defend during the dialogue. The initial conflict description consists of a set of O's initial concessions and P's initial thesis.

**Rigorous persuasion.** During the rigorous persuasion stage the agents exchange arguments to challenge or support a thesis. The following rules can be used to govern these moves adapted from [21]:

1. Starting with O the two parties move alternately according to the rules of the game.
2. Each move consists of either a challenge, a question, a statement, a challenge or question accompanied by a statement, or a final remark.
3. The game is highly asymmetrical. All P's statements are assertions, and called *theses*, all O's statements are called *concessions*. P is doing the questioning and O all the challenging.
4. The initial move by O challenges P's initial thesis. It is P's goal to make O concede the thesis. P can do this by questioning O and thus bridge the gap between the initial concessions of O and the thesis, or by making an assertion to clinch the argument if acceptable.
5. Each move for O is to pertain to P's preceding move. If this was a question, then O has to answer it. If it was an assertion, then O has to challenge it.
6. Each party may give up, using the final remark $\mathrm{ASS}_{a,i}(quit)$ for the initiator, or $\mathrm{ASS}_{i,a}(\mathrm{INT}(i, \varphi \wedge \mathrm{M\text{-}INT}_G(\varphi)))$.
   If O's concessions imply P's thesis, then P can end the dialogue by the final remark: $\mathrm{ASS}_{a,i}(won)$. In our system we assume to have the following rule:
   $[\mathrm{ASS}_{a,i}(won)]\mathrm{OBL}(\mathrm{ASS}_{i,a}(\mathrm{INT}(i, \varphi \wedge \mathrm{M\text{-}INT}_G(\varphi))))$, which means that agent $i$ is obliged to state that it has been persuaded and accepts its role in the team. This does not mean that $i$ will actually make this assertion! Just that there is an obligation (according to the rules of the persuasion "game"). The modal operator OBL is taken from deontic logic [1].
7. All challenges have to follow logical rules. For example, a thesis $A \wedge B$ can be challenged by challenging one of the two conjuncts. For a complete set of rules for the propositional part of the logic we refer to [21].

In the completion stage the outcome is made explicit, such that the agents either have a collective belief and/or intention or they know that they differ in opinion.

**Speech acts during persuasion.** In contrast to [21], we need to monitor the agent's informational and motivational attitudes during persuasion. We are concerned with assertions and challenges (wrt. informational attitudes), and concessions and requests (wrt. both informational and motivational attitudes).

As for assertions, after a speech act of the form $\mathrm{ASS}_{a,i}(B)$, agent $i$ believes that the initiator believes that $B$:

$$[\mathrm{ASS}_{a,i}(B)]\mathrm{BEL}(i, \mathrm{BEL}(a, B))$$

Let us assume that $i$ has only two rules for answering an assertion $B$. If $i$ does not have a belief that is inconsistent with $B$ then $i$ will concede (similarly as in default logic). If, on the other hand, $i$ does have a belief to the contrary it will challenge the assertion. Formally:

$$\neg\text{BEL}(i, \neg B) \rightarrow \text{DO}(i, \text{CONCEDE}_{i,a}(B))$$

$$\text{BEL}(i, \neg B) \rightarrow \text{DO}(i, \text{CHALLENGE}_{i,a}(B))$$

where the operator $\text{DO}(i, \alpha)$ indicates that $\alpha$ is the next action performed by $i$.

The CONCEDE action with respect to informational attitudes is basically an assertion plus a possible mental update of the agent. Thus, it does not only assert the proposition but actually believes it as well, even if it did not believe the proposition beforehand. Suppose that $i$ did not have a contrary belief, then $i$ concedes $B$ by the speech act $\text{CONCEDE}_{i,a}(B)$. The effect of this speech act is similar to that of ASS, except that $a$ can only assume that $i$ believes the formula $B$ during the dialogue and might retract it afterwards.

$$[\text{CONCEDE}_{i,a}(B)]\text{BEL}(a, \text{BEL}(i, B))$$

The CHALLENGE with respect to informational attitudes, on the other hand, is a combination of a denial (assertion of a belief in the negation of the proposition) and a request to prove the proposition. The exact form of the challenge depends on the logical form of the assertion [21]. For this reason, the complete effects of this speech act are quite complex to describe fully. We will give an example challenge in the next subsection.

With respect to motivational attitudes, the situation is different. For example, initiator $a$ requests $i$ to take on an intention $\psi$ by the following speech act:

$$\text{REQ}_{a,i}(\text{CONCEDE}_{i,a}(\text{INT}(i, \psi))).$$

Again, $i$ has only two rules for answering such a request. If $i$ does not have an intention $\neg\psi$ (that is inconsistent with $\psi$) then $i$ will concede. If, on the other hand $i$ does have an intention to the contrary it will assert that it intends $\neg\psi$:

$$\neg\text{INT}(i, \neg\psi) \rightarrow \text{DO}(i, \text{CONCEDE}_{i,a}(\text{INT}(i, \psi)))$$

$$\text{INT}(i, \neg\psi) \rightarrow \text{DO}(i, \text{ASS}_{i,a}(\text{INT}(i, \neg\psi)))$$

For example, suppose that $i$ did not have a contrary intention then $i$ concedes by the speech act $\text{CONCEDE}_{i,a}(\text{INT}(i, \psi))$. The effect of this speech act is:

$$[\text{CONCEDE}_{i,a}(\text{INT}(i, \psi))]\text{BEL}(a, \text{INT}(i, \psi))$$

## 5.2   Team Formation for the Example

In the travel example, the initiator tries to persuade the other agents $i$ in the potential team to take on the intention to achieve the overall goal of organizing the journey $(\text{INT}(i, \varphi))$, but also with respect to doing this as a team with the other agents $(\text{INT}(i, \text{M-INT}_G(\varphi)))$. To this end, the initiator exploits the theory of intention formation.

Intentions are formed on the basis of beliefs and previously formed intentions of a higher abstraction level by a number of formal rules (see [4]). For example, the built-in intention can be to obey the law, or avoid punishment. The (instrumental) belief is that driving slower than the speed limit is instrumental for obeying the law, and is its preferred way to do so. Together with the rule the new intention of driving slower than the speed limit is derived.

The general intention generation rule is represented as follows:

(8) $\text{INT}(i, \psi) \wedge \text{BEL}(i, \text{INSTR}(i, \chi, \psi)) \wedge \text{PREFER}(i, \chi, \psi) \rightarrow \text{INT}(i, \chi)$ It states that if an agent $i$ has a intention $\psi$ and it believes that $\chi$ is instrumental in achieving $\psi$ and $\chi$ is its preferred way of achieving $\psi$, then it will have the intention to achieve $\chi$. "$\chi$ is instrumental in achieving $\psi$" means that achieving $\chi$ gets the agent "closer" to $\psi$ in some abstract sense. We do not define this relation any further, but leave it as primitive.

The PREFER relation is based on an agent's individual beliefs about the utility ordering between its goals, collected here into a finite set $H$. We abstract from the specific way in which the agent may compute the relative utilities, but see the literature about (qualitative) decision theory [2].

$$\text{PREFER}(i, \chi, \psi) \leftrightarrow$$
$$\bigwedge_{\xi \in H} (\text{BEL}(i, \text{INSTR}(i, \xi, \psi)) \rightarrow \text{BEL}(i, ut(i, \chi) \geq ut(i, \xi)))$$

The mechanism sketched in subsection 5.1 can be used in our setting during persuasion. In our example, the initiator $a$ tries to get the other agent $i$ to concede to higher level intentions, instrumental beliefs and preferences that together with (8) imply the intention to achieve the overall goal $\varphi$. To be more concrete, we could choose the higher level intention $\psi$ to stand for "earn good money". Here follows an example move of the initiator:

$$\text{ASS}_{a,i}(\forall j(\text{INT}(j, \psi) \rightarrow \text{INSTR}(j, \varphi, \psi))).$$

After this speech act agent $i$ believes that the initiator believes that if an agent has the higher level intention to earn good money, then the overall intention $\varphi$ is instrumental to this. Formally (see also [7]):

$$[\text{ASS}_{a,i}(\forall j(\text{INT}(j, \psi) \rightarrow \text{INSTR}(j, \varphi, \psi)))]$$
$$\text{BEL}(i, \text{BEL}(a, \forall j(\text{INT}(j, \psi) \rightarrow \text{INSTR}(j, \varphi, \psi))))$$

According to the general rule about assertions there are two possibilities for $i$'s answer. Let us assume that the positive case holds, i.e. $i$ does not have a contrary belief, so it concedes: $\text{CONCEDE}_{i,a}(\forall j(\text{INT}(j, \psi) \rightarrow \text{INSTR}(j, \varphi, \psi)))$. The effect of this speech act on agent $a$ is given by the general rule:

$$[\text{CONCEDE}_{i,a}(\forall j(\text{INT}(j, \psi) \rightarrow \text{INSTR}(j, \varphi, \psi)))]$$
$$\text{BEL}(a, \text{BEL}(i, \forall j(\text{INT}(j, \psi) \rightarrow \text{INSTR}(j, \varphi, \psi))))$$

Now the formula is believed by both $a$ and $i$. Thus, the initiator's next aim in the persuasion will be to get $i$ to intend $\psi$ (earn good money) by the question:

$$\text{REQ}_{a,i}(\text{CONCEDE}_{i,a}(\text{INT}(i, \psi))).$$

By the general rule, $i$ is obliged to either concede it has the intention $\psi$ (if it is consistent with its other intentions) or to assert that it intends its negation. After $i$'s response, the initiator believes i's answer. Note that in the second case, it may be useful for $a$ to embed a negotiation dialogue in the persuasion, in order to get $i$ to revise some of its previous intentions. For the example, let us suppose that $a$ is successful in persuading $i$.

When the initiator has persuaded agent $i$ to take on high level intention $\psi$ and to believe the instrumentality of $\varphi$ with respect to $\psi$, it can go on to persuade the other that $\mathrm{PREFER}(i, \phi, \psi)$ by the speech act:

$$\mathrm{ASS}_{a,i}(\bigwedge_{\xi \in H} (\mathrm{BEL}(i, \mathrm{INSTR}(i, \xi, \psi)) \rightarrow \mathrm{BEL}(i, ut(i, \varphi) \geq ut(i, \xi))))$$

To make the example more interesting, let us suppose that $i$ does not yet prefer $\varphi$ as a means to earn good money; instead it believes that $\chi$, arranging some less complex holidays for another family, has a higher utility than $\varphi$. Thus $i$ does not concede to the initiator's speech act, but instead counters with a challenge. According to the logical structure of the definition of $\mathrm{PREFER}$, this challenge is a complex speech act consisting of three consecutive steps. First $i$ asserts the negation of $a$'s assertion, a conjunction of implications; then it concedes to the antecedent of the implication for the specific goal $\chi \in H$; and finally it requests $a$ to present a proof that $\varphi$ has a better utility for $i$ than $\chi$.

$\mathrm{CHALLENGE}_{i,a}$
$(\bigwedge_{\xi \in H}(\mathrm{BEL}(i, \mathrm{INSTR}(i, \xi, \psi)) \rightarrow \mathrm{BEL}(i, ut(i, \varphi) \geq ut(i, \xi)))) \equiv$
$\mathrm{ASS}_{i,a}(\neg(\bigwedge_{\xi \in H}(\mathrm{BEL}(i, \mathrm{INSTR}(i, \xi, \psi)) \rightarrow \mathrm{BEL}(i, ut(i, \varphi) \geq ut(i, \xi)))));$
$\mathrm{CONCEDE}_{i,a}(\mathrm{BEL}(i, \mathrm{INSTR}(i, \chi, \psi)));$
$\mathrm{REQ}_{i,a}(\mathrm{ASS}_{a,i}(\mathrm{PROOF}(ut(i, \varphi) \geq ut(i, \chi))))$

As a reply, $a$ could prove that the utility of $\varphi$ is in fact higher than that of $\chi$, because it generates a lot of good publicity, which will be profitable for $i$ in future – something of which $i$ was not yet aware. Let us suppose that $i$ is persuaded by the proof and indeed concedes to its new preference by the speech act:
$\mathrm{CONCEDE}_{i,a}(\mathrm{PREFER}(i, \varphi, \psi))$.

All these concessions, together with the general intention formation rule and the fact that agents are correct about their intentions, then lead to $\mathrm{INT}(i, \varphi)$. For intentions with respect to cooperation with other potential team members, the process to persuade the agent to take on $\mathrm{INT}(i, \mathrm{M\text{-}INT}_G(\varphi))$ is analogous.

## 6  Discussion and Conclusions

In previous work [9] it was shown how all four stages of CPS result in specific motivational attitudes that can be formally described. In this paper, we have shown for the first two stages, potential recognition and team formation, which rules govern the dialogues by which the motivational attitudes are formed, and how to represent the moves within the dialogues by formalized speech acts.

It is clear that, even though the dialogues are governed by strict rules, the reasoning needed to find an appropriate move is highly complex. This implies that the agents also have to contain complex reasoning mechanisms in order to execute the dialogues. It means that, although the result is much more flexible and refined than using a protocol like Contract Net, the process is also more time consuming. For practical cases one should carefully consider what carries more weight and choose the method of team formation accordingly.

Related work can be found in [17], who also presents an agent architecture and a representation for agent communication. In the discussion they note that their own "negotiation" in fact covers a number of Walton and Krabbe's different dialogue types. We find the more fine-grained typology to be very useful when designing agents for teamwork: one can use specific sets of rules governing each type of dialogue as well as the possible embeddings between the different types. Thus desired kinds of communication are allowed and harmful ones prevented, without completely fixing any protocol. Also [17] use multi-context logic whereas we stick to (multi-)modal logic.

In a sense, the work of [15] is also closely related to the work reported here. However, they concentrate on the reasoning part of how to construct a multi-agent plan, while we concentrate on the actual mechanism to establish the team after the agent has decided which plan to execute and which agents should be involved in that plan.

Our work is also related to that of [16] in that they also try to model communication as actions and not just information exchange. The context they use is that of delegation, which makes it almost complementary to our setting. They emphasize responsibilities of agents and organizational aspects to warrant the execution of a delegated task. We assume (in our setting) that tasks cannot just be delegated to other agents, but that the agents have to be persuaded to perform the task.

The emphasis on pre-planning (here in the stage of potential recognition) and establishing appropriate collective attitudes for teamwork is shared with [13]. Nevertheless, the intentional component in their definition of collective plans is much weaker than our collective intention: Grosz and Kraus' agents involved in a collective plan have individual intentions towards the overall goal and a collective belief about these intentions; intentions with respect to the other agents play a part only at the level of individual sub-actions of the collective plan. We stress, however, that team members' intentions about their colleagues' motivation to achieve the overall goal play an important role in keeping the team on track even if their plan has to be changed radically due to a changing environment (see also [9]).

The first issue for further research is to give a complete set of formal rules for all the types of dialogue and indicate how these are implemented through formal speech acts. This would make it possible to extend the framework to the next stages of cooperative problem solving, namely plan formation and execution.

A second issue is the further investigation of several aspects of the internal reasoning of the agents. One example is the concept of giving a proof as defense of an assertion during the rigorous persuasion. Finally, it should be investigated how actual proofs can be constructed in an efficient way to prove that the end results of a dialogue are formed through the speech acts given the rules of the dialogue.

**Acknowledgments.** We would like to thank Alexandru Baltag, Magnus Boman, Wiebe van der Hoek, Chris Reed, and the anonymous referees for their useful comments. Barbara Dunin-Kęplicz' research was supported by ESPRIT under the Grant CRIT-2 No. 20288.

# References

1. L. Aaqvist. Deontic logic. In: D. Gabbay and F. Guenthner (eds.), *Handbook of Philosophical Logic*, Vol. III, Reidel, Dordrecht, 1984, pp. 605–714.
2. C. Boutilier. Toward a logic for qualitative decision theory. In: *Proceedings KR'94*, 1994, pp. 75-86.
3. C. Castelfranchi and Y.-H. Tan (eds.). *Trust and deception in virtual societies*, Kluwer, Dordrecht, 2000.
4. F. Dignum and R. Conte. Intentional agents and goal formation. In: M. Singh et. al.(eds.), *Intelligent Agents IV (LNAI 1365)*, Springer Verlag, 1998, pp. 231–244.
5. F. Dignum, B. Dunin-Kęplicz, and R. Verbrugge. Dialogue in team formation: a formal approach. In: F. Dignum and B. Chaib-draa (eds.), *IJCAI Workshop on Agent Communication Languages*, Stockholm, 1999, pp. 39–50.
6. F. Dignum and R. Kuiper. Combining dynamic deontic logic and temporal logic for the specification of deadlines. In: Jr. R. Sprague (ed.), *Proceedings of thirtieth HICSS*, Wailea, Hawaii, 1997.
7. F. Dignum and H. Weigand. Communication and deontic logic. In: R. Wieringa and R. Feenstra (eds.), *Information Systems, Correctness and Reusability*, World Scientific, Singapore, 1995, pp. 242–260.
8. B. Dunin-Kęplicz and R. Verbrugge. Collective commitments. In: *Proc. Second International Conference on Multi-Agent Systems, ICMAS'96*, IEEE Computer Society Press, Kyoto, 1996, pp. 56–63.
9. B. Dunin-Kęplicz and R. Verbrugge. A Reconfiguration algorithm for distributed problem solving. In: *Journal of Electronic Modeling*, vol. 22, nr 2, 2000, pp. 68-86.
10. B. Dunin-Kęplicz and R. Verbrugge. Collective motivational attitudes in cooperative problem solving. In: V. Gorodetsky et al. (eds.), *Proceedings of The First International Workshop of Central and Eastern Europe on Multi-agent Systems (CEEMAS'99)*, St. Petersburg, 1999, pp. 22–41.
11. B. Dunin-Kęplicz and R. Verbrugge. The role of dialogue in collective problem solving. In: Mathias Petsch and Brian Lees (eds.) *Proceedings Workshop Intelligent Agents for Computer Supported Co-operative Work: Technology and Risks*, Barcelona, June 2000, pp. 1-8.
12. R. Fagin, J.Y. Halpern, Y. Moses, and M.Y. Vardi. *Reasoning about Knowledge*. MIT Press, Cambridge (MA), 1995.
13. B.J. Grosz and S. Kraus. Collaborative plans for group action. *Artificial Intelligence* 86 (1996) pp. 269-357.
14. B. van Linder, W. van der Hoek, and J.-J. Ch. Meyer. Formalising abilities and opportunities of agents. *Fundamenta Informaticae* 34 (1998) pp. 53-101.
15. M. Luck and M. d'Inverno. Plan analysis for autonomous sociological agents. In C. Castelfranchi and Y. Lespérance, editors, *Intelligent Agents VII. Agent Theories, Architectures and Languages-7th. International Workshop, ATAL-2000, Boston, MA, USA, July 7-9, 2000, Proceedings*, Lecture Notes in Artificial Intelligence. Springer-Verlag, Berlin, 2001. In this volume.
16. T. Norman and C. Reed. Delegation and responsibility. In C. Castelfranchi and Y. Lespérance, editors, *Intelligent Agents VII. Agent Theories, Architectures and Languages-7th. International Workshop, ATAL-2000, Boston, MA, USA, July 7-9, 2000, Proceedings*, Lecture Notes in Artificial Intelligence. Springer-Verlag, Berlin, 2001. In this volume.
17. S. Parsons, C. Sierra, and N. Jennings. Agents that reason and negotiate by arguing. *Journal of Logic and Computation*, 8(3) (1998), pp. 261-292.
18. T. Sandholm and V. Lesser. Issues in automated negotiation and electronic commerce: extending the contract net protocol. In: *Proceedings First International Conference on Multiagent Systems (ICMAS95)*, San Francisco, AAAI Press and MIT Press, 1995, pp. 328-335.

19. J.R. Searle and D. Vanderveken *Foundations of Illocutionary Logic*, Cambridge, Cambridge University Press, 1985.
20. A.S. Rao and M.P. Georgeff. Modeling rational agents within a BDI architecture. In: R. Fikes and E. Sandewall (eds.), *Proceedings of Knowledge Representation and Reasoning (KR&R-91)*, San Mateo, Morgan Kaufmann, 1991, pp.473-484.
21. D. Walton and E. Krabbe. *Commitment in Dialogue*, SUNY Press, Albany, 1995.
22. M. Wooldridge and N.R. Jennings. Cooperative Problem Solving. *Journal of Logic and Computation* 9 (4) (1999), pp. 563-592.

# Task Coordination Paradigms for Information Agents

Marian Nodine*, Damith Chandrasekara**, and Amy Unruh***

MCC, 3500 W. Balcones Ctr. Dr., Austin, TX 78759

**Abstract.** In agent systems, different (autonomous) agents collaborate to execute complex tasks. Each agent provides a set of useful capabilities, and the agent system combines these capabilities as needed to perform complex tasks, based on the requests input into the system. Agent communication languages (ACLs) allow agents to communicate with each other about how to partition these tasks, and to specify the responsibilities of the individual agents that are invoked. Current ACLs make certain assumptions about the agent system, such as the stability of the agents, the lifetime of the tasks and the intelligence of the agents in the system, etc. These assumptions are not always applicable in information-centric applications, since such agent systems contain unreliable agents, very long running tasks, agents with widely varying levels of sophistication, etc. Furthermore, not all agents may be able to support intelligent planning to work around these issues, and precanned interactions used in more component-based systems do not work well. Thus, it becomes important that proper support for task coordination be available to these agent systems. In this paper we explore issues related to coordinating large, complex, long running tasks in agent systems. We divide these issues into the following categories: tasks, roles, and conversations. We then discuss how these issues impose requirements on ACL, and propose changes to support these requirements.

## 1 Introduction

Agent systems [2] are groups of agents that work together as a single system to integrate their functionality. They consist of a group or groups of agents that interoperate, cooperating to execute large complex tasks. In these agent systems each agent has the capability to perform a particular set of tasks or subtasks. To execute a larger, more complex task, an agent system composes a solution to the task from the capabilities provided by the agents in the system. Naturally, a key piece in this picture is the need for the agent system to be able to coordinate the execution of these complex tasks via the messages between agents.

Proposed agent communication language (ACL) standards include FIPA [4] and various flavors of KQML [3,6,7]. These proposals are oriented towards speech act theory. Speech acts are utterances that perform some action or request some specification. An ACL message is a representation of a speech act, and thus provides guidelines as to the

---

* Current Affiliation: Telcordia Technologies Austin Research Center, 106 E. 6th St., Suite 415, Austin, TX, nodine@research.telcordia.com
** Current Affiliation: Enetica, Austin, TX, damith@enetica.com
*** Current Affiliation: Easytrieve, Inc., Austin, TX, aunruh@easytrieve.com

C. Castelfranchi, Y. Lespérance (Eds.): Intelligent Agents VII, LNAI 1986, pp. 167–181, 2001.
© Springer-Verlag Berlin Heidelberg 2001

interpretation of its contents. This facilitates openness by providing a structure on which patterns of discourse can be defined. These ACLs, while well-suited to knowledge-based applications, make certain assumptions about the system, such as:

1. The agents are stable, and therefore the set of available agents is stable, relative to the tasks that are input into the agent system.
2. Related to the above, the lifespan of the tasks are assumed to be much smaller than the lifespans of the agents that execute the tasks.
3. The agents have a certain level of intelligence, that allows them to reason to some degree about the other agents.
4. Tasks are service-oriented, so communication occurs in a request-response manner.

In this paper, we explore issues and requirements that information-centric agents place on an ACL. These agents focus their efforts on collecting, processing, analyzing, and monitoring large amounts of information, and presenting the information at appropriate levels and in appropriate ways to users interested in that information. This particular class of agent systems is interesting because of its eclecticism—cooperating information agents may span a wide range of capabilities, from simple file-accessing agents to agents implementing mathematically-intensive analytical tasks to intelligent agents with sophisticated reasoning engines. We note, however, that the issues we discuss are not necessarily confined to information-centric agent systems. Information-centric agents have several issues that clash with the above assumptions, including:

1. Long-running tasks may easily outlive the agents they run on.
2. Many of the agents do not incorporate any kind of reasoning mechanism.
3. Agents may be mobile, going to the information as opposed to pulling the information to themselves.
4. Communication may be sporadic and task-related, and may not follow a request-response paradigm.

The issues we address here have emerged from our extensive experiences with the InfoSleuth™ [1,8,10] system, an information-centric agent system that has been under development for over five years and in use for the last four years. Recently, we have begun to develop long-running tasks in the areas of competitive intelligence and genomic research. These tasks have placed unforeseen strains on both our agents and our ACL. Our issues both synergize with and extend some of the issues we had with shorter-lived, information-centric applications as discussed in Nodine et.al. [9].

We continue this paper with a discussion about terminology related to tasks and conversations within an agent system. This terminology serves as a framework for the discussions in the rest of this paper. We then discuss some language requirements for supporting *abstract tasks*, *tasks*, *roles* and *conversations* within agent systems. Following this, we note some impedance mismatch issues that come up in any eclectic agent system, and their impact on the ACL and on the agents themselves.

## 2   Terminology

We will begin with a set of definitions for terms about tasks in agent systems.

## 2.1  Tasks

In an agent system, a task is executed by multiple cooperating agents. The types of tasks that an agent system can execute are called *abstract tasks*, and are composed of a set of *abstract subtasks* that communicate among themselves using an *extended conversation*. The abstract subtasks form a hierarchy within the abstract task.

An abstract task is instantiated into a *task* by specifying some input from a user or external process. This instantiation can be either *fixed* at the time the input is received, or *emergent*, becoming defined from the context as the task execution unfolds in the agent system. Emergence is affected by the tasks themselves and the nature of the agents that run them; for the purposes of this paper we will largely ignore how the tasks themsleves are generated, including whether or not the task is emergent.

## 2.2  Roles and Conversations

A *role* is an abstract subtask that has been partially instantiated with input parameters based on a user request. During the execution of a task, roles within the task are further instantiated by taking information derived from the specific user input and using this information as input to a relevant abstract subtask. Different roles may be initiated and terminated as a task progresses; thus both tasks and roles occupy specific spans of *time*. Furthermore, both the task and its different roles potentially access various subsets of both the request and the environment the task is running in; this is the role's *space*. The task's space-time is naturally a superset of the space-time of all of its roles.

Within the agent system, different agents have different capabilities, and every role in the system (hopefully) corresponds to one or more agents' capabilities. An agent is assigned to a role by some (other) agent when there is a need for the role to execute, one of the agents' capabilities matches that role, and there is no other agent currently executing that role in the given space-time. This assignment may be done in a variety of ways. Once a role is assigned to some agent, we call the instantiation of that role on that agent an *activity*.

The roles in an agent system need to communicate with each other to coordinate the execution of a task. The set of all the communications regarding the task is the tasks' *extended conversation*. The extended conversation is broken up (conceptually) into a set of interrelated pairwise conversations between roles, which we call *localized conversations*. For any localized conversation, there is an *initiating role* and a *responding role*. The initiating role is the one that specified the particular (sub-)request that caused the instantiation of the responding role. A localized conversation is initiated at some point in the space-time of the initiating role, and can either be terminated explicitly or end implicitly when one of its roles terminates.

## 2.3  Activities

In an agent system where all of the agents are stably online for the execution of all of the tasks input by the users, each role is matched up to some agent in the system, and the localized conversations can be handled as structured exchanges of messages between the agents. However, there are agent systems where tasks are long-lived, often existing beyond the lifetimes of the agents that may be implementing the different roles. This may be because the agents are mobile (occasionally going offline to move), or they are unreliable (occasionally exiting precipitously), or they are inherently short-lived (due to the architecture of the agent system). In this case, a role is likely to execute on different agents in different areas of space-time, as a set of activities. If the role has multiple activities running at a given time, they must agree on how to partition the space of the role for the time they are running concurrently. If an activity is assigned to an agent that is online, then the activity is online and its role is online; otherwise, if the agent is offline, the activity is offline. If a role has only offline activities, then the role itself is offline. If a role is assigned to no agent at all, and the current time is within the time of the role, then the role is unassigned. Thus, a role can be in one of three states at any point in its life: *unassigned*, *offline*, or *online*.

### 2.4 Example

Suppose we have an agent system that supports an abstract subscription task that operates as follows: a user connects to the system via a *portal agent*, and specifies some subscription. The portal agent forwards the subscription to an agent capable of doing subscriptions. The class of subscription agents in the agent system executes the subscription by periodically querying for the information used to implement the subscription, and forwarding any change notifications. This means that periodically it looks for some information fusion agent that can merge information from different resources, and poses a query to it. The information fusion agent operates by decomposing the query, locating resource agents that can access databases for the query fragments, and forwarding the query fragments to those resource agents. It then merges the information and returns a response to the subscription agent. The subscription agent then computes the difference from the last query and forwards the results to the portal, which transmits them to the user. This is the abstract task.

Suppose we have a user Fred, who is interested in subscribing to information about companies that are developing recycling technologies. Since this is a subscription task that can be handled by the system, Fred's request instantiates a task based on the abstract subscription task. Each subtask in the abstract task gets mapped to one or more roles in the actual task, where each role is responsible for some piece of the input request (based on the nature of the subtask it is instantiated from).

As the task executes, each of the roles must be assigned as needed to capable agents. The matching process locates an agent that has the capability to execute a role, and starts up that role as an activity on that agent. This match may be time-dependent, in that the same role may be assigned to different agents at different times. At the current time $T$, the agents involved in the task are FredPortal, SubagentB, MQRelational1, CompanyResource and RecyclingResource. This scenario is summarized in Table 1.

## 3   Abstract Tasks (and Agent Capabilities)

Abstract tasks define the kind of work that a particular agent-based system can do. An abstract task consists of a set of abstract subtasks and the localized conversation types that

**Table 1.** Example abstract subtasks, roles, activities

| Abstract Subtasks (subscription) | Roles (Fred's request) | Activities (Fred's request Time T) |
|---|---|---|
| Portal Subtask | Portal Connected to Fred | FredPortal initiating subscription |
| Subscription Subtask | Subscription to Companies developing recycling technology | SubagentB executing that subscription and sending out queries |
| Information Fusion Subtask | Query fusing company information with recycling technology information | MQRelational1 decomposing the current query into subqueries for company information and recycling technology information |
| Database Access Subtask | Query for company information | CompanyResource retrieving company information |
| | Query for recycling technology companies | RecyclingResource retrieving recycling technology information |

link pairs of abstract subtasks. Note that these abstract tasks are arranged hierarchically, with some abstract tasks initiating and governing other abstract tasks.

The nature of the abstract tasks that an agent system can do is directly related to the capabilities of the agents within the agent system, in that for each abstract subtask there must be some agent in the agent system that has the capability of executing that type of subtask. The abstract subtask hierarchy of an abstract task mimics the patterns of interaction among these capabilities, because the different capabilities require help from other capabilities to fulfill their tasks. For instance, in our example from the previous section, the capability for information fusion in this case requires access to other agents that have the capability of database access.

# 4  Tasks

Tasks, with their associated roles and localized conversations, are instantiated based on some input request to the agent system. Recall that the extended conversation related to a task is the collection of localized conversations among the different roles in the task. The extended conversations associated with the different tasks can either follow deterministic interaction patterns among the capabilities in the system, or can emerge as the execution of each instance of the abstract task unfolds. For example, in the restricted scenario in the introduction, the interaction pattern associated with the abstract task is deterministic, in that its basic structure is known before it is instantiated into any tasks. Some agent(s) with the portal capability subscribes to some agent(s) with the subscription capability; each such agent in turn periodically queries some agent(s) with the information fusion capability. Each agent with the information fusion capability queries one or more agents with the database access capability (specifically, the set of all the database access agents that, at the given time, can provide information related to the query). The results are percolated back in an equally deterministic manner.

Suppose, however, that some other agent enters the system with a subscription capability that induces a different interaction pattern. The selection of which subscription agent to use happens dynamically, during the execution of a task involving subscriptions, at the time a particular agent is selected to fill the subscription role. If many such options exist, and some are unknown, then at any given time it will be difficult to predict how the execution of the task will unfold among the agents themselves, and the extended conversation emerges over the lifetime of the task.

### 4.1   Task Identification and Specification

An ACL needs to facilitate the management of the task-related services within the agent system. In this section, we discuss some general requirements for ACL support for tasks. Table 2 summarizes these requirements.

**Task-1: Each task in the system should have its unique identifier used in all messages pertaining to that task.**

From the perspective of a role within a task, the role may be responding to some localized conversation, and initiating one or more localized conversations. An ACL needs to support the ability to relate all conversations related to a specific role, especially if the task is monitored and/or controlled externally. To facilitate this, there should be some easy way of correlating all localized conversations with their roles; for instance, by associating a task identifier with all the task's messages and roles.

**Task-2: The ACL should support the ability in responses to explain what the response contains, where the response came from and how it was derived.**

One issue that comes up immediately in an agent system where different agents can come and go is that the same sort of task may be executed at different times using different sets of agents, and potentially returning different results. For instance, if an agent with the information fusion capability executes the same query at two separate times, it may get different results because the underlying database resources have changed. This may in turn affect the remainder of the task. As a consequence, results may be incomplete or inconsistent with the user's expectations. Therefore, for any type of task in a dynamic system, it may be important that it have the capability to return results with an associated *pedigree* to aid the requestor in determining where the result came from. Additionally, the result possibly might contain an *explanation* for what was done and not done with respect to the task. Ideas related to this have been explored, for instance, in Tomasic et.al.'s DISCO [11] system. Responses also should be able to be annotated with support for using or viewing that information; for instance, it may recommend that large amounts of numerical data be displayed as a graph or scatter plot.

Thus we see four aspects of support, one for requesting the type of support, and three for support returned with a result: its pedigree, its explanation, and its viewing annotations. The user should be able to specify which of these are needed, and this information should be able to be propagated to all the roles that are cooperating to execute the task. Table 2 includes required message properties to implement these options.

**Table 2.** Message properties related to task identification and specification.

| Property | Value semantics | Requirement |
|---|---|---|
| `:task-id` | unique task identifier | **Task-1** |
| `:request-annotations` | pedigree, explanation and/or viewing-annotation | **Task-2** |
| `:pedigree` | list of resources | **Task-2** |
| `:explanation` | explanation | **Task-2** |
| `:viewing-annotation` | annotation information | **Task-2** |

### 4.2   Task Monitoring and Control

There is a certain amount of monitoring and control that must be done at the task level to ensure the overall correct operation of the task as well as recovery when some unexpected event related to the task occurs. Note that all messages pertaining to the task should contain the task identifier, as specified in Requirement **Task-1**.

Task monitoring can either be done internally to the roles in the task, or externally using a specialist monitoring agent. Task monitoring requires that the agent system be able to supply information about task status and about the agents that are currently executing the different activities current in the task. This leads to the following requirements, summarized in the speech acts of Table 3:

**Task-3: All agents in the agent system should be able to respond to pinging for online status, both at the agent level and at the task level.**

There are many unforeseen events that can occur during the execution of a task. In a dynamic agent system, with potentially unreliable agents, one type of event that needs to be watched for is the unexpected failure of an agent or a specific activity. Usually, such failures are not accompanied by neat notifications, but must instead be detected by either the roles that are communicating with the activity, or by the monitoring agent. Pinging allows a role to generically ask whether some agent or activity is still running and responding. The `ping` speech act required to implement this is shown in Table 3.

**Task-4: The agent system should be able to respond to queries on task status.**

While a task is executing, there are several different entities that may be monitoring the task status and progress, including the user, the roles in the task, some monitoring or control agent, etc. For example, some long-running consumer role may be monitoring the progress of another role that feeds information to it. When there is no information available from the role producing the information, the consumer waits for the producer to produce some. Alternatively, a control agent may want to monitor how fast the role is progressing and whether it is falling behind, and move the role to a different agent if it suspects that this would cause an improvement.

**Task-5: The ACL should support the ability for tasks to control their roles and localized conversations, at the level of {initiate, start, stop, terminate} the role.**

As with task monitoring, task control may either be done internally to the roles in the task, or externally using an explicit control agent. At a minimum, the ACL must support issues related to setting up, starting and running long-running roles, and dealing with unexpected events by terminating or adjusting roles to deal with unforeseen circumstances. Types of role control are summarized in Table 3.

**Table 3.** Speech acts related to task monitoring and execution.

| Speech Act | Semantics | Requirement |
|---|---|---|
| `ping` | Tell me if you are really there | Task-3 |
| `status(query)` | Return the status information as requested by the query | Task-4 |
| `error(explanation)` | Indicates an error in the initiator that affects the role | Task-4 |
| `initiate (parameters)` | Set the role up to be ready to run | Task-5 |
| `start` | Begin executing the role | Task-5 |
| `stop` | Stop executing the role | Task-5 |
| `terminate` | Tear down the role so it is no longer ready to run | Task-5 |

### 4.3    Dealing with Instability at the Task Level

Instability issues arise when the task, and the roles that comprise the task, outlive or outgrow the agents that the roles are running on. Several requirements spring from the need to run these long-lived tasks, including:

**Task-6: If the task has roles that can go offline, the task should provide each such role with persistent storage space for saving task status (we call this a *locker*), and a method for leaving messages for the role (we call this a *mailbox*).**

If an activity has the potential to go offline, either expectedly or unexpectedly, then the task itself must provide information to enable the new activity to continue where the previous activity let off. One step in enabling a role to be taken offline is to provide it with a known location for saving any status information and intermediate state associated with the role. When a new agent picks up the role, it then knows exactly where to look for this information as it starts up. A second issue is that the role itself may be receiving messages while it is offline. These messages must be placed in some known mailbox as well, so that the role can process the messages that were received, in the order they were received. This ability to store up inputs and state is a necessary precondition for continuing the role seamlessly on the new agent.

**Task-7: The ACL should support the ability to suspend (take offline) a role, and later continue it under specified conditions, perhaps on another agent.**

Given that a role is suspendable and movable, and that the role itself is being controlled either by some control agent or by the role that initiated it, there must be some form of ACL support to enable the appropriate requests to be passed to the role itself. These messages need not contain information about the role, as that information can be retrieved from the role's locker and mailbox by the new activity, at its start-up time. New speech acts to support these features are shown in Table 4.

If a role can be suspended/continued or moved, then the control structure for the task may need to take on the job of determining when this role should be brought online. Factors involved in determining this timing include whether there is unproecessed input to the role, whether there are available agents to execute the role, and whether the timing is correct with respect to other roles in the task or other tasks in the agent system. Note that the suspension request may go from the agent running the activity to the initiating role, informing that role of when its continuation is appropriate.

**Task-8: The ACL should support the ability to reconfigure a role.**

**Table 4.** Speech acts related to controlling roles.

| Speech Act | Semantics | Requirement |
|---|---|---|
| `suspend(conditions)` | Suspend executing the role, take it offline until the conditions are met. | **Task-7** |
| `continue` | Continue operation, placing role online on a given agent | **Task-7** |
| `move(agent)` | Move the role from one agent to another | **Task-7** |
| `reconfigure(parms)` | Reconfigure the role for slightly different operation | **Task-8** |

One additional tactic to deal with unreliable and bursty operation is to replicate and/or partition the role to run over several agents. Also, if a task is not operating as expected or needed, the user may adjust its operation to optimize it. In either case, the task itself may wish to reconfigure the role's input parameters. ACL support for this requirement is shown in Table 4.

## 5  Roles

Recall that a role is an abstract subtask that has been partially instantiated with input parameters based on a user request. A role itself is fully instantiated into one or more activities by assigning it to run on one or more agents. In the previous section, we discussed issues of tasks and their related roles, and what the task needs to control the specifics of its roles and their localized conversations. In this section we deal with issues specific to roles: what information is needed to initiate them, how they are instantiated into activities, what must be done to support persistence across activities.

### 5.1  Role Initiation

**Role-1: The ACL should support the ability to specify how a role is to be executed and the results returned in its role-initiating messages.**

In an agent system, when one role asks another to execute some abstract subtask related to its request, there may be additional nuances about how the role is to be executed and how the results are to be returned. These nuances must be specified in addition to the computational inputs to that role related to the user request. For example, for all aspects of agent interaction relating to data – telling or updating, querying, and responding, there are nuances about how the information is requested or presented that should not necessarily show up at the layer of the speech act. For instance, if you want to subscribe to changes over certain information, a notification may either be sent periodically, or as soon as the information changes. The response may contain a fresh copy of all requested data, or only the changes. There are also issues related to the fact that resources may contain overlapping sets of data, and that there may be a number of relevant resources available, containing more information than is really needed by the requester. In this situation, it is helpful to constrain the set of agents accessed, and sometimes to return a

**Table 5.** Properties related to how to execute a role.

| Property | Value semantics |
|---|---|
| :ask-policy | change in data, periodic, all the data, modifications only, etc |
| :query-effort | best effort, complete result |
| :query-context | context of query |
| :reply-out-of-band | ftp, http, etc |
| :locator | URL locator for the result |

"best effort" result as opposed to a complete result. Some of the message properties that implement these options for query-type roles are shown in Table 5.

These tags may vary depending on the nature of the role. For instance, very long-running roles need to specify how the task should execute, whether or not it can move or be suspended, etc. Short-lived roles may need no additional properties.

## 5.2   Assigning Agents to Roles

**Role-2: An agent system must supply a capability to match agents to roles that the agents can execute.**

For correct matching of an agent to a role, some agent must consider the specifics of the role itself, and the capabilities of the agents that potentially may be assigned to the role, and filter through the possible agents to locate the best fit at the current time. This process is called *matching*. There are several methods by which matching can occur, summarized in Table 6. In one method, a role that needs to initiate another role, and understands its specifics, can send requests to other agents that it knows about. Those agents in turn can try to match the role requests to their own capabilities. If they think there is a match, then they can negotiate for the role with the requester. The requester can then select among the possibilities to select the agent to match to the role.

**Table 6.** Matching possibilities.

| Role requester | (Potential) responder | Third agent | Example |
|---|---|---|---|
| Requests | Matches, responds | | Bid/propose system |
| Matches, requests | Responds | | Gossip system |
| Requests | Responds | Matches | Facilitated system |

The second method implies that each agent has a repository of agents that it knows about and their capabilities. In this case, the requesting agent compares its role request with the capabilities of the agents in its repository, and selects one that matches. The role requestor then initiates the role on that agent. This process may need to be repeated. Naturally, the success of this method depends on the ability of each agent to keep an up-to-date repository of the agents it may need. This may be done by soliciting *advertisements* from the other agents that it knows about.

The third method places that repository instead in a specialist agent, called a *facilita-tor*. The facilitator takes active steps to ensure that its repository is up-to-date, possibly relying on the agents to advertise their capabilities when they come online. The facilitator receives requests for agents with specific replies, matches specific agents to those requests, and does what is needed to ensure that the requesting agent and responding agent get connected with each other. The speech acts required to implement these three possibilities are included in Table 7.

**Table 7.** Speech acts related to matching and negotiation.

| Speech Act | Semantics | Requirement |
|---|---|---|
| `request-match` | Requests a match for a particular role. | **Role-2** |
| `advertise` | Asserts information about the agent's capabilities either for the first time, or when the agent has updated information about its capabilities. | **Role-2** **Role-4** |
| `change-status` | Indicates that the agent has changed its status. Potential status values are {online, offline, out-of-service}. | **Role-4** |
| `rfp(role)` | Request for proposals for bids on a role. | **Role-5** |
| `propose` | Propose a match to my agent | **Role-5** |
| `accept` | Accept a role. | **Role-5** |
| `refuse` | Refuse a role. | **Role-5** |

**Role-3: Advertisements and requests for roles should not be required to use a specific content language, but rather should use a language appropriate to the needs of the system. The agent system should provide an ontology that specifies the vocabulary for describing agent capabilities.**

Many matching systems have been described that deal with matching at various levels. Many of these [5,7] deal with matching at an interface level—whether the interface to the agent matches the "call" to the interface in the role. However, the interface is merely one aspect of the service, and sometimes more detail is needed about the semantics of the role being matched or the capability of the agent, or their methods for executing and returning results. The clearer the specification of an agent advertisement or a request for a match to a role, the better the matching system can be. This means that an agent must be able to describe its capabilities in more depth than just advertising its service interface. This in turn impacts the ontology of capabilities as well as the content language of the advertisement and request methods.

**Role-4: An agent should be able update or delete its advertisement.**

An agent offers up its services to an agent system by advertising itself. Later, the agent may wish to change its advertisement, or even advertise that it is going offline or shutting down. This enables other agents to keep their repositories up-to-date. The speech acts needed to implement this are shown in Table 7.

**Role-5: An agent should be able to negotiate over or refuse to execute an activity.**

Agents are autonomous, which means that an initiating agent cannot assume that it can just tell an agent to take on a role, but rather it must request that the agent take the role. The responding agent in turn must have the option of being able to interact with the requesting agent over the terms and conditions under which it will execute the role. Thus, the ACL must support the ability to negotiate about roles with agents that it has matched. The speech acts in the ACL needed to implement this are shown in Table 7.

**Role-6: Roles should respond correctly to control directives from the task.**

The task model implied by the agent communication implies that the role should be able to respond to appropriate directives at any time, including both before it receives any results, during the middle of the computation, and during the transmission of results. For many short-lived roles such as responding to short queries for information, the expected control directives may be very simple. However, other long-lived tasks may need to deal with more complex control directives.

**Role-7: Roles that can be suspended and continued or moved must support the storing of state in the role's locker, the retrieval of information from the locker and mailbox, and the continuation of the role from where it left off.**

This requirements indicate that agents with the capability to execute suspendable roles must be designed with the need for storing and recovering role state in mind. The task itself merely provides locker and mailbox space in a commonly-accessible location, but places no requirements on the agents themselves for how that space is used. The role itself must encapsulate information about how this space is used, what information is kept in it, and how to resume a task given that information. This frees the ACL from the need to define a common format for communicating role state. This is appropriate because roles may differ vastly in what state they need to save.

## 6    Localized Conversations

Localized conversations occur between roles in a task as a part of the extended conversation. A localized conversation consists of one or more activity-activity conversations, where a new activity-activity conversation is started when the role is first assigned to an agent, and every ensuing time that a role moves from one agent to another.

### 6.1    Conversation Identification

**Conv-1: The ACL should support properties for transmitting identifiers for both the localized and the activity-activity conversation.**

These identifiers are useful both in sorting the messages by conversation, in determining where to send a response, and in monitoring the operation of the task itself. KQML ignores issues of conversation identification, relying instead on message chaining. This enforces a request-response mode on the conversational structure. Suppose however there are requirements for other sorts of modes of interaction, such the ability to cancel a long-running request before a response has been received. With a message-chaining conversation model, this conversation structure is at best awkward. We conclude rather that each message in the conversation should be explicitly related to a conversation, as in FIPA. However, our delineation of roles and activities requires additional identifiers.

**Table 8.** Message properties related to localized conversations.

| Property | Value semantics | Requirement |
|---|---|---|
| :local-conv-id | unique conversation identifier for localized conversation | **Conv-1** |
| :current-conv-id | unique conversation identifier for activity-activity conversation. | **Conv-1** |
| :sequence-number | identifier to place message in proper sequence in the localized conversation. | **Conv-2** |
| :sending-role | role that sent the message. | **Conv-3** |
| :sending-agent | agent that sent the message. | **Conv-3** |
| :receiving-role | role that the message is intended for. | **Conv-3** |
| :receiving-agent | agent that the message is intended for. | **Conv-3** |

### 6.2 Dealing with Instability at the Localized Conversation Level

**Conv-2: The ACL should support sequencing for messages within conversations, to ensure that messages are received in order even across agent activity transitions.**

Conversations with multiple messages add complexity and versatility to communication between agents but may be affected by incorrect message ordering. This problem is important when dealing with multimedia and internet retrieval information since the order of processing of the information in the messages becomes very important. The ACL needs to provide information for assembling the messages into the proper sequence if required, as indicated in Table 8.

While this problem certainly became apparent with large, ordered data sets in some of the early applications of InfoSleuth, it is becoming much more critical when agents can partition roles into a set of concurrent activities. It also becomes an issue when a role is taken offline for some period of time, the new activity must resume from some point in time, and some of the communication may have been lost. Then this sequence becomes important in determining from where in the execution to continue the role.

**Conv-3: The ACL should provide information about both the origin and destination roles and the origin and destination agents of the messages.**

This requires the message properties to include both the sending and receiving roles and agents, as shown in Table 8. Because the roles that sit at the ends of a localized conversation may be picked up by different agents in turn, the messages themselves should contain information on which role sent them, and where the sending role expected them to be delivered. This enables the roles to monitor when and to where a related role has moved, as well as enabling the forwarding of messages after a role has moved.

**Conv-4: Roles that can go offline must support the ability to receive messages while in the offline state, in the mailbox supplied by the task.**

Messages pertaining to some localized conversation do not necessarily get sent between the same two agents for the lifetime of the localized conversation, as different agents can assume the same role during the role's lifetime. In fact, at any given time, one or both of the roles involved in the conversation may be offline. Table 9 summarizes the various combinations of role states and the possible message-sending options. In addition to the use of a mailbox, the table also incorporates the alternatives of (1) posting

**Table 9.** Message sending options.

| Sending role | Receiving role | Localized conv. status | Message passing possibilities |
|---|---|---|---|
| online | online | online | Any |
| online | offline | partially offline | mailbox, blackboard |
| online | unassigned | partially offline | mailbox, blackboard, start an agent |
| offline or unassigned | online | offline | None |
| offline or unassigned | offline or unassigned | offline | None |

the message on a public blackboard to be picked up later by the role, and (2) starting a new agent to fill the role and receive the message.

## 7   Impedance Issues

Because of the eclectic nature of the agents sytems we are considering, there is not always a clean correlation between the capabilities and reliability of the agents in the system and the needs of the tasks requested of it by the users. Three separate areas where an agent system may encounter such impedance mismatches are:

*Capability mismatch.* The capabilities of the available agents may not exactly cover the roles needed to execute the task or the advertisements may not provide enough information to determine whether or not the agent can execute the task. This is detected when some agent attempts to assign some role to some other agent, but fails to locate an agent that can fill the role. In this case, either the agent assigning the role must either select an agent to fill the role that is "close enough", and provide some sort of glue functionality to compensate for the inadequacies, or fail to complete the task. If similar inadequacies occur across different tasks, this may indicate that either a new agent type needs to be inserted into the agent system or some existing agent needs to be enhanced.

*Localized conversation mismatch.* The localized conversations supported by the agents may not match the needs of the localized conversations between roles. This is detected when an agent looks inside its localized conversational model, and determines that its conversation support is inadequate. This can be, for example, as a consequence of trying to build more sophisticated behavior over less sophisticated behavior, such as implementing complex conversations over distributed object systems. In this case, the agents themselves may need to be designed to incorporate the intended conversational policy, and maintain conversational states and support mechanisms internally.

*Stability mismatch.* The stability of the individual agents may not match the stability needs of the roles that run on them. This happens when the application itself requires more stability than the agents that support it. This would occur, for example, if some task requires 24 hour a day, 7 day a week stability, and the computers the agents are running on are unreliable. In this case, also, the agent capabilities must include the ability to restart roles over agent failure by reassigning roles and by enabling task persistence through the saving and restoring of state.

## 8   Conclusions

In this paper we discussed task coordination for agent based systems. Task coordination requires support at two levels: one within the implementation of the agents themselves, and one within the ACL. In this paper, we present requirements that apply to agents and ACLs, based on our experiences in InfoSleuth running information-centric tasks.

We define a *task* as a collection of *roles* that can be instantiated on agents, and a set of conversations among those roles, used for coordination and information transfer. As tasks, and some of the roles that implement them, have the potential to outlive the agents running them, we define *activities* as the instantiations of a task's roles on specific agents at a given time. A particular role may execute as different activities on different agents at different times during its lifetime.

In this paper, we also discussed issues related to supporting the coordination of these large, complex, and possibly long running tasks. Current conversation support in ACLs is insufficient to support the communication necessary to execute these types of tasks. The key contribution of this paper is the suggestion of a general paradigm for decomposing and chaining together tasks, and a set of requirements for an ACL that support this paradigm.

## References

1. R. Bayardo et al. Semantic integration of information in open and dynamic environments. In *Proc. ACM SIGMOD Int'l Conf. on Management of Data*. ACM Press, 1997.
2. Jeffrey M. Bradshaw. An introduction to software agents. In J. Bradshaw, editor, *Software Agents*, chapter 1. MIT Press, AAAI Press, 1997.
3. T. Finin and G. Wiederhold. An overview of KQML: A knowledge query and manipulation language, 1991. (Available through the Stanford University Computer Science Department.).
4. FIPA. http://www.fipa.org.
5. Object Management Group and X/Open. *The Common Object Request Broker: Architecture and Specification, Revision 1.1*. John Wiley and Sons, 1992.
6. Y. Labrou. *Semantics for an Agent Communication Language*. PhD thesis, University of Maryland at Baltimore County, September 1996.
7. Y. Labrou and T. Finin. A proposal for a new KQML specification, 1997. http://www.cs.umbc.edu/kqml/kqmlspec.ps.
8. M. Nodine and A. Unruh. Facilitating open communication in agent systems. In Munindar Singh, Anand Rao, and Michael Wooldridge, editors, *Intelligent Agents IV: Agent Theories, Architectures, and Languages*. Springer-Verlag, 1998.
9. Marian Nodine and Damith Chandrasekhara.  Agent communication languages for information-centric agent communities. In *Proc. Hawaii Int'l Conf. on System Sciences*, 1999.
10. Marian Nodine et al. Active information gathering in InfoSleuth. *Int'l Journal of Cooperative Information Systems*, 9(1/2):3–28, 2000.
11. A. Tomasic, L. Raschid, and P. Valduriez. Scaling heterogeneous databases and the design of DISCO. In *Proc. Int'l Conf. of Distributed Computing Systems*, pages 449–457, 1996.

# Plan Analysis for Autonomous Sociological Agents

Michael Luck[1] and Mark d'Inverno[2]

[1] Dept of Electronics and Computer Science, University of Southampton, SO17 1BJ, UK
mml@ecs.soton.ac.uk
[2] Cavendish School of Computer Science, Westminster University, London W1M 8JS, UK
dinverm@westminster.ac.uk

**Abstract.** This paper is concerned with the problem of how effective social interaction arises from individual social action and mind. The need to study the *individual social mind* suggests a move towards the notion of *sociological* agents who can *model* their social environment as opposed to acting socially within it. This does not constrain social behaviour; on the contrary, we argue that it provides the requisite information and understanding for such behaviour to be effective. Indeed, it is not enough for agents to model other agents in isolation; they must also model the relationships between them. A *sociological agent* is thus an agent that can model agents *and* agent relationships. Several existing models use notions of autonomy and dependence to show how this kind of interaction comes about, but the level of analysis is limited. In this paper, we show how an existing agent framework leads naturally to the enumeration of a map of inter-agent relationships that can be modelled and exploited by sociological agents to enable more effective operation, especially in the context of multi-agent plans.

## 1  Introduction

Underlying all multi-agent systems are the notions of interaction and cooperation. Much research in the area of intelligent agents has thus sought to develop computational mechanisms for bringing about and sustaining these relationships in a dynamic and open world. The focus on mechanisms is just one part of the set of areas for investigation, however, and a separate and distinct strand of work aims to provide an understanding of the relationships themselves and how agents may influence each other through these relationships over the course of time. Over a number of years, one such effort has been in the work of Castelfranchi and Conte, which has focussed on issues relating to the *social foundations* of multi-agent systems. For example, they point out that the problem of how to allocate tasks and resources and how to coordinate actions is typically raised only after a collective or social problem or goal is assumed [3]. One key question in consideration of this is *how society is implemented in the minds of social agents*.

There are many definitions of a *social* agent. For example, Wooldridge states that any agent in a multi-agent system is necessarily social [14] and Moulin and Chaib-draa [10] take an agent to be social if it can model others. However, the term is more often associated with social *activity* such as provided by Wooldridge and Jennings [15] who refer to the process of interaction. Yet the need to study the *individual social mind* suggests a move towards the notion of *sociological* agents who can *model* their social environment as

C. Castelfranchi, Y. Lespérance (Eds.): Intelligent Agents VII, LNAI 1986, pp. 182–197, 2001.
© Springer-Verlag Berlin Heidelberg 2001

opposed to acting socially within it. This does not constrain social behaviour; on the contrary, we argue that it provides the requisite information and understanding for such behaviour to be effective. We argue that effective social agents must be sociological. These notions are implicit in the work of Castelfranchi, in particular, which has led to the construction and refinement of a theory of social relationships based on notions of inter-agent dependence[2,4]. Taking as a base his Social Power Theory (SPT), he has sought to provide a computational model of autonomy and inter-agent relationships through the Social Dependence Networks (SDN)[12] that implement the constructs of SPT.

The point of this work is to identify dependence situations in which one agent depends on another for actions or resources, or is autonomous with respect to these components, according to a particular plan. Using these notions of dependence, the *negotiation power* of an agent can be found to represent how well an agent can sell itself on a market. Underlying this very powerful theory are plans, yet the analyses possible, while revealing certain information about inter-agent relationships, are still rather crude. In order to provide a more detailed and precise account of these dependencies, further analysis is required. SDN provides the motivation from a very particular perspective for considering agent plans, while more general social interaction provides a broader base of direction.

It is not enough for agents to model other agents in isolation; they must also model the relationships between them. A *sociological agent* is an agent that can model agents *and* agent relationships. In this paper, we show how an existing agent framework leads naturally to the enumeration of a map of inter-agent relationships that can be modelled and exploited by sociological agents to enable more effective operation, especially in the context of multi-agent plans. Importantly, the resulting strong model of individual agents could be applied to clarify several issues in SDN. Constraints of space, however, limit the potential for showing the particular impact on SDN, but we illustrate the potential benefits of the analysis with a detailed example at the end. The paper begins with a brief review of an agent framework and the relationships that arise within it, and then proceeds to provide a detailed description of single and multi-agent plans, identifying useful categories of plans and agents.

## 2   Preliminaries

**Agent Framework.** Elsewhere, we have presented an agent framework to define entities, objects, agents and autonomous agents. Below we provide a brief overview of the main aspects of the framework [6,8], and the relationships that arise within it [9], but we omit a detailed exposition. We use the Z notation [13] to formalise these notions and, though we assume some familiarity, the meaning should be clear.

As specified in Figure 1, an *entity* comprises a set of *motivations*, a set of *goals*, a set of *actions*, and a set of *attributes* such that the attributes and actions are non-empty. Entities can be used to group together attributes into a whole without any *functionality*. They serve as a useful abstraction mechanism by which they are regarded as distinct from the remainder of the environment, to organise perception. An *object* is then an entity with abilities that can affect the environment in which it is situated. Now, an *agent* is just an object either that is useful to another agent in terms of satisfying that agent's goals,

$Entity$
$attributes : \mathbb{P} \, Attribute$
$capabilities : \mathbb{P} \, Action$
$goals : \mathbb{P} \, Goal$
$motivations : \mathbb{P} \, Motivation$

$attributes \neq \{ \, \}$

$Object == [Entity \mid capableof \neq \{ \, \}]$
$Agent == [Object \mid goals \neq \{ \, \}]$

$AutoAgent == [Agent \mid motivations \neq \{ \, \}]$
$NeutralObject == [Object \mid goals = \{\}]$
$ServerAgent == [Agent \mid motivations = \{\}]$

$MultiAgentSystem$
$entities : \mathbb{P} \, Entity$
$objects : \mathbb{P} \, Object$
$agents : \mathbb{P} \, Agent$
$autonomousagents : \mathbb{P} \, AutoAgent$
$neutralobjects : \mathbb{P} \, NeutralObject$
$serveragents : \mathbb{P} \, ServerAgent$

**Fig. 1.** Formal specification of the agent framework

or that exhibits independent purposeful behaviour. In other words, an agent is an object with an associated set of goals, but one object may give rise to different instantiations of agents with different goals. This notion of agency relies upon the existence of other agents to provide the goals that are adopted to instantiate an agent. In order to escape an infinite regress of goal adoption, however, we can define *autonomous agents*, which are just agents that generate their own goals from motivations (not dissimilar to Antunes's notion of values [1]). We can also distinguish objects that are not agents, and agents that are not autonomous, as *neutral-objects* and *server-agents* respectively. An agent is then either a server-agent or an autonomous agent, and an object is either a neutral-object or an agent, and a multi-agent system simply contains a collection of these entities.

**Agent Relations.** When an agent uses another non-autonomous entity, the entity adopts or satisfies the agent's goals and creates a *social* relationship [2] known as an *engagement*. In a *direct engagement*, a neutral-object or a server-agent adopts the goals of another. Chains of engagements are also possible, explicitly representing the goal and all the agents involved in the sequence of direct engagements. Since goals are grounded by motivations, the agent at the head of the chain must be autonomous.

Now, since it can generate its goals and decide when to adopt the goals of others, an autonomous agent is said to be *cooperating* with another autonomous agent if it has adopted the goal or goals of the other. This notion of autonomous goal acquisition applies both to the origination of goals by an autonomous agent for its own purposes, and the *adoption* of goals from others. A *cooperation* describes a goal, the autonomous agent that generated the goal, and those autonomous agents who have adopted that goal from the generating agent. (At any point in time, such autonomous agents may then be cooperating with others as well as attempting to satisfy their own self-motivated goals.) Further details of these relationships, specified in Figure 2, may be found elsewhere [9].

These inter-agent relationships are not imposed, but arise naturally from our view of agents as they interact (regardless of the manner of their initiation) and therefore underlie all multi-agent systems. They provide a means for analysing the interdependence of agents in terms of the goals some agents achieve for others. Moreover, from this basic

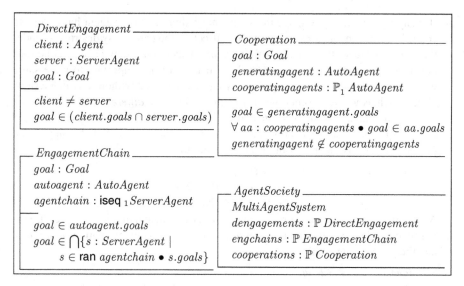

**Fig. 2.** Formal specification of agent relationships

set of constructions, we can derive a detailed map of the relationships between individual agents for a better understanding of their current social interdependence. In particular, different situations of interdependence each suggest different possibilities for interaction. Below, we enumerate the various possible relations that might result in this view. Each relation is described and defined formally.

- The direct engagement relationship specifies the situation in which there is a direct engagement for which the first agent is the client and the second agent is the server. Thus, an agent, $c$, *directly engages* another server-agent, $s$, if, and only if, there is a direct engagement between $c$ and $s$.

$$\forall c : Agent;\ s : ServerAgent \bullet (c, s) \in dengages \Leftrightarrow$$
$$\exists d : dengagements \bullet d.client = c \wedge d.server = s$$

- The notion of direct engagement implies a tight coupling between the behaviours of the agents involved without an intermediate entity. However, there may be entities an agent engages that indirectly serve some purpose for it. An agent $c$ *engages* another (server) agent $s$ if there is some engagement chain $ec$ that includes $s$, such that either $c$ is *before* $s$ in the chain or $c$ is the autonomous agent of $ec$. (This requires the *before* relation, which holds between a pair of elements and a sequence of elements if the first element of the pair precedes the second element in the sequence. The details are omitted here.)

$$\forall c : Agent, s : ServerAgent \bullet (c, s) \in engages \Leftrightarrow$$
$$\exists ec : engchains \bullet (s \in (\mathsf{ran}\ ec.agentchain) \wedge c = ec.autoagent) \vee$$
$$(((c, s), ec.agentchain) \in before)$$

- To distinguish engagements involving an intermediate agent we introduce the indirect engagement relation *indengages*. An agent *indirectly* engages another if it engages it, but does not *directly* engage it.

$$indengages = engages \setminus dengages$$

- If many agents directly engage the same entity, then no single agent has complete control over it. Any actions an agent takes affecting the entity may destroy or hinder the engagements of the other engaging agents. This in turn, may have a deleterious effect on the engaging agents themselves. It is therefore important to understand *when* the behaviour of an engaged entity can be modified without any deleterious effect (such as when no other agent uses the entity for a *different* purpose). In this case we say that the agent *owns* the entity. An agent, $c$, owns another agent, $s$, if, for every sequence of server-agents in an engagement chain, $ec$, in which $s$ appears, $c$ precedes it, or $c$ is the autonomous client-agent that initiated the chain.

$$\forall \, c : Agent; \; s : ServerAgent \bullet (c, s) \in owns \Leftrightarrow$$
$$(\forall \, ec : engchains \mid s \in \mathsf{ran} \; ec.agentchain \bullet$$
$$ec.autoagent = c \; \vee \; ((c, s), ec.agentchain) \in before)$$

- An agent, $c$, *directly owns* another agent, $s$, if it owns it, and directly engages it. Formally, this relation is the intersection of the direct engagement relation, *dengages*, and the generic ownership relation, *owns*.

$$downs = owns \cap dengages$$

- A further distinction of direct ownership can be made. Either no other agent directly owns the entity, or there is another agent who is also directly engaging that entity for the same purpose. The first case occurs normally but the second situation can occur if the entity is engaged by two agents, each for the same purpose as generated by a single autonomous agent. To distinguish these situations we define the *uniquely owns* relation, which holds when an agent *directly* and *solely* owns another. An agent $c$ *uniquely owns* another $s$, if it directly owns it, and no other agent is engaging it.

$$\forall \, c : Agent; \; s : ServerAgent \bullet (c, s) \in uowns \Leftrightarrow$$
$$(c, s) \in downs \wedge \neg (\exists \, a : Agent \mid a \neq c \bullet (a, s) \in engages)$$

- An agent may own another with respect to either multiple distinct goals (which may conflict) or a single goal. The distinction is important because achieving one goal may affect the achievement of another. An agent, $c$, *specifically owns* another agent, $s$, if it owns it, and $c$ has only one goal.

$$\forall \, c : Agent; \; s : ServerAgent \bullet$$
$$(c, s) \in sowns \Leftrightarrow (c, s) \in owns \wedge \#(s.goals) = 1$$

- Finally, an agent, $b$, *cooperates* with agent, $a$, if and only if both agents are autonomous, and there is some cooperation in which $a$ is the generating agent and $b$ is in the set of cooperating agents. Notice that the relationship is not symmetric: if $b$ is cooperating with $a$, $a$ need not be cooperating with $b$.

$$\forall \, a, b : AutoAgent \bullet (a, b) \in cooperates \Leftrightarrow$$
$$\exists \, c : cooperations \bullet a = c.generatingagent \wedge$$
$$b \in c.cooperatingagents$$

This analysis of the relationships between *agents* provides computational entities with a means of determining how they should approach interactions with those agents. For example, if I own an entity, I can do as I please, and other agents would be ill-advised to attempt to use this entity for another purpose. If I only engage it, then I may be more constrained in my interaction and may anticipate other agents engaging it.

The framework described above, together with the relationships arising from it, are suitable for reasoning both *about* entities in the world, and *with* entities in the world. That is to say that in addition to providing us with a way of understanding and analysing agents, agents themselves can also use the entity hierarchy as a basis for reasoning about other agents within their environment. It may be relevant, for example, for them to consider the functionality of other agents and the likelihood, that these others may or may not be predisposed to help in the completion of certain tasks. In this section we describe how we enable the possibility within agents of such reasoning.

**Models.** If agents are to model their environment, they need more than just actions, goals and motivations; they require an *internal store*. Agents without internal stores are extremely limited since their past experience cannot direct behaviour, and actions can only be selected *reflexively*. A store exists as part of an agent's state in an environment but it must also have existed *prior* to that current state. We call this feature an *internal store* or *memory*, and define *store agents* as those with memories. Formally, a store-agent is a refinement of an agent, with the addition of a *store* variable represented as a non-empty set of attributes. We omit this simple schema due to space constraints.

The most obvious things to represent in such models are other agents. Thus we need to describe agents who can model others in their environment and, for sufficiently advanced agents, the autonomy of others. However, it is inadequate to model entities in isolation; the relationships between them must also be modelled. Unlike *social* agents that engage in interaction with others (or social activity), *sociological* agents also model agent relationships. It is a simple matter to define the model an agent has of another agent (*AgentModel*), or its model of a cooperation relationship (*CoopModel*) by re-using the agent framework components.

$$\ldots \textit{AgentModel} == \textit{Agent} \ldots$$
$$\ldots \textit{CoopModel} == \textit{Cooperation} \ldots$$

Even though the types of these constructs are equivalent to those presented earlier, it is useful to distinguish physical constructs from mental constructs such as models, as it provides a conceptual aid. Similarly, we can define the models agents have of entities, objects and autonomous agents as well as models of other relationships we have described (though only the model of a cooperation is given above). A sociological agent is thus specified as a refinement of the *Agent* schema.

```
┌─ SociologicalAgent ──────────────────────────────────────
│  Agent
│  ... agentmodels : ℙ AgentModel;  ... coopmodels : ℙ CoopModel ...
└───────────────────────────────────────────────────────────
```

# 3  Plans

In this section we develop our models of agents further to consider multi-agent plans. Sometimes, agents may select an action, or a set of concurrent actions, to achieve goals directly. At other times, however, there may not be such a simple correspondence between goals and actions, and appropriately designed agents may perform *sequences* of actions, or *plans*, to achieve their goals. In multi-agent systems, agents have at their disposal not only their own capabilities but, potentially, the capabilities of others. Agents with plans requiring actions outside their competence need models of others to consider making use of their capabilities. If these agents are sociological then they can evaluate plans with respect to their model of current agent relationships. For example, agents can decide to what extent plans can exploit current relationships as well as consider how they may *impinge* on them. In general, agents must reason about exploiting existing and potential relationships without inadvertently or unnecessarily destroying them.

In this work, we do not model the *process* of planning, but instead consider how plans can be modelled and how agents can evaluate plans using these models. Similar to the BDI view, we take an agent to have a repository of goals and a repository of plans that have either been designed before the agent starts executing [7] or acquired and developed over the course of the agent's life [11]. Each plan may be associated with one or more goals, identifying the plan as a potential means of achieving those goals, as used for example, by Georgeff [7].

There are many different notions of agent plans both at the theoretical and the practical level, and in order to substantiate the claim that the agent framework and ensuing models can be generally applied it is necessary that different representations of plans can all be equally accommodated. Whilst we do not specify every type of plan of which we are aware, we do intend to show *how* the agent framework can be extended to describe familiar notions of plans, and to impress upon the reader how other models of plans can be similarly accommodated. We aim to achieve this by specifying general theoretical plan representations that we call *total* plans, *partial* plans and *tree* plans.

One methodological characteristic of our work is the *incremental* development of the models in it. Therefore, we first construct a high-level model of *plan-agents*, which applies equally well to reactive or deliberative, single-agent or multi-agent, planners. It represents a high-level of abstraction because nothing is decided about the nature of the agent, the plan representation, or of the agent's environment; we simply distinguish *categories* of plan and possible relationships between an agent's plans and goals. Specifically, we define *active* plans as those identified as candidate plans not yet selected for execution; and *executable* plans as those active plans that have been selected for execution.

Formally, we initially define the set of all agent plans to be a given set ($[Plan]$), so that at this stage we abstract out any information about the nature of plans themselves. Our highest-level description of a *plan-agent* can then be formalised in the *PlanAgent* schema below. Since plans must be encoded as aspects of an internal store, the *StoreAgentState* schema is included.

---

$PlanAgent$ _____

$StoreAgent$
$goallib : \mathbb{P}\ Goal$
$planlib, activeplans, executableplans : \mathbb{P}\ Plan$
$activeplangoal, plangoallib : Goal \nrightarrow \mathbb{P}\ Plan$

---

**dom** $activeplangoal \subseteq goals \ \wedge\ \bigcup(\text{ran } activeplangoal) = activeplans$
**dom** $plangoallib \subseteq goallib \ \wedge\ \bigcup(\text{ran } plangoallib) \subseteq planlib$
$goals \subseteq goallib \ \wedge\ executableplans \subseteq activeplans \subseteq planlib$

---

The variables *goallib*, *planlib*, *activeplans* and *executableplans* represent the agent's repository of goals, repository of plans, active plans and executable plans, respectively. Each active plan is necessarily associated with one or more of the agent's current goals as specified by *activeplangoal*. For example, if the function contains the pair $(g, \{p_1, p_2, p_3\})$, it indicates that $p_1$, $p_2$ and $p_3$ are competing active plans for $g$. Whilst active plans must be associated with at least one active goal the converse is not true, since agents may have goals for which no plans have been considered. Analogously the *plangoallib* function relates the repository of goals, *goallib*, to the repository of plans, *planlib*. However, not necessarily all library plans and goals are related by this function.

A plan consisting of a total order of plan-actions is a *total plan*, which is represented as a sequence of plan-actions. (Other types of plan can be defined similarly and accommodated easily within our specification.) In *single*-agent systems, all the actions of such plans must be within the agent's capabilities. However, plan-agents in *multi*-agent systems can consider executing plans containing actions not within their capabilities as long as they can model the capabilities of others as we have described. It is our claim that if plan agents are also *sociological* agents then they can make more informed choices about plan selection. (Of course, while this describes how an agent can consider its use of plans involving others, it does not impact the issues involved in whether those others choose to cooperate or not.) Agents can be constrained in their design by including additional predicates. For example, it is possible to restrict the active plans of an agent, with respect to a current goal, to those which are related to that goal by the function *plangoallib*. This can be achieved in the specification of such an agent by including the following predicate.

$$\forall ag : PlanAgent;\ g : Goal;\ ps : \mathbb{P}_1\ Plan \bullet (g, ps) \in ag.activeplangoal \Rightarrow$$
$$(\exists qs : \mathbb{P}\ Plan \mid qs \subset ag.planlib \bullet (g, (ps \cup qs)) \in ag.plangoallib)$$

**Multi-agent Plans.** In order for agents to reason about plans involving others it is necessary to analyse the nature of the plans themselves. This involves defining first the *components* of a plan, and then the *structure* of a plan, as shown in Figure 3. The components, which we call *plan-actions*, each consist of a *composite-action* and a set of related entities as described below. The structure of plans defines the relationship of the component plan-actions to one another. For example, plans may be *total* and define a sequence of plan-actions, *partial* and place a partial order on the performance of plan-actions, or *trees* and, for example, allow choice between alternative plan-actions at every stage in the plan's execution.

$$TotalPlan == \textsf{seq}\ PlanAction$$

$Primitive == Action$

$Template == \mathbb{P}\ Action$

$ConcPrimitive == \mathbb{P}\ Action$

$ConcTemplate == \mathbb{P}(\mathbb{P}\ Action)$

$ActnComp ::= Prim\langle\!\langle Primitive \rangle\!\rangle$
$\quad | \ Temp\langle\!\langle Template \rangle\!\rangle$
$\quad | \ ConcPrim\langle\!\langle ConcPrimitive \rangle\!\rangle$
$\quad | \ ConcTemp\langle\!\langle ConcTemplate \rangle\!\rangle$

$TreePlan ::= Tip\langle\!\langle PlanAction \rangle\!\rangle$
$\quad | \ Fork\langle\!\langle \mathbb{P}_1(PlanAction \times TreePlan) \rangle\!\rangle$

$Plan ::= Part\langle\!\langle PartialPlan \rangle\!\rangle$
$\quad | \ Total\langle\!\langle TotalPlan \rangle\!\rangle$
$\quad | \ Tree\langle\!\langle TreePlan \rangle\!\rangle$

$planpairs : Plan \to \mathbb{P}\ PlanAction$

$planentities : Plan \to \mathbb{P}\ EntityModel$

$planactions : Plan \to \mathbb{P}\ Action$

$$PlanAction == \mathbb{P}(ActnComp \times \mathbb{P}\ EntityModel)$$
$$PartialPlan == \{ps : PlanAction \leftrightarrow PlanAction \mid \forall a, b : PlanAction \bullet$$
$$(a, a) \notin ps^+ \wedge (a, b) \in ps^+ \Rightarrow (b, a) \notin ps^+ \bullet ps\}$$

**Fig. 3.** Plan components and structure

We identify four types of action that may be contained in plans, called *primitive*, *template, concurrent-primitive* and *concurrent-template*. There may be other categories and variations on those we have chosen but not only do they provide a starting point for specifying systems, they also illustrate how different representations can be formalised and incorporated within the same model. A primitive action is simply a base action as defined in the agent framework. An action template provides a high-level description of what is required by an action, defined as the set of all primitive actions that may result through an instantiation of that action-template. For example, in dMARS [5], template actions represent action formulae containing free variables, and become primitive actions when bound to values. Concurrent-primitive and concurrent-template actions are primitive actions and action templates performed concurrently. We define a new type, *ActnComp*, as a *compound-action* to include all four of these types.

Actions must be performed by entities, so we associate every compound-action in a plan with a set of entities, such that each entity in the set can potentially perform the action. At some stage in the planning process this set may be empty, indicating that no choice of entity has yet been made. We define a *plan-action* as a set of pairs, where each pair contains a compound-action and a set of those entities that could potentially perform the action. Plan-actions are defined as a *set* of pairs rather than *single* pairs so that plans containing simultaneous actions can be represented.

The following examples illustrate this representation. First, action $a_1$ is to be performed by either the plan-agent itself or the entity $entity1$. The second example describes the two separate actions, $a_{2_1}$ and $a_{2_2}$, being performed simultaneously by the two entities $entity1$ and $entity2$ respectively. Then, the third example states that the actions $a_{3_1}$ and $a_{3_2}$ are to be performed simultaneously. No entity has been established as a possibility to perform $a_{3_1}$, and $a_{3_2}$ is to be performed by either $entity2$ or $entity3$.

1. $\{(a_1, \{self, entity1\})\}$
2. $\{(a_{2_1}, \{entity1\}), (a_{2_2}, \{entity2\})\}$
3. $\{(a_{3_1}, \{\ \}), (a_{3_2}, \{entity2, entity3\})\}$

We specify three commonly-found categories of plan according to their structure as discussed earlier. Other types may be specified similarly. A partial plan imposes a partial order on the execution of actions, subject to two constraints. First, an action cannot be performed before itself and, second, if plan-action $a$ is before $b$, $b$ cannot be before $a$. A plan consisting of a total order of plan-actions is a total plan. Formally, this is represented as a sequence of plan-actions. A plan that allows a choice between actions at every stage is a tree. In general, a tree is either a leaf node containing a plan-action, or a fork containing a node, and a (non-empty) set of branches each leading to a tree. These are formalised in Figure 3, replacing the definition of *Plan* as a given set by a free-type definition to include the three plan categories thus defined. For *single*-agent systems all the actions of an executable plan must be within its capabilities:

$$\forall\, sap : PlanAgent;\; plan : Plan \mid plan \in sap.planlib \bullet$$
$$planactions\; plan \subseteq sap.capabilities$$

However, plan-agents in *multi* agent systems can consider executing plans containing actions not within their capabilities as long as they can model the capabilities of others. If such agents are also *sociological*, then we claim that they can make more informed choices about plan selection, through a better analysis of situations, as discussed below.

```
__ SPAgent _____
  SociologicalAgent
  PlanAgent
_____
```

# 4   Sociological Agents

Sociological agents with the capacity to model agents, relationships and plans (especially multi-agent plans) have available to them an appropriate level of detail to coordinate their actions in order to achieve their local goals more effectively. This bold claim arises from the increased awareness and appreciation not of the agents in their environment, but of the *impact* of those agents. In particular, the description of the multi-agent environment advanced so far enables an analysis to reveal opportunities to exploit existing relationships and how to minimise effort and avoid conflict.

To illustrate this greater reasoning capacity of sociological agents, we describe below some examples of categories of goals, agents and plans (with respect to the models of the sociological plan-agent), that may be relevant to an agent's understanding of its environment. Each of the categories is formally defined in Figures 4 and 5, in which the sociological plan-agent is denoted as *spa*. Any variable preceded by *model* denotes the models that *spa* has of some specific type of entity or relationship. For example, *spa.modelneutralobjects* and *spa.modelowns* are the set of neutral objects and ownership relations the sociological agent models in its environment.

- A *self-sufficient plan* is any plan that involves only neutral-objects, server-agents the plan-agent owns, and the plan-agent itself. Self-sufficient plans can therefore be executed without regard to other agents, and exploit current agent relationships. (The formal definition makes use of the relational image operator: in general, the relational image $R(\!|\ S\ |\!)$ of a set $S$ through a relation $R$ is the set of all objects $y$ to which $R$ relates some member $x$ of $S$.)

- A *self-sufficient goal* is any goal in the goal library that has an associated self-sufficient plan. These goals can then, according to the agent's model, be achieved independently of the existing social configuration.
- A *reliant-goal* is any goal that has a non-empty set of associated plans that is not self-sufficient.

For each plan that is not self-sufficient, a sociological plan-agent can establish the autonomous agents that may be affected by its execution, which is an important criterion in selecting a plan from competing active plans. An autonomous agent $A$ may be affected by a plan in one of two ways: either it is required to perform an action directly, or it is engaging a server-agent $S$ required by the plan. In this latter case, a sociological plan-agent can reason about either persuading $A$ to share or release $S$, taking $S$ without permission, or finding an alternative server-agent or plan. To facilitate such an analysis, we consider the following categories of agents and plans, formally defined in Figure 5.

- The *cooperating autonomous agents* of a plan are those autonomous agents, other than the plan-agent itself, that are involved in performing actions of that plan. They will need to cooperate with the plan-agent for the plan to be executed. Formally, an agent is a cooperating autonomous agent with respect to a plan, if it is contained in the set entities required for the plan. Note that an agent cannot guarantee that the identified cooperating agents of a plan will cooperate, only that cooperation is necessary for the plan to be performed.
- The *affected autonomous agents* of a plan are those autonomous agents, other than the plan-agent itself, that are engaging an entity required in the plan. Formally, an autonomous agent is *affected* with respect to a plan if a server-agent, contained in the set of entities required by the plan, is currently engaged by the autonomous agent. These agents *may* need to cooperate with the plan-agent. Notice that the affected autonomous agents do not include the cooperating agents.
- The *least-direct-fuss plans* for any reliant-goal are those plans that require the fewest number of cooperating agents.
- The *least-fuss plans* for any reliant-goal are those plans that require the fewest number of affected autonomous agents.

---

**s-suff plan** $\forall\, p \in spa.planlib \bullet selfsuff(p) \Leftrightarrow spa.planentities(p) \subseteq$
$spa.modelneutralobjects \cup spa.modelself \cup spa.modelowns(\!|\ spa.modelself\ |\!)$

**s-suff goal** $\forall\, g \in spa.goallib \bullet selfsuffgl(g) \Leftrightarrow (\exists\, p \in sag.plangoallib(g) \bullet p \in selfsuff)$

**rel goal** $\forall\, g \in spa.goallib \bullet reliantgoal(g) \Leftrightarrow spa.plangoallib\ g \neq \{\ \}\ \wedge$
$\neg\,(\exists\, p : spa.plangoallib\ g \bullet p \in selfsuff)$

**Fig. 4.** Sociological Agent Categories I

$$\begin{array}{ll}
\textbf{coop} \\
\textbf{agents}
\end{array} \quad \forall\, p : spa.planlib \bullet cooperatingagents(p) = \\
\qquad\qquad \{a : spa.modelautoagents \mid a \in spa.planentities\ p \bullet a\} \setminus spa.modelself$$

$$\begin{array}{ll}
\textbf{affected} \\
\textbf{agents}
\end{array} \quad \forall\, p : spa.planlib \bullet affectedagents\ p = \\
\qquad\qquad \{a : spa.modelautoagents \mid (\exists\, s : ServerAgent \bullet s \in spa.planentities\ p\ \wedge \\
\qquad\qquad\qquad (a, s) \in spa.modelengages) \setminus spa.modelself$$

$$\begin{array}{ll}
\textbf{least} \\
\textbf{direct} \\
\textbf{fuss} \\
\textbf{plans}
\end{array} \quad \forall\, g \in spa.goallib \bullet leastdirectfuss\ g = \\
\qquad\qquad \{p : Plan \mid (p \in spa.plangoallib\ g)\ \wedge \\
\qquad\qquad\quad \neg\, (\exists\, q : Plan \mid q \in spa.plangoallib\ g \bullet \\
\qquad\qquad\qquad \#(cooperatingagents\ q) < \#(cooperatingagents\ p)) \bullet p\}$$

$$\begin{array}{ll}
\textbf{least} \\
\textbf{fuss} \\
\textbf{plans}
\end{array} \quad \forall\, g \in spa.goallib \bullet leastfuss\ g = \\
\qquad\qquad \{p : Plan \mid (p \in spa.plangoallib\ g)\ \wedge \\
\qquad\qquad\quad \neg\, (\exists\, q : Plan \mid q \in spa.plangoallib\ g \bullet \\
\qquad\qquad\qquad \#(affectedagents\ q) < \#(affectedagents\ p)) \bullet p\}$$

**Fig. 5.** Sociological Agent Categories II

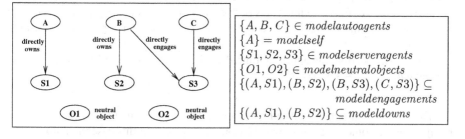

**Fig. 6.** Example: A Sociological Agent's Model

The categories described above are useful to an agent both at planning time and at run time. In the example below we consider their importance in the former case.

## 5    An Illustrative Example

To illustrate the value to an autonomous sociological plan-agent of being able to analyse plans using the categories above, consider an autonomous sociological plan-agent, $A$, and suppose that it models the agent relationships in its environment as follows. Autonomous agent $B$ directly owns the server-agent $S2$ and directly engages $S3$; autonomous agent $C$ directly engages $S3$; and $A$ directly owns $S1$. In addition, in $A$'s view, $O1$ and $O2$ are neutral-objects. This agent configuration can be seen in Figure 6 and would be represented in $A$'s models as shown.

Consider also that agent $A$ generates the goal, $g_A$, and activates four *total* plans $p_1$, $p_2$, $p_3$ and $p_4$ to achieve $g_A$ as follows. The four plans are then in the set of active plans,

$\{g_A\} \subseteq goals$
$\{p_1, p_2, p_3, p_4\} \subseteq activeplans$
$(g_A, \{p_1, p_2, p_3, p_4\}) \in activeplangoal$

$p_1 = Total\ \{\{(a_1, \{B, C\}), (a_2, \{A\})\}, \{(a_3, \{S2, S3\})\}\}$

$p_{1_1} = Total\ \{\{(a_1, \{B\}), (a_2, \{A\})\}, \{(a_3, \{S2\})\}\}$
$p_{1_2} = Total\ \{\{(a_1, \{B\}), (a_2, \{A\})\}, \{(a_3, \{S3\})\}\}$
$p_{1_3} = Total\ \{\{(a_1, \{C\}), (a_2, \{A\})\}, \{(a_3, \{S2\})\}\}$
$p_{1_4} = Total\ \{\{(a_1, \{C\}), (a_2, \{A\})\}, \{(a_3, \{S3\})\}\}$

$p_2 = Total\ \{\{(a_{11}, \{O1\}), (a_1, \{A\})\}, \{(a_{12}, \{S1\}), (a_2, \{A\})\},$
$\quad \{(a_{13}, \{O1\}), (a_3, \{A\})\}, \{(a_{14}, \{S1\}), (a_4, \{A\})\}, \{(a_{15}, \{O1\}), (a_5, \{A\})\}\}$
$p_3 = Total\ \{\{(a_1, \{A\})\}, \{(a_2, \{S3\})\}\}$
$p_4 = Total\ \{\{(a_1, \{A\})\}, \{(a_2, \{S2\})\}\}$

**Fig. 7.** Example agent goals and plans

and the pair $(g_A, \{p_1, p_2, p_3, p_4\})$ is in the function *activeplangoal* relating current goals to candidate active plans. These goals and plans are shown in Figure 7. Notice that since in plan $p_1$, action $a_1$ can be performed by either agents $B$ or $C$, and action $a_3$ by either $S2$ or $S3$, there are four possible ways of executing it, represented by $p_{1_1}$, $p_{1_2}$, $p_{1_3}$ and $p_{1_4}$ at the end of the figure. The agent then has seven alternative plans for execution selection.

Now, by inspection, the entities required by the plan $p_2$ are $A$, $S1$ and $O1$.

*planentities* $p_2 = \{A, S1, O1\}$

The previous definition of a self-sufficient plan for an agent $A$ is any plan that only requires neutral-objects, agents owned by $A$, and $A$ itself. In this case the union of the set of neutral-objects, owned agents and $A$ itself is simple to calculate.

*modelneutralobjects* $\cup$ *modelself* $\cup$ *modelowns*$(\!$ *modelself* $)\!) = \{O1, O2, A, S1\}$

The set of entities required by $p_2$ is a subset of this set which means that $p_2$ is self-sufficient, as is the associated goal $g_A$.

$\{A, S1, O1\} \subseteq \{O1, O2, A, S1\} \Rightarrow p_2 \in selfsuff$
$p_2 \in selfsuff \Rightarrow g_A \in selfsuffgl$

$A$ is thus able to achieve $g_A$ without affecting other autonomous agents and can act without regard to them whilst exploiting the current set of agent relationships. However, it may decide that, even though $p_2$ is self-sufficient, it is too costly, dismisses this possibility, and evaluates the six other alternatives to give the information shown in Table 1. It can be seen that the least-fuss and least-direct-fuss plans are as follows. Each of the least fuss plans affects only the one agent (in fact agent $B$ in each case) as a result of requiring the server-agent S2 which is engaged by $B$. Both the direct least fuss plans require no cooperating agents.

*leastfuss* $g_A = \{p_{1_1}, p_{1_3}, p_4\} \wedge$ *leastdirectfuss* $g_A = \{p_3, p_4\}$

Based on this analysis, $p_4$ may seem like the best candidate plan for execution since it does not involve the direct cooperation of other entities, and only affects one autonomous agent, $B$. The plan-agent can then analyse options concerning how to engage $S2$. Clearly, the final choice of plan must also consider other factors such as the motivations of the plan-agent, and its models of the motivations of others affected by plans. Nevertheless, this brief example illustrates just how sociological agents can use the plan, goal and agent categories defined in this section as important criteria in evaluating alternative active plans. If agents can model the plans of others, or produce agreed *multi-agent plans*, then they can *coordinate* their actions in order to achieve their local goals more effectively. Agents can then take advantage of the plans of others to avoid duplication of effort and to avoid *conflict*, which arises, for example, when two agents require direct ownership of the same entity at the same time.

Once agents are designed with the ability to reason about the plans of other agents, bargaining can take place between agents able to help each other in their plans. As an example, suppose agent $A$ has a plan that necessarily involves the cooperation of $B$. It may be appropriate for $A$ to consider the plans of $B$ that involve $A$'s cooperation since $A$ may then realise that $B$ has a high-priority plan that can only be achieved with $A$'s cooperation. In this case $A$ would consider herself to be in a strong bargaining position. The actual level at which other agents are modelled is clearly critical in directing behaviour. For example, a sociological agent with models of other agents as non-sociological may realise that these agents are unable to recognise agent relationships. The sociological agent may then be concerned that these other agents may use entities that destroy their own existing agent relationships.

# 6    Conclusions

As Castelfranchi has shown in his work on Social Power Theory, the relationships between agents are critical for effective behaviour in dynamic and open environments composed of multiple autonomous agents. Without an adequate appreciation of them, opportunities for interaction to enhance and improve individual agent performance may be missed, and agents may not be duly exploited. In this paper we have extended previous work to show how detailed models of plans, and the categories that may be derived from them, can be used to map the social landscape effectively. This is vital — in our view, autonomy is an absolute, but it means that agents will seek to exert power over others. Just as Castelfranchi's notion of negotiation power provides a *measure* of the independence or autonomy of an agent in his view of the world, so it provides us with a test of whether an agent is autonomous. Power *will* be used by an agent that can influence

**Table 1.** Example: A Sociological Agent's Evaluation of its Plans

| Plan | $p_{1_1}$ | $p_{1_2}$ | $p_{1_3}$ | $p_{1_4}$ | $p_3$ | $p_4$ |
|---|---|---|---|---|---|---|
| cooperatingagents | $\{B\}$ | $\{B\}$ | $\{C\}$ | $\{C\}$ | $\{\}$ | $\{\}$ |
| affectedagents | $\{B\}$ | $\{B, C\}$ | $\{B\}$ | $\{B, C\}$ | $\{B, C\}$ | $\{B\}$ |

others — an autonomous agent, in seeking to maximise its benefit, must make use of the information available in its models of agents and relationships.

The analysis we provide is not tailored to any pre-existing model, and is generally applicable, though it does arise naturally from our clean and simple agent framework. However, the particular value can be seen in applications that embody critical notions of dependence among agents such as, for example, Social Power Theory and its computational counterpart, Social Dependence Networks [12]. Our work provides two key benefits: first, it addresses some of the weaknesses in the SDN model in relation to the ambiguity of some constructs such as the nature of an *owned resource*, which we have clarified and tightened; second, it balances that earlier work which focussed on the problem *situations*, such as dependencies, by considering configurations of *solutions* to minimise effort and take advantage of opportunities in dealing with dependencies (through self-sufficient plans, for example). The next step is to explore the space of plans, goals and agents in more detail, based on the inter-agent relationships described above, and to show how further, more refined categories in the manner of those above, impact an agent's capacity to understand its environment and the agents within it.

# References

1. L. Antunes, J. Faria, and H. Coelho. Improving choice mechanisms within the BVG architecture. In *Intelligent Agents VII. Agent Theories, Architectures and Languages–7th International Workshop, ATAL-2000, Proceedings.* LNAI, Springer-Verlag, 2001. In this volume.
2. C. Castelfranchi. Social power. In Y. Demazeau and J.-P. Müller, editors, *Decentralized AI — Proceedings of the First European Workshop on Modelling Autonomous Agents in a Multi-Agent World*, pages 49–62. Elsevier, 1990.
3. C. Castelfranchi and R. Conte. Distributed artificial intelligence and social science: Critical issues. In G. M. P. O'Hare and N. R. Jennings, editors, *Foundations of Distributed Artificial Intelligence*, pages 527–542. Wiley, 1996.
4. C. Castelfranchi, M. Miceli, and A. Cesta. Dependence relations among autonomous agents. In E. Werner and Y. Demazeau, editors, *Decentralized AI 3: Proceedings of the Third European Workshop on Modelling Autonomous Agents in a Multi-Agent World*, pages 215–231. Elsevier, 1992.
5. M. d'Inverno, D. Kinny, M. Luck, and M. Wooldridge. A formal specification of dMARS. In *Intelligent Agents IV: Proceedings of the Fourth International Workshop on Agent Theories, Architectures and Languages*, volume 1365, pages 155–176. Springer-Verlag, 1998.
6. M. d'Inverno and M. Luck. Development and application of a formal agent framework. In M. G. Hinchey and L. Shaoying, editors, *ICFEM'97: First IEEE International Conference on Formal Engineering Methods*, pages 222–231. IEEE Press, 1997.
7. M. P. Georgeff and F. F. Ingrand. Decision-making in an embedded reasoning system. In *Proceedings of the Eleventh International Joint Conference on Artificial Intelligence (IJCAI-89)*, pages 972–978, Detroit, MI, 1989.
8. M. Luck and M. d'Inverno. A formal framework for agency and autonomy. In *Proceedings of the First International Conference on Multi-Agent Systems (ICMAS-95)*, pages 254–260. AAAI Press / MIT Press, 1995.
9. M. Luck and M. d'Inverno. Engagement and cooperation in motivated agent modelling. In C. Zhang and D. Lukose, editors, *Distributed Artificial Intelligence Architecture and Modelling: Proceedings of the First Australian Workshop on Distributed Artificial Intelligence*, LNAI 1087, volume 1087, pages 70–84. Springer Verlag, 1996.

10. B. Moulin and B. Chaib-draa. An overview of distributed artificial intelligence. In G. M. P. O'Hare and N. R. Jennings (eds), editors, *Foundations of Distributed Artificial Intelligence*, pages 3–56. John Wiley and Sons, 1996.

11. J. S. Rosenschein. Multiagent planning as a social process: Voting, privacy, and manipulation. In *Proceedings of the First International Conference on Multi-Agent Systems (ICMAS-95)*, page 431, June 1995.

12. J. S. Sichman, R. Conte, C. Castelfranchi, and Y. Demazeau. A social reasoning mechanism based on dependence networks. In *ECAI 94. 11th European Conference on Artificial Intelligence*, pages 188–192. John Wiley and Sons, 1994.

13. J. M. Spivey. *The Z Notation: A Reference Manual*. Prentice Hall, Hemel Hempstead, 2nd edition, 1992.

14. M. Wooldridge. *The Logical Modelling of Computational Multi-Agent Systems*. PhD thesis, Department of Computation, UMIST, Manchester, UK, October 1992. (Technical Report MMU–DOC–94–01, Department of Computing, Manchester Metropolitan University, UK).

15. M. J. Wooldridge and N. R. Jennings. Intelligent agents: Theory and practice. *Knowledge Engineering Review*, 10(2), 1995.

# Multiagent Bidding Mechanisms for Robot Qualitative Navigation

Carles Sierra, Ramon López de Màntaras, and Dídac Busquets

Artificial Intelligence Research Institute (IIIA),
Spanish Council for Scientific Research (CSIC)
Campus UAB, 08193 Bellaterra, Barcelona, Spain
{sierra, mantaras, didac}@iiia.csic.es

**Abstract.** This paper explores the use of bidding mechanisms to coordinate the actions requested by a group of agents in charge of achieving the task of guiding a robot towards a specified target in an unknown environment. This approach is based on a qualitative (fuzzy) approach to landmark-based navigation.

## 1  Introduction

Navigating in outdoor unknown environments is a difficult open problem in robotics. Existing approaches assume that an appropriately detailed and accurate metric map can be obtained through sensing the environment. Even landmark-based navigation approaches assume unrealistically (except if a GPS system is available) accurate distance and direction information between the robot and the landmarks (see Section 6). In this work we propose a fuzzy set based approach to landmark-based navigation in outdoor environments that assumes only very rough vision estimation of the distances and therefore does not rely on GPS information. The motivation being to test the feasibility of animal-like qualitative navigation in machines. Our approach is implemented by means of a multiagent architecture.

The navigation system uses a camera for landmark identification and recognition and has to compete with other systems for the control of the camera. This control is achieved through a bidding mechanism (see Section 3).

Another partner in the project is building a six legged robot with an on board camera. When available, we will test our approach with the real robot. Right now, the navigation system is tested over a simulation of an outdoor environment composed of elements such as buildings, trees, rivers, etc.

The map of the environment is represented by a labelled graph whose nodes represent triangular shaped regions delimited by groups of three non-collinear landmarks and whose arcs represent the adjacency between regions, that is, if two regions share two landmarks, the corresponding nodes are connected by an arc. The arcs are labelled with costs that reflect the easiness of the path between the two corresponding regions. A blocked path would have an infinite cost whereas a flat, hard paved path would have a cost close to zero. Of course these costs can only be assigned after the robot has moved (or tried to move) along the path connecting the two regions. Therefore, the map is built

C. Castelfranchi, Y. Lespérance (Eds.): Intelligent Agents VII, LNAI 1986, pp. 198–212, 2001.

while the robot is moving towards the target. The only a priori assumption is that the target is visible from the initial robot location. Of course, the target can be lost during the navigation and is when the navigation system will need to compute its location with respect to a set of previously seen landmarks whose spatial relation with the target is qualitatively computed both in terms of fuzzy distance and direction.

This paper is structured as follows. Section 2 discusses the map representation, Section 3 the multiagent architecture and bidding mechanism for cooperation and competition among the agents. In Section 4 we describe each individual agent. Section 5 contains an example and Section 6 is devoted to relevant related work. Finally, the paper is concluded in Section 7.

## 2  Map Representation

For map representation and wayfinding, we will use the model proposed by Prescott in [15]. This model is based on the relative positions of landmarks in order to estimate the location of a target. The method is named the *beta-coefficient system*.

We will firstly describe how this method works when the robot is able to have exact information about its environment, and then we will explain how we have adapted it to work with imprecise information.

### 2.1  Beta-Coefficient System

Having seen three landmarks and a target (which is also a landmark) from a viewpoint (i.e., landmarks $A$, $B$ and $C$ and target $T$ from viewpoint $V$, as shown in Figure 1), then seeing only the three landmarks, but not the target, from another viewpoint (i.e., $V'$), the system is able to compute the position of the target. The only calculation needed to do this is

$$\beta = X^{-1}X_T$$

where $X = [X_A X_B X_C]$ with $X_i = (x_i, y_i, 1)^T, i \in \{A, B, C, T\}$, are the homogeneous coordinates of object $i$ from the viewpoint $V$. The resultant vector, $\beta$, is called the $\beta$-vector of landmarks A, B, C and T. This relation is unique and invariant for any viewpoint, with the only restriction for the landmarks to be distinct and non collinear.

The target's new location from viewpoint $V'$ is computed by

$$X'_T = X'\beta$$

This method can be implemented with a two-layered network. Each layer contains a collection of units, which can be connected to units of the other layer. The lowest layer units are *object-units*, and represent the landmarks the robot has seen. Each time the robot recognizes a new landmark, a new object-unit is created. The units of the highest layer are *beta-units* and there is one for each $\beta$-vector computed. When the robot has four landmarks in its viewframe, it selects one of them to be the target, a new beta-unit is created, and the $\beta$-vector for the landmarks is calculated. This beta-unit will be connected to the three object-units associated with the landmarks (as incoming connections) and to the object-unit associated with the target landmark (as an outgoing connection). Thus,

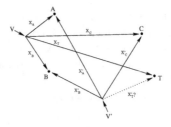

**Fig. 1.** Possible landmark configuration and points of view.

a beta-unit will always have four connections, while an object-unit will have as many connections as the number of beta-units it participates to. An example of the network can be seen in Figure 2b. In this figure there are six object-units and three beta-units. The notation ABC/D is understood as the beta-unit that computes the location of landmark D when knowing the locations of landmarks A, B and C.

This network has a propagation system that permits to compute the location of the non-visible landmarks. The system works as follows: when the robot sees a group of landmarks, it activates (sets the value) of the associated object-units with the egocentric locations of these landmarks. When an object-unit is activated, it propagates its location to the beta-units connected to it. On the other hand, when a beta-unit receives the location of its three incoming object-units, it gets active and computes the location of the target it encodes using its $\beta$-vector, and propagates the result to the object-unit representing the target. Thus, an activation of a beta-unit will activate an object-unit that can activate another beta-unit, and so on. For example, in the network of Figure 2b, if landmarks A, B and C are visible, their object-units will be activated and this will activate the beta-unit ABC/D, computing the location of D, which will activate BCD/E, activating E, and causing BDE/F also to be activated. Knowing the location of only three landmarks, the network has computed the location of three more landmarks that were not visible. This propagation system makes the network compute all possible landmarks locations. Obviously, if a beta-unit needs the location of a landmark that is neither in the current view nor activated through other beta-units, it will not get active.

The network created by object and beta units is implicitly defining an adjacency graph of the topology of the landmarks. It can be converted to a graph where the nodes represent regions (delimited by a group of three landmarks), and the arcs represent paths. These arcs can have an associated cost, representing how difficult it is to move from one region to another. An example of how the topology is encoded in a graph is shown in Figure 2c.

This topological graph will be useful when planning routes to the target. Sometimes, when the position of the target is known, the easiest thing to do is to move in a straight line towards it, but sometimes it is not (the route can be blocked, the cost too high...). With the topological graph, a route to the target can be computed. This route will consist in a sequence of regions through which the robot will have to go.

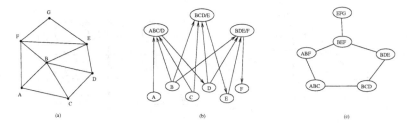

**Fig. 2.** (a) Landmark configuration (b) Associated network (partial view) and (c) Associated topo-logical map.

## 2.2 Moving to Fuzzy

However, this method assumes that the robot will have the exact position of every landmark, in order to create the beta-units and use the network. But this is not our case. The vision system of our robot will provide us with inexact information about the locations of landmarks. To work with this uncertain information we will use fuzzy numbers.

To use the beta-coefficient system with fuzzy numbers, we simply perform the calculations using the fuzzy operators as defined in [2]. However, because of the nature of fuzzy operators, some landmark configurations may not be feasible (because of the division by 0) and alternative landmarks might be needed.

When using the network to compute the position of a landmark, we obtain a fuzzy polar coordinate $(r, \phi)$, where $r$ and $\phi$ are fuzzy numbers, giving us qualitative information about its location.

## 3   Robot Architecture

Navigation, as the general activity of leading a robot to a target destination, is naturally intermingled with other low-level activities of the robot such as actual leg co-ordination or obstacle avoidance (that is, piloting) and high-level activities such as landmark identification. All these activities *co-operate* and *compete*. They co-operate because they need one another in order to fulfill their tasks. For instance, the navigation system needs to identify the known landmarks in a particular area of the environment or to find new ones; or, the vision system needs the pilot to move in a particular direction to change the point of view on a landmark. These activities compete for the use of the most important resource, the camera. For instance, the pilot needs the camera to have a close view in front of a leg to safely avoid and obstacle, the navigation system needs sometimes to look behind in order to position the robot by seeing known landmarks, or the vision system may need to look to the right of the robot to track an already identified landmark.

We propose a model for co-operation and competition based on a simple mechanism: *bidding*. We can see each of the activities (services), from an engineering point of view, as a system (represented as a square in Figure 3), that is, systems require and offer services one another. The model works as follows, each system generates bids for the services offered by the other systems according to the internal expected utility associated to the

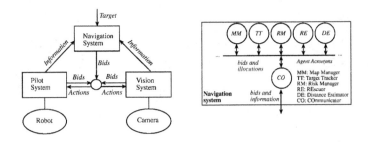

**Fig. 3.** Robot architecture and multiagent view of the navigation system.

provisioning of such service. Each system provides a number of services and waits for bids for them. Each system decides which service to engage on based on the active bids that have been received.

This modular view conforms an extensible architecture. To extend this architecture with a new capability we would just have to plug in a new system. Not only that, it also permits recursively to have a modular view of each one of the systems.

### 3.1   Pilot System

In this paper we do not focus on the algorithmics of the pilot system. We asseume the pilot is able to safely command the motors that control the robot legs to move in a given direction. When the sensors detect problems: a leg is blocked, or slips, for instance, the pilot bids for the control of the camera to inspect the surroundings of the robot in order to perform a local planning to avoid the obstacle. This system is being currently developed in parallel by another partner in the project (IRI [1]).

### 3.2   Vision System

We neither focus on the vision system description, although we build upon the results for landmark identification obtained by [11]. The vision system is able to recognise new landmarks in the vision field of the camera and is also able to identify previously recognised landmarks. It will also provide information about the movement performed by the robot. The algorithmics of the vision system may need a complementary view in order to perform a correct landmark identification. In those cases, it will bid for the control of the pilot to momentaneously divert the robot to take a new perspective on a landmark. This system is also being developed in parallel by another partner in the project.

### 3.3   Navigation System

We have used the modular view inspiring the overall robot architecture in the design of the navigation system. Again, the overall activity of leading the robot to the target

---

[1] Institut de Robòtica i Informàtica Industrial, http://www.iri.csic.es

destination is decomposed into a set of simple *agents* that bid for services provided by other robot systems. This system has a communication agent that gathers the different biddings and determines which one to select at any given time. Thus, the navigation system is defined to be a multiagent system where each agent is competent in a particular task. The co-ordination between the agents is made through a common representation of the map. Agents consult the map and suggest changes to it. Other robot systems provide information about the environment —position of landmarks, obstacles, difficulty of terrain, ... — which is also used to update the map.

The local decisions of agents take the form of bids for services and are combined into a group decision: which set of compatible services to require, and hence gives us a handle on the difficult combinatorial problem of deciding *what to do next*. In the next section we describe in detail the society of agents that models the navigation process.

## 4    The Group of Bidding Agents

In the model reported in this paper we present a group of five agents that take care of different tasks that, when co-ordinated through the bidding mechanism, provide the overall desired behaviour of leading the robot to a target landmark. The tasks are: to *keep the target located* with minimum uncertainty, to *keep the risk* of losing the target low, to *recover* from blocked situations, to *keep the error distance* to landmarks low, and to *keep the information on the map* consistent and up-to-date.

An agent has been designed to fulfill each one of these goals, plus a communicator agent, that will be the responsible of communicating the navigation system with the other robot systems.

The services —actions— that agents can bid for, in order to fulfill their tasks are: Move(*direction*), instructs the pilot system to move the robot in a particular *direction*; Look_for_target(*angle, error*), instructs the vision system to look for the target that can be found in the area at *angle* ± *error* radians from the current body orientation; and, Identify_landmarks(*number, area*), instructs the vision system to identify a certain number of landmarks in a particular area represented as an angle arc.

Finally, agents may question one another with respect to the different capabilities they have. For instance, any agent in the society may request the agent responsible of keeping the uncertainty low, which is the current level of uncertainty, or request from the map manager whether the target is currently visible or not. When describing the algorithm schemas these speach acts will appear as expressions in a KQML-style type of language.

Agents have a hybrid architecture. We will use the following construct to model the reactive component of agents:

**On** *condition* **do** *action*

Whenever the *condition* holds (typically an illocution arriving to the agent) the *action* is executed immediately. Agents will refer to themselves by the special symbol "self". When referring to all the agents of the society, they will use the symbol "all".

The code schemas of the agents can be found in Table 1.

## 4.1  Map Manager

This agent is responsible of maintaining the information of the explored environment as a map. It also maintains the information of the current view frame. As explained in Section 2, a map is a graph where each node corresponds to a group of three landmarks and where arcs are labelled with a passability cost. An arc labelled with an infinite cost represents a non-passable section of the terrain —for instance, an obstacle, a wall, a river ...The activity of this agent consists on processing the information associated with the incoming view frames – expanding the graph and possibly changing the beta-vectors, and asynchronously changing arcs' cost labels when informed by other agents or by other robot systems.

Each time a new view frame arrives, it permits to compute the difference in angle from the last view frame for each landmark. This angle is used to determine the distance to the landmark, $d_{l_i}$, and also the overall distance error, $\epsilon_{l_i}$, in the following way:

$$d_{l_i} = d\frac{\sin\beta}{\sin\alpha_{l_i}} \qquad\qquad \epsilon_{l_i} = \frac{\epsilon_d}{d}\frac{\sin\beta}{\sin\alpha_{l_i}}$$

where $\epsilon_d$ is half of the support of the fuzzy number representing the distance in the direction of the movement of the robot, $d$ is the most confident value for the distance, $\alpha_{l_i}$ is the difference in angle for $landmark_i$ from the last frame and the current frame and $\beta$ is the actual angle of the movement performed by the robot (see Figure 4).

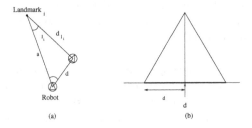

**Fig. 4.** (a) Robot movement and angle variation and (b) Fuzzy distance and error

This agent will use the fuzzy beta-coefficient system described in Section 2 to answer questions about landmark and target positions, coming from the *target tracker* and the *distance estimator*. It will activate the network with the information of the current view frame, and the propagation system will compute the positions of the non visible landmarks.

It will also be the responsible of computing the quality of the landmarks in the current view frame, when required by the *risk manager*. This quality will be a function of the collinearity of the landmarks. Having a set $S$ of landmarks, their quality is computed as: $q_s = \max\{1 - Col(S')|S' \subseteq S, |S| = 3\}$ where $Col(S') = 1 - \frac{\alpha\beta\gamma}{(\frac{\pi}{3})^3}$, and $\alpha$, $\beta$ and $\gamma$ are the three angles of the triangle formed by the landmarks in $S'$. The best quality is associated to equilater triangles, where $\alpha = \beta = \gamma = \frac{\pi}{3}$, and hence their collinearity is 0. When one of the angles is 0, landmarks would be maximally collinear and $Col(S') = 1$.

Another responsibility of this agent is to compute diverting targets when asked for by the *rescuer*, possibly backtracking from the current situation. To do this it uses the map where all path costs and previous navigation decisions are recorded. We have explored two ways of computing a new target. With the first method, we select the target that makes the diverting path shorter. With the second, we select the target that minimizes the direction change of the robot.

## 4.2  Target Tracker

The goal of this agent is to keep the target located at any time. Ideally, the target should be always within the current view of the camera. If it is not, the uncertainty associated to its location is computed by this agent using the map and the current view. Actions of other systems are requested to keep the uncertainty as low as possible.

We model uncertainty as a function on the angle arc, $\epsilon_\alpha$, from the robot's current position, where the target is thought to be located. When we are sure of the position of the target we have a crisp direction and hence, $\epsilon_\alpha = 0$ and the uncertainty is 0. When we are completely lost, any direction can be correct, $\epsilon_\alpha = 2\pi$, and the uncertainty level is 1. Thus, the uncertainty level is computed as: $U_a = (\frac{\epsilon_\alpha}{2\pi})^\beta$, where $\beta$ gives a particular increasing shape to the uncertainty function. If $\beta$ is much smaller than 1, we are going to increase uncertainty very quickly as the imprecision in angle grows. For $\beta$ values well over 1, uncertainty will grow very slowly until the error angle gets very big.

The actions required by this agent are to move towards the target and to look at the place where the target is assumed to be. Bids for moving towards the target start at a value $\kappa_1$ and decrease polinomically (depending on a parameter $\alpha$) to 0 when the uncertainty increases. Bids for looking at the target follow a sinusoidal increasing from 0, reaching a maximum of $\kappa_2$ for uncertainty equal to 0,5 and then decreasing again until 0. This is so because there is no need to look at the target when the uncertainty is very low, and it does not make sense to bid high to look at the target when the uncertainty is already too high.

## 4.3  Distance Estimator

The goal of this agent is to keep the distance error to the neighboring landmarks as low as possible. This agent will play a very important role at the beginning of the navigation. When analysing the first view frame to obtain the initial landmarks, the error in distance will be maximal, there will be no reference view to obtain an initial estimation of the distance to the target. This agent will generate high bids to move, preferably orthogonally, with respect to the line connecting the robot and the target in order to get another view on it and establish an initial estimation of the distances to the visible landmarks. Similarly, when a target switch is produced (by the intervention of the rescuer) this agent may become relevant again if the distance value to the new selected target is very imprecise. Again, the same process will have as consequence a decrease in the new target distance error.

We model distance uncertainty as the size of the support of the fuzzy number modeling distance. As already mentioned in Subsection 4.1, we will note $\epsilon_{l_i}$ the imprecision error in distance to $landmark_i$ and $\epsilon_t$ the imprecision error to the current target. Thus, the uncertainty in distance to the target can be modeled as $U_d = 1 - \frac{1}{e^{\kappa \epsilon_t}}$, where $\kappa$ is a parameter that changes the shape of $U_d$; high values of $\kappa$ will give faster increasing shapes. At the beginning of a run the *distance* is the fuzzy number $[0, \infty]$, $\epsilon_t = +\infty$ and hence $U_d = 1$.

This agent will be relevant when this value is very high. Its action will be to bid to move the robot in an orthogonal direction using as bid the value of $U_d$.

The single action required by this agent is to move orthogonally to the line connecting the robot and the target ($a$ in Figure 4).

This agent will also be the responsible of deciding (up to a certainty degree $\phi$) whether the robot is *at target*. It will consider that the robot has reached the target if the upper bound of the $\alpha$-cut of level $\phi$ of fuzzy number modeling the distance to the target is less than three times the body size of the robot.

## 4.4    Risk Manager

The goal of this agent is to keep the risk of losing the target as low as possible. The way to satisfy this goal is by keeping a reasonable amount of landmarks, as non collinear as possible, in the surroundings of the robot. The less landmarks we keep around the more risky is our current exploration and the higher the probabilities of losing the target. Also, the more collinear are the landmarks the higher is the error in the location of the target and thus the higher the uncertainty on its location.

We will model the risk as a function that combines several variables: 1) the number of landmarks ahead (elements in set $A$), 2) the number of landmarks around (elements in set $B$), and 3) their "quality"($q_A$ and $q_B$). $A$ and $B$ are the sets of landmarks ahead and around of the robot, respectively. We understand by "quality" how collinear they are. A lowest risk of 0 will be assessed when we have at least four visible landmarks in the direction of the movement with the minimum collinearity between them. A highest risk of 1 is given to the situation when there are neither landmarks ahead nor around us.

$$R = 1 - \min(1, q_A \left(\frac{|A|}{4}\right)^{\gamma_A} + q_B \left(\frac{|B|}{4}\right)^{\gamma_B})$$

The values $\gamma_A$ and $\gamma_B$ determine the relative importance of the type of landmarks. Having landmarks ahead should be privileged somehow, so normally $\gamma_A > \gamma_B$.

Given that the robot has little to do in order to increase the quality of the landmarks, the only way to decrease the risk level is by increasing the number of landmarks ahead and around. We privilege the fact of having landmarks ahead by bidding $\gamma_r R$ for that action and $\gamma_r R^2$ (which is obviously smaller that $\gamma_r R$) for the action of identifying landmarks around the robot, where $\gamma_r$ is a parameter to control the shape of the bid function.

## 4.5    Rescuer

The goal of the rescuer agent is to rescue the robot from problematic situations. These situations may happen due to three reasons. First, the pilot can lead the robot to a position with an obstacle ahead. Second, the uncertainty of the location of the target is too high, over a threshold $\overline{U}_a$. Finally, we can be at a very risky place, that is a place where we can get easily lost, a value of R over a threshold $\overline{R}$. If any of these situations happen, the rescuer agent asks the map manager for a diverting target. The algorithm uses a stack where the different diverting targets are stacked.

### 4.6  Communicator

The multiagent system implementing the navigation algorithm communicates with the remaining robot systems through the communicator agent. This agent receives bids for services from the other agents. The services required may be conflicting or not. For instance, an agent that requires the camera to look behind and another that requires it to identify a new landmark on the right end up with conflicting service biddings, that is services that cannot be fulfilled at the same time. On the contrary, an agent requiring the robot to move forward, and an agent requiring the camera to look behind might be perfectly non-conflicting. The communicator agent combines the bids for the different services, determines the service with highest bid for each group of conflicting services and outputs service bids accordingly.

We note the set of services, or actions, as $\mathcal{A}$. If two actions cannot be performed at the same time, we say that they conflict, and we note it as $Conflict(a_i, a_j)$. A bid is a pair of the form $(a_i, b)$ such that $a_i \in \mathcal{A}$ and $b \in [0, 1]$. The set of active bids in a given moment is a set of bids received from the remaining agents in the multiagent system since the last decision taken by the communicator agent. The communicator generates as output to the other systems a set of feasible bids.

Given a set of active biddings $B$, a feasible bidding is a set $F$ of bids $\{(a_1, b_1), \ldots,$ $(a_i, b_i), \ldots, (a_n, b_n)\}$ such that for all $a_i$ and $a_j$, $a_i \neq a_j$, $Conflict(a_i, a_j)$ is false and $b_i = \bigvee\{b_j | (a_i, b_j) \in B\}$. The combination function $\bigvee$ being any form of disjunctive operator, such as $max$. We note by $B^*$ the set of feasible biddings of $B$.

Given a set of bids, the agent will select the feasible bidding associated to them that maximises the welfare of the society. Understanding the value in a bid as a measure of the expected utility of the action in that bid to a particular agent, we use the sum of the bids as the function to maximise. Thus, the actual output is:

$$F = arg\ max\{\sum_{i=1}^{j} b_i | \{(a_1, b_1), \ldots, (a_j, b_j)\} \in B^*\}$$

## 5   A Navigation Example

We are currently implementing the agents of the navigation system and testing the algorithm on the Webots[2] simulator. Since we do not have the real robot yet, we also simulate the pilot and vision systems.

The system is being implemented in Youtoo[3] connected to the Webots simulator. Each agent is executed as an independent thread, and they use shared memory to simulate messages passing.

---

[2] Cyberbotics, http://www.cyberbotics.com
[3] A multi-threaded dialect of Lisp, http://www.maths.bath.ac.uk/~jap/ak1/youtoo

**Table 1.** Agents code schemas

```
Agent MM(initial_target)=
  Begin
    target = initial_target
    On inform(CO,self,current_view(CV,movement)) do
      update_map(CV,movement)
    On ask(X,self,position-landmark(L)?) do
      ⟨angle,ε_α,d,ε_d⟩ = compute_landmark_position(L)
      inform(self,X,position-landmark(L,angle,ε_α,d,ε_d))
    On ask(X,self,landmarks?) do
      ⟨|A|,|B|,q_A,q_B⟩ = compute_landmarks_quality
      inform(self,X,landmarks(|A|,|B|,q_A,q_B))
    On ask(X,self,diverting-target?) do
      T = compute_diverting_target
      inform(self,X,diverting-target(T))
    On inform(RE,self,target(T)) do target = T
  end
```

```
Agent TT(α, β, κ_1, κ_2, initial_target, initial_angle)=
  Begin
    ⟨target,angle,ε_α⟩ = ⟨initial_target,initial_angle,0⟩
    Repeat
      ask(self,MM,position-landmark(target)?)
      When inform(MM,self,position-landmark(target,
          angle,ε_α,dist,ε_{dist})) do
        U_a = (ε_α/2π)^β
        inform(self,all,uncertainty(U_a))
        inform(self,CO,
          {(Move(angle), κ_1(1 − (U_a^{1/α}))),
          (Look_for_target(angle, ε_α),
          κ_2 sin (πU_a))})
      endwhen
    Until inform(DE,self,at_target(initial_target))
    On inform(RE,self,target(T)) do target = T
  end
```

```
Agent DE(initial_target, κ, φ)=
  Begin
    target = initial_target
    d = [0, ∞]
    ε_t = +∞
    U_d = 1
    Repeat
      ask(self,MM,position-landmark(target)?)
      [min,max]={d}_φ
      at_target = max ≤ 3*bodyshape
      If at_target then inform(self,all,at_target(target))
      When inform(MM,self,
          position-landmark(target,angle,ε_α,dist,ε_t)) do
        U_d = 1 − 1/(e^{κε_t})
        d = dist
        inform(self,CO, {(Move(angle + π/2), U_d)})
      endwhen
    Until inform(self,self,at_target(initial_target))
    On inform(RE,self,target(T)) do target = T
  end
```

```
Agent RM(γ_A, γ_B, γ_r, initial_target)=
  Begin
    target = initial_target
    R = 0
    Repeat
      ask(self,MM,landmarks?)
      When inform(MM,self,
          landmarks(|A|,|B|,q_A,q_B) do
        R = 1 − min(1, q_A(|A|/4)^{γ_A} +
          q_B(|B|/4)^{γ_B})
        inform(self,all,risk(R))
        If |A| < 4 then inform(self,CO,
          {(Identify_landmarks(4, ahead),
          γ_r R)})
        If |B| < 4 then inform(self,CO,
          {(Identify_landmarks(4, around),
          γ_r R^2)})
      endwhen
    Until inform(DE,self,at_target(initial_target))
    On inform(RE,self,target(T)) do target = T
  end
```

```
Agent RE(U̅_a, R̅, initial_target)=
  Begin
    stack = push(emptystack,initial_target)
    Repeat
      When inform(CO,self,Blocked) or (inform(TT, self, uncertainty(U_a)) and U_a > U̅_a)
        or (inform(RM, self, risk(R)) and R > R̅) do
        ask(self,MM,diverting_target?)
      endwhen
    Until inform(DE,self,at_target(initial_target))

    On inform(DE,self,at_target(T)) do
      pop(stack)
      if not empty(stack) then
        T := top(stack)
        inform(self, all, target(T))
    On inform(MM,self,diverting_target(T)) do
      push(stack, T)
      inform(self, all, target(T))
  end
```

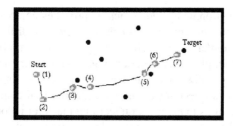

**Fig. 5.** Robot's path from starting point to the target

We will explain a navigation run as shown in Figure 5. It shows the path followed by the robot from a starting point to a target landmark. The environment is very simple, it is composed only of landmarks (drawn as black circles), and the obstacles are the landmarks themselves.

When the robot starts its search, in point (1), it sees the target, but as there is no distance estimation, the agent DE bids very high to move orthogonally with respect to the target. The agent TT will also bid high to move towards the target, but DE wins and the robot turns. When the robot reaches point (2) the angle to the target has varied enough to compute its distance, so the bids of DE to move in that direction decrease. Since the robot is looking at the target, there is no uncertainty about its location, so TT will bid high to move towards it. As bids of DE are low, TT wins and the robot starts moving to the target. In point (3) the pilot detects an obstacle so it takes the control to avoid it. Once the obstacle is avoided, in point (4), TT's bid wins again and the robot continues moving to the target. The same situation is encountered in point (5). There, the pilot takes the control for a while, and TT resumes it in point (6). The robot finally reaches the target in point (7).

## 6 Related Work

Mapping for robot navigation dates back to the famous SRI Shakey robot [14]. Recent research on modeling unknown environments is based on two main approaches: occupancy grid-based (or metric), proposed among others by Elfes [4] and Moravec [13], and topological such as those proposed by Chatila [3], Kuipers and Byun [9], Mataric [12] and Kortenkamp [8] among others. Cells in a occupancy grid contain information about the presence or not of an obstacle. The position of the robot is incrementally computed using odometry and information from sensors. One problem with this approach is that it requires an accurate odometry to disambiguate among positions that look similar. Besides, grids are computationally very expensive, specially in large outdoor environments, because the resolution of the grid (cell's size) cannot be too large. Contrarily to grid-based representations, topological representations are computationally cheaper. They use graphs to represent the environment. Each node corresponds to an environment feature or landmark and arcs represent direct paths between them. In our work, however, nodes are regions defined by groups of three landmarks and they are connected by arcs if the regions are adjacent. This graph is incrementally built while the robot is moving within the environment. Topological approaches compute the position of the robot relative to the known landmarks, therefore they have difficulties to determine if two places that look similar are or not the same place unless a robust enough landmark recognition system is in place. Landmark recognition is a very active field of research in vision and very promising results are being obtained [11]. In this work we assume that the vision system can recognize landmarks. Thrun [19] combines grid-based and topological representations in his work on learning maps for indoor navigation. This is indeed a good idea for indoor environments but for large-scale outdoor environments may not be worth the computational effort of maintaining a grid representation under a topological one.

The incremental map building approach presented here is based on previous work by Prescott [15] that proposed a network model that used barycentric coordinates, also called beta-coefficients by Zipser [20], to compute the spatial relations between landmarks for robot navigation. By matching a perceived landmark with the network, the robot can find its way to a target provided it is represented in the network. Prescott's approach is quantitative whereas our approach uses a fuzzy extension of the beta-coefficient coding system in order to work with fuzzy qualitative information about distances and directions. Levitt and Lawton [10] also proposed a qualitative approach to the navigation problem but assumes an unrealistically accurate distance and direction information between the robot and the landmarks. Another qualitative method for robot navigation was proposed by Escrig and Toledo [5], using constraint logic. However, they assume that the robot has some a priori knowledge of the spatial relationship of the landmarks, whereas our system builds these relationships while exploring the environment.

Regarding the related work on multi-agent architectures, Liscano et al [6] use an activity-based blackboard consisting of two hierarchical layers for strategic and reactive reasoning. A blackboard database keeps track of the state of the world and a set of activities to perform the navigation. Arbitration between competing activities is accomplished by a set of rules that decides which activity takes control of the robot and resolves conflicts. Other hierarchical centralized architectures similar to that of Liscano et al are those of Stentz [17] to drive CMU's Navlab and Isik [7] among others. Our approach is completely decentralized which means that the broadcast of information is not hierarchical. This approach is easier to program and is more flexible and extensible than centralized approaches. Arkin [1] also emphasized the importance of a nonhierarchical broadcast of information. Furthermore, we propose a model for cooperation and competition between activities based on a simple bidding mechanism. A similar model was proposed by Rosenblatt [16] in the CMU's DAMN project. A set of modules cooperated to control a robot's path by voting for various possible actions, and an arbiter decided which was the action to be performed. However the set of actions was pre-defined, while in our system each agent can bid for any action it wants to perform. Moreover, in the experiments carried out with this system (DAMN), the navigation system used a grid-based map and did not use at all landmark based navigation. Sun and Sessions [18] have also proposed an approach for developing multi-agent reinforcement learning systems that uses a bidding process to segment sequences (and divided up among agents) in sequential decision tasks, their goal being to facilitate the learning of the overall task based on reinforcements received during task execution.

# 7   Concluding Remarks and Future Work

This paper presents a new approach to robot navigation based on the combination of fuzzy representation and multiagent coordination based on a bidding mechanism. The implementation is finished on top of a simulator and we are starting the phase of experimentation.

Experimentation will be carried out along three dimensions: number of environments (one or several), number of points in each environment where to start a run (one or several), and number of samplings of robot parameters per starting point (one or several). This gives eight increasingly more complex experimental scenarios for which the results will be given as path length averages compared either with optimal results or with human obtained results.

The goal of the experimentation will be to tune the different parameters of the agents, which define the overall behaviour of the robot through the combination of the individual behaviours of each agent, in order to achieve the best behaviour of the robot in any environment. Of course, it can be the case that such a "best robot" does not exist, and it would then be necessary to distinguish between different types of environments, so we would end up with a set of robot configurations, each one useful in a concrete situation. These configurations could be used to a priori set up the robot for a certain task, or the robot could dynamically change its configuration while it is performing its task, depending on the situations it encounters. For this latter case, we plan to develop a new agent that would be the responsible of recognising the different situations and deciding which configuration to use. We will use genetic algorithms to carry out this tuning.

Once the simulation results are satisfactory enough, and the real robot is available, we plan to test the navigation algorithm in real environments.

New methods of computing the quality of the landmarks will also be developed. One of these methods takes into account how close are the landmarks from being lost from the current view and how far has the robot moved since the last view frame ahead was taken. For instance, the closer the landmarks to the margins of the frame corresponding to the front view, the less quality associated to them.

We will also explore more complex types of interaction, such as negotiation, between the different agents of the navigation system.

**Acknowledgments.** This research has been supported by CICYT Project number TAP97-1209 and CIRIT project CeRTAP. Dídac Busquets enjoys the CIRIT doctoral scholarship 2000FI-00191. We acknowledge the discussions held with Thomas Dietterich during his sabbatical stay at IIIA, at the early stage of this research work.

# References

1. R.C. Arkin. Motor schema-based mobile robot navigation. *Int. J. Robotics research*, 8(4):92–112, 1989.
2. G. Bojadziev and M. Bojadziev. *Fuzzy sets, fuzzy logic, applications*, volume 5 of *Advances in Fuzzy Systems*. World Scientific, 1995.
3. R. Chatila. Path planning and environment learning in a mobile robot system. In *Proceedings of the 1982 European Conference on Artificial Intelligence (ECAI-82)*, 1982.

4. A. Elfes. Sonar-based real-world mapping and navigation. *IEEE J. Robotics and Automation*, 3(3):249–265, 1987.

5. M. Teresa Escrig and F. Toledo. Autonomous robot navigation using human spatial concepts. *Int. Journal of Intelligent Systems*, 15:165–196, 2000.

6. R. Liscano et al. Using a blackboard to integrate multiple activities and achieve strategic reasoning for mobile-robot navigation. *IEEE Expert*, 10(2):24–36, 1995.

7. C. Isik and A.M. Meystel. Pilot level of a hierarchical controller for an unmanned mobile robot. *IEEE J. Robotics and Automation*, 4(3):242–255, 1988.

8. D. M. Kortenkamp. *Cognitive maps for mobile robots: A representation for mapping and navigation*. PhD thesis, University of Michigan, Computer Science and Engineering Department, Michigan, 1993.

9. B.J. Kuipers and Y.-T. Byun. A robust qualitative method for spatial learning in unknown environments. In *Proceedings AAAI-88*, Menlo Park, CA, 1988. AAAI Press/MIT Press.

10. T.S. Levitt and D.T. Lawton. Qualitative navigation for mobile robots. *Artificial Intelligence Journal*, 44:305–360, 1990.

11. E. Martinez and C. Torras. Qualitative vision for the guidance of legged robots in unstructured environments. *Pattern Recognition*, In press, 2000.

12. M.J. Mataric. Navigating with a rat brain: a neurobiologically-inspired model for robot spatial representation. In J.-A. Meyer and S.W. Wilson, editors, *From Animals to Animats*, Cambridge, MA, 1991. MIT Press.

13. H.P. Moravec. Sensor fusion in certainty grids for mobile robots. *AI Magazine*, 9(2):61–74, 1988.

14. N.J. Nilsson. A mobile automaton: An application of AI techniques. In *Proceedings of the 1969 International Joint Conference on Artificial Intelligence*, 1969.

15. T.J. Prescott. Spatial representation for navigation in animats. *Adaptive Behavior*, 4(2):85–125, 1996.

16. Julio Rosenblatt. Damn: A distributed architecture for mobile navigation. In *Proceedings of the 1995 AAAI SpringSymposium on Lessons Learned from Implemented Software Architectures for Physical Agents*. AAAI Press, March 1995.

17. A. Stentz. The codger system for mobile robot navigation. In C.E. Thorpe, editor, *Vision and Navigation, the Carnegie Mellon Navlab*, pages 187–201, Boston, 1990. Kluwer Academic Pub.

18. R. Sun and C. Sessions. Bidding in reinforcement learning: A paradigm for multi-agent systems. In J.P. Müller O. Etzioni and J.M. Bradshaw, editors, *Proceedings 3d Annual Conference on Autonomous Agents*, pages 344–345, Seattle, 1999.

19. S. Thrun. Learning metric-topological maps for indoor mobile robot navigation. *Artificial Intelligence Journal*, 99(2):21–72, 1998.

20. D. Zipser. Biologically plausible models of placerecognition and place location. In J.L. McClelland and D.E. Rumelhart, editors, *Parallel Distributed Processing: Explorations in the Micro-Structure of Cognition*, Vol. 2, pages 432–470, Cambridge, MA, 1986. Bradford Books.

# Performance of Coordinating Concurrent Hierarchical Planning Agents Using Summary Information*

Bradley J. Clement and Edmund H. Durfee

Artificial Intelligence Laboratory, University of Michigan
1101 Beal Avenue, Ann Arbor, MI 48109-2110, USA
+1-734-764-2138
{bradc, durfee}@umich.edu

**Abstract.** Recent research has provided methods for coordinating the individually formed concurrent hierarchical plans (CHiPs) of a group of agents in a shared environment. A reasonable criticism of this technique is that the summary information can grow exponentially as it is propagated up a plan hierarchy. This paper analyzes the complexity of the coordination problem to show that in spite of this exponential growth, coordinating CHiPs at higher levels is still exponentially cheaper than at lower levels. In addition, this paper offers heuristics, including "fewest threats first" (FTF) and "expand most threats first" (EMTF), that take advantage of summary information to smartly direct the search for a global plan. Experiments show that for a particular domain these heuristics greatly improve the search for the optimal global plan compared to a "fewest alternatives first" (FAF) heuristic that has been successful in Hierarchical Task Network (HTN) Planning.

## 1   Introduction

In a shared environment with limited resources, agents may have enough information about the environment to individually plan courses of action but may not be able to anticipate how the actions of others will interfere with accomplishing their goals. Prior techniques have enabled such agents to cooperatively seek merges of individual plans that will accomplish all of their goals if possible [7]. This is done by identifying conflicts and adding synchronization actions to the plans to avoid conflicts. Agents can also interleave planning and merging, such that they propose next-step extensions to their current plans and reconcile conflicts before considering extensions for subsequent steps. By formulating extensions in terms of constraints rather than specific actions, a "least commitment" policy can be retained [5]. In addition, recent research has provided these agents with tools to coordinate their hierarchical plans resulting in more flexible abstract solutions that allow the agents to choose refinements of their actions during execution that can withstand some amount of failure and uncertainty [3]. In addition to adding ordering constraints, agents may need to eliminate choices of subplans for accomplishing subgoals. In order to reason about abstract plans to identify and resolve conflicts, information about how the abstract plans must or may be refined into lower level actions

---

* This work was supported by DARPA (F30602-98-2-0142).

C. Castelfranchi, Y. Lespérance (Eds.): Intelligent Agents VII, LNAI 1986, pp. 213–227, 2001.

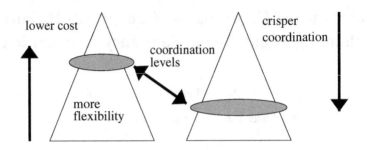

**Fig. 1.** Hierarchical plan coordination at multiple levels.

must be available. This information can be summarized from the conditions of subplans in its potential refinements.

It was previously shown that using this strategy to find abstract solutions to the coordination problem can improve the overall performance of coordinating and executing plans [3]. As depicted in Figure 1, coordination is cheaper at higher levels in the hierarchy because there are fewer plan steps to reason about. Although anecdotal evidence was given to show this, in this paper we reinforce the result with a more rigorous complexity analysis. At lower levels in the hierarchy, however, more detailed solutions of potential greater quality can be found, but only after greater coordination effort. Depending on how costly computation time is compared to the cost of executing the coordinated plans, coordinating at levels in between the top and bottom could likely result in better overall performance. On the other hand, only coordinating at the lowest level can guarantee finding the optimal solution.

If the goal is to find the optimal solution, a reasonable criticism might be that using summary information to reason at abstract levels will be more costly than just coordinating at the lowest level of primitive actions because of the overhead of deriving and using summary information. The experimental results given here contradict this criticism and show how reasoning about plans at abstract levels can better focus the search to much more quickly find detailed solutions at the level of primitive actions.

This paper makes the following contributions:

- complexity analysis showing that finding global plans at higher levels can be exponentially less expensive than at lower levels;
- search techniques and heuristics, including Fewest Threats First (FTF) and Expand Most Threats First (EMTF), that take advantage of summary information;
- a description of a search algorithm that uses these heuristics for coordinating concurrent hierarchical plans; and
- preliminary experiments showing how these heurisitics can greatly save computation time in finding the optimal plan compared to a Fewest Alternatives First (FAF) heuristic [4] that has been successful in Hierarchical Task Network (HTN) Planning [8].

In addition, of potential interest to the planning community, we prove that resolving threats among a set of unordered STRIPS operators is NP-complete. This result is necessary our complexity analysis.

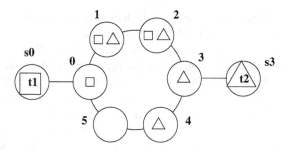

**Fig. 2.** Transports $t1$ and $t2$ must pick up square and triangle evacuees respectively.

Reasoning about abstract plans with conditions of lower-level subplans has also been used to efficiently guide the search through hierarchical plan spaces (HTN planning) for single agents [9]. This technique computes the *external conditions* of abstract plans, which are the preconditions required external to the abstract plans in order for them to be executed successfully. We redefine these as *external preconditions* and additionally employ *external postconditions*, the effects seen external to an abstract plan. Since the coordination problem requires reasoning about the concurrent execution of actions, we also derive *summary inconditions*, the intermediate, or internal, conditions that must or may be required to hold during an abstract plan step for the execution to be successful. We have detailed a procedure for deriving these summary conditions, proofs of their properties, and sound and complete mechanisms for determining legal interactions of abstract plans based on summary conditions elsewhere in [2].

## 1.1   A Simple Example

This example illustrates how agents can coordinate their actions using summary information to guide the search for a global plan that resolves conflicts and optimizes the total completion time of the agents' plans. In a non-combative evacuation operation (NEO) domain, transport agents are responsible for visiting certain locations along restricted routes to pick up evacuees and bring them back to safety points. To avoid the risk of oncoming danger (from a typhoon or an enemy attack), the transports need to coordinate in order to avoid collisions along the single lane routes and must accomplish their goals as quickly as possible.

Suppose there are two transport agents, $t1$ and $t2$, located at safety points $s0$ and $s3$ respectively, and they are responsible for visiting the locations 0-2 and 1-4 respectively as shown in Figure 2. Because there is overlap in the locations they must visit, they must synchronize their individual plans in order to avoid a collision. The hierarchical plan of $t1$ at the highest level is to evacuate the locations for which it is responsible. This decomposes into a primitive action of moving to location 0 on the ring and then to traverse the ring. It can choose to adopt a plan to travel in one direction around the ring without switching directions, or it can choose to switch directions once. $t1$ can then choose to either go clockwise or counterclockwise and, if switching, can choose to switch directions at any location and travel to the farthest location it needs to visit from where it switched. Once it has visited all the locations, it continues around until it can go to the first safety point it finds. $t2$ has a similar plan.

Now let us say $t1$ collects summary information about $t2$'s plan and attempts to coordinate it with its plan. Looking just at the highest level, $t1$ can determine that if it finishes its plan before $t2$ even begins execution, then there will be no conflicts since the external postconditions of its *evacuate* plan reveal that none of the routes are being traversed. $t1$ then tells $t2$ to add a plan step to the beginning of its plan to *wait* for $t1$'s signal, and $t1$ can append a *signal* subplan to the end of its plan. However, this coordinated global plan is inefficient since there is no parallel action—the length ranges from 12 to 26 steps depending on how the agents decompose their plans during execution. If the agents wish to get more concurrency, then they must expand the top-level plans into more detailed plans and resolve conflicts there. At a mid-level expansion where both agents move clockwise without switching directions, the algorithm finds a solution with a length of only eight steps. Now the search algorithm can eliminate the need to resolve threats for any global plan whose length can be no shorter than eight. To find the optimal solution, the agents must almost completely expand their hierarchies. This is a plan of length seven where $t1$ moves clockwise until it reaches location $s3$, and $t2$ starts out clockwise, switches at location 4, and then winds up at $s0$.

## 1.2   Overview

In the next section, we describe how concurrent hierarchical plans can be coordinated using summary information. Then we explain why it is easier to compute abstract solutions at higher levels than at lower levels with a complexity analysis of the coordination algorithm. Next we show experimental results verifying that summary information can greatly improve the search for the optimal global plan even when it exists at the lowest level of primitive actions.

## 2   Top-Down Coordination of Concurrent Hierarchical Plans

Our approach to coordinating concurrent hierarchical plans (CHiPs) is to first try to coordinate the plans at the top-level of the hierarchies, then consider their subplans, and iteratively expand selected subplans until a "feasible" solution is found. A general algorithm for doing this is described in [3]. Here we briefly explain the basic mechanisms for deriving and using summary information and then describe a specific algorithm we use to evaluate the effectiveness of coordinating using summary information. All terms and mechanisms mentioned here are formalized in [2].

### 2.1   CHiPs

As described here, hierarchical plans are non-primitive plans that each have their own sets of conditions, a set of subplans, and a set of ordering constraints over the subplans. These ordering constraints can be conjunctions of temporal interval relations [1] or point relations over endpoints of plan execution time intervals. A primitive plan is only different in that it has an empty set of subplans. In the style of STRIPS planning operators [6],

**external preconditions**  the conditions that must be met external to the execution of an abstract plan for any decomposition of the plan in order for the execution to succeed

**external postconditions**  the effects of a successful execution of an abstract plan for any decomposition of the plan that are not *undone* by its execution (which includes any execution of subplans in its decomposition)

**summary preconditions**  the external preconditions computed for an abstract plan along with *existence* (*must* or *may*) information for each condition[2]

**summary inconditions**  the internal conditions computed for an abstract plan that include any required conditions or effects that must hold within the interval of execution for some decomposition of the plan along with *existence* (*must* or *may*) and *timing* (*always* or *sometimes*) information for each condition

**summary postconditions**  the external preconditions computed for an abstract plan along with *existence* (*must* or *may*) information for each condition[2]

**must**  property of a summary condition where the condition must hold for the execution of the plan for *any* decomposition

**may**  property of a summary condition where the condition must hold for the execution of the plan for *some* decomposition

**always**  property of a summary incondition where the condition must hold throughout the execution of the plan for any decomposition

**sometimes**  property of a summary incondition where the condition must hold at some point during the execution of the plan for some decomposition

**clobber**  the effects of one plan's execution negates a condition required by another plan causing the plan to fail

**achieve**  the effects of one plan's execution asserts a condition required for another plan to be successful

**undo**  the effects of one plan's execution negates a condition asserted by another plan

**CanAnyWay**(*plans, order*)  every plan in *plans* can be decomposed and executed in any way according to the ordering constraints in *order*, and all executions will succeed

**MightSomeWay**(*plans, order*)  there is some decomposition and execution of each plan in *plans* according to the ordering constraints in *order* such that all executions succeed

**Fig. 3.** A review of terminology formalized in [2].

each of these plans has sets of preconditions and effects.[1] However, since we necessarily worry about agents performing tasks in parallel, we also associate a set of inconditions with each plan so that threats during the execution of a task can be represented.

An agent's plan library is a set of CHiPs, any of which could be part of the agent's current plan, and each plan in the hierarchy is either a primitive plan, an *and* plan, or an *or* plan. An *and* plan decomposes into a set of plans that each must be accomplished according to specified temporal constraints. An *or* plan decomposes into a set of plans of which only one must be accomplished. So, for the example given in Section 1.1, there is an *or* plan that would have subplans for traveling clockwise or counterclockwise, and there are *and* plans for chaining primitive level movements between locations to get a transport around the ring.

---

[1] These are not summary conditions.

## 2.2   Plan Summary Information

We derive summary conditions for CHiPs by propagating the conditions from the primitive level up the hierarchy. The procedure is quick ($O(n^2c^2)$) for $n$ plans in the hierarchy each with $c$ conditions) because the summary conditions of a plan are derived only from its own conditions and the summary conditions of its immediate subplans. As mentioned in the Section 1, summary preconditions, inconditions, and postconditions are computed for each plan to represent the external preconditions, internal conditions, and external postconditions respectively. Modal information about whether these conditions *must* or *may* hold and whether they must hold throughout the plan's execution (*always* or *sometimes*) is kept to reason about whether certain plan interactions must or may occur.

## 2.3   Temporal Interactions of CHiPs

In conventional planning, we often speak of *clobbering* and *achieving* preconditions of plans [10]. With CHiPs these notions are slightly different since inconditions can clobber and be clobbered. We use these concepts to determine whether a summary precondition of a plan should be a summary condition of its parent. A summary precondition is an *external* precondition of its subplans, and what makes the precondition external is that it is not *achieved* by another subplan—it needs to be met outside the scope of the parent plan. A summary postcondition is external because it is a net effect of the execution of the subplans. Thus, we need to also determine when a postcondition is *undone* by another subplan since a postcondition is not external if it is undone.

Determining these relationships helps us derive summary information, but it also helps identify threats across the plan hierarchies of the agents. For example, plan $p$ of one agent cannot clobber a condition $c$ of plan $q$ of another agent if there is another plan $r$ ordered between $p$ and $q$ that achieves $c$ for $q$. However, if plan $r$ only *may* achieve $c$ because $c$ is a *may* postcondition of $r$, then $p$ threatens $q$. Reasoning about these kinds of interactions, we can determine that a set of temporal relations can hold among plans no matter how they are decomposed ($CanAnyWay$) or that certain relations cannot hold for any decomposition ($\neg MightSomeWay$). As the procedure for determining these relations is similar to propagating summary information, its complexity is also $O(n^2c^2)$ for $n$ plans with $c$ conditions each [2].[3]

## 2.4   Top-Down Search Algorithm

Since an agent can determine whether a set of the agents' abstract plans $CanAnyWay$ or $MightSomeWay$ be executed successfully under particular ordering constraints, we can integrate this into an algorithm that smartly searches for a consistent global plan for a group of agents. The particular algorithm we describe here is sound and complete and returns the optimal global plan if it exists. The search starts out with the top-level

---

[3] The algorithm for determining $\neg MightSomeWay$ looks at all pairs of plans to detect if one must clobber another. This is not a complete algorithm because it does not consider impossibilities of satisfying combinations of threatened conditions. In Section 3 we show that this is an intractable problem.

plans of each agent, which together represent the global plan. The algorithm tries to find a solution at this level and then expands the hierarchies deeper and deeper until the optimal solution is found or the search space has been exhausted. A pseudocode description of the algorithm is given later in this section.

A state of the search is a partially elaborated global plan that we represent as a set of *and* plans (one for each agent), a set of temporal constraints, and a set of blocked plans. The subplans of the *and* plans are the leaves of the partially expanded hierarchies of the agents. The set of temporal constraints includes synchronization constraints added during the search in addition to those dictated by the agents' individual hierarchical plans. Blocked subplans keep track of pruned *or* subplans.

While one agent can be responsible for coordinating the plans of all agents in the system, the agents can use the summary information to determine which subsets of agents have locally conflicting plans and designate a coordinator for each localized group. In addition, the decisions made during the search could be made decentrally. The agents can negotiate over ordering constraints imposed, choices subplans to accomplish higher level plans, and which decompositions to explore first. While the algorithm described here does not comment specific negotiation techniques, it does provide the mechanics for identifying the choices over which the agents can negotiate.

The operators of the search are expanding non-primitive plans, blocking *or* subplans, and adding temporal constraints on pairs of plans. When the agents expand one of their plans, it is replaced by its subplans, and the ordering information is updated in the global plan. *Or* plans are only replaced by a subplan when all other subplans are blocked. Blocking an *or* subplan can be effective in resolving a constraint in which the other *or* subplans are not involved. This can lead to least commitment abstract solutions that leave the agents flexibility in selecting among the multiple applicable remaining subplans. The agents can take another approach by selecting subplans (effectively blocking the others) to investigate choices that are given greater preference or are more likely to resolve conflicts.

In the pseudocode below, the coordinating agent collects summary information about the other agents' plans as it decomposes them. The *queue* keeps track of expanded search states. If the $CanAnyWay$ relation holds for the search state, the Dominates function determines if the current solutions are better for every agent than the solution represented by the current search state and keeps it if the solution is not dominated. If $MightSomeWay$ is false, then the search space represented by the current search state can be pruned; otherwise, the operators mentioned above are applied to generate new search states. Nondeterministic "Choose" functions determine how these operators are applied. Our implementation uses heuristics specified in Section 2.5 to determine what choices are made. When a plan is expanded or selected, the ordering constraints for that plan must be updated for the subplans that replace it. The UpdateOrder function accomplishes this.

Hierarchical Plan Coordination Algorithm

$plans = \emptyset$
for each agent $a_i$
    $p_i$ = get summary information for top-level plan of $a_i$
    $plans = plans \cup \{p_i\}$
end for

```
queue = {(plans, ∅, ∅)}
solutions = ∅
loop
   if queue == ∅
      return solutions
   end if
   (plans, order, blocked) = Pop(queue)
   if CanAnyWay(initial_state, plans, order, blocked)
      solution = (plans, order, blocked)
      if Dominates(solutions, solution) == false
         solutions = solutions ∪ {solution}
      end if
   end if
   if MightSomeWay(initial_state, plans, order, blocked)
      operator = Choose({expand, select, block, constrain})
      if operator == expand
         plan = ChooseAndPlan(plans)
         if Exists(plan)
            plan.subplans = get summary information for
               subplans of plan
            plans = plans ∪ plan.subplans - plan
            UpdateOrder(order, plan, plan.subplans, plan.order)
         end if
      end if
      if operator == select
         plan = ChooseOrPlan(plans)
         if Exists(plan)
            plan.subplans = get summary information for
               subplans of plan
            for each subplan ∈ plan.subplans
               newblocked = blocked ∪ plan.subplans - {subplan}
               newplans = plans ∪ {subplan} - plan
               neworder = order
               UpdateOrder(neworder, plan, {subplan}, ∅)
               InsertStateInQueue(queue, newplans, neworder,
                  newblocked)
            end for
         end if
      end if
      if operator == block
         plan = ChooseOrPlan(plans)
         if Exists(plan)
            plan.subplans = get summary information for
               subplans of plan
            for each subplan ∈ plan.subplans where subplan ∉ blocked
               newblocked = blocked ∪ subplan
               neworder = order
               if ∃! subplan' ∈ plan.subplans, subplan' ∉ blocked
                  newplans = plans ∪ {subplan'} - plan
                  UpdateOrder(neworder, plan, {subplan'}, ∅)
               else
                  newplans = plans
               end if
               InsertStateInQueue(queue, newplans, neworder,
                  newblocked)
```

```
          end for
        end if
      end if
    if operator == constrain
      plan = ChoosePlan(plans)
      plan' = ChoosePlan(plans - {plan})
      constraint = ChooseConstraint({Start, End} ×
          {<, ≤, =, ≥, >} × {Start, End})
      neworder = order ∪ constraint
      if Consistent(neworder)
        InsertStateInQueue(queue, plans, neworder, blocked)
      end if
    end if
  end if
end if
end loop
```

Adding temporal constraints should only generate new search nodes when the ordering is consistent with the other global and local constraints. In essence, this operator performs the work of merging non-hierarchical plans since it is used to find a synchronization of the individual agents' plans that are one level deep. In the pseudocode above, the ChooseConstraint function nondeterministically investigates all orderings (represented by point algebra constraints over the "Start" and "End" points of action intervals), and inconsistent ordering constaints are pruned. However, in our implementation, we only investigate legal ordering constraints that resolve threats that are identified by algorithms determining must/may achieves and clobbers relations among CHiPs. In our experiments, we separated the search for synchronizations from the expansion and selection of subplans. An outer search was used to explore the space of plans at different levels of abstraction. For each state in the outer search, an inner search explores the space of plan merges by resolving threats with ordering constraints.

The soundness and completeness of the coordination algorithm depends on the soundness and completeness of identifying solutions and the complete exploration of the search space. Each search state is tested by the $CanAnyWay$ procedure to determine whether it is a solution. The $CanAnyWay$ procedure is shown to be sound and complete in [2]. Although the algorithm for determining $\neg MightSomeWay$ is only complete for a total ordering of CHiPs, it is used to prune invalid branches in the search space, so it is enough that it is sound [2]. In order to explore the search space completely, the coordinator would need to consider all synchronizations of all possible decompositions of each of the agents' top-level plans. We assume that the plan hierarchy of each agent is finite in its decomposition, so when the coordinator nondeterministically expands abstract plans, eventually all abstract plans will be replaced with primitive decompositions. Likewise, eventually all *or* plans will be replaced with subplan choices, and since new search states are generated and added to the queue for each subplan of an *or* plan, all possible decompositions of the agents' top-level plans are explored. The Choose function for selecting operators nondeterministically explores any synchronization of the expanded plans in conjunction with the ChooseConstraint function, so the search is complete.

## 2.5   Heuristics Using Summary Information

As discussed in [3], summary information is valuable for finding coordinated plans at abstract levels. However, this information can also be valuable in directing the search to avoid branches in the search space that lead to inconsistent or suboptimal global plans. Inconsistent global plans can be pruned away at the abstract level by doing a quick check to see if $MightSomeWay$ is false. In terms of the number of states expanded during the search, employing this technique will always do at least as well as not using it. Another strategy that is employed is to first expand plans involved in the most threats. For the sake of completeness, the order of plan expansions does not matter as long as they are all expanded at some point when the search trail cannot be pruned. But, employing the "expand on most threats first" (EMTF) heuristic aims at driving the search down through the hierarchy to find the subplan(s) causing conflicts with others so that they can be resolved more quickly. This is similar to a most-constrained variable heuristic often employed in constraint satisfaction problems. Another heuristic used in parallel in our experiments is "fewest threats first" (FTF). Here the search orders nodes in the outer search queue by ascending numbers of threats to resolve. By trying to resolve the threats of global plans with fewer conflicts, it is hoped that solutions can be found more quickly. So, EMTF is a heurisitic ordering plans to expand, and FTF orders subplan choices and, thus, search states to investigate. In addition, in trying to find optimal solutions in the style of a branch-and-bound search, we use the cost of abstract solutions to prune away branches of the search space whose minimum cost is greater than the maximum cost of the current best solution. This technique can be used without summary information, but then only solutions at the primitive level can be used to prune the search space. Again, pruning abstract plans can only help improve the search. We report experimental results in Section 4 that show that these techniques and heuristics can greatly improve coordination performance.

## 3   Complexity

In [3], anecdotal evidence was given to show that coordinating at higher levels of abstraction is less costly because there are fewer plan steps. But, even though there are fewer plans at higher levels, those plans have greater numbers of summary conditions to reason about because they are collected from the much greater set of plans below. Here we argue that even in the worst case where summary conditions increase exponentially up the hierarchy, finding solutions at abstract levels is expected to be exponentially cheaper than at lower levels.

The procedure for deriving summary conditions works by basically propagating the conditions from the primitives up the hierarchy to the most abstract plans. Because the conditions of any non-primitive plan depend only on those of its immediate subplans, deriving summary conditions can be done quickly. In [2], it was reported that the complexity of this is $O(n(log^2 n)c^2)$ for $n$ non-primitive plans with $c$ conditions in each plan's *summary* pre-, in-, and postconditions. This, however, does not tell us how the complexity grows as a result of summary conditions accumulating in greater and greater sets as they are propagated up the hierarchy. If $c'$ is the greatest number of literals in any plan's pre-, in-, and postconditions, then the complexity is $O(n^2 c'^2)$. Here, the worst case is when all plans are *and* plans, and the conditions of each plan are completely different than those of any other plan. In this way, the maximum number of conditions are propagated up the hierarchy and all of the expanded plans must be synchronized to avoid conflicts. Consider a global hierarchy with $n$ total plans, $b$ subplans for each non-primitive plan, and depth $d$.[4] At each level, the procedure tests each condition in each summary condition set of the $b$ subplans of each plan at that level to see if they are achieved/clobbered/undone by any other subplan attempting to assert that condition. Thus, a constant number of operations must be performed when comparing each condition in each subplan with every other condition in every other subplan resulting in $O(b^2 c^2)$ operations for each plan with $b$ subplans each having $O(c)$ summary conditions. So, as shown in Figure 4, at the next-to-bottom depth level $d - 1$, each of the $b^{d-1}$ plans has $b$ primitive subplans each with $O(c')$ conditions. Thus, $O(b^2 c'^2)$ operations are performed for each of the $b^{d-1}$ plans for a total of $O(b^{d-1}b^2 c'^2)$ operations for that level. At level $d - 2$, there are $b^{d-2}$ plans, and the number of conditions that must be compared among their subplans at level $d-1$ additionally includes those propagated from the primitive level for a total of $3c' + b3c'$ conditions. Thus, $O(b^{d-2}b^2(c' + bc')^2)$ operations are performed at level $d - 2$. This generalizes to $O(\sum_{i=0}^{d-1} b^i b^2 (b^{d-i-1}c')^2)$ operations for the entire hierarchy. We can reduce this to $O(b^2 c'^2 \sum_{i=0}^{d-1} b^{2d-i-2}) = O(b^{2d}c'^2)$, and since $n = O(b^d)$, the complexity can be simply stated as $O(n^2 c'^2)$.

In this worst case, the number of summary conditions for an abstract plan grows exponentially as you go up the hierarchy as shown in the second column of Figure 4. At the primitive level $d$, each plan has only $3c' = O(c')$ conditions, and there are $c' + bc' = O(bc')$ summary conditions for each plan at level $d - 1$ and $O(b^2 c')$. There are at most $3nc'$, or $O(b^d c')$, summary conditions at the root of the hierarchy—this is the total number of pre-, in-, and postconditions in the hierarchy. One might argue that in such cases deriving summary information only increases computation. But, actually, exponential computation time is saved when decisions based on summary information can be made at abstract levels because the complexity from exponential growth in the number of plans down the hierarchy outweighs the complexity of conditions growing exponentially up the hierarchy. This is because, as will be shown, the only known algorithms for synchronizing plan steps to avoid conflicts are exponential with respect to the number of plans expanded in the hierarchy, which also grows exponentially with the depth. This exponential growth down the hierarchy outweighs the exponential growth of summary conditions in plans up the hierarchy. So the improvements made using summary information can yield exponential savings while only incurring a small polynomial overhead in deriving and using summary information.

Let's make this more clear. At the $i$th depth level in the hierarchy, each of the $O(b^i)$ plans has $O(b^{d-i}c'^2)$ summary conditions in the worst case. As described in [2], the algorithm to check whether a particular ordering of $n$ plan steps (each with $c$ summary conditions) results in all plans executing successfully is similar to deriving their collective summary information and has a complexity of $O(n^2 c^2)$. Checking such a synchronization for the plans at any level $i$ in a plan hierarchy is, thus, $O(b^{2i}b^{2d-2i}c'^2) = O(b^{2d}c'^2)$. So, since $i$ drops out, the complexity of doing this check is *independent of the depth level*. In Figure 4, this is shown in the fifth column of the table where the number of operations

---

[4] We consider the root at depth level 0 and the leaves at level $d$.

is the same at each level. But, there is a huge space of $n! = O((b^i)!)$ sequential order-ings[5] of the $n$ plans at level $i$ to potentially check to find a valid synchronization.[6] Thus, the search space grows doubly exponentially down the hierarchy despite the worst case when the number of conditions grows exponentially up the hierarchy. This argument assumes that finding a valid synchronization is intractable for larger numbers of plan steps, so we show that it is actually NP-complete. We reduce HAMILTONIAN PATH to the THREAT RESOLUTION problem for STRIPS planning and claim that a similar reduction can be done for our problem that allows concurrent execution.

| level | #plans | #conds / plan | #operations to derive summ. info. | #test operations / solution candidate | solution space |
|---|---|---|---|---|---|
| 0 | 1 | $O(b^d c')$ | $O(b^2(b^{d-1}c')^2)$ $= O(b^{2d}c'^2)$ | $O(1)$ | 1 |
| 1 | $b$ | $O(b^{d-1}c')$ | $O(bb^2(b^{d-2}c')^2)$ $= O(b^{2d-1}c'^2)$ | $O(b^2(b^{d-1}c')^2)$ $= O(b^{2d}c'^2)$ | $O(b!)$ |
| 2 | $b^2$ | $O(b^{d-2}c')$ | $O(b^2b^2(b^{d-3}c')^2)$ $= O(b^{2d-2}c'^2)$ | $O(b^4(b^{d-2}c')^2)$ $= O(b^{2d}c'^2)$ | $O(b^2!)$ |
| d-2 | $b^{d-2}$ | $O(b^2c')$ | $O(b^{d-2}b^2(bc')^2)$ $= O(b^{d+2}c'^2)$ | $O(b^{2(d-2)}(b^2c')^2)$ $= O(b^{2d}c'^2)$ | $O(b^{d-2}!)$ |
| d-1 | $b^{d-1}$ | $3c'+b3c'$ $= O(bc')$ | $O(b^{d-1}b^2c'^2)$ $= O(b^{d+1}c'^2)$ | $O(b^{2(d-1)}(bc')^2)$ $= O(b^{2d}c'^2)$ | $O(b^{d-1}!)$ |
| d | $b^d$ | $3c'$ | $O(1)$ | $O(b^{2d}c'^2)$ | $O(b^d!)$ |

**Fig. 4.** The table gives the number of plans and summary conditions for each plan at some level of expansion of a global plan hierarchy (with branching factor $b$) where each plan has $c'$ conditions in each set of pre-, in-, and postconditions. The number of operations to derive summary information for all of the plans at a particular depth level is the product of the number of plans at that level, the square of the number of subplans per plan, and the square of the number of conditions per subplan. The number of operations to check if a candidate expansion under particular ordering constraints is a solution is on the order of the square of the product of the number of plans and the number of summary conditions per plan at that level of expansion. The solution space is the number of temporal orderings of the expanded plans (approximated by the factorial).

**Theorem.** THREAT RESOLUTION is NP-complete. This is the problem of determining whether there is a set of ordering constraints that can be added to a partial order STRIPS plan such that no operator's preconditions are threatened by another operator's effects.

**Proof.** If there is a set of ordering constraints that will resolve all threats, then there is at least one corresponding total order where there are no threats. Thus, the problem is

---

[5] There are more for other orderings allowing for concurrent execution.

[6] This is why Georgeff[7] chose to cluster multiple operators into "critical regions" and synchro-nize the (fewer) regions since there would be many fewer interleavings to check. By exploiting the hierarchical structure of plans, we use the "clusters" predefined in the hierarchy to this kind of advantage without needing to cluster from the bottom up.

in NP since orderings of operators can be chosen non-deterministically, and threats can be identified in polynomial time.

Given a directed graph $G = (V, E)$ with nodes $v_1, v_2, \ldots, v_n \in V$ and edges $e_1, e_2, \ldots, e_m \in E$ (a set of ordered pairs of nodes), HAMILTONIAN PATH is the problem that asks if there is a path that visits each node exactly once. We build an instance of THREAT RESOLUTION (a partial order plan) by creating an operator for each node $v_i$. The only precondition of the operator is $A(i)$, representing the *accessibility* of the node. There is a postcondition $A(j)$ for each edge $e_k = (v_i, v_j)$, and a postcondition $\overline{A(l)}$ for all other nodes for which there is no edge from $v_i$. All operators are unordered and the initial state and goal state is empty.

If there is a Hamiltonian path for the graph, then the operators for the nodes can be ordered the same as the nodes in the path because the accessibility preconditions of each operator will be satisfied by the previous operator. If there is no Hamiltonian path for the graph, then there is no consistent ordering of the operators. We know this because there is a one-to-one mapping from an ordering of nodes to an ordering of operators. If the ordering of the nodes is such that there is no edge from one to a succeeding node, then the accessibility precondition of the corresponding operator will be clobbered. In addition, for any walk through the graph, there eventually will be an unvisited node for which there is no edge from the last node visited. In this case, the unvisited node will be clobbered because its accessibility precondition will not be met. Thus, THREAT RESOLUTION is NP-hard, and since it was shown to be in NP, it is NP-complete. □

In order to show that resolving threats among CHiPs is also NP-complete, we only need to add inconditions to each operator that prevent concurrent action. This can be done by adding $A(i)$ for $v_i$ and $\overline{A(j)}$ for every other $v_j \in V$ to the inconditions of the operator corresponding to $v_i$ for each $v_i \in V$. This ensures that the only temporal relations that can hold between any pair of operators are *before*, *after*, *meets*, or *imeets*, and the one-to-one mapping from paths in the graph to sequences of operators is preserved.

There are only *and* plans in this worst case. In the case that there are *or* plans, by similar argument, being able to prune branches at higher levels based on summary information will greatly improve the search despite the overhead of deriving and using summary conditions. Obviously, the computational savings of using summary information will be even greater when there are conditions common to plans on the same level, and the number of summary conditions does not grow exponentially up the hierarchy. Still, surely there are cases where none of the details of the plan hierarchy can be ignored, and summary information would incur unnecessary overhead, but when the size of problem instances are scaled, dealing with these details will likely be infeasible anyway.

## 4    Experiments

The experiments described here used the coordination algorithm described in Section 2.4 with all of the stated heuristics. It was compared to another top-down search algorithm that did not use summary information but used a FAF ("fewest alternatives first") heuristic [4] to decide the order in which *or* subplans are investigated. This simply means we chose to expand the *or* subplan that had the fewest number of subplan choices. Since no

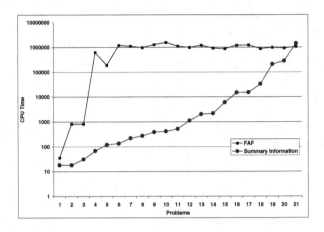

**Fig. 5.** CPU time measurements comparing summary information heuristics to FAF for finding optimal solutions. FAF only solved problems 1-5 and 7; others were killed when the search queue was too large to fit in memory.

summary information was used, threats could only be resolved at primitive levels. The FAF heuristic has been shown to be effective in the HTN planning domain to get large improvements in search time [8], and a similar approach to ours shows how heuristics using external conditions can be used to get exponential improvements over FAF [9]. We show here that summary information can also be used to gain significant improvements over FAF. Certainly, a comparison of our approach with that in [9] could help shed light on the benefits and disadvantages of varying amounts of summary information. This is a future consideration of this work.

The problems were hand-crafted from the NEO domain, described in the example in the Introduction. Agents had plans to either visit their specified locations by traveling in one direction only or switching directions at some location. These choices expand into choices to begin traveling clockwise or counterclockwise. For the branch where the agent switches directions, it can choose to change directions at any location it is specified to visit. Primitive actions are to move between adjacent locations without running into another agent. Optimality is measured as the total completions time where each move has a uniform time cost. We chose problems with four, six, and eight locations; with two and three agents; and with no, some, and complete overlap in the locations the agents visited. Results of the experiments are given in Figure 5.

For problems with only four locations and two agents, both algorithms found the optimal solution quickly. For more complex algorithms, the heuristics using summary information appear to make great improvements over FAF, which could only solve six of the 21 problems within memory constraints. These results are by no means conclusive, but they do show promise for search based on summary information. For most of these problems, coordinating at the primitive level was intractable. In most cases, the algorithm using summary information was able to find an abstract solution quickly.

## 5  Conclusions and Future Work

We have shown that summary information can can find solutions at higher levels exponentially more quickly than at lower levels; and we have identified heuristics and search techniques that can take advantage of summary information in finding coordinated plans. In addition, we have characterized a coordination algorithm that takes advantage of these search techniques and experimentally shown how it can make large improvements over an FAF heuristic in finding optimal coordinated plans. More work is needed to show that these results translate to different domains, and future considerations include comparing this approach to other planning heuristics that capitalize on domain knowledge in order to better understand the relationship between plan structure and search performance. We expect the benefits of using summary information to also apply to hierarchical planning and wish to compare these techniques with current heuristics for concurrent hierarchical planning.

## References

1. J. F. Allen. Maintaining knowledge about temporal intervals. *Communications of the ACM*, 26(11):832–843, November 1983.
2. B. Clement and E. Durfee. Theory for coordinating concurrent hierarchical planning agents. In *Proc. AAAI*, 1999.
3. B. Clement and E. Durfee. Top-down search for coordinating the hierarchical plans of multiple agents. In *Proc. Intl. Conf. Autonomous Agents*, 1999.
4. K. Currie and A. Tate. O-plan: The open planning architecture. *Artificial Intelligence*, 52:49–86, 1991.
5. E. Ephrati and J. Rosenschein. Divide and conquer in multi-agent planning. In *Proc. AAAI*, pages 375–380, July 1994.
6. R. E. Fikes and Nilsson N. J. Strips: A new approach to the application of theorem proving to problem solving. *Artificial Intelligence*, 2:189–208, 1971.
7. M. P. Georgeff. Communication and interaction in multiagent planning. In *Proc. AAAI*, pages 125–129, 1983.
8. R. Tsuneto, J. Hendler, and D. Nau. Space-size minimizationin refinement planning. In *Proc. Fourth European Conference on Planning*, 1997.
9. R. Tsuneto, J. Hendler, and D. Nau. Analyzing external conditions to improve the efficiency of htn planning. In *Proc. AAAI*, pages 913–920, 1998.
10. D. Weld. An introduction to least commitment planning. *AI Magazine*, 15(4):27–61, 1994.

# Agent Programming with Declarative Goals

Koen V. Hindriks, Frank S. de Boer, Wiebe van der Hoek, and John-Jules Ch. Meyer

Institute of Information & Computing Sciences, University Utrecht
P.O. Box 80 089, 3508 TB Utrecht
{koenh,frankb,wiebe,jj}@.cs.uu.nl

**Abstract.** A long and lasting problem in agent research has been to close the gap between agent logics and agent programming frameworks. The main reason for this problem of establishing a link between agent logics and agent programming frameworks is identified and explained by the fact that agent programming frameworks have not incorporated the concept of a *declarative goal*. Instead, such frameworks have focused mainly on plans or *goals-to-do* instead of the end goals to be realised which are also called *goals-to-be*. In this paper, a new programming language called GOAL is introduced which incorporates such declarative goals. The notion of a *commitment strategy* - one of the main theoretical insights due to agent logics, which explains the relation between beliefs and goals - is used to construct a computational semantics for GOAL. Finally, a proof theory for proving properties of GOAL agents is introduced. An example program is proven correct by using this programming logic.

## 1 Goal-Oriented Agent Programming

In the early days of agent research, an attempt was made to make the concept of agents more precise by means of *logical systems*. This effort resulted in a number of - mainly - modal logics for the specification of agents which formally defined notions like *belief, goal, intention*, etc. associated with agents [14,12,3]. The relation of these logics with more practical approaches remains unclear, however, to this day. Several efforts to bridge the gap have been attempted. In particular, a number of *agent programming languages* have been developed to bridge the gap between theory and practice [13,7]. These languages show a clear family resemblance with one of the first agent programming languages Agent-0 [17,8], and also with the language ConGolog [5,6,10].

These programming languages define agents in terms of their corresponding beliefs, goals, plans and capabilities. Although they define similar notions as in the logical approaches, there is one notable difference. In logical approaches, a goal is a *declarative* concept, whereas in the cited programming languages goals are defined as sequences of actions or *plans*. The terminology used differs from case to case. However, whether they are called commitments (Agent-0), intentions (AgentSpeak), or goals (3APL) makes little difference: all these notions are structures built from *actions* and therefore similar in nature to *plans*. The PLACA language [18] also focuses more on extending AGENT0 to a language with complex planning structures (which are not part of the programming language itself!) than on providing a clear theory of declarative goals of agents as part of a programming language and in this respect is similar to AgentSpeak and 3APL.

C. Castelfranchi, Y. Lespérance (Eds.): Intelligent Agents VII, LNAI 1986, pp. 228–243, 2001.
© Springer-Verlag Berlin Heidelberg 2001

In contrast, a *declarative* perspective on goals in agent languages is still missing. This is also true of attempts to directly execute agent logics like [4]. Because of this mismatch it has not been possible so far to use modal logics which include both belief and goal modalities for the specification and verification of programs written in agent languages and it has been impossible to close the gap between agent logics and programming frameworks. The value of adding declarative goals to agent programming lies both in the fact that it offers a new abstraction mechanism as well as that agent programs with declarative goals more closely approximate the intuitive concept of an intelligent agent. To fully realise the potential of the notion of an intelligent agent, a declarative notion of a goal, therefore, should also be incorporated into agent languages. In this paper, we introduce the new agent programming language GOAL, which takes the declarative concept of a goal seriously and which provides a concrete proposal to bridge the gap between theory and practice. We offer a complete theory of agent programming in the sense that our theory provides both for a programming framework and a programming logic for such agents. In contrast with other attempts [17,19] to bridge the gap, our programming language and programming logic are related by means of a formal semantics. Only by providing such a formal relation it is possible to make sure that statements proven in the logic concern properties of the agent.

## 2   The Programming Language GOAL

In this Section, we introduce the programming language GOAL (for Goal-Oriented Agent Language). The programming language GOAL is inspired by work in concurrent programming, in particular by the language UNITY designed by Chandy and Misra [2]. The basic idea is that a set of actions which execute in parallel constitutes a program. However, whereas UNITY is a language based on assignment to variables, the language GOAL is an agent-oriented programming language which incorporates more complex notions as belief, goal, and agent capabilities that operate on high-level information instead of simple values.

As in most agent programming languages, GOAL agents select actions on the basis of their current mental state. A mental state is a pair $\langle \sigma, \gamma \rangle$ where $\sigma$ are the beliefs and $\gamma$ are the goals of the agent. However, in contrast to most agent languages, GOAL incorporates a *declarative* notion of goal which is used by the agent to decide what to do. That is, both the beliefs $\sigma$ and goals $\gamma$ are drawn from one and the same logical language, $\mathcal{L}$, with associated consequence relation $\models$. In this paper, we assume that this *content language* $\mathcal{L}$ is a propositional language. Our motivation for this assumption is the fact that we want to present the main ideas in their simplest form and do not want to clutter the definitions below with details. We impose a constraint on mental states and insist that an agent cannot have a goal to achieve $\phi$ if the agent already believes that $\phi$ is the case. This constraint is derived from the default commitment strategy that agents use, and is explained in detail below. Formally, the constraint on mental states $\langle \sigma, \gamma \rangle$ means that no $\psi \in \gamma$ can be inconsistent nor can $\psi$ be entailed by $\sigma$ ($\sigma \not\models \psi$), and $\sigma$ must be consistent.

A mental state does *not* contain a program or plan component in the 'classical' sense. Although both the beliefs and the goals of an agent are drawn from the same logical language, as we will see below, the semantics of beliefs and goals are quite different. This difference in meaning derives from the different features of beliefs and goals of agents. The goals of an agent in this paper are best thought of as *achievement goals*, that is, they describe a goal state that the agent desires to reach. Mainly due to the temporal aspects of such goals many properties of beliefs fail for goals. For example, the fact that an agent has the goal to *be at home* and the goal to *be at the movies* does not allow the conclusion that this agent also has the conjunctive goal to *be at home and at the movies* at the same time. As a consequence, less stringent consistency requirements are imposed on goals than on beliefs. An agent may have the goal to be at home and the goal to be at the movies simultaneously; assuming these two goals cannot consistently be achieved at the same time does not mean that an agent cannot have adopted both in the language GOAL.

To express conditions on mental states, the language $\mathcal{L}_M$ of mental state formulas is introduced. The language $\mathcal{L}_M$ consists of boolean combinations of the basic mental state formulas $\mathsf{B}\phi$, which expresses that $\phi$ is believed to be the case, and $\mathsf{G}\psi$, which expresses that $\psi$ is a goal of the agent. Here, both $\phi$ and $\psi$ range over the content language $\mathcal{L}$.

Besides beliefs and goals, a third basic concept in GOAL is that of an agent *capability*. The capabilities of an agent consist of a set of so called *basic actions* which are interpreted as updates on the agent's belief base. An example of a capability is the action $\mathsf{ins}(\phi)$ which inserts $\phi$ in the belief base. The capabilities of an agent do not modify the agent's goals. Two special actions $\mathsf{adopt}(\phi)$ and $\mathsf{drop}(\phi)$ are introduced to respectively adopt a new goal or drop an old goal. We use *Bcap* to denote the set of all belief update capabilities of an agent. The set of all capabilities is then defined by: $Cap = Bcap \cup \{\mathsf{adopt}(\phi), \mathsf{drop}(\phi) \mid \phi \in \mathcal{L}\}$.

A *GOAL agent* is a triple $\langle \Pi, \sigma_0, \gamma_0 \rangle$ that consists of the specification of an *initial mental state* $\langle \sigma_0, \gamma_0 \rangle$ and a set of actions built from the capabilities associated with the agent. Actions derived from the capabilities are *conditional actions* of the form $\varphi \to do(\mathsf{a})$, where $\mathsf{a} \in Cap$, and $\varphi \in \mathcal{L}_M$ is a mental state condition. The mental state condition specifies when the action $\mathsf{a}$ may be considered for execution by the agent. Note the most salient differences between GOAL agents and, for example, AgentSpeak or 3APL agents: whereas AgentSpeak and 3APL agents have planning capabilities (by means of plan rules), GOAL agents do not; whereas GOAL agents have declarative goals, neither AgentSpeak nor 3APL has such goals.

One of the key ideas in the semantics for GOAL is to incorporate into the semantics a particular *commitment strategy* (cf. [15,3]). The semantics is based on a particularly simple and transparent commitment strategy, called *blind commitment*. An agent that acts according to a blind commitment drops a goal if and only if it believes that that goal has been achieved. By incorporating this commitment strategy into the semantics of GOAL, a default commitment strategy is built into agents. It is, however, only a default strategy and a programmer can overwrite this default strategy by means of the drop action. It is not possible, however, to adopt a goal $\psi$ in case the agent believes that $\psi$ is already achieved.

The semantics of action execution should now be defined in conformance with this basic commitment principle. To get started, we must assume that some specification of the belief update semantics of all capabilities (except for the two special actions adopt and drop which are allowed to explicitly update goals) is given. From this specification, then, we must construct a semantics for updating goals for each action. That is, we must specify how an action updates the complete current mental state of an agent given only a specification of the belief update it performs.

From the default blind commitment strategy, we conclude that a goal is dropped *only* if the agent *believes* that the goal has been accomplished. The revision of goals thus is based on the beliefs of the agent, which comprises all the information available to an agent to decide whether or not to drop or adopt a goal. So, in case the agent believes a goal has been achieved, this goal is to be removed from the current goals of the agent. Besides the default commitment strategy, only the two special actions adopt or drop can result in a change to the goal base.

Formally, the update on the current mental state - and not just the belief base - due to an action is derived from a given partial transition function $\mathcal{T}$ of type : $Bcap \times \wp(\mathcal{L}) \to \wp(\mathcal{L})$. $\mathcal{T}$ specifies how a capability updates a belief base. The update function $\mathcal{M}$ on mental states $\langle \sigma, \gamma \rangle$ is derived from $\mathcal{T}$. Like $\mathcal{T}$, $\mathcal{M}$ is a *partial* function representing the fact that an action may not be executable or *enabled* in some mental states. Also, $\mathcal{M}$ defines the semantics of adopt and drop. An adopt($\phi$) adopts $\phi$ as a goal if $\phi$ is consistent. A drop($\phi$) removes every goal which entails $\phi$ from the goal base. As an example, consider the two extreme cases: drop(false) removes no goals, whereas drop(true) removes all current goals.

$$\mathcal{M}(\mathsf{a}, \langle \sigma, \gamma \rangle) = \langle \mathcal{T}(\mathsf{a}, \sigma), \gamma \setminus \{\psi \in \gamma \mid \mathcal{T}(\mathsf{a}, \sigma) \models \psi\} \rangle$$
for $\mathsf{a} \in Bcap$ if $\mathcal{T}(\mathsf{a}, \sigma)$ is defined,
$\mathcal{M}(\mathsf{a}, \langle \sigma, \gamma \rangle)$ is undefined for $\mathsf{a} \in Bcap$ if $\mathcal{T}(\mathsf{a}, \sigma)$ is undefined,
$\mathcal{M}(\mathsf{drop}(\phi), \langle \sigma, \gamma \rangle) = \langle \sigma, \gamma \setminus \{\psi \in \gamma \mid \psi \models \phi\} \rangle$,
$\mathcal{M}(\mathsf{adopt}(\phi), \langle \sigma, \gamma \rangle) = \langle \sigma, \gamma \cup \{\phi\} \rangle$ if $\sigma \not\models \phi$ and $\not\models \neg\phi$,
$\mathcal{M}(\mathsf{adopt}(\phi), \langle \sigma, \gamma \rangle)$ is undefined if $\sigma \models \phi$ or $\models \neg\phi$.

The semantic function $\mathcal{M}$ maps an agent capability and a mental state to a new mental state. The capabilities of an agent thus are *mental state transformers*. Note that the semantics of the adopt action allows that an agent adopts a new goal inconsistent with its old goals. For example, if the current goal base $\gamma = \{p\}$ contains $p$, it is legal to execute the action adopt($\neg p$) resulting in a new goal base $\{p, \neg p\}$. Although inconsistent goals cannot be achieved at the same time, they might be achieved in some temporal order. Individual goals in a goal base, however, are required to be consistent. Thus, whereas local consistency is imposed (i.e., individual goals must be consistent), global consistency is not required (i.e., $\{p, \neg p\}$ is a legal goal base).

The second idea incorporated into the semantics concerns the *selection of conditional actions*. A conditional action $\varphi \to do(\mathsf{a})$ may specify conditions on the beliefs as well as conditions on the goals of an agent. As is usual, conditions on the beliefs are taken as a precondition for action execution: only if the agent's current beliefs entail the belief conditions associated with $\varphi$ the agent will select a for execution. The goal condition, however, is used in a different way. It is used as a means for the agent to determine whether or not the action will help bring about a particular goal of the agent. Bluntly put, the goal condition specifies where the action is good for. This does not mean that the action necessarily establishes the goal immediately, but rather may be taken as an indication that the action is helpful in bringing about a particular state of affairs. To make this discussion more precise, we introduce a formal definition of a *formula* $\phi$ *that partially fulfils a goal in a mental state* $\langle \sigma, \gamma \rangle$, notation: $\phi \leadsto_\sigma \gamma$. By definition, we have

$$\phi \leadsto_\sigma \gamma \text{ iff for some } \psi \in \gamma : \psi \models \phi \text{ and } \sigma \not\models \phi$$

Informally, the definition of $\phi \leadsto_\sigma \gamma$ can be paraphrased as follows: the agent needs to establish $\phi$ to realise one of its goals, but does not believe that $\phi$ is the case. The formal definition of $\phi \leadsto_\sigma \gamma$ entails that the realisation of $\phi$ would also bring about at least part of one of the goals in the goal base $\gamma$ of the agent. The restriction that the agent does not already believe that $\psi$ is the case ($\sigma \not\models \psi$) prevents an agent from performing an action without any need to do so. The same condition also implies that the goals of an agent are never tautologies. Our definition of $\leadsto$ provides for a simple and clear principle for action selection: an action can only be selected in case the goal condition associated with that action partially fulfils some goal in the current goal base of the agent.

From the formal definition of $\leadsto$ we derive the semantics of mental state formulas. Formally, for a mental state $\langle \sigma, \gamma \rangle$, the semantics of a mental state formula is defined by:

| | |
|---|---|
| $\langle \sigma, \gamma \rangle \models \mathbf{B}\phi$ iff $\sigma \models \phi$ | $\langle \sigma, \gamma \rangle \models \mathbf{G}\psi$ iff $\psi \leadsto_\sigma \gamma$ |
| $\langle \sigma, \gamma \rangle \models \neg\varphi$ iff $\langle \sigma, \gamma \rangle \not\models \varphi$ | $\langle \sigma, \gamma \rangle \models \varphi_1 \wedge \varphi_2$ iff $\langle \sigma, \gamma \rangle \models \varphi_1$ and $\langle \sigma, \gamma \rangle \models \varphi_2$. |

Now we know what it means that a mental condition holds in a mental state, we are able to formalise the selection and execution of a conditional action by an agent. In the definition below, we assume that the action component $\Pi$ of an agent $\langle \Pi, \sigma_0, \gamma_0 \rangle$ is fixed. The execution of an action gives rise to a *computation step* formally denoted by the transition relation $\xrightarrow{b}$ where $b$ is the conditional action executed in the computation step. More than one computation step may be possible in a current state and the step relation $\longrightarrow$ thus denotes a *possible* computation step in a state. A computation step updates the current state and yields the next state of the computation. Note that because $\mathcal{M}$ is a partial function, a conditional action can only be successfully executed if both the condition is satisfied and the basic action is enabled.

**Definition 1.** (action selection)
Let $\langle \sigma, \gamma \rangle$ be a mental state and $b = \varphi \rightarrow do(\mathsf{a}) \in \Pi$. Then, as a rule, we have that if the mental condition $\varphi$ holds in $\langle \sigma, \gamma \rangle$, i.e., $\langle \sigma, \gamma \rangle \models \varphi$, and $\mathsf{a}$ is enabled in $\langle \sigma, \gamma \rangle$, i.e., $\mathcal{M}(\mathsf{a}, \langle \sigma, \gamma \rangle)$ is defined, then $\langle \sigma, \gamma \rangle \xrightarrow{b} \mathcal{M}(\mathsf{a}, \langle \sigma, \gamma \rangle)$ is a possible computation step. The relation $\longrightarrow$ is the smallest relation closed under this rule.
We say that a conditional action $b$ is *enabled* in a mental state $\langle \sigma, \gamma \rangle$ in case $\mathcal{M}(\mathsf{a}, \langle \sigma, \gamma \rangle)$ is defined. The special predicate *enabled* is introduced to denote that a conditional action $b$ (*enabled*($b$)) or a capability $\mathsf{a}$ (*enabled*($\mathsf{a}$)) is enabled.

## 3    A Personal Assistant Example

In this Section, we give an example to show how the programming language GOAL can be used to program agents. The example concerns a shopping agent that is able to buy books on the Internet on behalf of the user. The example provides for a simple illustration of how the programming language works. The agent in our example uses a standard procedure for buying a book. It first goes to a bookstore, in our case Amazon.com. At the web site of Amazon.com it searches for a particular book, and if the relevant web page with the book details shows up, the agent puts the book in its shopping cart. In case the shopping cart of the agent contains some items, it is allowed to buy the items on behalf of the user. The set of capabilities of the agent is defined by $Bcap = \{goto\_website(site), search(book), put\_in\_shopping\_cart(book), pay\_cart\}$. In the example, relevant web pages are the home page of the user, Amazon.com, web pages with information about books, and a web page that shows the current items in the shopping cart of the agent (called *ContentCart*).

In the program text below, we assume that *book* is a variable referring to the specifics of the book the user wants to buy (in the example, we use variables as a means for abbreviation; variables should be thought of as being instantiated with the relevant arguments in such a way that predicates with variables reduce to propositions). We also assume that the user has provided the agent with the goals to buy *The Intentional Stance* by Daniel Dennett (abbreviated to 'T') and *Intentions, Plans, and Practical Reason* by Michael Bratman (abbreviated to 'I').

$$
\begin{aligned}
\Pi = \{ & \\
& \mathsf{B}(current\_website(page(user)) \vee current\_website(ContentCart)) \wedge \\
& \qquad \mathsf{G}(bought(book)) \rightarrow do(goto\_website(Amazon.com)), \\
& \mathsf{B}(current\_website(Amazon.com)) \wedge \neg\mathsf{B}(in\_cart(book)) \wedge \\
& \qquad \mathsf{G}(bought(book)) \rightarrow do(search(book)), \\
& \mathsf{B}(current\_website(book)) \wedge \mathsf{G}(bought(book)) \rightarrow \\
& \qquad do(put\_in\_shopping\_cart(book)), \\
& \mathsf{B}(in\_cart(book)) \wedge \mathsf{G}(bought(book)) \rightarrow do(pay\_cart)\}, \\
\sigma_0 = \{ & current\_webpage(page(user)), \\
& \qquad \forall s, s'(s \neq s' \wedge current\_webpage(s)) \rightarrow \neg current\_webpage(s')\}, \\
\gamma_0 = \{ & bought(T) \wedge bought(I)\}
\end{aligned}
$$

Some of the details of this program will be discussed in the sequel, when we prove some properties of the program. The agent basically follows the recipe for buying a book outlined above. A number of web pages are named and distinguished; the agent is capable of browsing through these web pages and selecting actions associated with these web pages. For now, however, just note that the program is quite flexible, even though the agent more or less executes a fixed recipe for buying a book. The flexibility results from the agent's knowledge state and the non-determinism of the program. In particular, the ordering in which the actions are performed by the agent - which book to find first, buy a book one at a time or both in the same shopping cart, etc. is not determined by the program. The scheduling of these actions thus is not fixed by the program, and might be fixed arbitrarily on a particular agent architecture used to run the program.

## 4    Temporal Logic for GOAL

On top of the language GOAL and its semantics, we now construct a temporal logic to prove properties of GOAL agents. The logic is similar to other temporal logics but its semantics is derived from the operational semantics of GOAL. Moreover, the logic incorporates the belief and goal modalities used in GOAL agents, and thus can be classified as an complete agent logic (incorporating the basic notions of time, belief and goals).

The semantics of GOAL agents is derived directly from the operational semantics as presented above. The meaning of a GOAL agent consists of a set of so-called *traces*. A trace is an infinite computation sequence of consecutive mental states and actions performed in those mental states.

**Definition 2.** A trace $s$ is an infinite sequence $s_0, b_0, s_1, b_1, s_2, \ldots$ where $s_i$ are states, $b_i$ are conditional actions, and for every $i$ we have: $s_i \xrightarrow{b_i} s_{i+1}$, or $b_i$ is not enabled in $s_i$ and $s_i = s_{i+1}$.

An important assumption in the programming logic for GOAL is a *fairness* assumption. Fairness assumptions concern the fair selection of actions during the execution of a program. In our case, we make a *weak fairness* assumption [11]. A trace is weakly fair if it is not the case that an action is always enabled from some point in time on but is never selected to be executed. This weak fairness assumption is built into the semantics by imposing a constraint on traces. By definition, a *fair trace* is a trace in which each of the actions occurs infinitely often. In a fair trace, there always will be a future time point at which an action is scheduled (considered for execution) and so a fair trace implements the weak fairness assumption. However, note that the fact that an action is scheduled does not mean that the action also is enabled (and therefore, the selection of the action may result in an idle step which does not change the state).

By definition, the *meaning of a GOAL agent* $\langle \Pi, \sigma_0, \gamma_0 \rangle$ is the set of *fair* traces $S$ such that for $s \in S$ we have $s_0 = \langle \sigma_0, \gamma_0 \rangle$.

### 4.1  Basic Action Theories and Hoare Triples

The specification of basic actions provides the basis for the programming logic and, as we will show below, is all we need to prove properties of agents. Because they play such an important role in the proof theory of GOAL, the specification of the basic agent capabilities requires special care. In the proof theory of GOAL, Hoare triples of the form $\{\varphi\}\, b\, \{\psi\}$, where $\varphi$ and $\psi$ are *mental state formulas*, are used to specify actions. The use of Hoare triples in a formal treatment of traditional assignments is well-understood [1]. Because the agent capabilities of GOAL agents are quite different from assignment actions, however, the traditional predicate transformer semantics is not applicable. GOAL agent capabilities are mental state transformers and, therefore, we require more extensive basic action theories to formally capture the effects of such actions. Hoare triples are used to specify the *preconditions*, the *postconditions* (effects) and the *frame conditions* of actions. Conditions on the initial state can simply be specified by mental state formulas.

The formal semantics of a Hoare triple for conditional actions is derived from the semantics of a GOAL agent and is defined relative to the set of traces $S_A$ associated with the GOAL agent $A$. A Hoare triple for conditional actions thus expresses a property of an agent and not just a property of an action. The semantics of the basic capabilities are assumed to be fixed, however, and are not defined relative to an agent. Below, we write $\varphi[s_i]$ to denote that a mental state formula $\varphi$ holds in state $s_i$.

**Definition 3.** A *Hoare triple for conditional actions* $\{\varphi\}\ b\ \{\psi\}$ means that for all traces $s \in S_A$ and time points $i$, we have that $(\varphi[s_i] \wedge b = b_i \in s) \Rightarrow \psi[s_{i+1}]$ where $b_i \in s$ means that action $b_i$ is taken in state $i$ of trace $s$.
A *Hoare triple for basic capabilities* $\{\varphi\}\ \mathsf{a}\ \{\psi\}$ means that for all $\sigma, \gamma$

- if $\langle \sigma, \gamma \rangle \models \varphi$ and $\mathsf{a}$ is enabled in $\langle \sigma, \gamma \rangle$, then $\mathcal{M}(\mathsf{a}, \langle \sigma, \gamma \rangle) \models \psi$, and
- if $\langle \sigma, \gamma \rangle \models \varphi$ and $\mathsf{a}$ is *not* enabled in $\langle \sigma, \gamma \rangle$, then $\langle \sigma, \gamma \rangle \models \psi$.

Conclusions about changes to the beliefs of an agent at a next state because of the execution of a basic capability requires a set of axioms that specify how each capability updates the beliefs of an agent. In this paper, however, our concern is not so much with the structure and specification of basic action theories , but with providing a programming framework for agents in which such theories can be plugged in. For this reason, we only provide some example specifications of the capabilities in the personal assistant example.

As an illustration and a definition of the meaning of the basic agent capabilities, we provide an effect axiom for each capability of the shopping agent that specifies the effects of that capability given some preconditions. But first, we introduce some notation. Instead of *current_website(sitename)* we simply write *sitename*; e.g., we write *ContentCart* instead of *current_website(ContentCart)*. These conventions can result in formulas like $B(T)$, which means that the agent is at the web page concerning the book *The Intentional Stance*.
The action *goto_website* results in moving to the relevant web page:

$\{\mathsf{true}\}\ goto\_website(site)\ \{Bsite\}$,

At Amazon.com, searching for a(n existing) book results in finding a page with relevant information about the book: $\{BAmazon.com\}\ search(book)\ \{Bbook\}$. On the page with information about a particular book, selecting the action *put_in_shopping_cart* results in the book being put in the cart; also, the web page is updated and shows the content of the cart: $\{Bbook\}\ put\_in\_shopping\_cart(book)\ \{B(in\_cart(book) \wedge ContentCart)\}$. In case *book* is in the cart, and the current web page presents a list of all the books in the cart, the action *pay_cart* may be selected resulting in the buying of all listed books:

$\{B(in\_cart(book) \wedge ContentCart)\}$
   *pay_cart*
$\{\neg Bin\_cart(book) \wedge B(bought(book) \wedge Amazon.com)\}$

Besides these effect axioms, we need a number of frame axioms which specify which properties are not changed by each of the capabilities of the agent. For example, both the capabilities *goto_website* and *search* do not change any beliefs about *in_cart*. Thus we have, e.g.: $\{Bin\_cart(book)\}\ goto\_website(site)\ \{Bin\_cart(book)\}$. It is important to realise that the only (frame) axioms for capabilities of an agent that we require the user to specify concern the *beliefs* of the agent. Effects on and persistence of goals after performing an action can be derived with rules and axioms below that are specifically designed to reason about changes to goals. Finally, our basic action theories require a set of user specified axioms that axiomatise the predicate *enabled*(a) for each agent capability. For example, we have:

*enabled*(*search*(*book*)) ↔ (B(*Amazon.com*)),
*enabled*(*put_in_shopping_cart*(*book*)) ↔ B(*book*),
*enabled*(*pay_cart*) ↔ ((B*in_cart*(T) ∨ B*in_cart*(I)) ∧ B*ContentCart*)

These axioms define when a capability can be executed and should correspond with the formal semantics of the predicate *enabled*, which is defined for basic capabilities by: $\langle \sigma, \gamma \rangle \models$ *enabled*(a) iff $\mathcal{T}(\mathsf{a}, \sigma)$ is defined.

For a more extensive treatment of basic action theories, we refer the reader to [9]. A theory of the basic actions and their effects on an agent's beliefs which needs to be specified by the user is complemented with a theory that specifies how the goals of an agent change. This theory about actions and their effects on goals consist of a special set of (frame) axioms for goals. These axioms need to capture both the effects of the default commitment strategy as well as give a specification of the effects of the drop and adopt actions.

We first list some general properties of the belief and goal modalities. First, from the definition of the semantics of the goal modality, it is easy to see that $\mathsf{B}\phi \rightarrow \neg \mathsf{G}\phi$ is valid. In case an agent believes a proposition to be the case, that agent does not have a goal of achieving that same proposition. In particular, an agent never has the goal to achieve a tautology, that is, $\neg \mathsf{G}(\mathsf{true})$ is valid. By definition of a mental state, an agent also cannot have an inconsistent goal. As a consequence, we have that $\neg \mathsf{G}(\mathsf{false})$ is an axiom.

The goal modality is a weak logical operator. In particular, it does not distribute over implication, and we do not have $(\mathsf{G}p \wedge \mathsf{G}(p \rightarrow q)) \rightarrow \mathsf{G}q$. This is due to the fact that two independent goals $\gamma = \{p, p \rightarrow q\}$ are adopted or it is due to the fact that the agent believes $q$. In the case that $\mathsf{B}q$, we even do not have $\mathsf{G}(p \wedge (p \rightarrow q)) \rightarrow \mathsf{G}q$ because $\mathsf{B}q \rightarrow \neg \mathsf{G}q$. From a given goal $\mathsf{G}\phi$ it is possible to conclude that the agent also has goal $\mathsf{G}\psi$ if $\psi$ is entailed by $\phi$ and the agent does not already believe that $\psi$ is the case (otherwise the axiom $\mathsf{B}\phi \rightarrow \neg \mathsf{G}\phi$ would be contradicted). Finally, we *cannot* conclude from two goals $\mathsf{G}\phi$ and $\mathsf{G}\psi$ that an agent has the conjunctive goal $\mathsf{G}(\phi \wedge \psi)$. That is, $(\mathsf{G}\phi \wedge \mathsf{G}\psi) \rightarrow \mathsf{G}(\phi \wedge \psi)$ is *not* valid. In sum, most of the usual problems that many logical operators for motivational attitudes suffer from do not apply to our $\mathsf{G}$ operator (cf. also [12]).

Conditional actions and capabilities are formalised by means of Hoare triples in our framework. A set of rules to derive Hoare triples for capabilities from *Cap* and conditional actions is listed below. The Rule for Infeasible Capabilities allows to derive frame axioms for a capability in case it is not enabled in a particular situation. The Rule for Conditional Actions allows the derivation of Hoare triples for conditional actions from Hoare triples for capabilities. Finally, there are three rules for combining Hoare triples and for strengthening the precondition and weakening the postcondition.

Rule for Infeasible Capabilities:  Rule for Conditional Actions:

$$\frac{\varphi \rightarrow \neg enabled(\mathsf{a})}{\{\varphi\} \; \mathsf{a} \; \{\varphi\}} \qquad\qquad \frac{\{\varphi \wedge \psi\} \; \mathsf{a} \; \{\varphi'\}, (\varphi \wedge \neg\psi) \rightarrow \varphi'}{\{\varphi\} \; \psi \rightarrow do(\mathsf{a}) \; \{\varphi'\}}$$

Consequence Rule:  Conjunction Rule:

$$\frac{\varphi' \rightarrow \varphi, \{\varphi\} \; \mathsf{a} \; \{\psi\}, \psi \rightarrow \psi'}{\{\varphi'\} \; \mathsf{a} \; \{\psi'\}} \qquad \frac{\{\varphi_1\} \; b \; \{\psi_1\}, \{\varphi_2\} \; b \; \{\psi_2\}}{\{\varphi_1 \wedge \varphi_2\} \; b \; \{\psi_1 \wedge \psi_2\}}$$

Disjunction Rule:

$$\frac{\{\varphi_1\} \; b \; \{\psi\}, \{\varphi_2\} \; b \; \{\psi\}}{\{\varphi_1 \vee \varphi_2\} \; b \; \{\psi\}}$$

The default commitment strategy can also be captured by a Hoare triple. In case $\mathsf{a} \neq \mathsf{drop}(\psi)$, we have that $\{\mathsf{G}\phi\} \; \varphi \rightarrow do(\mathsf{a}) \; \{\mathsf{B}\phi \vee \mathsf{G}\phi\}$ which expresses that after execution of an action an agent either believes it has achieved $\phi$ or it still has the goal $\phi$ in case $\phi$ was a goal before action execution. The next Hoare triple formalises a similar kind of statement for the absence of goals. In principle, no other action than an **adopt** action can add a goal to the goals of an agent. However, in case an agent believes that $\phi$ has been achieved before an action is executed, but after execution no longer believes this to be the case, it may adopt $\phi$ as a goal again. Formally, we have $\{\neg\mathsf{G}\phi\} \; b \; \{\neg\mathsf{B}\phi \vee \neg\mathsf{G}\phi\}$. (This Hoare triple can be derived with the consequence rule and axiom $\mathsf{B}\phi \rightarrow \neg\mathsf{G}\phi$). Adopting goals again when it is believed they are not established anymore, provides for a mechanism similar to that of maintenance goals.

The remaining axioms and derivation rules concern the special actions **drop** and **adopt**. Neither of these actions changes anything with respect to the current beliefs of an agent. This is captured by the following four Hoare triples:

- $\{\mathsf{B}\phi\} \; \mathsf{adopt}(\psi) \; \{\mathsf{B}\phi\}, \{\neg\mathsf{B}\phi\} \; \mathsf{adopt}(\psi) \; \{\neg\mathsf{B}\phi\}$,
- $\{\mathsf{B}\phi\} \; \mathsf{drop}(\psi) \; \{\mathsf{B}\phi\}, \{\neg\mathsf{B}\phi\} \; \mathsf{drop}(\psi) \; \{\neg\mathsf{B}\phi\}$.

Concerning the changes to goals, if an agent does not believe $\psi$ and $\psi$ is not a contradiction, then $\mathsf{adopt}(\psi)$ results in a (new) goal $\mathsf{G}\psi$. Formally, $\{\neg\mathsf{B}\psi\} \; \mathsf{adopt}(\psi) \; \{\mathsf{G}\psi\}$. An adopt action does not have any effect on current goals of the agent. That is, if $\phi$ is a goal before the execution of an adopt action, it is still a goal after the execution of the adopt action: $\{\mathsf{G}\phi\} \; \mathsf{adopt}(\psi) \; \{\mathsf{G}\phi\}$. On the other hand, an $\mathsf{adopt}(\psi)$ action does not result in the adoption of a new goal $\phi$ in case $\phi$ is not entailed by $\psi$:

$$\frac{\not\models \psi \rightarrow \phi}{\{\neg\mathsf{G}\phi\} \; \mathsf{adopt}(\psi) \; \{\neg\mathsf{G}\phi\}}$$

A drop action $\mathsf{drop}(\psi)$ does never result in the adoption of new goals. Therefore, the absence of a goal $\neg\mathsf{G}\phi$ persists when a drop action is executed: $\{\neg\mathsf{G}\phi\} \; \mathsf{drop}(\psi) \; \{\neg\mathsf{G}\phi\}$. A drop action $\mathsf{drop}(\psi)$ results in the removal of all goals that entail $\psi$. This is captured by the next derivation rule.

$$\frac{\models \phi \rightarrow \psi}{\{\mathsf{true}\} \; \mathsf{drop}(\psi) \; \{\neg\mathsf{G}\phi\}}$$

Persistence of a goal with respect to a drop action is harder to formalise. Since a drop action removes goals which entail $\psi$, if we can make sure that a current goal of an agent does not depend on a goal which entails $\psi$, we may conclude that the goal persists. This is formalised in the following Hoare triple: $\{\neg G(\phi \wedge \psi) \wedge G\phi\}$ drop$(\psi)$ $\{G\phi\}$.

## 4.2  Temporal Logic

On top of the Hoare triples for specifying basic actions, a temporal logic is used to specify and verify properties of a GOAL agent. The temporal logic language $\mathcal{L}_T$ based on $\mathcal{L}$ is defined by: (i) **init** $\in \mathcal{L}_T$, (ii) if $\phi \in \mathcal{L}$, then $B\phi, G\phi \in \mathcal{L}_T$, (iii) if $\varphi, \psi \in \mathcal{L}_T$, then $\neg\varphi, \varphi \wedge \psi \in \mathcal{L}_T$, (iv) if $\varphi, \psi \in \mathcal{L}_T$, then $\varphi$ **until** $\psi \in \mathcal{L}_T$.

**init** is a proposition which states that the agent is at the beginning of execution, i.e., nothing has happened yet. The **until** operator is a weak until operator. $\varphi$ **until** $\psi$ means that $\psi$ eventually becomes true and $\varphi$ is true until $\psi$ becomes true, or $\psi$ never becomes true and $\varphi$ remains true forever. The usual abbreviations for the propositional operators $\vee, \rightarrow$, and $\leftrightarrow$ are used. In case we just write false as a formula, this should be taken as an abbreviation for $B(p \wedge \neg p)$ for some $p$. The *always* operator $\Box\varphi$ is an abbreviation for $\varphi$ **until** false, and the *eventuality* operator $\Diamond\varphi$ is defined as $\neg\Box\neg\varphi$ as usual. As already was explained in the previous Section, the atoms $B\phi$, $G\psi$ and any other state formula are evaluated with respect to mental states. The semantics of temporal formulas, relative to a trace $s$ and time point $i$ is defined by:

$$
\begin{array}{l}
s, i \models \mathbf{init} \text{ iff } i = 0 \quad s, i \models B\phi \text{ iff } B\phi[s_i] \; s, i \models G\phi \text{ iff } G\phi[s_i] \\
s, i \models \neg\varphi \text{ iff } s, i \not\models \varphi, \; s, i \models \varphi \wedge \psi \text{ iff } (s, i \models \varphi \text{ and } s, i \models \psi) \\
s, i \models \varphi \text{ \textbf{until} } \psi \text{ iff } \exists j \geq i(s, j \models \psi \wedge \forall k(i \leq k < j(s, k \models \varphi))) \text{ or } \forall k \geq i(s, k \models \varphi)
\end{array}
$$

For a set of traces $S$, we define: (i) $S \models \varphi$ iff $\forall s \in S, i(s, i \models \varphi)$, and (ii) $\models \varphi$ iff $S \models \varphi$ where $S$ is the set of all traces. Temporal formulas evaluated with respect to the traces of a GOAL agent express properties of that agent. Let $A$ be a GOAL agent and $S_A$ be the set of traces associated with $A$. Then, if $S_A \models \varphi$, $\varphi$ is a property of $A$. Recall that the semantics of a GOAL agent was defined in terms of a set of fair traces. This property of fairness is important in this context for proving liveness and safety properties of agents.

In general, two important types of temporal properties are distinguished. Temporal properties are divided into *liveness* and *safety* properties. Liveness properties concern the progress that an agent makes and express that a (good) state eventually will be reached. Safety properties, on the other hand, express that some (bad) states are never entered. In the rest of this Section, we discuss a number of specific liveness and safety properties of an agent $A = \langle \Pi_A, \sigma_0, \gamma_0 \rangle$ and show how these properties can be proven on the basis of the program text only. The fact that proofs can be constructed from just the program text is important because it avoids the need to reason about individual traces of a program. Reasoning from the program text is more economical since the number of traces associated with a program in general is exponential in the size of the program.

The first property we discuss concerns a safety property. Informally, the property states that if $\varphi$ ever becomes true, then it remains true until $\psi$ becomes true. Formally, this property can be written as $\varphi \rightarrow (\varphi \text{ \textbf{until} } \psi)$, which is abbreviated as: $\varphi$ **unless** $\psi \overset{df}{=}$

$\varphi \rightarrow (\varphi \textbf{ until } \psi)$. **unless** properties of an agent $A$ can be proven by proving Hoare triples for conditional actions in $\Pi_A$ only. In case we can prove that after execution of an arbitrary action either $\varphi$ persists or $\psi$ becomes true, we can conclude that $\varphi$ **unless** $\psi$. The proofs of theorems can be found in the full paper [9].

**Theorem 1.** $\forall b \in \Pi_A(\{\varphi \wedge \neg\psi\}\, b\, \{\varphi \vee \psi\})$ iff $S_A \models \varphi$ **unless** $\psi$

An important special case of an **unless** property is $\varphi$ **unless** false, which expresses that if $\varphi$ ever becomes true, it will remain true. The Hoare triples which are needed to prove $\varphi$ **unless** false simplify to $\{\varphi\}\, b\, \{\varphi\}$. In case we also have **init** $\rightarrow \varphi$, where **init** denotes the initial starting point of execution, $\varphi$ is always true and $\varphi$ is an *invariant* of the program.

Liveness properties involve eventualities stating that some state will be reached given some condition. To express a special class of such properties, we introduce the operator $\varphi$ **ensures** $\psi$ which informally means that condition $\varphi$ guarantees the realisation of $\psi$. The operator **ensures** is defined by: $\varphi$ **ensures** $\psi \overset{df}{=} \varphi$ **unless** $\psi \wedge (\varphi \rightarrow \diamond\psi)$. From this operator, below we derive a somewhat less constrained operator 'leads to'. Again, we can show that **ensures** properties can be derived by inspecting the program text only.

**Theorem 2.**
$\forall b \in \Pi_A(\{\varphi \wedge \neg\psi\}\, b\, \{\varphi \vee \psi\}) \wedge \exists b \in \Pi_A(\{\varphi \wedge \neg\psi\}\, b\, \{\psi\}) \Rightarrow S_A \models \varphi$ **ensures** $\psi$

From the **ensures** operator, we can derive a new operator $\mapsto$ which is defined as the transitive, disjunctive closure of **ensures**, where $\varphi \mapsto \psi$ informally means that when $\varphi$ is the case, $\psi$ will be the case at some future moment.

| $\varphi$ **ensures** $\psi$ | $\varphi \mapsto \chi, \chi \mapsto \psi$ | $\varphi_1 \mapsto \psi, \ldots, \varphi_n \mapsto \psi$ |
|---|---|---|
| $\varphi \mapsto \psi$ | $\varphi \mapsto \psi$ | $(\varphi_1 \vee \ldots \vee \varphi_n) \mapsto \psi$ |

## 5   Proving Correctness

In this Section, we use the programming logic to prove the correctness of our agent program. A simple and intuitive correctness property, which is natural in this context and applicable to our example agent, states that a GOAL agent is *correct* when the agent realises its initial goals. For this subclass of correctness properties, we may consider the agent to be finished upon establishing the initial goals and in that case the agent could be terminated. Of course, it is also possible to continue the execution of such agents. This class of correctness properties can be expressed by means of temporal formulas like $G\phi \rightarrow \diamond\neg G\phi$. From this discussion, we conclude that the interesting property to prove for our example program is the following property:

$Bcond \wedge \mathsf{G}(bought(T) \wedge bought(I)) \mapsto \mathsf{B}(bought(T) \wedge bought(I))$

where $Bcond$ is some condition of the initial beliefs of the agent. More specifically, $Bcond$ is defined by:

$\mathsf{B}current\_webpage(page(user)) \wedge \neg\mathsf{B}in\_cart(T) \wedge \neg\mathsf{B}in\_cart(I) \wedge$
$\mathsf{B}(\forall s, s'((s \neq s' \wedge current\_webpage(s)) \rightarrow \neg current\_webpage(s')))$

The correctness property states that the goal to buy the books *The Intentional Stance* and *Intentions, Plans and Practical Reason*, given some initial conditions on the beliefs of the agent, leads to buying (or believing to have bought) these books. Note that this property expresses a *total correctness* property. It states both that the agent behaves as desired and that it will eventually reach the desired goal state.

*Invariants and Frame Axioms.* In the correctness proof, we need a number of frame axioms. A special case of such axioms involves properties that, once true, remain true whatever action is performed. In case such a property holds initially, the property is an *invariant* of the program. In our example program, we have one invariant which states that it is impossible to be at two web pages at the same time: $inv = B \forall s, s'((s \neq s' \wedge current\_webpage(s)) \rightarrow \neg current\_webpage(s'))$.

To prove that *inv* is an invariant of the agent, we need frame axioms stating that when *inv* holds before the execution of an action it still holds after execution of that action. Formally, for each $a \in Cap$, we have: $\{inv\}$ a $\{inv\}$. Because initially we have *inv* since $\langle \sigma_0, \gamma_0 \rangle \models inv$, we have that **init** $\rightarrow inv$. From the frame axioms, the Rule for Conditional Actions and Theorem 1 it then follows that (**init** $\rightarrow inv) \wedge (inv$ **unless** false), which expresses that *inv* is an invariant and holds at all times during the execution of the program. Because of this fact, we will not mention *inv* explicitly anymore in the proofs below, but will freely use the property when we need it.

A second property that remains true once it is true is the property that once a book is in the cart and it is a goal to buy the book, it remains in the cart and is only removed from the cart when it is bought. So, if either one of these two things holds, the disjunction of these two properties, abbreviated by *status(book)*, holds from that point on. (The proof can be found in the full paper.)

$$status(book) \overset{df}{=} (Bin\_cart(book) \wedge Gbought(book)) \vee Bbought(book)$$

*Proof Outline.* The main proof steps to prove our agent example program correct are listed next. The proof steps below consist of a number of **ensures** formulas which together prove that the agent reaches its goal in a finite number of steps.

(1) $Bpage(user) \wedge \neg Bin\_cart(T) \wedge Gbought(T) \wedge \neg Bin\_cart(I) \wedge Gbought(I)$ **ensures**
$BAmazon.com \wedge \neg Bin\_cart(T) \wedge Gbought(T) \wedge \neg Bin\_cart(I) \wedge Gbought(I)$

(2) $BAmazon.com \wedge \neg Bin\_cart(T) \wedge Gbought(T) \wedge \neg Bin\_cart(I) \wedge Gbought(I)$ **ensures**
$[(B(T) \wedge Gbought(T) \wedge \neg Bin\_cart(I) \wedge Gbought(I)) \vee$
$(B(I) \wedge Gbought(I) \wedge \neg Bin\_cart(T) \wedge Gbought(T))]$

(3) $B(T) \wedge Gbought(T) \wedge \neg Bin\_cart(I) \wedge Gbought(I)$ **ensures**
$Bin\_cart(T) \wedge Gbought(T) \wedge \neg Bin\_cart(I) \wedge Gbought(I) \wedge BContentCart$

(4) $Bin\_cart(T) \wedge Gbought(T) \wedge \neg Bin\_cart(I) \wedge Gbought(I)$ **ensures**
$BAmazon.com \wedge \neg Bin\_cart(I) \wedge Gbought(I) \wedge status(T)$

(5) $B(Amazon.com) \wedge \neg Bin\_cart(I) \wedge Gbought(I) \wedge status(T)$ **ensures**
$B(I) \wedge Gbought(I) \wedge status(T)$

(6) $B(I) \wedge Gbought(I) \wedge status(T)$ **ensures**
$Bin\_cart(I) \wedge Gbought(I) \wedge BContentCart \wedge status(T)$

(7) $Bin\_cart(I) \wedge Gbought(I) \wedge BContentCart \wedge status(T)$ **ensures**
$Bbought(T) \wedge Bbought(I)$

At step 3, the proof is split up into two subproofs, one for each of the disjuncts of the disjunct that is ensured in step 2. The proof for the other disjunct is completely analogous. By applying the rules for the 'leads to' operator the third to seventh step result in:

$(a)$ $B(T) \wedge$ G$bought(T) \wedge \neg$B$in\_cart(I) \wedge$ G$bought(I) \mapsto$ B$bought(T) \wedge$ B$bought(I)$
$(b)$ $B(I) \wedge$ G$bought(I) \wedge \neg$B$in\_cart(T) \wedge$ G$bought(T) \mapsto$ B$bought(T) \wedge$ B$bought(I)$

Combining (a) and (b) by the disjunction rule for the 'leads to' operator and by using the transitivity of 'leads to' we then obtain the desired correctness result:

$B cond \wedge$ G$(bought(T) \wedge bought(I)) \mapsto$ B$(bought(T) \wedge bought(I)).$

## 6  Conclusion

Although a programming language dedicated to agent programming is not the only viable approach to building agents, we believe it is one of the more practical approaches for developing agents. Several other approaches to the design and implementation of agents have been proposed. One such approach promotes the use of *agent logics* for the specification of agent systems and aims at a further refinement of such specifications by means of an associated design methodology for the particular logic in use to implementations which meet this specification in, for example, an object-oriented programming language like Java. In this approach, there is no requirement on the existence of a natural mapping relating the end result of this development process - a Java implementation - and the formal specification in the logic. It is, however, not very clear how to implement these ideas for agent logics incorporating both informational and motivational attitudes and some researchers seem to have concluded from this that the notion of a motivational attitude (like a goal) is less useful than hoped for. Yet, others like [16] still built on this work. They develop a specification language called CASL which includes a declarative notion of goal. The presentation of CASL suggests a closer link between the language itself and an executable agent program, although it is not quite clear how such a program should be obtained from a specification. Still another approach promotes the construction of *agent architectures* to 'implement' the different mental concepts. Such an architecture provides a template which can be instantiated with the relevant beliefs, goals, etc. Although this second approach is more practical than the first one, our main problem with this approach is that the architectures proposed so far tend to be quite complex. As a consequence, it is quite difficult to predict the behaviour that an instantiated architecture will generate.

Our own research concerning intelligent agents has focused on the *programming language* 3APL which supports the construction of intelligent agents, and reflects in a natural way the intentional concepts used to design agents (in contrast with the approach discussed above which promotes the use of logic, but at the same time suggests that such an intermediate level is not required). Nevertheless, in previous work the incorporation of declarative goals in agent programming frameworks has, to our knowledge, not been established. It has been our aim in this paper to show that it is feasible to construct a programming framework that incorporates declarative goals. The language GOAL has an operational semantics which can rather straightforwardly be implemented. GOAL, however, lacks planning and communication features and the ideal would be to combine GOAL and some other agent programming language like 3APL, which does include such features.

In this paper, we provided a complete programming theory. Many insights were drawn from concurrent programming semantics and temporal logics for such programs. The programming theory includes a concrete proposal for a programming language and a formal, operational semantics for this language as well as a corresponding proof theory based on temporal logic. The logic enables reasoning about the dynamics of agents and about the beliefs and goals of the agent at any particular state during its execution. The semantics of the logic is provided by the GOAL agent semantics which guarantees that properties proven in the logic are properties of a GOAL agent. By providing such a formal relation between an agent programming language and an agent logic, we were able to bridge the gap between theory and practice. In future research, we aim to extend GOAL - for example, to allow the nesting of belief and goal modalities.

# References

1. Gregory R. Andrews. *Concurrent Programming: Principles and Practice*. The Benjamin/Cummings Publishing Company, 1991.
2. K. Mani Chandy and Jayadev Misra. *Parallel Program Design*. Addison-Wesley, 1988.
3. Philip R. Cohen and Hector J. Levesque. Intention is choice with commitment. *Artificial Intelligence*, 42:213–261, 1990.
4. Michael Fisher. Implementing BDI-like Systems by Direct Execution. In *Proceedings of the Fifteenth International Joint Conference on Artificial Intelligence (IJCAI)*. Morgan Kaufmann, 1997.
5. Giuseppe De Giacomo, Yves Lespérance, and Hector Levesque. *ConGolog*, a Concurrent Programming Language Based on the Situation Calculus. *Artificial Intelligence, accepted for publication*.
6. K. Hindriks, F. de Boer, W. van der Hoek, and J.-J. Meyer. A Formal Embedding of AgentSpeak(L) in 3APL. In G. Antoniou and J. Slaney, editors, *Advanced Topics in Artificial Intelligence*, pages 155–166. Springer-Verlag, 1998.
7. K. Hindriks, F. de Boer, W. van der Hoek, and J.-J. Meyer. An Operational Semantics for the Single Agent Core of AGENT-0. Technical Report UU-CS-1999-30, Department of Computer Science, University Utrecht, 1999.
8. K. Hindriks, F. de Boer, W. van der Hoek, and J.-J. Meyer. Agent Programming in 3APL. *Autonomous Agents and Multi-Agent Systems*, 2(4):357–401, 1999.
9. Koen V. Hindriks, Frank S. de Boer, Wiebe van der Hoek, and John-Jules Ch. Meyer. Agent Programming with Declarative Goals. Technical Report UU-CS-2000-16, Department of Computer Science, University Utrecht, 2000.
10. Koen V. Hindriks, Yves Lespérance, and Hector J. Levesque. An Embedding of ConGolog in 3APL. In Werner Horn, editor, *Proceedings of the 14th European Conference on Artificial Intelligence*, pages 558–562, 2000.
11. Zohar Manna and Amir Pnueli. *The Temporal Logic of Reactive and Concurrent Systems*. Springer-Verlag, 1992.
12. John-Jules Ch. Meyer, Wiebe van der Hoek, and Bernd van Linder. A Logical Approach to the Dynamics of Commitments. *Aritificial Intelligence*, 113:1–40, 1999.
13. Anand S. Rao. AgentSpeak(L): BDI Agents Speak Out in a Logical Computable Language. In W. van der Velde and J.W. Perram, editors, *Agents Breaking Away*, 1996.

14. Anand S. Rao. Decision procedures for propositional linear-time belief-desire-intention logics. In M.J. Wooldridge, J.P. Müller, and M. Tambe, editors, *Intelligent Agents II*. Springer-Verlag, 1996.
15. Anand S. Rao and Michael P. Georgeff. Intentions and Rational Commitment. Technical Report 8, Australian Artificial Intelligence Institute, Melbourne, Australia, 1990.
16. Steven Shapiro and Yves Lespérance. Modeling Multiagent Systems with CASL — A Feature Interaction Resolution Application. In C. Castelfranchi and Y. Lespérance, editors, *Intelligent Agents VII (LNAI)*. Springer-Verlag, 2001. In this volume.
17. Yoav Shoham. Agent-oriented programming. *Artificial Intelligence*, 60:51–92, 1993.
18. Sarah Rebecca Thomas. *PLACA, An Agent Oriented Programming Language*. PhD thesis, Department of Computer Science, Stanford University, 1993.
19. Wayne Wobcke. On the Correctness of PRS Agent Programs. In N.R. Jennings and Y. Lespérance, editor, *Intelligent Agents VI (LNAI 1757)*. Springer-Verlag, 2000.

# Modeling Multiagent Systems with CASL – A Feature Interaction Resolution Application[*]

Steven Shapiro[1] and Yves Lespérance[2]

[1] Department of Computer Science, University of Toronto
Toronto, ON M5S 3G4, Canada
steven@ai.toronto.edu
[2] Department of Computer Science, York University
Toronto, ON M3J 1P3, Canada
lesperan@cs.yorku.ca

**Abstract.** In this paper, we describe the Cognitive Agents Specification Language (CASL), and exhibit its characteristics by using it to model the multiagent feature interaction resolution system described by Griffeth and Velthuijsen [7]. We discuss the main features of CASL that make it a useful language for specifying and verifying multiagent systems. CASL has a nice mix of declarative and procedural elements with a formal semantics to facilitate the verification of properties of CASL specifications.

## 1 Introduction

The use of proper design methods is just as important for multiagent systems as for non-agent-based software. In this paper, we present a formal specification language for multiagent systems called the Cognitive Agents Specification Language (CASL). CASL combines a theory of action [13] and mental states [14,15] based on the situation calculus [11] with ConGolog [6], a concurrent, nondeterministic programming language that has a formal semantics. The result is a specification language that contains a rich set of operators to facilitate the specification of *complex* multiagent systems. Specifications in this language can exploit the higher level of abstraction that comes from expressing constraints in terms of mental attitudes.

An earlier version of CASL was described in [16], where the use of the formalism was illustrated with a simple meeting scheduling multiagent system example. The motivation for our approach was discussed in further detail there. In this paper, we extend the formalism to support communication with encrypted speech acts and incorporate a simpler account of goals. But foremost, we use the formalism to model a somewhat more complex multiagent system taken from the literature. In [7], Griffeth and Velthuijsen present a feature interaction resolution system for telecommunication applications

---

[*] This research was funded by Communications and Information Technology Ontario and the Natural Science and Engineering Research Council of Canada. We thank Fawzi Daoud for suggesting that we look at feature interaction applications and Griffeth and Velthuijsen's work in particular.

C. Castelfranchi, Y. Lespérance (Eds.): Intelligent Agents VII, LNAI 1986, pp. 244–259, 2001.
© Springer-Verlag Berlin Heidelberg 2001

that involves negotiating, autonomous agents with explicit goals. This is an attractive approach in the context of rapidly expanding telecommunication services, open environments, and the need for client customization. In CASL, agents' goals (and knowledge) can be represented explicitly, making CASL an ideal formalism for specifying systems such as the one described by Griffeth and Velthuijsen. They informally state a property of their system and (also informally) show that the property holds for their system. Since CASL is a formal language, it is possible to *formally* state and prove such properties. We use Griffeth and Velthuijsen's system as an example of the modeling capabilities of CASL, and give a formal statement of the property discussed by Griffeth and Velthuijsen.

## 2    The Model of Domain Dynamics

In CASL, a dynamic domain is represented using an action theory [13] formulated in the situation calculus [11], a predicate calculus language for representing dynamically changing worlds. A situation represents a snapshot of the domain. There is a set of initial situations corresponding to the ways the agents believe the domain might be initially. The actual initial state of the domain is represented by the initial situation constant, $S_0$. The term $do(a, s)$ denotes the unique situation that results from the agent performing action $a$ in situation $s$. Thus, the situations can be structured into a set of trees, where the root of each tree is an initial situation and the arcs are actions. The initial situations are defined as those situations that do not have a predecessor: $Init(s) \stackrel{\text{def}}{=} \neg \exists a, s'.s = do(a, s')$.

Predicates and functions whose value may change from situation to situation (and whose last argument is a situation) are called *fluents*. For instance, in our model of Griffeth and Velthuijsen's system, we use the fluent $\text{TwoWayIP}(x, y, s)$ to represent the property that a two-way phone connection is in progress between agents $x$ and $y$. The effects of actions on fluents are defined using successor state axioms [13], which provide a solution to the frame problem; see below for an example.

There is a distinguished predicate $Poss(a, s)$, denoting that action $a$ is executable in situation $s$. $s \preceq s'$ means that $s'$ results from performing a (possibly empty) executable sequence of actions in $s$. We use a theory containing the following kinds of axioms [13] to specify a dynamic domain:

- Action precondition axioms, one for each action, which characterize *Poss*.
- Successor state axioms, one for each fluent.
- Initial state axioms, which describe the initial state of the domain and the initial mental states of the agents. These are axioms that only describe initial situations.
- Unique names axioms for the actions.
- Domain-independent foundational axioms (similar to the ones given by Lakemeyer and Levesque [9]).

### 2.1    Modeling the Environment

In the feature interaction resolution system, the agents are negotiating to establish telephone connections on behalf their human users. We consider two types of connections:

a regular two-way telephone connection and a recording connection, during which one person leaves a message for another. These two types of connections are established by the actions TWOWAY$(x, y)$ ($x$ sets up a two-way connection with $y$) and RECORD$(x, y)$ ($x$ records a message for $y$), resp. In addition, once a connection is established, the agent initiating the connection may identify its user to the other agent. The initiating agent may send its user's name or telephone number. The corresponding actions are: NAME$(x, y)$ and NUMBER$(x, y)$, resp. There is also the DISCONNECT$(x, y)$ action, which terminates a connection between $x$ and $y$.

Once a connection of a certain type is established, we say that the connection is in progress until the connection is terminated. For each of the connection and identification actions, we have a corresponding fluent that becomes true when the action is executed. An example of this is the TwoWayIP$(x, y, s)$ fluent discussed above. Similarly, we have the fluent RECORDINGIP$(x, y, s)$, which means that a recording is in progress between $x$ and $y$ in situation $s$. For the identification actions, we have the fluents NAMEIP$(x, y, s)$ and NUMBERIP$(x, y, s)$ whose intuitive meanings are that $x$'s owner's name (number, resp.) is being displayed for $y$'s owner in situation $s$. Any of these fluents that are true become false when the DISCONNECT$(x, y)$ action is executed.

We must give precondition axioms and successor state axioms for these actions and fluents. For example, the precondition axiom for TWOWAY is:

$$Poss(\text{TWOWAY}(x, y), s) \equiv \neg \text{TwoWayIP}(x, y, s) \land \neg \text{RECORDINGIP}(x, y, s).$$

The successor state axiom for TwoWayIP is:

$$\text{TwoWayIP}(x, y, do(a, s)) \equiv$$
$$a = \text{TWOWAY}(x, y) \lor (\text{TwoWayIP}(x, y, s) \land a \neq \text{DISCONNECT}(x, y)).$$

As mentioned earlier, successor state axioms provide a solution to the frame problem. The other precondition and successor state axioms are similar to these, so we omit them.

### 2.2    Modeling Agents' Mental States

We model two aspects of the mental states of agents: knowledge and goals. These are represented with a possible worlds semantics in the situation calculus using situations as possible worlds, following Scherl and Levesque [14]. The accessibility relation for knowledge, $K(agt, s', s)$[1], holds if situation $s'$ is compatible with what $agt$ knows in situation $s$. An agent knows a formula $\phi$, if $\phi$ is true in all the $K$-accessible worlds:

$$\textbf{Know}(agt, \phi, s) \stackrel{\text{def}}{=} \forall s'(K(agt, s', s) \supset \phi[s']).$$

Here $\phi$ is a formula that may contain a free variable $now$. This variable is used as the situation argument of the fluents in $\phi$. $\phi[s]$ denotes the formula that results from

---

[1] Scherl and Levesque only consider a single agent; we [16] generalize the framework to handle multiple agents by adding an agent argument to the accessibility relations.

substituting $s$ for $now$ in $\phi$. We also say that an agent knows whether $\phi$ holds if it either knows $\phi$ or its negation: $\mathbf{KWhether}(agt, \phi, s) \stackrel{\text{def}}{=} \mathbf{Know}(agt, \phi, s) \vee \mathbf{Know}(agt, \neg\phi, s)$.

Scherl and Levesque formulated a successor state axiom for $K$ that describes how an agent's knowledge is affected by actions, including expansion due to *sensing* actions. We [16] adapted the axiom to handle the INFORM$(informer, agt, \phi)^2$ action, i.e., *informer* informs $agt$ that $\phi$ holds. A limitation of the formalization is that all agents are aware of all actions, as in a broadcast model of communication. Here, we modify the representation of speech acts to accommodate *encrypted messages*. We model the encryption and decryption of messages using the functional fluents ENCODE and DECODE, resp. The value of ENCODE$(sender, rec, \phi, s)$ is a code, and the value of DECODE$(sender, rec, c, s)$— where $c$ is a code— is a formula. These functions have to be fluents in order to be able to model the fact that only $rec$ knows the value of DECODE$(sender, rec, c, s)$ and only $sender$ knows the value of ENCODE$(sender, rec, \phi, s)$. That is the only reason these functions are fluents as their values are unchanged by actions as shown in the following successor state axioms:

$$\text{ENCODE}(sender, rec, \phi, do(a, s)) = \text{ENCODE}(sender, rec, \phi, s)$$
$$\text{DECODE}(sender, rec, c, do(a, s)) = \text{DECODE}(sender, rec, c, s)$$

The content of messages will be codes instead of formulae, e.g., we will use INFORM$(informer, agt, c)$ instead of INFORM$(informer, agt, \phi)$.

We modify the successor state axiom for $K$ to handle encrypted messages:

$$K(agt, s'', do(a, s)) \equiv$$
$$\exists s'(K(agt, s', s) \wedge s'' = do(a, s') \wedge Poss(a, s') \wedge$$
$$\forall informer, \phi, c(a = \text{INFORM}(informer, agt, c) \wedge$$
$$\mathbf{Know}(agt, \phi = \text{DECODE}(informer, agt, c), s) \supset \phi(s'))).$$

This axiom states the conditions under which a situation $s''$ will be $K$-accessible from $do(a, s)$. If $a$ is not an INFORM action, then the predecessor of $s''$ (i.e., $s'$) must be $K$-accessible from $s$ and the action that takes $s'$ to $s''$ must be $a$ and executable in $s'$. If $a$ is the action of *informer* informing $agt$ that $c$, where $c$ is a code, and $agt$ knows that $\phi$ is the decoding of $c$, then, in addition to the previous conditions, it must be the case that $\phi$ holds in $s'$. Thus, this axiom ensures that after any action, the agents know that the action has occurred and that it was executable, and if the action is an INFORM action, and the recipient of the message can decode the message, then the recipient knows that the decrypted content of the message holds. This axiom defines the $K$ relation at non-initial situations. The $K$ relation at initial situations is specified by the axiomatizer of the domain using initial state axioms, subject to the constraint that initial situations can only be $K$-related to other initial situations. This framework only handles knowledge expansion. In [17], we give an account of belief revision that is compatible with this framework.

We model the goals of an agent using another accessibility relation on situations, $W(agt, s', s)$. This relation holds if $s'$ is compatible with what the agent *wants* in $s$.

---

[2] Since we have functions and relations that take formulae as arguments, we need to encode formulae as first-order terms. For example, we could use the encoding given by De Giacomo et al. [6]. For notational simplicity, we suppress this encoding and use formulae as terms directly.

Unlike with the $K$ relation, we allow the $W$ relation to relate situations that have different histories. The reason for this is that an agent may want things that do not currently hold, but that it wants to hold in the future. Therefore, we allow future situations to be among the $W$-accessible situations.

An agent may want something that it knows to be impossible to obtain, but we want the *goals* of the agent to be consistent with what the agent knows. Therefore, we define the goals of an agent to be those formulae that are true in all $W$-accessible situations that have a $K$-accessible situation in their past:

**Goal**$(agt, \psi, s) \overset{\text{def}}{=}$
$\forall now, then(K(agt, now, s) \wedge W(agt, then, s) \wedge now \preceq then \supset \psi[now, then])$.

Here $\psi$ is a formula that has two free variables, $now$ and $then$. $then$ can be thought of as defining a finite path of situations, namely, the sequence of situations up to situation $then$. $now$ corresponds to the current situation along that path. In the definition of **Goal**, the $K$ relation is used to pick out the current situation ($now$) along the path defined by the $W$-related situation ($then$) as well as to filter out the situations that are incompatible with what the agent knows to be the case. $\psi[s', s'']$ denotes the formula that results from substituting $s'$ for $now$ and $s''$ for $then$ in $\psi$.

The successor state axiom for $W$ is similar to the one for $K$:

$W(agt, then, do(a, s)) \equiv [W(agt, then, s) \wedge$
$\quad \forall requester, \psi, c, now(a = \text{REQUEST}(requester, agt, c) \wedge$
$\quad\quad \textbf{Know}(agt, \psi = \text{DECODE}(requester, agt, c), s) \wedge K(agt, now, s) \wedge$
$\quad\quad now \preceq then \wedge \neg\textbf{Goal}(agt, \neg\psi, s) \supset \psi[do(a, now), then)]].$

A situation $then$ is $W$-accessible from $do(a, s)$ iff it is $W$-accessible from $s$ and if $a$ is the action of *requester* requesting $agt$ that the decoding of $c$ obtain, and $agt$ knows that $\psi$ is the decoding of $c$, and $now$ is the current situation along the path defined by $then$, and the agent does not have the goal that $\neg\psi$ in $s$ then $\psi$ holds at $(do(a, now), then)$. If the agent gets a request for $\psi$ and it already has the goal that $\neg\psi$, then it does not adopt the goal that $\psi$, otherwise its goal state would become inconsistent and it would want everything. This is a simple way of handling goal conflicts. It should be possible to cancel requests. A more sophisticated handling of conflicting requests will be presented in [15].

In order to execute an INFORM action, an agent must know how to encode the message and also know that the content of the message is true. Therefore, after receiving the message, the recipient of the message knows that the sender knew that the content of the message was true. Similarly, in order to execute a REQUEST action, an agent must know how to encode the message and not have any goals that conflict with the request. This is a somewhat simplistic model for these communicative acts, and we plan to refine it in the future. Here are the precondition axioms for INFORM and REQUEST:

$Poss(\text{INFORM}(informer, agt, c), s) \equiv$
$\quad \exists\phi.\textbf{Know}(informer, (\text{ENCODE}(informer, agt, \phi) = c \wedge \phi), s).$
$Poss(\text{REQUEST}(reqr, agt, c), s) \equiv$
$\quad \exists\psi.\textbf{Know}(reqr, \text{ENCODE}(reqr, agt, \psi) = c, s) \wedge \neg\textbf{Goal}(reqr, \neg\psi, s).$

We also use the following definitions adapted from Lakemeyer and Levesque [9]. A formula $\phi$ describes *all* that $agt$ knows initially:

$$\textbf{OKnow}_0(agt, \phi) \stackrel{\text{def}}{=} \forall s'(K(agt, s', S_0) \equiv Init(s') \wedge \phi(s')).$$

A formula $\psi$ describes *all* the paths that are consistent with $agt$'s initial goals:

$$\textbf{OGoal}_0(agt, \psi) \stackrel{\text{def}}{=} \forall now, then.(K(agt, now, S_0) \wedge now \preceq then \supset$$
$$(W(agt, then, S_0) \equiv \psi[now, then])).$$

We need to put constraints on the accessibility relations in order to yield mental attitudes with desirable properties. For example, we want positive and negative introspection of knowledge and of goals. Due to lack of space, we will not discuss the constraints that need to be placed on the $K$ and $W$ in order to yield these properties. Let us simply assume that these properties hold.

In our formalization of goals, goals are evaluated relative to finite paths. Thus, we cannot represent that an agent wants that $\psi$ always be true because the path relative to which the proposition is evaluated ends, so there is no way of knowing whether $\psi$ holds "after" the end of the path. However, we can model maintenance goals that are time bounded: $\psi$ is true until time $\tau$. If $\tau$ is chosen suitably far in the the future, time-bounded maintenance goals can replace unbounded maintenance goals. However, this requires adding a notion of time. We formalize time in the situation calculus as we did in [16]. That is, we add a functional fluent $time(s)$ whose value is a natural number that represents the time at situation $s$. To simplify the formalization of time, here, we assume that all actions have duration of 1 and that the time at all initial situations is 1.

We will express maintenance goals using the predicate $\textbf{Always}(\psi, now, then)$, which says that $\psi$ always holds, from $now$ until the end of time, denoted by the constant $\tau$:
$$\textbf{Always}(\psi, now, then) \stackrel{\text{def}}{=} \text{TIME}(then) = \tau \wedge \forall s.now \preceq s \preceq then \supset \psi[s, then].$$

## 3   The Behavior Specification

We specify the behavior of agents with the notation of the process specification language ConGolog [6], the concurrent version of Golog [10]. We take a ConGolog program[3] to be composed of a sequence of procedure declarations, followed by a complex action. Complex actions are composed using the following constructs:

| | |
|---|---|
| $a$, | primitive action |
| $\phi?$, | wait for a condition |
| $\delta_1; \delta_2$, | sequence |
| $\delta_1 \mid \delta_2$, | nondeterministic choice between actions |
| $\delta^*$, | nondeterministic iteration |
| **if** $\phi$ **then** $\delta_1$ **else** $\delta_2$ **endIf**, | conditional |
| **for** $x \in \Sigma$ **do** $\delta$ **endFor**, | for loop |
| **while** $\phi$ **do** $\delta$ **endWhile**, | while loop |

---

[3] We retain the term *program* even though it is not our intention to execute the programs directly.

$$\delta_1 \parallel \delta_2, \qquad \text{concurrency with equal priority}$$
$$\delta_1 \rangle\!\rangle \delta_2, \qquad \text{concurrency with } \delta_1 \text{ at a higher priority}$$
$$\langle \, x : \phi \rightarrow \delta \, \rangle, \qquad \text{interrupt}$$
$$\beta(p), \qquad \text{procedure call.}$$

$a$ denotes a situation calculus primitive action, as described earlier. The ConGolog spec-ification can be for a single agent or multiple agents, depending on whether the primitive actions contain an argument for the agent of the action. $\phi$ denotes a situation calculus formula with the situation argument of its fluents suppressed. $\delta$, $\delta_1$, and $\delta_2$ stand for complex actions, $\Sigma$ is a set, $x$ is a set of variables, $\beta$ is a procedure name, and $p$ denotes the actual parameters to the procedure. These constructs are mostly self-explanatory. Intuitively, the interrupts work as follows. Whenever $\exists x.\phi$ becomes true, then $\delta$ is exe-cuted with the bindings of $x$ that satisfied $\phi$; once $\delta$ terminates, the interrupt can trigger again.

Procedures are defined with the following syntax: **proc** $\beta(y)$ $\delta$ **endProc**, where $\beta$ is the procedure name, $y$ denotes the formal parameters to the procedure, and $\delta$ is the procedure body, a complex action. The semantics of ConGolog programs are defined using the $Do$ predicate (see [6] for details). Informally, $Do(\rho, s, s')$ holds if situation $s'$ is a legal terminating situation of program $\rho$ starting in situation $s$.

## 4    Modeling the Feature Interaction Resolution System

In the feature interaction resolution system, there are two types of agents: those that represent the interests of humans, which we call *personal* agents and the *negotiator*, which coordinates the negotiation of a solution for the personal agents. The personal agents negotiate to create telephone connections. One personal agent is the initiating agent. The initiating agent has an *aim* for the negotiation. Any solution to the negotiation will be a specialization of this aim. The negotiator receives proposals from the personal agents and forwards them to the other personal agents and waits for their responses. If everyone agrees to a proposal (or if there are no more proposals to try) then the negotiator terminates the negotiation successfully (unsuccessfully, resp.). When a personal agent receives a proposal it answers whether it agrees to it. If it does not agree to the proposal then it can make a counterproposal.

We implement proposals as complex actions in our system. For this example, the possible proposals will be any of the primitive actions listed earlier or any of the following complex actions:

$$\text{CONNECT}(x, y) \overset{\text{def}}{=} \text{TWOWAY}(x, y) \mid \text{RECORD}(x, y)$$
$$\text{ANONYMOUSCALL}(x, y) \overset{\text{def}}{=} \text{CONNECT}(x, y); \text{DISCONNECT}(x, y)$$
$$\text{IDENTITY}(x, y) \overset{\text{def}}{=} \text{NAME}(x, y) \mid \text{NUMBER}(x, y).$$
$$\text{IDENTIFIEDCALL}(x, y) \overset{\text{def}}{=} \text{CONNECT}(x, y); \text{IDENTITY}(x, y); \text{DISCONNECT}(x, y)$$
$$\text{CALL}(x, y) \overset{\text{def}}{=} \text{ANONYMOUSCALL}(x, y) \mid \text{IDENTIFIEDCALL}(x, y)$$

Note that these complex actions represent the simplest possible sequence of events that can occur for each proposal. Normally, one would expect that, for example, in an anonymous call other actions would occur between the connect and a disconnect action, namely the agents (or, rather, the humans the agents represent) would speak to each other. However, for the purposes of negotiation, these simpler specifications suffice because they include the actions of each proposal that are relevant to the negotiations.

In order to simplify the presentation of the system, we have a fixed initiating agent with a fixed aim and a fixed initial proposal. The initiator may not accept all specializations of its aim, so it initially suggests a specialization of its aim that it accepts, which is its initial proposal. We have a functional fluent, AIM, to represent the initiator's aim in order to allow other agents to be ignorant of the initial aim. The aim remains fixed over time, therefore, only one negotiation will take place. It would not be difficult to generalize the system to handle multiple negotiations.

We now list some definitions that will be used in the remainder of the paper:

$\text{SENDREC}(x, y, a) \stackrel{\text{def}}{=} \text{SENDEROF}(a) = x \wedge \text{RECIPIENTOF}(s) = y$
The sender in the action $a$ is $x$ and the recipient in $a$ is $y$. The definitions of $\text{SENDEROF}(a)$ and $\text{RECIPIENTOF}(a)$ are straightforward and we omit them.

**Eventually**$(\phi, now, then) \stackrel{\text{def}}{=} \exists s'. now \preceq s' \preceq then \wedge \phi(s')$
Eventually $\phi$ holds in the path defined by $(now, then)$.

**Next**$(seq, now, then) \stackrel{\text{def}}{=} now \preceq do(seq, now) \preceq then$
The sequence of actions $seq$ occurs next in the path defined by $(now, then)$. For this definition, the $do$ function is overloaded to handle sequences of actions, but we leave out the new definition here.

**Previously**$(\alpha, s) \stackrel{\text{def}}{=} \exists s', s''. s' \preceq s'' \preceq s \wedge Do(\alpha, s', s'')$
The complex action $\alpha$ occurred in the history of $s$.

$\text{PROPOSAL}(\tau) \stackrel{\text{def}}{=}$
$\exists x, y(\tau = \text{TWOWAY}(x, y); \text{DISCONNECT}(x, y)) \vee$
$\exists x, y(\tau = \text{RECORD}(x, y); \text{DISCONNECT}(x, y)) \vee$
$\exists x, y(\tau = \text{TWOWAY}(x, y); \text{IDENTITY}(x, y); \text{DISCONNECT}(x, y)) \vee$
$\exists x, y(\tau = \text{RECORD}(x, y); \text{IDENTITY}(x, y); \text{DISCONNECT}(x, y)) \vee$
$\exists x, y(\tau = \text{TWOWAY}(x, y); \text{NAME}(x, y); \text{DISCONNECT}(x, y)) \vee$
$\exists x, y(\tau = \text{TWOWAY}(x, y); \text{NUMBER}(x, y); \text{DISCONNECT}(x, y)) \vee$
$\exists x, y(\tau = \text{RECORD}(x, y); \text{NAME}(x, y); \text{DISCONNECT}(x, y)) \vee$
$\exists x, y(\tau = \text{RECORD}(x, y); \text{NUMBER}(x, y); \text{DISCONNECT}(x, y)) \vee$
$\exists x, y(\tau = \text{ANONYMOUSCALL}(x, y)) \vee \exists x, y(\tau = \text{IDENTIFIEDCALL}(x, y)) \vee$
$\exists x, y(\tau = \text{CALL}(x, y))$
$\tau$ is a complex action that can be used as a proposal.

$\text{SPECIALIZATION}(\tau, \rho) \stackrel{\text{def}}{=}$
$(\forall s, s'. Do(\tau, s, s') \supset Do(\rho, s, s')) \wedge \text{PROPOSAL}(\tau) \wedge \text{PROPOSAL}(\rho) \wedge \tau \neq \rho$
The proposal $\tau$ is a (strict) specialization of the proposal $\rho$.

$\text{COUSIN}(\tau, \rho) \stackrel{\text{def}}{=} \exists \delta(\text{SPECIALIZATION}(\tau, \delta) \wedge \text{SPECIALIZATION}(\rho, \delta))$
The proposal $\tau$ is a cousin of the proposal $\rho$, if both $\tau$ and $\rho$ are specializations of another proposal $\delta$ (i.e., $\delta$ is a common ancestor of $\tau$ and $\rho$ in the specialization tree of proposals). When a non-initiating agent does not accept any of the specializations

of a proposal (e.g. $\tau$), it will try to find an acceptable proposal by generalizing $\tau$ and finding a specialization of the generalization that it accepts. In other words, it will suggest an acceptable cousin of $\tau$.

$\text{ACCEPTABLE}(agt, \tau, s) \overset{\text{def}}{=}$

$\forall seq[\mathbf{Know}(agt, Do(\tau, now, do(seq, now)), s) \supset \neg\mathbf{Goal}(agt, \neg\mathbf{Next}(seq), s)] \wedge$
$\forall\rho[\mathbf{Know}(agt, \text{AIM} = \rho, s) \supset \mathbf{Know}(agt, \text{SPECIALIZATION}(\tau, \rho), s)]$

The proposal $\tau$ is acceptable to $agt$ in $s$. This holds if every sequence of actions that $agt$ thinks is a legal execution of $\tau$ is compatible with $agt$'s goals, and if $agt$ knows the initial aim ($\rho$) of the negotiation (i.e., $agt$ is the initiator) then $agt$ also knows that $\tau$ is a specialization of $\rho$.

$\text{NIAACCEPT}(\tau, s) \overset{\text{def}}{=} \forall agt \in \text{AGENTS}(\tau) - \{initiator\}.\text{ACCEPTABLE}(agt, \tau, s)$

All the non-initiating agents accept the proposal $\tau$. $\text{AGENTS}(\tau)$ is a function, whose definition we omit, that returns the set of agents involved in proposal $\tau$. $initiator$ is a free variable in this definition and will be bound by an outer construct.

$\text{ALLACCEPT}(\tau, s) \overset{\text{def}}{=} \forall agt \in \text{AGENTS}(\tau).\text{ACCEPTABLE}(agt, \tau, s)$

All the agents accept $\tau$.

$\text{POSSIBLESOLUTION}(\tau, agt, s) \overset{\text{def}}{=}$

$\mathbf{Know}(self, \text{ACCEPTABLE}(agt, \tau), s) \wedge \neg\mathbf{Know}(self, \neg\text{ALLACCEPT}(\tau), s)$

This definition is used by the negotiator to select possible solutions to propose to the agents. A proposal $\tau$ is a possible solution for $agt$ if the negotiator knows that $\tau$ is acceptable to $agt$, i.e., $\tau$ has already been suggested to the negotiator by $agt$, and the negotiator does not know that $\tau$ is not acceptable to another agent.

$\text{INFORM}(informer, agt, \phi) \overset{\text{def}}{=}$

$\text{INFORM}(informer, agt, \text{ENCODE}(informer, agt, \phi, now))$

$\text{REQUEST}(requester, agt, \psi) \overset{\text{def}}{=}$

$\text{REQUEST}(requester, agt, \text{ENCODE}(requester, agt, \psi, now))$

All messages are encrypted. To simplify the notation, we will have formulae as arguments to INFORM and REQUEST actions, but the formulae are replaced by their encodings according to these definitions.

## 4.1    Agent Behaviors and Example Scenario

In Griffeth and Velthuijsen's example scenario, there are two personal agents, UN and CND, and the negotiator, N. UN is the initiator and its AIM is to initiate a call with CND, i.e., CALL(UN, CND). UN's owner has an unlisted number, so UN has the constraint that it never wants to send its number to another agent. CND's owner always wants to know who is calling, so CND never wants to accept an unidentified connection. Here is the axiom that specifies CND's initial goals:

$\mathbf{OGoal}_0(\text{CND}, \forall x(\mathbf{Always}(\forall a_1, a_2, s_2\{do(a_1, now) \prec then \wedge$
$\quad Do(\text{CONNECT}(x, \text{CND}), now, do(a_1, now)) \wedge \text{SENDREC}(x, \text{CND}, a_2) \wedge$
$\quad do(a_1, now) \preceq do(a_2, s_2) \preceq then \wedge$
$\quad [\forall a^*, s^*.do(a_1, now) \prec do(a^*, s^*) \preceq do(a_2, s_2) \supset \neg\text{SENDREC}(x, \text{CND}, a^*)] \supset$
$\qquad Do(\text{IDENTITY}(x, \text{CND}), s_2, do(a_2, s_2))\}))).$

In all paths consistent with CND's goals, whenever an agent $x$ initiates a connection with CND, the next action performed by $x$ towards CND identifies $x$ to CND.

If an agent has any other initial goals, they will have to be included in the **OGoal$_0$** axiom for that agent. In our example, UN is the initiator agent, so we take it to want to know the result of the negotiation, i.e. whether some proposal is acceptable to all, and if so what that proposal is. Since UN's owner has an unlisted number, UN also wants it to be the case that it never divulges its owner's phone number. We state UN's initial goals with the following axiom:

$\quad$ **OGoal$_0$**(UN, [$\forall y$.**Always**($\neg$NUMBERIP(UN, $y$)) $\wedge$ **Eventually**(
$\quad\quad \exists \tau$ **Know**(UN, ALLACCEPT($\tau$)) $\vee$ **Know**(UN, $\neg \exists \tau$ ALLACCEPT($\tau$)))]).

We also need to specify what the agents know initially. We want to assert that initially, all agents only know how to encode and decode messages addressed to them. In order to do this, we need functions to represent the actual encoding and decoding of messages. Therefore, we introduce ENC($sender, rec, \phi$), whose value is the encoding of $\phi$, and DEC($sender, rec, c$), whose value is the decoding of $c$, i.e., a formula. We need an axiom to ensure that DEC is the inverse of ENC:

$$\text{DEC}(sender, rec, \text{ENC}(sender, rec, \phi)) = \phi.$$

Here is the axiom that defines the non-initiating agents' initial knowledge:

$\forall agt.agt \neq$ UN $\supset$
$\quad$ **OKnow$_0$**($agt$, [($\forall rec, \phi$.ENCODE($agt, rec, \phi$) = ENC($agt, rec, \phi$)) $\wedge$
$\quad\quad\quad\quad\quad\quad$ ($\forall sender, c$.DECODE($sender, agt, c$) = DEC($sender, agt, c$))]).

The initiator also needs to know the value of AIM, which in this example is CALL(UN, CND), as stated in the following axiom:

$\quad$ **OKnow$_0$**(UN, [($\forall rec, \phi$.ENCODE(UN, $rec, \phi$) = ENC(UN, $rec, \phi$)) $\wedge$
$\quad\quad\quad\quad$ ($\forall sender, c$.DECODE($sender$, UN, $c$) = DEC($sender$, UN, $c$)) $\wedge$
$\quad\quad\quad\quad$ AIM = CALL(UN, CND)]).

The procedures that specify the behavior of the agents are shown in Figures 1 and 2. A system with an initiator whose initial proposal is *initProp*, one other negotiating agent *agt*, and a negotiator *negot* can be specified with the following complex action, which we will call FIR(*initiator, agt, negot, initProp*):

$\quad$ INITIATE(*initiator, negot, initProp*) $\|$ PERSONAL(*agt, negot*) $\|$
$\quad$ NEGOTIATOR(*negot*)

For example, we can specify the scenario given in Griffeth and Velthuijsen, where UN initiates a negotiation with CND with N as the negotiator, and with TWOWAY(UN, CND); DISCONNECT(UN, CND) as UN's initial proposal, as follows:

$\quad$ FIR(UN, CND, N, TWOWAY(UN, CND); DISCONNECT(UN, CND)).

We will now go through a trace of this scenario, in order to explain how the agent procedures work. UN is running the INITIATE procedure. UN's first action is to request the negotiator to ensure that UN eventually knows a proposal that is acceptable to all:

$\quad$ REQUEST(UN, N, **Eventually**($\exists \tau$(**Know**(UN, ALLACCEPT($\tau$))))).

Then UN informs the negotiator that it accepts its own initial proposal:

**proc** INITIATE(*self*, *negotiator*, *initProp*)
  REQUEST(*self*, *negotiator*, **Eventually**($\exists\tau$.**Know**(*self*, ALLACCEPT($\tau$))));
  INFORM(*self*, *negotiator*, ACCEPTABLE(*self*, *initProp*));
  [$\langle$**Know**(*self*, $\neg\exists\tau$.ALLACCEPT($\tau$)) $\wedge$
    $\neg$**Previously**(INFORM(*self*, *negotiator*, $\neg\exists\tau$.ALLACCEPT($\tau$))) $\rightarrow$
      INFORM(*self*, *negotiator*, $\neg\exists\tau$.ALLACCEPT($\tau$))$\rangle$
  $\rangle\rangle$
  PERSONAL(*self*, *negotiator*)]
**endProc**

**proc** PERSONAL(*self*, *negotiator*)
  $\langle\tau$ : **Goal**(*self*, **Eventually**(**KWhether**(*negotiator*, ACCEPTABLE(*self*, $\tau$)))) $\wedge$
    **Know**(*self*, $\neg$**Previously**(INFORMWHETHER(*self*, *negotiator*,
                        ACCEPTABLE(*self*, $\tau$)))) $\rightarrow$
      **if Know**(*self*, ACCEPTABLE(*self*, $\tau$)) **then**
        INFORM(*self*, *negotiator*, ACCEPTABLE(*self*, $\tau$))
      **else**
        INFORM(*self*, *negotiator*, $\neg$ACCEPTABLE(*self*, $\tau$)) ;
        COUNTERPROPOSE(*self*, $\tau$, *negotiator*)
      **endIf**$\rangle$
**endProc**

**proc** COUNTERPROPOSE(*self*, $\tau$, *negotiator*)
  **if** $\exists\tau'$.**Know**(*self*, SPECIALIZATION($\tau'$, $\tau$) $\wedge$ ACCEPTABLE(*self*, $\tau'$) $\wedge$
      $\neg$PREVIOUSLY(INFORM(*self*, *negotiator*, ACCEPTABLE(*self*, $\tau'$)))) **then**
    $\pi\tau'$.**Know**(*self*, SPECIALIZATION($\tau'$, $\tau$) $\wedge$ ACCEPTABLE(*self*, $\tau'$) $\wedge$
      $\neg$PREVIOUSLY(INFORM(*self*, *negotiator*, ACCEPTABLE(*self*, $\tau'$))))?;
      INFORM(*self*, *negotiator*, ACCEPTABLE(*self*, $\tau'$))
  **elsif** $\exists\tau'$.**Know**(*self*, COUSIN($\tau'$, $\tau$) $\wedge$ ACCEPTABLE(*self*, $\tau'$) $\wedge$
      $\neg$**Previously**(INFORM(*self*, *negotiator*, ACCEPTABLE(*self*, $\tau'$)))) **then**
    $\pi\tau'$.**Know**(*self*, COUSIN($\tau'$, $\tau$) $\wedge$ ACCEPTABLE(*self*, $\tau'$) $\wedge$
      $\neg$**Previously**(INFORM(*self*, *negotiator*, ACCEPTABLE(*self*, $\tau'$))))?;
      INFORM(*self*, *negotiator*, ACCEPTABLE(*self*, $\tau'$))
  **endIf**
**endProc**

**Fig. 1.** Procedures run by the initiator and other personal agents.

**proc** NEGOTIATOR(*self*)
   ⟨*initiator* : **Goal**(*self*, **Eventually**(∃τ.**Know**(*initiator*, ALLACCEPT(τ)))) →
     **while** (¬∃τ.**Know**(*self*, ALLACCEPT(τ)) ∧
          ¬**Know**(*self*, ¬∃τ.ALLACCEPT(τ))) **do**
      **if** ∃τ, *agent*.POSSIBLESOLUTION(τ, *agent*) **then**
        πτ, *agent*.POSSIBLESOLUTION(τ, *agent*)?;
          **if** *agent* ≠ *initiator* ∧
            ¬**KWhether**(*self*, ACCEPTABLE(*initiator*, τ)) **then**
            REQUEST(*self*, *initiator*, **Eventually**(
                   **KWhether**(*self*, ACCEPTABLE(*initiator*, τ))));
            **KWhether**(*self*, ACCEPTABLE(*initiator*, τ))?;
            **if Know**(*self*, ¬ACCEPT(*initiator*, τ)) **then**
              INFORMALL(*self*, AGENTS(τ), ¬ALLACCEPT(τ))
            **endIf**
          **else**
            **for** *agt* ∈ AGENTS(τ) − {*initiator*, *agent*} **do**
              REQUEST(*self*, *agt*, **Eventually**(
                   **KWhether**(*self*, ACCEPTABLE(*agt*, τ))))
            **endFor**;
            **KWhether**(*self*, NIAACCEPT(τ))?;
            **if Know**(*self*, NIAACCEPT(τ)) **then**
              TERMINATESUCCESSFULLY(*self*, τ)
            **else**
              INFORMALL(*self*, AGENTS(τ), ¬ALLACCEPT(τ))
            **endIf**
          **endIf**
        **endIf**
     **endWhile**;
     **if** ¬∃τ.**Know**(*self*, ALLACCEPT(τ)) **then**
       TERMINATEUNSUCCESSFULLY(*self*)
     **endIf**⟩
**endProc**

**proc** INFORMALL(*self*, *agts*, φ)
  **for** *agt* ∈ *agts* **do** INFORM(*self*, *agt*, φ) **endFor**
**endProc**

**proc** TERMINATESUCCESSFULLY(*self*, τ)
  INFORMALL(*self*, AGENTS(τ), ALLACCEPT(τ));
  INFORMALL(*self*, ALLAGENTS − AGENTS(τ), FINISHEDNEGOTIATION)
**endProc**

**proc** TERMINATEUNSUCCESSFULLY(*self*)
  INFORMALL(*self*, ALLAGENTS, ¬∃τ.ALLACCEPT(τ))
**endProc**

**Fig. 2.** Procedures run by the negotiator agent.

$$\text{INFORM}(\text{UN}, \text{N}, \text{ACCEPTABLE}(\text{UN}, \text{TWOWAY}(\text{UN}, \text{CND});$$
$$\text{DISCONNECT}(\text{UN}, \text{CND}))).$$

In order to satisfy UN's request, the negotiator—whose behavior is described by the NEGOTIATOR procedure—will start a negotiation process between UN and CND and then inform them of the results of this process. CND is running the PERSONAL procedure, in which it waits for and responds to proposals from the negotiator. After executing the two actions above, UN also runs the PERSONAL procedure, but at a higher priority it executes an interrupt. In the interrupt, if UN comes to know that there are no untried proposals that it accepts, then it informs the negotiator of this and the negotiation terminates unsuccessfully.

UN's request described above causes the negotiator to have the appropriate goal and its interrupt fires. The first action in the interrupt is a while-loop to try possible solutions. Since the negotiator has not yet found a proposal that everyone accepts, and it does not know that there are no acceptable proposals, and UN has suggested a proposal to the negotiator, and the negotiator does not know that anyone rejects this proposal, the negotiator enters its while-loop with UN's proposal as a possible solution. Since UN is the initiator, the negotiator will ask the non-initiating agents whether they accept UN's proposal. In this case, the only non-initiating agent is CND:

$$\text{REQUEST}(\text{N}, \text{CND}, \textbf{Eventually}(\textbf{KWhether}(\text{N},$$
$$\text{ACCEPTABLE}(\text{CND}, \text{TWOWAY}(\text{UN}, \text{CND}); \text{DISCONNECT}(\text{UN}, \text{CND}))))).$$

Then, the negotiator waits to find out if CND accepts the proposal. The negotiator's request causes CND's interrupt to fire. The proposal is not acceptable to CND because TWOWAY(UN, CND) is an implementation of CONNECT(UN, CND) and the next action whose agent is UN and whose recipient is CND (which happens to be the next action in the proposal, i.e., DISCONNECT(UN, CND)) is not a specialization of IDENTITY(UN, CND). Therefore, CND informs the negotiator that UN's proposal is not acceptable:

$$\text{INFORM}(\text{CND}, \text{N}, \neg\text{ACCEPTABLE}(\text{CND}, \text{TWOWAY}(\text{UN}, \text{CND});$$
$$\text{DISCONNECT}(\text{UN}, \text{CND}))).$$

Next, CND enters the COUNTERPROPOSE procedure. There are no specializations of the proposal, so CND seeks an acceptable cousin. For example, suppose CND chooses IDENTIFIEDCALL(UN, CND). CND then suggests its choice as a proposal to the negotiator:

$$\text{INFORM}(\text{CND}, \text{N}, \text{ACCEPTABLE}(\text{CND}, \text{IDENTIFIEDCALL}(\text{UN}, \text{CND}))).$$

CND exits COUNTERPROPOSE and then exits the body of the interrupt and waits for further proposals from the negotiator.

The negotiator now has its answer from CND. CND did not accept UN's proposal, so it informs UN and CND that not everyone accepted the proposal and goes back to the top of the while-loop. Now, CND's proposal is a possible solution. Since CND is not the initiator and the negotiator does not know whether UN accepts CND's proposal, the negotiator asks UN whether it accepts the proposal and awaits UN's answer:

REQUEST(N, UN, **Eventually**(**KWhether**(N,
$$\text{ACCEPTABLE}(\text{UN}, \text{IDENTIFIEDCALL}(\text{UN}, \text{CND}))))).$$

This request causes the interrupt in UN's instantiation of the PERSONAL procedure to fire. CND's proposal is not acceptable to UN because TWOWAY(UN, CND); NUMBER(UN, CND); DISCONNECT(UN, CND) is a specialization of the proposal that clashes with UN's goals. So, UN indicates to the negotiator that it does not accept CND's proposal:

$$\text{INFORM}(\text{UN}, \text{N}, \neg\text{ACCEPTABLE}(\text{UN}, \text{IDENTIFIEDCALL}(\text{UN}, \text{CND}))).$$

TWOWAY(UN, CND); NAME(UN, CND); DISCONNECT(UN, CND) is a specialization of the proposal that UN accepts, so UN counterproposes it to the negotiator:

$$\text{INFORM}(\text{UN}, \text{N}, \text{ACCEPTABLE}(\text{UN}, \text{TWOWAY}(\text{UN}, \text{CND}); \text{NAME}(\text{UN}, \text{CND});$$
$$\text{DISCONNECT}(\text{UN}, \text{CND}))).$$

The execution then continues in a similar way, with the negotiator suggesting UN's latest proposal to CND, who responds by informing the negotiator that it accepts the proposal. The negotiator then knows that all the agents accepted this last proposal, so it enters the TERMINATESUCCESSFULLY procedure where it informs UN and CND of the successful proposal. At this point, no interrupts fire for any agent, so the program terminates.

## 4.2   Verification

Griffeth and Velthuijsen informally state and show that their system has the property that if there is a proposal to which all the agents involved agree, it will eventually be found. Since our system is defined formally, we can also formally state and verify its properties. Here is a formal statement of the property suggested by Griffeth and Velthuijsen:

$$Do(\text{FIR}(initiator, agt, negot, initProp), S_0, s) \supset$$
$$(\exists \tau.\text{ALLACCEPT}(\tau, S_0)) \supset$$
$$\exists \tau.\forall agt \in \text{AGENTS}(\tau).\textbf{Know}(agt, \text{ALLACCEPT}(\tau), s)).$$

That is, for any legal execution of FIR($initiator, agt, negot, initProp$) that ends in $s$, if there is a proposal that is acceptable to all agents, then in $s$, there will be a proposal that is known by all agents concerned to be acceptable to all.

Conversely, we might want to show that if there is no proposal that is acceptable to all, then this fact becomes known to all:

$$Do(\text{FIR}(initiator, agt, negot, initProp), S_0, s) \supset$$
$$(\neg\exists \tau.\text{ALLACCEPT}(\tau, S_0)) \supset$$
$$\forall agt \in \text{ALLAGENTS}.\textbf{Know}(agt, \neg\exists \tau.\text{ALLACCEPT}(\tau), s).$$

We [15] are currently developing an environment to facilitate the verification of properties of CASL specifications using the PVS verification system [12]. The environment has been used to prove properties of simpler multiagent systems. We plan to use it to verify properties of this example as well.

## 5   Conclusions and Future Work

We feel that using a formal specification language, such as CASL, to model multiagent systems such as this feature interaction resolution system is advantageous for several reasons. Firstly, since the language has a formal semantics, it is possible to formally state and verify properties of the system. The use of a theory of action with complex actions allows us great flexibility in defining agents' preferences. Also, modeling agents' preferences with mental state operators (i.e., knowledge and goals) allows us to abstract over the representation of these preferences. Moreover, it also allows us to model the communication between agents as speech acts (i.e., informs and requests), which abstracts over the messaging mechanism.

There has been a lot of work in the past on formal specification languages for software engineering [1,18]. But these formalisms did not include any notions of agents and mental attitudes. Only recently have such notions started to be incorporated into requirements engineering frameworks such as KAOS [4], Albert-II [2], and $i^*$ [20]. But the general view has been that goals and other mentalistic notions must be operationalized away by the time requirements are produced.

Within the agents community, there has been some recent work on agent-oriented software design methodologies [3,8,19]. In [5], a formal specification language for multiagent systems based on temporal epistemic logic is described, and techniques for specifying and verifying such systems in a compositional manner are proposed. While compositionality is clearly an important issue for verification, the specification language in [5] is less expressive than CASL; there is no goal modality and the specification of complex behaviors appears to be more difficult. In future work, we hope to address the connection between our specification language and methodologies for designing multiagent systems.

We would also like to verify the properties discussed in Sec. 4.2 as well as other properties of the system using the verification environment that we are developing. As mentioned in Sec. 2.2, we want to develop a more sophisticated method for handling conflicting requests. We would like to expand the example presented here and our model of communicative interaction to make them more realistic.

## References

1. D. Bjorner and C. B. Jones. *The Vienna Development Method: The Metalanguage*, volume 61 of *LNCS*. Springer-Verlag, 1978.
2. Ph. Du Bois. *The Albert II Language – On the design and the Use of a Formal Specification language for Requirements Analysis*. PhD thesis, Department of Computer Science, University of Namur, 1995.
3. F. Brazier, B. Dunin-Keplicz, N. R. Jennings, and Jan Treur. Formal specifications of multi-agents systems: A real-world case study. In *Proceedings of the First International Conference on Multi-Agent Systems (ICMAS'95)*, pages 25–32, San Francisco, CA, June 1995. Springer-Verlag.
4. A. Dardenne, S. Fickas, and A. van Lamsweerde. Goal-directed requirements acquisition. *Science of Computer Programming*, 20:3–50, 1993.

5. Joeri Engelfriet, Catholijn M. Jonker, and Jan Treur. Compositional verification of multi-agent systems in temporal multi-epistemic logic. In J. P. Müller, M. P. Singh, and A. S. Rao, editors, *Intelligent Agents V: Proceedings of the Fifth International Workshop on Agent Theories, Architectures and languages (ATAL'98)*, volume 1555 of *LNAI*, pages 177–194. Springer-Verlag, 1999.

6. Giuseppe De Giacomo, Yves Lespérance, and Hector J. Levesque. ConGolog, a concurrent programming language based on the situation calculus. To appear in *Artificial Intelligence*.

7. Nancy D. Griffeth and Hugo Velthuijsen. Win/win negotiation among autonomous agents. In *Proceedings of the 12th International Workshop on Distributed Artificial Intelligence*, pages 187–202, Hidden Valley, PA, May 1993.

8. D. Kinny, M. Georgeff, and A. S. Rao. A methodology and modelling technique for systems of BDI agents. In W. Van der Velde and J. W. Perram, editors, *Agents Breaking Away*, pages 56–71. LNAI 1038, Springer-Verlag, 1996.

9. Gerhard Lakemeyer and Hector J. Levesque. AOL: a logic of acting, sensing, knowing, and only knowing. In *Proceedings of Knowledge Representation and Reasoning (KR-98)*, pages 316–327, 1998.

10. Hector J. Levesque, Raymond Reiter, Yves Lespérance, Fangzhen Lin, and Richard B. Scherl. GOLOG: A logic programming language for dynamic domains. *Journal of Logic Programming*, 31:59–84, 1997.

11. John McCarthy and Patrick J. Hayes. Some philosophical problems from the standpoint of artificial intelligence. In Bernard Meltzer and Donald Michie, editors, *Machine Intelligence 4*. Edinburgh University Press, 1969.

12. S. Owre, S. Rajan, J. M. Rushby, N. Shankar, and M. K. Srivas. PVS: Combining specification, proof checking, and model checking. In Rajeev Alur and Thomas A. Henzinger, editors, *Computer-Aided Verification, CAV '96*, volume 1102 of *Lecture Notes in Computer Science*, pages 411–414, New Brunswick, NJ, July/August 1996. Springer-Verlag.

13. Raymond Reiter. The frame problem in the situation calculus: A simple solution (sometimes) and a completeness result for goal regression. In Vladimir Lifschitz, editor, *Artificial Intelligence and Mathematical Theory of Computation: Papers in Honor of John McCarthy*, pages 359–380. Academic Press, San Diego, CA, 1991.

14. Richard B. Scherl and Hector J. Levesque. The frame problem and knowledge-producing actions. In *Proceedings of the Eleventh National Conference on Artificial Intelligence*, pages 689–695, Washington, DC, July 1993. AAAI Press/The MIT Press.

15. Steven Shapiro. PhD thesis. In preparation.

16. Steven Shapiro, Yves Lespérance, and Hector J. Levesque. Specifying communicative multi-agent systems. In Wayne Wobcke, Maurice Pagnucco, and Chengqi Zhang, editors, *Agents and Multi-Agent Systems — Formalisms, Methodologies, and Applications*, volume 1441 of *LNAI*, pages 1–14. Springer-Verlag, Berlin, 1998.

17. Steven Shapiro, Maurice Pagnucco, Yves Lespérance, and Hector J. Levesque. Iterated belief change in the situation calculus. In A. G. Cohn, F. Giunchiglia, and B.Selman, editors, *Principles of Knowledge Representation and Reasoning: Proceedings of the Seventh International Conference (KR2000)*, pages 527–538, San Francisco, CA, 2000. Morgan Kaufmann Publishers.

18. J. M. Spivey. *The Z Notation: A Reference Manual*. Prentice Hall, 1989.

19. M. Wooldridge, N. R. Jennings, and D. Kinny. A methodology for agent-oriented analysis and design. In O. Etzioni, J. P. Müller, and J. Bradshaw, editors, *Agents '99: Proceedings of the Third International Conference on Autonomous Agents*, Seattle, WA, May 1999.

20. Eric S. K. Yu. *Modelling Strategic Relationships for Process Reengineering*. PhD thesis, Dept. of Computer Science, University of Toronto, 1995.

# Generalised Object-Oriented Concepts for Inter-agent Communication

Rogier M. van Eijk, Frank S. de Boer, Wiebe van der Hoek, and John-Jules Ch. Meyer

Utrecht University, Department of Computer Science
P.O. Box 80.089, 3508 TB Utrecht, The Netherlands
{rogier, frankb, wiebe, jj}@cs.uu.nl

**Abstract.** In this paper, we describe a framework to program open societies of concurrently operating agents. The agents maintain a subjective theory about their environment and interact with each other via a communication mechanism suited for the exchange of information, which is a generalisation of the traditional rendez-vous communication mechanism from the object-oriented programming paradigm. Moreover, following object-oriented programming, agents are grouped into agent classes according to their particular characteristics; viz. the program that governs their behaviour, the language they employ to represent information and most interestingly the questions they can be asked to answer. We give and operational model of the programming language in terms of a transition system for the formal derivation of computations of multi-agent programs.

## 1 Introduction

The field of multi-agent systems is a rapidly growing research area. Although in this field there is no real consensus on what exactly constitutes an agent (in fact, this also applies to the notion of an object, which nonetheless has proven to be a successful concept for the design of a new generation of programming languages), there are some generally accepted properties attributed to it [14]. An *agent* is viewed upon as an *autonomous* entity that shows both a *reactive* and *proactive* behaviour by perceiving and acting in the environment it inhabits. Moreover, it has a *social* ability to interact with other agents in a multi-agent context. In the stronger conception of agency, an agent is additionally assumed to have a mental state comprised of *informational* attitudes (like knowledge and belief) and *motivational* attitudes (like goals, desires and intentions).

What this enumeration of properties shows, is that rather than being thought of as a computational entity in the traditional sense, an agent is viewed upon as a more elaborate software entity that embodies particular human-like characteristics. For instance, an important issue in the rapidly growing research area of electronic commerce, is the study of whether agents can assist humans in their tedious tasks of localising, negotiating and purchasing goods. The negotiation activities, for example, in general comprise the exchange of information of a highly complex nature, requiring the involved parties to employ high-level modalities as knowledge and belief about the knowledge and belief of the other parties.

The emerging novel application areas such as electronic commerce require the development of new *programming paradigms*, as the emphasis of programming involves a

C. Castelfranchi, Y. Lespérance (Eds.): Intelligent Agents VII, LNAI 1986, pp. 260–274, 2001.

shift from performing *computations* towards the more involved concepts of *interaction* and *communication*. The object-oriented languages, for instance, as the term indicates, are primarily designed to program systems consisting of a collection of objects. In general, such an *object* is modelled as an entity whose state is stored in a set of variables and that is assigned a set of methods that can be invoked to operate on these variables. In fact, it constitutes a type of *data encapsulation*; other objects can inspect and change the state of the object through the invocation of one of its methods. The central interaction mechanism of this paradigm is thus one that proceeds via method invocations, which in our opinion, is not a mechanism suited to the communication of high-level types of information. Moreover, the field of multi-agent systems is not so concerned with programming objects, but, if we draw the classical philosophical distinction, more with programming *subjects*. That is, in this paradigm the subjective point of view of computational entities is explicated: the state of an agent is not given by an objective state mapping variables to values, but constitutes a mental state that expresses the agent's subjective view on itself and its environment. Hence, the object-oriented languages, in their current forms, are not well-suited to program multi-agent systems.

Among multi-agent programming languages like AgentSpeak [13] and DESIRE [3], in previous research, we have developed an abstract multi-agent programming framework that has a well-defined *formal semantics* [4,5,6]. The framework is fit to program open societies of concurrently operating agents, which maintain a subjective theory about their environment, and which interact with each other via a communication mechanism for the *exchange of information* rather than the communication of values (like in [10]). In this paper, we further extend this framework with generalisations of concepts from the object-oriented programming paradigm such as *agent classes*, communication based on a *rendez-vous* mechanism and the introduction of *questions*.

## 2    Inter-agent Communication

We view an agent has a computational entity that operates together with a collection of other agents in some environment. It maintains a private, subjective theory about its environment, given by its specific expertise and reasoning capabilities, and interacts with other agents via the communication of information. In particular, we explicate the following constituents of an agent.

First of all, an agent has its own activity given by the execution of a private *program*, which describes the agent's reasoning patterns and its behaviour. The program is executed in the context of a *mental state* that consists of motivational attitudes (as goals) and informational attitudes (as beliefs). In this paper, we only consider the second category of mental attitudes; the motivational attitudes are outside the scope of the present paper and studied in other papers in this volume [9,12]. That is, we assume that each agent has its own belief base. Additionally, the agent has a private *first-order system* to represent and process information. In addition to a first-order language, this system comprises an entailment relation $\vdash$ (e.g., a prolog interpreter, theorem-prover) to decide whether formulae constitute a consequence of the current belief base. This operator for instance indicates how the agent deals with negations; i.e., whether it employs a negation-as-failure strategy, a finite-failure strategy, and so on. Moreover, it can be thought of representing the agent's decision-making capabilities. Finally, the first-order system comprises an operation ∘ to *update* the agent's belief base with newly acquired information and newly established conclusions. That is, we assume that each agent employs its private belief revision strategy [8].

*Communication via Questions.* Let us give a sketch of a communication mechanism that is based upon the notion of a *question*, by analogy with the notion of a *method* from object-oriented programming. Given a first-order system that comprises a set $C$ of first-order formulae and an entailment relation $\vdash$, a question is of the form:

$$q(\mathbf{x}) \leftarrow \varphi,$$

where $q$ constitutes the name of the question, $\mathbf{x}$ is a sequence of formal parameters and $\varphi$ denotes a formula in $C$. Consider for instance the following question to ask whether a particular liquid $x$ has reached its boiling point:

$$boiling(x) \leftarrow Hydrogen\_oxide(x) \wedge temp(x) \geq 100°C) \vee$$
$$Hydrogen\_sulfide(x) \wedge temp(x) \geq -60°C).$$

According to this definition, a liquid $x$ has reached its boiling point in case it concerns hydrogen oxide (water) and its current temperature is at least 100 degrees Celcius, or the liquid is hydrogen sulfide (hepatic acid) in which case the temperature should be equal to or higher than $-60$ degrees Celcius. A question $q$ is also assigned an *interface signature* $\Sigma_q$ that determines which details of the vocabulary of the body of the question are visible from the outside. Let us consider the following two instances $\Sigma_1 = \{Hydrogen\_oxide, Hydrogen\_sulfide\}$ and $\Sigma_2 = \Sigma_1 \cup \{temp, \ldots, -2°C, -1°C, 0°C, 1°C, 2°C, \ldots\}$ of the signature $\Sigma_{boiling}$. In case $\Sigma_{boiling} = \Sigma_1$ the details of the question that are visible from the outside are the types of liquids for which the question is defined. In case $\Sigma_{boiling} = \Sigma_2$ the function $temp$ and the constants to denote temperatures are also visible.

An *invocation* of the above question $q(\mathbf{x}) \leftarrow \varphi$ is of the form:

$$q(\mathbf{t} \mid \psi),$$

where $\mathbf{t}$ is a sequence of closed terms of the same length as $\mathbf{x}$ and $\psi$ is a formula that is expressed in the interface signature $\Sigma_q$ of the question. The purpose of $\psi$ is to give additional information about the actual parameters $\mathbf{t}$. The invocation amounts to checking that the following holds: $B \wedge (\mathbf{x} = \mathbf{t}) \wedge \psi \vdash \varphi$, where $B$ denotes the current information store of the answering agent. Thus, the body $\varphi$ of the question should follow from the current information store $B$ together with the instantiation of the formal parameters $\mathbf{x}$ with the actual parameters $\mathbf{t}$ and the additional information $\psi$ as provided in the invocation.

For instance, a possible invocation of the question *boiling* in the situation its interface signature is given by $\Sigma_1$, is the following: $boiling(c \mid Hydrogen\_oxide(c))$. This invocation amounts to testing that the following holds:

$$B \wedge x = c \wedge \quad \vdash \quad (Hydrogen\_oxide(x) \wedge temp(x) \geq 100°C) \vee$$
$$Hydrogen\_oxide(c) \qquad (Hydrogen\_sulfide(x) \wedge temp(x) \geq -60°C),$$

where $B$ denotes the answering agent's information store. Thus the invocation is successful if the information state $B$ contains information that confirms the temperature of the fluid $c$ to be at least 100 degrees Celcius.

In case the signature $\Sigma_{boiling}$ is equal to $\Sigma_2$, information about the temperature of the liquid $c$ can also be included in the invocation of the question, such that it does not need to be contained in the answering agent's belief state. For instance, the following is then a possible invocation: $boiling(c \mid Hydrogen\_oxide(c) \wedge temp(c) = 102°C)$, in which the additional information $temp(c) = 102°C$ is supplied.

We make one more refinement: we admit the signature of the invocation to be different from the signature of the question. That is, we allow agents to invoke a question with a distinct signature, after which a translation takes place, in which the symbols in the invocation are mapped to the symbols of the question. An example is the following invocation: $boiling(c \mid Water(c) \wedge temp(c) = 215°F)$. We assume a translation function that maps the predicate $Water$ to the predicate $Hydrogen\_oxide$ and the temperature $215°F$ in degrees Fahrenheit to the corresponding temperature $102°C$ in degrees Celcius.

An important feature of the communication mechanism is that it not only allows us to define *what* questions an agent can be asked, but also allows us to hide the details of the underlying first-order system by analogy with the ideas of object-oriented programming. Consider for instance an alternative definition of the question *boiling* like the following:

$$boiling(x) \leftarrow (Hydrogen\_oxide(x) \wedge temp(x) \geq 212°F) \vee$$
$$(Hydrogen\_sulfide(x) \wedge temp(x) \geq -76°F),$$

where the interface signature is given by $\{Hydrogen\_oxide,\ Hydrogen\_sulfide\}$. This question is associated with agents that represent the temperature in degrees Fahrenheit instead of degrees Celcius. From the outside however, this difference in implementation is not visible. That is, an asking agent is not concerned with the representation of the temperature, that is, it does not need to know whether the temperature is measured in degrees Celcius or in degrees Fahrenheit.

## 3   Concepts from Object-Oriented Programming

In defining the above communication mechanism, we adapt and generalise mechanisms and techniques from the object-oriented programming paradigm.

*Object Classes.* An important characteristic of the object-oriented programming paradigm is that object populations are structured into *object classes*. That is, each object in a population is an *instance* of a particular class, which is of the form: $C = \langle \mathbf{x}, M \rangle$ where $C$ is the name of the class, $\mathbf{x}$ is comprised of the variables each object of the class employs and $M$ collects the methods that are used to operate on these variables. That is to say, each object has its *own* set of variables and methods, but the names of these variables and the code that implements these methods are the same among all objects in the class. The class thus defines a *blueprint* for the creation of its instances.

*Active Objects.* In several languages, like for instance the parallel object-oriented programming language POOL [1], rather than being *passive* entities, objects are assigned an activity of their own. That is, in these languages, object classes are of the form: $C = \langle \mathbf{x}, M, S \rangle$ where the additional constituent $S$ denotes a program which governs the behaviour of the objects of the class. The main purpose of this program $S$ is to maintain control over the invocation of the object's methods. That is, these methods cannot be invoked at any arbitrary point in the execution, but only at certain points, which are controlled by the program $S$. Moreover, at each point, the invokable methods typically constitute a *subset* of the entire set of methods.

One of the issues in the field of object-oriented programming is the design of programming languages for *concurrent* systems in which the object population *dynamically evolves* over time. An illustrative representative of these languages is the above mentioned language POOL [1]. A program in this language is comprised of a set of object class definitions, in which one class is identified as the *root class*. The execution of the program starts with the creation of an instance of the root class, which is marked as the *root object*. This root object executes the program that is defined in its class during which it creates new objects of the other classes. In this manner, a dynamically evolving population of concurrently operating objects is attained.

*Communication between Objects.* The interaction mechanism that is used in object-oriented languages like POOL, is based on the classical notion of a *rendezvous* [2]. This constitutes a communication mechanism in which a process, say $A$, executes one of its procedures on behalf of another process $B$. In particular, the rendezvous can be viewed upon as to consist of three distinct stages. First, the process $B$ *calls* one of the procedures of the process $A$. This is followed by the *execution* of the corresponding procedure by $A$, during which the execution of the calling process $B$ is suspended. Finally, there is the communication of the *result* of the execution back to $A$, upon which $A$ resumes its execution. It follows that a rendezvous comprises two points of synchronisation. First, there is the call involving the exchange of the actual procedure parameters from the caller to the callee and secondly, there is the communication of the results back from the callee to the caller

## 4  Programming Language

In this section, we define the syntax of our multi-agent programming language, in which we adapt and generalise the above concepts from the object-oriented programming paradigm in the light of communication between agents. It is important to keep in mind that the driving motivation of this generalisation is the fact that, in contrast to the notion of an object, agents are viewed upon as computational entities that process and reason with high-level forms of *information* rather than with low-level data as expressions and values.

First, we introduce the notion of a *first-order system*. We assume a set $Var$ of logical variables with typical element $x$, where we use the notation $Vec$ to denote the set of finite sequences over $Var$, with typical element $\mathbf{x}$.

**Definition 1** (*First-order systems*)

A first-order system $C$ is a tuple $C = (C, \vdash, \circ)$, where $C$ is a set $form(\Sigma)$ of formulae from a sorted first-order language over a particular signature $\Sigma$. A signature is comprised of constant, function and relation symbols. We use the notation $term(\Sigma)$ to denote the set of terms over the signature $\Sigma$ and $cterm(\Sigma)$ to denote the set of closed terms, which are the terms that do not contain variables from $Var$. Additionally, $\vdash \subseteq C \times C$ constitutes an entailment relation, and $\circ : (C \times C) \to C$ denotes a belief update operator, such that $\varphi \circ \psi$ constitutes the belief base $\varphi$ that has been updated with the information $\psi$.

We assume a global set $Q$ that consists of *question names*. Questions templates and question invocations are then defined as follows.

**Definition 2** (*Question templates and question invocations*)

Given a first-order system $C = (C, \vdash, \circ)$ over a signature $\Delta$, the set $Q_t(C)$ of question *templates* and the set $Q_i(C)$ of question *instances* over $C$, are defined as follows:

$$Q_t(C) = \{q(\mathbf{x}, \mathbf{y}) \leftarrow \varphi \mid q \in Q, \ \mathbf{x}, \mathbf{y} \in Vec, \ \varphi \in C\}$$

$$Q_i(C) = \{q(\mathbf{s}, \mathbf{t} \mid \psi) \mid q \in Q, \ \mathbf{s}, \mathbf{t} \in cterm(\Delta), \ \psi \in C\}.$$

A question template is of the form $q(\mathbf{x}, \mathbf{y}) \leftarrow \varphi$, where the *head* $q(\mathbf{x}, \mathbf{y})$ is comprised of the name $q$ of the question and the sequences $\mathbf{x}$ and $\mathbf{y}$ of variables constitute the formal parameters that in a communication step are to be instantiated with actual values. The difference between the sequences is that the variables $\mathbf{x}$ are global variables of which the scope extends over the boundaries of the question, whereas the variables $\mathbf{y}$ are strictly local to the question. As we will see later on, the purpose of the parameters $\mathbf{x}$ is to support the communication of dynamically generated agent names. The *body* of the question is a logical formula $\varphi$ that comes from the underlying first-order system $C$. Moreover, each question $q$ is also assigned an interface signature $\Sigma_q$ that defines the visible vocabulary of the question body.

A question invocation is of the form $q(\mathbf{s}, \mathbf{t} \mid \psi)$, where $q$ denotes the name of the question, the sequences $\mathbf{s}$ and $\mathbf{t}$ of closed terms denote the actual parameters that are to be substituted for the formal parameters $\mathbf{x}$ and $\mathbf{y}$ of the question, respectively, and the formula $\psi$ constitutes additional information regarding these actual parameters, which is either already expressed in the interface signature $\Sigma_q$ or will be translated into this signature (via a translation function).

By analogy with the object-oriented programming paradigm, we introduce the notion of an agent class.

**Definition 3** (*Agent classes*)

An *agent class* $A$ is defined to be a tuple of the following form $A ::= (C, Q, D, S, \varphi)$, where $C$ is a first-order system, $Q \subseteq Q_t(C)$ is a set of question templates, $S$ denotes a programming statement in which procedures that are declared in the set $D$ can be invoked, and $\varphi \in C$ constitutes an information store.

A class $A$ thus consists of a first-order system $C$ describing the language and operators the agents in the class employ to represent and process information. Secondly, it comprises a set $Q$ of question templates that the agents in the class can be asked to answer, where for technical convenience we require that $Q$ does not contain two questions with the same name. Thirdly, the class definition contains a statement $S$ that describes the behaviour of the agents in the class; that is, upon its creation each agent of the class will start to execute this statement. The syntax of atomic statement is given in Definition 5, while the syntax of complex statements is discussed in Definition 6. The set $D$ collects the declarations of the procedures that can be invoked in $S$, which, in case it is clear from the context, is usually omitted from notation. Finally, $\varphi$ denotes the initial information store of the agents in the class.

A program then simply consists of a collection of agent classes.

**Definition 4** (*Multi-agent programs*)
A *multi-agent program* $\mathcal{P}$ is a tuple $(\mathcal{A}_0, \mathcal{A}_1, \ldots, \mathcal{A}_k)$ of agent classes.

Each class in a multi-agent program $\mathcal{P}$ defines a blueprint for the creation of its instances. The execution of the program consists of a dynamically evolving agent population in which *existing instances* have the ability to integrate new instances. Additionally, we can think of the possibility to extend the population with agents that have been created *outside* the system (for instance, by a particular user). However, the latter type of agent integration falls outside the scope of the current framework, as it requires an outer layer of user interfaces on top of the programming language.

We assume that each class $\mathcal{A}$ in the program also makes up a *sort* $\mathcal{A}$, which we will refer to as an *agent sort*. We assume that the first-order system of each class in the program includes constants and variables of the different agent sorts, which are used to denote instances of the corresponding classes. In particular, we assume that there is a constant *self* that is used by an agent to refer to itself.

**Definition 5** (*Actions*)
For each class $\mathcal{A} = (\mathcal{C}, Q, D, S, \psi)$ in a multi-agent program $\mathcal{P}$, the *atomic actions* $a$ of the complex statement $S$ and the procedures in $D$ are defined as follows.

*Actions for information processing*  $a ::= \text{update}(\varphi) \mid \text{query}(\varphi)$
The action $\text{update}(\varphi)$ denotes the update of the agent's information store with the information $\varphi$, while the action $\text{query}(\varphi)$ denotes a test that the formula $\varphi \in \mathcal{C}$ is a consequence of the current information store.

*Action for integration*  $a ::= \text{new}(x)$
An action of the form $\text{new}(x)$ denotes the act of integrating a new agent in the system. This new agent will be an instance of the agent class $\mathcal{B}$, where $\mathcal{B}$ denotes the sort of the variable $x$. Moreover, the action constitutes a *binding* operation in the sense that it binds the free occurrences of the variable $x$ in the subsequent program.

*Action for asking*  $a ::= \text{ask}(x, q(\mathbf{s}, \mathbf{t} \mid \varphi))$
This action denotes the act of asking the agent $x$ the question $q(\mathbf{s}, \mathbf{t} \mid \varphi)$ in the set $\mathcal{Q}_i(\mathcal{C})$. If the class $\mathcal{B}$ denotes the sort of the variable $x$, it is required that the set of question templates defined in $\mathcal{B}$ includes a template with the head $q(\mathbf{x}, \mathbf{y})$, for some formal parameters $\mathbf{x}$ and $\mathbf{y}$ that are of the same length as $\mathbf{s}$ and $\mathbf{t}$, respectively. Additionally, we require the variable $x$ to be *bound*, that is, the action should occur in the scope of the

binding action $\mathtt{new}(x)$ or of the binding action of the form $\mathtt{answer}(p(\mathbf{u}, \mathbf{v}))$, where $x$ is an element of $\mathbf{u}$.

*Action for answering* $a ::= \mathtt{answer}(q(\mathbf{x}, \mathbf{y}))$
This action denotes the act of answering a question template $q(\mathbf{x}, \mathbf{y}) \leftarrow \varphi$ in $Q$, where the sequence $\mathbf{x}$ collects the global formal parameters, $\mathbf{y}$ denotes the local formal parameters and $\varphi$ denotes the body of the question.

Like the operation $\mathtt{new}(x)$, the action $\mathtt{answer}(q(\mathbf{x}, \mathbf{y}))$ constitutes a *binding* operator that binds the global variables $\mathbf{x}$ (but not the local variables $\mathbf{y}$) in the subsequent agent program. In fact, it gives rise to a *block construction*; that is, the variables can be referred to inside the scope of the operator, but outside the scope these variables do not exist. In particular, the idea is that the variables $\mathbf{x}$ are used to store the actual parameters of the question, which can referred to in the agent's subsequent program. Since the names of dynamically integrated agents are unknown at compile-time, it is indispensable that these identifiers are communicated at run-time. Consider for instance the following programming statement: $\mathtt{answer}(q_1(x, y)) \cdot \mathtt{ask}(x, q_2)$. In the statement, the occurrence of $x$ in the second action is bound by the first action. That is, in answering the question $q_1$ the agent comes to know about a particular agent which name will be substituted for the variable $x$, after which this agent is asked the question $q_2$. So, in answering questions an agent can extend its circle of acquaintances with new agents that it had not been aware of before.

In the communication mechanism, after answering a question, the actual parameters of a question can thus be referred to in the subsequent agent program. In the literature, this technique is also known as *scope extrusion*: the feature to extend the original scope of variables to larger parts of a program, like for instance in the $\pi$-calculus [11].

**Definition 6** *(Statements)*

$$S ::= a \cdot S \mid S_1 + S_2 \mid S_1 \& S_2 \mid \mathtt{loc}_x S \mid p(\mathbf{x}) \mid \mathtt{skip}.$$

Complex statements are composed by means of the sequential composition operator $\cdot$, the non-deterministic choice operator $+$ and the internal parallelism operator $\&$. Additionally, there is the possibility to define local variables and to have procedure calls. Finally, the statement $\mathtt{skip}$ denotes the empty statement that has no effects.

**Example 7** We illustrate the syntax of the programming language by means of the following example. Consider a multi-agent program $\mathcal{P}$ that consists of two classes: (*Booksellers, Bookbuyers*). Let us first describe in detail how the class of book-selling agents is defined: *Booksellers* $= (\mathcal{C}, Q, D, \mathtt{HandleOffer}, \varphi)$. The first constituent of this class is a first-order system $\mathcal{C} = (C, \vdash, \circ)$, which contains formulae over a signature $\Delta$. The predicates in this signature $\Delta$ are given by the ordering relations $<$ and $\geq$, a predicate $Customer(x)$ to denote that the agent $x$ is a customer, a predicate $Defaulter(x)$ to denote that the agent $x$ is notorious for not paying for its purchases, predicates $Novel(y)$ and $Comic(y)$ to denote that the book $y$ is a novel and a comic, respectively, and finally a relation $Sold(x, y)$ to denote that the book $x$ has been sold to agent $y$. Additionally, $\Delta$ contains a set $\Sigma$ of constants: $\Sigma = \Sigma_1 \cup \Sigma_2 \cup \Sigma_3$, which is comprised of a set $\Sigma_1$ of constants to denote *agents* with typical element $n$, a set $\Sigma_2$ of constants to denote *books* with typical element $b$ and finally, a set $\Sigma_3$ to denote the *prices* of books in euros with typical element €$m$. Furthermore, the entailment relation $\vdash$ implements a negation-as-failure strategy; that is, for all $\varphi, \psi \in \mathcal{C}$, the following holds: $\varphi \nvdash \psi \Rightarrow \varphi \vdash \neg\psi$. The set $Q$ of the class consists of the following question templates:

$$
\begin{aligned}
NewBuyer(x, \epsilon) \quad &\leftarrow \neg Customer(x) \\
AcceptOffer(xy, z) \quad &\leftarrow Customer(x) \wedge \\
&\quad \neg Defaulter(x) \wedge \neg\exists u(Sold(y, u)) \wedge \\
&\quad ((Novel(y) \wedge z \geq €20) \vee (Comic(y) \wedge z \geq €4)) \\
RefuseOffer(\epsilon, xyz) \quad &\leftarrow Customer(x) \wedge \\
&\quad (Defaulter(x) \vee \exists u(Sold(y, u)) \vee \\
&\quad (Novel(y) \wedge z < €20) \vee (Comic(y) \wedge z < €4)).
\end{aligned}
$$

Moreover, the interface signature of the question *NewBuyer* is given by $\Sigma_1$, while the signatures of the other two questions is given by $\Sigma$. So, the question $NewBuyer(x, \epsilon)$ amounts to asking that the agent $x$ is not already a customer. This question is typically asked for its side-effects, as we will see below. The question $AcceptOffer(xy, z)$ is employed to ask that $z$ is an acceptable offer from the agent $x$ for the book $y$, while $RefuseOffer(\epsilon, xyz)$ is used to ask that such an offer is unacceptable.

The procedure `HandleOffer`, which is declared in the set $D$, is defined as follows:

```
HandleOffer :-
    (answer(AcceptOffer(xy, z))·
        update(Sold(y, x))·
        HandleOffer)
    +
    ((answer(RefuseOffer(ε, xyz))·
        HandleOffer)
    +
    (answer(NewBuyer(x, ε))·
        update(customer(x))·
        HandleOffer))
```

Thus, the procedure loops over the non-deterministic choice between the acceptance of an offer, the refusal of an offer and the registration of a new customer. Note that the question *NewBuyer* is typically answered for its side effect, namely the binding of the global formal parameter $x$ to an actual parameter. In particular, the scope of the variable $x$ is extruded to the next action of the program in which the information $customer(x)$ about $x$ is added to the information store. Provided that a buyer has been registered as a customer, novels and comics are sold in case the offered price exceeds 20 euros and 4 euros, respectively. In the other cases, including the situation that the customer is known to be a defaulter and the situation that the book has been sold already, offers are refused.

Finally, the information store $\varphi$ of the class is a conjunction of atomic formulae of the form $Novel(b)$ and $Comic(b)$, where $b$ ranges over the elements of $\Sigma_2$. The store thus defines for each of the books whether it is a novel or a comic. In particular, we assume it to contain the information $Novel(b_{737})$.

Additionally, there is the following class of agents that buy want to buy a book $b_{737}$ from the booksellers: $Bookbuyers = (\mathcal{D}, R, F, \texttt{BuyBook737}, true)$. The first-order system $\mathcal{D}$ is defined over a signature that is comprised of a relation $Bought(x, y)$ to denote that the book $x$ has been bought from agent $y$. Additionally, it contains the subsignatures $\Sigma_1$ of constants to denote *agents* with typical element $n$, a set $\Sigma_2$ of constants to denote *books* with typical element $b$ and thirdly, instead of constants to denote the price of books in euros, a set $\Sigma_4$ of constants to represent the prices of books in *dollars* with typical element $\$m$. The set $R$ consists of the following question:

$$NewSeller(x, \epsilon) \leftarrow true,$$

where $x$ is a variable of the sort *Booksellers*. This question is typically employed for its side effect, namely to come to know about a selling agent $x$.

The procedure `BuyBook737`, which is declared in the set $F$, is defined as follows:

```
BuyBook737 :−
   answer(NewSeller(x, ε)).
      ask(x, NewBuyer(self, ε | true)).
         ask(x, AcceptOffer((self, b737), $22) | true)).
            update(Bought(b737, x))
      +
         ask(x, RefuseOffer(ε, (self, b737, $22) | true)).
            BuyBook737
```

So, in this procedure, the agent comes to know about a bookselling agent $x$, with which it registers itself through an invocation of the question *NewBuyer*. Subsequently, the bookseller $x$ is asked whether or not it sells the book $b_{737}$ for a price of 22 dollars. If this offer is accepted the information store is subsequently updated with the information $Bought(b_{737}, x)$ upon which the procedure terminates. On the other hand, if it is refused, the procedure is recursively invoked in order to come to know about (another) bookselling agent. It is important to note here that the price $\$22$ in dollars needs to be translated into a price in euros. For instance, one can think of a translation function that multiplies a price in dollars with a factor 0.95, yielding the corresponding price €21 in euros.

## 5 Operational Semantics

In this section, we define the operational semantics of multi-agent programs. Let us first consider the notion of an agent, which is an instance of a particular agent class.

**Definition 8** (*Agents*)
An instance of an agent class is called an *agent*. Given a class $\mathcal{A} = (\mathcal{C}, Q, D, S, \varphi)$, the initial configuration of an agent is the tuple $\langle n, S, \varphi \rangle$, where $n$ is a unique constant of sort $\mathcal{A}$.

An agent is assigned a unique name $n$, which can be used by other agents in a system to address it. Upon integration in the system, the initial information store of the agent is given by the store $\varphi$ from the class and its initial programming statement is $S$. Moreover, the agent uses the first-order system $C$ to represent and process information, while the questions it can be asked to answer are collected in the set $Q$. Additionally, the procedures that can be invoked in $S$ are collected in the set $D$. As the constituents $C$, $Q$ and $D$ remain invariant under execution and can be inferred from the class, they are not included in the agent's configuration. Although also the name $n$ of the agent stays the same during execution, it is still included in the agent's configuration simply because it allows us to distinguish between the different instances of the same class.

**Definition 9** (*Multi-Agent Systems*)
Given a program $\mathcal{P} = (\mathcal{A}_0, \mathcal{A}_1, \ldots, \mathcal{A}_k)$, a *multi-agent system* is a set of instances of the agent classes $\mathcal{A}_i$ $(0 \leq i \leq k)$.

A multi-agent system is a population of agents that dynamically evolves itself through the dynamic integration of new instances of the classes of the program.

The operational semantics of the programming language is defined in terms of transitions between multi-agent systems. Such a *transition* is of the form:

$$A \longrightarrow A' \quad \text{if } cond,$$

which denotes a computation step of the multi-agent system $A$, where $A'$ constitutes the part of the agent system that still needs to be executed. This computation step is only allowed to take place in case the condition *cond* is satisfied.

In order to be able to define the transition rules, we use the notation $S[\mathbf{t}/\mathbf{x}]$ to denote the simultaneous substitution of the terms $\mathbf{t}$ for the variables $\mathbf{x}$ in the statement $S$. We define the transition rules for the integration of agents, communication and parallel execution. The transition rules for the other actions and for statements are similar to those in [5,4,6] and therefore omitted here.

**Definition 10** (*Transition for agent integration*)
Let the class $\mathcal{A} = (C, Q, D, T, \psi)$ be the agent sort of the variable $x$, and let $m$ be a *fresh* agent constant of sort $\mathcal{A}$, we have the transition:

$$\langle n, \mathtt{new}(x) \cdot S, \varphi \rangle \longrightarrow$$

$$\langle n, S[m/x], \varphi \rangle, \langle m, T[m/self], \psi \rangle$$

In this transition, a new agent $m$ of the class $\mathcal{A}$ is created that starts to execute the statement $T$ defined in its class, and which has an information store that is given by the formula $\psi$. In the program $S$ of the integrating agent $n$, the variable $x$ is substituted by the actual name $m$ of the integrated agent. Additionally, in the program of the new agent, the constant *self* is replaced by its actual name $m$. Note that we assume a global naming mechanism: the constant $m$ is not only fresh with respect to the above local transition rule, but fresh with respect to the entire agent population. This assumption ensures that all agents in the population are assigned a distinct name.

**Definition 11** (*Transition for rendezvous*)
Given the question template $q(\mathbf{x}, \mathbf{y}) \leftarrow \psi$ with interface signature $\Sigma$, let $\Delta$ denote the

signature (excluding agent constants) of a formula $\varphi$ and terms $\mathbf{s}$ and $\mathbf{t}$. The transition is as follows:

$$\begin{array}{ll} \langle n, \mathtt{ask}(m, q(\mathbf{s}, \mathbf{t} \mid \varphi)) \cdot S, B_1 \rangle, & \langle n, S, B_1 \rangle, \\ \langle m, \mathtt{answer}(q(\mathbf{x}, \mathbf{y})) \cdot T, B_2 \rangle & \longrightarrow \quad \langle m, T[\mathbf{s}/\mathbf{x}], B_2 \rangle \end{array}$$

- if $B_1 \vdash \varphi$ and
- $B_2 \circ ((\mathbf{x} = f(\mathbf{s})) \wedge (\mathbf{y} = f(\mathbf{t})) \wedge f(\varphi)) \vdash \psi$, for some $f : \Delta \to \Sigma$.

Let us explain this transition. A rendezvous between an agent that asks the question $q(\mathbf{s}, \mathbf{t} \mid \varphi)$ and an agent that answers the question $q(\mathbf{x}, \mathbf{y})$, takes place in case the body $\psi$ of the question follows from the answering agent's belief base $B_2$ in conjunction with the instantiation $\mathbf{x} = \mathbf{s}$ of the global parameters, the instantiation $\mathbf{y} = \mathbf{t}$ of the local parameters and the additional information $\varphi$, which is required to be a consequence of the asking agent's belief base $B_1$. As the actual parameters $\mathbf{s}$ and $\mathbf{t}$ and the information $\varphi$ are expressed in the signature of the asking agent, they need to be translated into the interface signature of the question. This is achieved via a translation function $f$ that maps the symbols in $\Delta$ into the symbols of the signature $\Sigma$, where it is required that the function $f$ does *not* translate agent constants. Consequently, in the transition, the vocabulary of the answering agent $m$ is *extended* with the agent constants that occur in $\mathbf{s}$, as these are not translated into the interface signature of the question. Note that possible inconsistencies need to be resolved by the update operator $\circ$.

Moreover, the transition reflects how the scope of the global formal parameters of a question is extended to the agent's subsequent program; that is, the formal parameters $\mathbf{x}$ of the question $q$ can be referred to in the subsequent statement $T$ of the answering agent. As mentioned before, this technique of extending the original scope of variables, is in the literature known as *scope extrusion*. In fact, these variables are replaced by the actual parameters $\mathbf{s}$.

**Definition 12** (*Transition rule for external parallelism*) If $A_1 \cap A_2 = \emptyset$, we have:

$$\frac{A_2 \longrightarrow A_2'}{A_1 \cup A_2 \longrightarrow A_1 \cup A_2'}$$

The rule defines that the computation steps of a multi-agent system are derivable from the computation steps of its subsystems. That is, if a subsystem $A_2$ evolves itself to the system $A_2'$, the resulting configuration of the overall multi-agent system $A_1 \cup A_2$ is given by the system $A_1 \cup A_2'$.

**Example 13** (*Selling and buying books*)
Recall the multi-agent program $\mathcal{P} = (Booksellers, Bookbuyers)$ from the previous section. Consider the initial system $\{(n_1, \mathtt{IntegrateSellerAndBuyer}, true)\}$, which consists of an agent with name $n_1$ that has an empty information store $true$ and executes the procedure $\mathtt{IntegrateSellerAndBuyer}$ that is defined as follows:

```
IntegrateSellerAndBuyer :-
    loc_y(new(y)·
        loc_z(new(z)·
            ask(z, NewSeller(y, ε | true))))·
            IntegrateSellerAndBuyer,
```

where $y$ is a variable of the sort *Booksellers* and $z$ a variable of the sort *Bookbuyers*. Thus, in this procedure, a seller $y$ and a buyer $z$ are integrated, after which the name of the seller is communicated to the buyer by means of an invocation of the buyer's question *NewSeller*.

Using the transition for agent integration this system evolves itself in one step to the multi-agent system:

$$\{(n_1, \texttt{loc}_z(\texttt{new}(z) \cdot S), true),$$
$$(n_2, \texttt{HandleOffer}, \varphi)\},$$

in which a selling agent $n_2$ has been integrated. The statement $S$ abbreviates the remainder of the procedure `IntegrateSellerAndBuyer`, in which the variable $y$ is substituted by the constant $n_2$.

Subsequently, the agent $n_1$ integrates an instance of the class *Bookbuyers*. Using the rules for integration and external parallelism, we derive the system:

$$\{(n_1, \texttt{ask}(n_3, NewSeller(n_2, \epsilon \mid true)) \cdot S', true),$$
$$(n_2, \texttt{HandleOffer}, \varphi),$$
$$(n_3, \texttt{BuyBook737}, true)\},$$

where $S'$ abbreviates the remainder of the program of agent $n_1$.

After that, a rendezvous between the agent $n_1$ and the buying agent $n_3$ takes place through an invocation of the question *NewSeller*, which has the side-effect that the name of the selling agent $n_2$ is communicated. By means of the rules for rendezvous and parallel execution, this results in the following configuration of the program:

$$\{(n_1, \texttt{IntegrateSellerAndBuyer}, true),$$
$$(n_2, \texttt{HandleOffer}, \varphi),$$
$$(n_3, \texttt{ask}(n_2, NewBuyer(n_3, \epsilon \mid true)) \cdot (U_1 + U_2), true)\},$$

where $U_1$ and $U_2$ abbreviate the corresponding parts of the program of agent $n_3$.

In the next two steps of the program, a rendezvous between the buyer $n_3$ and the seller $n_2$ takes place through an invocation of the question *NewBuyer*. After that the information store of the seller is updated with the information *Customer*$(n_3)$. These two steps lead to the following multi-agent system:

$$\{(n_1, \texttt{IntegrateSellerAndBuyer}, true),$$
$$(n_2, \texttt{HandleOffer}, \varphi \circ Customer(n_3)),$$
$$(n_3, (\texttt{ask}(n_2, AcceptOffer((n_3, b_{737}), \$22 \mid true)) \cdot U_3), true)\},$$

where $U_3$ abbreviates the remainder of the program of agent $n_3$.

Finally, as we assume that $\varphi$ contains the information *novel*$(b_{737})$, a rendezvous between the buyer $n_3$ and the seller $n_2$ takes place through an invocation of the question *AcceptOffer*. This results in the following configuration:

$$\{(n_1, \texttt{IntegrateSellerAndBuyer}, true),$$
$$(n_2, \texttt{update}(Sold(b_{737}, n_3)) \cdot \texttt{HandleOffer}, \varphi \circ Customer(n_3)),$$
$$(n_3, \texttt{update}(Bought(b_{737}, n_2)), true)\}.$$

Let us examine whether the requirements of the rendezvous are satisfied: the body of the question *AcceptOffer* should be implied by the information store of the answering agent together with the information provided by the asking agent, modulo a translation into the signature of the question. This condition is the following:

$$Customer(n_3) \wedge Novel(b_{737})$$
$$x = n_3 \wedge y = b_{737} \wedge z = f(\$22) \wedge$$
$$\vdash$$
$$Customer(x) \wedge \neg Defaulter(x) \wedge \neg \exists u (Sold(y, u)) \wedge$$
$$((Novel(y) \wedge z \geq €20) \vee (Comic(y) \wedge z \geq €4))$$

where $f$ denotes the translation function that maps dollars to euros using the equality $\$1 = €0.95$. Hence, $f(\$22)$ stands for $€21$. The condition holds as $\neg Defaulter(x)$ and $\neg \exists u (Sold(y, u))$ follow from the fact that $\vdash$ is a negation-as-failure operator.

## 6  Conclusions and Future Research

One of the benefits of following the structuring mechanisms of object-oriented programming is that it allows us to study how the Unified Modeling Language (UML) [7], which has become a significant software engineering tool, can be applied for the modeling of agent communication. Moreover an interesting topic of feature research is the study of the concept of *inheritance* in the context of agent communication, which denotes the reuse of code, and the concept of *subtyping*, which denotes the specialistion of behaviour. That is, agent classes can be organised into hierarchical classifications, which describe what constituents classes inherit from other classes. An important ingredient of this study is the development of a semantic characterisation of the subtyping relation, which describes under what circumstances agents from a particular class specialise the behaviour of agents from an other class. One of the conditions of this relation is for example the condition that agents of the subtype can be asked the same questions as the agents of the supertype and moreover, provide the same answers. Subtyping is a very significant concept from a software-engineering point of view, as in modifying existing multi-agent programs, it allows the local replacement of agents by agents from a subtype, without affecting the overall behaviour of the system. A subsequent step is the development of an equivalent *syntactic* characterisation of the subtyping relation, possibly based on a refinement calculus, which yields a method of formally proving subtype relations. An additional interesting issue of future research is to extend the framework with mechanisms that can be used by agents to *advertise* the questions they can be asked to answer.

## References

1. P.H.M. America, J. de Bakker, J.N. Kok, and J. Rutten. Operational semantics of a parallel object-oriented language. In *Conference Record of the 13th Annual ACM Symposium on Principles of Programming Languages*, pages 194–208, St. Petersburg Beach, Florida, 1986.
2. G.R. Andrews. *Concurrent Programming, Principles and Practice*. The Benjamin Cummings Publishing Company, Inc., Redwood City, California, 1991.

3. F. Brazier, B. Dunin-Keplicz, N. Jennings, and J. Treur. Formal specification of multi-agent systems: a real-world case. In *Proceedings of International Conference on Multi-Agent Systems (ICMAS'95)*, pages 25–32. MIT Press, 1995.

4. R.M. van Eijk, F.S. de Boer, W. van der Hoek, and J.-J.Ch. Meyer. Systems of communicating agents. In Henri Prade, editor, *Proceedings of the 13th biennial European Conference on Artificial Intelligence (ECAI'98)*, pages 293–297. John Wiley & Sons, Ltd, 1998.

5. R.M. van Eijk, F.S. de Boer, W. van der Hoek, and J.-J.Ch. Meyer. Information-passing and belief revision in multi-agent systems. In J. P. M. Müller, M. P. Singh, and A. S. Rao, editors, *Intelligent Agents V, Proceedings of 5th International Workshop on Agent Theories, Architectures, and Languages (ATAL'98)*, volume 1555 of *Lecture Notes in Artificial Intelligence*, pages 29–45. Springer-Verlag, Heidelberg, 1999.

6. R.M. van Eijk, F.S. de Boer, W. van der Hoek, and J.-J.Ch. Meyer. Open multi-agent systems: Agent communication and integration. In N.R. Jennings and Y. Lespèrance, editors, *Intelligent Agents VI, Proceedings of 6th International Workshop on Agent Theories, Architectures, and Languages (ATAL'99)*, volume 1757 of *Lecture Notes in Artificial Intelligence*, pages 218–232. Springer-Verlag, Heidelberg, 2000.

7. A. Evans, S. Kent, and B. Selic, editors. *The Unified Modeling Language (UML 2000)*, volume 1939 of *Lecture Notes in Computer Science*. Springer-Verlag, Heidelberg, 2000.

8. P. Gärdenfors. *Knowledge in flux: Modelling the dynamics of epistemic states*. Bradford books, MIT, Cambridge, 1988.

9. Koen V. Hindriks, Frank S. de Boer, Wiebe van der Hoek, and John-Jules Ch. Meyer. Agent programming with declarative goals. In C. Castelfranchi and Y. Lespérance, editors, *Intelligent Agents VII. Agent Theories, Architectures, and Languages — 7th. International Workshop, ATAL-2000, Boston, MA, USA, July 7–9, 2000, Proceedings*, Lecture Notes in Artificial Intelligence. Springer-Verlag, Berlin, 2001. In this volume.

10. Simone Marini, Maurizio Martelli, Viviana Mascardi, and Floriano Zini. Specification of heterogeneous agent architectures. In C. Castelfranchi and Y. Lespérance, editors, *Intelligent Agents VII. Agent Theories, Architectures, and Languages — 7th. International Workshop, ATAL-2000, Boston, MA, USA, July 7–9, 2000, Proceedings*, Lecture Notes in Artificial Intelligence. Springer-Verlag, Berlin, 2001. In this volume.

11. R. Milner. *Communicating and Mobile Systems: the π-Calculus*. Cambridge University Press, 1999.

12. Steven Shapiro and Yves Lespérance. Modeling multiagent systems with CASL — a feature interaction resolution application. In C. Castelfranchi and Y. Lespérance, editors, *Intelligent Agents VII. Agent Theories, Architectures, and Languages — 7th. International Workshop, ATAL-2000, Boston, MA, USA, July 7–9, 2000, Proceedings*, Lecture Notes in Artificial Intelligence. Springer-Verlag, Berlin, 2001. In this volume.

13. D. Weerasooriya, A. Rao, and K. Ramamohanarao. Design of a concurrent agent-oriented language. In M. Wooldridge and N.R. Jennings, editors, *Intelligent Agents - Workshop on Agent Theories, Architectures, and Languages (ATAL'94)*, volume 890 of *Lecture Notes in Artificial Intelligence*, pages 386–401. Springer-Verlag, 1995.

14. M. Wooldridge and N. Jennings. Intelligent agents: theory and practice. *The Knowledge Engineering Review*, 10(2):115–152, 1995.

# Specification of Heterogeneous Agent Architectures

Simone Marini[1], Maurizio Martelli[1], Viviana Mascardi[1], and Floriano Zini[2]

[1] DISI - Università di Genova
Via Dodecaneso 35, 16146, Genova, Italy.
marini@educ.disi.unige.it
{martelli, mascardi}@disi.unige.it
[2] ITC-IRST
Via Sommarive 18, 38050 Povo (Trento), ITALY
zini@itc.it

**Abstract.** Agent-based software applications need to incorporate agents having heterogeneous architectures in order for each agent to optimally perform its task. HEMASL is a simple meta-language used to specify intelligent agents and multi-agent systems when different and heterogeneous agent architectures must be used. HEMASL specifications are based on an agent model that abstracts several existing agent architectures. The paper describes some of the features of the language, presents examples of its use and outlines its operational semantics. We argue that adding HEMASL to CaseLP, a specification and prototyping environment for MAS, can enhance its flexibility and usability.

## 1 Introduction

Intelligent agents and multi-agent systems (MAS) are increasingly being acknowledged as the "new" modelling techniques to be used to engineer complex and distributed software applications [17,9]. *Agent-based* software development is concerned with the realization of software applications modelled as MAS. A two-phase approach can be adopted to develop agent applications at the *macro-level* before implementing the final application.

1. *Specification of the MAS*:
   - describe the *services* each agent provides other agents or human beings with;
   - describe the environmental *events* that each agent can perceive;
   - describe agent-agent, agent-human and agent-environment interactions, abstracting from the agents' internal structure;
   - provide each agent with domain-dependent procedural knowledge, so it can supply its services and respond to stimuli from the environment.

   If a *prototype* of the final application is being developed additional specifications of the environment (and its evolution due to the agents' actions) as well as specifications of the communication media among agents can be given.

2. *Proof of the specification correctness*:
   - specification properties are formally verified, and/or
   - informal testing of the system behaviour by means of a working prototype is performed.

C. Castelfranchi, Y. Lespérance (Eds.): Intelligent Agents VII, LNAI 1986, pp. 275–289, 2001.

The first phase leaves the *architecture* of each agent implicit and profitably abstracts from the internal organization and structure of single agents. Thus, the application developer is not burdened with the modelling of too many details and the specification phase is clearer and more modular. On the other hand, the services that an agent provides are usually variegated and complex and generally involve management of heterogeneous information using different kinds of behaviour. This diversity has to be taken into account and the developer must identify "the right agent to do the right thing" [14]. In other words, an application needs to incorporate agents having heterogeneous architectures in order for each agent to optimally perform its task.

One good approach is certainly to provide the application developer with a predefined library of architectures from which he/she can choose the most appropriate ones. Obviously, the architectures in the library have to be specified, verified and tested before being employed. This process concerns *micro-level* agent development, i.e., building software systems that include some of the main features of an agent.

The declarative nature of *logic programming* makes it very suitable for the interactive development and testing of macro and micro-level agent applications. Logic programming languages can be used to specify agents and MAS at the proper level of abstraction. They can be executed, thus providing a working prototype "for free", and thanks to their well-founded semantics they can be used to formally verify properties of programs, which is fundamental when safety critical applications are developed. Nevertheless, two considerations have to be made:

- Industries and programmers mostly use implementation languages such as C, C++, Visual Basic or Java, and specification languages (mainly non-executable) such as UML or even less formal ones.
- Logic languages which are most suitable for formal verification of system properties are definitely not user-friendly. This makes their use even harder than the "simple" and "user-friendly" Prolog!

Since 1997 the Logic Programming Group at the Computer Science Department of Genova University has been working on the development of a specification and prototyping environment for MAS. CaseLP (*Complex Application Specification Environment based on Logic Programming*) [13,12] provides a macro and micro-level development method for agent applications, as well as tools and languages which support the development steps. In our methodology the more formal and abstract specification of the MAS can be given using the executable linear logic programming language $\mathcal{E}_{hhf}$ [4], which provides constructs for concurrency and state-updating. Even if $\mathcal{E}_{hhf}$ has been successfully adopted as a specification language both at the inter-agent (macro) [1] and intra-agent (micro) [2] levels of abstraction, its use requires a profound knowledge of the linear logic [7] syntax and semantics and the language is definitely difficult to adopt.

One of the initial ideas in the design of CaseLP was to create an environment which could accommodate various specification and implementation languages as well as legacy software so that a MAS prototype could be built using a range of techniques integrated into a common framework. In this paper we attempt to bridge the gap between the above mentioned users' habits and our tool for rapid prototyping.

We present HEMASL (*HEterogeneous Multi-Agent Systems Language*) which is a simple, imperative, meta-language for the specification of agent architectures and the configuration of MAS and which is much closer to widespread existing specification and implementation languages than logic languages. The basic features of HEMASL make it suitable for agent architecture specification and for incorporation of heterogeneous agents into the same MAS. The operational semantics of HEMASL is based on the concepts of "MAS configuration" and "configuration transition". It defines an abstract interpreter for the language that can be used to animate specifications within the CaseLP framework.

HEMASL can be considered as a first step towards defining an "intermediate" language which could make it much easier to animate and incorporate traditional specification languages into CaseLP. The possibility to formally verify MAS specifications using $\mathcal{E}_{hhf}$, a feature of CaseLP, can be obviously obtained by an implementation of HEMASL in $\mathcal{E}_{hhf}$. A formal mapping between HEMASL and $\mathcal{E}_{hhf}$ constructs is under study to make this possibility more valuable.

Some important characteristics of HEMASL are presented below.

**Agent model.** The agent model supported by HEMASL is an abstraction of many existing architectures. This facilitates the development of the architecture specification. Moreover, since this model is the same as the one we adopted to develop agents in CaseLP, integration of HEMASL specifications into CaseLP is facilitated.

**Hierarchy of abstraction levels.** HEMASL provides constructs for specifying a MAS through four different levels of abstraction which support a modular and flexible representation of the system based on the concepts of abstract and concrete architecture, agent class and agent instance. This helps to model the heterogeneity of agent services and architectures.

**Situatedness and social ability.** The ability of an agent to interact with the surrounding environment consists in perceiving the events which take place in the environment and in performing actions which modify it. HEMASL provides an explicit model of the environment as well as primitives that can be used by agents to sense and modify it. It also provides constructs for modelling the message exchange among agents.

In the following sections we expand the concepts outlined above. Section 2 describes the computational model of our agents and the hierarchy of abstraction levels. Section 3 shows the main features of HEMASL through the specification of two agent architectures and one MAS embedding agents having these architectures. Section 4 outlines the operational semantics of HEMASL. Sections 5 and 6 compare our approach to other proposals, and conclude the paper by identifying future research possibilities.

# 2   Agent Model and Structure of a MAS

Since we want to model MAS with agents having different architectures, we need a simple abstraction which can encompass several of the existing architectures. The agents we model with our language are characterized, from a computational point of view, by:

- a **state**,
- a **program** and
- an **engine**.

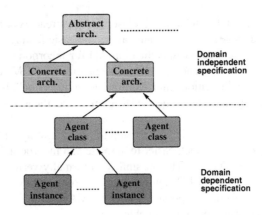

**Fig. 1.** Abstraction hierarchy.

The *state* includes data that may change during the execution of the agent. For example, the state of a BDI agent [15] contains its beliefs, goals and intentions. The *program* contains the information that does not change during the execution of the agent. The program of a BDI agent is determined by its plans. Lastly, the *engine* controls the execution of the agent. A typical BDI engine should be characterized by *a)* perceiving an event, *b)* identifying a set of plans which can be used to manage the perceived event according to the current beliefs, *c)* selecting one plan from the set, *d)* adding the selected plan to the intention set, *e)* selecting one intention and executing one instruction of the selected intention, and *f)* dropping successful goals.

The engine and the program belong to different abstraction levels: the engine is a meta-interpreter for the program and the data (state) on which the program operates. The behaviour of the agent is determined by the application of the agent program on the agent state by means of the agent engine.

The architecture of an agent is characterized by components which contain its state, components for the program, and an engine operating on them. The content of the agent components will be expressed using some architecture dependent object language for which the engine provides an interpreter. In this paper we do not commit to any particular object language.

A specification language for heterogeneous MAS should ensure modularity and flexibility in the definition of agent architectures. Therefore, we introduce a four abstraction level hierarchy, illustrated in Fig 1.

*Abstract architecture.* The abstract architecture defines the components in the architecture and the basic structure of the engine. It is possible to provide guidelines on the realization of any "macro-instruction" (procedure) present in the engine without necessarily giving all the implementation details.

*Concrete architecture.* Concrete architecture is defined by starting from an abstract architecture: each component is assigned a type chosen among the ones the language provides; each macro-instruction of the engine is implemented.

*Agent class.* A class is defined by instantiating the components in the concrete architecture which contain the program of the agent.

*Agent instance.* Starting from an existing class, the initialization of the architecture components containing the state identifies an agent instance.

HEMASL allows the definition of all these abstraction levels. Intuitively, an abstract architecture defines the data structures and the engine that organize agent internal activities without going into too many details. For example, the way data structures are implemented or how an intention is selected in a BDI architecture are irrelevant details at this level. An abstract architecture can give rise to several concrete architectures. This level of abstraction makes the data structures used for architecture components as well as the detailed functioning of the agent concrete. The same concrete architecture can be employed for agents that work on various application domains. Domain dependent behavioural patterns are given by defining the agent program at the class level. Finally, a MAS may require several instances of the same agent class that work by starting from different initial states. This is captured in our hierarchy by defining an agent instance level in which state components are filled.

Besides its internal representation, an agent is also characterized by the ability to perceive the surrounding environment and to interact with other agents in the system. In HEMASL the *environment* ($env$) is modelled as a collection of facts representing the physical environment features which are relevant to the application domain. Agents are able to directly perceive the environment, but they can only modify it by interacting with an "environment agent". Suppose that an agent *robot* is able to perform the action turn_the_engine_on. There are several consequences of the action on the environment, for example, noise, temperature and pollution will increase. It is not realistic that the robot would know all the consequences of its actions, thus it could not directly modify the environment. Therefore we employ a domain-dependent "environment agent" whose task is to evaluate all the relevant consequences of primitive agent actions, and to update the environment consequently.

As far as communication is concerned, an agent interacts with the "environment agent" and with other agents by means of the *ether* ($eth$), a data structure where messages are collected, and from which they are retrieved. HEMASL provides primitives for communication.

# 3   Syntax and Examples of Use

## 3.1   Primitive Instructions and Statements

HEMASL provides primitive instructions for managing the information contained in the architecture components, for delivering and receiving messages, for perceiving events from the environment, for generating events which modify it, and for performing actions in it. These basic instructions can be composed with the statements: *variable declaration* and *assignment*; *procedure call*; *deterministic choice* (**if-then-else**); *loop* (**while**); *concatenation* (;); *non deterministic choice* (|); *concurrent execution* (||).

The instructions which operate on the agent's internal components are

- **get_comp**($c$, $m$, $v$),
- **put_comp**($c$, $m$, $e$), and
- **del_comp**($c$, $m$)

where $c$ stands for the name of the component, $v$ is a variable, $e$ is an expression and $m$ is the mode of insertion, extraction or deletion of an element into/from a component, that depends on the component type. For example, if the component is a list, $m$ can assume head and `tail` as values.

The instructions for message exchange are

- **send**($r$, $m$),
- **rec**($s$, $m$), and
- **block_rec**($s$, $m$)

where $r$, $m$, and $s$ represent respectively the receiver, the message, and the sender. When a blocking reception is performed, execution of the agent program is blocked until agent $s$ sends a message. In the not-blocking reception, the execution goes on even if no message coming from $s$ may be retrieved from the ether.

The instructions for perception and generation of an event $e$ in the MAS environment are

- **perceive**($e$),
- **put_event**($e$), and
- **remove_event**($e$).

Insertion and deletion of an event into/from the environment are reserved operations that can be executed only by the "environment agent". Perception operations can be performed by all the agents in the system.

Lastly, any agent can execute an action $a$ using the primitive

- **exec**($a$).

The effect of this primitive is to send a message with content $a$ to the "environment agent". This agent evaluates the consequences of performing $a$ in the environment and modifies it by means of **put_event**($e$) and **remove_event**($e$) primitives.

### 3.2    Abstract Architecture Definition

To define an abstract architecture, we declare its components, its engine and the engine procedures. As an example, consider a BDI-like architecture. As previously described, it is characterized by four components: one for beliefs, one for goals, one for intentions and one for plans.

The definition of an abstract BDI architecture is depicted in Figure 2. The keyword **class** means that the *plans_component* will be instantiated during the definition

```
abstract_architecture {bdi} {
    components {
        class plans_component;
        agent beliefs_component, goals_component, intentions_component;
    };
    procedures
        { ... definition of the engine's procedures ... }
    engine {
        decl event, selected_event, triggered_plans, selected_plans;
        while true do
            perceive_event();
            plan_triggering();
            plan_selection();
            upgrade_intentions_component();
            exec_intention();
            drop_succesful_goals();
        endwhile
    }
}
```

**Fig. 2.** BDI abstract architecture.

```
upgrade_intentions_component() {
    decl plan, empty;
    is_empty_selected_plans(!empty);
    if not(empty) then
        select_plan(!plan);
        put_intentions_component(gettupla(plan,3))
    else skip
}
```

**Fig. 3.** A partially defined procedure.

of the agent class, and thus that the data contained in it represent the *program* of the agent. The keyword **agent** suggests that *beliefs_component*, *goals_component* and *intentions_component* will contain information representing the agent's state.

The engine consists in a "while" loop continuously executing a sequence of macro-instructions defined as procedure calls. *Global variables* declarations can be included in the engine body. The body of a procedure may be only partially specified in the abstract architecture. This means that the implementation details of the macro-instruction defined by the procedure will be completely described when defining the concrete architecture. A macro-instruction can also be left completely undefined. In this example, *perceive_event()* is not defined at all, while *upgrade_intentions_component()* is partially defined, as depicted in Figure 3.

The procedure body contains declarations of *local variables* at the beginning. The procedures *is_empty_selected_plans(!empty)*, *select_plan(!plan)*[1], and *put_intentions_component(**gettupla**(plan,3))* are not defined at the abstract architecture level.

### 3.3 Concrete Architecture Definition

In the definition of the concrete architecture, all the components are assigned a type, the global variables are initialized, and the definitions of partially specified procedures are completed. To illustrate two different implementation choices, we consider two concrete BDI architectures, $bdi_1$ and $bdi_2$, obtained from the previously defined abstract BDI architecture $bdi$.

In concrete architecture $bdi_1$, *plans_component* is assigned a type stack, *beliefs_component* has type set, *goals_component* has type set and *intentions_component* has a type queue. External events are either events generated by the environment or messages sent by other agents in the system. An agent which is implemented using this architecture will have both reactivity and social ability.

In the architecture $bdi_2$, *plans_component, beliefs_component* and *goals_component* are sets, while *intentions_component* is a stack[2]. The only perceived events are those generated by the environment. This architecture gives origin to strongly reactive agents without the ability to receive messages. In both concrete architectures, perceived events are collected in the global variable *event* which has type queue.

The implementation of the BDI concrete architectures is depicted in Figure 4 and 5. In $bdi_1$, an event is perceived from the environment by means of the **perceive**(e_1) procedure. The global variable *event* is updated by inserting the perceived event into it. A message from *sender* is received in parallel with the perception of the environment, and the received message is also put into the event queue. In $bdi_2$, only events taking place in the environment are perceived and inserted in the event queue.

### 3.4 Definition of Agent Classes and Instances

After the concrete architectures have been defined the MAS is instantiated (Figure 6). The classes of agents are defined, the environment *env* and the ether *eth* are initialized and finally the instances of the agents are created. Due to space constraints we will not go into further detail on this aspect of the language.

## 4    Operational Semantics

The operational semantics of HEMASL specifications is given by a tree that represents the transitions between tuples of *MAS configurations*. A full account of the semantics can be found in [10], while a brief account is given here. A MAS configuration has the form

---

[1] The symbol "!" in the procedure call means that the argument is passed by reference.

[2] These types are probably not the most reasonable to assign to BDI components. They have been chosen to demonstrate language flexibility.

```
architecture {bdi₁} is a {bdi} {
    components {
        plans_component: stack;
        belief_component, goals_component: set;
        intention_component: queue
    };
    init_global_vars { ... };
    procedures {
        perceive_event() {
            decl sender, e_1, e_2;
            ( perceive(e_1); event := insqueue(event, e_1) ) ||
            ( get_belief_component("sender", !sender); rec(sender, e_2);
            event := insqueue(event, e_2) )
        };
        ...
    }
}
```

Fig. 4. Definition of concrete architecture $bdi_1$.

$$[env, \ eth, \ s_{a_1}, \ ..., \ s_{a_n}, \ s_{env\_agt}]$$

where $env$ and $eth$ represent respectively the state of the MAS environment and the state of the MAS ether, $s_{a_1}, \ ..., \ s_{a_n}$ represent the states of the "common" agents and $s_{env\_agt}$ is the state of the "environment agent".

The environment $env$ is a set of pairs $\langle fact, \ value \rangle$, where $fact$ is a string representing a relevant fact characterizing the MAS environment (for example, "temperature"), and $value$ is a string representing the current value of the observed fact (for example, "25"). The ether $eth$ is a set of triples of strings $\langle sender, \ receiver, \ content \rangle$. The term $sender$ must be instantiated by the name of the sender and $receiver$ may be instantiated by an agent name or with the string "all", to model broadcast communication. The ether contains all the messages that have been delivered but have yet to be received by an agent.

The state of the agent $a$ is a pair $\langle ex\_env_a, \ cmp_a \rangle$. It contains information about the architecture components content ($cmp_a$) and about the execution environment of the agent engine ($ex\_env_a$)[3]. Coherently with the meaning assigned to the execution environment in the imperative languages semantics, $ex\_env_a$ is a function which associates values to variables and local execution environments to procedure identifiers.

The relation $\overset{MAS}{\longmapsto}$ defines the transitions between MAS configurations. The actions of the "environment agent" may affect its state, the ether and the MAS environment, and thus the relation $\overset{env\_agt}{\longmapsto}$ is defined over *environment agent configurations* of the form $(s_{env\_agt}, \ eth, \ env)$. Conversely, the actions of a "common agent" $a$ cannot

---

[3] Some confusion could arise due to the presence of the agents' execution environment $ex\_env_a$ and the MAS environment $env$. The context always clarifies the meaning of the term "environment".

```
architecture {bdi₂} is a {bdi} {
    components {
        plans_component, belief_component, goals_component: set;
        intention_component: stack
    };
    init_global_vars { ... };
    procedures {
        perceive_event() {
            decl e;
            perceive(e); event := insqueue(event, e)
        };
        ...
    };
}
```

**Fig. 5.** Definition of concrete architecture $bdi_2$.

```
MAS {
    class_agent {arch_name₁, classagent_name₁} {
        init_comp comp_name₁ [elem₁₁, ..., elem₁ᵢ]; ...
    };
    ⋮

    init_ENV [event₁, ..., eventₑ];
    init_ETH [msg₁, ..., msgₘ];
    create_agent(classagent_nameₜ₁, agent_name₁) {
        init_comp comp_name₁ [elem₁₁, ..., elem₁ᵢ]; ...
    };
    ⋮

}
```

**Fig. 6.** MAS definition schema.

directly modify the MAS environment, and thus $\overset{agt}{\underset{a}{\longmapsto}}$ is defined over *agent configurations* $(s_a, eth)$. Let $\mathcal{A}$ be the set of names of the agents in the MAS. The above concepts are formalized by the meta-rules

$$\frac{(s_{env\_agt}, eth, env) \overset{env\_agt}{\longmapsto} (s'_{env\_agt}, eth', env')}{[env, eth, S, s_{env\_agt}] \overset{MAS}{\longmapsto} [env', eth', S, s'_{env\_agt}]}$$

$$\frac{(s_a, eth) \overset{agt}{\underset{a}{\longrightarrow}} (s'_a, eth')}{[env, eth, S, s_{env\_agt}] \overset{MAS}{\longmapsto} [env, eth', S', s_{env\_agt}]} \quad a \in \mathcal{A}$$

where $S'$ is obtained by substituting $s_a$ with $s'_a$ in $S$.

To give an overview of the language semantics we will describe some meta-rules governing the execution of "common" agents. The meta-rules for the "environment agent" execution are similar to the following ones; in addition, they also define the semantics of **put_event** and **remove_event**. The relation $\xrightarrow[a]{agt}$ is defined by the meta-rule

$$\frac{(\langle ex\_env_a, cmp_a \rangle,\ eth) \xrightarrow[a,i]{ins} (\langle ex\_env_a', cmp_a' \rangle,\ eth')}{(\langle ex\_env_a, cmp_a \rangle,\ eth) \xrightarrow[a]{agt} (\langle ex\_env_a', cmp_a' \rangle,\ eth')} \quad \begin{array}{l} a \in \mathcal{A} \\ N\_I(a) = i \end{array}$$

The function $N\_I(a)$ returns the next instruction which agent $a$ must execute. The relation $\xrightarrow[a,i]{ins}$ is defined over agent configurations and depends on the agent performing the instruction and on the instruction itself. We give its definition for some **HEMASL** basic constructs.

*Event perception*

$$\frac{f \xrightarrow[ex\_env_a]{e\_exp} f'}{(\langle ex\_env_a, cmp_a \rangle,\ eth) \xrightarrow[a,\mathbf{perceive}((f,x))]{ins} (\langle ex\_env_a[v/x],\ cmp_a \rangle,\ eth)} \quad \begin{array}{l} a \in \mathcal{A} \\ (f', v) \in env \\ x \in d(ex\_env_a) \end{array}$$

The relation $\xrightarrow[ex\_env_a]{e\_exp}$ evaluates an expression according to the current execution environment of agent $a$. The function $d(ex\_env_a)$ returns the domain of the function $ex\_env_a$ and $ex\_env_a[v/x]$ is obtained by composing $ex\_env_a$ with the function which associates $v$ to $x$. The effect of a perception instruction is to modify the agent's state by creating a new association between the variable argument of **perceive** and the value associated to the perceived fact.

*Message delivery*

$$\frac{r \xrightarrow[ex\_env_a]{e\_exp} r' \qquad c \xrightarrow[ex\_env_a]{e\_exp} c'}{(\langle ex\_env_a, cmp_a \rangle,\ eth) \xrightarrow[a,\mathbf{send}(r,c)]{ins} (\langle ex\_env_a, cmp_a \rangle,\ eth \cup \{(a,\ r',\ c')\})} \quad a \in \mathcal{A}$$

The effect of a **send** is the insertion of a new triple in the ether.

*Message reception*

$$\frac{s \xrightarrow[ex\_env_a]{e\_exp} s'}{(\langle ex\_env_a, c_a \rangle,\ eth) \xrightarrow[a,\mathbf{rec}(s,x)]{ins} (\langle ex\_env_a[c/x], c_a \rangle,\ eth/\{(s', a, c)\})} \quad \begin{array}{l} a \in \mathcal{A} \\ (s',\ a,\ c) \in eth \\ x \in d(ex\_env_a) \\ a \neq "all" \end{array}$$

This meta-rule can be applied when the receiver of the message is a particular agent and not the string "all". The effect of a **rec** is to associate the content of the received message to the variable argument of **rec** and to remove the read message from the ether. If the receiver is "all", the message is not removed from the ether until all the agents in the system have read it[4].

---

[4] The ether takes care that the receivers of a broadcast message read it only once, and that the message is removed when all the recipients have read it.

The same rules are also given for the blocking reception instruction. The difference between not-blocking and blocking reception semantics is that for non-blocking reception a third meta-rule exists. It can be applied when the desired message is not present in the ether. In this case the effect of a **rec** is to create an association between the variable argument of **rec** and the string "null", with no side-effects on the ether. Conversely, the semantics of the blocking reception is undefined if the message is not present in the ether thus forcing the agent to block its execution.

*Action execution*

$$\frac{act \; \overset{e\_exp}{\underset{ex\_env_a}{\longmapsto}} \; act'}{(\langle ex\_env_a, cmp_a \rangle, \; eth) \; \overset{ins}{\underset{a, \mathbf{exec}(act)}{\longmapsto}} \; (\langle ex\_env_a, cmp_a \rangle, \; eth \cup \{ (a, \; env\_ag, \; act') \})} \; a \in \mathcal{A}$$

The semantics of an **exec** instruction is to send a message to the "environment agent" containing the action to be performed. This is achieved by modifying the ether.

## 5   Comparison

In this section we compare our approach to the specification of heterogeneous agent architectures with other proposals: [5], by Fisher; [8], by Hindriks et al.; [3], by Treur et al., [6] by De Giacomo et al. and [16] by van Eijk et al.. The proposals will be compared with respect to their capabilities to specify architectures that comply with the model of the agent presented in Section 2, i.e., in terms of state, program and engine.

In [5], Fisher presents the specification of an "abstract agent architecture" using Concurrent MetateM, a specification language based on temporal logics. The architecture model allows us to encompass different kinds of *behaviour*, performed by *groups* of sub-agents. Each behaviour is described as a set of temporal logics rules that specify how the future state of agent computation should be obtained by starting from its present state. Examples are presented on the specification of *reactive*, *deliberative*, and *social* behaviour and on the composition of these types of behaviour in different kinds of layered architectures. This approach seems highly suitable to represent the agent program thanks to the expressiveness of temporal logic. On the other hand, this approach does not give explicit representation of agent state and engine which are implicitly maintained in the *interpreter* for Concurrent MetateM, that executes Concurrent MetateM specifications.

Hindriks et al. follow a different approach. They mainly focus on specifications of agent engines that can be used as meta-interpreters for many different object level languages used to give agent programs. They assume that agent computation may be well expressed using programming languages based on the concept of *beliefs*, *goals* and *rules* and define an imperative meta language that is used to describe a "standard" engine cycle which includes *sensing*, *rule application*, and *goal execution*. They argue that a *glass box* approach for defining agent engines which makes internal functioning of engines visible to the MAS developer, is the "right" approach. In such a way the developer can directly program the control of the agent's internal activities. Following the approach by Hindriks et al., the development of agent engines is natural and immediate. However, it constrains the agent state to be composed by beliefs and goals, and the agent program to be composed by rules. Even if most of the agent architectures are designed in terms of these abstractions, the approach could not be as general as needed to fit some agent applications.

The DESIRE research focuses on the study of compositional MAS for complex tasks and development methods for these systems. The structure of DESIRE specifications is based on the notion of compositional architecture: an architecture composed of components with hierarchical relations among themselves. This approach flexibly supports the definition of different heterogeneous architectures. Some architecture components may contain the agent's state and some others the agent's program. The different purposes of these two kinds of components do not arise, however, either from a syntactical or from a semantical point of view. The flow of information among the components is described by the specification of communication links. There is not an engine governing the execution flow inside the agent's components. Even if the DESIRE framework does not provide explicit support for defining agent architectures in terms of state, program and engine, it has been successfully adopted to develop a library of heterogeneous architectures ranging from reactive and proactive ones, to reflective and BDI ones.

ConGolog specifies the agent's behaviour based on the actions an agent can execute. The language adopted for this purpose is the *situation calculus*, a first-order language (with some second order features) for representing dynamic domains. ConGolog also includes facilities for prioritizing the execution of concurrent processes, interrupting the execution when certain conditions become true, and dealing with exogenous actions. These features make adoption of the language for implementing reactive agents possible. On the other hand, the ascription of mental attitudes to agents can easily be achieved by adapting the possible worlds model of knowledge to the situation calculus. Communicative capabilities can also be modelled in the framework. ConGolog provides the means for describing both the declarative and the procedural knowledge of agents with very different capabilities ranging from reactivity to rationality. Nevertheless, this is always done at the "program" level. The engine for these programs is always the same, as is the agent architecture.

Finally, [16] defines a multi-agent programming language in which concepts from the object-oriented paradigm are adapted and generalized in the light of communication among agents. An agent class $\mathcal{A}$ is a tuple $(C, Q, D, S, \phi)$. $C$ is a first-order system describing the language and operators the agents in the class employ to represent and process information. $Q$ is a set of question templates the agents in the class can answer, and represents the interface of the class. $S$ denotes a programming statement in which procedures that are declared in $D$ can be invoked: upon its creation each agent of the class will start to execute this statement. $\phi \in C$ constitutes the initial information store of the agents in the class. There are many similarities between HEMASL and this language: as far as the agent model is concerned, $C$ resembles the *architecture engine*, which can be different for different classes, $S$ corresponds to the *agent program* and $\phi$ to the *agent state*. The language for composing statements provides, like HEMASL does, atomic operations for updating the information store and for communication, as well as nondeterministic choice and parallelism operators. The semantics of the language is given in terms of transition rules quite similar to the ones given for HEMASL.

HEMASL lets the architecture designer choose the most suitable components and agent programming languages, in order for the agent state and program to encompass a great variety of representations, and for the architecture to provide a high degree of flexibility. Furthermore, the HEMASL primitives allow the architecture designer to build the engine as he/she wants. We argue that an "opaque box" approach is the best solution for agent-based software development. The MAS developer should know the main characteristics of the architectures he/she can use for the applications, but he/she is not usually an expert and does not need to be burdened with implementation details about architecture control. By giving a great deal of freedom in architecture development, we can obtain a library including architectures with several data structures and control flows. In such a way, the MAS developer can (hopefully) find the architectures that fits his/her needs in the library.

## 6    Conclusions

The realization of MAS often involves the choice of agents with heterogeneous architectures, so that each agent can optimally provide its services. HEMASL is a simple meta-language which is used to specify heterogeneous agent architectures, in terms of the components that form the agent state and program, and the engine that implements the mechanisms concerning control of the agent's internal activities. These specifications can be subsequently implemented into a library of architectures that MAS developers can use.

Adding HEMASL to CaseLP, our specification and prototyping environment for MAS, enhances its flexibility and usability. In fact, HEMASL can be the "intermediate language" through which non-executable specification languages (both formal and commercial) can be integrated into CaseLP and thus animated using CaseLP working prototypes. Moreover, we think that HEMASL can be used as a specification language for the development of agents which will be implemented into commercial, object-oriented programming languages. Translation of HEMASL specifications into Java programs is presently being investigated [11].

**Acknowledgments.** The authors thank Valeria Perricone for her helpful contribution in improving the presentation of the paper, and the anonymous referees for their useful comments.

This research was carried out while Floriano Zini was at DISI, Università di Genova, Italy.

## References

1. A. Aretti. Semantica di Sistemi Multi-Agente in Logica Lineare. Master's thesis, DISI – Università di Genova, Genova, Italy, 1999. In Italian.
2. M. Bozzano, G. Delzanno, M. Martelli, V. Mascardi, and F. Zini. Multi-Agent Systems Development as a Software Engineering Enterprise. In G. Gupta, editor, *Proc. of First International Workshop on Practical Aspects of Declarative Languages (PADL'99)*, number 1551 in Lecture Notes in Computer Science. Springer-Verlag, 1999.

3. F. Brazier, B. Dunin Keplcz, N. R. Jennings, and J. Treur. Formal Specification of Multi-Agent Systems: a Real-World Case. In *Proc. of International Conference on Multi Agent Systems (ICMAS'95)*, San Francisco, CA, USA, 1995.

4. G. Delzanno and M. Martelli. Proofs as Computations in Linear Logic. *Theoretical Computer Science*. To appear.

5. M. Fisher. Representing Abstract Agent Architectures. In M. P. Singh J. P. Mueller and A. S. Rao, editors, *Intelligent Agents V*, number 1555 in Lecture Notes in Artificial Intelligence. Springer-Verlag, 1999.

6. G. De Giacomo, Y. Lespérance, and H. J. Levesque. ConGolog, a concurrent programming language based on the situation calculus. *Artificial Intelligence*, 121(1-2):109–169, 2000.

7. J. Y. Girard. Linear logic. *Theoretical Computer Science*, 50:1:1–102, 1987.

8. K. V. Hindriks, F. S. de Boer, W. van der Hoek, and J. C. Meyer. Control Structures of Rule-Based Agent Languages. In M. P. Singh J. P. Mueller and A. S. Rao, editors, *Intelligent Agents V*, number 1555 in Lecture Notes in Artificial Intelligence. Springer-Verlag, 1999.

9. N. R. Jennings, K. Sycara, and M. Wooldridge. A Roadmap of Agent Research and Development. *Autonomous Agents and Multi-Agent Systems*, 1:7–38, 1998.

10. S. Marini. Specifica di Sistemi Multi-Agente Eterogenei. Master's thesis, DISI - Università di Genova, Genova, Italy, 1999. In Italian.

11. S. Marini, M. Martelli, V. Mascardi, and F. Zini. HEMASL: A Flexible Language to Specify Heterogeneous Agents. In A. Corradi, A. Omicini, and A. Poggi, editors, *WOA 2000. Dagli Oggetti agli Agenti*, Parma, Italy, 2000.

12. M. Martelli, V. Mascardi, and F. Zini. Towards Multi-Agent Software Prototyping. In H. S. Nwana and D. T. Ndumu, editors, *Proc. of The Third International Conference and Exhibition on The Practical Application of Intelligent Agents and Multi-Agent Technology (PAAM'98)*, London, UK, 1998.

13. M. Martelli, V. Mascardi, and F. Zini. Specification and Simulation of Multi-Agent Systems in CaseLP. In M. C. Meo and M. Vilares Ferro, editors, *Proc. of Appia–Gulp–Prode 1999*, L'Aquila, Italy, 1999.

14. J. P. Müller. The Right Agent (Architecture) to Do the Right Thing. In M. P. Singh J. P. Mueller and A. S. Rao, editors, *Intelligent Agents V*, number 1555 in Lecture Notes in Artificial Intelligence. Springer-Verlag, 1999.

15. A. S. Rao and M. Georgeff. BDI Agents: from Theory to Practice. In *Proc. of International Conference on Multi Agent Systems (ICMAS'95)*, San Francisco, CA, USA, 1995.

16. R. M. van Eijk, F. S. de Boer, W. van der Hoek, and J. C. Meyer. Generalised Object-Oriented Concepts for Inter-Agent Communication. In C. Castelfranchi and Y. Lespérance, editors, *Intelligent Agents VII*, Lecture Notes in Artificial Intelligence. Springer-Verlag, 2001. In this volume.

17. M. Wooldridge. Agent-based Software Engineering. *IEE Proc. of Software Engineering*, 144(1), 1997.

# Improving Choice Mechanisms within the BVG Architecture

Luis Antunes, João Faria, and Helder Coelho

Faculdade de Ciências, Universidade de Lisboa
Campo Grande, 1749-016 Lisboa, Portugal
Ph: +351-21-7500087
Fax: +351-21-7500084
{xarax@di., jfaria@, hcoelho@di.}fc.ul.pt

**Abstract.** The BVG agent architecture relies on the use of values (multiple dimensions against which to evaluate a situation) to perform choice among a set of candidate goals. Choice is accomplished by using a calculus to collapse the several dimensions into a function that serialises candidates. In our previous experiments, we have faced decision problems only with perfect and complete information. In this paper we propose new experiments, where the agents will have to decide in the absence of all the needed and relevant information. In the BVG model, agents adjust their scale of values by feeding back evaluative information about the consequences of their decisions. We use the exact same measures to analyse the results of the experiments, thus providing a fair trial to the agents: they are judged with the same rules they can use for decision. Our method, based on values, is a novel approach for choice and an alternative to classical utilitarian theories.

## 1 Introduction

We consider a setting in which multiple agents interact in a shared environment. Usually, this environment is computer-simulated. Sometimes it is self-contained and agents are used in experiments to draw conclusions about socially relevant phenomena; in other cases, there is a user to whom the agent responds to, and a certain amount of subservience is expected from the agent.

Whichever the complexity of agents, they must possess a flexible decision component to clarify all the deliberation processes. Even a compile-time pre-specified agent will be of little use if it is not ready for a certain extent of non-forecast possibilities. As the environment gets more demanding in terms of unpredictability (at least a priori unpredictability), more complex should our agent be in what respects to decision adaptability. The designer must have the means to specify what is expected from the agent even in a new environment s/he has never considered. With the advent of mobile computation and huge, varied artificial environments (such as the Internet), we have to enhance our agents with autonomous and reliable decision skills.

When confronted with a situation, an agent is defined as rational if he decides in such a way that pursues his self-interest. A classical way of defining self-interest is by adopting utility theory [11], that requires the agent to know in advance all possible

C. Castelfranchi, Y. Lespérance (Eds.): Intelligent Agents VII, LNAI 1986, pp. 290–304, 2001.
© Springer-Verlag Berlin Heidelberg 2001

situations and be prepared to express his preference between any two states of the world. Not only do these conditions seem difficult to be fulfilled, but also this theory leads to interesting decision paradoxes that show its limitations [9, 8].

An attempt to escape from this kind of rationality was the BDI (Belief, Desire, Intention) agent model [10]. Here, commitment to past decisions is used as a way to decrease complexity, since committed intentions constrain the possibilities for the future, and are only abandoned when fulfilled or believed impossible to fulfil. The preferences of the agents are represented by their desires, and these will be transformed in intentions through a deliberation process. In [13], nothing is said about how this deliberation is done. Most BDI approaches consider the problem of commitment, but choice is seldom addressed.

Simon [12] proposed the idea of aspiration levels along multiple, non comparable dimensions that characterise a decision problem. Aspirations are the minimum standards that some solution must meet in order to be adopted. The agent adopts and selects for execution the first solution that meets all of the aspiration levels. In a similar line of reasoning, we have addressed the issue of choice, as one of the central components in the agent's decision machinery [1, 2, 3]. We have proposed the use of multiple values to assess a decision situation. A value is a dimension against which a situation can be evaluated. By dimension we mean a non empty set endowed with an order relation. Most interesting situations from the decision standpoint will have several such dimensions, and so most decisions are based on multiple evaluations of the situation and alternative courses of action. The agent's choice machinery becomes more clear, as agents express their preferences through the use of this multiple value framework. Choice is performed by collapsing the various assessments into a choice function, that cannot be considered equivalent to a utility function, since it is computed in execution time. The multiple values framework we defend can encompass Simon's aspiration levels, but it is more general, allowing for further flexibility, as is shown in [2].

The coexistence of these values in a mind further allows the enhancement of the adaptability decision capabilities by feeding back assessments of the quality of the previous decision into the agent's decision process. Our agents' decisions no longer depend solely on the past events as known at design time. Instead, events are incorporated into the decision machinery as time passes, and the components of those processes evolve continuously to be aggregated just when a decision is needed. This is done by feeding back evaluative information about the results of the decision taken by the agent. In [2] this assessment of (the results of) the decision was done by using some measure of goodness (an abstract higher value). We also suggested other alternatives, such as the agent's own values, or the designer's values (which amounts to looking for emergent features in the agent's behaviour, that is, agents decide by using some system of values, but the designer is interested in what happens to *another* set of values, to which the agents do not have access). Even in the simplest version, the power of adaptability shown by this schema surpasses by far that of choice based on the maximisation of expected utility. It is enough to remember the demands made on the agents by utility theory: they must know *in advance* all available alternatives and preferences between any two of them [7, 11].

In this paper we expand on the functionality of the BVG (Beliefs, Values, Goals) architecture to enhance the decision mechanism to cope with more complex situations, namely the agent has to decide in absence of all the relevant evaluations. We also propose functions for the several kinds of update of the decision process, and experimentally assess them. In section 2 we briefly present the BVG agent architecture, while in section 3 agent autonomy is address with a special focus on choice. Section 4 presents a case study that is explored through sections 5 and 6, where the choice calculus is presented. Section 7 concludes by pointing out the most important contributions.

## 2   The BVG Architecture

The BVG architecture roughly follows Castelfranchi's principles for autonomy contained in his „Double Filter Architecture" [6]. We include herein the main ideas behind this architecture, for a more exhaustive description refer to [1, 2, and 3].

The reference schema of the BVG architecture for decision-making includes goals, candidate actions to be chosen from, beliefs about states of the world, and values about several things, including desirability of those states. Values are dimensions along which situations are evaluated, and appropriate actions selected.

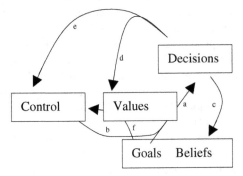

**Fig. 1.** The BVG architecture. (a) value-informed decision making; (b) control over decision; (c) watching consequences of decisions; (d) feeding back information to enhance decision machinery; (e) getting emotional information about the results of decisions; (f) cognitive evaluations.

Decision is a complex, multi-staged process in an agent's mind. One stage deals with the origin of goals. Agents can either adopt goals from other agents or generate goals as a result of internal processes. In another stage, goals are considered against other objects in the agent's mind, such as beliefs (which include plans about their feasibility) and classified accordingly. For instance, we can have suspended goals, active goals, etc. Finally, among the active goals, the agent has to serialise them into execution. This is the choice phase, our primary focus in this paper. We don't want to over-determine the behaviour of the agent. However, it is fundamental to reduce its deliberation time, which is possible by having several partial ordered sets of actions, and computing the final order only when the moment arrives.

In the model proposed in [3], emotions have a determinant role in the control of the choice process (see fig. 1). One main role of emotions is to set the amount of time available for a decision to be made. We proposed a cumulative method, that improves the quality of the decision when time allows it. The idea is based on the different importance of the relevant values. Options are evaluated against the most important values first.

The other key issue in the BVG architecture is the update of the choice machinery based on assessments of the consequences of the previous decisions. These assessments can be made in terms of (1) some measure of goodness (the quality of the decision, measured through its consequences on the world); (2) the same dimensions that the agent used for decision; and (3) a different set of dimensions, usually the dimensions that the designer is interested in observing, what amounts to look for emergent behaviour (cf. [2]).

## 3   Autonomy and Character: Focus on Choice

When we want to define autonomous agents, we must address three processes: creation, selection and choice, which raises the issue of the agent's character. The character can be defined as the set of collective qualities, especially mental and moral, that distinguish a person or entity. Autonomy implies difference, the agents should be free to decide differently from one another even in the same situation: agents can have different characters. Either in the creation or in the choice, the reasons can vary from agent to agent. It is in this two phases that we can locate the personality traits that define the character. In the creation phase, some agents will adopt goals whereas others don't, some agents will generate goals in one way, while others may not generate goals at all, and only obey goals from their creator. In the choice phase, we look at different rationalities in different agents. Some choice is not necessarily irrational just because we cannot identify the reasons that led to it [7]. Even considering agents endowed with the same set of goals and beliefs, their different sets of values should be enough to produce differentiated behaviours.

We sustain that the multiple values approach represents a step towards autonomy. Here we will be more concerned with executive autonomy [6], in [3] we further addressed „cognitive mediation" issues, by proposing a mechanism for value-based goal acquisition, thus assuring goals autonomy. Autonomy should pay no tribute to a super-imposed rationality: autonomy means exactly the liberty to adopt one's own rationality.

In [2], our agent had a goal to fulfil that was characterised by some values. The candidate actions were all comparable according to the same values, so choice was straightforward. The agent just computed a real function of those values for all the alternatives, and the highest scorer was chosen. Afterwards, the agent looked at the results of his action by assessing the resulting state of the world against a dimension of goodness, and updated the values appropriately.

We now propose to tackle choice situations where the agent doesn't have all the relevant information. Imagine some goal G is characterised by targets for three (out of five) values: $V_1 = {}_1$, $V_2 = {}_2$, $V_3 = {}_3$. Let the candidate actions be represented by sub-goals $G_1$ and $G_2$, with associated values, respectively: $V_1 = {}_{11}$, $V_4 = {}_{14}$, and $V_1 = {}_{21}$, $V_2 = {}_{22}$, $V_5 = {}_{25}$.

As long as choice is performed by using a linear combination of some function of the paired (e.g. ${}_1$, ${}_{11}$) values, like in [2], one can just omit the values outside of the intersection of the goal and the candidate characterisation, thus rendering them not redundant. Or we can assign mean values to the unknown fields. If other types of choice functions are used one must proceed with more care. Anyway, even in the simple case above, there are open problems to be dealt with. First of all, it is necessary to characterise the new adopted goal, say $G_2$. Should $G_2$ include values for $V_3$? Should it keep values for $V_5$? We think that the answer to both questions is positive: $V_3$ should be kept (with target ${}_3$) because we are adopting $G_2$ *just because* of G. So it is only fair that we keep whatever guides the attempts at achieving G, and those are the values $V_1$, $V_2$, and $V_3$. For an analogous reason we should include $V_5$. It could be the case that $V_5$ represents important evaluative notions to be considered during the attempts at $G_2$, and so we mustn't give up $V_5$ for our future execution. In both cases, these values will help control the execution of the agent towards his goals, possibly allowing for revisions and recalculations if the chosen goals no longer serve the relevant values at stake.

Another key and general purpose issue is the necessity of multidimensional assessment of the quality of decisions. There is only limited adaptation one can perform over his decision processes when considering unidimensional measures. This does not mean optimisation of the decision model to better react to some reward function. The truth is that we assume no reward function to be learnt, unlike in reinforcement learning. The world is just out there and our agents need to constantly adapt. Multidimensional information is shown to enrich this adaptation process.

## 4   A Case-Study: Choosing Wines

We put our model to trial by using an experimental setting where choice has to be performed in purchasing a product, with later assessment of this decision. We simulate the case of wine selection (in the future we will have our agents going to virtual shops and selecting wines for us, yet hopefully not drinking them). Note that this example, because of the generality of its multidimensional form, is quite meaningful for tackling other problem domains.

### 4.1   An Instance of BVG to Select Wines

Some consumer wants to purchase a bottle of wine, and so goes to a wine merchant. He has some knowledge about wine, but naturally does not know every wine that is available to him. He will evaluate candidate wines using a fixed set of five dimensions: $V_1$ is the knowledge and trust he has of the producer; $V_2$ is the quality of the region in the given vintage; $V_3$ is the price of the wine; $V_4$ is the ideal consumption time window (with $v_4 = (v_{4,1}, v_{4,2})$     $V_4$); and $V_5$ is the quality of the specific wine. Domains for these dimensions will be $D_1=$ $D_2=$ $\{0,*,**,***,****,*****\}$, $D_3=N$, $D_4=N\ N$, and $D_5=[0..20]$.

Now imagine our buyer has the goal of giving a formal dinner this evening, and wants to impress his guests with a nice bottle of wine. So, he specifies as minimum standards (4, 4, 1000, (0,5), 16), meaning that the wine should come from a known and trustworthy producer, price is no matter, should be ready to drink, and a quality of at least 16 points. Notice that different things could be tried: for instance, his guests might be impressed by a wine fulfilling this specification: (1, 5, 75, (0,5), 18), meaning that a very expensive wine from an unknown producer turns out to be very good. In any case, there could be lacking information at the time the choice must be performed.

## 4.2 Goals and Alternatives

We propose to iterate the process just illustrated, and let the consumer adjust his choice machinery. In a first row of experiments, we will test the power of quantitative assessments by making this adjustment by feeding back the grade the wine achieves when it eventually gets tasted. Afterwards, we enhance the choice machinery update by feeding back multiple assessments of the quality of the decision (for instance, after several bad bottles from a given region in a given vintage, we can decide to downgrade the impression we had on that region/vintage, or even to pay less importance to this dimension in the future).

Goals to buy are those characterised as follows:

$G_1$: Goal ($V_1=$****, $V_2=$****, $V_3=20$, $V_4=(5,10)$, $V_5=16$) Buy(wine)
(good wine, from top producer in a good vintage, to hold)
$G_2$: Goal ($V_1=$**, $V_2=$*****, $V_3=10$, $V_4=(1,4)$, $V_5=14$) Buy(wine)
(medium wine, from new producer in a very good vintage, to drink)
$G_3$: Goal ($V_1=$*****, $V_2=$*****, $V_3=100$, $V_4=(20,30)$, $V_5=19$) Buy(wine)
(excellent wine, from star producer in an excellent vintage, to hold a long time).

Goals to drink include these characterisations:

$G_4$: Goal ($V_1=$*, $V_2=$****, $V_3=0$, $V_4=(0,1)$, $V_5=14$) Drink(wine)
(everyday drinking)
$G_5$: Goal ($V_1=$****, $V_2=$*****, $V_3=200$, $V_4=(0,10)$, $V_5=17$) Drink(wine)
(special occasion)
$G_6$: Goal ($V_1=$*, $V_2=$*, $V_3=200$, $V_4=(10,50)$, $V_5=10$) Drink(wine)
(wine tasting)

We have included about thirty wines in our wine shop, and will look first at what our agent buys, to see how he builds his initial wine cellar. This allows us to tune up the choice function by hand. When he starts drinking, the process enters a new phase, with updates to the choice mechanism.

## 5  A Calculus for Choice

Let us start by presenting the functions we have selected to tackle the decision problem we have just described, before we go into their makings with some detail.

The function that performs choice is (for $v_k$ features of the goal, and $v_{ki}$ features of alternative i; and where $\|(x,y)-(a,b)\| = \sqrt{(x-a)^2+(y-b)^2}$, (the Euclidean norm), and $(u)=\dfrac{1+u}{2}$):

$$F_{buy}(v_k, v_{ki}) =$$

$$c_1 \frac{v_1-v_{1i}}{2+|v_1-3|} +c_2 \frac{v_2-v_{2i}}{2+|v_2-3|} +c_3 \frac{1}{1+e^{-\frac{v_{3i}-v_3}{v_3}}}{}^3 +c_4\ 1-e^{-\frac{\|v_{4i}-v_4\|}{10}} +c_5 \frac{1}{1+e^{\frac{v_{5i}-v_5}{2}}}$$

$F_{drink}(v_k, v_{ki}) = F_{buy}(v_k, v_{ki})$ with $c_4$ altered to have more importance in the final decision (for instance, $c_4$ twice what it was above).

### 5.1  Designing the Choice Function

Let us look into the design of the choice function F with some detail. For simplicity reasons, we opted to keep the structure of this function a linear combination of several components. F is meant to be minimised, so is each of its components (call them $F_k$). All $F_k$s will be scaled to the interval [0, 1] by appropriate linear transformations (e.g. from [-1, 1] to [0, 1] we use $(u)=\dfrac{1+u}{2}$). It seemed natural to keep F also inside [0, 1].

So we kept the linear combination convex ( $c_k$=1). Several choices were possible, and we are conscious that the choice we've made ($c_k$=1/n) corresponds only to a possible attitude of the buyer. We can easily model other attitudes by changing these coefficients (see discussion in section 6).

$F_1$ and $F_2$ share the same structure. In both, we compare our goal with the alternative, and then bring this difference to a scale of [-1, 1] by dividing by a quantity that relates the scale of the difference with the scale of the goal. For instance, in $F_1$, it is preferable to obtain 5 when aspiring to 3 (with the best of scores, -1), than to obtain 3 when aspiring to 1 (with score -0.5).

For field $F_3$ (rating price discrepancies), and after a lot of discussion and experimentation, we opted for a sigmoid curve, $f(x)=\dfrac{1}{1+e^{-x}}$, which has the advantage of being approximately stationary behaviour in the neighbourhood of the origin. Its possibly not ideal symmetrical behaviour to the left and to the right of the origin could be corrected by using another branch for the function. However, we didn't think it was necessary, because the numerical significance is negligible. It suffices to notice that f will be applied to $\frac{v_{3i}-v_3}{v_3}$, and price $v_{3i}$ is always greater or equal to 0, so when the argument is negative, it always is in the interval [-1, 0[. With this design of $F_3$, we slightly overlook the behaviour in face of discounts. However, the behaviour in face of high prices is fully modelled (the case when x   [0, + [). When the price is exactly what we look for (x=0), f is 1/2, that is, the medium point of the target interval. For small aggravations of the price, f grows slowly; f grows faster for prices far superior to the desired one, but refrains this growth rate when prices are very high, meaning that when the price is already much higher than the one we want, further increases only aggravate the choice function infinitesimally.

$F_5$ rates quality discrepancies and is similar to $F_3$, although it doesn't suffer the cubic aggravation. The argument is only divided by a constant (2), in order to get a less steep curve. For example, for a goal of 15 points, $F_5$ will compute 0.182 for getting 18, 0.269 for getting 17, 0.378 for getting 16, 0.5 for getting 15 and 0.818 for getting 12.

Finally, field $F_4$ is only a reduction to the interval [0, 1] of the Euclidean distance between the two time-intervals (goal and alternative). The distance is divided by a factor 10 (supposed to be a common value for the maximum norm) as a way of avoiding too much concentration of the function around 1.

Some of the values $v_{ki}$ can be directly observed on the alternatives (e.g. price). Others depend from prior knowledge, and are assigned to each alternative by the consumer on the basis of previous contacts with the same product. We thought it was adequate to value the number of previous contacts, and so consider the pair (x, n) to represent respectively the rating for the value at stake, and the number of observations that gave rise to that rating. In the next section we will check on the scope of this representation.

## 5.2  The Update Mechanism

We have several alternatives to update the choice mechanism. First, we consider the result $r(s_j)$ of the selected alternative $(s_j)$, to be an unidimensional classification of the tasted wine, in the scale of 0 to 20.

The update of the choice mechanism is thus done by function G, as follows:
$$G(r(s_j), v_{kj}) = [G_1(r(s_j), v_{kj}), G_2(r(s_j), v_{kj}), id, id, G_5(r(s_j), v_{kj})]^T,$$
where id is the identity function projected onto the appropriate component, and

$$G_1(r(s_j), v_{1j}) = \frac{scale(r(s_j)) + no.\ observations\ rating}{1 + no.\ observations}, \text{ with } v_{1i} = \frac{rating}{no.\ observations}.$$

$$G_2(r(s_j), v_{2j}) = \frac{scale(r(s_j)) + no.\ observations\ rating}{1 + no.\ observations}, \text{ with } v_{2i} = \frac{rating}{no.\ observations}.$$

$$G_5(r(s_j), v_{5j}) = \frac{r(s_j) + no.\ observations\ grade}{1 + no.\ observations}, \text{ with } v_{5i} = \frac{grade}{no.\ observations}.$$

where *scale* performs the adequate transformation from [0..20] to [1..5].

We should note that some of these updates (namely $G_1$ and $G_2$) must be applied to all alternatives containing the same information (e.g. one must update the producer rating not only for the wine just tasted, but also in all other wines of the same producer). Note also that we chose to perform a complete average of all the observations, although other options could be used (e.g., moving averages, or filtering through a degradation function, like in [4]).

Another alternative to perform this update operation would be to distribute credit equally among all the components of choice. This amounts to linearly transform the result $r(s_j)$ into the interval [0, 1] (the interval where all $F_k$s have co-domains), and then incorporate this classification into the alternative, for instance by computing an average like we have done above, for all of the multidimensional components (or using some moving average to include memory dissipation effects). However, it is easily shown that this would amount to collapse all dimensions into one unique dimension, because the iteration of such an update process would quickly lead to equal values in every dimension (the weight of the initial values would be weaker and weaker with the addition of new values to the average).

One of the main theses of our work rests upon the use of multiple values to perform also the update of the choice machinery. This was only pointed out in [3] so here we propose another update function H to compare results of the two simulations. In the following definition of H, $r(s_i)$ will then be a vector of multiple assessments. We consider the same dimensions that were used for choice itself (cf. also [2]), although some things are not assessable, price for instance. So, we let $r(s_i)$ be $[r_k(s_i)]$, but consider only k=4 and k=5:

$$H([r_k(s_i)], v_{ki}) = [H_1(r_k(s_i), v_{ki}), H_2(r_k(s_i), v_{ki}), id, H_4(r_k(s_i), v_{ki}), H_5(r_k(s_i), v_{ki})]^T;$$

$$H_1(r_4(s_i), r_5(s_i), \frac{rating}{no.\ obs.}, v_{2i}, v_{3i}, v_{4i}, v_{5i}) = \frac{(1+\|r_4(s_i)-v_{4i}\|)\ scale(r_5(s_i))+no.\ obs.}{1+\|r_4(s_i)-v_{4i}\|+no.\ obs.}, \frac{rating}{},$$

$$H_4(r_4(s_i), r_5(s_i), v_{1i}, v_{2i}, v_{3i}, v_{4i}, v_{5i}) = \frac{r_4(s_i)+v_{4i}}{2}.$$

$H_2$ and $H_5$ are respectively obtained from $G_2$ and $G_5$, in such a way as $H_1$ was from $G_1$. Note that for $V_4$ we perform an outright average with previous value, because the most recent assessment reports on the current condition of the wine, and so should have a quicker impact on our decisions. The factor $(1+\|r_4(s_i)-v_{4i}\|)$ put on the quality is meant to represent the urgency of change. The more the wine is not to be consumed when we imagined it should be, the more weight the new assessment should have in the update.

### 5.3  Further Enhancing Choice Procedures

As we describe the genesis of the choice function F, we should observe that values $V_1$ to $V_5$ are considered a priori, in design-time. Much as we want our choice model to tackle any situation in execution-time, it is to be expected that situations come around where our model doesn't cope. The BVG architecture encompasses methods for adaptation to enhance choice performance. Adaptation is done by updating the values along the relevant dimensions, but another possibility would have been to modify the choice function.

This option would amount to incorporate some realism into the model, in the sense that our agent would always consider observations of the alternatives at stake to be perfect, and would change the choice function in order to optimise its behaviour. We prefer the alternative idealist view: the choice function is not perfect, rather as good as we can get; it is always possible to improve on the perception we have of alternatives, illuminated by the assessment of our previous choices. A combination of both alternatives would be preferable, but the one we picked seems more intuitive, and allows for a more parsimonious calculus.

Once chosen a model of choice and respective values, we can raise the point if those are the appropriate values, all of the appropriate values, what are the correct functions to account for the role of each of those values in the problem at hand, etc. Can our model ever be closed up and considered ready for every eventuality? We think not. The world is highly dynamic and unpredictable, and choice must conform to that. Decision if often time-dependent, and an additive form for the choice function allows for the process to be interrupted (or even pre-emptive) and some anytime character to be achieved (cf. [3]). On the other hand, mechanisms must be included to avoid ties between alternatives (for instance, in the case of major absence of evaluative information). Some choice must be done, whatsoever.

Usually, when people are confronted with massive lack of information and have to choose all the same, they recur to analogies with other lived situations. For instance, to pick some wine just because the bottle has a nice label is not irrational, it amounts to invoke the analogy upon which the whole Marketing discipline is based: if the producer cares about the quality of the packaging then *for sure* he cares about the quality of his product. Could it be then that we should always include the beauty of the label as a pointer of the wine's quality? Perhaps, but when information about the real quality is available why should we trust the label?

The conclusion is: when we don't have information, we can use the *Principle of Insufficient Reason* [5] to assign a mean value to this field. When we have information, whatever its origin, we just use it. Although we cannot at this time detail all of the mechanisms here involved, in the next section we present one such mechanism. We include a new field in the choice function that uses non-linearity to account for positive or negative effects of lacking information.

## 5.4 The Effect of Surprise

After we analysed values $V_1$ to $V_5$ and corresponding fields in the function F (let's call them $F_1$ to $F_5$), where common-sense and intuition set the optimisation rules, it was apparent to us that we needed to introduce a further dimension, $V_6$, to account for features not grabbed by the initial fields. Broadly speaking, this new value accounts for the „surprise-effect." Let us explain through an example.

An unknown brand of automobiles issues a new model with a price far above the average for that market segment. A possible buyer's attention is drawn by the publicity effort and is surprised by the price. Probably, he will not buy this car, since the amount at stake is high. If, on the contrary, the new model costs much less than its competitors, the effect on the image of the product can also lead the careful customer not to buy it. If we consider a box of chocolates instead of a car, this „surprise-effect" can more easily lead the customer to a purchase: the potential loss is much less. In this case, the expectations caused by the high price (and other factors, for instance, a good presentation) surpass the negative effects.

Going back to our case study, the same wine can rise different expectations (and decisions) in different agents. H and A both see on the shelves a wine from a new producer, with good presentation, and slightly higher price than the average for its region. Naturally, for some of the $F_k$s there is no information. Then H buys the wine and A doesn't. Clearly, our original F was disregarded by H. The surprise-effect of the high price caused different evaluations (of attraction and of repulse) in the two agents.

F was built in such a way (with all $F_k$s increasing) that this behaviour of H could never occur. But the $F_k$s must be increasing, at the risk of arbitrarily loosing transitivity in choice (cf. section 5.1). We propose to add a new component to F, called $F_6$, to account for this strange effect. $F_6$ is sensitive to lacking information in the other $F_k$s. When this happens, $F_6$ sets up the agent's preference for novelty, by conceding extra points for big discrepancies in whatever evaluative information is available. For instance, in H's case, $F_6$ will give a positive contribution to F, for the simple reason that $v_{3i}$ is high, and $v_{5i}$ is low (in the absence of information about quality, H naturally assigns an average grade to $v_{5i}$).

The default value of $F_6$ is 0.5. When the surprise effect is triggered by lacking information, we'll have:

$F_6(v_k, v_{ki}) = 0$ if $v_3/3 < v_{3i} - v_3 \leq v_3$ and $v_1 \leq 2$ and $v_2 \leq 2$ and $v_5 \leq 10$;

$F_6(v_k, v_{ki}) = 0.25$ if $v_3/3 < v_{3i} - v_3 \leq v_3$ and ($v_1 \leq 2$ or $v_2 \leq 2$ or $v_5 \leq 10$).

## 6  Results

The first results we collected concern the effect of surprise (field $F_6$). To this end, we decided to use the very example that led to the inclusion of this field, that is, H and A behave differently in face of a possible purchase of a bottle of red wine Quinta da Ponte Pedrinha, Dão, 1997. H buys the wine, and A doesn't. We evaluated this particular wine, assuming the real conditions of insufficient information that H and A had to stand against. So we considered default mean values for the lacking information, and computed the choice function for goal $G_2$ with and without the surprise-effect, in a universe of 25 other wines. Obviously, we didn't expect surprise to put it into pole-position, but it jumped 5 positions up, from $23^{rd}$ to $18^{th}$ in the ordered list. Further positions could have been gained if the particular parameters for either the wine or the goal would have made it possible to get the maximum possible score for surprise.

In table 1, we list the best five wines to be chosen for each of the goals $G_1$ to $G_3$. We had previous made the choice ourselves, based on the text description of those goals (see section 4.2). The wines from our list that are present in the BVG choice are underlined in the table. Some interesting results occur, especially in what concerns goal $G_3$. Since this goal requires wines of great longevity, and the contenders weren't particularly adapted to that requirement, four out of the five best wines benefited from insufficient information leading to the assignment of mean default values (0.5) to the respective field of the choice function ($F_4$). This unavailability of information also sustains the results of three of the five wines for $G_1$. Castello Banfi manages to get in the top for all three goals as a result of having already a non-default quality assessment of 15, whereas most candidates have a default quality of 10. Nevertheless, other candidates with good quality grades didn't make that well, since had poorer grades on other values. A good fit between goals and characteristics of the candidates also favours a good score (e.g. Quinta de Pancas has a perfect fit with goal $G_2$ with respect to consumption time).

**Table 1.** Top-scorers for buying goals.

| $G_1$ | $G_2$ | $G_3$ |
|---|---|---|
| Castello Banfi, Chianti '98 | Castello Banfi, Chianti '98 | Castello Banfi, Chianti '98 |
| Quinta do Côtto 1997 | Quinta das Caldas 1996 | Quinta Baceladas 1997 |
| Quinta das Caldas 1996 | Herd. Esporão, Arag. 1997 | Tapada Coelheiros 1996 |
| Herd. Esporão, Arag. 1997 | Quinta da Terrugem 1996 | Capela-Mor 1997 |
| Ad. Coop. Portalegre 1997 | Qta. Pancas, Cab. S. 1997 | Quinta do Côtto 1997 |

Table 2 shows the five top-scorers (for goal $G_2$) when we progressively changed weights. As we increase the weight of $V_4$ in the final decision, we watch the candidates with the most approximate fit to $G_2$ in what concerns $V_4$ do better and better. We did some other experiments with $V_1$ and $V_2$ and the results were similar. Setting up weights seems to be a good way of fine-tuning the choice model.

**Table 2.** Fine-tuning by changing weights.

| (1/6, 1/6, 1/6, 1/6, 1/6, 1/6) | (.1,.1,.1,.5,.1,.1) | (.05,.05,.05,.75,.05,.05) |
|---|---|---|
| Castello Banfi, Chianti '98 | Castello Banfi, Chianti '98 | Qta. Pancas, Cab. S. 1997 |
| Quinta das Caldas 1996 | Qta. Pancas, Cab. S. 1997 | Castello Banfi, Chianti '98 |
| Herd. Esporão, Arag. '97 | Quinta da Terrugem 1996 | Quinta da Terrugem 1996 |
| Quinta da Terrugem 1996 | Herd. Esporão, Arag. '97 | Falcoaria 1997 |
| Qta. Pancas, Cab. S. 1997 | Falcoaria 1997 | Borges 1996 |

Now we invert terms, and try to induce better results for Quinta da Ponte Pedrinha, by exaggerating the weight of the surprise-effect in the calculus of F. We kept $c_1=c_2=c_3=c_4=c_5=(1-c_6)/5$, and ranged $c_6$ through $\{0.15, 1/6, 0.2, 0.25, 0.4, 0.5\}$, and the position of Ponte Pedrinha changed respectively from 20th to 18th, 17th, 17th, 5th and 2nd. So, one way of getting different attitudes with respect to surprise (and so emulate our example buyers H and A) is to consider a heterogeneous distribution of weights $c_k$. This conclusion is extendable to any other field of F (e.g. different importance of money for different agents, including some function $F_3$ (price) that depends on exogenous variables, for instance agent's wealth). Note that we didn't set any desirability for the state of surprise, although this is easily done. The idea would be to simulate the consumer's curiosity, by giving a premium to options not yet tried and assessed.

In a similar line of reasoning, there is another way of adapting the agent's choice machinery without changing the function F at all: by judiciously setting up the goal specifications. We isolated value $V_3$ (price), and run several experiments with goal $G_2$. The first thing we realised is that setting up a very low aim for $V_3$ is pretty much the same as setting up a very high one, and amounts to making $F_3$ irrelevant. This is caused by the shape of function $F_3$: both very big or very small discrepancies between $v_3$ and each of the $v_{3i}$ tend to cause $F_3$ to equalise all alternatives. So we watched the ordering of alternatives when small variations were made around the original aim price of $G_2$. For a significant number of wines, the non-linear shape of $F_3$ determines trajectories from the $V_3$-irrelevant initial ordering ($v_3=1$) to that same order (resulting from $v_3$=1000), passing through several progressive changes. Table 3 summarises some interesting cases, where price is quoted after the name of the wine.

**Table 3.** Some order trajectories determined by aim-price change.

| $v_3$ | 1 | 8 | 9 | 10 | 11 | 12 | 15 | 20 | $\infty$ |
|---|---|---|---|---|---|---|---|---|---|
| Poças, Res. 1992 (9.85) | 13 | 13 | 14 | 14 | 14 | 16 | 16 | 16 | 13 |
| Qta. Maias, Res. '91 (4.8) | 16 | 16 | 16 | 16 | 15 | 14 | 13 | 13 | 16 |
| Qta Terrugem '96 (11.22) | 5 | 4 | 4 | 4 | 4 | 5 | 6 | 5 | 5 |
| Qta. Pancas,C.S.'97 (6.7) | 6 | 5 | 5 | 5 | 6 | 6 | 4 | 4 | 6 |
| Ad. Portalegre '97 (14.9) | 4 | 9 | 6 | 6 | 5 | 4 | 5 | 6 | 4 |

It is sometimes difficult to predict the results of a change in the goal values. So preferably, the set up of the decision functions will be made before-hand by correctly judging the weight of the various dimensions in the final decision. Moreover, some preliminary experimentation is recommended with goal specifications, before decisions are taken. The power of this decision model remains in its capacity for performing updates.

**Table 4.** Top-scorers for buying goals after G-update.

| $G_1$ | $G_2$ | $G_3$ |
|---|---|---|
| Quinta do Côtto 1997 | Poças, Reserva 1992 | Finca Flichman, C. S. '97 |
| Vallado 1998 | Castello Banfi, Chianti '98 | Quinta do Côtto 1997 |
| Herd. Esporão, Arag. '97 | Herd. Esporão, Arag. '97 | #Capela-Mor 1997 |
| Quinta das Caldas 1996 | Casa de Santar, Res. 1996 | #Quinta Baceladas '97 |
| Castello Banfi, Chianti '98 | Quinta do Côtto 1997 | #Tapada Coelheiros '96 |

Our last results are obtained by letting the choice machinery decide purchases and tastings. Their results are taken from real world tastings. After 28 tastings of 17 (of the 26) wines, and without further calibration, updates were performed as described in section 5.2. Table 4 shows the top five scorers after updates are made, and is meant to be compared with table 1.

The fall of Quinta das Baceladas (with respect to $G_1$) from position 14 to position 20, (while, say, Castello Banfi has fallen only slightly), is partially explained by the fact that its producer, Caves Aliança, was assessed through other wines. So despite Baceladas wasn't tasted, it was penalised all the same. It is interesting that the top scores for goal $G_3$ are kept by wines that didn't get tasted (marked with #). So the fact that some wines got tasted and even got good scores might not be enough to score highly with such an out of the way goal. Also the fact that updates aren't performed on $V_4$ allows for good scoring for $F_4$ on basis of unknown information. Since updates are progressive and cumulative, changes in ordering are gradual and depend on the quantity of samplings for each wine. This is the reason why the medium-scorer Castello Banfi decays from his top position rather slowly. A solution for quicker adjustment could be to assign other type of default values (like the average of a set of somehow related wines, e.g. from the same producer, or the same region/year), or the use of moving averages to disregard older observations.

These comments lead us to the conclusion that there is a clear need for another type of update, based on a richer set of information, like we proposed above with update function H. Experiments with this function are still being conducted, but we present in table 5 some preliminary results. We have redone experiment reported in table 4, but now using update function H.

**Table 5.** Top-scorers for buying goals after H-update.

| $G_1$ | $G_2$ | $G_3$ |
| --- | --- | --- |
| Quinta do Côtto 1997 | Poças, Reserva 1992 | Quinta do Côtto 1997 |
| Herd. Esporão, Arag. '97 | Casa Santar, Res. 1996 | Herd. Esporão, Arag. '97 |
| Vallado 1998 | Herd. Esporão, Arag. '97 | #Capela-Mor 1997 |
| Quinta das Caldas 1996 | Castello Banfi, Chianti '98 | #Qta. das Baceladas 1997 |
| Poças, Reserva 1992 | Quinta do Côtto 1997 | #Tapada Coelheiros 1996 |

We compared this final ordering with our initial intuitive choices, to discover that the top five we had chosen for each goal had an average position of 15, 8, and 5, respectively for $G_1$, $G_2$, and $G_3$. We explain the rather poor results for $G_1$ with the fact that most of the wines in our group weren't tasted at all, and so did not have the chance of improving position. Anyway, we don't find the results unsatisfactory, since it was obvious that this new way of performing update will lead to much faster adaptation to the user's tastes as accounted. If these accounts are accurate, the choice function will eventually reflect the user's preferences.

Perhaps the main problem we found whilst conducting these experiments was the evaluation of their results. Unless some drastic surprise occurred, this could be (and in fact was) easily foreseen; the question is 'how should one evaluate the results of his evaluations?' These experiments succeed in exhibiting the potential of the BVG model, but they don't go far beyond that. The idea of looking for emergence as a result of the agent using exogenous values to update his decisions (cf. section 2) may provide help in escaping from this riddle.

# 7  Concluding Remarks

We have restated the fundamentals of the BVG architecture, namely the use of multiple values to inform choice, and the feedback of assessment information to recalibrate the choice machinery. We have proposed an instance of BVG that performs decisions in a case domain, and a corresponding calculus for choice. The update prescribed in BVG was done by feeding back both unidimensional and multidimensional information. The latter proved experimentally to accomplish further adaptability and reactivity to important new information coming from the environment.

The choice of the interval [0, 1] for co-domain of F was not naïve. In the future, we will study a stochastic approach concerning the agent's decisions. We will also test the thesis that patterns of consumption grow also out of habit (by letting the choice mechanism update itself), as opposed to 'rational' assessment of previous decisions. Further experimentation is also needed to assess emotion-driven control. We will be trying this approach in a multiple agent scenario, with incidence on the expansion of an agent's system of values as a result of interaction with other agents.

**Acknowledgements.** This research has been carried out within the research unit LabMAC, and partially supported by projects Praxis 2/2.1/TIT/1662/95 (SARA) and Praxis XXI/Feder/FCT. We wish to express our thanks to the anonymous referees.

# References

1. Antunes, L., Towards a model for value-based motivated agents, in Proceedings of MASTA'97 (EPIA'97 Workshop on Multi-Agent Systems: Theory and Applications), Coimbra, October, 1997.
2. Antunes, L. and Coelho, H., Decisions based upon multiple values: the BVG agent architecture, in Barahona, P. and Alferes, J. (eds.), Progress in Artificial Intelligence, Proceedings of EPIA'99, Springer-Verlag, Lecture Notes on AI no. 1695, September, 1999.
3. Antunes, L. and Coelho, H., Redesigning the agents' decision machinery, in Proceedings of IWAI'99, Siena, October 1999; extended and revised version will appear in Paiva, A. (ed.) Affective Interactions, Springer-Verlag, Lecture Notes on AI no. 1814, 2000.
4. Antunes, L., Moniz, L. and Azevedo, C., RB+: The dynamic estimation of the opponent's strength, in Proceedings of the AISB Conference, IOS Press, Birmingham, 1993.
5. Bernoulli, J., Ars Conjectandi, (posthumous publication, Basel, 1713), reprint in Culture et Civilisation, Bruxelles 1986.
6. Castelfranchi, C., Guarantees for autonomy in cognitive agent architecture, in Wooldridge, J. and Jennings, R., Intelligent Agents, Agent Theories, Architectures, and Languages, ECAI'94 Workshop (ATAL), Springer-Verlag, Lecture Notes in AI no. 890, 1995.
7. Doyle, J., Rationality and its roles in reasoning, Computational Intelligence, 8 (2), 1992.
8. Faria, J., A Discussion with Kolmogorov; a Survey in Defence of the Axiomatic Approach towards Subjective Probability, Tech. Rep. 1/89, CEAUL, Lisboa, 1989.
9. Hollis, M., The Philosophy of Social Science - An Introduction. Cambridge: Cambridge University Press, 1994.
10. Rao, A. S. and Georgeff, M. P., Modeling Rational Agents within a BDI-Architecture, in Proceedings of the 2nd International Conference on Principles of Knowledge Representation and Reasoning, Morgan Kaufmann, 1991.
11. Russell, S. and Norvig, P., Artificial intelligence: a modern approach, Prentice Hall, 1995.
12. Simon, H., The Sciences of the Artificial (3rd edition), the MIT Press, Cambridge, 1996.
13. Wooldridge, M. and Parsons, S., Intention Reconsideration Reconsidered, in Proceedings of ATAL'98, 4-7 July, Paris, 1998.

# Planning-Task Transformations for Soft Deadlines

Sven Koenig

College of Computing, Georgia Institute of Technology
Atlanta, GA 30305, USA
skoenig@cc.gatech.edu

**Abstract.** Agents often have preference models that are more complicated than minimizing the expected execution cost. In this paper, we study how they should act in the presence of uncertainty and immediate soft deadlines. Delivery robots, for example, are agents that are often confronted with immediate soft deadlines. We introduce the additive and multiplicative planning-task transformations, that are fast representation changes that transform planning tasks with convex exponential utility functions to planning tasks that can be solved with variants of standard deterministic or probabilistic artificial intelligence planners. Advantages of our representation changes include that they are context-insensitive, fast, scale well, allow for optimal and near-optimal planning, and are grounded in utility theory. Thus, while representation changes are often used to make planning more efficient, we use them to extend the functionality of existing planners, resulting in agents with more realistic preference models.

## 1 Introduction

To determine how agents should act, one has to know their preference model. This is an often neglected research topic in agent theory and artificial intelligence in general. Many artificial intelligence planners, for example, assume that agents want to minimize the expected cost or maximize the expected reward. Unfortunately, agents often have preference models that are more complicated than that. They have, for example, to trade-off between different resource consumptions (such as money, energy, and time), take risk attitudes in high-stake decision situations into account, or act in the presence of deadlines. Our research program aims at building agents with these preference models. In this paper, we study planning tasks for delivery robots in the presence of uncertainty and immediate soft deadlines. Uncertainty can be caused by actuator and sensor noise, limited sensor ranges, map uncertainty, uncertainty about the initial pose of the robot, and uncertainty about the dynamic state of the environment (such as people opening and closing doors or moving furniture around). Immediate soft deadlines are caused by delivery requests that are not made in advance but the goods are needed right away and their utility declines over time, for example because the goods become obsolete or lose their value over time (coffee, for example, gets cold). While artificial intelligence planners usually determine plans that achieve the goal with minimal expected execution time, here they have to determine plans that achieve the goal with maximal expected utility for the convex exponential utility functions that model the immediate soft deadlines. Maximizing expected utility and minimizing expected execution time result in the same plans

C. Castelfranchi, Y. Lespérance (Eds.): Intelligent Agents VII, LNAI 1986, pp. 305–319, 2001.

if either the domain is deterministic or the utility function is linear, but these properties rarely hold. The goal of this paper is to develop a planning methodology for planning in the presence of uncertainty and immediate soft deadlines that determines optimal or near-optimal plans for agents and scales up to large domains. To this end, we combine constructive planning approaches from artificial intelligence with more descriptive approaches from utility theory [1,18], utilizing known properties of exponential utility functions [17,10]. In particular, we develop efficient representation changes that transform planning tasks with convex exponential utility functions to planning tasks that can be solved with variants of standard deterministic or probabilistic artificial intelligence planners such as [5,3,8,7,13,2,16]. Our planning-task transformations provide alternatives to the few existing approaches to planning with non-linear utility functions, namely approximate planners [9], planners with limited look-ahead [11], intelligent branch-and-bound methods [19], and hill-climbing methods [15]. Advantages of our planning-task transformations include that they are simple context-insensitive representation changes that are fast, scale well, allow for optimal and near-optimal planning, and are grounded in utility theory. While we use delivery robots to illustrate the problem and our solution, our insights apply to other agents as well, including agents that have to make decisions in high-stake decision situations.

## 2    Immediate Soft Deadlines

Delivery robots are agents that are often confronted with deadlines [6]. Immediate deadlines coincide with the time at which the execution of a plan begins. Soft deadlines are those whose utility does not drop to zero immediately after the deadline has passed but rather declines slowly. Immediate soft deadlines can often be modeled either exactly or approximately with convex exponential utility functions, where a utility function maps rewards $r$ (here: the negative of the execution times) to the resulting real-valued utilities $u(r)$. Convex exponential utility functions are of the form $u(r) = \gamma^r$ with parameter $\gamma > 1$ or linear transformations thereof. The smaller $\gamma$, the softer the deadline. An example is the utility function $u(r) = (2^{1/300})^r$, where the reward $r$ is the negative of the execution time, measured in seconds. In this particular case, the utility of the delivery halves every five minutes. A simple example of an immediate soft deadline occurs when coffee is delivered. Coffee gets colder during the delivery and one therefore often wants to maximize its expected temperature at the time of delivery. The utility function expresses how the temperature of the coffee depends on the execution time. Since the rate of cooling is proportional to the temperature difference between the cup and its environment, the utility function is convex exponential in the negative of the execution time. A more complex example of an immediate soft deadline occurs when printouts are delivered on demand. Imagine, for example, that you are debugging a program on your computer. To get a better overview of the program, you print it out and send your office delivery robot to fetch the printout from the remote printer room. In this case, the printout is needed right away, but you do not need it any longer once you determine the problem with the program. The probability that you have not found the problem decreases during the delivery and one therefore often wants to maximize the expected probability that the problem has not been found at the time of delivery. The utility function expresses how this probability depends on the execution time. If the probability that the problem is found in any period of time $\Delta t$ is $p$, then the probability that it has not been found after $n$ such time periods (assuming probabilistic independence) is $(1 - p)^n$. Thus, the utility function is convex exponential in the negative of the execution time, just like in the coffee-delivery example.

## 3   Utility Theory

In this paper, we make use of the following concepts from utility theory [1,18]: If the execution of some plan $plan$ leads with probability $p_i$ to reward $r_i$, then its expected reward is $er(plan) := \sum_i [p_i r_i]$ and its expected utility is $eu(plan) := \sum_i [p_i u(r_i)]$ for the convex exponential utility function $u(r) = \gamma^r$ with parameter $\gamma > 1$ that models the immediate soft deadline. (If the utility function that models the immediate soft deadline is a linear transformation of this utility function, we can use this utility function instead.) The certainty equivalent of the plan is $ce(plan) := u^{-1}(eu(plan))$. A decision maker is indifferent between a plan and a deterministic plan (that is, obtaining a certain reward for sure) if and only if the reward of the deterministic plan is the same as the certainty equivalent of the other plan. This explains the name of this concept from utility theory. It is easy to see that maximizing the certainty equivalent and maximizing the expected utility are equivalent.

## 4   Approximation Error

Traditional artificial intelligence planners determine plans that achieve the goal with minimal expected execution time or, equivalently, with maximal expected reward. Our planners, on the other hand, have to determine plans that achieve the goal with maximal expected utility. We first show that, in general, plans that achieve the goal with maximal expected reward cannot be used to closely approximate plans that achieve the goal with maximal expected utility. To determine the approximation error of choosing a plan with maximal expected reward over a plan with maximal expected utility, let $plan_{eu}$ denote a plan that achieves the goal with maximal expected utility and $plan_{er}$ a plan that achieves the goal with maximal expected reward. We quantify the approximation error $err$ of choosing $plan_{er}$ over $plan_{eu}$ as the amount of time by which we have to delay the execution of $plan_{eu}$ so that the resulting expected utility equals the expected utility of $plan_{er}$. This is the idle time that is available for other tasks. Thus, if the execution of plan $plan_{eu}$ leads with probability $p_i$ to reward $r_i$, then the approximation error $err$ satisfies the equation

$$eu(plan_{er}) = \sum_i p_i u(r_i - err). \tag{1}$$

It follows that

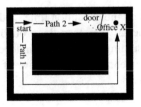

**Fig. 1.** A Simple Planning Example

$$ce(plan_{er}) = u^{-1}(eu(plan_{er}))$$
$$= u^{-1}\left(\sum_i p_i u(r_i - err)\right) \quad \text{see (1)}$$
$$= \log_\gamma\left(\sum_i p_i \gamma^{r_i - err}\right)$$
$$= -err + \log_\gamma\left(\sum_i p_i \gamma^{r_i}\right)$$
$$= -err + u^{-1}\left(\sum_i p_i u(r_i)\right)$$
$$= -err + u^{-1}(eu(plan_{eu}))$$
$$= -err + ce(plan_{eu}). \tag{2}$$

Consequently, the approximation error is $err = ce(plan_{eu}) - ce(plan_{er}) \geq 0$. To construct an example with a large approximation error, assume that the utility function is $u(r) = (2^{1/300})^r$ (as before). Consider a plan $plan_{bad}$ that leads with probability 0.37 to an execution time of 80.00 seconds and with the complementary probability to an execution time of 800.00 seconds. The expected utility of $plan_{bad}$ is $eu(plan_{bad}) = 0.41$, its certainty equivalent is $ce(plan_{bad}) = -389.31$ seconds, and its expected reward is $er(plan_{bad}) = -533.60$ seconds. Also consider a plan $plan_{worse}$ that leads with probability 1.00 to an execution time of 533.60 seconds. The expected utility of $plan_{worse}$ is $eu(plan_{worse}) = 0.29$, its certainty equivalent is $ce(plan_{worse}) = -533.60$ seconds, and its expected reward is $er(plan_{worse}) = -533.60$ seconds as well. The approximation error of choosing $plan_{worse}$ over $plan_{bad}$ calculates to roughly 2.5 minutes (144.29 seconds) for this delivery task whose expected execution time is only about 9 minutes (533.60 seconds). This example might appear to be constructed but delivery robots face indeed similar planning tasks. Assume, for example, that a robot operates in the corridor environment from Figure 1 and has to reach office X, at which point execution stops. There are only two candidate plans that are not clearly dominated by some other plan. The robot can either follow path 1 or path 2. Path 1 is known not to be blocked and thus results in a deterministic execution time, just like $plan_{worse}$ in the worst-case example above. Path 2 leads through a door that the robot is not able to open. Furthermore, the robot cannot sense whether the door is open or closed until it is close to the door. Thus, it has to move towards the door and, if the door is closed, return to its start location

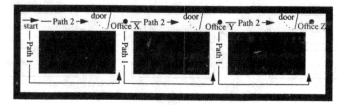

**Fig. 2.** Another Simple Planning Example

and then take the long path to office X. Consequently, path 2 can result in different execution times depending on whether the door is open or closed, just like $plan_{bad}$ in the worst-case example above.

## 5 Optimal Planning

The previous section showed that it is important to directly determine plans that achieve the goal with maximal expected utility. Unfortunately, utility theory is a purely descriptive theory that specifies only what optimal plans are, but not how plans that achieve the goal with maximal expected utility can be obtained other than by enumerating every chronicle of every possible plan, where a chronicle is a specification of the state of the world over time, representing one possible course of execution of the plan. Operations research and control theory have picked up on the results from utility theory and use dynamic programming methods to determine plans that achieve the goal with maximal expected utility in the context of risk-sensitive Markov decision process models [14] and risk-sensitive control [20]. These methods do not utilize available domain knowledge. Artificial intelligence has investigated knowledge-based planners that promise to scale up to larger domains, but traditionally do not determine plans that achieve the goal with maximal expected utility. In the following, we therefore extend the range of planners that determine plans that achieve the goal with maximal expected utility for convex exponential utility functions from methods of operations research to variants of standard deterministic or probabilistic artificial intelligence planners. We limit our attention to plans that are mappings from states to actions and planning tasks where the chronicles of all plans have a bounded reward. In other words, they always terminate after a bounded execution time. We also assume that all rewards are negative, which is the case if the rewards correspond to resource consumptions.

### 5.1 The Additive Planning-Task Transformation

The additive planning-task transformation applies to special cases of planning tasks, namely those for which every action is deterministic in the sense that its execution always ends in the same state although it can result in different rewards. This requirement is similar to assumptions sometimes made in the literature [19]. For example, the plans that we studied in the context of the example from Figure 1 satisfy it because the actions correspond to plans (or "macro actions") for getting from one office to another and

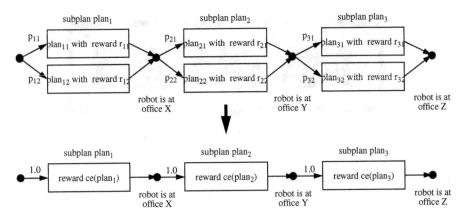

**Fig. 3.** Additive Planning-Task Transformation

move the robot to its destination, although the robot can take different paths depending on whether the door is open or closed and thus incur different execution times. The additive planning-task transformation converts the planning tasks by modifying all of their actions (everything else remains the same): If an action can be executed in state $s$ and its execution leads with probability $p_i$ and reward $r_i$ to state $s'$ (for all $i$), then it is replaced with a deterministic action. This action can be executed in state $s$ and its execution leads with probability one and reward $u^{-1}(\sum_i[p_i u(r_i)])$ (= the certainty equivalent of the original action) to state $s'$. We illustrate the additive planning-task transformation using the planning task from Figure 2. This example is the simplest example we could devise that allows us to demonstrate the advantages of the additive planning-task transformation. It is similar to the example from Figure 1 but consists of three parts. The robot has to first visit office X to pick up a form, then obtain a signature in office Y, and finally deliver the signed form to office Z, at which point plan execution stops. We assume throughout this paper that the probabilities with which doors are open when the robot visits them are independent (even if the robot visits the same door multiple times). Consider the action that corresponds to trying to take path 2 to get from office X to office Y. If the robot reaches office Y in 120.00 seconds with probability 0.50 (= the door is open) and in 576.00 seconds with probability 0.50 (= the door is closed), then the action is replaced with a deterministic action that can be executed when the robot is at office X and whose execution moves the robot with probability one and reward $u^{-1}(0.50\,u(-120.00) + 0.50\,u(-576.00)) = \log_\gamma(0.50\,\gamma^{-120.00} + 0.50\,\gamma^{-576.00})$ to office Y. The other actions are transformed similarly.

We now explain why the additive planning-task transformation is such that a plan that achieves the goal with maximal reward for the transformed planning task corresponds to a plan that achieves the goal with maximal expected utility for the original planning task, see Figure 4. Exponential utility functions satisfy the Markov property, which implies that it is unimportant how much reward has already been accumulated for acting optimally in the future. This property of exponential utility functions is also known as the delta property [10] or, equivalently, constant local risk aversion [17]. Now consider

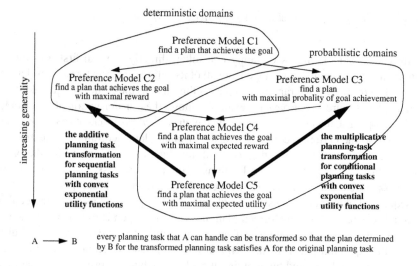

A ——→ B     every planning task that A can handle can be transformed so that the plan determined by B for the transformed planning task satisfies A for the original planning task

**Fig. 4.** Preference Models for Planning Tasks

the certainty equivalent of any sequential plan for the original planning task. As an example, we use the plan from Figure 3 (top) that solves the planning task from Figure 2 by trying to take path 2 for all three parts of the planning task. We use the following notation: The first action $plan_1$ corresponds to reaching office X. It has two possible subchronicles $plan_{11}$ and $plan_{12}$. Subchronicle $plan_{11}$ denotes the case where the door is open, whereas subchronicle $plan_{12}$ corresponds to the door being closed. Subchronicle $plan_{11}$ has reward $r_{11}$ and occurs with probability $p_{11}$, subchronicle $plan_{12}$ has reward $r_{12}$ and occurs with probability $p_{12}$ (where $p_{11} + p_{12} = 1$), and similarly for the other actions and subchronicles. Then, the certainty equivalent of plan $plan_1 \cdot plan_2 \cdot plan_3$ (the concatenation of the three actions) is

$$
\begin{aligned}
&ce(plan_1 \cdot plan_2 \cdot plan_3) \\
&= u^{-1}(eu(plan_1 \cdot plan_2 \cdot plan_3)) \\
&= u^{-1}(\sum_{i=1}^{2}\sum_{j=1}^{2}\sum_{k=1}^{2}[p_{1i}p_{2j}p_{3k}u(r_{1i} + r_{2j} + r_{3k})]) \\
&= \log_\gamma \sum_{i=1}^{2}\sum_{j=1}^{2}\sum_{k=1}^{2}[p_{1i}p_{2j}p_{3k}(\gamma^{r_{1i}+r_{2j}+r_{3k}})] \\
&= \log_\gamma \sum_{i=1}^{2}[p_{1i}(\gamma^{r_{1i}})] + \log_\gamma \sum_{j=1}^{2}[p_{2j}(\gamma^{r_{2j}})] + \log_\gamma \sum_{k=1}^{2}[p_{3k}(\gamma^{r_{3k}})] \\
&= u^{-1}(\sum_{i=1}^{2}[p_{1i}u(r_{1i})]) + u^{-1}(\sum_{j=1}^{2}[p_{2j}u(r_{2j})]) + u^{-1}(\sum_{k=1}^{2}[p_{3k}u(r_{3k})]) \\
&= u^{-1}(eu(plan_1)) + u^{-1}(eu(plan_2)) + u^{-1}(eu(plan_3))
\end{aligned}
$$

$$= ce(plan_1) + ce(plan_2) + ce(plan_3). \tag{3}$$

Instead of calculating its certainty equivalent directly, we can first transform the plan. Its structure remains unchanged, but all of its actions are transformed (as described above). The reward of the transformed plan is the same as the certainty equivalent of the original plan. Figure 3 (bottom), for example, shows the transformation of the plan from Figure 3 (top). The reward of the transformed plan is $ce(plan_1)+ce(plan_2)+ce(plan_3)$, which is also the certainty equivalent of the original plan according to Equation 3. To determine a plan that achieves the goal with maximal expected utility for the original planning task, one can transform all actions of the planning task. Since there is a one-to-one correspondence between the sequential plans of the original planning task and the sequential plans of the transformed planning task, a plan that achieves the goal with maximal reward for the transformed planning task corresponds to a plan that achieves the goal with maximal certainty equivalent (and thus also maximal expected utility) among all sequential plans for the original planning task. To summarize, the original planning task can be solved by applying the additive planning-task transformation and then solving the transformed planning task with any planner that determines plans that achieve the goal with maximal reward.

The additive planning-task transformation, although simple, can solve standard kinds of delivery tasks. We give two examples in the following. The first example is the planning task from Figure 3. It can be solved as follows:

$$\max_{plan_1, plan_2, plan_3} ce(plan_1 \cdot plan_2 \cdot plan_3)$$
$$= \max_{plan_1, plan_2, plan_3} [ce(plan_1) + ce(plan_2) + ce(plan_3)] \quad \text{see (3)}$$
$$= \max_{plan_1} ce(plan_1) + \max_{plan_2} ce(plan_2) + \max_{plan_3} ce(plan_3).$$

Thus, to determine a plan that achieves the goal with maximal expected utility for the original planning task, a planner can determine separate actions for the three parts of the planning task, each of which achieves its subgoal with maximal certainty equivalent and thus also with maximal expected utility. This can be done by transforming each part of the planning task individually with the additive planning-task transformation and solving the transformed planning task. The three resulting actions combined then form a plan that achieves the goal with maximal expected utility for the original planning task. This is no longer true in the next example, that is similar to the previous one. This time, however, the robot starts at the secretary's office with the task of collecting ten signatures on a form and returning it to the secretary. This planning task is essentially one of task sequencing. The additive planning-task transformation converts the planning task to a traveling-salesman problem on a directed graph with deterministic edge rewards. The reward of an edge is the certainty equivalent of a plan with maximal expected utility that moves from the office at the beginning of the edge to the office at its end. The traveling-salesman problem can then be solved with traveling-salesman problem methods or standard deterministic artificial intelligence planners. While these examples show that the additive planning-task transformation is useful, it cannot be used to solve

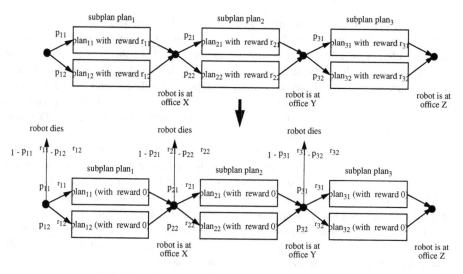

**Fig. 5.** Multiplicative Planning-Task Transformation

all planning tasks because it is often not the case that each action is atomic and always ends in the same state. As an example, consider again a robot that has to collect ten signatures. The actions move the robot to a specified office. They are not atomic in practice because their execution can be interrupted. For example, while the robot moves to some office, it might have to take a detour because a door is closed. If this detour leads past another office, it can be advantageous for the robot to go first to that office in order to obtain another signature on the way to its original destination. This suggests considering "move to the door" as an action because this would allow the robot to re-plan and change its destination when it recognizes that the door is closed. However, this action can end in two different states: the robot being at an open door or the robot being at a closed door. Thus, it does not satisfy the assumption of the additive planning-task transformation and we have to consider ways of determining conditional (rather than sequential) plans that achieve the goal with maximal expected utility.

## 5.2    The Multiplicative Planning-Task Transformation

The multiplicative planning-task transformation is more general than the additive planning-task transformation. It extends our previous work on planning with exponential utility functions [12] from reactive planning in high-stake decision situations to deliberative planning in the presence of immediate soft deadlines. The multiplicative planning-task transformation applies to planning tasks that can be solved optimally with conditional plans and converts them by modifying all of their actions (everything else remains the same): If an action can be executed in state $s$ and its execution leads with probability $p_i$ and reward $r_i$ to state $s_i$ (for all $i$), then it is replaced with an action that can be executed in state $s$ and whose execution leads with probability $p_i \gamma^{r_i}$ to state $s_i$ (for all $i$) and with probability $1 - \sum_i [p_i \gamma^{r_i}]$ to a new nongoal state ("death") in which execution stops. The rewards do not matter. We illustrate the multiplicative planning-task transformation using the planning task from Figure 2 (as before). Consider the action that corresponds to trying to take path 2 to get from office X to office Y. If the robot reaches office Y in 120.00 seconds with probability 0.50 (= the door is open) and in 576.00 seconds with probability 0.50 (= the door is closed), then the action is replaced with an action that can be executed when the robot is at office X and whose execution moves the robot with probabilities $0.5\gamma^{-120.00}$ and $0.5\gamma^{-576.00}$ to office Y and with probability $1 - 0.5\gamma^{-120.00} - 0.5\gamma^{-576.00}$ to the new nongoal state "death." The other actions are transformed similarly.

We now explain why the multiplicative planning-task transformation is such that a plan that achieves the goal with maximal probability for the transformed planning task and always stops in the goal states or "death" corresponds to a plan that achieves the goal with maximal expected utility for the original planning task, see Figure 4. We first consider sequential plans as a special case and then conditional plans in general. As an example, we use again the sequential plan $plan_1 \cdot plan_2 \cdot plan_3$ from Figure 5 (top). It solves the planning task from Figure 2 by trying to take path 2 for all three parts of the planning task. Its expected utility for the original planning task is

$$eu(plan_1 \cdot plan_2 \cdot plan_3)$$
$$= \sum_{i=1}^{2}\sum_{j=1}^{2}\sum_{k=1}^{2}[p_{1i}p_{2j}p_{3k}u(r_{1i} + r_{2j} + r_{3k})]$$
$$= \sum_{i=1}^{2}\sum_{j=1}^{2}\sum_{k=1}^{2}[p_{1i}p_{2j}p_{3k}\gamma^{r_{1i}+r_{2j}+r_{3k}}]$$
$$= \sum_{i=1}^{2}[p_{1i}\gamma^{r_{1i}}] \times \sum_{j=1}^{2}[p_{2j}\gamma^{r_{2j}}] \times \sum_{k=1}^{2}[p_{3k}\gamma^{r_{3k}}]$$
$$= \sum_{i=1}^{2}\bar{p}_{1i} \times \sum_{j=1}^{2}\bar{p}_{2j} \times \sum_{k=1}^{2}\bar{p}_{3k}, \tag{4}$$

where the parameters $\bar{p}_{mn}$ are new values with $\bar{p}_{mn} := p_{mn}\gamma^{r_{mn}}$. These values satisfy $0 \leq \bar{p}_{mn} \leq p_{mn}$ according to our assumption that the utility function is convex exponential ($\gamma > 1$) and all rewards are negative ($r_{mn} < 0$). Thus, the parameters $\bar{p}_{mn}$ can be interpreted as probabilities of not dying during the execution of the transformed action, one probability for each of its subchronicles. The complementary probability $1 - \sum_{n}\bar{p}_{mn} \geq 0$ is the probability of dying during the execution of the transformed action. Instead of calculating the expected utility of the original plan directly, we can first transform it. Its structure remains unchanged, but all of its actions are transformed (as described above). The expected utility of the original plan is the same as the probability of not dying while executing the transformed plan, which is the product of the probabilities of not dying while executing its actions (due to probabilistic independence). Figure 5 (bottom), for example, shows the transformation of the plan from Figure 5 (top). The probability of not dying during the execution of the transformed plan is $\sum_{i=1}^{2}[p_{1i}\gamma^{r_{1i}}] \times \sum_{j=1}^{2}[p_{2j}\gamma^{r_{2j}}] \times \sum_{k=1}^{2}[p_{3k}\gamma^{r_{3k}}]$, which is also the expected utility of the original plan according to Equation 4. Now consider an arbitrary conditional plan for the original planning task. We can use the multiplicative planning-task transformation on the plan and it remains true that the expected utility of the original plan is the same as the probability of not dying while executing the transformed plan. This is so because the expected utility of the original plan is the sum of the utility contributions over all of its chronicles, where the utility contribution of a chronicle is the product of its probability and utility. A chronicle is a sequence of subchronicles. If subchronicle $i$ of the chronicle has probability $p_i$ and reward $r_i$, then the utility contribution of the chronicle is

$$\left(\prod_i p_i\right) u\left(\sum_i r_i\right) = \left(\prod_i p_i\right) \gamma^{\sum_i r_i} = \prod_i [p_i \gamma^{r_i}] = \prod_i \bar{p}_i. \tag{5}$$

A chronicle of the original plan corresponds to several chronicles of the transformed plan, only one of which does not end in "death." Equation 5 is the probability of this chronicle. The sum of these probabilities over all chronicles of the original plan is the probability of not dying during the execution of the transformed plan. To determine plans that achieve the goal with maximal expected utility for the original planning task one can transform all actions of the planning task. Then, a plan that achieves the goal with maximal probability for the transformed planning task and always stops in only the goal states or "death" also achieves the goal with maximal expected utility for the original planning task. This is so because there is a one-to-one correspondence between the plans of the transformed planning task that always stop in only the goal states or "death" and the plans that achieve the goal for the original planning task. The expected utility of a plan for the original planning task is the same as the probability of not dying during the execution of the corresponding plan for the transformed planning task, which is the same as the probability with which the transformed plan achieves the goal if it stops in only the goal states or "death." To summarize, the original planning task can be solved by applying the multiplicative planning-task transformation and then solving the transformed planning task with any planner that determines plans that achieve the goal with maximal probability and always stop in the goal states or "death" or, synonymously, correspond to plans for the original planning task that achieve the goal. It is not a problem for planners to only consider plans with this property. Thus, perhaps surprisingly, planners that do not reason about rewards at all can be used, in conjunction with the multiplicative planning-task transformation, to determine plans that achieve the goal with maximal expected utility. Weaver [3], for example, is an artificial intelligence planner based on Bayesian networks, and standard software for Bayesian networks often performs only inferences on probabilities, not rewards. Other artificial intelligence planners that reason only with probabilities include [5,8,7,13,2,16]. However, the transformed planning task cannot only be solved with planners that determine plans that achieve the goal with maximal probability. After another transformation, it can also be solved with planners that determine plans that achieve the goal with maximal expected reward (as long as they are able to handle rewards that are zero), such as many standard artificial intelligence planners including those based an Markov models [4], by declaring "death" another goal state and making the rewards for stopping in goal states other than "death" one and all other rewards zero.

# 6  Near-Optimal Planning

We have assumed so far that planners are available that determine optimal plans for the transformed planning tasks. However, both the additive and multiplicative planning-task transformation have the following desirable property: the better the plan that planners find for the transformed planning task, the better the corresponding plan is for the original planning task. Thus, both planning-task transformations can be used in conjunction with planners that can determine only near-optimal ("satisficing") plans for the transformed planning tasks. In this section, we analyze the worst-case approximation error of planners that are used in conjunction with the additive and multiplicative planning-task transformation. Remember from Section 4 that the approximation error of a plan that attempts to maximize expected utility is the difference between the certainty equivalent of a plan with maximal expected utility and the certainty equivalent of the plan in question. The worst-case approximation error of a planner is the largest possible difference between the certainty equivalent of a plan with maximal expected utility and the certainty equivalent of the plan found by the planner, over all planning tasks. While the multiplicative planning-task transformation is more general than the additive one, it turns out that the multiplicative planning-task transformation can magnify the worst-case approximation error of a planner whereas the additive one does not. This is a disadvantage of the multiplicative planning-task transformation because, even if a planner has a small worst-case approximation error when used in isolation, its worst-case approximation error can be large when it is used in conjunction with the multiplicative planning-task transformation.

## 6.1  The Multiplicative Planning-Task Transformation

For the multiplicative planning-task transformation, the probability of not dying during the execution of any plan for the transformed planning task is the same as the expected utility of the corresponding plan for the original planning task. Thus, the larger the probability of not dying during the execution of a plan for the transformed planning task, the larger the expected utility of the corresponding plan for the original planning task, and a near-optimal plan for the transformed planning task corresponds to a near-optimal plan for the original planning task. However, a near-optimal planner with a given worst-case approximation error for the transformed planning task can have a larger worst-case approximation error for the original planning task. Assume, for example, that the optimal plan for the transformed planning task achieves the goal with probability $p$ and stops in only the goal states or "death." Consequently, the expected utility of the optimal plan that achieves the goal for the original planning task is $p$ and its certainty equivalent is $\log_\gamma p$. Case 1: Consider a near-optimal planner with absolute (= additive) approximation error for the transformed planning task. This means that the planner determines a plan whose quality is at least $x - \epsilon$ for a constant $\epsilon > 0$ if the quality of the best plan is $x$. If this planner is used to solve the transformed planning task, it can potentially determine a plan that stops in only the goal states or "death" and whose probability of goal achievement is only $p - \epsilon$ (but not worse). Thus, the corresponding plan for the original planning task achieves the goal but its expected utility is only $p - \epsilon$ and its certainty equivalent is only $\log_\gamma [p - \epsilon]$. To determine the approximation error of this plan for the original planning task, we need to consider how close its certainty equivalent is to the certainty equivalent of the plan that achieves the goal with maximal expected utility. Table 1 summarizes this data.

**Table 1.** Approximation Error for Case 1

|  | probability of goal achievement for the transformed planning task | certainty equivalent for the original planning task |
|---|---|---|
| optimal plan | $p$ | $\log_\gamma p$ |
| found plan (worst case) | $p - \epsilon$ | $\log_\gamma [p - \epsilon]$ |

Thus, the resulting approximation error for the original planning task, $\log_\gamma p - \log_\gamma [p - \epsilon] = \log_\gamma \frac{p}{p-\epsilon}$, increases as $p$ and $\gamma$ decrease. It can get arbitrarily large. Case 2: Now consider a near-optimal planner with relative (= multiplicative) approximation error for the transformed planning task. This means that the planner determines a plan whose quality is at least $(1 - \epsilon)x$ for a constant $\epsilon > 0$ if the quality of the best plan is $x$. Table 2 summarizes the resulting data.

**Table 2.** Approximation Error for Case 2

|  | probability of goal achievement for the transformed planning task | certainty equivalent for the original planning task |
|---|---|---|
| optimal plan | $p$ | $\log_\gamma p$ |
| found plan (worst case) | $(1 - \epsilon)p$ | $\log_\gamma [1 - \epsilon] + \log_\gamma p$ |

Thus, the resulting approximation error for the original planning task, $\log_\gamma p - \log_\gamma [1 - \epsilon] - \log_\gamma p = \log_\gamma \frac{1}{1-\epsilon}$, is additive. Figure 6 shows its graph.

## 6.2   The Additive Planning-Task Transformation

For the additive planning-task transformation, the reward of any sequential plan for the transformed planning task is the same as the certainty equivalent of the corresponding plan for the original planning task. Thus, the larger the reward of a plan for the transformed planning task, the larger the certainty equivalent of the corresponding plan for the original planning task, and a near-optimal plan for the transformed planning task corresponds to a near-optimal for the original planning task. Furthermore, a near-optimal planner that has a given absolute or relative worst-case approximation error for the transformed planning task has the same absolute or relative worst-case approximation error, respectively, for the original planning task.

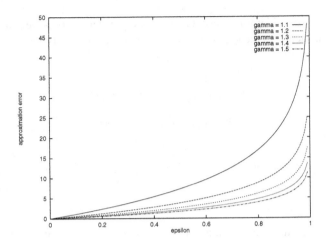

**Fig. 6.** Approximation Error for Case 2

## 7    Conclusions

Many existing artificial intelligence planners attempt to determine plans that achieve
the goal with maximal probability or minimal expected execution time, but agents often
need to determine plans that achieve the goal with maximal expected utility for nonlinear
utility functions. In this paper, we developed a planning methodology for determining
plans that achieve the goal with maximal expected utility for convex exponential utility
functions. These utility functions are necessary to model the immediate soft deadlines
often encountered in the context of delivery tasks. Our planning methodology combines
constructive approaches from artificial intelligence with more descriptive approaches
from utility theory. It is based on simple representation changes, that we call the additive and multiplicative planning-task transformations. Advantages of the planning-task
transformations are that they are fast, scale well, allow for optimal and near-optimal
planning, and are grounded in utility theory. Future work includes studying planning
for agents with even more general preference models, including trading-off between
different resource consumptions (such as money, energy, and time).

**Acknowledgments.** The Intelligent Decision-Making Group is supported by an NSF
Career Award to Sven Koenig under contract IIS-9984827. The views and conclusions
contained in this document are those of the author and should not be interpreted as representing the official policies, either expressed or implied, of the sponsoring organizations
and agencies or the U.S. Government.

## References

1. D. Bernoulli. Specimen theoriae novae de mensura sortis. *Commentarii Academiae Sci-
   entiarum Imperialis Petropolitanae*, 5, 1738. Translated by L. Sommer, *Econometrica*, 22:
   23–36, 1954.

2. A. Blum and J. Langford. Probabilistic planning in the graphplan framework. In *Proceedings of the European Conference on Planning*, 1999.

3. J. Blythe. Planning with external events. In *Proceedings of the Conference on Uncertainty in Artificial Intelligence*, pages 94–101, 1994.

4. C. Boutilier, T. Dean, and S. Hanks. Decision-theoretic planning: Structural assumptions and computational leverage. *Journal of Artificial Intelligence Research*, 11:1–94, 1999.

5. J. Bresina and M. Drummond. Anytime synthetic projection: Maximizing the probability of goal satisfaction. In *Proceedings of the National Conference on Artificial Intelligence*, pages 138–144, 1990.

6. T. Dean, J. Firby, and D. Miller. Hierarchical planning involving deadlines, travel times, and resources. *Computational Intelligence*, 4(4):381–398, 1988.

7. D. Draper, S. Hanks, and D. Weld. Probabilistic planning with information gathering. In *Proceedings of the International Conference on Artificial Intelligence Planning Systems*, pages 31–37, 1994.

8. R. Goldman and M. Boddy. Epsilon-safe planning. In *Proceedings of the Conference on Uncertainty in Artificial Intelligence*, pages 253–261, 1994.

9. P. Haddawy and S. Hanks. Representation for decision-theoretic planning: Utility functions for deadline goals. In *Proceedings of the International Conference on Principles of Knowledge Representation and Reasoning*, 1992.

10. R. Howard and J. Matheson. Risk-sensitive Markov decision processes. *Management Science*, 18(7):356–369, 1972.

11. K. Kanazawa and T. Dean. A model for projection and action. In *Proceedings of the International Joint Conference on Artificial Intelligence*, pages 985–990, 1989.

12. S. Koenig and R.G. Simmons. How to make reactive planners risk-sensitive. In *Proceedings of the International Conference on Artificial Intelligence Planning Systems*, pages 293–298, 1994.

13. N. Kushmerick, S. Hanks, and D. Weld. An algorithm for probabilistic planning. *Artificial Intelligence*, 76(1–2):239–286, 1995.

14. S. Marcus, E. Fernàndez-Gaucherand, D. Hernàndez-Hernàndez, S. Colaruppi, and P. Fard. Risk-sensitive Markov decision processes. In C. Byrnes et. al., editor, *Systems and Control in the Twenty-First Century*, pages 263–279. Birkhauser, 1997.

15. R. Neuneier and O. Mihatsch. Risk sensitive reinforcement learning. In *Proceedings of the Neural Information Processing Systems*, pages 1031–1037, 1999.

16. N. Onder and M. Pollack. Conditional, probabilistic planning: A unifying algorithm and effective search control machanisms. In *Proceedings of the National Conference on Artificial Intelligence*, 1999.

17. J. Pratt. Risk aversion in the small and in the large. *Econometrica*, 32(1-2):122–136, 1964.

18. J. von Neumann and O. Morgenstern. *Theory of games and economic behavior*. Princeton University Press, second edition, 1947.

19. M. Wellman, M. Ford, and K. Larson. Path planning under time-dependent uncertainty. In *Proceedings of the Conference on Uncertainty in Artificial Intelligence*, pages 523–539, 1995.

20. P. Whittle. *Risk-Sensitive Optimal Control*. Wiley, 1990.

# An Architectural Framework for Integrated Multiagent Planning, Reacting, and Learning

Gerhard Weiß

Institut für Informatik, Technische Universität München
D-80290 München, Germany
weissg@in.tum.de

**Abstract.** Dyna is a single-agent architectural framework that integrates learning, planning, and reacting. Well known instantiations of Dyna are Dyna-AC and Dyna-Q. Here a multiagent extension of Dyna-Q is presented. This extension, called M-Dyna-Q, constitutes a novel coordination framework that bridges the gap between plan-based and reactive coordination in multiagent systems. The paper summarizes the key features of Dyna, describes M-Dyna-Q in detail, provides experimental results, and carefully discusses the benefits and limitations of this framework.

## 1   Introduction

Dyna (e.g., [31,32] and [33, Chapter 9]) is an architectural framework that integrates learning, planning, and reacting in single agents. This integration is based on two fundamental observations that can be summarized as follows:

- "Learning is a valuable basis for both planning and reacting." Through learning an agent acquires information that enables him to plan and react more effectively and efficiently. More specifically, according to Dyna an agent plans on the basis of an incrementally learnt world model and reacts on the basis of incrementally learnt values that indicate the usefulness of his potential actions.
- "Both planning and reacting are a valuable basis for learning." An agent uses the outcomes of his planning and reacting activities for improving his world model and the estimates of their actions' usefulness. More specifically, according to Dyna planning serves as a basis for trial-and-error learning from hypothetical experience, while reacting serves as a basis for trial-and-error learning from real experience.

Figure 1 summarizes this interwining of learning, planning, and reacting. This figure is complemented by Figure 2 which overviews the general flow of control and information within a Dyna agent. Both real and hypothetical experience are used for updating the action values. Additionally, real experience (reacting) is employed for learning a world model which helps to handle hypothetical experience (planning). Two well known instantiations of the Dyna framework are Dyna-AC (Dyna plus actor-critic learning) and Dyna-Q (Dyna plus Q-learning); see e.g. [31]. An advantage of Dyna-Q over Dyna-AC is that it is simpler to realize. In particular, Dyna-AC requires two learning rules and two memory structures (evaluation function and policy), while Dyna-Q requires only

C. Castelfranchi, Y. Lespérance (Eds.): Intelligent Agents VII, LNAI 1986, pp. 320–330, 2001.

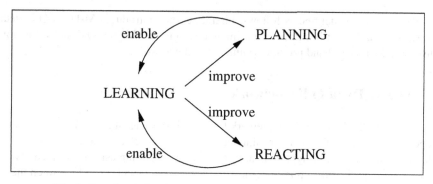

**Fig. 1.** Dyna's relationships between learning, planning, and reacting.

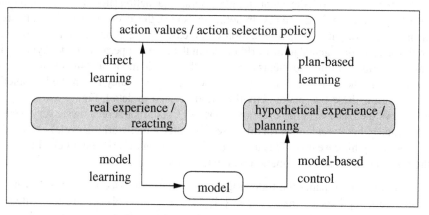

**Fig. 2.** Dyna's internal flow of control and information.

one learning rule and one memory structure (which is a cross between Dyna-AC's two memory structures).

This paper describes work that extends the Dyna framework to multiagent settings. Based on Dyna-Q a general coordination framework called M-Dyna-Q for multiagent systems is proposed that integrates joint learning, joint planning, and joint reactivity. M-Dyna-Q bridges the gap between two contrary main approaches to multiagent coordination, namely, plan-based coordination (see e.g. [4,5,6,9,12,15,23,28,16]) and reactive coordination (see e.g. [2,8,10,18,20,22,25,27] and also [7]). The basic idea behind the former approach is that the agents jointly generate hypothetical activity sequences on the basis of their world model in order to find out in advance (i.e., before acting in the real world) what actions among all possible actions are most promising. Against that, the basic idea behind the latter approach is that the agents jointly generate rapid reactions on the basis of simple stimulus-response rules that can be carried out by the agents. A unique key feature of M-Dyna-Q is that it brings together these two contrary ideas.

The paper is structured as follows. First, Section 2 introduces M-Dyna-Q in detail. Next, Section 3 describes initial experimental results on M-Dyna-Q. Finally, Section 4 discusses M-Dyna-Q and provides pointers to related work.

## 2    The M-Dyna-Q Framework

According to the M-Dyna-Q framework the overall multiagent activity results from the repeated execution of two major joint activities—action selection and learning—, each running either in real or hypothetical mode. In the most simplest form (which also underlies the experiments reported in the next section), the agents switch between the two modes at a fixed and predefined rate. The real mode corresponds to (fast) "reactive behavior," whereas the hypothetical mode corresponds to (slower) "plan-based behavior." During action selection, the agents jointly decide what action should be carried out next (resulting in the next real or a new hypothetical state); this decision is made on the basis of the agents' distributed value function in the case of operating in the real mode, and on the basis of the agents' joint world model in the case of operating in the hypothetical mode.[1] During learning the agents adjust both their world model and their value function if they act in the real mode, and just their world model if they act in the hypothetical mode. Below these two major activities are described in detail. Figure 3 conceptually overviews the basic working cycle of M-Dyna-Q. As this figure shows, every working cycle runs either in real mode (in this case it is called a real working cycle) or hypothetical mode (in this case it is called a hypothetical working cycle). The Figure 4 illustrates the flow of control and information within this framework.

Throughout the paper the following simple notation is used and the following elementary assumptions are made. $Ag = \{A_1, \ldots, A_n\}$ ($n \in \mathsf{N}$) denotes the finite set of agents available in the MAS under consideration. The environment in which the agents act can be described as a discrete state space, and the individual real and hypothetical states are denoted by $\mathcal{S}, \mathcal{T}, \mathcal{U}, \ldots$ $Ac_i^{poss} = \{a_i^1, \ldots, a_i^{m_i}\}$ ($m_i \in \mathsf{N}$) denotes the set of all possible actions of the agent $A_i$, and is called his *action potential*. Finally, $Ac_i^{poss}[\mathcal{S}]$ denotes the set of all actions that $A_i$ could carry out (identifies as "executable") in the environmental state $\mathcal{S}$ ($Ac_i^{poss}[\mathcal{S}] \subseteq Ac_i^{poss}$).

**Joint Action Selection.** According to M-Dyna-Q each agent $A_i$ maintains state-specific estimates of the usefulness of his actions for goal attainment. More specifically, an agent $A_i$ maintains, for every state $\mathcal{S}$ and each of his actions $a_i^j$, a quantity $Q_i^j(\mathcal{S})$ that expresses his estimate of $a_i^j$'s state-specific usefulness with respect to goal attainment. Based on these estimates, action selection works as follows. If the agents operate in the "real mode", then they analyze the current real state $\mathcal{S}$, and each agent $A_i$ identifies and announces the set $Ac_i^{poss}[\mathcal{S}]$ of actions it could carry out immediately (assuming the availability of a standard blackboard communication structure and a time-out announcement mechanism). The action to be carried out is then selected among all announced

---

[1] In accordance with common usage in the field of reinforcement learning, here "model" refers to a mapping from state-action pairs to state-reward pairs, and "value function" refers to a mapping from state-action pairs to values expressing the estimated usefulness of carrying out actions in given states.

1. **Joint Action Selection:**
   - the agents choose among $mode = real$ and $mode = hypo(thetical)$
   - if $mode = real$: $state$ = current real state
   - if $mode = hypo$: $state$ = any previously observed real state
   - each agent announces the actions it could carry out in $state$
   - if $mode = real$: an action is selected from all actions announced in
     $state$ with probability proportional to their estimated usefulness,
     the selected action is carried out (resulting in a new real state)
   - if $mode = hypo$: an action is randomly choosen from all actions
     previously carried out in $state$ (resulting in a hypothetical
     successor state)

2. **Joint Learning:**
   - if $mode = real$: the agent that carried out the selected action
     adjusts this action's estimated usefulness dependent on the usefulness
     of the actions applicable in the new real state, and the agents
     update their world model
   - if $mode = hypo$: the agent that could carry out the selected hypo-
     thetical action adjusts this action's estimated usefulness dependent
     on the usefulness of the actions applicable in the hypothetical suc-
     cessor state

   Goto 1

**Fig. 3.** The basic working cycle of M-Dyna-Q.

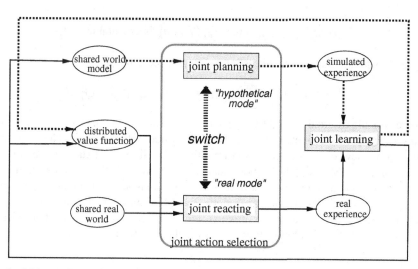

**Fig. 4.** M-Dyna-Q's flow of control and information in the real (solid lines) and hypothetical (dotted lines) mode.

actions dependent on the agents' action selection policy. A standard policy (which was also used in the experiments reported below) is that the probability of selecting an announced action $a_i^j$ is proportional to the estimated usefulness of all actions announced in $S$, i.e.,

$$\frac{e^{Q_i^j(S)}}{e^{\sum_{a_i^j} Q_i^j(S)}} \tag{1}$$

where the sum ranges over all currently announced actions (i.e., over $\bigcup_{i=1}^n \mathcal{A}c_i^{poss}[S]$). If the agents operate in the "hypothetical mode," then they *(i)* randomly choose an environmental state $S$ from those real states which they already encountered in the past and *(ii)* select an action $a_i^j$ from those already carried out in this state according to Equation (1). This means that in the hypothetical mode the agents simulate real activity and do as if $S$ is the current real state and $a_i^j$ had been selected for execution. Because the agents only choose hypothetical states that they already know from experience, they avoid to be forced to make speculative activity decisions under unknown hypothetical environmental circumstances. Note that the agents do single-step planning when operating in the hypothetical mode. This "planning in very small steps" has been adopted from the single-agent Dyna-Q framework with the intention to enable the agents to redirect their course of activity without unnecessarily wasted computation and communication whenever necessary.

**Joint Learning.** Learning is realized by the agents through adjusting the estimates of their actions' usefulness. Suppose that $a_i^j$ has been selected in the real or hypothetical state $S$ and $T$ is the resulting successor state. All agents that could carry out actions in $T$ inform the agent $A_i$ about these actions' estimated usefulness. $A_i$ determines the maximum

$$maxQ_k^l(T) \quad =_{\text{def}} \quad \max\{Q_k^l(T) : a_k^l \text{ is executable in } T\} \tag{2}$$

of these estimates and adjusts his estimate $Q_i^j(S)$ according to

$$Q_i^j(S) \quad = \quad Q_i^j(S) + \alpha \cdot [R + \beta \cdot maxQ_k^l(T) - Q_i^j(S)] \tag{3}$$

where $R$ is the external reward (if any) and $\alpha$ and $\beta$ are small constants called learning rates. ($maxQ_k^l(T)$ defines, so to say, the global value of the state $T$.) This adjustment rule can be viewed as a straightforward multiagent realization of standard single-agent Q-learning [34,35] in which the individual Q-values and thus the value function is distributed over and maintained by several agents. Whereas the adjustment rule is applied in both the real and the hypothetical mode, the world model is updated by the agents only if they act in the real mode; this is reasonable because the most reliable way to improve a world model obviously is to observe the effects of real actions.

## 3   Experimental Results

We made initial experiments with several synthetic state-action spaces that allow to efficiently obtain indicative results. This paper describes the results for the state-action spaces shown in the Tables 1 (SAS1) and 2 (SAS2). SAS1 consists of 18 world states $(0, \ldots, 17)$ and 32 actions that can be carried out by 5 agents. Most of the actions can

**Table 1.** State-action space SAS1.

| $a_i^j$ | $S$ | $T$ | $a_i^j$ | $S$ | $T$ | $a_i^j$ | $S$ | $T$ |
|---|---|---|---|---|---|---|---|---|
| $a_1^1$ | 0 | 1 | $a_2^3$ | 1 | 7 | $a_5^1$ | 3 | 5 |
| $a_1^1$ | 6 | 11 | $a_2^3$ | 15 | 10 | $a_5^1$ | 5 | 10 |
| $a_1^1$ | 7 | 10 | $a_2^4$ | 6 | 9 | $a_5^2$ | 3 | 8 |
| $a_1^2$ | 4 | 8 | $a_2^4$ | 10 | 16 | $a_5^2$ | 5 | 8 |
| $a_1^3$ | 8 | 9 | $a_2^4$ | 4 | 7 | $a_5^3$ | 0 | 2 |
| $a_1^3$ | 10 | 14 | $a_2^4$ | 12 | 17 | $a_5^3$ | 2 | 7 |
| $a_1^3$ | 11 | 17 | $a_3^3$ | 6 | 12 | $a_5^3$ | 8 | 10 |
| $a_1^3$ | 12 | 16 | $a_4^1$ | 2 | 5 | $a_5^4$ | 12 | 13 |
| $a_2^1$ | 0 | 3 | $a_4^1$ | 7 | 8 | $a_5^4$ | 4 | 6 |
| $a_2^1$ | 3 | 7 | $a_4^1$ | 0 | 4 | $a_5^5$ | 1 | 5 |
| $a_2^2$ | 5 | 9 | $a_4^2$ | 2 | 6 | $a_5^5$ | 9 | 14 |
| $a_2^2$ | 14 | 9 | $a_4^2$ | 9 | 15 | $a_5^5$ | 11 | 15 |

| start state: 0 | goal state: 17 | reward: 1000 |
|---|---|---|

**Table 2.** State-action space SAS2.

| $a_i^j$ | $S$ | $T$ | $a_i^j$ | $S$ | $T$ | $a_i^j$ | $S$ | $T$ | $a_i^j$ | $S$ | $T$ |
|---|---|---|---|---|---|---|---|---|---|---|---|
| $a_1^1$ | 0 | 1 | $a_2^1$ | 14 | 18 | $a_3^3$ | 9 | 14 | $a_6^4$ | 12 | 18 |
| $a_1^1$ | 1 | 10 | $a_2^1$ | 0 | 2 | $a_4^1$ | 0 | 4 | $a_6^4$ | 17 | 3 |
| $a_1^1$ | 6 | 15 | $a_2^2$ | 19 | 3 | $a_5^1$ | 4 | 9 | $a_7^1$ | 3 | 9 |
| $a_1^2$ | 11 | 20 | $a_2^2$ | 5 | 9 | $a_5^1$ | 5 | 10 | $a_7^1$ | 8 | 14 |
| $a_1^2$ | 2 | 6 | $a_2^2$ | 10 | 14 | $a_5^1$ | 8 | 13 | $a_7^1$ | 13 | 19 |
| $a_1^2$ | 7 | 11 | $a_2^2$ | 15 | 19 | $a_5^1$ | 10 | 15 | $a_7^2$ | 0 | 5 |
| $a_1^3$ | 12 | 16 | $a_3^1$ | 1 | 6 | $a_5^1$ | 13 | 18 | $a_7^2$ | 18 | 4 |
| $a_1^3$ | 0 | 21 | $a_3^1$ | 0 | 21 | $a_5^1$ | 0 | 21 | $a_7^2$ | 14 | 20 |
| $a_1^4$ | 17 | 1 | $a_3^1$ | 2 | 7 | $a_5^1$ | 14 | 19 | $a_7^2$ | 4 | 10 |
| $a_1^4$ | 3 | 7 | $a_3^2$ | 6 | 11 | $a_6^1$ | 15 | 20 | $a_7^2$ | 9 | 15 |
| $a_1^4$ | 8 | 12 | $a_3^2$ | 7 | 12 | $a_6^1$ | 1 | 7 | $a_7^3$ | 0 | 21 |
| $a_1^4$ | 13 | 17 | $a_3^2$ | 11 | 16 | $a_6^2$ | 6 | 12 | $a_7^3$ | 19 | 5 |
| $a_1^4$ | 18 | 2 | $a_3^3$ | 12 | 17 | $a_6^3$ | 11 | 17 | $a_7^3$ | 5 | 6 |
| $a_1^4$ | 0 | 21 | $a_3^3$ | 21 | 6 | $a_6^3$ | 21 | 9 | $a_7^4$ | 21 | 5 |
| $a_1^5$ | 4 | 8 | $a_3^3$ | 3 | 8 | $a_6^3$ | 2 | 8 | $a_7^4$ | 10 | 11 |
| $a_1^5$ | 9 | 13 | $a_3^3$ | 0 | 3 | $a_6^3$ | 7 | 13 | $a_7^4$ | 15 | 16 |

| start state: 0 | goal state 1: 16 | goal state 2: 20 |
|---|---|---|
| reward in state 16: 500 | reward in state 20: 1000 | |

be carried out in different states (e.g., action $a_1^1$ in the states 0, 6, and 7), and different actions can be carried out in the same state (e.g., the actions $a_2^2$, $a_5^1$, and $a_5^3$ can be carried out in state 5). The learning task is to find a sequence of at most 5 actions that transform the start state 0 into the goal state 17. (An example of a solution sequence of length $L = 4$ is $< a_5^3, a_4^2, a_3^1, a_2^4 >$.) Reward is provided only if the goal state is reached. SAS2 is designed analogously, except that there are two goal states with different reward levels.

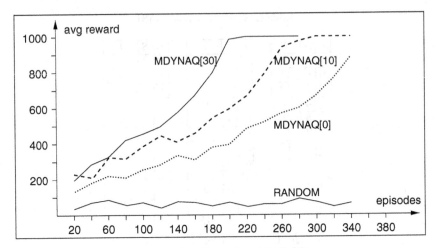

**Fig. 5.** Experimental results for SAS1.

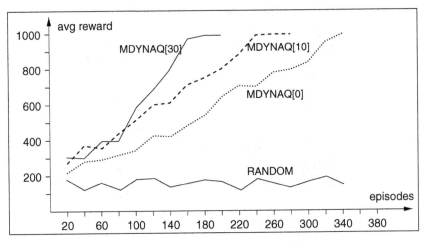

**Fig. 6.** Experimental results for SAS2.

Figures 5 and 6 show the results for SAS1 and SAS2, respectively. Learning proceeds by the repeated execution of episodes, where an episode is defined as any sequence of at most 5 real working cycles that transform the start state into the goal state (successful sequence) or into a non-goal state (unsuccessful sequence). The parameter setting was as follows: $\alpha = 0.2$, $\beta = 0.9$, and $R = 1000$ (SAS1 in state 17), $R = 500/1000$ (SAS2 in states 16/20). The initial Q-values were all zero. Each figure shows four curves: RANDOM (random walk of maximum length 5 through the state-action space); MDY-NAQ[30] (30 hypothetical working cycles after each real working cycle), MDYNAQ[10] (10 hypothetical experiences after each real experience), and MYDNA[0] (no hypothetical experiences at all). Each data point shows the mean reward obtained in the previous 20 episodes, averaged over 5 independent runs. The main observations are as follows.

First, MDYNAQ clearly performed better than uninformed RANDOM search which achieved an average reward level of 64 in the case of SAS1 and 156 in the case of SAS2. This indicates the general performance capacity of M-Dyna-Q. Second, MDYNA always reached the maximum reward level, even if there are different reward levels as it is the case with SAS2. This indicates the robustness of M-Dyna-Q against local performance maxima. Third, MDYNAQ[30] performed better than MDYNAQ[10] which performed better than MDYNAQ[0]. On the average, MDYNAQ[30] (MDYNAQ[10], MDYNAQ[0]) reached the maximum reward level after about 190 (300, 400) episodes in the case of SAS1 and after about 160 (240, 340) cycles in the case of SAS2. This indicates how learning based on hypothetical experiences contributes to M-Dyna-Q's overall performance.

## 4  Discussion

This paper described a multiagent extension of a single-agent architecture known as Dyna-Q. This extension, M-Dyna-Q, constitutes a coordination framework that combines the ideas of two contrary main approaches to coordination in multiagent systems, namely, plan-based and reactive coordination. Each of these two approaches has its specific advantages and disadvantages:

- An advantage of plan-based coordination is that the probability of carrying out unsuccessful activity sequences, which additionally may be expensive and perhaps even irreversible, is kept low. A disadvantage of this approach is that it is limited by the accuracy of the world model used by the agents. Another disadvantage is that it tends to be rather time-consuming and that the computation and communication costs for coordinating planning activities of multiple agents can grow enormously with the length of the planning sequences. Both disadvantages are directly correlated with the dynamics of the world in which the agents act and with the number of agents involved in the planning process—the more dynamic the world is and/or the more agents are involved, the more challenging it is to cope with these disadvantages.
- An advantage of reactive coordination is that it enables agents to rapidly respond to environmental changes without requiring to equip the agents a priori with complex and often difficult-to-obtain knowledge about their environment. A disadvantage of this approach is that concerted interaction and overall coherence can hardly be achieved through simply applying stimulus-response rules, especially in environments in which there are inherent dependencies among the agents' potential actions. Another disadvantage is that it can lead rather poor performance in environments in which it is hard (costly, time-consuming, and so forth) to undo the effects of actions.

Obviously, M-Dyna-Q aims at merging plan-based and reactive coordination such that there advantages are retained while their disadvantages are avoided.

M-Dyna-Q explicitly integrates joint planning, joint reacting, and joint learning. It is this integration that makes the M-Dyna-Q unique and different from a number of related approaches to multiagent activity coordination, including approaches that rely on either pure planning or pure reaction (see the references provided in Section 1), approaches that rely on a combination of planning and learning (e.g., [29,30,38]), and approaches that rely on a combination of reacting and learning (e.g., [3,17,19,21,26,24,36,37]). M-Dyna-Q can be considered as a generalization of these approaches, and as such it aims at offering "maximum coordination flexibility." This is not to say that M-Dyna-Q is the best choice for every application. However, due to its potential flexibility this framework seems to be a very promising candidate especially in environments whose dynamics and coordination requirements are not know in advance.

M-Dyna-Q, in its current form, is limited as follows. First, and most important, M-Dyna-Q requires the agents to strictly synchronize their action selection and learning activities. In particular, it requires the agents to sequentialize their actions such that only one action per working cycle is executed. Obviously, this restricts multiagent systems in the parallel capabilities they might have in a given application domain, and further research is necessary to identify and analyze methods for weakening this limitation. A possible solution may be to take *sets* of compatible actions rather than individual actions as the agents' basic activity units, as done in our previous work (e.g. [37]). Second, M-Dyna-Q realizes just a very simple form of planning consisting of one-step lookahead activities of the individual agents. Although this makes sense in a variety of situations (especially in unknown and highly complex environments), in general it is desirable and necessary that the agents possess more advanced planning capabilities. Improvement is necessary both w.r.t. a more flexible handling of the planning depth and a more efficient exploitation of the planning results. Several sophisticated distributed planning mechanisms have been described in the literature (e.g., see [1]), and to explore the use of these mechanisms within M-Dyna-Q is another interesting issue for future research. Third, M-Dyna-Q assumes that the agents can maintain and use a joint world model without remarkable efforts. This is not necessarily the case in application domains in which the agents are not aware of all the effects of their actions or in which they sense different parts of their environment. This limitation requires an extension of M-Dyna-Q toward distributed modeling and diagnosis, as investigated in e.g. [11,13,14]. And fourth, switching between real mode (reactivity) and hypothetical mode (planning) is done in a very simple way, and in view of more complex environments there is a need for a more sophisticated switch control. For instance, switching may occur in dependence on the overall performance and may be itself subject to learning. "Optimal switching" constitutes a research theme that is not only of relevance to M-Dyna-Q, but to any multiagent as well as single-agent approach that aims at bringing together reactivity and planning.

To summarize, M-Dyna-Q offers a novel perspective of multiagent coordination based on a unified view of concerted learning, planning, and reacting. What makes M-Dyna-Q additionally interesting is that it has been directly derived from a single-agent architectural framework. We think that these features and the encouraging intitial experimental results clearly justify to say that it is worth to further explore M-Dyna-Q along the research directions outlined above.

**Acknowledgments.** The research reported in this paper has been supported by Deutsche Forschungsgemeinschaft DFG (German National Science Foundation) under contract We1718/6-3.

# References

1. AI Magazine. Special Issue on Distributed Continual Planning, Vol. 20, No. 4, Winter 1999.
2. T. Bouron, J. Ferber, and F. Samuel. A multi-agent testbed for heterogeneous agents. In Y. Demazeau and J.-P. Müller, editors, *Decentralized A.I. 2*, pages 195–214. North-Holland, Amsterdam et al., 1991.
3. R.H. Crites and A.G. Barto. Elevator group control using multiple reinforcement learning agents. *Machine Learning*, 33(2/3):235–262, 1998.
4. K.S. Decker and V.R. Lesser. Generalized partial global planning. *International Journal of Intelligent Cooperative Information Systems*, 1(2):319–346, 1992.
5. E.H. Durfee, P.G. Kenny, and K.C. Kluge. Integrated premission planning and execution for unmanned ground vehicles. In *Proceedings of the First International Conference on Autonomous Agents (Agents'97)*, pages 348–354, 1997.
6. E.H. Durfee and V.R. Lesser. Partial global planning: A coordination framework for distributed hypothesis formation. *IEEE Transactions on Systems, Man, and Cybernetics*, SMC-21(5):1167–1183, 1991.
7. J. Ferber. Reactive distributed artificial intelligence: Principles and applications. In G.M.P. O'Hare and N.R. Jennings, editors, *Foundations of Distributed Artificial Intelligence*, pages 287–314. Wiley, New York et al., 1996.
8. J. Ferber and E. Jacopin. The framework of ECO-problem sloving. In Y. Demazeau and J.-P. Müller, editors, *Decentralized A.I. 2*, pages 181–194. North-Holland, Amsterdam et al., 1991.
9. M. Georgeff. Communication and interaction in multi-agent planning. In *Proceedings of the Third National Conference on Artificial Intelligence (AAAI-83)*, pages 125–129, 1983.
10. D. Goldberg and M.J. Matarić. Coordinating mobile robot group behavior using a model of interaction dynamics. In *Proceedings of the Third International Conference on Autonomous Agents (Agents'99)*, pages 100–107, 1999.
11. B. Horling, V. Lesser, R. Vincent, A. Bazzan, and P. Xuan. Diagnosis as an integral part of multi-agent adaptability. Technical Report 99-03, Computer Science Department, University of Massachussetts at Amherst, 1999.
12. M.J. Huber and E.H. Durfee. An initial assessment of plan-recognition-based coordination for multi-agent systems. In *Proceedings of the 2nd International Conference on Multi-Agent Systems (ICMAS-96)*, pages 126–133, 1996.
13. E. Hudlická and V.R. Lesser. Modeling and diagnosing problem-solving system behavior. *IEEE Transactions on Systems, Man, and Cybernetics*, SMC-17(3):407–419, 1987.
14. E. Hudlická, V.R. Lesser, A. Rewari, and P. Xuan. Design of a distributed diagnosis system. Technical Report 86-63, Computer Science Department, University of Massachussetts at Amherst, 1986.
15. F. Kabanza. Synchronizing multiagent plans using temporal logic. In *Proceedings of the First International Conference on Multi-Agent Systems (ICMAS-95)*, pages 217–224, 1995.
16. F. von Martial. *Coordinating plans of autonomous agents*. Lecture Notes in Artificial in Artificial Intelligence, Vol. 610. Springer-Verlag, Berlin et al., 1992.
17. M. Matarić. Reinforcement learning in the multi-robot domain. *Autonomous Robots*, 4(1):73–83, 1997.
18. M.J. Matarić. Designing and understanding adaptive group behavior. *Adaptive Behavior*, 4(1):51–80, 1995.
19. N. Ono and Y. Fukuta. Learning coordinated behavior in a continuous environment. In G. Weiß, editor, *Distributed Artificial Intelligence Meets Machine Learning*, Lecture Notes in Artificial in Artificial Intelligence, Vol. 1221, pages 73–81. Springer-Verlag, Berlin et al., 1997.

20. L.E. Parker. On the design of behavior-based multi-robot teams. *Advanced Robotics*, 10(6):547–578, 1996.

21. L.E. Parker. L-alliance: Task-oriented multi-robot learning insystems. *Advanced Robotics*, 11(4):305–322, 1997.

22. C. Reynolds. Flocks, herds, and schools: A distributed behavioral model. *Computer Graphics*, 21(4):25–34, 1987.

23. A.E.F. Seghrouchni and S. Haddad. A recursive model for distributed planning. In *Proceedings of the 2nd International Conference on Multi-Agent Systems (ICMAS-96)*, pages 307–314, 1996.

24. S. Sen and M. Sekaran. Multiagent coordination with learning classifier systems. In G. Weiß and S. Sen, editors, *Adaption and Learning in Multiagent Systems*, Lecture Notes in Artificial in Artificial Intelligence, Vol. 1042, pages 218–233. Springer-Verlag, Berlin et al., 1996.

25. L. Steels. Cooperation between distributed agents through self-organization. In Y. Demazeau and J.-P. Müller, editors, *Decentralized A.I.*, pages 175–196. North-Holland, Amsterdam et al., 1990.

26. P. Stone and M. Veloso. Collaborative and adversarial learning: A case study in robotic soccer. In S. Sen, editor, *Adaptation, Coevolution and Learning in Multiagent Systems. Papers from the 1996 AAAI Symposium*, Technical Report SS-96-01, pages 88–92. AAAI Press, Menlo Park, CA, 1996.

27. T. Sueyoshi and M. Tokoro. Dynamic modeling of agents for coordination. In Y. Demazeau and J.-P. Müller, editors, *Decentralized A.I. 2*, pages 161–176. North-Holland, Amsterdam et al., 1991.

28. T. Sugawara. Reusing past plans in distributed planning. In *Proceedings of the First International Conference on Multi-Agent Systems (ICMAS-95)*, pages 360–367, 1995.

29. T. Sugawara and V. Lesser. On-line learning of coordination plans. In *Working Papers of the 12th International Workshop on Distributed Artificial Intelligence*, 1993.

30. T. Sugawara and V. Lesser. Learning to improve coordinated actions in cooperative distributed problem-solving environments. *Machine Learning*, 33(2/3):129–153, 1998.

31. R.S. Sutton. Dyna, an integrated architecture for learning, planning, and reacting. *SIGART Bulletin*, 2:160–163, 1991.

32. R.S. Sutton. Planning by incremental dynamic programming. In *Proceedings of the Eigth International Workshop on Machine Learning*, pages 353–357, 1991.

33. R.S. Sutton and A.G. Barto. *Reinforcement Learning. An Introduction*. MIT Press/A Bradford Book, Cambridge, MA, 1998.

34. C.J.C.H. Watkins. *Learning from Delayed Rewards*. PhD thesis, King's College, Cambridge University, 1989.

35. C.J.C.H. Watkins and P. Dayan. Q-learning. *Machine Learning*, 8:279–292, 1992.

36. G. Weiß. Action selection and learning in multi-agent environments. In *From Animals to Animats 2 – Proceedings of the Second International Conference on Simulation of Adaptive Behavior*, pages 502–510, 1993.

37. G. Weiß. Learning to coordinate actions in multi-agent systems. In *Proceedings of the 13th International Joint Conference on Artificial Intelligence (IJCAI-93)*, pages 311–316, 1993.

38. G. Weiß. Achieving coordination through combining joint planning and joint learning. Technical Report FKI-232-99, Institut für Informatik, Technische Universität München, 1999.

# Panel Summary: Agent Development Tools

Joanna Bryson[1], Keith Decker[2], Scott A. DeLoach[3], Michael Huhns[4], and
Michael Wooldridge[5]

[1] Department of Computer Science
Massachusetts Institute of Technology, Cambridge, MA 00000
joanna@ai.mit.edu
[2] Department of Computer and Information Sciences
University of Delaware, Newark, DE 19716-2586
decker@cis.udel.edu
[3] Department of Electrical and Computer Engineering, Air Force Institute of Technology
2950 P Street, Wright-Patterson AFB, OH 45433-7765
sdeloach@computer.org
[4] Electrical and Computer Engineering Department
University of South Carolina, Columbia, SC 29208
huhns@ece.sc.edu
[5] Department of Computer Science
University of Liverpool Liverpool L69 7ZF, UK
m.j.wooldridge@csc.liv.ac.uk

## 1 Introduction

This panel (and a corresponding paper track) sought to examine the state of the art (or lack thereof) in tools for developing agents and agent systems. In this context, "tools" include complete agent programming environments, testbeds, environment simulators, component libraries, and specification tools. In the past few years, the field has gone from a situation where almost all implementations were created from scratch in general purpose programming languages, through the appearance of the first generally available public libraries (for example, the venerable Lockeed "KAPI" (KQML API) of the mid-90's [10]), to full-blown GUI-supported development environments. For example, http://www.agentbuilder.com/AgentTools/ lists 25 commercial and 40 academic projects, many of which are publicly available. The sheer number of projects brings up many questions beyond those related to the tools themselves, and we put the following to our panel members:

- What are useful metrics or simply feature classes for comparing and contrasting agent development tools or methodologies (especially features that are unique to agent systems)?
- How does a tool suggest/support/enforce a particular design methodology, theory of agency, architecture, or agent language?
- Why, as more and more development tools and methodologies become available, do most systems still seem to be developed without any specialized tools?
- What are the differences in development tools oriented toward the research community versus the agent application community, and are we already seeing a significant lag between theory and practice?

C. Castelfranchi, Y. Lespérance (Eds.): Intelligent Agents VII, LNAI 1986, pp. 331–338, 2001.

- Are there obvious development tools, that are unique to agent-based system development, that have yet to be built?
- Given the resources available to the average basic researcher, what do you think can be done to improve reuse of agent infrastructure / software?
- Is there any evidence that agent development tools actually increase programmer productivity and/or the quality of the resulting systems?
- What do you see as the largest time-sink (wasted time) in your research and in the agent software you have developed (e.g., having to write one's own compiler would be a waste of time)?
- What infrastructure have you succeeded in reusing? Why do you think you were able to do this?
- What (if any) stumbling blocks have you encountered in distributing your technology, e.g., legal, platform dependence, etc.?
- What do you see as the current infrastructure limitations in establishing large agent communities for real world applications?

## 2   Statement by Mike Wooldridge

Historically, the main obstacle to be overcome in developing multi-agent systems has been one of *infrastructure*. By this, I mean that in order to reach a state where two agents can communicate, (let alone cooperate, coordinate, negotiate, or whatever), there needs to be an underlying, relatively robust communications infrastructure that the agents can make use of. Moreover, simply providing such an infrastructure is not usually enough; as Gasser and colleagues suggested as long ago as 1987, there also needs to be some way of visualizing and monitoring ongoing communication in the system [3]. Until very recently, the provision of such an infrastructure represented a significant challenge for multi-agent system developers.

As an example of this, back in the late 1980s, we developed a multi-agent system platform called MADE (the Multi-Agent Development Environment) [15]. MADE allowed agents implemented using several different AI-oriented languages (LISP, PROLOG, and POP-I I) to communicate using performatives such as request and inform, provided some simple tools to monitor and track the behavior of the system, and provided support for distributing agents across a local area network. MADE was implemented in C, on Sun 3/50 and Sun 3/60 UNIX workstations. Agents in MADE were UNIX processes, (which rather limited the number of agents it was possible to run at any one time), and communication between agents was handled using a mixture of UNIX SVID interprocess communication mechanisms (for communication between agents on the same physical machine), and sockets (for communication between different machines). Our experience with MADE was that handling communications, and the problems of handling a system composed of multiple processes, took up the vast majority of our time. We implemented a stream of utilities that were intended to help us launch our agents, and even such apparently trivial tasks as stopping the system were complicated by the distributed, multi-process nature of the system. In addition, the cost of computer hardware at the time meant that developing a multi-agent system was an expensive process.

In the past decade, three things have happened to change this situation fundamentally:

- The first is that computer power today is considerably cheaper than it was even a decade ago.
- The second is that, whereas in the late 1980s comparatively few computers had network connections, today it is rather rare to find computers that are *not* networked.
- The third is that high-power communications and programming environments are available much more cheaply and widely than they were previously (I am thinking here of, for example, the Java language and its associated packages, as well as communication frameworks such as CORBA and RMI).

This means that many of the infrastructure hurdles that were in place a decade ago are no longer present: any medium power PC sold today has the software and the processing capability to run a respectably sized multi-agent system. There are also many powerful, freely available software platforms for implementing sophisticated agent systems, and these can be leveraged to develop agent systems in a time scale that was unthinkable even five or six years ago.

Looking to the future, perhaps the most important trend I anticipate is that the "non-agent" part of computing (in which I include the object-oriented world) will gradually expand to encompass more and more agent features. There are several good examples of this already. Sun's Jini system is one; the ability of software components to advertise their capabilities to other components, as provided by Jini, was until recently the province of the agent community. Another good example is the reflection API provided by the Java language, which allows objects to reflect on their capabilities; again, this type of behavior, which is now provided in the Java language for free, would until recently have been regarded as an agent-like feature. In much the same way, we can expect software development platforms and tools to provide ever more "agent-like" features, thus blurring the line between what is an what is not an agent even more (as if the line needed more blurring).

## 3   Statement by Joanna Bryson

The questions Keith set are all interesting and important, but the one I will concentrate on is "Why aren't more systems developed with established tools?" The answers to this question have serious implications for the others.

For tool sets to be successful, *tools need to be needed.* There are two sides to this statement. The first is an issue of user education. People who don't understand a problem won't recognize its solution, and people that don't know solutions exist won't bother to purchase or download them. The other side is of course design. Tools that don't address frequently occurring problems in clear ways can't be useful.

A major problem with utility is this: *Needs change.* Our field moves very quickly. Consumer demands change, applications change, new methodological insights occur. Consequently, tools need to be easy to update and extend. Also, we should expect that throwing out old toolsets should happen regularly. This means that for tools to be useful, they have to be quick to write and quick to learn. For any ongoing project, there should be developers dedicated to the tools' continuous updating and support.

A surprisingly large problem is that *Productivity has to matter.* You wouldn't think this would be a problem, but it is. Of course, productivity matters ultimately, but it also has to matter in the heads of decision makers. People who budget money have to think buying tools is worthwhile. This means software engineers have to tell these decision makers the value of tools. With decent tools, a developer can be three to ten times more productive, so tool budgets should be considered part of staffing budgets. How much more would you pay to have an excellent programmer rather than a pretty good one? That's how much a good tool set is worth. And don't forget the lessons of the Mythical Man-Month [7]. It's better to have a few excellent programmers than a lot of pretty good ones, because of the inefficiencies involved in teams and communication.

Unfortunately, programmers themselves don't always value learning and using tools. For some of them, this is due to past experience with tool benches, which is a serious consideration, but not the one I'm addressing right here. I'm still complaining about people not recognizing that you have to take time to save time, or spend money to make money. People who budget time have to think learning tools is worthwhile. Getting stuff done well and quickly has to matter more than early milestones, product loyalty or inertia.

Now I will get back to the issue of programmers who have experienced tool sets and don't find them worth the effort of learning. *Tool developers have to do good work.* We need to know what's already out there, and what the alternatives are. We need to understand and minimize the costs of transitioning to our tools. No one should design a tool set that hasn't tried to use at least two of the sets that are already out there, and also already tried to do the work from scratch. And *any* product developer needs to know the work habits and latent knowledge of their target users.

Being on the ATAL tools panel made me very aware that both the problems of tool quality *and* of getting people to use tools are enormous. Here's a suggestion for debugging your own toolbench: try using someone else's. Then go back and think about how many of the problems you had a novice user of your system would share. Common problems are: poor accessibility, poor documentation, no source code, no examples, and not facilitating users to help each other (I can't believe tool sets that don't have mailing lists).

But there has to be more to the underutilization of tool sets than these problems. Some products get these things right, and they still struggle. In mainstream software engineering, I would swear by Center Line C/C++ (formerly Saber), PARC Place Smalltalk VisualWorks80, NextStep (ObjectiveC — now possibly resurrected in Mac X), and to a lesser extent XANALYS (formerly Harlequin) LispWorks. These are all excellent programming tool sets, and they are all struggling or bankrupt. Why??? Is it because the Microsoft antitrust action came too late? In an incredible coincidence—do all these companies lack basic business skills? Or is there something fundamental lacking in corporate culture that can't recognize, value or use good tool sets? I don't know the answer, but I know it matters. I wouldn't expect *any* agent toolkit to succeed if a product like Center Line can't. A lot more people use C/C++ than use agents, and Center Line is probably the best software product I've ever used.

To end on a positive note, I'd like to suggest that the best thing we can do to address these issues is to set up an agent toolset comparison server. This way, for those of us who have used more than one agent toolset (at least 20% of the people who attended ATAL said they have), if we stumble on a good one, we can let people know. New users would then have a better chance of having a good first experience, if they could make an informed choice. Comments on the server might also provide information for toolmakers: they could see what users valued or disparaged in various toolkits. As a community, we should cooperate to both police and promote all of our agent toolkits. This is the best way to make sure we make targeted, useful, easy-to-adopt tools, and that these tools get to their intended consumers.

# 4    Statement by Scott DeLoach

Multi-agent systems development methodologies and tools to support them are still in their infancy. While there have been several methods proposed for analyzing, designing, and building multi-agent systems, most of these have come out of the academic community [1,2,5,6,8,9,13] and there has not been wide-spread industry support for any particular approach. Because agents provide a unique perspective on distributed, intelligent systems, our traditional ways of thinking about and designing software do not fit the multi-agent paradigm. These unique characteristics cry out for methodologies, techniques, and tools to support multi-agent systems development. Providing this capability requires a three part solution: an appropriate agent modeling language, a set of agent-unique methodologies for analyzing and designing multi-agent systems, and a set of automated tools to support modeling language and methodologies.

Developing an agent modeling language that can capture the wide range of concepts associated with multi-agent systems is a challenge at best. One place to start is with the Unified Modeling Language (UML), which is rapidly becoming the standard in the analysis and design of object-oriented systems [12]. There are many similarities including the encapsulation of state and services within a single entity and the passing of messages between these entities. While much of the syntax of UML can be adapted to multi-agent systems, the semantics would be inherently different. The concept of an object class can be equated to an agent class; however, there are many differences. First of all, classes are not decomposable. They have attributes and methods, but no internal architecture that further describes them. Agents, on the other hand, can, and often are, decomposed into more detailed, often complex, architectures. Also, in object-orientation, messages almost always become method calls between objects whereas in multi-agent systems there usually are messages that are transmitted between distributed systems and have all the associated problems. Therefore, multi-agent systems must include the ability to define message passing protocols that include such things as error handling and timeout conditions.

A concept associated with many of the proposed agent methodologies is the use of roles and role models. These concepts are lacking in the object-oriented paradigm and require a special modeling component. An issue related to the modeling language is that of how to evolve the models of multi-agent systems from the requirements specification into a detailed design. This is the area of agent methodologies. Modeling of agent capabilities is a start; however, a methodology provides a map that shows the multi-agent system developer how to move from a set of requirements to design to implementation. Most of the current methodologies focus either on high-level multi-agent aspects, such as the organization and coordination of the agents, or on low-level issues such as how to develop internal agent reasoning. The key to modeling the internal reasoning of agents in a multi-agent system is that it must be consistent with the external interface defined at the organizational level. For instance, if the external interface of an agent states that the agent will respond to a particular message type with either message type A or B, the internal design of the agent must adhere to this as well. This can be much more complex than it first appears. Since an agent, by popular definition, is autonomous, it must be able reason about its actions. The problem comes in guaranteeing that the reasoning will adhere to the external interface definition. Learning brings with it even more difficulties in this area.

The last area necessary for advancement of multi-agent methodologies and techniques is the tools themselves. Many toolsets have been developed to support the development of individual agents as well as multi-agent systems [1,11]. However, most of these tools are either implementation toolkits or limited tools that support only a particular agent architecture working within a specific agent environment or framework. What is needed are tools that support the developer in using an appropriate modeling language and methodology. Generally, tools that support particular methodologies are more useful than simple drawing tools. Good methodologies define relationships between modeling components that can be enforced by a toolset. The methodology should not only describe the order in which the models should be developed, but should define how to derive information from one model to the next. While the existence of tools would greatly increase the ability of developers to design and build multi-agent systems, the development of the languages and methodologies must precede the development of the tools. Once a language is defined for expressing multi-agent designs, development of rudimentary, drawing level, toolsets can be undertaken. However, it is not until complete multi-agent system development methodologies are defined that the power of such toolsets can be realized. Toolsets can then go far beyond the current crop of tools to actually help the designer by making suggestions and actually performing many of the mundane steps while allowing the designer to concentrate on the more critical analysis and design decisions.

## 5   Conclusion by Keith Decker

Our panelists attacked different areas of the questions surrounding agent development tools—the "agentization" of traditional software; quality, support and distribution issues; the need for tools to complement a development methodology. At Delaware, our own experiences with building the DECAF toolkit bears out many of these observations[4]. While the earliest publicly available agent implementation toolkits focussed mostly on providing increasingly well-thought-out APIs for agent communications, in order to actually build agents, programmers needed to piece together those APIs to create some kind of complete agent architecture from scratch. While this made supporting different research goals easy, it also made it harder for students, multi-agent application programmers, or researchers interested in only some agent architectural components to develop their ideas quickly and efficiently. From the standpoint of non-researchers or those new to the field, the focus of an agent toolkit might just as well be on programming agents and building multi-agent systems, and not on designing new internal agent architectures from scratch for each project.[1] Another important goal for an agent toolkit is to support that which makes agents different from arbitrary software objects: flexible (reactive, proactive, and social) behavior [14]. The other goals of toolkits may be to develop a modular platform suitable for research activities, allow for rapid development of third-party domain agents, and provide a means to quickly develop complete multi-agent solutions using combinations of domain-specific agents and standard middle-agents. All in all, the toolkit should both take advantage of the features of the underlying programming language and provide an efficient framework that adds value for the developer.

# References

1. Scott A. DeLoach and Mark Wood. Developing multiagent systems with agentTool. In C. Castelfranchi and Y. Lespérance, editors, *Intelligent Agents VII. Agent Theories, Architectures, and Languages — 7th. International Workshop, ATAL-2000, Boston, MA, USA, July 7–9, 2000, Proceedings*, Lecture Notes in Artificial Intelligence. Springer-Verlag, Berlin, 2001. In this volume.

2. A. Drogoul and A. Collinot. Applying an agent oriented methodology to the design of artificial organizations: A case study in robotic soccer. *Autonomous Agents and Multi-Agent Systems*, 1(1):113–129, 1998.

3. L. Gasser, C. Braganza, and N. Hermann. MACE: A flexible testbed for distributed AI research. In M. Huhns, editor, *Distributed Artificial Intelligence*, pages 119–152. Pitman/Morgan Kaufmann, 1987.

4. J. Graham and K.S. Decker. Towards a distributed, environment-centered agent framework. In N.R. Jennings and Y. Lespérance, editors, *Intelligent Agents VI*, LNAI-1757, pages 290–304. Springer Verlag, 2000.

5. C. Iglesias, M. Garijo, and J. González. A survey of agent-oriented methodologies. In J. P. Muller, M. P. Singh, and A. S. Rao, editors, *Intelligent Agents V. Agents Theories, Architectures, and Languages*. Springer-Verlag, 1998. Lecture Notes in Computer Science, vol. 1555.

6. C. Iglesias, M. Garijo, J. González, and J. Velasco. Analysis and design of multiagent systems using MAS-CommonKADS. In *INTELLIGENT AGENTS IV: Agent Theories, Architectures, and Languages*. Springer Verlag, 1998.

7. Frederick P. Brooks Jr. *The Mythical Man-month: Essays on Software Engineering*. Addison-Wesley Publishing Company, Reading, MA, 20th anniversary edition edition, 1995.

8. E. Kendall, U. Palanivelan, and S. Kalikivayi. Capturing and structuring goals: Analysis patterns. In *Proceedings of the Third European Conference on Pattern Languages of Programming and Computing*, July 1998.

9. D. Kinny, M. Georgeff, and A. Rao. A methodology and modelling technique for systems of BDI agents. In *Agents Breaking Away: Proceedings of the Seventh European Workshop on Modelling Autonomous Agents in a Multi-Agent World, MAAMAW '96*. Springer-Verlag, 1996. Lecture Notes in Artificial Intelligence, vol. 1038.

10. D. Kuokka and L. Harada. On using KQML for matchmaking. In *Proceedings of the First International Conference on Multi-Agent Systems*, pages 239–245, San Francisco, June 1995. AAAI Press.

11. H. Nwana, D. Ndumu, L. Lee, and J. Collis J. ZEUS: A toolkit for building distributed multi-agent systems. *Applied Artificial Intelligence Journal*, 13(1):129–185, 1999.

---

[1] Designing new agent architectures is certainly an important *research* goal, but fraught with peril for beginning students and programmers wanting to work with the agent concept.

12. J. Odell, H. V. D. Parunak, and B. Bauer. Representing agent interaction protocols in UML. In *Proceedings of the First International Workshop on Agent-Oriented Engineering*, June 2000.

13. M. Wooldridge, N. Jennings, and D. Kinny. The gaia methodology for agent-oriented analysis and design. *Journal of Autonomous Agents and Multi-Agent Systems*, 3(3), 2000.

14. M. Wooldridge and N.R. Jennings. Intelligent agents: Theory and practice. *The Knowledge Engineering Review*, 10(2):115–152, 1995.

15. M. Wooldridge, G. M. P. O'Hare, and R. Elks. FELINE — a case study in the design and implementation of a co-operating expert system. In *Proceedings of the Eleventh European Conference on Expert Systems and Their Applications*, Avignon, France, May 1991.

# Again on Agents' Autonomy: A Homage to AlanTuring — Panel Chair's Statement

Cristiano Castelfranchi

University of Siena - Dep. of Communication Sciences
castel@ip.rm.cnr.it

## 1  Some Introductory Remarks

"Autonomy"? Why wasting time with such a philosophical notion, such a ridiculous pretence typical of the arrogant ambitions of "Artificial Intelligence"? Is this a real scientific (and interesting) problem, or just "blah, blah"? Is this a relevant practical, technical issue? The answers to these questions are not obvious at all. Consider for example the animated discussion on the agents-list initiated by the following stimulating and radical intervention:

> >Can you folks now please stop **this nonsense about autonomy?**
> >As long as humanity is in the driver seat, software cannot and should
> >not be autonomous. The idiots that concocted "autonomous agents" are even more
> >irresponsible than the folks that mangled the language by substituting: methodology
> >for method; method for operation; technology for techniques **computer science** for
> >whatever, **but it is definitely not a science.** Thanks! (July 20 - Agents-list)

Although I disagree with such a view, at least it paradoxically shows some awareness of the significance of our issue. We should be conscious of the non merely technical import of our research. Personally, I still believe (wishful thinking?) that AI is a science and that Autonomy is central in the very notion, theory, and practice of Agents. Let me very briefly observe that:

1.  In fact, some form of autonomy is (explicitly or implicitly) implied in any Agent definition and use.
2.  Autonomy is crucial for understanding the "philosophy" of what is happening in computing and in Human-Machine interaction.
3.  Autonomy is both dangerous and useful , and in any case unavoidable.

I will say nothing here about the theory of autonomy: what autonomy is; how to identify its dimensions; its social nature and relations with dependence, power, control, and trust (see [2; 3; 4] and Falcone, this volume) [1]. I will also not argue on the

---

[1] Our theory of autonomy based on dependence/reliance on other agents for some lacking resource and on the idea of "agents in the loop of other agents" is rather close to Hexmoor's and to Barber's view (this volume). Such a convergence is a good premise for the development of a shared ontology and a good operational definition.

C. Castelfranchi, Y. Lespérance (Eds.): Intelligent Agents VII, LNAI 1986, pp. 339–342, 2001.
© Springer-Verlag Berlin Heidelberg 2001

first claim which is rather evident. Let me say something on the other two, taking inspiration from some of Turing's hints. I think in fact that *the Agents paradigm is leading AI back to its original challenges.*

## 2    Autonomy Is Crucial for Understanding the "Philosophy" of What Is Happening in Computing and in HM Interaction

In distributed computing and especially within the *Agent paradigm* we are beyond Lady Lovelace's limits. I mean beyond her claim that *Machine can do everything ... we know how to instruct it to do.*

In 1947 Alan Turing, challenging this famous truism,[2] said that our intention in building computers had been that of treating them like slaves, of giving them tasks that are so completely specified that the user may know at each instant what is being done. Until now he says, machines have been used only in this way; but *must this remain the case forever?*

Agents are, in fact, beyond Lady Lovelace's limits, and this comes precisely from their "autonomy": autonomy in *evolving* and *learning*, in *directly accessing information* from the world, in *moving*, planning and *solving problems*,  in taking *initiatives*, in having *their own goals*, etc. It seems to me that in the Agents paradigm nobody knows not only - obviously - *where*, but also *if, when, who* (human or software), and especially *HOW* a program is executed, a task is accomplished, an information is processed or provided.

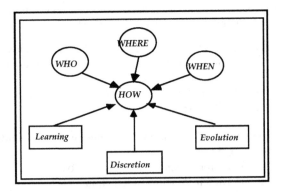

This is mainly due to autonomy in moving, negotiating, delegating, learning, evolving, acquiring local or new information, reacting...

---

[2] To be true it seems to me that Lady Lovelace's dictum is always misinterpreted as *"Machine can do **only**...what we know how to instruct it to do"*

Autonomy is obviously dangerous because it implies a number of risks, such as lack of control, unpredictable effects, intrusiveness. But it is also very useful and probably unavoidable. I think that it is necessary because of:

> Limited knowledge, competence, time and capability of the user/client Agent, that make 'delegation' (reliance) necessary and in particular open delegation i.e., the delegation to "bring it about that..." without specifying the necessary actions or plans.
>
> Local and updated information to be taken into account in reasoning and problem solving (open and uncertain world; moving around)
>
> Required local and timely reaction and learning

Not only we have to discuss about autonomy, but we have to work also on "initiative", because we need initiative too (which is a form of autonomy) in our machines; both initiative in HC interaction and initiative in the world. This leads us back to Turing.

One day, he was talking on the radio and he issued the challenge, claiming something like "Describe me what - in your view- a computer cannot do, ... and I will build one on purpose". The famous philosopher Karl Popper was rather scandalised and wrote him a letter claiming that there is something in particular that computers do not have and cannot have: initiative! We cannot 'describe' initiative, although it is something that any little child and animal has.

Now in fact, while modelling autonomous Agents (robots or software Agents), we are precisely trying to model several forms of initiative. This is why for example, we worry about 'mixed initiative' in human-computer interaction [1], or about 'adjustable autonomy'.

We should be aware of the range and significance of our objectives; we should not deal with such foundational and very committing issues just involuntarily or under the counter.

Given this general framework for our debate, let me introduce some questions for the panellists.

# 3    Questions for the Panel

Autonomy is *a foundational notion for Agents*, but:

> Do we really need autonomous software Agents and why?
>
> What exactly is autonomy? How can we characterise it?
>
> Which are the main gaps in the theory of autonomy (what should be defined and formalised)?
>
> Are there different dimensions of autonomy and measures of degrees of autonomy?
>
> Can we distinguish among autonomy with respect to the user, with respect to other Agents, or with respect to a "role" in an organisation?
>
> How is autonomy related to initiative, discretion, and responsibility?

How can we control, intervene on, and adjust the Agents' autonomy during their collective activity in order to obtain the desired services or global result?

What is the trade-off between autonomy, trust, and lack of control?

Which are the most urgent or important problems in Agents applications relatively to their autonomy?

# References

1. AA.VV. Mixed-initiative interaction. *IEEE Intelligent Systems*, September/October 1999, 14-23
2. C. Castelfranchi, Guaranties for Autonomy in Cognitive Agent Architecture. In M.J. Woolridge and N. R. Jennings (eds.) *Intelligent Agents I*, Berlin, Springer, 1995
3. C. Castelfranchi, Towards an Agent Ontology: Autonomy, Delegation, Adaptivity. *AI*IA Notizie.* 11, 3, 1998; Special issue on "Autonomous Intelligent Agents", Associazione Italiana per l'Intelligenza Artificiale, Roma, 45-50.
4. C. Castelfranchi, Founding Agent's 'Autonomy' On Dependence Theory. *ECAI'00*, Berlin, August 2000.

# Autonomy as Decision-Making Control

K. Suzanne Barber and Cheryl E. Martin

The Laboratory for Intelligent Processes and Systems
The University of Texas at Austin, Department of Electrical and Computer Engineering
201 East 24th Street, ACE 5.402, Austin, TX 78712
{barber,cemartin}@mail.utexas.edu

## Defining Autonomy

Autonomy is a very complex concept. This discussion develops a definition for one dimension of autonomy: decision-making control. The development of this definition draws salient features from previous work. Each stage in the development of this definition is highlighted by bold text.

The general concept of agent autonomy is often interpreted as **freedom from human intervention, oversight, or control** [2;5-7;9]. This type of definition corresponds well to the concept of autonomy in domains that involve single-agent-to-human-user interaction. However, in multi-agent systems, a human user may be far removed from the operations of any particular agent. Some researchers have defined autonomy in a more general sense as a property of self-motivation and self-control for the agent [3;4;7;8]. This sense of the word autonomy captures the concept of **freedom from intervention, oversight, or control by *any other agent***, including, but not limited to, a human.

Unfortunately, this broad statement fails to account for many characteristics often considered necessary for the realization of autonomous agents. For example, the behavior of autonomous agents is generally viewed as *goal-directed* [3-5;8]. That is, autonomous agents act with the purpose of achieving their goals. In addition, many researchers consider *pro-activeness* to be a defining property of autonomous agents [2;5;7]. Autonomous agents must consider their goals, make decisions about how to achieve those goals, and act on these decisions. Incorporating these properties, autonomy becomes **an agent's active use of its capabilities to pursue its goals without intervention, oversight, or control by any other agent.**

No agent can be completely free from all types of intervention with respect to any goal. This discussion distinguishes among three types of intervention as illustrated in the figure and described below:

1. modification of an agent's environment – other agents modify the environment in which agent $a_0$ operates,
2. influence over an agent's beliefs – other agents assert facts or, in general, provide information to agent $a_0$ in order to change or influence beliefs held by agent $a_0$, and
3. control over the decision-making process determining which goals, sub-goals, or intentions the agent will pursue – other agents participate to a greater or lesser degree in telling agent $a_0$ how to pursue its higher-level goals.

C. Castelfranchi, Y. Lespérance (Eds.): Intelligent Agents VII, LNAI 1986, pp. 343–345, 2001.
© Springer-Verlag Berlin Heidelberg 2001

Extending and modifying the argument presented in [3], the figure below depicts these three ways that other agents may intervene in the operation of agent $a_0$. The solid arrows in the figure represent interventions that primarily affect an agent's environment, belief base, or goals, respectively. The dotted arrows represent effects of secondary interactions. This discussion suggests that agent designers attempt to classify each agent interaction as one of the three types of intervention based on its primary effect, as pictured in the figure. For example, a task assignment message from agent $a_x$ to agent $a_0$ should be classified as an intervention of type "goal/task determination" because its most salient effect is to change agent $a_0$'s goals. Certainly, such a message would also affect agent $a_0$'s beliefs (agent $a_0$ first believes agent $a_x$ wants agent $a_0$ to perform the new task) and environment (the sending, propagation, and reception of the message imply environmental change). However, these other effects do not capture the nature of the interaction as completely.

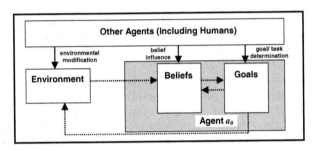

Due to the interplay among an agent's goals, its beliefs, and its environment (pictured in the figure by dotted arrows), it can be difficult to ascribe causality for any particular internal agent modification to a specific intervention occurrence. Establishing this causality becomes especially difficult if the internal agent implementation is unknown. This discussion argues that task assignments creating internal goal changes are useful to model for the purposes of describing autonomy. In any system where agent $a_x$ has authority over agent $a_y$ (e.g. military command structure, employer/employee, etc.), agent $a_x$ need not convince agent $a_y$ that some goal needs to be done. Agent $a_x$ simply assigns the goal to $a_y$. Much future work is required to develop classification algorithms for agent interactions, which may ultimately depend on knowledge of the internal design of the particular agents under study. Nevertheless, these suggested categories are useful at this stage to frame discussions of agent autonomy. Because autonomy relates directly to intervention, it is important to be able to identify the nature and impact of these interventions.

This discussion suggests that freedom from intervention of the type "goal/task determination" is the primary dimension of agent autonomy [1]. Goal/task determination is modeled as the process of deciding and assigning which subgoals or subtasks an agent should perform in order to carry out its higher-level goal or inherent purpose. Since any actionable "oversight" or "control" would require such intervention, those terms can be removed from the proposed definition. Therefore, the primary dimension of **autonomy is an agent's active use of its capabilities to pursue its goals, without intervention by any other agent in the decision-making processes used to determine how those goals should be pursued**. This statement presents autonomy as an absolute value (i.e. either an agent is autonomous or it is not). However, it is more useful to model agents as able to possess different degrees of autonomy, allowing the representation of stronger or weaker intervention.

In addition, it is important to recognize that agents often have multiple goals, some of which may be implicit. This discussion considers an agent's degree of autonomy on a goal-by-goal basis, rather than attempt to discuss an agent's overall autonomy as an indivisible top-level concept. This view recognizes that an agent's autonomy may be different for each goal. For example, some would argue that a thermostat is autonomous and others would argue that it is not. This argument actually hinges on which goal is most important in the assessment of the thermostat's overall autonomy. It should be quite easy to agree that the thermostat does autonomously carry out the goal to maintain a particular temperature range but that it does not autonomously determine its own set point. Once an agent's level of autonomy has been specified for each of its goals, the argument can focus (properly) on determining how important each goal is in the assessment of the agent's overall autonomy. The final proposed definition of autonomy follows: **An agent's degree of autonomy, with respect to some goal that it actively uses its capabilities to pursue, is the degree to which the decision-making process, used to determine how that goal should be pursued, is free from intervention by any other agent.**

# References

1. Barber, K. S. and Martin, C. E.: Dynamic Adaptive Autonomy in Multi-Agent Systems: Representation and Justification. International Journal of Pattern Recognition and Artificial Intelligence. Special Issue on Intelligent Agent Technology, (2000). To appear.
2. Beale, R. and Wood, A.: Agent-based Interaction. In Proceedings of People and Computers IX: Proceedings of HCI'94 (Glasgow, UK, 1994) 239-245.
3. Castelfranchi, C. Guarantees for Autonomy in Cognitive Agent Architecture. In Intelligent Agents: ECAI-94 Workshop on Agents Theories, Architectures, and Languages, Wooldridge, M. J. and Jennings, N. R., (eds.). Springer-Verlag, Berlin, (1995) 56-70.
4. Covrigaru, A. A. and Lindsay, R. K. Deterministic Autonomous Systems. AI Magazine 12 (3): 110-117. 1991.
5. Etzioni, O. and Weld, D. S.: Intelligent Agents on the Internet: Fact, Fiction, and Forecast. IEEE Expert, 10, 4 (1995) 44-49.
6. Evans, M., Anderson, J., and Crysdale, G.: Achieving Flexible Autonomy in Multiagent Systems Using Constraints. Applied Artificial Intelligence, 6 (1992) 103-126.
7. Jennings, N. R., Sycara, K., and Wooldridge, M.: A Roadmap of Agent Research and Development. Autonomous Agents and Multi-agent Systems, 1, 1 (1998) 7-38.
8. Luck, M. and D'Inverno, M. P.: A Formal Framework for Agency and Autonomy. In Proceedings of First International Conference on Multi-Agents Systems (San Francisco, CA, 1995) AAAI Press / The MIT Press, 254-260.
9. Wooldridge, M. J. and Jennings, N. R.: Intelligent Agents: Theory and Practice. Knowledge Engineering Review, 10, 2 (1995) 115-152.

# Autonomy: Theory, Dimensions, and Regulation

Rino Falcone

IP-CNR Rome, Group of "Artificial Intelligence, Cognitive Modeling and Interaction"
falcone@ip.rm.cnr.it

The notion of *autonomy* is becoming a central and relevant topic in Agent and Multi Agent theories and applications. In very simple terms we can say that the concept of autonomy implies three main subjects (each of which should be thought in a very general sense): the *main agent* (the autonomy *of which* is considered), the *resource* (*about which* the first subject is considered autonomous), and a *secondary agent* (*from which* the main agent is considered autonomous). More in general, there are two main meanings of the concept of autonomy:

- autonomy as *self-sufficiency* (where the *resource* includes all things the main agent needs, and the *secondary agent,* might be any agent in the same world);
- autonomy as implied in *cooperation* (where the *resource* includes all things the main agent needs in that specific relationship, and the *secondary agent* is any cooperative agent in that relationship).

The first meaning tries to cope with the more general and abstract sense of the autonomy notion, considering such questions as: is an agent independent of others for achieving its own goals? Is the agent allowed to have or formulate its own goals? The second meaning is more relative and restricted to a specific relation (*cooperation*) between the main agent and the secondary one, and considers problems of levels and types of delegation/help: what is the agent autonomy when he is working with/for another agent, exploited by it, helping it, collaborating with it, obeying it, etc.?

In this intervention we will focus on the second meaning. We start from the claim that any collaboration or cooperation is based on some task allocation which, in turn, requires an action of delegation/adoption [1]. There are many kinds and levels of delegation and adoption (with respect to the task specification, to the interaction between the cooperating agents, and so on), and for each of these dimensions it is possible to establish various levels of autonomy: the important thing is to identify these levels, to individuate the reasons for choosing them, and possibly for changing them during the interaction. Following our theory [1] (see fig.1) we can say that in *reliance/delegation*, an agent (client) needs or likes an action of another agent (contractor) and includes it in its own plan; in *help/adoption*, an agent (contractor) performs an action for a given goal, as (long as) this action (or the goal) is included in the plan of another agent (client). On the one hand, the delegated task could be specified at different levels of abstraction, and this specification determines/influences the level of autonomy of the delegated agent. On the other hand, the autonomy of the contractor determines the level of adoption of the contractor itself.

C. Castelfranchi, Y. Lespérance (Eds.): Intelligent Agents VII, LNAI 1986, pp. 346–348, 2001.
© Springer-Verlag Berlin Heidelberg 2001

With respect to the delegated agent we can characterize:

- *Realization autonomy*: that means that the agent has more or less discretion in finding a solution to an assigned problem, or a plan for an assigned goal.
- *Meta-level autonomy*: that denotes how much the agent is able to and in condition of negotiating about the delegation itself or of changing it.

Both are forms of goal-autonomy, the former at the sub-goals (instrumental) level, the latter at the higher level.

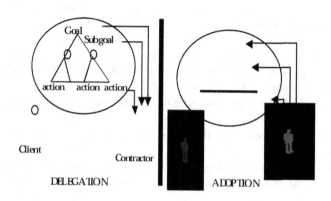

**Fig.1**

We would like to emphasize that autonomy and initiative are not simply optional features in collaboration/cooperation, but rather they are necessary requirements, and directions of study: in fact, a collaborator (contractor) is not only useful for relieving an agent (client) from boring and repetitive tasks; it is mainly useful for situations where delegation and autonomy are necessary ('strong dependence') because the client does not have the local, decentralized and updated knowledge, or the expertise, or the just-in-time reactivity, or some physical skill that requires some local control-loop. However, control cannot be completely lost and delegation cannot be complete, not only because of lack of confidence and trust, but also for reasons of distribution of goals, knowledge, and competence, and for an effective collaboration. In this sense it is very important that the level of an agent's autonomy could be changed (adjusted) during the interaction. Adjustable autonomy [2] is a desirable agent characteristic because:

- it allows the client to gradually increase a contractor's autonomy as the client becomes more confident in the contractor's competence and performance (from the client's view, to adjust the autonomy means to modify the level of delegation);
- it allows the contractor to dynamically change its own autonomy on the basis of its needs, external constraints, etc.

So, the autonomy adjustment could be done from both sides: the client and the contractor (*bilateral*); and by either increasing or decreasing the amount of autonomy itself (*bidirectional*) [3].

How can the client control, intervene on, and adjust the contractor's autonomy during their interaction in order to obtain the desired services or global/collective result? What is the tradeoff between autonomy, trust, and lack of control? Our claim is that an explicit theory of delegation (and of trust, that is the mental counterpart of the delegation itself [4]) — specifying different dimensions and levels of delegation and consequently determining different levels of autonomy — is fundamental to adjust the level of autonomy and to arrive to a dynamic level of control. For an analysis of the complex relationships among trust, control, autonomy and delegation see [4]. The main causes of Autonomy Adjustment are the following ones:

- there is a change of the contractor's entitlement at the meta-level (contractor can refuse, negotiate, change the delegation); or it is not entitled but in fact takes such an initiative (*meta-autonomy adjustment*);
- a new task is more or less specified than the former (*adjustment of realization autonomy*);
- there is more or less control on the contractor (*control-dependent autonomy adjustment*);
- there is a change in strength of delegation (in other terms, in the strength of the commitments between client and contractor) (*interaction-dependent autonomy adjustment*).

Each of these autonomy adjustments can be both *bilateral* (realized by either the client or the contractor) and *bidirectional* (either augmenting or reducing the autonomy itself).

# References

1. Castelfranchi, C., Falcone, R., (1998) Towards a Theory of Delegation for Agent-based Systems, *Robotics and Autonomous Systems*, Special issue on Multi-Agent Rationality, Elsevier Editor, Vol 24, Nos 3-4, , pp.141-157.
2. Musliner, D., Pell, B., (Eds) (1999), Proceedings of the AAAI 1999 Spring Symposium Series on Agents with Adjustable Autonomy, Stanford University, CA.
3. Falcone, R., Castelfranchi, C., (2000), Levels of Delegation and Levels of Adoption as the basis for Adjustable Autonomy, *Lecture Notes in Artificial Intelligence* n°1792, pp.285-296.
4. Castelfranchi C., Falcone R., (2000), Trust and Control: A Dialectic Link, *Applied Artificial Intelligence* journal, Special Issue on "Trust in Agents" Part1, Castelfranchi C., Falcone R., Firozabadi B., Tan Y. (Editors), Taylor and Francis 14 (8).

# Situated Autonomy

Henry Hexmoor

Dept. of Computer Science, University of North Dakota, Grand Forks, ND, USA
hexmoor@cs.und.edu

Our interest in autonomy is grounded in the context of an agent, a situation, and a goal. We limit our view of autonomy to an agent's moment-to-moment action selection instead of a long-lived agent characteristic. Autonomy of an agent maps an agent, a situation, and a goal to a stance towards the goal such that the stance will be used to generate the most appropriate or the most relevant action for the agent [3]. At a coarse level the agent's stance towards the goal will be whether to abandon it or to decide its overall position toward the goal: to make it an entirely personal goal, to make a goal for another agent, to collaborate with other agents with some level of responsibility, or to have some responsibility about it that is less than total responsibility. Responsibility for a goal is the amount of effort an agent is willing to spend on seeing to its accomplishment. At a finer level the agent's stance will go beyond an overall position to include a degree of autonomy.

Time affects the autonomy of an agent. Consider an agent that must have fast action selection decisions. This agent does not have time for deliberation and will use instinctual means to produce its stance. An agent with more leisurely action selection requirements can use reasoning and perhaps examines its Beliefs, Desires, and Intentions before producing a stance. An agent's stance may have a temporal dimension that includes external cues. External cues might be observation of a second agent's actions or autonomies it exhibits. For instance, an agent's stance to pay for dinner for two might be "If the dinner bill is less than $20, I will offer to pay unless the other guy offers to pay".

Teamwork provides context for an agent's autonomy. Once an agent is motivated to form or to participate in a team toward a common goal, its stance will be to share the goal. Such a stance will require the agent to dynamically monitor and adjust its stance relative to teammates. Situation in autonomy consideration must not only include the state of the world as it pertains to the agent's goal but also the agent's model of teammate situations and autonomies.

Next, I make brief remarks about concepts that are discussed alongside autonomy and point out the differences and misunderstandings.

Control and autonomy are often conflated. A system with ability to operate at several different control regimes is said to have adjustable autonomy. Whereas, autonomy produces a stance, control is a skill. An agent who ponders autonomy with respect to a goal has not fully committed to the goal. An agent who is concerned with control of a goal, has largely finished its consideration of autonomy. Variable or changing control is desirable but that is not the same as the ability for adjustable autonomy. An agent's capacity or power for choice and commitment to a control level is autonomy. This view of "capacity or power for choice and commitment" can be taken too far as in the idea of *free will,* which requires an independence from natural, social, or divine restraints. From the *free will* perspective, a program or a robot would

C. Castelfranchi, Y. Lespérance (Eds.): Intelligent Agents VII, LNAI 1986, pp. 349–350, 2001.

never have autonomy. However, we consider "capacity or power for choice and commitment" as a relational notion and in the context of a goal and a situation.

Experiencing independence or self-sufficiency seems to be proportionally related to the experience of autonomy. Autonomy is proactive in that it is an agent stance whereas dependence or reliance is a perception. "I feel independent, so I choose to be autonomous." However, if I decide on being autonomous, it does not make me feel independent. Castelfranchi points out that Social Dependence is a sub-set of Non-Autonomy [1]. We agree with his position that autonomy is related to the computational and representational powers of an agent's architecture.

Unlike the purported paradox that autonomy is lowered with cooperation [2], we believe that an agent's cooperative attitude is not at odds with its autonomy. Autonomy and cooperative attitude are independent. Consider the example of race-drivers in a "draft' who mutually benefit from the aerodynamics of the drafting. In this example, drivers keep their autonomy fairly high and their cooperation is not with any specific driver but a driver that is at the right position for "drafting".

# References

1. C. Castelfranchi (2000). Founding Agent's 'Autonomy' On Dependence Theory, European Conference in Artificial Intelligence, ECAI 2000, Berlin.
2. C. Castelfranchi (1995). Guarantees for Autonomy in a Cognitive Agent Architecture, In Agent Theories, Languages, and Languages (**ATAL**), p. 56-70, (LNAI volume 890), Springer-Verlag.
3. H. Hexmoor, (2000). A Cognitive Model of Situated Autonomy, In Proceedings of PRICAI-2000 Workshop on Teams with Adjustable Autonomy, Australia.

# Autonomy: A Nice Idea in Theory

Michael Luck[1] and Mark d'Inverno[2]

[1] Dept. of Electronics and Computer Science, University of Southampton, SO17 1BJ, UK
mml@ecs.soton.ac.uk
[2] Cavendish School of Computer Science, Westminster University, London W1M 8JS, UK
dinverm@westminster.ac.uk

## 1 Introduction

Autonomy is perplexing. It is recognisably and undeniably a critical issue in the field of intelligent agents and multi-agent systems, yet it is often ignored or simply assumed. For many, agents are autonomous by definition, and they see no need to add the tautologous prefix in explicitly considering *autonomous* agents, while for others autonomy in agents is an important yet problematic issue that demands attention. The difficulty when considering autonomy, however, is that there are different conceptual levels at which to reason and argue, including the philosophical and the practical.

The notion of *autonomy* has associated with it many variations of meaning. According to Steels, autonomous systems must be automatic systems and, in addition, they must have the capacity to form and adapt their behaviour while operating in the environment. Thus traditional AI systems and most robots are automatic but not autonomous — they are not independent of the control of their designers [7].

## 2 What Is Autonomy?

A dictionary definition will tell us, among other things, that autonomy amounts to freedom of will (and we will add that it includes the ability to exercise that will). In short, this means that it provides the ability to exercise choice, which is particularly relevant in the context of goals and goal-directed behaviour, as in Castelfranchi's notions of goal (or motivational) autonomy [1]. In this view, autonomous agents are able to generate their own goals, to select between multiple alternative goals to pursue, and to decide to adopt goals from others (to further their own ends). Franklin and Graesser's definition of an *autonomous agent* as a system that pursues "its own agenda" reinforces this perspective [4].

Now, from a purely *conceptual* or theoretical point of view removed from practical considerations, autonomy can naturally be regarded as absolute, without dimension or measure of degree. Yet, this *strong view* of autonomy contrasts with much of the practical work with agents in which autonomy is taken to be the same as *independence*, a very distinctly relative notion. In what might be called this *weak view*, a non-autonomous agent either depends on others or is fixed (eg an automaton), while an autonomous agent can either be independent or depend on others. It is this last point that seems to suggest that autonomy is not the same as independence — an agent does not simply

C. Castelfranchi, Y. Lespérance (Eds.): Intelligent Agents VII, LNAI 1986, pp. 351–353, 2001.

lose its autonomy by virtue of depending on another for a particular goal; situations of dependence occur also for autonomous agents.

Practically then, the notion of independence can be used as an approximation for autonomy with the added benefit that it admits the dimensions and measures of degree that are missing from the strong view. In this sense it might be considered as a valuable practical realisation of autonomy, and provides a way to characterise different dependence situations.

## 3   Autonomy through Motivation

For all the difficulty in pinning down autonomy, it is in our view key to understanding the nature and behaviour both of individual agents, and of interactions between them. In a series of papers, we have described and formally specified an extended theory of agent interaction, based on *goals* and *motivations*, which takes exactly this standpoint. The theory describes a framework for categorising different agents [5], and has been used as a basis for investigating aspects of the relationships between agents [6], providing an operational account of their invocation and destruction [3], as well as for reformulating existing systems and theories, including those relating to dependence situations [2].

In essence, autonomous agents possess goals that are *generated* within rather than *adopted* from other agents. These goals are generated from *motivations*, higher-level non-derivative components characterizing the nature of the agent that can be regarded as any desires or preferences affecting the outcome of a given reasoning or behavioural task. For example, *greed* is not a goal in the classical artificial intelligence sense since it does not specify a state of affairs to be achieved, nor is it describable in terms of the environment. However, it may give rise to the generation of a goal to rob a bank. The distinction between the motivation of greed and the goal of robbing a bank is clear, with the former providing a reason to do the latter, and the latter specifying what must be done.

This view of autonomous agents is based on the generation and transfer of goals between agents. More specifically, something is an agent if it can be viewed as satisfying a goal that is first created and then, if necessary and appropriate, transferred to another. It is the adoption of goals that gives rise to agenthood, and it is the *self-generation* of goals that is responsible for autonomy. Thus an *agent* is just something either that is useful to another agent in terms of satisfying that agent's goals, or that exhibits independent purposeful behaviour. Importantly, agents rely on the existence of others to provide the goals that they adopt for instantiation as agents. In order to escape an infinite regress of goal adoption, however, we define *autonomous agents* to be just agents that generate their own goals from motivations.

## 4   Conclusion

The answer to whether we can control autonomy depends on the viewpoint adopted. In the strong view, it is by definition impossible to control autonomy externally. At the same time, however, we can design agents with appropriate motivations and motivational mechanisms that constrain and guide agent behaviour as a result of internal imposition.

In this way, control is *on-board*, and more and better processing of environmental information is required.

We must also question the *need* for autonomy. Certainly, there is value in the flexibility and robustness that autonomy can bring in a dynamic and open world, but many problems which merit an agent approach do not necessarily require autonomous behaviour. Indeed, the strong view of autonomy can be very dangerous if used for example in military applications for tank or missile control; independence with respect to a user or designer can often be bad. Thus, we also need to consider the kinds of situations to which autonomy is suited.

While we have offered an absolute theoretical viewpoint of autonomy as well as a weaker alternative that provides a practical realisation of it that is useful for many, it is important to understand the difference in purpose and context of these notions, and not to be dogmatic in practical situations. Clearly there is value in studying the general concept of autonomy, regardless of practical concerns, but we must also address ourselves to the practical imperative. It matters little what we call it (just as it matters little whether we call a program an agent) as long as it gives us the required robustness and flexibility we desire.

## References

1. C. Castelfranchi. Guarantees for autonomy in cognitive agent architecture. In M. Wooldridge and N. R. Jennings, editors, *Intelligent Agents: Theories, Architectures, and Languages, LNAI 890*, pages 56–70. Springer-Verlag, 1995.
2. M. d'Inverno and M. Luck. A formal view of social dependence networks. In C. Zhang and D. Lukose, editors, *Distributed Artificial Intelligence Architecture and Modelling: Proceedings of the First Australian Workshop on Distributed Artificial Intelligence, Lecture Notes in Artificial Intelligence*, volume 1087, pages 115–129. Springer Verlag, 1996.
3. M. d'Inverno and M. Luck. Making and breaking engagements: An operational analysis of agent relationships. In C. Zhang and D. Lukose, editors, *Multi-Agent Systems Methodologies and Applications: Proceedings of the Second Australian Workshop on Distributed Artificial Intelligence, Lecture Notes in Artificial Intelligence*, volume 1286, pages 48–62. Springer Verlag, 1997.
4. S. Franklin and A. Graesser. Is it an agent, or just a program?: A taxonomy for autonomous agents. In J. P. Müller, M. J. Wooldridge, and N. R. Jennings, editors, *Intelligent Agents III — Proceedings of the Third International Workshop on Agent Theories, Architectures, and Languages (ATAL-96)*, Lecture Notes in Artificial Intelligence, 1193. Springer-Verlag, 1996.
5. M. Luck and M. d'Inverno. Engagement and cooperation in motivated agent modelling. In *Distributed Artificial Intelligence Architecture and Modelling: Proceedings of the First Australian Workshop on Distributed Artificial Intelligence, Lecture Notes in Artificial Intelligence, 1087*, pages 70–84. Springer Verlag, 1996.
6. M. Luck and M. d'Inverno. Plan analysis for autonomous sociological agents. In *Proceedings of the Third International Workshop on Agent Theories, Architectures, and Languages*, 2000.
7. L. Steels. When are robots intelligent autonomous agents? *Journal of Robotics and Autonomous Systems*, 15:3–9, 1995.

# Adjustable Autonomy: A Response

Milind Tambe, David Pynadath, and Paul Scerri

Information Sciences Institute, University of Southern California
4676 Admiralty Way, Marina del Rey, CA 90292

tambe@isi.edu

Gaining a fundamental understanding of adjustable autonomy (AA) is critical if we are to deploy multi-agent systems in support of critical human activities. Indeed, our recent work with intelligent agents in the "Electric Elves" (E-Elves) system has convinced us that AA is a critical part of any human collaboration software. In the following, we first briefly describe E-Elves, then discuss AA issues in E-Elves.

## Electric Elves: A Deployed Multi-agent System

The past few years have seen a revolution in the field of software agents, with agents now proliferating in human organizations, helping individuals in information gathering, activity scheduling, managing email, etc. The E-Elves effort at USC/ISI is now taking the next step: dynamic teaming of all such different heterogeneous agents, as well as proxy agents for humans, to serve not just individuals, but to facilitate the functioning of entire organizations. The ultimate goal of our work is to build agent teams that assist in all organization activities, enabling organizations to act coherently, to robustly attain their mission goals and to react swiftly to crises, e.g., helping a disaster rescue organization to coordinate movement of personnel and equipment to the site of a disaster. The results of this work could potentially be relevant to all organizations.

As a step towards this goal, we have had an agent team of 15 agents, including 10 proxies (for 10 people) running 24/7 for the past four months at USC/ISI. Each proxy is called Friday (from Robinson Crusoe's Friday), and it acts on the behalf of its user in the agent team. Thus, if a user is delayed to a meeting, then Friday will reschedule that meeting, by informing other Fridays, which in turn will inform the humans users. If there is a research presentation slot open, Friday may volunteer or decline the invitation for that slot. In addition, Friday can also order a user's meals — a user can say "order my usual" and Friday will select a nearby restaurant such as *California Pizza Kitchen* and send over a fax to order the meal from the user's usual favorites. Friday communicates with a user using different types of mobile wireless devices, such as PALM VIIs and WAP enabled mobile phones. By connecting a PALMVII to a GPS, Friday can also track our locations using wireless transmission.

Each Friday is based on a teamwork model called STEAM[3], which helps it communicate and coordinate with other Fridays. One interesting new development wrt STEAM is that roles in teamwork are now auctioned off. In particular, some meetings have a presenter role. Given a topic of presentation, Friday bids on behalf of its user, indicating if its user is capable and/or willing for that topic. Here, a Friday bids autonomously on capability by looking up user's capability in a capability database, but its willingness decision is not autonomous. The highest bidder wins the auction and gets the preseter role.

C. Castelfranchi, Y. Lespérance (Eds.): Intelligent Agents VII, LNAI 1986, pp. 354–356, 2001.

## Adjustable Autonomy in Electric Elves

AA is of critical importance in Friday agents. Clearly, the more decisions that Friday makes autonomously, the more time its user saves. Yet, given the high uncertainty in Friday's beliefs about its user's state, it could potentially make very costly mistakes while acting autonomously, e.g., it may order an expensive dinner when the user is not hungry, or volunteer a busy user for a presentation. Thus, each Friday must make intelligent decisions about when to consult its user and when to act autonomously.

One key problem here is that a Friday agent faces significant uncertainty in its autonomous decision, e.g., if a user is not at the meeting location at meeting time, does he/she plan to attend? To address such uncertainty, our initial attempt at AA in E-Elves was inspired by CAP[1], the well-known agent system for advising a human user on scheduling meetings. As with CAP, Friday learned user preferences using C4.5[2] decision-tree learning, although Friday's focus was on rescheduling meetings. Thus, in the training mode, Friday recorded values of a dozen carefully selected attributes and also the user's preferred action (by querying him/her using a dialog box as shown in Figure 1). This recorded data and user response was used to learn a decision tree, e.g., *if* the user has a meeting with his/her advisor, but the user is not at ISI at meeting time, *then* delay the meeting 15 minutes. Simultaneously, Friday queried the user if s/he wanted Friday to take the decision autonomously or not; C4.5 was again used to learn a second decision tree from these responses.

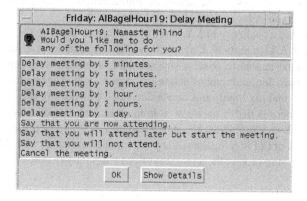

**Fig. 1.** Dialog boxes used in Electric Elves.

Initial tests based on the above setup were successful, as reported in [4]. Soon thereafter however, one key problem became apparent: a user would suggest Friday to not take some specific decision autonomously, but then s/he would not be available to provide any input. Thus, a Friday would end up waiting for user input, and miscoordinate with its team. To address this *team miscoordination* problem, timeouts were introduced: if a user did not respond within a time-limit, Friday used its own decision tree to take autonomous action. In our initial tests, the results still looked promising. Unfortunately, when the resulting system was deployed for real, it led to some dramatic failures:

1. Tambe's (a user) Friday incorrectly cancelled a meeting with his division's director. C4.5 had overgeneralized, incorrectly taking an autonomous action from the initial set of training examples.
2. Pynadath's (another user) Friday incorrectly cancelled the group's weekly research meeting. The time-out forced an incorrect autonomous action when Pynadath was unavailable to respond in time.
3. One of the Fridays delayed a meeting almost 50 times, each in 5 minute increments. The agent was applying its learned rule to cause a small delay each time, but ignoring the nuisance to the rest of the meeting participants.
4. Tambe's proxy automatically volunteered him for a presentation, even though he was not willing. Again, C4.5 had overgeneralized from a few examples and with timeout, taken an undesirable autonomous action.

From the growing list of failures, it became increasingly clear that our original approach faced some fundamental problems. The first problem is clearly that agents must balance the possibility of team miscoordination against effective team action. Learning from user input combined with timeouts, failed to address this challenge: the agent was sometimes forced to take autonomous actions when it was ill-prepared, causing problems as seen in example 2 and 4. Second, C4.5 was not considering the cost to the team due to erroneous autonomous actions, e.g., an erroneous cancellation, as seen in example 1 and 2. Third, decision-tree learning lacked the ability to look-ahead, to plan actions that would work better in the longer term. For instance, in example 3, each 5 minute delay is appropriate for its corresponding state *in isolation*, but the C4.5 rules did not take into account the consequences of one action on future actions. Such planning could have preferred a one hour delay instead of several 5 minute delays.

Thus, one major challenge in AA, based on our experience with C4.5 is guaranteeing *safe learning* in AA. In particular, agents may often learn in the presence of noisy data, e.g., they may be unable to observe that a user is attending a meeting on time. Yet, the increased need for autonomous action in teams may lead agents to act despite such faulty learning, making highly inaccurate decisions and causing drastic team failures. One argument here is that if agents wait long enough to collect a lot more data, they would overcome such problems; but in rich domains, it would be difficult to first gather the required amount of training data in any reasonable amount of time. Thus, we need a safety mechanism to protect the agent team from temporary distortions in learning.

# References

1. Tom Mitchell, Rich Caruana, Dayne Freitag, John McDermott, and David Zabowski. Experience with a learning personal assistant. *Communications of the ACM*, 37(7):81–91, July 1994.
2. J. R. Quinlan. *C4.5: Programs for machine learning*. Morgan Kaufmann, San Mateo, CA, 1993.
3. M. Tambe. Towards flexible teamwork. *Journal of Artificial Intelligence Research (JAIR)*, 7:83–124, 1997.
4. Milind Tambe, David V. Pynadath, Nicolas Chauvat, Abhimanyu Das, and Gal A. Kaminka. Adaptive agent integration architectures for heterogeneous team members. In *Proceedings of the International Conference on MultiAgent Systems*, pages 301–308, 2000.

# Author Index

# Lecture Notes in Artificial Intelligence (LNAI)

Vol. 1952: M.C. Monard, J. Simão Sichman (Eds.), Advances in Artificial Intelligence. Proceedings, 2000. XV, 498 pages. 2000.

Vol. 1955: M. Parigot, A. Voronkov (Eds.), Logic for Programming and Automated Reasoning. Proceedings, 2000. XIII, 487 pages. 2000.

Vol. 1967: S. Arikawa, S. Morishita (Eds.), Discovery Science. Proceedings, 2000. XII, 332 pages. 2000.

Vol. 1968: H. Arimura, S. Jain, A. Sharma (Eds.), Algorithmic Learning Theory. Proceedings, 2000. XI, 335 pages. 2000.

Vol. 1972: A. Omicini, R. Tolksdorf, F. Zambonelli (Eds.), Engineering Societies in the Agents World. Proceedings, 2000. IX, 143 pages. 2000.

Vol. 1979: S. Moss, P. Davidsson (Eds.), Multi-Agent-Based Simulation. Proceedings, 2000. VIII, 267 pages. 2001.

Vol. 1986: C. Castelfranchi, Y. Lespérance (Eds.), Intelligent Agents VII. Proceedings, 2000. XVII, 357 pages. 2001.

Vol. 1991: F. Dignum, C. Sierra (Eds.), Agent Mediated Electronic Commerce. VIII, 241 pages. 2001.

Vol. 1994: J. Lind, Iterative Software Engineering for Multiagent Systems. XVII, 286 pages. 2001.

Vol. 2003: F. Dignum, U. Cortés (Eds.), Agent-Mediated Electronic Commerce III. XII, 193 pages. 2001.

Vol. 2007: J.F. Roddick, K. Hornsby (Eds.), Temporal, Spatial, and Spatio-Temporal Data Mining. Proceedings, 2000. VII, 165 pages. 2001.

Vol. 2014: M. Moortgat (Ed.), Logical Aspects of Computational Linguistics. Proceedings, 1998. X, 287 pages. 2001.

Vol. 2019: P. Stone, T. Balch, G. Kraetzschmar (Eds.), RoboCup 2000: Robot Soccer World Cup IV. XVII, 658 pages. 2001.

Vol. 2033: J. Liu, Y. Ye (Eds.), E-Commerce Agents. VI, 347 pages. 2001.

Vol. 2035: D. Cheung, G.J. Williams, Q. Li (Eds.), Advances in Knowledge Discovery and Data Mining – PAKDD 2001. Proceedings, 2001. XVIII, 596 pages. 2001.

Vol. 2036: S. Wermter, J. Austin, D. Willshaw (Eds.), Emergent Neural Computational Architectures Based on Neuroscience. X, 577 pages. 2001.

Vol. 2039: M. Schumacher, Objective Coordination in Multi-Agent System Engineering. XIV, 149 pages. 2001.

Vol. 2056: E. Stroulia, S. Matwin (Eds.), Advances in Artificial Intelligence. Proceedings, 2001. XII, 366 pages. 2001.

Vol. 2062: A. Nareyek, Constraint-Based Agents. XIV, 178 pages. 2001.

Vol. 2070: L. Monostori, J. Váncza, M. Ali (Eds.), Engineering of Intelligent Systems. Proceedings, 2001. XVIII, 951 pages. 2001.

Vol. 2080: D.W. Aha, I. Watson (Eds.), Case-Based Reasoning Research and Development. Proceedings, 2001. XII, 758 pages. 2001.

Vol. 2083: R. Goré, A. Leitsch, T. Nipkow (Eds.), Automated Reasoning. Proceedings, 2001. XV, 708 pages. 2001.

Vol. 2086: M. Luck, V. Mařík, O. Stěpánková, R. Trappl (Eds.), Multi-Agent Systems and Applications. Proceedings, 2001. X, 437 pages. 2001.

Vol. 2087: G. Kern-Isberner, Conditionals in Non-monotonic Reasoning and Belief Revision. X, 190 pages. 2001.

Vol. 2099: P. de Groote, G. Morrill, C. Retoré (Eds.), Logical Aspects of Computational Linguistics. Proceedings, 2001. VIII, 311 pages. 2001.

Vol. 2100: R. Küsters, Non-Standard Inferences in Description Logics. X, 250 pages. 2001.

Vol. 2101: S. Quaglini, P. Barahona, S. Andreassen (Eds.), Artificial Intelligence in Medicine. Proceedings, 2001. XIV, 469 pages. 2001.

Vol. 2103: M. Hannebauer, J. Wendler, E. Pagello (Eds.), Balancing Reactivity and Social Deliberation in Multi-Agent Systems. VIII, 237 pages. 2001.

Vol. 2109: M. Bauer, P.J. Gmytrasiewicz, J. Vassileva (Eds.), User Modeling 2001. Proceedings, 2001. XIII, 318 pages. 2001.

Vol. 2111: D. Helmbold, B. Williamson (Eds.), Computational Learning Theory. Proceedings, 2001. IX, 631 pages. 2001.

Vol. 2116: V. Akman, P. Bouquet, R. Thomason, R.A. Young (Eds.), Modeling and Using Context. Proceedings, 2001. XII, 472 pages. 2001.

Vol. 2117: M. Beynon, C.L. Nehaniv, K. Dautenhahn (Eds.), Cognitive Technology: Instruments of Mind. Proceedings, 2001. XV, 522 pages. 2001.

Vol. 2120: H.S. Delugach, G. Stumme (Eds.), Conceptual Structures: Broadening the Base. Proceedings, 2001. X, 377 pages. 2001.

Vol. 2123: P. Perner (Ed.), Machine Learning and Data Mining in Pattern Recognition. Proceedings, 2001. XI, 363 pages. 2001.

Vol. 2132: S.-T. Yuan, M. Yokoo (Eds.), Intelligent Agents: Specification, Modeling, and Application. Proceedings, 2001. X, 237 pages. 2001.

# Lecture Notes in Computer Science

Vol. 2081: K. Aardal, B. Gerards (Eds.), Integer Programming and Combinatorial Optimization. Proceedings, 2001. XI, 423 pages. 2001.

Vol. 2082: M.F. Insana, R.M. Leahy (Eds.), Information Processing in Medical Imaging. Proceedings, 2001. XVI, 537 pages. 2001.

Vol. 2083: R. Goré, A. Leitsch, T. Nipkow (Eds.), Automated Reasoning. Proceedings, 2001. XV, 708 pages. 2001. (Subseries LNAI).

Vol. 2084: J. Mira, A. Prieto (Eds.), Connectionist Models of Neurons, Learning Processes, and Artificial Intelligence. Proceedings, 2001. Part I. XXVII, 836 pages. 2001.

Vol. 2086: M. Luck, V. Mařík, O. Stěpánková, R. Trappl (Eds.), Multi-Agent Systems and Applications. Proceedings, 2001. X, 437 pages. 2001. (Subseries LNAI).

Vol. 2087: G. Kern-Isberner, Conditionals in Nonmonotonic Reasoning and Belief Revision. X, 190 pages. 2001. (Subseries LNAI).

Vol. 2089: A. Amir, G.M. Landau (Eds.), Combinatorial Pattern Matching. Proceedings, 2001. VIII, 273 pages. 2001.

Vol. 2091: J. Bigun, F. Smeraldi (Eds.), Audio- and Video-Based Biometric Person Authentication. Proceedings, 2001. XIII, 374 pages. 2001.

Vol. 2092: L. Wolf, D. Hutchison, R. Steinmetz (Eds.), Quality of Service – IWQoS 2001. Proceedings, 2001. XII, 435 pages. 2001.

Vol. 2093: P. Lorenz (Ed.), Networking – ICN 2001. Proceedings, 2001. Part I. XXV, 843 pages. 2001.

Vol. 2094: P. Lorenz (Ed.), Networking – ICN 2001. Proceedings, 2001. Part II. XXV, 899 pages. 2001.

Vol. 2095: B. Schiele, G. Sagerer (Eds.), Computer Vision Systems. Proceedings, 2001. X, 313 pages. 2001.

Vol. 2096: J. Kittler, F. Roli (Eds.), Multiple Classifier Systems. Proceedings, 2001. XII, 456 pages. 2001.

Vol. 2097: B. Read (Ed.), Advances in Databases. Proceedings, 2001. X, 219 pages. 2001.

Vol. 2098: J. Akiyama, M. Kano, M. Urabe (Eds.), Discrete and Computational Geometry. Proceedings, 2000. XI, 381 pages. 2001.

Vol. 2099: P. de Groote, G. Morrill, C. Retoré (Eds.), Logical Aspects of Computational Linguistics. Proceedings, 2001. VIII, 311 pages. 2001. (Subseries LNAI).

Vol. 2100: R. Küsters, Non-Standard Inferences in Description Logics. X, 250 pages. 2001. (Subseries LNAI).

Vol. 2101: S. Quaglini, P. Barahona, S. Andreassen (Eds.), Artificial Intelligence in Medicine. Proceedings, 2001. XIV, 469 pages. 2001. (Subseries LNAI).

Vol. 2102: G. Berry, H. Comon, A. Finkel (Eds.), Computer-Aided Verification. Proceedings, 2001. XIII, 520 pages. 2001.

Vol. 2103: M. Hannebauer, J. Wendler, E. Pagello (Eds.), Balancing Reactivity and Social Deliberation in Multi-Agent Systems. VIII, 237 pages. 2001. (Subseries LNAI).

Vol. 2104: R. Eigenmann, M.J. Voss (Eds.), OpenMP Shared Memory Parallel Programming. Proceedings, 2001. X, 185 pages. 2001.

Vol. 2105: W. Kim, T.-W. Ling, Y-J. Lee, S.-S. Park (Eds.), The Human Society and the Internet. Proceedings, 2001. XVI, 470 pages. 2001.

Vol. 2106: M. Kerckhove (Ed.), Scale-Space and Morphology in Computer Vision. Proceedings, 2001. XI, 435 pages. 2001.

Vol. 2109: M. Bauer, P.J. Gymtrasiewicz, J. Vassileva (Eds.), User Modeling 2001. Proceedings, 2001. XIII, 318 pages. 2001. (Subseries LNAI).

Vol. 2110: B. Hertzberger, A. Hoekstra, R. Williams (Eds.), High-Performance Computing and Networking. Proceedings, 2001. XVII, 733 pages. 2001.

Vol. 2111: D. Helmbold, B. Williamson (Eds.), Computational Learning Theory. Proceedings, 2001. IX, 631 pages. 2001. (Subseries LNAI).

Vol. 2116: V. Akman, P. Bouquet, R. Thomason, R.A. Young (Eds.), Modeling and Using Context. Proceedings, 2001. XII, 472 pages. 2001. (Subseries LNAI).

Vol. 2117: M. Beynon, C.L. Nehaniv, K. Dautenhahn (Eds.), Cognitive Technology: Instruments of Mind. Proceedings, 2001. XV, 522 pages. 2001. (Subseries LNAI).

Vol. 2118: X.S. Wang, G. Yu, H. Lu (Eds.), Advances in Web-Age Information Management. Proceedings, 2001. XV, 418 pages. 2001.

Vol. 2119: V. Varadharajan, Y. Mu (Eds.), Information Security and Privacy. Proceedings, 2001. XI, 522 pages. 2001.

Vol. 2120: H.S. Delugach, G. Stumme (Eds.), Conceptual Structures: Broadening the Base. Proceedings, 2001. X, 377 pages. 2001. (Subseries LNAI).

Vol. 2121: C.S. Jensen, M. Schneider, B. Seeger, V.J. Tsotras (Eds.), Advances in Spatial and Temporal Databases. Proceedings, 2001. XI, 543 pages. 2001.

Vol. 2123: P. Perner (Ed.), Machine Learning and Data Mining in Pattern Recognition. Proceedings, 2001. XI, 363 pages. 2001. (Subseries LNAI).

Vol. 2126: P. Cousot (Ed.), Static Analysis. Proceedings, 2001. XI, 439 pages. 2001.

Vol. 2132: S.-T. Yuan, M. Yokoo (Eds.), Intelligent Agents: Specification, Modeling, and Application. Proceedings, 2001. X, 237 pages. 2001. (Subseries LNAI).